Himalaya and Tibet:
Mountain Roots to Mountain Tops

Edited by

Allison Macfarlane*
Department of Geography and Earth Systems Science
George Mason University
Fairfax, Virginia 22030-4444

Rasoul B. Sorkhabi*
Department of Geology
Arizona State University
Tempe, Arizona 85287-1404

and

Jay Quade
Department of Geological Sciences
University of Arizona
Tucson, Arizona 85721

SPECIAL PAPER

328

1999

*Present addresses: Macfarlane, Belfer Center for Science and International Affairs, Kennedy School of Government, Harvard University, 79 JFK Street, Cambridge, Massachusetts 02138; Sorkhabi, Japan National Oil Corporation, Technology Research Center, 2-2 Hamada, 1-chome, Mihama-ku, Chiba-shi 261, Japan.

Published by The Geological Society of America, Inc.
3300 Penrose Place, P.O. Box 9140, Boulder, Colorado 80301

Printed in U.S.A.

GSA Books Science Editor Abhijit Basu

Library of Congress Cataloging-in-Publication Data
Himalaya and Tibet : mountain roots to mountain tops / edited by
    Allison Macfarlane. Rasoul B. Sorkhabi and Jay Quade.
        p.   cm.   --   (Special paper : 328)
    Includes bibliographical references and index.
    ISBN 0-8137-2328-0
    1. Geology--Himalaya Mountains Region. 2. Geology--China--Tibet.
I. Macfarlane, Allison. II. Sorkhabi, Rasoul B., 1961-
III. Quade, Jay, 1955-   . IV. Series: Special paper (Geological
Society of America) : 328.
QE319.H5H512   1999
555.496--DC21   98-43984
                                                                CIP

Cover: Mount Everest (8,848 m); photo by Rasoul Sorkhabi, Nepal, 1994.

10   9   8   7   6   5   4   3   2

Contents

PLATE
(in pocket)

Geological Society of America
Special Paper 328
1999

Himalaya and Tibet:
Mountain roots to mountain tops

Rasoul B. Sorkhabi*
Department of Geology, Arizona State University, Tempe, Arizona 85287-1404
Allison Macfarlane*
Department of Geography and Earth Systems Science, George Mason University, Fairfax, Virginia 22030-4444

> *The richest and most varied elements for pursuing an analysis of this nature present themselves to the eyes of the traveler in the scenery of Southern Asia, ... where the same subterranean forces that once raised these mountain chains still shake them to their foundation and threaten their downfall.*
> —Alexander von Humboldt in Cosmos (1854, v. 1, p. 27)

INTRODUCTION

High mountains and plateaus of south-central Asia form the largest, loftiest, and youngest highland topography on Earth. Persian geographers called it "Bâm-i Dunyâ"—the Roof of the World. The Tibetan Plateau has an area of 2.5×10^6 km^2 and an average elevation of 5000 m, and is surrounded by high mountains of the Himalaya to the south, the Kunlun to the north, and the Karakoram and Pamir to the west (Fig. 1). In the "Pamir Knot," several major mountain ranges—Tian Shan, Karakoram, and Hindu Kush—merge with the Pamir mountains. These remote highlands hold crucial keys to understanding the tectonic and geomorphic processes shaping the Earth and contribute in many ways to the natural resources and environment. In the first half of the nineteenth century, explorers, surveyors, and geologists working for the British East India Company conducted preliminary mapping in the western Himalaya. Systematic geological work in the region began with the establishment of the Geological Survey of India in Calcutta in 1851. In the mid-nineteenth century, the Survey of India (established in 1800 in southern India) extended its cartographic work to the Himalayan foothills. This century-old field work provided the foundation for our present-day research on the Himalaya-Tibet geology. Some of the fundamental discoveries in the earth sciences, such as monsoon meteorology, isostasy, Tethys, *Ramap-*

ithecus and other Miocene hominoids, Gondwanaland, continental collision, postcollisional leucogranite genesis, inverted metamorphism, and crustal extension coeval with compression in collision zones have arisen largely from studies in south-central Asia. The classic knowledge of Himalayan geology has been synthesized in several volumes (Burrard and Hayden, 1934; Pascoe, 1964; Gansser, 1964; Wadia, 1975; Thakur, 1992). Sorkhabi (1997) reviewed the historical development of Himalayan geology as a scientific activity.

The Himalaya-Karakoram-Tibet orogenic system may be the highest and largest culmination of Earth's crust since the early Paleozoic "Pan African" mountains, as evidenced from strontium isotope analyses of the Phanerozoic marine sedimentary rocks (indicative of the magnitude of continental denudation) (e.g., Edmond, 1992). Large rivers originating in the Himalaya-Tibetan region account for 25% of the global sedimentation budget, although they drain only 4.2% of the land surface (Raymo and Ruddiman, 1992). Fed by perpetual snow and monsoon rains, these rivers provide fresh water for more than one billion people in south Asia, nearly one-fifth of the world's population. Sediments shed from the Himalaya and Tibet have formed the world's largest marine fan (the Bengal Fan) and river delta (the Ganges Delta), as well as the most extensive, fertile agricultural lands in northern India and China which have supported human settlements for millennia. The influence of the Himalaya-Tibet highland on the Asian monsoon system and mid-latitude atmospheric circulations, and perhaps on the development of late Cenozoic glacial climate in the Northern Hemisphere, has drawn much interest in recent years (e.g., Quade et al., 1989, 1995; Prell and Kutzbach, 1992; Raymo and Ruddiman, 1992).

*Present address: Sorkhabi, Japan National Oil Corporation, Technology Research Center, Geology and Geochemistry Section, 2-2 Hamada, 1-chome, Mihama-ku, Chiba-shi 261, Japan; Macfarlane, Belfer Center for Science and International Affairs, Kennedy School of Government, Harvard University, 79 JFK Street, Cambridge, Massachusetts 02138.

Sorkhabi, R. B., and Macfarlane, A., 1999, Himalaya and Tibet: Mountain roots to mountain tops, in Macfarlane, A., Sorkhabi, R. B., and Quade, J., eds., Himalaya and Tibet: Mountain Roots to Mountain Tops: Boulder, Colorado, Geological Society of America Special Paper 328.

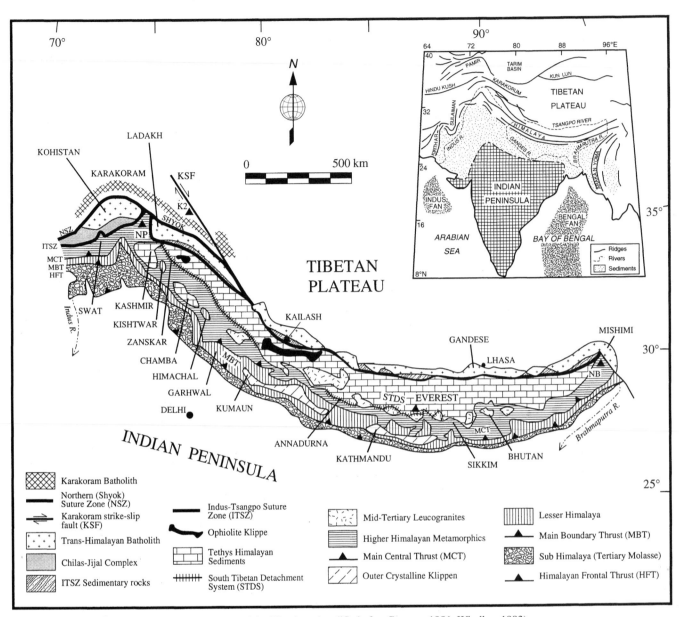

Figure 1. A geological map of the Himalaya (modified after Gansser, 1981; Windley, 1983).

Fundamental geological processes have been shaping the Himalaya-Tibet region throughout the Cenozoic. Investigating the nature of these processes and their operation in space and time has far-reaching implications for our understanding of how the crust of this planet functions and how it has evolved.

India-Asia Collision Tectonics

A major advance in our understanding of Asian tectonics is the notion that the Asian continent has been built up from the accretion of fragments of Gondwanaland with the Siberian shield (Angaraland) over the past 500 m.y., following the closure of "Tethyan" (sensu lato) oceanic basins (see Sengör and Natal'in, 1996, for a recent review).

The collision of India (as the latest fragment of Gondwanaland) with Asia resulted in the formation of the Himalaya along the leading edge of the Indian continental plate and in the reactivation, deformation, and uplift of a large tract of south-central Asian crust. This concept of collision tectonics and crustal reactivation due to continental drift was eloquently developed by Argand (1924), and revived in a plate tectonic framework (Dewey and Bird, 1970; Powell and Conaghan, 1973; Molnar and Tapponnier, 1975).

Over the past two decades unprecedented international attention has focused on the geology of the Himalaya and Tibet. This has been partly due to the opening of many parts of this remote region to foreign visitors, and partly due to the advent of the plate tectonic theory, which recognizes the Himalaya-Tibet orogenic system as the type example of continent-to-continent collision tectonics for the following reasons (see also Mattauer, 1986).

1. The geneses of the Himalaya and Tibetan Plateau are clearly linked (both in terms of tectonic setting and timing of events) to the Cenozoic convergence between India and Asia, following the closure of the Mesozoic Neo-Tethys ocean.

2. Compared to many ancient eroded orogens, there is a complete record of precollisional and postcollisional events in the Himalaya.

3. Orogenic and geomorphic activities in the Himalaya are continuing, making the region a natural field laboratory for studying the processes of continental deformation, crustal thickening, and landscape evolution.

4. Due to high rates of uplift and denudation and incision of deep valleys perpendicular to the strike of mountains, the Himalaya offer excellent exposures of rocks and structures for investigating a diverse array of geological phenomena.

5. Despite local complexities, the overall structure and lithology of the Himalaya are fairly uniform; thus deriving and applying testable theories on fundamental orogenic processes can be done with increased confidence.

It is significant that plate tectonic theory grew out of studies of the structure and dynamics of oceanic lithosphere rather than continental lithosphere. Continental deformation is too diffuse and the thermotectonic behavior of continents too complex to be subjected to the simple motion of rigid plates, wherein deformation is confined to narrow plate boundaries (McKenzie, 1977). The India-Asia collision zone provides unique opportunities to better understand the processes of continental tectonics. A major challenge is to quantify the response of the Asian lithosphere to the stress regime induced by the convergence of India: considering the great expanse of the region, much more geological, geochemical, and geophysical data are required.

Geophysical surveys give key constraints on the deep structures of the double-normal continental crust in the India-Asia convergence zone (see Molnar, 1988, for a review). In the 1990s, the INDEPTH Project obtained seismic profiles in southern Tibet (Zhao et al., 1993; Nelson et al., 1996). Gao et al. (this volume) present results of a 900 km seismic profile conducted by Chinese scientists in northernmost Tibet that constrains the crustal structure from the northern margin of the Kunlun as far as the Mongolian border.

Since India collided with Asia 55 ± 10 Ma, it has moved northward 3,000 m (Klootwijik, 1984; Patriat and Achache, 1984; Searle et al., 1987). Some of the intriguing tectonic questions concern the mechanisms to accommodate this "missing continental crust." Various models such as whole-scale continental subduction of Greater India beneath Asia, ductile deformation and basement reactivation in the Himalaya as well as the entire region of Tibet, and lateral escape or extrusion tectonics of the Indochina block have been proposed (see Dewey et al., 1989; Le Pichon et al., 1992, for reviews). Other questions concern the kinematics and uplift history of Tibet and the Himalaya (e.g., Harrison et al., 1992; Sorkhabi and Stump,

1993). Xu et al. (this volume) argue that the thermotectonics of the interior of the Tibetan Plateau is controlled by a mantle diapir while the margins of the plateau are subjected to intra-continental subduction.

A Geological Framework of the Himalaya

The Himalaya extend for about 2,500 km in a northwest-northeast direction along the leading margin of the Indian continental plate and are bounded by the Nanga Parbat syntaxis in the northwest and the Namche Barwa syntaxis in the northeast. The syntaxial bends of the Himalaya join the lineaments of Burma (the Arakan Yoma) on the east and of Pakistan (the Sulaiman and Kirther Ranges) on the west. These circum-Indian mountains also resulted from the India-Asia collision, although they are much less studied. Schelling discusses the structure of southern Kirthar Range in Pakistan.

The Himalaya have been traditionally divided into six lithotectonic zones extending in parallel belts (Gansser, 1964; Le Fort, 1975; Windley, 1983; Thakur, 1992) (Fig. 1). From north to south, they are as follows: (1) the Trans-Himalayan batholith; (2) the Indus-Tsangpo suture zone; (3) the Tethyan (Tibetan) Himalaya; (4) the Higher (Greater) Himalaya; (5) the Lesser (Lower) Himalaya; and (6) the Sub-Himalaya.

The Trans-Himalaya is essentially composed of a large, linear plutonic complex (the Trans-Himalayan batholith) covered partly by forearc and continental molasse sedimentary rocks derived from the uplift and erosion of magmatic rocks. The Trans-Himalayan batholith is a composite I-type plutonic complex ranging from gabbro through diorite to granite. It formed in several magmatic phases from 110 to 40 Ma due to partial melting of the subducting Neo-Tethyan slab beneath the southern margin of Asia (Honegger et al., 1982). The Trans-Himalaya is divided into the Kohistan block (to the west of the Nanga Parbat syntaxis), the Ladakh block (between Nanga Parbat and the Karakoram strike-slip fault), Kailas, Gandese (southern Tibet), and Mishimi (to the east of the Namche Barwa syntaxis). In the Kohistan block, the Jijal-Chilas complex is regarded as the tilted base of a Cretaceous island arc. Mikoshiba et al. report new geochemical and Rb-Sr age data from the arc-type Chilas intrusive rocks.

Gansser (1964) first defined the "Indus Suture Line" as the tectonic boundary between India and Asia along which the Tethys was consumed. The Indus-Tsangpo suture zone crops out in the upper valleys of the Indus and Tsangpo (Brahmaputra) rivers, and is composed of deep-sea and flysch sedimentary rocks, blueschist metamorphic rocks, ultrabasic and submarine volcanic rocks, and plutonic intrusions. In the western parts of the Himalaya, a second suture zone to the north, the Northern suture zone (or the Shyok-Chalt suture zone, named after the Shyok and Chalt Rivers in Kohistan and Ladakh, respectively), separates the Kohistan-Ladakh blocks from the Karakoram mountains. The Shyok-Chalt suture formed in mid-Cretaceous time from the collision of the Kohistan-Ladakh island arc with the Karakoram block, before the early Eocene collision of India along the Indus-Tsangpo suture zone (Searle, 1991, and references therein).

The less-accessible Karakoram mountains have had a complex thermotectonic history in Mesozoic and Cenozoic time. Searle (1991) ended his book with the remark that one-half of the total area of the Karakoram Range may still be labeled as unexplored. This is especially true of the eastern Karakoram of India. Sinha et al. present the results of their mapping and stratigraphic work in this area.

The Tethyan (Tibetan) Himalaya has an apparent thickness of 10–17 km and has preserved highly fossiliferous Tethyan marine rocks deposited on the shelf and slope of the Indian continental margin from Late Proterozoic–Cambrian through early Eocene time. Except in the Pakistan Himalaya, the Paleozoic-Mesozoic Tethys Himalaya rocks are largely unmetamorphosed, and occur in synclinorium-type basins to the south of the Indus-Tsangpo suture zone. Hughes and Jell provide important data on the Cambrian trilobite faunas from the western Himalaya of India. Liu and Einsele present a detailed sedimentologic and paleogeographic study of the Indian passive margin during the Jurassic.

Another study of pre-Himalayan events in the less-investigated region of Balochistan of northeastern Pakistan is documented by Khan et al., who suggest that the 76–66 Ma Parh Group basalts mark the passage of the Tethyan floor over the Reunion hotspot prior to movement of the Indian shield over the same hotspot at ca. 66 Ma, as represented by the Deccan Traps.

The postcollisional culmination of India-Asia tectonics is best revealed in the Higher Himalayan Crystalline sequence (also called the Greater Himalaya or Central Crystalline zone in the Indian Himalaya and the Tibetan Slab in Nepal). This zone constitutes the metamorphic core of the Himalaya affected by ductile deformation and is the axis of maximum uplift of the orogen. The High Himalayan Crystalline sequence comprises a 10–15-km-thick assemblage of mica schist, quartzite, paragneiss, orthogneiss, migmatite, and Miocene leucogranite bodies. The regional metamorphism seems to have been polyphase, an early Barrovian type followed by a Buchan type, and finally localized retrograde events. Thermobarometric analyses reveal pressures of 500–800 MPa and temperatures of 475–825 °C for the peak metamorphic conditions (see Hodges et al., 1989, for a review; Macfarlane, 1995). The metamorphism is recorded by mineral assemblages of upper greenschist to amphibolite facies; index minerals are biotite to sillimanite. The deformation fabric shows a consistent top-to-south sense of movement, in accordance with the northward dip of the Main Central thrust, which brings the Higher Himalayan Crystalline sequence atop the Lesser Himalaya. The MCT, a longitudinal thrust fault first mapped by Heim and Gansser (1939) in the Garhwal Himalaya, is in many traverses a several kilometer-thick deformed zone affected by varying degrees of shearing and imbrication (e.g., Hashimoto et al., 1973; Macfarlane et al., 1992).

The collision of India may have occurred first in the north-western part of the Himalaya at 65-55 Ma and then terminated on the eastern part at 50-45 Ma (Klootwijik, 1984; Patriat and Achache, 1984). This diachronous, oblique convergence should also have differential impact on the metamorphic and crustal melting history of the Higher Himalayan Crystalline sequence. Guillot et al. explore this possibility using the pressure-temperature paths of metamorphic rocks and geochronological data from the anatectic leucogranites in various sectors of the Himalaya.

The well-known Miocene two-mica tourmaline-bearing leucogranites of the Higher Himalaya crop out predominantly near the contact the Crystalline sequence with the Tethyan Himalaya. While it is widely agreed that the leucogranites were formed by the partial melting of the Indian continental crust (e.g., Le Fort et al., 1987), the heat source for their genesis remains controversial. In recent years, a more complex history of the leucogranites has emerged in the Nanga Parbat area of Pakistan Himalaya, which yield both very old (Eocene) and very young (Pliocene) leucogranites (Zeitler and Chamberlain, 1991). Whittington et al. present field and geochemical data on the contrasting anatectic processes at Nanga Parbat.

The geology of Nanga Parbat has drawn much attention due to reports of extremely rapid exhumation rates and very young tectonothermal events (e.g., Zeitler et al., 1982; Zeitler and Chamberlain, 1991). The geology has, however, proved to be extremely complex due to multiple syntaxial structures, necessitating detailed studies. DiPietro et al. present such a detailed map for the Indus syntaxis in the Swat area to the west of the Nanga Parbat syntaxis. The contact between the Nanga Parbat syntaxis and the Karakoram is explored by Pêcher and Le Fort.

The nature of the contact between the Higher Himalayan Crystalline sequence and the Tethyan Himalaya has a history of controversy. Mapping in southern Tibet (Burg et al., 1984; Burchfiel et al., 1992) and India (Herren, 1987; Valdiya, 1989) indicates that this contact is a low-angle normal fault system referred to as the South Tibetan detachment system (Burchfiel et al., 1992). This extensional structure extends parallel to the strike of the Main Central thrust and dips to the north. It has been interpreted as dorsal collapse of a Himalayan topographic high in the early Miocene when the wedge of the Higher Himalayan Crystalline sequence extruded by coincident movement on both the Main Central thrust and the South Tibetan detachment system (Burg et al., 1984; Burchfiel and Royden, 1985; Hodges et al., 1992). The kinematic and temporal links between compressional and extensional structures in the Himalaya have drawn much attention in recent years. Godin et al. analyze the complex deformational history of the hanging wall of the South Tibetan detachment system (locally called the Annapurna detachment fault by the authors) in central Nepal. Carosi et al. present field evidence of widespread extensional features in the footwall of the South Tibetan detachment system in the Mount Everest region of Nepal. Manickavasagam et al. present new structural and metamorphic data from several sections of the western Himalayan of India and argue that the entire Higher Himalayan Crystalline sequence should be viewed as a distributed shear zone affected by both compressional and extensional tectonics. They then use the distributed shear model to explain the long-standing problem of the inverted metamorphic sequence that is observed from the Lesser Himalaya through the Main Central thrust zone to the High Himalaya.

The Lesser Himalaya is delimited by the Main Central thrust in the north and the Main Boundary thrust in the south. The Lesser Himalaya mainly consists of the Proterozoic and lower Paleozoic sedimentary rocks of the Indian platform, some of which were metamorphosed to greenschist facies. Scattered capping of Paleocene-Eocene limestone and shale (the Subathu Formation), synclinal outliers (klippen) of the Higher Himalaya metamorphic rocks intruded by the Cambrian-Ordovician ("Pan African") granites are also in this zone. Due to the lack of fossils, the ages of lithostratigraphic formations and displacement history of rock units in the Lesser Himalaya are poorly constrained. Upreti and Le Fort argue against a one-to-one relationship between the crystalline outliers in the Lesser Himalaya and their supposed "root zones" in the Higher Himalayan Crystalline sequence; they base their arguments on variations in lithology and metamorphic grade, and alternatively hypothesize that the root zones may be concealed beneath the Main Central thrust.

HIMALAYAN FORELAND: THIN-SKINNED TECTONICS, SEDIMENTS, AND LANDFORMS

The crustal structures of the Himalaya inferred from microearthquake studies (Seeber et al., 1981), reflection seismic profiles (Zhao et al., 1993), and structural cross sections (Schelling and Arita, 1991) demonstrate both thick-skinned (basement reactivation of the Crystalline sequence) and thin-skinned tectonics in the Himalayan fold and thrust belt. All of the major Himalayan faults seem to join a mid-crustal decollement (the Main Himalayan thrust of Zhao et al., 1993). The sequence of thrusting appears to become younger from north to south, toward the Himalayan foreland, which also reflects the temporal pattern of uplift in the Himalaya (Gansser, 1981; Sorkhabi and Stump, 1993).

The active tectonics of the Himalayan foreland are conspicuous in the Sub-Himalayan zone, which consists of clastic sediments derived from the uplift and erosion of the Himalaya and deposited by rivers in a foreland basin. The Sub-Himalayan molasse has been faulted and folded, and forms the low-altitude Siwalik Hills skirting the Lesser Himalaya. The sediments have been grouped into the Murree (Dharamsala) Group (late Eocene?–early Miocene) which is overlain by the Siwalik (Churia) Group (early Miocene–Pleistocene). The Sub-Himalaya is overthrust by the Lesser Himalaya along the Main Boundary thrust. To the south, the Sub-Himalaya overthrusts the Holocene alluvial tracts of the Indo-Gangetic plains along an active fault system called the Himalayan Frontal thrust.

Kumar et al. discuss basin evolution and sedimentation in the Siwalik zone of India and controls of south-verging Himalayan thrust tectonics during the Pliocene-Pleistocene. Jadoon et al. present a seismic profile that constrains the thin-skinned tectonics of the Pliocene-Pleistocene Siwalik formations in Potwar Plateau (north Pakistan), a region well known for its petroleum resources; these authors calculate shortening and uplift rates for an overthrust wedge from structural cross sections and stratigraphic constraints. Pogue et al. report their research on the structural and stratigraphic relations between the cover sediments and basement rocks in a section of the Pakistan Himalaya.

The geomorphic consequences of active tectonics is an important field of study, and in this respect, the Himalayan region is second to none. Uhlir and Schram document large-scale landslides in the Ganesh Himal, northwest of Kathmandu. Their study makes a case for hazard mapping that is badly needed for the populous areas of the Himalaya.

Bendick and Bilham touch on an important issue that the Indian shield may not be as rigid and passive as it is commonly supposed. They examine "buckles" in the Malabar coast of southwest India and relate these structures to the effects of the ongoing Indian collision.

ABOUT THIS VOLUME

Since 1985, a series of international annual meetings, the Himalaya-Karakoram-Tibet (HKT) Workshops, have been held; Leicester, United Kingdom (U.K.) (1985); Nancy, France (1986); London, U.K. (1987); Lausanne, Switzerland (1988); Milan, Italy (1990); Grenoble, France (1991); Oxford, U.K. (1992); Vienna, Austria (1993); Kathmandu, Nepal (1994); Ascona, Switzerland (1995). The 11th HKT Workshop was held in Flagstaff, Arizona, in April 1996 (Sorkhabi et al., 1996). This first HKT Workshop in America was the logical outcome of an increasing involvement of North American geologists in the studies of the Himalaya and Tibet over the past two decades.

Some of the past HKT Workshops have resulted in the publication of the following proceedings volumes: Barnicoat and Treloar (1989); Baud (1989); Treloar and Searle (1993); Upreti and Dhital (1995); Burg (1996a, 1996b).

In keeping this useful tradition, this *special paper* contains a collection of selected, refereed papers presented at the 11th HKT Workshop in Arizona. In editing this volume, we have paid special attention to the novelty of data and ideas. Another feature of this volume is the attempt to integrate both "hard-rock" and "soft-rock" geology, paleotectonic and neotectonic history, and endogenic (tectonic) and exogenic (geomorphic) processes in the Himalaya. No single volume can offer solutions to the numerous problems of Himalayan geology. Nevertheless, we hope that this collection of papers presenting new data and integrating diverse fields of research in a regional framework is a step forward in our scientific journey.

ACKNOWLEDGMENTS

The 11th Himalaya-Karakoram-Tibet Workshop was held at the Du Bois Center of Northern Arizona University, Flagstaff, from April 28 to May 2, 1996. As organizers of the workshop, we thank all of the nearly 120 participants at the workshop, which made this a successful meeting with their punctual attendance, presentations (both oral and poster), comments, and discussions.

Financial support for the workshop came largely from a grant from the Continental Dynamics Program of the U.S. National Science Foundation (NSF). The NSF grant supported travel funds for some researchers from the Himalayan countries (China, India, Nepal, and Pakistan) and students from Europe, as well as the production of this proceedings volume.

George Mason University generously provided much of the initial financial and clerical help to the workshop. In particular, the staff in the Geography and Earth Systems Science Department gave their time to support the Workshop. Elenore Lavender of Travel World ably handled the accommodation, banquet party, and may other chores. The field trip to the Grand Canyon was led by Troy Péwé and Edmund Stump, and the Basin and Range field trip was led by Stephen Reynolds, all at Arizona State University. We thank friends at University of Arizona—Jan Price, Lois Roe, Clark Isachsen, Tom Moore, and David Richards—for help with, for example, transportation vehicles, registration desk, and projectors. We also thank David Spencer for his help in many ways, including sharing with us his files of the 10th workshop. Sorkhabi acknowledges a grant from the NSF Tectonics Program and an Invited Fellowship from the Japan Society for the Promotion of Science (JSPS) at Hokkaido University.

We would like to thank Abhijit Basu (Books Editor, GSA) and for his time, advice, and official handling of the publication. We thank Jay Quade and Kazunori Arita for critically reading this introduction.

We are grateful to the following colleagues and friends who kindly reviewed the papers submitted for this volume: David Applegate, Kazunori Arita, Gary Axen, Loren Babcock, Asish Basu, Aymon Baud, Sam Bowring, John Bridge, Michael Brookfield, John Carter, C. Page Chamberlain, Margaret Coleman, Brian Currie, Peter DeCelles, Steve Ellen, Maurizio Gaetani, Bernhard Grassemann, Brad Hacker, Michael Hauck, Kip Hodges, Mary Hubbard, Robert Lawrence, Robert Lillie, Yizhaq Makovsky, Gautam Mitra, C. J. Northrup, David Pivnik, Carolyn Ruppel, Daniel Schelling, John Shroder, Jr., Michael Searle, Albrecht Steck, Peter Treloar, K. S. Valdiya, Igor Villa, David Waters, Robert Webb, Neil Wells, Stephen Westrop, John Wheeler, Brian Willis, Robert Yeats, An Yin, Mitsuo Yoshida, and George Zandt.

REFERENCES CITED

Argand, E., 1924, La tectonique de l'Asie: Compte-Rendu XIII Congrès Géologique International, Belgique, 1922: Liège, France, Vaillant-Carmanne, p. 171–372.

Barnicoat, A. C., and Treloar, P. J., eds., 1989, Himalayan metamorphism: Journal of Metamorphic Geology, v. 7, no. 1, 149 p.

Baud, A., ed., 1989, Colloque Himalaya-Karakoram-Tibet, Lausanne, 1988: Eclogae Geologicae Helvetiae, v. 82, part 2, p. 583–715.

Burchfiel, C., and Royden, L. H., 1985, North-south extension under the convergent Himalayan regime: Geology, v. 13, p. 679–682.

Burchfiel, B. C., Chen, Z., Hodges, K. V., Liu, Y., Royden, L. H., Deng, C., and Xu, J., 1992, The south Tibetan detachment system, Himalayan orogen: Extension contemporaneous with and parallel to shortening in a collisional mountain belt: Geological Society of America Special Paper 269, 41 p.

Burg, J.-P., ed., 1996a, Uplift and exhumation of metamorphic rocks, the Himalayan Tibet region: Tectonophysics, v. 260, 226 p.

Burg, J.-P., ed., 1996b, Special issue: Geodinamica Acta, v. 9, no. 2-3, 233 p.

Burg, J.-P., Brunel, M., Gapais, D., Chen, G. M., and Liu, G. H., 1984, Deformation of leucogranites of the crystalline Main Central Sheet in southern Tibet (China): Journal of Structural Geology, v. 6, p. 535–542.

Burrard, S. G., and Hayden, H. H., 1934, A sketch of the geography and geology of the Himalaya Mountains and Tibet: (revised by S. G. Burrard and A. M. Herron) Calcutta, Government of India Press, 359 p.

Dewey, J. F., and Bird, J. M., 1970, Mountain belts and the new global tectonics: Journal of Geophysical Research, v. 75B, p. 2625–2647.

Dewey, J. F., Cande, S., and Pitman, W. C., 1989, Tectonic evolution of the India-Eurasia collision zone: Eclogae Geologicae Helvetiae, v. 82, p. 717–734.

Edmond, J., 1992, Himalayan tectonics, weathering processes, and the strontium isotope record in marine limestones: Science, v. 256, p. 1594–1597.

Gansser, A. 1964, Geology of the Himalayas: London, Interscience Publishers, 289 p.

Gansser, A., 1981, The geodynamic history of the Himalaya, in Gupta, H. K., and Delany, F. M., eds., Zagros, Hindu Kush, Himalaya, geodynamic evolution: American Geophysical Union Geodynamic Series 3, p. 111–121.

Harrison, T. M., Copeland, P., Kidd, W. S. F., and Yin, A., 1992, Raising Tibet: Science, v. 255, p. 1663–1670.

Hashimoto, S., Ohta, Y., and Akiba, C., eds., 1973, Geology of the Nepal Himalayas: Tokyo, Saikon Publishing Co., 286 p.

Heim, A., and Gansser, A., 1939, The Central Himalayas—Geological observations of the Swiss Expedition of 1936: Mémoires de la Société Helvétique des Sciences Naturelles, v. 73, 245 p.

Herren, E., 1987, The Zanskar shear zone: Northeast-southwest extension within the Higher Himalayas (Ladakh, India): Geology, v. 15, p. 409–413.

Hodges, K. V., Hubbard, M. S., and Silverberg, D. S., 1989, Metamorphic constraints on the thermal evolution of the central Himalayan orogen: Royal Society of London Philosophical Transactions, v. A326, p. 257–280.

Hodges, K. V., Parrish, R. R., Housh, T. B., Lux, D. R., Burchfiel, B. C., Royden, L. H., and Chen, Z., 1992, Simultaneous Miocene extension and shortening in the Himalayan orogen: Science, v. 258, p. 1466–1470.

Honegger, K., Dietrich, V., Frank, W., Gansser, A., Thöni, M., and Trommsdorff, V., 1982, Magmatism and metamorphism in the Ladakh Himalayas (the Indus-Tsangpo suture zone): Earth and Planetary Science Letters, v. 60, p. 253–292.

Klootwijik, C., 1984, A review of Indian Phanerozoic paleomagnetism; implications for the India-Asia collision: Tectonophysics, v. 105, p. 331–353.

Le Fort, P., 1975, Himalayas—The collided range: Present knowledge of the continental arc: American Journal of Science, v. 275A, p. 1–44.

Le Fort, P., Cuney, M., Deniel, C., Frances-Lonard, C., Sheppard, S. M. F., Upreti, B. N., and Vidal, P., 1987, Crustal generation of the Himalayan leucogranites: Tectonophysics, v. 134, p. 39–57.

Le Picheon, X., Fourier, M., and Julivet, L., 1992, Kinematics, topography, shortening and extrusion in the India-Eurasia collision: Tectonics, v. 11, p. 1085–1098.

Macfarlane, A. M., 1995, An evaluation of the inverted metamorphic gradient at Langtang National Park, central Nepal Himalaya: Journal of Metamorphic Geology, v. 13, p. 595–612.

Macfarlane, A. M., Hodges, K. V., and Lux, V., 1992, A structural analysis of the Main Central Thrust zone, Langtang National Park, central Nepal Himalaya: Geological Society of America Bulletin, v. 104, p. 1389–1402.

Mattauer, M., 1986, Intracontinental subduction, crust-mantle decollement and crustal-stacking wedge in the Himalayas and other collision belts, *in* Coward, M. P., and Ries, A. C., eds., Collision tectonics: Geological Society of London Special Publication No. 19, p. 37–50.

McKenzie, D., 1977, Can plate tectonics describe continental deformation?, *in* Biju-Duval, B., and Jarvis, G. T., eds., Structural history of the Mediterranean basins: Paris, Editions Technip, p. 189–196.

Molnar, P., 1988, A review of geophysical constraints on the deep structure of the Tibetan plateau, the Himalaya and the Karakoram, and their tectonic implications: Royal Society of London, Philosophical Transactions, v. A326, p. 33–88.

Molnar, P., and Tapponnier, P., 1975, Cenozoic tectonics of Asia: Effects of a continental collision: Science, v. 189, p. 419–426.

Nelson, K. D., Zhao, W., and INDEPTH Team, 1996, Partially molten middle crust beneath southern Tibet: Synthesis of Project INDEPTH results: Science, v. 274, p. 1684–1688.

Pascoe, E. H., 1964, A manual of the geology of India and Burma (v. III): Calcutta, Geological Survey of India.

Patriat, P., and Achache, J., 1984, India-Eurasia collision chronology has implications for crustal shortening and driving mechanism of plates: Nature, v. 311, p. 615–621.

Powell, C. M. A., and Conaghan, P. J., 1973, Plate tectonics and the Himalayas: Earth and Planetary Science Letters, v. 20, p. 1–12.

Prell, W. L., and Kutzbach, J. E., 1992, Sensitivity of the Indian monsoon to forcing parameters and implications for its evolution: Nature, v. 360, p. 646–650.

Quade, J., Cerling, T. E., and Bowman, J. R., 1989, Development of Asian monsoon revealed by marked ecological shift during the latest Miocene in northern Pakistan: Nature, v. 342, p. 163–166.

Quade, J., Cater, J. M. L., Ohja, T. P., Adam, J., and Harrison, T. M., 1995, Late Miocene environmental change in Nepal and the northern Indian subcontinent: Stable isotopic evidence from paleosols: Geological Society of America Bulletin, v. 107, p. 1381–1397.

Raymo, M. E., and Ruddiman, W. F., 1992, Tectonic forcing of late Cenozoic climate: Nature, v. 359, p. 117–122.

Schelling, D., and Arita, K., 1991, Thrust tectonics, crustal shortening, and the structure of the far-eastern Nepal Himalaya: Tectonics, v. 10, p. 851–862.

Searle, M. P., 1991, Geology and tectonics of the Karakoram Mountains: Chichester, John Wiley, 358 p.

Searle, M. P., Windley, B. F., Coward, M. P., Cooper, D. J. W., Rex, A. J., Rex, D., Li, T., Xiao, X., Jan, M. Q., Thakur, V. C., and Kumar, S., 1987, The closing of Tethys and the tectonics of the Himalaya: Geological Society of America Bulletin, v. 98, p. 678–701.

Seeber, L., Armbruster, J. G., and Quittmeyer, R. C., 1981, Seismicity and continental subduction in the Himalayan arc, *in* Gupta, H. K., and Delany, F. M., eds., Zagros, Hindu Kush, Himalaya, geodynamic evolution: American Geophysical Union Geodynamic Series 3, p. 215–242.

Sengör, A. M. C. and Natal'in, B. A., 1996, Paleotectonics of Asia: Fragments of a synthesis, *in* Yin, A., and Harrison, M., eds., The tectonic evolution of Asia: Cambridge, Cambridge University Press, p. 486–640.

Sorkhabi, R. B., 1997, Historical development of Himalayan geology: Geological Society of India Journal, v. 49, p. 89–108.

Sorkhabi, R. B. and Stump, E., 1993, Rise of the Himalaya: A geochronologic approach: GSA Today, v. 3, p. 85, 88–92.

Sorkhabi, R. B., Macfarlane, A., and Quade, J., 1996, 'Roof of the Earth' offers clues about how our planet was shaped: Eos (Transactions, American Geophysical Union), v. 77, p. 385–387.

Thakur, V. C., 1992, Geology of Western Himalaya: Oxford, Pergamon Press, 363 p.

Treloar, P. J., and Searle, M. P., eds., 1993, Himalayan Tectonics: Geological Society of London Special Publication 74, 630 p.

Upreti, B. N., and Dhital, M. R., eds., 1995, Proceedings of the 9th Himalaya-Karakoram-Tibet Workshop: Nepal Geological society Journal, v. 11, 298 p.

Valdiya, K. S., 1989, Trans-Himadri intracrustal fault and basement upwarps south of Indus-Tsangpo suture zone, *in* Malinconico, L. L., and Lillie, R. J., eds., Tectonics of Western Himalayas: Geological Society of America Special Paper 232, p. 153–168.

Wadia, D. N., 1975, Geology of India (fourth edition): New Delhi, Tata-McGraw-Hill, 508 p.

Windley, B. F., 1983, Metamorphism and tectonics of the Himalaya: Geological Society of London Journal, v. 140, p. 849–865.

Zeitler, P. K., and Chamberlain, C. P., 1991, Petrogenetic and tectonic significance of young leucogranites from the northwestern Himalaya, Pakistan: Tectonics, v. 10, p. 729–741.

Zeitler, P. K., Johnson, N. M., Naeser, C. W., and Tahirkheli, R. A. K., 1982, Fission-track evidence for Quaternary uplift of the Nanga Parbat region, Pakistan: Nature, v. 298, p. 255–257.

Zhao, W., Nelson, K. D., and INDEPTH Team, 1993, Deep seismic reflection evidence for continental underthrusting beneath southern Tibet: Nature, v. 366, p. 557–559.

MANUSCRIPT ACCEPTED BY THE SOCIETY FEBRUARY 3, 1998

Geological Society of America
Special Paper 328
1999

Lithospheric structure and geodynamic model of the Golmud-Ejin transect in northern Tibet

Gao Rui, Cheng Xiangzhou, and Wu Gongjian*
Lithosphere Research Center, Chinese Academy of Geological Sciences, Beijing 100037

ABSTRACT

This chapter summarizes the general geological setting and the lithospheric structure of the Golmud-Ejin transect, in a suggested preliminary geodynamic model. The transect has been divided into five terranes; the names of these terranes and their boundaries are (from south to north) the North Kunlun–Qaidam terrane, bordered by the North Jun Ul fault; the Central-South Qilian terrane, bordered by the Central Qilian fault; the North Qilian terrane, bordered by the North Border thrust; the South Beishan terrane, bordered by the Shibanjing-Xiaohuangshan fault; and the North Beishan terrane. The Moho beneath the transect corridor is in the range of about 40–73 km in depth; it is deepest beneath the Central-South Qilian terrane and shallowest beneath Ejin in the North Beishan terrane. There is a continuous low-velocity layer in the crust along the transect, about 20 km deep and generally 5–10 km thick, having a velocity from 5.80 km/s to 6.05 km/s. Slight changes in velocity of the layer are observed in the Beishan area (only 0.05–0.10 km/s). The northern Qaidam belt and the North Qilian terrane are characterized by high geotemperatures, and the South Beishan terrane and Qaidam terrane have low geotemperatures: the geothermal regime of the Central-South Qilian terrane is between the two. The depth of the high conductivity layer in the upper mantle varies locally within 10 km of the transect, and has an average value of 140–150 km. Recent deformation in northern Tibet has been caused by the major northward movement of the Indian plate and the minor southward indentation of the Siberian plate, resulting in a double-sense compressive stress state. We speculate that the convergent force on the plates results from uneven flow in the mantle. We observe that the compression occurs mainly in the middle and lower crust. Thrusting complicated by strike-slip faulting has occurred in the upper crust, followed by extensional faulting. The significant North Border thrust fault has been discovered by deep seismic reflection profiling in the Hexi corridor in the north Qilian Mountains; the corridor is very important in the dynamics of northern Tibet. The North Border thrust is interpreted as evidence that the Alxa landmass is underthrusting the Qilian Mountains.

* Other researchers: Cui Z.Z., Wu X.Z., (CAGS, Beijing 100037), Meng L.S., Zhu R.X., (Changchun Univ. of Earth Sci., Changchun 130026), Yu Q.F., (Chinese Univ. of Geosci., Beijing 100083), Shen X.J., (Institute of Geology, Academy Sinica, Beijing 100029), Zhu, J.S., (Chengdu Institute of Technology, Chengdu 610059).

Gao Rui, Cheng Xiangzhou, and Wu Gongjian, 1999, Lithospheric structure and geodynamic model of the Golmud-Ejin transect in northern Tibet, *in* Macfarlane, A., Sorkhabi, R. B., and Quade, J., eds., Himalaya and Tibet: Mountain Roots to Mountain Tops: Boulder, Colorado, Geological Society of America Special Paper 328.

LOCATION AND TECTONIC SETTING

The Golmud-Ejin transect traverses about 900 km across northern Tibet (Fig. 1). It begins at the northern margin of the Kunlun Mountains, crossing northerly through the Qaidam basin, Har Lake, the Qilian Mountains, the Hexi corridor, and Beishan, and ending in Ejin Qi near the Sino-Mongolian border. The transect is continuous with the Yadong-Golmud transect in the south (Wu, Gongjian et al., 1991a, 1993). Most geoscientists believe that the continuous northward motion of the Indian plate causes the uplift of the Himalayas and the Tibetan Plateau (Harrison et al., 1992). Results from the Yadong-Golmud transect have shown that the Indian plate has underthrusted Tibet and the crust of the Tibetan block has shortened and thickened (Gao, 1990; Wu, Gongjian et al., 1991b; Gao and Wu, 1995). However, the tectonics of the northern margin of Tibet have not been studied. In particular, the role of the Eurasian plate in the formation of Tibet is not known. The Golmud-Ejin transect crosses four structural belts in northern Tibet; from south to north these are the Qaidam basin, the Qilian Mountains, the Hexi corridor basin, and the Beishan. The consolidation of the basement of the Qaidam basin (about 1,400 Ma) was earlier than that of several terranes of the Qinghai-Tibet Plateau in the south (Li et al., 1982), and

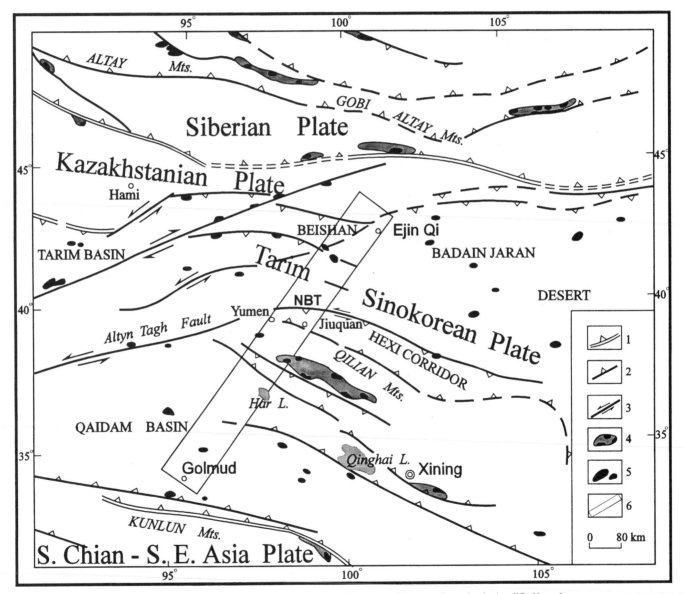

Figure 1. Location and tectonic setting of the Golmud-Ejin transect. The tectonic setting is simplified based on the map of Asian plate tectonics compiled by Li Chunyu et. al (1982). 1—Suture line, 2—crystalline thrust-system (dashed where inferred), 3—strike-slip fault, 4—ophiolite zone, 5—basic and ultrabasic volcanic rocks, 6—Golmud-Ejin transect strip. Note that the Badain Jaran Desert is the main body of the Alxa landmass.

later than that of the North China platform. New data show that (1) Cenozoic strata of the Qaidam basin are strongly folded, (2) the Qilian Mountains are uplifting rapidly in the Quaternary at a rate of 1.5–1.8 mm/yr, and (3) the northern Qilian Mountains reach their highest elevations, but the crustal root is deepest beneath the southern Qilian Mountains; all of these indicate that the present-day tectonic activities of northern Tibet, its basins and mountains, are affected by the Himalayan orogeny (Bureau of Geology and Mineral Resources of Gansu Province, 1989). Beishan is at the intersection of the Tianshan and the Kelameili tectonic belts, along which the Kazakhstanian block, Siberian block, and the North China platform (the main body of the Sino-Korean plate) converged (Zuo Guochao and He Guoqi, 1990). The Yadong-Golmud and Golmud-Ejin transects together extend north from Yadong in southern Tibet to the southern margin of the Siberian block, so we are able to study the interaction between the Indian plate and Eurasian plate and the deformation and dynamics of the entire continental lithosphere (crust and mantle lithosphere), and its evolution over space and time.

FIELD SURVEY AND PRELIMINARY INTERPRETATION

During 1992–1993, multidisciplinary field surveys of geology, geochemistry, and geophysics were undertaken for the Golmud-Ejin transect. Geophysical studies included wide-angle reflection and deep refraction sounding, magnetelluric sounding (MT), as well as gravimetry, magnetics, and heat-flow measurements. In addition, from the North Qilian Mountains to the Hexi corridor, a deep seismic reflection profile was collected; its location is shown in Figure 2.

The Bouguer gravity anomaly map is compiled by means of the unified data reduction and processing based on the 1:2,500,000 Bouguer gravity map of the People's Republic of China (accomplished jointly by the Institute of Geophysical and Geochemical Exploration and the Regional Gravity Surveying Center of the Ministry of Geology and Mineral Resources, 1989); the data measured at 199 effective physical points (Meng et al., 1995). The mean square error of the Bouguer anomaly is less than $3.0 \times 10^{-5} m/s^2$.

The average point spacing is 10 km and the normal field correction is based on the international gravity formula of 1967:

$$\gamma_0 = 978,031.85 \times (1 + 0.00530233 \sin^2 \psi \\ - 0.00000589 \sin^2 2\psi) \times 10^{-5} m/s^2, \quad (1)$$

where ψ is the latitude of the station. The mean density of the crust is taken as $2.67 \times 10^3 kg/m^3$.

The heat flow profile of the Golmud-Ejin transect is made up of the data measured in 18 boreholes (Shen Xianjie et al., 1995), which are mainly located in the area from the eastern margin to northern margin of the Qaidam basin and the area from northern Qilian to the Hexi corridor. There are two 200 km long zones with no heat flow values in the Central-South Qilian and the North Beishan terranes. The distribution area of

regional heat flow can be tentatively divided into three parts: (1) the belt of low heat flows in the eastern Qaidam basin; (2) the belt of high heat flows in the northern margin of the Qaidam basin or the entire (?) Qilian area; and (3) a belt of low heat flow in the Hexi corridor. The Baishantang heat flow is high in the southern Beishan area, and is unclear in the northern Beishan area.

The total aeromagnetic anomaly (ΔT) was extracted from ΔT Contour Map of Northeastern China, compiled by the Center of Airborne Geophysical Exploration and Remote-Sensing in 1986. This map is on the scale of 1:1,000,000; the contour interval is 10 nT. The International Geomagnetic Reference Field of 1980 is taken as the normal field, the total measuring accuracy is ± 2.0 nT (in the Qaidam basin) and ± 4.9 nT (in the Qilian area), and the clearance is 900–1300 m (in the Qaidam basin), 100 m (in the Beishan area), and 500–1000 m (in the Qilian area).

The transect has been divided into five terranes, based on preliminary results of the surveys, a comprehensive interpretation of seismic tomography using regional earthquakes, remote sensing images, regional gravity and magnetic fields, and geological data (Chen et al., 1995). The names of these terranes (and their boundaries) are (from south to north): North Kunlun-Qaidam terrane (North Jun Ul fault), Central-South Qilian terrane (Central Qilian fault), North Qilian terrane (North Border thrust), South Beishan terrane (Shibanjing-Xiaohuangshan fault), and North Beishan terrane. The principal structures crossed by the Golmud-Ejin transect are shown in Figure 3 (top). The lithosphere structure of the transect is shown in Figure 3B (bottom).

The analysis of modern earthquake epicenters (Fig. 3, item 8) shows that the Altyn Tagh Mountains and the Qilian Mountains form the northern boundary of a zone of intense seismicity in the Qinghai-Tibet Plateau, whereas few earthquakes have occurred in the Tarim basin and Alxa landmass to the north, which thus have the nature of a stable block (see Editorial Board of Seismic Zoning Map of China, 1991). This boundary also coincides with the edge of the plateau defined by filtered imagery of the gravity field and the morphology of the plateau shown by stereoscopic topographic imagery. The rapid uplift of the Altyn Tagh Mountains and the Qilian Mountains in the late Quaternary is coincident with the most recent stages of Himalayan orogeny. We interpret that they are both controlled by the same geodynamic process.

A deep seismic reflection profile (Wu Xyanzhi, et al., 1995; Fig. 4) shows that since the Cenozoic, the North Qilian terrane has been thrust northward over the Hexi corridor. In the early Quaternary, molasse developed extensively at the southern edge of the Hexi corridor (Xiang and Lu, 1990). The sediments beneath the southern edge of the Hexi corridor are much thicker than those beneath the northern edge. A large thrust fault termed the North Border thrust has been discovered by deep seismic reflection profiling in the Hexi corridor of the north Qilian Mountains. We think that it has great

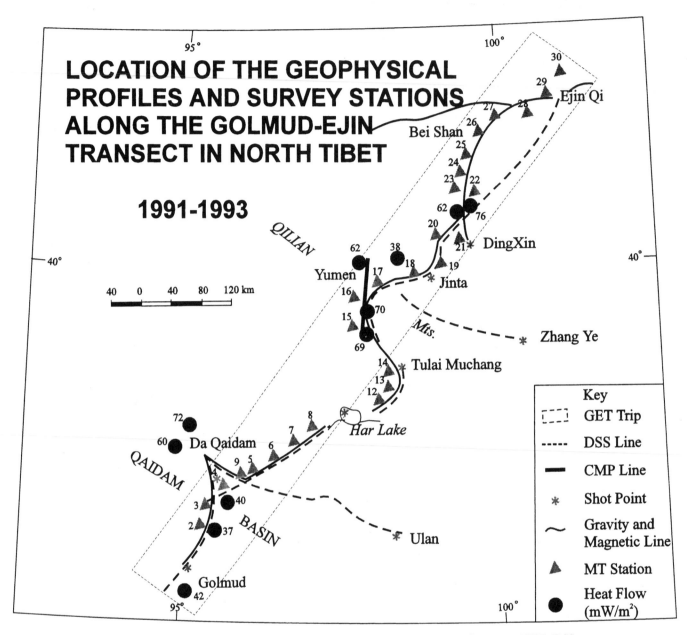

Figure 2. Map showing location of the geophysical profiling along the Golmud-Ejin transect (GET) (DSS: deep seismic sounding, CMP: common mid point vertical reflection profile, MT: magnetotelluric sounding.

importance for understanding the geodynamics of northern Tibet (Fig. 5).

Deep seismic sounding indicates that the Moho under the Qilian Mountains is deeper than it is beneath the basins on either side (Cui et al., 1995; Fig. 3, item 4). The tomographic analysis of seismic body waves also shows that there is a deep root under the Qilian Mountains. The unevenly distributed seismic velocity indicates segmentation in the Qilian Mountains reflecting different types of deformation. In the Beishan area a series of Late Jurassic south-vergent thrusts are present; the transportation distance is more than 100 km (Zheng et al., 1991,

1996; Zuo Guochao and He Guoq, 1990). The seismic reflection profiling (Fig. 4) discovered several weaker north-dipping reflections beneath the Hexi corridor basin that probably represent older structures, whereas strongly south dipping reflections are indicative of Cenozoic north-vergent thrusts. These observations imply that the North Border thrust is a boundary fault between the North Qilian terrane and the Beishan terrane.

The lithosphere can be divided into three particular areas of deformation, Beishan, Qilian, and Qaidam, on the basis of a comprehensive comparison of the gravity and magnetic fields, filtered remote sensing imagery, surficial deformation, and structural

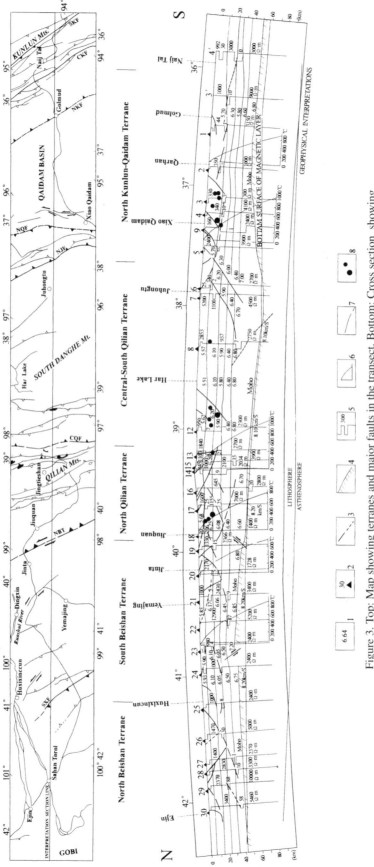

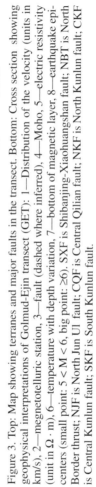

Figure 3. Top: Map showing terranes and major faults in the transect. Bottom: Cross section showing geophysical interpretations of Golmud-Ejin transect (GET): 1—Distribution of the velocity (units in km/s), 2—megnetotelluric station, 3—fault (dashed where inferred), 4—Moho, 5—electric resistivity (unit in Ω · m), 6—temperature with depth variation, 7—bottom of magnetic layer, 8—earthquake epicenters (small point: $5 < M < 6$, big point: ≥ 6). SXF is Shibanjing-Xiaohuangshan fault; NBT is North Border thrust; NJF is North Jun Ul fault; CQF is Central Qilian fault; NKF is North Kunlun fault; CKF is Central Kunlun fault; SKF is South Kunlun fault.

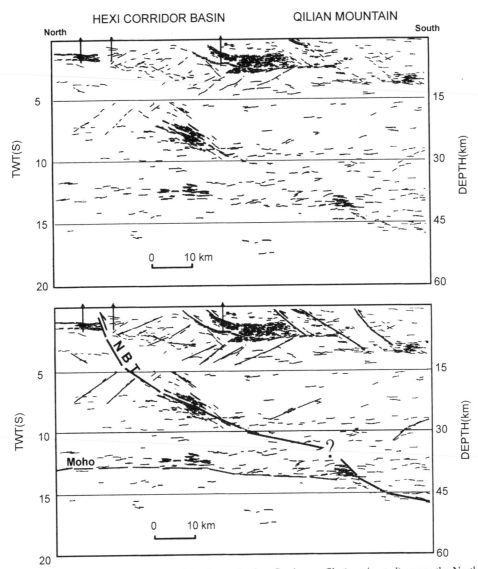

Figure 4. Interpretive line drawings of the deep seismic reflection profile (unmigrated) across the North Qilian Mountains. The south-dipping North Border thrust (NBT) is interpreted as an important north-vergent thrust fault along which the Alxa landmass underthrusts northern Tibet. TWT = two-way traveltime.

traces. The Beishan area is characterized by nearly east-west extension and north-south shortening. The Qilian area shows complicated northeast-southwest thrusting. The basement of the western part of the Qaidam basin tilts to the west. The northeastward trace of the Altyn Tagh fault may diverge west of the Golmud-Ejin transect. One possible continuation of the Altyn Tagh fault across the transect corresponds with the North Border thrust (Fig. 1).

FRAMEWORK OF THE LITHOSPHERE

Variations in the thickness of the crust

The Moho as interpreted from deep seismic data; deep seismic reflection profiling extends beneath the entire transect with the exception of a small offset at the northern end. The deepest Moho is located at 74 km depth beneath the Qilian Mountains on the Gol-

mud-Ejin transect, in the area of Juhongtu (near lat 38° N), south of Har Lake in the Southern Qilian, away from the highest mountains (near lat 39°20′N, north Qilian). The crust beneath the Qaidam basin is 52 km thick on average, but the crust in the center of basin is slightly less thick. The Moho deepens beneath the Qilian Mountains and the basins on both sides and dips toward the interior mountains; in the south (at the contact with Qaidam basin) it dips more steeply than in the north. In two places, beneath the northern margin (near lat 41°N) and southern margin (near lat 40°N) of the Hexi corridor basin, the Moho is locally offset by 2–3 km.

Thickness of the lithosphere

The variation in the thickness of the lithosphere along the transect is interpreted from the inversion of surface waves from

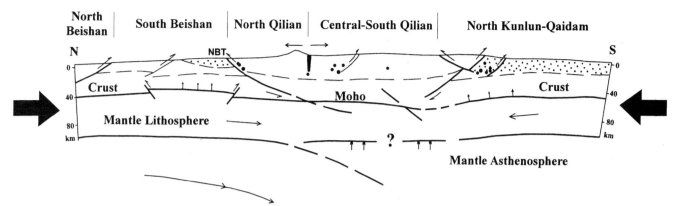

Figure 5. Preliminary geodynamic model for northern Tibet that is consistent with the Golmud-Ejin transect (GET) geophysical data and existing geological data.

earthquakes, and the depth of a high conductivity layer in the upper mantle is given by the inversion of MT data (Zhu and Hu, 1995). The two data sets show different results.

The bottom of lithosphere defined by the inversion of surface waves varies and deepens gently in the middle of the transect, as shown in Figure 3. The thickest lithosphere, 130 km, is located in the center of the Qilian Mountains. The lithosphere thins toward the basins on both sides of the transect. The thickness of lithosphere is 100 km in the Qaidam basin and 90 km beneath Beishan.

The depth of the high conductivity layer in the upper mantle is greater than the thickness of the lithosphere, as determined from the inversion of surface wave. The depth of the high-conductivity layer in the upper mantle varies locally within 10 km within the transect and has an average value of 140–150 km.

A low-velocity (high-conductivity) layer in the crust

A low-velocity layer was discovered near 20 km depth beneath the entire transect, on the basis of the interpretation of deep seismic sounding. The thickness of the low-velocity layer is generally 5–10 km. Its velocity varies between 5.80 and 6.05 km/s, which is typically 0.3–0.5 km/s lower than the layer above it (only about 0.05–0.10 km/s in the area of Beishan). A high-conductivity layer was also discovered by MT: it extends along the entire transect, but its depth and thickness change greatly. The high-conductivity layer is very pronounced (5–10 $\Omega \cdot$ m).

Lateral variations of physical properties

Velocity variations. The crust can be divided into three parts: upper crust (velocity is <6.0 km/s), middle crust, and lower crust. The velocity of the lower crust in Beishan is high, 6.50–6.75 km/s in the north and 6.45–7.20 km/s in the south. The Pn (head wave) value (8.20 km/s) of the top of the upper mantle in Beishan is also higher than that of all the terranes (8.10 km/s) to the south. The velocity of the lower crust in the North Qilian terrane is the lowest, 6.40–6.60 km/s. The velocity of the lower crust in the

Northern Qaidam belt is also low, 6.40–6.70 km/s. The velocity of lower Qaidam terrane and Central-Southern Qilian terrane crust is normal, 6.60–6.80 km/s. The upper crust of Qaidam basin consists of a huge thickness of sedimentary rocks having an average velocity of 5.7 km/s. The velocity of the upper crust beneath the Qilian Mountains (5.51–5.60 km/s) is lower than that of the Qaidam basin. The velocity of the upper crust in Beishan is 5.85–5.93 km/s, the average velocity of the middle crust of the Qaidam is 6.30 km/s and the velocity of the middle crust of the Qilian Mountains is 6.25 km/s; the lowest value (6.10 km/s) is under Har Lake. The velocity of the middle crust of Beishan is 6.10–6.19 km/s; the lowest value (6.10 km/s) is under the North Beishan terrane.

Temperature variation at depth. We calculated the temperature at the bottom of the crust (40–60 km depth) on the basis of surface heat-flow measurements. The base of the crust beneath the Northern Qaidam structural zone and the North Qilian terrane is warm; temperatures are 688–850 °C. The Southern Beishan terrane and the Qaidam terrane have lower temperatures of 424–600 °C. The geothermal regime of the Central-Southern Qilian terrane is between the two; i.e., slightly lower than normal.

Electrical resistivity variations in the lower lithosphere. The electrical resistivity of the lower lithosphere of Beishan is generally high (3,000–5,000 $\Omega \cdot$ m); the highest value, 5,000–10,000 $\Omega \cdot$ m, is under the Northern Beishan terrane. The electrical resistivity of the lower lithosphere under the Hexi corridor and Qaidam basin is generally lower (3150 $\Omega \cdot$ m); the lowest value, 300–1,000 $\Omega \cdot$ m, is under Zhaerhan Lake. The electrical resistivity of the lower lithosphere in the Qilian Mountains appears to be higher under the margins of ranges (4,000–10,000 $\Omega \cdot$ m) and lower under the central (2,034–2,750 $\Omega \cdot$ m) part.

OUTLINE OF THE GEODYNAMIC MODEL

Figure 5 is a sketch of the geodynamic model for the Golmud-Ejin transect. It is compiled from a preliminary analysis in conjunction with the previous results. It outlines the kinetics and dynamics of major structural units in northern Tibet, and illustrates how the crust is shortened and thickened. Our model shows compression resulting from major northward motion of the Indian plate and minor southward motion of the Siberian plate. Convergence of the plates results from uneven flow in the mantle. Compression occurs mainly in the middle and lower crust, while the upper crust undergoes strike-slip faulting and extension.

In the light of Golmud-Ejin transect geophysical data and our interpretation, the model can be generalized as follows.

Bidirectional underthrusting

Northward motion of the Indian plate and passive wedging of the Siberian plate moving relatively southward provide the dynamic setting for the latest deformation of Tibet's lithosphere. The Indian plate underthrust the Himalayas and compressed the Tibetan plateau from the south, as has been shown by the first completed deep seismic reflection profile (Zhao et al., 1993; Zeng and Gao, 1995). Deep seismic reflection profiles along the Northern Qilian show that the Alashan massif similarly underthrust the northern plateau, compressing the plateau from the north.

Extensional structures in a compressive setting

Our model shows extensional structures in upper crust in the central part of the Qilian Mountains (see Fig. 5), according to comprehensive geophysical interpretation. Anisotropy of seismic waves also indicates horizontal extension in shallow central Qilian crust (Song et al., 1991; Wang et al., 1991). Earthquake mechanisms have normal fault solutions in the shallow crust of the Qinghai-Tibet Plateau (Molnar and Lyon-Caen, 1989) and they exhibit a regular band distribution on the inner side of the reversed fault belt on the plateau margin (Xu et al., 1994). Due to outward thrusting on both southern and northern sides of the Qilian Mountains, the central part of the Qilian Mountains becomes the inner side of the southward and northward thrusting movement, so the existence of extensional structures is easily understood in this case. Geological observations (Avouac and Tapponnier, 1993; Gaudemer et al., 1995) suggested the existence of strike-slip and thrust faulting in a compressive setting in the Qilian Mountains. A study by Chen et al. (1996) on the source of the earthquake measuring 6.9 in magnitude in the Gonghe basin in the Central-South Qilian terrane in 1990, reveals the extensional structure developed in a compressive setting.

Do buoyant forces exist in the mantle?

Our model indicates the existence of buoyant forces in the mantle under the Qilian Mountains, but questions remain. A study of seismic wave anisotropy indicated uplift of the lithospheric mantle under the Qilian Mountains (Song et al., 1991; Molnar et al., 1993). This may be caused by a buoyant force from

bilateral compression, but more probably is caused by uplift of asthenospheric mantle (Gao and Wu, 1995).

Flow direction of the mantle

Our model shows subduction of the north Qilian continent beneath the Qilian Mountains. This proposed subduction may involve entire lithospheric movement and asthenospheric flow (Gao, 1995a, 1995b). We speculate that the convection is caused by lateral variation of upper mantle density. The northern Qilian Mountains are situated in the gradient belt of the isostatic gravity anomaly and the variation belt of seismic wave velocity (Wu and Levshin, 1994). Convection might occur below these belts, and its flow direction would be close to the subduction direction of the lithospheric plate (Arnaud et al., 1992).

Numerical simulation of stress field along the Golmud-Ejin transect

A numerical simulation of the state of stress of the lithosphere has been made using an improved finite element method, constrained by physical properties and structural boundaries. We used it to test the Golmud-Ejin transect geodynamic model. It shows that deformation of the lithosphere is caused by bilateral compression resulting in horizontal shortening, vertical thickening, and detachment faulting in the lower crust.

CONCLUSION AND DISCUSSION

We have offered a comprehensive geophysical interpretation of the structure and tectonics of northern Tibet based on the Golmud-Ejin transect lithospheric geotransect. We have also created a generalized geodynamic model that has been tested by finite-element modeling. It is consistent with results of geophysical observation, including gravimetry and magnetics, and remote sensing images, as well as geological data. The model explains the tectonics of the main structural units of the Qaidam basin–Qilian–Beishan areas, and the deformation of the Tibetan lithosphere. The main cause of deformation of the Tibetan lithosphere is bilateral compression, principally from the Indian plate pushing north and partly from the Siberian plate pushing south. Compression develops mainly in the lower crust, and thrust-slip movement and sluggish extension occur in the shallow crust. The most recent lithospheric deformation and late Cenozoic uplift in the Qilian Mountains developed in this dynamic setting.

ACKNOWLEDGMENTS

We express our deep appreciation to A. M. Macfarlane, M. Hauck, and an anonymous reader for their critical reviews of the first version of the manuscript, and to Zhang Zhaoyuan and A. M. Macfarlane for reviews of the second version of the manuscript. This research is financially supported by the Ministry of Geology and Mineral Resources of China and the China National Natural Science Foundation.

REFERENCES CITED

Arnaud, N. O., Vidal, P., Tapponnier, P., Matte, P., and Deng, W. M., 1992, The high K_2O volcanism of northwestern Tibet: Geochemistry and tectonic implications: Earth and Planetary Science Letters, v. 111, p. 351–367.

Avouac, J. P., and Tapponnier, P., 1993, Kinematic model of active deformation in Central Asia: Geophysical Research Letters, v. 20, p. 895–898.

Bureau of Geology and Mineral Resources of Gansu Province, 1989, Regional geology of Gansu Province: Beijing, Geological Publishing House, p. 625 (in Chinese with English abstract).

Chen Bingwei, Wang Yanbin, and Zuo Guochao, 1995, Terrain subdivision of the northern Qinghai-Xizang (Tibet) plateau and its tectonic evolution: Acta Geophysica Sinica, v. 38, supplement, p. 98–112 (in Chinese with English abstract).

Chen, Y. T., Xu, L. S., Li, X., and Zhao, M., 1996, Source process of the 1990 Gonghe, China, earthquake and tectonic stress field in the northeastern Qinghai-Xizang (Tibet) Plateau: PAGEOPH, v. 146, no. 3/4, p. 697–715.

Cui Zuozhou, Li Qiusheng, Wu Chaodong, Yin Zhouxun, and Liu Hongbing, 1995, The crustal and deep structures in Golmud-Ejin Qi GGT: Acta Geophysica Sinica, v. 38, supplement, p. 15–28 (in Chinese with English abstract).

Editorial Board of Seismic Zoning Map of China, compilers, 1991, Map of earthquake epicenters in China and its adjacent areas: Beijing, State Seismological Bureau, Seismological Press, 2 sheets, scale 1: 4,000,000.

Gao Rui, 1990, The deformation of lithosphere and continental crust movement in the Qinghai-Tibet Plateau [abs.], *in* Annual of the Chinese Geophysical Society: Beijing, Seismological Press, p 121 (in Chinese).

Gao Rui, 1995a, Recent progress in the geophysical investigation of the upper mantle-crust of the Qinghai-Tibet plateau: Chinese Geology, no. 215, p. 26–28 (in Chinese).

Gao Rui, 1995b, Recent progress in the geophysical investigation of the upper mantle-crust of the Qinghai-Tibet plateau: Chinese Geology, no. 216, p. 20–22 (in Chinese).

Gao Rui and Wu Gongjian, 1995, Geophysical model and geodynamic process of Yadong-Ge'ermu geoscience tansect in Qinghai-Tibet plateau: Changchun University of Earth Sciences Journa , v. 25, p. 241–250.

Gaudemer, Y., Tapponnier, P., Meyer, B., Peltzer, G., Guo, S., Chen, Z., Dai, H., and Cifuentes, I., 1995, Partitioning crustal slip between linked, active faults in the eastern Qilian Shan, and evidence for major seismic gap, the 'Tianzhu Gap', on the western Haiyuan Fault, Gansu (China): Geophysical Journal International, v. 120, p. 599–645.

Harrison, T. M., Copeand, P., Kidd, W. S. F., and Yin, A., 1992, Raising Tibet: Science, v. 255, p. 1663–1670.

Li Chunyu, Wang Quan, Liu Xueya, and Tang Yaoqing, 1982, Explanatory notes to the tectonic map of Asian: Beijing Cartographic Publishing House, Beijing, p. 8-11.

Meng Lingshun, Guan Ye, Qi Li, and Gao Rui, 1995, Gravity field and deep crustal structure in Golmud-Ejin Qi geoscience transect and nearby area: Acta Geophysica Sinica, v. 38, supplement , p. 36–45 (in Chinese with English abstract).

Molnar, P., and Lyon-Caen, H., 1989, Fault plane solutions of earthquakes and active tectonics of the Tibetan plateau and its margins: Geophysical Journal International, v. 99, p. 123–153.

Molnar, P., England, P., and Martinod, J., 1993, Mantle dynamics, uplift of the Tibetan plateau, and the Indian monsoon: Review of Geophysics, v. 31, p. 357–396.

Shen Xianjie, Yang Shuzhen, and Shen Jiying, 1995, Heat flow study and analysis along the Golmud-Ejin Qi geotransect: Acta Geophysica Sinica, v. 38, supplement, p. 86–97 (in Chinese with English abstract).

Song Zhonghe, An Changqiang, Chen Guoying, Chen Lihua, Zhuang Zhen, Fu Zhuwu, Lu Zhiling, and Hu Jiafu, 1991, Study on 3D velocity structure and anisotropy beneath the west China from the love wave dispersion:

Acta Geophysica Sinica, v. 34, p. 694–707 (in Chinese with English abstract).

Wang Xuyun, Xu Zhonghuai, and Gao Ajia, 1991, Earthquake mechanisms map in China and its adjacent areas: Beijing, Seismological Press, 1 sheet, scale 1:10,000,000.

Wu, F. T., and Levshin, A., 1994, Surface-wave group velocity tomography of East Asia: Physics of the Earth and Planetary Interiors, v. 84, p. 59–77.

Wu Gongjian, Gao Rui, Yu Qinfan, Cheng Qingyun, Meng Lingshun, Dong Xuebin, Cui Zuozhou, Yin Zhouxun, Shen Xianjie, and Zhou Yauxiu, 1991a, Integrated investigations of the Qinghai-Tibet Plateau along the Yadong-Golmud geoscience transect: Acta Geophysical Sinica, v. 34, p. 552–562 (in Chinese with English abstract).

Wu Gongjian, Xiao Xuchang, Li Tingdong, Cheng Qingyun, Cui Junwen, Cue Zuozhou, Dong Xuebin, Gao Rui, Huang Huaizheng, Liu Xun, Meng Lingshun, Shen Xianjie, Yin Zhouxun, Yu Qinfan, and Zhou Yaoxiu, 1991b, Yadong to Golmud Transect Qinghai-Tibet Plateau, China (International Lithosphere Program Publication 189: Washington, D.C., International Committee of Lithosphere and American Geophysical Union, 1 sheet, scale 1:1,000,000.

Wu Gongjian, Xiao Xuchang, Li Tingdong, Cheng Qingyun, Cui Junwen, Cue Zuozhou, Dong Xuebin, Gao Rui, Huang Huaizheng, Liu Xun, Meng Lingshun, Shen Xianjie, Yin Zhouxun, Yu Qinfan, and Zhou Yaoxiu, 1993, Lithosphere structure and evolution of the Tibetan Plateau: The Yadong-Golmud geoscience transect: Tectonophysics, v. 219, p. 213–221.

Wu Xuanzhi, Wu Chunling, Lu Jie, and Wu Jie, 1995, Research on the fine crustal structure of the northern Qilian-Hexi Corridor by deep seismic reflection: Acta Geophysica Sinica, v. 38, supplement, p. 29–35 (in Chinese with English abstract).

Xiang Guangzhong and Lu Dehui, 1990, Formation, evolution and geodynamics of Hexi corridor basin [abs.], *in* Annual of the Chinese Geophysical Society: Beijing, Seismological Press, p. 128 (in Chinese).

Xu Zhonghuai, Wang Suyun, Gao Ajia, and Guo Ying, 1994, Redetermination, examination and compilation of focal mechanism of Chinese earthquakes, *in* Annual of the Chinese Geophysical Society: Beijing, Seismological Press, p. 133 (in Chinese).

Zeng Rongsheng and Gao Rui, 1995, A review on the studies of lithosphere structures and dynamics in Tibetan Plateau, *in* China National Report on Seismology and Physics of the Earth's Interior for the XXIth General Assembly of International Union of Geodesy and Geophysics: Beijing, China Meteorological Press, p. 41–53.

Zhao W., Nelson K. D., and Project INDEPTH Team, 1993, Deep seismic reflection evidence for continental underthrusting beneath southern Tibet: Nature, v. 366, p. 557–559.

Zheng Yadong, Wang Shizheng, and Wang Yufang, 1991, An enormous thrust nappe and extensional metamorphic core complex newly discovered in Sino-Mongolian boundary area: Science in China, Ser. B, v. 34, p. 1145–1152.

Zheng, Y., Zhang, Q., Wang, Y., Liu, R., Wang, S. G., Zuo, G., Wang, S. Z., Lkaasugen, B., Badarch, G., and Badamgarav, Z., 1996, Great Jurassic thrust sheets in Beishan (North Mountains)-Gobi areas of China and southern Mongolia: Journal of Structural Geology, v. 18, p. 1111–1126.

Zhu Renxue and Hu Xiangyun, 1995, Study on the resistivity structure of the lithosphere along the Golmud-Ejin Qi geoscience transect: Acta Geophysica Sinica, v. 38, supplement, p. 46–57 (in Chinese with English abstract).

Zuo Guochao and He Guoqi, 1990, Plate tectonics and metallogenic regularities in Beishan region: Beijing, Beijing University Publishing House, 194 p.

MANUSCRIPT ACCEPTED BY THE SOCIETY FEBRUARY 3, 1998.

Geological Society of America
Special Paper 328
1999

Mantle diapir and inward intracontinental subduction: A discussion on the mechanism of uplift of the Qinghai-Tibet Plateau

Xu Zhiqin
Institute of Geology, Chinese Academy of Geological Sciences, 26 Beiwanzhuang Road, Beijing 100037, China
Jiang Mei
Institute of Mineral Resources, Chinese Academy of Geological Sciences, Beijing 100037, China
Yang Jingsui
Institute of Geology, Chinese Academy of Geological Sciences, 26 Beiwanzhuang Road, Beijing 100037, China
Zhao Guoguang
Institute of Crustal Dynamics, State Seismological Bureau, Beijing 100085, China
Cui Junwen and Li Haibing
Institute of Geology, Chinese Academy of Geological Sciences, 26 Beiwanzhuang Road, Beijing 100037, China
Lu Qingtian and Xue Guangqi
Institute of Mineral Resources, Chinese Academy of Geological Sciences, Beijing 100037, China

ABSTRACT

In this chapter, we account for the mechanism of uplift of the Qinghai-Tibet Plateau beyond the subduction model of the Himalayas, through studies of features of Cenozoic deformation and the accompanying geological events, with a combination of results from geophysical exploration and experiments at the interior and hinterland of the plateau. Extensive alkaline volcanic rocks of Cenozoic age in the interior of the plateau are shoshonitic and high-K, formed by the partial melting of the lower crust and upper mantle in an extensional tectonic setting. A seismic converted-waves study from Golmud to Wenquan further shows that the lithosphere at the northern interior of the plateau has a multisandwich structure and lithospheric faults with sinistral strike-slip sense. The large low-velocity anomaly at the depths from 210 to 360 km beneath the Hoh Xil region, detected by seismic tomographic data, is interpreted to be a mantle diapir responsible for the genesis of the alkaline volcanic activity. A seismic reflection profile across the northern hinterland of the plateau shows that the North China craton was subducted southward beneath the Qilian Mountains. In the eastern hinterland, a wedge of the Yangtze craton embedded into the lower crust at the Longmenshan indicates that intracontinental subduction existed between the eastern Qinghai-Tibet Plateau and the Yangtze craton. The noncoaxial compression and oblique crustal shortening in the Qinghai-Tibet Plateau caused by northwest-southeast–trending compression at the northern margin and the south-north–trending compression at the southern margin are most likely responsible for the formation of strike-slip faults and rotation of blocks. We suggest a new model for the uplift of the Qinghai-Tibet Plateau: a mantle diapir in the interior and inward intracontinental subduction at the margin.

Xu Zhiqin, Jiang Mei, Yang Jingsui, Zhao Guoguang, Cui Junwen, Li Haibing, Lu Qingtian, and Xue Guangqi, 1999, Mantle diapir and inward intracontinental subduction: A discussion on the mechanism of uplift of the Qinghai-Tibet Plateau, *in* Macfarlane, A., Sorkhabi, R. B., and Quade, J., eds., Himalaya and Tibet: Mountain Roots to Mountain Tops: Boulder, Colorado, Geological Society of America Special Paper 328.

INTRODUCTION

After the collision between the Indian and Eurasian plates, extensive convergence has apparently caused the formation of the Himalaya orogenic belt and much of the observed Cenozoic deformation in Central Asia (Gansser, 1964; Dewey and Bird, 1970; Powell and Conaghan, 1973, 1975; Le Fort, 1975; Molnar and Tapponnier, 1975). This huge deformation domain ~2,400 km long and 1,500 km wide, extends northward from the foreland basin of the Himalayan orogen to the Tianshan-Qilian mountains, and earthward to the Longmenshan mountains. We named the deformation domain the Tethys-Himalaya orogenic composite (Xu et al., 1996). It is surrounded by the Indian, Yangtze, and North China cratons, and consists of four parts: the Himalayan foreland superimposed thrust zone, the interior of the Qinghai-Tibet Plateau, the Tarim-Qaidam hinterland basins, and the Tianshan-Qilianshan-Longmenshan hinterland thrust zone (Fig. 1). The interior of the Qinghai-Tibet Plateau includes four terrains: the Kunlun, Bayan Har, Qiangtang, and Gangdise terrains (Fig. 1).

Since Argand (1924) proposed the subduction model on the mechanism of uplift of the Qinghai-Tibet Plateau, a number of geologists have tried to address the role of continent-continent collision at the southern Qinghai-Tibet Plateau. For example, it is proposed that the Indian plate subducted beneath the Qinghai-Tibet Plateau at a low angle, which formed a two-layer crust and caused uplift of the plateau by gravity equilibrium (Barazangi and Ni, 1982; Beghoul et al., 1993). It has also been suggested that the lithospheric shortening and thickening of the Qinghai-Tibet Plateau occurred contemporaneously with the collision between the Indian and Eurasian plates (Dewey and Burke, 1973; England and Houseman, 1986). Different models of subduction and large-scale delamination were suggested to explain the uplift of the Qinghai-Tibet Plateau (Molnar and Deng, 1984; Zhao and Morgan, 1985; Zhao and Yuen, 1987; Mattews and Hirn, 1984; England and Houseman, 1986). Eastward extrusion of the Eurasian plate resulting from northward subduction of the Indian wedge was proposed by Tapponnier et al. (1982) to explain the formation of the huge deformation domain caused by the long-distance effect of the collision between the Indian and Eurasian plates. Some geologists considered that intracontinental subduction may also take place at

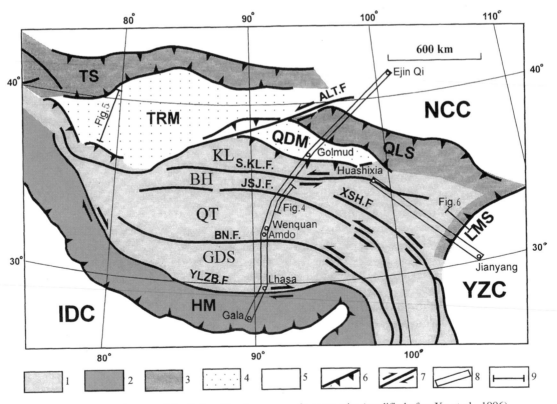

Figure 1. Tectonic map of the Tethys-Himalaya orogenic composite (modified after Xu et al., 1996), showing: 1—interior of the Qinghai-Tibet Plateau (QTP), including Kunlun (KL), Bayan Har (BH), Qiangtang (QT), and Gangdise (GDS) terrains; 2—Himalaya foreland superimposed thrust zone (HM); 3—Tarim (TRM)-Qaidam (QDM) hinterland basins; 4—Tianshan (TS)-Qilianshan (QLS)-Longmenshan (LMS) hinterland thrust zones; 5—North China craton (NCC), Yangtze craton (YZC), and Indian craton (IDC); 6—thrust; 7—strike-slip faults: Altyn-Tagh fault (ALT.F), South Kunlun fault (S.KL.F), Jinshajiang fault (JSJ.F.), Xianshuihe fault (XSH.F), Bangong-Nujiang fault (BN.F); Yarlung Zangbo Fault (YLZB.F); 8—geophysical profiles, 9—location of geological section.

the northern Qinghai-Tibet Plateau (Deng, 1978; Mattauer, 1992). Mattauer (1990) suggested a mantle diapir beneath the plateau as well.

We believe that the driving force for the uplift of the Qinghai-Tibet Plateau is complex and constrained by many factors, such as: (1) complicated fabrics of the Tethys-Himalaya orogenic composite; (2) the effect of the rigid cratons at the margins of the Qinghai-Tibet Plateau; and (3) direct deep factors of Cenozoic alkaline volcanic-magmatic activity, high heat flow and rifting at the interior of the Qinghai-Tibet Plateau.

However, until now most of the studies have mainly concentrated on the Himalayas, the southern interior of the plateau, and Karakoram, and not on the northern interior and hinterland of the plateau, e.g., the East Kunlun, Bayan Har, Qiangtang, Qaidam, and Qilian regions. Thus, we take account of the mechanism of the uplift of the Qinghai-Tibet Plateau, in particular the geodynamics of the formation of hinterland and interior of the plateau, through studies of features of Cenozoic deformation and the accompanying geological events at the interior and the hinterland of the Qinghai-Tibet Plateau; we also combine our results from geophysical experiments, including Sino-French geophysical exploration from Golmud to Gala in 1992–1995, and the geoscientific transects at the northern and eastern margins of the Qinghai-Tibet Plateau by Gao et al. (1995), and Cui et al. (1996), respectively.

CENOZOIC GEOLOGICAL EVENTS IN THE INTERIOR OF THE QINGHAI-TIBET PLATEAU

After the collision between Indian and Eurasian plates, the Qinghai-Tibet Plateau was subjected to heterogeneous uplift during Cenozoic time. Available data indicate that extensive uplift of the Qinghai-Tibet Plateau occurred after Miocene and Pliocene time, especially after Pleistocene time (Xiao, 1995). We focus on sedimentation, magmatism, structural deformation, and other geological events accompanying the uplift within the plateau since Cenozoic time.

Formation of Eocene pull-apart basins and Quaternary rifting basins

There are a number of small continental Eocene-Oligocene basins filled with red lacustrine sandstone and mudstone having thicknesses to 2,000 m (Bureau of Geology and Mineral Resources of Qinghai Province, 1991), distributed along sinistral strike-slip faults that trend east-west in the northern Qinghai-Tibet Plateau (Tapponnier and Molnar, 1977). Most of the basins are rhombohedral in shape (plane geometry) (Fig. 2). We consider that the formation of pull-apart basins is probably related to sinistral strike-slip movement. According to our study, the east-west–trending Dongqiao basin at the south of the Bangonghu-Nujiang fault is an Eocene-Oligocene basin devel-

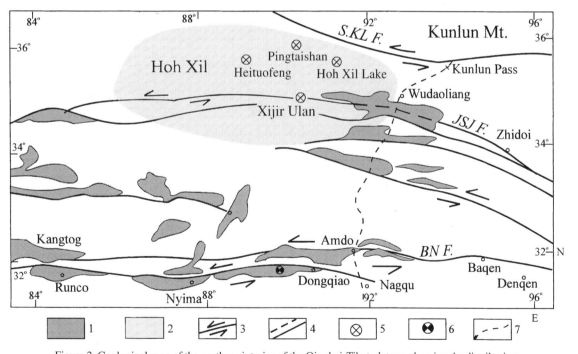

Figure 2. Geological map of the northern interior of the Qinghai-Tibet plateau, showing the distribution of Cenozoic alkaline volcanic rocks, Eocene-Oligocene sedimentary basins, and sinistral strike-slip faults. 1—Eocene-Oligocene sedimentary basin; 2—regions of Cenozoic alkaline volcanic rocks; 3—strike-slip fault; 4—fault and inferred fault; 5—sites of volcanics quoted in this chapter; 6—Eocene-Oligocene basins; 7—road.

oped on the Jurassic-Cretaceous folded strata. The Eocene sedimentary sequence is thicker in the west (1,400 m) and the north (1,100 m), and thinner in the east (1,000 m) and the south (100–200 m). The sedimentary center was located at the northwest part of the basin and controlled by normal faults during Eocene time, and then moved to the center of the basin during Oligocene time. This implies that the Dongqiao basin was a pull-apart basin along the east-west–trending sinistral strike-slip fault during Eocene time.

North-south–trending Quaternary extensional systems are well developed within the southern interior of the plateau, where grabens bounded by normal faults control the distribution of Quaternary sedimentation, north-south–trending lakes, and large earthquakes, and form a rifting system (Tapponnier and Molnar, 1977; Peltzer and Tapponnier, 1988). The Quaternary rifting region in the southern plateau (Gangdise terrain) is characterized by remarkable variations of heat flow ranging from 66 mW/m² to 364 mW/m² and an abrupt change in heat-flow types, from pure conductive to conductive-convective transition within a short distance. The peak value in the former type may reach 140 mW/m², whereas that in the latter exceeds 300 mW/m². The heat-flow anomaly demonstrates an obviously shallow heat source (Shen, 1996).

Alkaline volcanic activity

There are some alkaline volcanic rocks of Cenozoic age in the northern interior of the plateau, mainly in the Hoh Xil region (Fig. 2). Most of the volcanic rocks in Hoh Xil belong to a shoshonitic association (Fig. 3), including latite, shoshonite, and trachyte (Deng, 1991; Deng et al., 1996; Zhang and Zheng, 1994; Yang et al., 1996; Xu et al., 1996). The shoshonite at the

Heituofeng-Pingtaishan-Hoh Xil Lake, north of Hoh Xil, is characterized by enrichment in K, large ion lithophile elements (LILE), and light rare earth elements (REE), and depletion in Nb and Ta (Deng et al., 1996). A recent study on the shoshonite association at the Xijir Ulan Lake, at the center of Hoh Xil, by Yang et al. (1998) indicates that the SiO_2 content varied between 58 and 70 wt%, and TiO_2 and MgO increase with decreasing SiO_2. The rock has an initial $^{87}Sr/^{86}Sr$ ratio of 0.708 and $^{143}Nd/^{144}Nd$ ratio of 0.512, and almost constant Pb ratios ($^{206}Pb/^{204}Pb$ = 18.61–18.74, $^{207}Pb/^{204}Pb$ = 15.62–15.77, and $^{208}Pb/^{204}Pb$ = 38.72–39.10). It is inferred that the shoshonitic magma originated by the partial melting of the lower crust or crust-mantle boundary material and are related to the heat flow of the K-rich materials due to magmatism in the mantle (Xu et al., 1996). The olivine-bearing leucite and the alkaline basalt (Zhang and Zheng, 1994) discovered in Hoh Xil may be derived directly from partial melting of the mantle.

The K-Ar method yielded ages of 7–56 Ma for the volcanic rocks in Hoh Xil (Zhang and Zheng, 1994; Deng, 1991; Deng et al., 1996; Xu et al., 1996), and among them ages of 10–20 Ma predominated. In addition, three new K-Ar ages (15.66, 14.05, and 33.37 Ma) were obtained from samples at the Xijir Ulan Lake (Yang et al., 1998), and ages of 6.95–7.5 Ma were obtained from samples in northern Hoh Xil (Deng et al., 1996).

Crustal shortening

The crustal deformation and shortening occur extensively in the northern and central interior of the plateau; in different parts of the region, they have different deformational forms and strengths and directions of stress.

1. In the Bayan Har–Qiangtang region at the central inte-

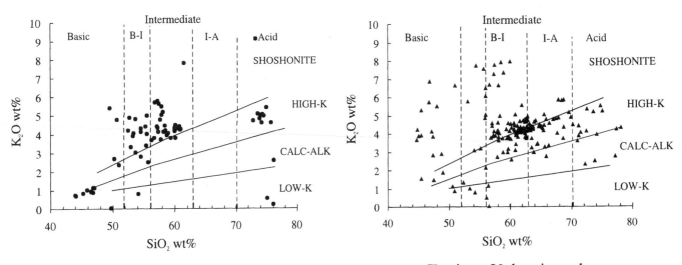

Figure 3. K2O vs. SiO2 plots show that most of the Quaternary and Tertiary volcanic rocks in the interior of the Qinghai-Tibet Plateau shoshonite association (after Yang et al., in press).

rior, crustal deformation is characterized by crustal shortening rather than faulting. The Eocene and Oligocene strata formed west-northwest–trending gentle concentric folds and are discordantly covered by Miocene sediments. The pre-Cenozoic strata in the region were thrust onto the Miocene strata along a high angle fault. A crustal shortening rate of 13% is inferred for the region (Xu and Cui, 1996) (Fig. 4). These features, coupled with the development of east-west–trending sinistral strike-slip faults, suggest that the compressional stresses in the region were relatively weak, trended north-northeast, and the compression occurred mainly in two periods: between Oligocene and Miocene time, and between Miocene and Quaternary time.

2. Because the Kunlun Mountains at the northern interior are mainly composed of lower Paleozoic folded basement and a large number of rigid granitic plutons, the crustal shortening is expressed by thrust faults. A series of west-northwest–striking ductile and brittle thrust faults have overthrust Proterozoic metamorphosed strata to the south-southwest onto Paleozoic, Mesozoic, and Cenozoic age strata, forming klippe and a stretching lineation trending 210°. In addition, there are some small north-northwest–striking dextral strike-slip faults and a few pull-apart basins of Oligocene age along these faults. The small dextral strike-slip faults cut off folded Mesozoic strata and displace some granitic bodies by less than 10 km. These deformational features, coupled with the sinistral sense of the east-west–trending South Kunlun fault, indicate that the Kunlun terrain has undergone northeast–southwest commpression since Cenozoic time.

Strike-slip faulting

Large-scale shearing forces gave rise to the relative movement of the blocks in the northern plateau (Tapponnier and Molnar, 1977). The major strike-slip faults are described as follows (Fig. 1).

1. The Altyn Tagh fault strikes 060°–070° and shows sinistral motion. The total displacement in Quaternary time is 39–50 km, which was estimated from the horizontal offset of the Miocene basins at an average slip rate of 13–16.7 mm/yr (Ge, 1992). Peltzer and Tapponier (1988) calculated that the displacement rate was ~12 ± 2 mm/yr in the western section and 15 ± 5 mm/yr in the central section of the Altyn Tagh fault.

2. The South Kunlun fault zone consists of a series of sinistral faults, trending west-northwest for ~1,600 km. Along the fault zone there are a number of broad valleys, pull-apart basins, and push-up structures. The total ductile displacement along the fault zone since Triassic time is 110 km, and in Quaternary time it is ~30 km (Li et al., 1998). Kidd and Molnar (1988) proposed that the Holocene slip rate of the South Kunlun fault was between 10 and 20 mm/yr, but more likely 13–15 mm/yr. Detailed data of geomorphic offsets, evidence of paleo-earthquakes in relation to the slip rates, and results of ^{14}C and thermoluminescence (TL) dating give estimated slip rates of 11.5 mm/yr for the western, 9.5–11.5/mm for the central, and 7.0 mm/yr for the eastern sections of this fault (Zhao et al., 1996).

3. The Xianshuihe fault trends northwest-southeast in the eastern plateau and changes strike to north-south at the eastern margin of the plateau. The age of the Xianshuihe fault can be inferred by the ages of a syntectonic granite located at the southern end of the fault. This granite has an emplacement U-Pb age of 12.8 ± 1.4 Ma and a cooling Rb-Sr age of 11.6 ± 0.4 Ma (Calassou, 1994). The cumulative displacement by sinistral strike-slip movement is ~80 km (Xu et al., 1992). In a study of the regional history of late Quaternary fluviation and glaciation, Zhao et al. (1991) made geomorphic profiles and more than 80 measurements of ^{14}C and TL dating. The refined averages of left-lateral slip rates are 14 ± 2 mm/yr, 2–5 mm/yr, 10 ± 2 mm/yr for the northwest, central, and southeast sections, respectively, in late Quaternary time.

The large strike-slip faults at the northern margin and central interior of the Qinghai–Tibet Plateau are therefore characterized by a sinistral sense, and, as a result of the faulting, blocks in the interior of the plateau have been rotated and extruded eastward or southeastward.

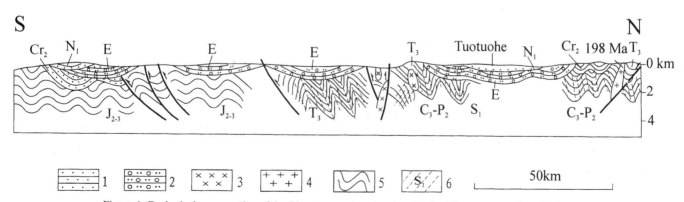

Figure 4. Geological cross-section of the Qiangtang region showing that the Miocene strata discordantly cover the gently folded Eocene strata. 1—Miocene strata; 2—Eocene strata; 3—gabbro; 4—granite; 5—folds; 6—cleavage. S_1—Lower Silurian; C_3—Upper Carboniferous; P_2—Upper Permian; T_3—Upper Triassic; J_{2-3}—Middle and Upper Jurassic; K_2—Upper Cretaceous; E—Eogene; N_1—Miocene.

CENOZOIC DEFORMATION IN THE HINTERLAND OF THE QINGHAI-TIBET PLATEAU

Tarim-Qaidam hinterland basins

The Tarim and Qaidam basins are located in the northern hinterland of the Qinghai-Tibet Plateau, and are separated by the Altyn Tagh fault. The basins contain Mesozoic-Cenozoic marine to continental facies sediments.

In the Qaidam basin, the sedimentary sequence is as thick as 6,000 m, and the basin is characterized by high-angle thrust faults and west-northwest–trending folds (Fig. 5). The folding in the basin migrated from the west to the center of the basin during Eocene and Holocene time (Xu et al., 1996). Both the southern and northern margins of the Qaidam basin are bounded by reverse faults. According to a magnetotelluric section (Zhang et al., 1992), the Qaidam basin plunged along the east-west–trending North Kunlun fault at its south margin at an intermediate angle southward beneath the Kunlun Mountains to a depth of 15 km. At the northern margin of the basin, the Paleozoic and Proterozoic metamorphic rocks from the southern Qilianshan have been thrust southward onto the Cenozoic sediments of the basin. Xu et al. (1996) estimated that the crust of the Qaidam basin has shortened since Cenozoic time by at least 50–60 km.

To the west of the Altyn Tagh fault, there are two well-developed faulting depressions separated by a central dome in the Tarim basin; sediment thicknesses are as much as 6,000 m in the south and 9,000 m in the north. Symmetrical ramp faults are developed at both the northern and southern margins of the basin, suggesting that compression was transferred from the marginal mountains (South Tianshan and Karakoram) to the basin (Fig. 5). The Tiekelike nappe at the northern Karakoram is displaced 70 km northward by thrusting (Ding and Tang, 1996).

Hinterland thrust zone of the Tianshan-Qilianshan-Longmenshan

The Tianshan, Qilianshan, and Longmenshan thrust zones are at the northwestern, northeastern, and eastern margins, respectively, of the orogenic composite. The extensive convergence and deformation in Cenozoic time resulted in the overturned fan-like thrust system in the Tianshan-Qilianshan orogenic belt. As a result, the Tianshan was thrust southward onto the Tarim basin and northeastward onto the Junggar basin, whereas the Qilianshan was thrust southward onto the Qaidam basin and northward onto the Hexi corridor basin. The crustal shortening since 20 Ma has been estimated to be ~120 km (Ding and Tang, 1996), and the shortening rate is about 13 mm/yr for the Tianshan and 15 mm/yr for the Qilianshan during Holocene (Molnar and Deng, 1984; Avouac, 1991).

The northeast-southwest–trending Longmenshan thrust zone at the eastern margin of the plateau consists of a series of superimposed thrust sheets (Fig. 6). The Proterozoic metamorphic complex at the front of the Longmenshan nappe has been overthrust eastward onto the continental Sichuan basin of Cretaceous-Eocene age. The lag ductile normal fault formed at 13–20 Ma, as determined by $^{39}Ar/^{40}Ar$ dating of retrograde metamorphic biotite (Xu et al., 1992; Calassou, 1994). The uplift of the Longmenshan Proterozoic metamorphic complex is considered to be closely related to the vertical extrusion caused by the formation of both the thrust and normal faults (Fig. 6). This is similar to the uplift and exhumation of the High Himalaya metamorphic belt associated with the formation of the Main Central thrust and the south Tibetan detachment fault at 20 Ma (Burg and Chen, 1984; Burchfiel and Royden, 1985; Mattauer and Brunel, 1989; Cui et al., 1992; Chemenda et al., 1995). Therefore, vertical extrusion is probably one of the most important factors related to the uplift of old

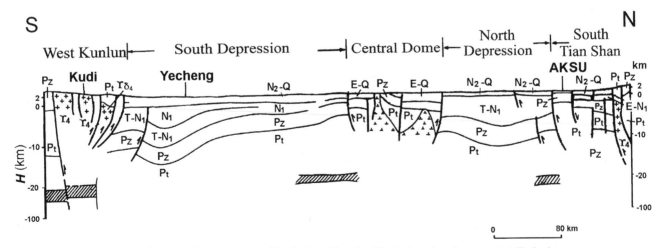

Figure 5. Geological cross-section of the Qaidam hinterland basin based on the magnetotelluric data (MT) (modified after Ding and Tang, 1996) showing tectonic units of the basin: north depression, central dome, and south depression; high-angle reverse faults, well developed in the basin, and marginal mountains thrusted on to the Tarim basin. Shaded parts represent low-resistant layers. Pz—Palaeozoic; Pt—Proterozoic; P—Permian; T—Triassic; N₁—Miocene; N₂—Pliocene; E—Eogene; Q—Quaternary. λ₄—Variscan granite; γδ₄—Variscan granodiorite.

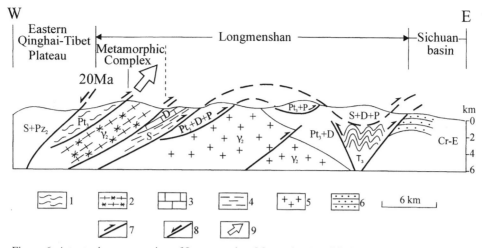

Figure 6. A tectonic cross-section of Longmenshan Mountains (modified after Xu et al., 1992), displaying Longmen Shan thrusts and nappe structure. This section shows that the uplift of the upper Proterozoic metamorphic complex is related to vertical extrusion, which is caused by thrusts and normal faults. 1—Schist; 2—granitic mylonite; 3—limestone; 4—phyllite; 5—migmatited granite; 6—sandstone and conglomerate; 7—thrust; 8—normal fault; 9—vertical extrusion. Pz_2—upper Paleozoic; Pt_3—upper Proterozoic; S—Silurian; D—Devonian; P—Permian; T—Triassic; Cr—Cretaceous; E—Eogene; γ_2—Proterozoic granite.

metamorphic terrain in the orogenic belts and is the result of intracontinental subduction of lithospheric plate material (Chemenda, 1994).

In general, the hinterland of the Qinghai-Tibet Plateau has been subjected to extensive compression for at least 20 Ma, and the compression direction is north-south at the Tianshan, northeast-southwest at the Qilianshan, and northwest-southeast at the Longmenshan. The Mesozoic and Cenozoic basins on the North China and Yangtze cratons at the margins of the Tethys-Himalaya orogenic composite have been embedded beneath the hinterland thrust zones. The compression at the hinterland thrust zones was stronger than that at the hinterland basins and the interior of the Qinghai-Tibet Plateau, but weaker than that at the Himalaya foreland superimposed thrust zone, where the crustal shortening rate reached 18 mm/yr in Holocene time (Molnar and Deng, 1984; Avouac, 1991). In addition, the rapid uplift and exhumation of the old metamorphic terrain at the margins of the Qinghai-Tibet Plateau is probably attributable to vertical extrusion, a result of intracontinental subduction. Thus the Qinghai-Tibet Plateau formed a particular topography, that is, high mountains at the margins and relatively flat in the interior of the plateau, as we see today.

GEOPHYSICAL INVESTIGATION OF THE INTERIOR AND THE HINTERLAND OF THE QINGHAI-TIBET PLATEAU

The data quoted here are from the Sino-French natural earthquake experiment section (Golmud–Kunlun Pass–Wudaoliang–Tuotuohe through Amdo-Lhasa-Rikaze-Gala) at the interior and the foreland of the Qinghai-Tibet Plateau, carried out in 1992–1994, using 110 seismometers. In this project, proper-

ties of anisotropy of the lithospheric mantle from Golmud to Gala were measured based on the splitting features of SKS, PKS, and PS (converted) waves (Hirn et al., 1995; Shi et al., 1998). Velocity images down to 400 km in depth were obtained by seismic tomography and the lithospheric structure from Golmud to Gala was mapped using converted phases from natural earthquakes (Jiang et al., 1995; Xu et al., 1996; Wittlinger et al., 1996).

Lithospheric structure of the northern Qinghai-Tibet Plateau

The lithospheric structure of the northern Qinghai–Tibet Plateau was obtained by earthquake converted wave experiments. The arrival times of the PS (converted waves) at the section from Golmud to Wenquen (Fig. 7) show the following features.

1. The depth of the Moho changes from 70 km to 60 km from south to north.

2. There are three low-velocity layers dipping northward at a low angle within the upper 30 km of crust in the region.

3. The 140-km-thick multisandwich structure of lithosphere consists of alternating high- and low-velocity layers. It is well accepted that the high-velocity and low-velocity layers represent the materials of high and low density, respectively. The low-velocity layer at the lower lithosphere may be explained by the properties of partial melting, high heat flow, and low rheologic strength (Xu et al., 1996).

4. The lithospheric faults (or zones of discontinuity) correspond to the northern marginal faults of the Kunlun Mountains, the South Kunlun fault and the Jinshajiang fault, and these are characterized by sinistral movement (Xu et al., 1996).

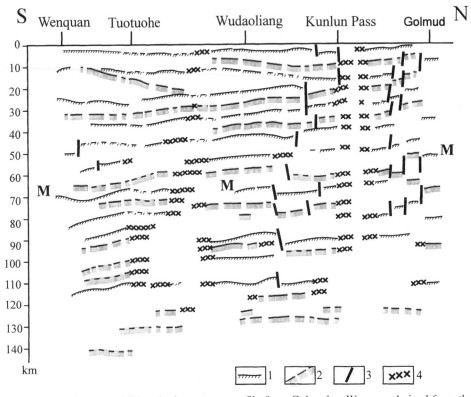

Figure 7. An interpreted lithospheric structure profile from Golmud to Wenquan derived from the arrival time of PS converted waves, showing the multisandwich structure, which consists of alternating high- and low-velocity layers, and lithospheric faults. 1—converting interface of high velocity; 2—converting interface of low-velocity; 3—inferred fault; 4—zone of discontinuity.

Seismic tomographic section transversing the northern Qinghai-Tibet Plateau and Himalayas

The seismic tomographic section of Golmud-Gala (Jiang et al., 1995; Hirn et al., 1995; Wittlinger et al., 1996) has provided velocity images to 400 km in depth shown in Figures 8 and 9.

Golmud-Wenquen seismic tomography section. The lithosphere above 100 km in depth in the Bayan Har terrain between the Kunlun Pass to the Jinshajing fault is of high velocity, and inferred to be cold, whereas in the northern Qiantang terrain between the Jinshajiang fault and Tuotuohe it is low velocity and inferred to be hot. Under the Hoh Xil region in the central part of the interior of the plateau, there is a large low-velocity anomaly between the depths of 200 and 360 km. It is ~250 km long, 250 km wide, and 160 km thick. This low-velocity anomaly is inferred to be associated with high heat flow, high conductivity, and low creep strength, corresponding to the Cenozoic alkaline volcanic activity in the Hoh Xil region. The large low-velocity anomaly may indicate a mantle plume or mantle diapir (Xu et al., 1996; Wittlingen et al., 1996; Jiang et al., 1998), and the smaller low-velocity bodies located in the shallow region south of the Jinshajiang fault may correspond to a hotspot group (Xu et al., 1996).

Amdo-Gala seismic tomographic section. In this section, a high-velocity zone from the south of Gala plunges northward at an intermediate angle to 200 km beneath the Himalayas, but not beyond the Yarlung Zangbo suture, and it is interpreted to be the result of the intracontinental subduction of the lithospheric mantle of the Indian plate under the Eurasian plate. Above this high-velocity zone, an obvious low-velocity anomaly zone (A in Fig. 9) occurs at depths of 50 to 100 km north of Gala, and probably formed in response to the subduction. The small northward-dipping low-velocity block (B in Fig. 9) below the Yarlung Zangbo suture zone is explained as the result of partial melting produced by the continuous activity on this suture zone. The shallow (0–50 km) low-velocity layer (C in Fig. 9) from Yangbajain to Gala is considered to be related to the Quaternary rifting. There are two high-velocity bodies within the lower velocity section at depths from 80 to 150 km in the mantle, which are located below the low-velocity layer C (Fig. 9) north of Yangbajain, and these are suggested to be evidence for delamination of the lithosphere (England and Houseman, 1989).

A comparison of the seismic tomography sections in Figures 8 and 9 shows that the low-velocity anomaly region beneath the southern plateau and Himalaya is at a shallow level (<100 km), whereas the low-velocity anomaly region beneath the central interior (Hoh Xil region) of the plateau is at a deep level (200–300 km). The low-velocity region in the southern part was related to intracontinental subduction caused by the collision of

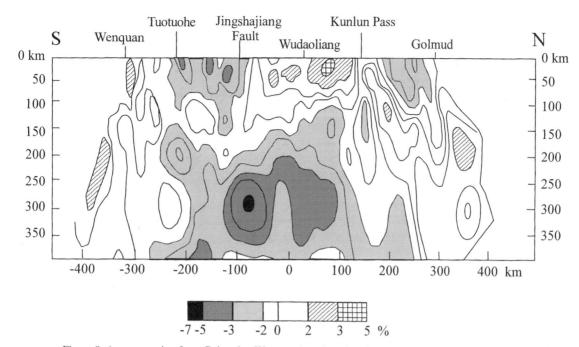

Figure 8. A cross section from Golmud to Wenquan based on data from seismic tomographic inversion (after Jiang et al., 1998), showing a large low-velocity anomaly from 200 to 360 km depth beneath the Hoh Xil region. The lithosphere above 100 km, north of the Jinshajiang fault, is high velocity, whereas it is low velocity south of the Jinshajiang fault. Units represent relative seismic velocity ratio (%).

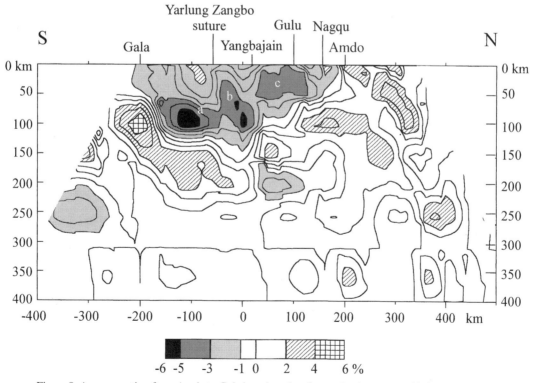

Figure 9. A cross section from Amdo to Gala based on data from seismic tomographic inversion shows a high-velocity zone plunging northward beneath the Himalayas 200 km in depth at the south of Gala, and three low-velocity anomalies (a, b, c) from Gala to Nagqu above the high-velocity zone. Units represent relative seismic velocity ratio (%).

the Indian and Eurasian plates. Previous seismic data for the northern part indicated a Sn-poor zone (Barazangi and Ni, 1982), a poor high-velocity upper mantle cover, thinner lithosphere, high heat-flow values, and a low-velocity zone (Molnar and England, 1990), as well as a large-magnitude anisotropy, all of which represent upper mantle flow beneath the Hoh Xil region and are related to alkaline volcanic activity since 20 Ma. However, the interpretation of the presence of a mantle diapir located in the upper part of the lower mantle can be considered as genetically related with these features.

Geophysical data from the hinterland of the Qinghai-Tibet Plateau: Explosive seismic profile from Huashixia to Jianyang at the eastern margin of the Qinghai-Tibet Plateau. The deep structure of the crust at the eastern margin of the Qinghai-Tibet Plateau and the nearby Yangtze craton was recently revealed by the Huashixia-Jianyang explosive seismic section (Fig. 10) (Cui et al., 1996). The northwest-southeast–trending Huashixia-Jianyang section is about 770 km long, and crosses the eastern margin of the Qinghai-Tibet Plateau, the Longmenshan, and the western Sichuan basin. The section shows the following features.

1. The crustal thickness is progressively augmented from east to west, from 40 km to 68 km.

2. Two detachments composed of low-velocity materials at a depth of 20 km beneath the eastern Qinghai-Tibet Plateau have been recognized, and are associated with the normal fault at the west of the Longmenshan Mountains.

3. Thrusts at the front of the Longmenshan Mountains caused the Longmenshan strata to overlap the Sichuan basin.

4. The Moho at 40 km depth below the Longmenshan has been offset by a gently east dipping reverse fault. As a result, the

Yangtze craton acted as a wedge and was embedded into the lower crust of the eastern Qinghai-Tibet Plateau (Cui et al., 1996).

Golmud-Ejin Qi geotransect at the northern margin of the Qinghai-Tibet Plateau. The Golmud-Ejin Qi geotransect (Fig. 11) (Wu et al., 1995) shows that thrusting occurs at the both sides of the Qilian Mountains and, as a result, the Qilian mountains have been overthrust onto the Hexi corridor basin, and Qaidam basin. On the basis of the fine crustal structure of the northern Qilianshan and Hexi corridor obtained by the seismic reflection survey (Fig. 11), it is apparent that the front thrust of north Qilianshan is dipping to the south, steeply at shallow levels and gently at deeper levels. This thrust fault connects with a low-angle decollement zone, represented by a reflection zone at the depth of ~10 km beneath the Qilian mountains. In the north, the major North Boundary thrust in the Hexi corridor extends southward at a low angle (~20°) for 100 km, reaching a depth of 30 km beneath the Qilian mountains (Gao et al., 1995). This fault acts as a boundary between the seismic region to the south and the aseismic region to the north (Yan et al., 1979). Natural earthquake activity is distributed at 60–130 km depth south of the North Boundary thrust and the focal depth is not deeper than 30 km (Wu et al., 1995). Thus, it is inferred that the North China craton has been subducted southward beneath the Qilian mountains.

DISCUSSION ON MECHANISM OF THE UPLIFT OF THE QINGHAI-TIBET PLATEAU

Several lines of evidence show that intracontinental deformation occurred in the Cenozoic time, particularly since 20 Ma, after the collision between the Indian and Eurasian plates. Crustal deformation and geophysical properties of the interior and margin of the Qinghai-Tibet Plateau show significant differences during the Cenozoic geological events. Therefore, it is necessary to take the constraints on various factors, obtained from different sections and depths of the Qinghai-Tibet Plateau, into consideration.

Mantle diapir below the northern Qinghai-Tibet Plateau

The existence of the mantle diapir beneath the interior of the plateau suggests that it is an important dynamic source at depth. The genetic relationship between the mantle diapir and alkaline volcanic activities hints that the dynamic source is probably produced initially from a cohesive thermal flow, and the dynamic driving force probably originates from radioactivity and heat energy from the upper mantle. The thermal upflow moves horizontally along the lower part of lithosphere and forms an extensional setting. In contrast, along lithospheric faults, it flows up to the Earth's surface, and produces large-scale volcanic eruptions in the Hoh Xil region. The thermal upflow in the mantle is probably the cause of the multisandwich structure in which high- and low-velocity layers alternate in the lithosphere around this region.

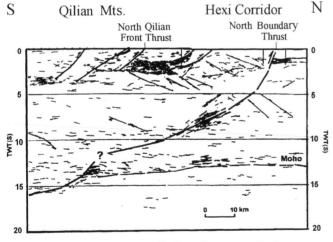

Figure 10. Explosive seismic profile from Jianyang to Aba (eastern section of Jianyang-Huashixia, after Cui et al., 1996), showing two low-velocity layers at 10 and 20 km depth beneath the eastern Qinghai-Tibet Plateau. The Yangtze craton was embedded as a wedge into the lower crust of the Longmenshan forming a "crocodile" structure between the Longmenshan, and the Yangtze Craton. 1—thrust; 2—normal fault; 3—Moho; 4—low-velocity layer; 5—wedged Yangtze craton. TWT: two-way traveltime.

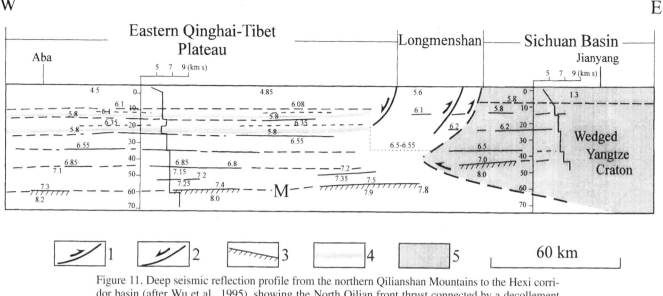

Figure 11. Deep seismic reflection profile from the northern Qilianshan Mountains to the Hexi corridor basin (after Wu et al., 1995), showing the North Qilian front thrust connected by a decollement zone represented by a reflection zone at 10 km depth beneath the Qilianshan, and the North Boundary thrust in the Hexi corridor extending southward at a low angle to 30 km depth beneath the Qilianshan. 1—Thrust fault; 2—normal fault; 3—Moho; 4—decollement zone; 5—wedged Yangtze craton.

Inward subduction at the margins of the Qinghai-Tibet Plateau

That the Indian plate subducted northward beneath the Eurasian plate has been further confirmed by the Sino-American INDEPTH I seismic profile across the Himalayas (Zhao and Nelson, 1993; Zhao et al., 1996). The result of the Sino-French seismic tomographic profile shows that the Indian lithospheric mantle subducted northward at an intermediate angle to a depth of 220 km beneath the Himalayas, but does not go beyond the Yarlung Zangbo suture. This is consistent with the results of the seismic anisotropy section, in which obvious different anisotropic directions are represented by flow of upper mantle on both sides of the Yarlung Zangbo suture (Jiang et al., 1995; Shi et al., 1998).

Some geologists have proposed that the volcanism of Hoh Xil, in the interior of the Qinghai-Tibet Plateau, is related to intracontinental subduction from the north, which would suggest that the Qaidam block and the Tarim block underlie the Kunlun mountains. However, we have not obtained any geophysical data to prove this. Instead, we propose that the North China craton plunged southwestward at a low angle beneath the Qilianshan. The intensive crustal shortening of the Qilianshan and earthquake activity since Cenozoic time support this hypothesis.

At the eastern margin of the Qinghai-Tibet Plateau, the lithospheric structure represented by the geoscientific transect data suggests the existence of intracontinental subduction between the eastern Qinghai-Tibet Plateau and the Yangtze craton. Thus, we propose a hypothesis of inward intracontinental subduction at the margins of the Qinghai-Tibet Plateau.

Significance of strike-slip faults

A number of sinistral strike-slip faults are in the interior of the Qinghai-Tibet Plateau, and these have been considered to be the result of collision between the Indian plate and the Eurasian plate (Tapponnier and Molnar, 1977; Molnar and England, 1990).

We suggest that noncoaxial compression and oblique crustal shortening in the Qinghai-Tibet Plateau, which are caused by northeast-southwest compression at the north margin and the south-north compression at the southern margin, are most likely responsible for the formation of sinistral strike-slip faults in the interior of the Qinghai-Tibet Plateau.

In conclusion, we suggest a new model to explain the mechanism of uplift of the Qinghai-Tibet Plateau, that is, a mantle diapir in the interior and inward subduction at the margins of the Qinghai-Tibet Plateau (Fig. 12). However, questions about (1) the original relationship between a mantle diapir at the interior of the plateau and inward subduction at the margins of the plateau, and (2) whether the inward subduction of the margin is active or passive remain.

ACKNOWLEDGMENTS

We acknowledge strong and continuous support given by the Ministry of Geology and Mineral Resources of the People's Republic of China and the Institut National de Science l'Univers, Center National de la Recherche Scientifique of France during the previous East Kunlun (1992–1994) and undergoing Altyn-Qilianshan (1995–1998) collaborative projects between Chinese and French scientists. We thank A. M. Macfarlane, George Zandt, Yang Wencai, and an anonymous reader for thorough and constructive reviews.

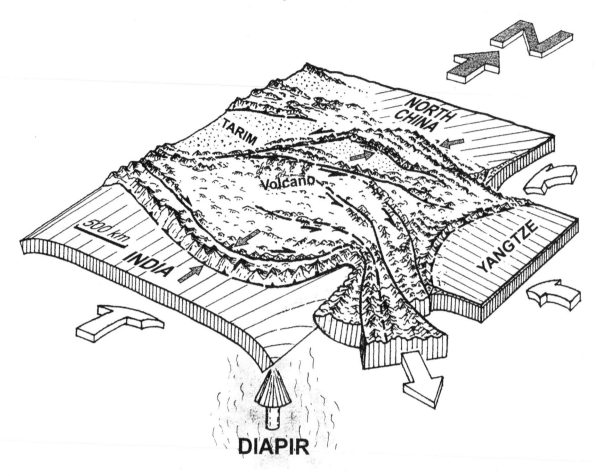

Figure 12. A model of the Qinghai-Tibet Plateau shows a mantle diapir and deep thermal spreading beneath northern interior of the plateau, suggested to be responsible for the alkaline volcanic activity of in the region. Inward intracontinental subduction occurs at the south, east, and northeast margins of the plateau, as shown by the arrows. Strike-slip faults cause eastward or southeastward extrusion of the blocks under noncoaxial compression. The spear shows the direction of high heat flow from the mantle diapir.

REFERENCES CITED

Argand, E., 1924, La tectonique de l'Asie: International Geological Congress, 13th, Brussels, 1922, Reports, v. 1, p. 170–372.

Avouac, J. P., 1991, Application des methods de morphologie quantitative a la Neotectonique: Model Cinematique des deformations actives en Asia Centrale [Ph.D. thesis]: Paris, Universite Paris VII, 50 p.

Barazangi, M., and Ni, J., 1982, Propagation characteristics of Pn beneath the Himalayan arc and Tibetan plateau: Possible evidence for underthrusting of Indian continental lithosphere beneath Tibet: Geology, v. 10, p. 179–185.

Beghoul, N., Barazangi, M., and Isacks, B. L., 1993, Lithospheric structure of Tibet and western north America: Mechanisms of uplift and a comparative study: Journal of Geophysical Research, v. 98, p. 1997–2016.

Burchfiel, B. C., and Royden, L. H., 1985, North-south extension within the convergent Himalayan region: Geology, v. 13, p. 653–679.

Bureau of Geology and Mineral Resources of Qinghai Province, 1991, Regional Geology of Qinghai Province: Beijing, Geological Publishing House, p. 206–227.

Burg, J. P., and Chen, G. M., 1984, Tectonics and structural zonation of southern Tibet, China: Nature, v. 311, p. 219–223.

Calassou, S., 1994, Etude Tectonique d'une chaine de Decollement [thesis]: Uni-

versite de Montpellier II-Sciences et Technigues du Langnedoc, 373 p.

Chemenda, A. I., 1994, Subduction, insights from physical modeling: Dordrecht, Kluwer Academic Publishers, 193 p.

Chemenda, A. I., Mattauer, M., Malavieille, J., and Bokun, A. N., 1995, A mechanism for syn-collisional rock exhumation and associated normal faulting: Results from physical modeling: Earth and Planetary Science Letters, v. 132, p. 225–232.

Cui Junwen, Zhu Hong, and Wu Chande, 1992, Yadong-Golmud GGT, Deformation and dynamics of the lithosphere in Qinghai-Xizang (Tibet) plateau: Beijing, Geological Publishing House, 164 p.

Cui Zuozhou, Chen Jiping, and Wu Ling, 1996, Altay-Taiwan GGT, texture and structure of Huashixia-Shaoyang deep crust: Beijing, Geological Publishing House, 192 p.

Deng Wanming, 1978, The Quaternary volcanic petrology and geochemistry in the Northern Tibet—A preliminary study: Acta Geologica Sinica, v. 2, p. 148–162.

Deng Wanming, 1991, Cenozoic volcanism and intraplate subduction in northern margin of the Tibet plateau: Journal of Geochemistry, v. 10, p. 140–152.

Deng Wenming, Zheng Xilan, and Yukio Matsumoto, 1996, Petrological characteristics and ages of Cenozoic volcanic rocks from the Hoh Xil Mts.,

Qinghai province: Acta Petrologica et Mineralogica, v. 15, p. 289–298.

Dewey, J., and Bird, J., 1970, Mountain belts and the new global tectonics: Journal of Geophysical Research, v. 75, p. 2625–2647.

Dewey, J., and Burke, K., 1973, Tibetan, Variscan and Precambrian basement reactivation: Products of continental collision: Journal of Geology, v. 81, p. 683–692.

Ding Daogui and Tang Liangjie, 1996, Formation and evolution of the Tarim basin: Hehai University Press House, 302 p.

England, P., and Housemen, G., 1986, Finite strain calculations of continental deformation. Comparison with the India-Asia collision zones: Journal of Geophysical Research, v. 91, p. 3664–3676.

England, P., and Houseman, G., 1989, Extension during continental convergence, with application to the Tibetan plateau: Journal of Geophysical Research, v. 94, p. 17561–17579.

Gansser, A., 1964, Geology of the Himalayas: London, Interscience Publication, John Wiley, 289 p.

Gao Rui, Cheng Xiangzhou, and Ding Qian, 1995, Preliminary geodynamic model of Golmud-Ejin Qi Geoscience transact: Acta Geophysica Sinica, v. 38, supplement II, p. 3–14.

Ge Shumo, ed., 1992, The Altyn-Tagh active fault zone: Beijing, Seismological Press, 319 p.

Hirn, A., Jiang, M., Diaz, J., Nercessian, A., Lu, Q. T., Lepine, J. C., Shi, D. N., Sachpazi, M., Pandey, M. R., Ma, K., and Gallart, J., 1995, Seismic anisotropy as an indicator of mantle flow beneath the Himalayas and Tibet: Nature, v. 375, p. 571–574.

Jiang, M., Hirn, A., and Poupinet, G., 1995, Tibetan Plateau Seismic Experiment: Design and preliminary results, 1992–1993: Global Tectonics and Metallogeny, v. 4, p. 199–201.

Jiang Mei, Lu, Q. T., Shi, D. N., Xue, G. D., Poupinet, G., and Hirn, A., 1998, Research on crust-upper mantle structure under the central Tibetan plateau by means of teleseismic experiment: Acta Geophysica Sinica (in press).

Kidd, W. S. F., and Molnar, P., 1988, Quaternary and active faulting observed on the 1985 Academia Sinica–Royal Society Geotraverse of Tibet: Royal Society of London Philosophical Transactions, ser. A, v. 327, p. 337–363.

Le Fort, P., 1975, Himalayas—the collided range, present knowledge of the continental arc: American Journal of Science, v. 275A, p. 1–44.

Li Haibing, Xu Zhiqin, and Chen Wen, 1998, Important style of introcontinental deformation: The South Kunlun strike-slip fault zone in the East Kunlun Mts.: Continental Dynamics, v. 1, no. 2 (in press).

Mattauer, M., 1990, Arguments en faveur d'un diapir mantellique sous le plateau Tibetan: Science de la Terre, v. 310, p. 1695–1700.

Mattauer, M., 1992, Continental subductions and large strike-slip faults in Tibetan-Himalayan system [abs.], *in* International symposium on the Karakoram and Kunlun Mountains, Kashi, China, June 5–9, 1992: Paris, Inst. National. Sci. Univers., p. 2.

Mattauer, M., and Brunel, M., 1989, La faille normale Nord-Himalaynne (FNNH) consequence probable d'un dispirisme granitique: Paris, Académie des Sciences Comptes Rendus, v. 308, p. 1285–1289.

Mattews, D., and Hirn, A., 1984, Crust thickening in Himalayas and Caledinides: Nature, v. 308, p. 497–498.

Molnar, P., and Deng, Q. D., 1984, Faulting associated with large earthquakes and the average rate of deformation in central and eastern Asia: Journal of Geophysical Research, v. 89, p. 6203–6228.

Molnar, P., and England, P., 1990, S-wave residuals from earthquakes in the Tibetan and lateral variations in the upper mantle: Earth and Planetary Science Letters, v. 101, p. 68–77.

Molnar, P., and Tapponnier, P., 1975, Cenozoic tectonics of Asia: Effects of a continental collision: Science, v. 74, p. 419–462.

Peltzer, G., and Tapponnier, P., 1988, Formation and evolution of strike-slip faults, rifts, and basins during the India-Asia collision: An experimental approach: Journal of Geophysical Research, v. 93, p. 15085–15117.

Powell, C., and Conaghan, P. J., 1973, Plate tectonics and the Himalayas: Earth and Planetary Science Letters, v. 20, p. 1–12.

Powell, C., and Conaghan, P. J., 1975, Tectonics models of the Tibetan Plateau: Geology, v. 3, p. 727–732.

Shen Xianjie, 1996, Plate-kinematics origin of the N-S heterogeneity of the Tibetan crustal-mantle thermal structure and its dynamic implications: Continental Dynamics, v. 1, p. 38–48.

Shi Danian, Gong Yingjun, and Jiang Mei, 1998, Shear wave anisotropy beneath the Tibetan plateau: Global Tectonics and Metallogeny, v. 5 (in press).

Tapponnier, P., and Molnar, P., 1977, Active faulting and Cenozoic tectonics of China: Journal of Geophysical Research, v. 82, p. 2905–2930.

Tapponnier, P., Peltzer, G., and Le Dain, A. Y., 1982, Propagating extrusion tectonics in Asia: New insights from simple experiments with plasticine: Geology, v. 10, p. 611–616.

Wittlinger, C., Masson, F., Tappnnier, P., Jiang Mei, Herquel, G., and Achauer, U., 1996, Seismic tomography of northern Tibet and Kunlun: Evidence for crustal blocks and mantle velocity contrasts: Earth and Planetary Science Letters, v. 139, p. 263–279.

Wu Xuanzhi, Wu Chunling, Lu Jie, and Wu Jie, 1995, Research on the fine crustal structure of the northern Qilian-Hexi Corridor by deep seismic reflection: Acta Geophysica Sinica, v. 38, supplement II, p. 29–35.

Xiao Xuchang, 1995, Tectonic evolution and uplift of the Himalaya-Tibet plateau: 10th Himalaya-Karakoram-Tibet Workshop (Abstract volume): Eidgenössischen Technischen Hochschule Conference Center Monte Verita (Ascona), Canton Ticino Switzerland: p. 45–46.

Xu Zhiqin and Cui Junwen, 1996, Deformation and dynamics of continental mountain chains: Beijing, Metallurgic Publishing House, 246 p.

Xu Zhiqin, Hou Liwei, and Wang Zongxiu, 1992, Orogenic processes of the Songpan-Ganze orogenic belt of China: Beijing, Geological publishing House, 190 p.

Xu Zhiqin, Jiang Mei, and Yang Jingsui, 1996, Tectonophysical process at depth for the uplift of the northern part of the Qinghai-Tibet Plateau: Illustrated by the geological and geophysical comprehensive profile from Golmud to the Tanggula mountains, Qinghai Province, China: Acta Geologica Sinica, v. 70, p. 195–206.

Yan Jiaquan, Shi Zhenglian, Wang Suyun, and Huan Wenlin, 1979, The regional characteristics of present-day tectonic stress field in China and adjacent region: Acta Seismologica Sinica, v. 1, p. 9–24.

Yang, J.-S., Bai, W., and Hu X., 1996, Basin subduction model for the uplift of the Qinghai-Tibet Plateau: Evidence from the Cenozoic volcanism in Hoh Xil, North Tibet: International Geological Congress, 30th, Beijing, China, 4–14 August 1996, Abstracts v. 1, p. 205.

Yang Jingsui, Xu Zhiqin, Bai Wenji, and Zhao Rongli, 1998, Cenozoic volcanism on the Qinghai-Tibetan plateau and its genesis: Continental Geodynamics (in press).

Zhang, Q. R., Xie, M. Q., and Xue, C., 1992, Statistical analysis of the structural evolution of western Qaidam basin: Geological Society of Malaysia Newsletter, v. 18, p. 265–266.

Zhang Yifu and Zheng Jian Kang, 1994, Geological overview in Hoh Xil, Qinghai and adjacent Areas: Beijing, Seismic Publishing House, 177 p.

Zhao Guoguang, Liu Dequang, Wei Wei, He Qunlu, and Su Gang, 1991, The late Quaternary slip rate and segmentation of the Xian Shuihe active fault zone, *in* Proceedings of the PRC-USA Bilateral Symposium on the Xianshuihe fault zone, Chengdu, China, October 1990: Beijing, Seismological Press, p. 41–57.

Zhao, W. J., and Nelson, K. D., 1993, Project INDEPTH Team, deep seismic reflection evidence for continental underthrusting beneath south Tibet: Nature, v. 366, p. 557–559.

Zhao Wenjin, Nelson, K. D., Che Jingkai, Brown, L. D., Xu Zhongxin, and Kuo, J.T., 1996, Deep seismic reflection in Himalaya region reveals the complexity of the crust and upper mantle structure: Acta Geophysica Sinica, v. 39, p. 615–628.

Zhao, W. L., and Morgan, W. J., 1985, Uplift of the Tibetan Plateau: Tectonics, v. 4, p. 359–369.

Zhao, W. L., and Yuen, D. A., 1987, Injection of Indian crust into Tibetan lower crust: A temperature-dependent viscous model: Tectonics, v. 6, p. 505–514.

MANUSCRIPT ACCEPTED BY THE SOCIETY FEBRUARY 3, 1998

Geological Society of America
Special Paper 328
1999

Contribution to the geology of the eastern Karakoram, India

Anshu K. Sinha,* Hakim Rai, Rajeev Upadhyay, and Rakesh Chandra
Wadia Institute of Himalayan Geology, 33 General Mahadeo Singh Road, Dehradun 248006, India

ABSTRACT

The Shyok suture zone to the north of the Trans-Himalayan Ladakh batholith delimits the southern extent of the Karakoram batholith. The two mica-granites of the Karakoram batholith contain mafic xenoliths. The Ladakh batholith intrudes the sediments of the Shyok Group, and the Karakoram batholith intrudes the Permian-Carboniferous Tethyan sequence of the Karakoram. Magmatic intrusion gave rise to metasedimentary rocks and sulfide mineralization in the Carboniferous-Permian Saser Brangsa Formation. Carbonaceous, turbidite-type, deeper water sediments of the Saser Brangsa and Chhongtash Formations are cut by post-Triassic dikes associated with the terminal phase of intrusion. The deeper water sediments are black shale, slates, and sandstone deposited under a reducing environment. These sediments contain a rich assemblage of trace fossils. The upper part of the Chhongtash Formation is marked by plant fossils bearing sandstones, some of which are calcareous in nature. Pillow lava of the Chhongtash Formation is also associated with the intrabasinal tectonic event, which may have been during Permian time.

Pink-gray-white limestone and red shale of the Morgo and Burtsa Formations have yielded a rich assemblage of shallow to deeper marine fossils. They include bivalves, gastropods, cephalopods, and corals ranging in age from Triassic to Cretaceous. This fossil assemblage indicates the extent of the basin conditions, from shallow to deeper marine during the Triassic and Cretaceous. Red-yellow conglomerates, mudstone, and sandstone of the Qazil Langer Formation suggest that deposition occurred in shallow-water continental conditions during Late Cretaceous and Paleogene time. Large clasts of these conglomerates are fossiliferous, suggesting that transportation was from a southern provenance. Continental deposits of the Qazil Langer Formation formed in an intermontane foreland basin and may be linked to the initial closing of a basin by the end of the Cretaceous. The overall geological signatures suggest that the eastern Karakoram rocks are similar to the geological formations of the Shaksgam valley of Gaetani et al. and the western Qiangtang block of Matte et al.

INTRODUCTION

During the summer of 1995, an expedition was conducted in the eastern extension of the Karakoram mountain region of Indian territory (elevations of 3,000–6,000 m) to unravel the intricacies and complex geological history of this inaccessible area bounded by the Nubra-Shyok river valleys to the south and

the Karakoram Pass to the north (Fig. 1). The field work was carried out following a traverse from Sasoma in the Nubra valley as far as the Karakoram Pass through Saser Brangsa, Chhongtash, Morgo, Burtsa, Qazil Langer, the Depsang Plain, and Daulet Beg Oldi (Figs. 1 d and e). The geographical limits of this inaccessible region are between the upper Yarkand river in the Chinese territory of the Kun-Lun range of Tibet in the north and the Ladakh Himalayan ranges in the south (Fig. 1c).

Since the mid-nineteenth century many expeditions have

---

*Present address: Birbal Sahni Institute of Palaeobotany, 53 University Road, Lucknow 226007, India.

Sinha, A. K., Rai, H., Upadhyay, R., and Chandra, R., 1999, Contribution to the geology of the eastern Karakoram, India, *in* Macfarlane, A., Sorkhabi, R. B., and Quade, J., eds., Himalaya and Tibet: Mountain Roots to Mountain Tops: Boulder, Colorado, Geological Society of America Special Paper 328.

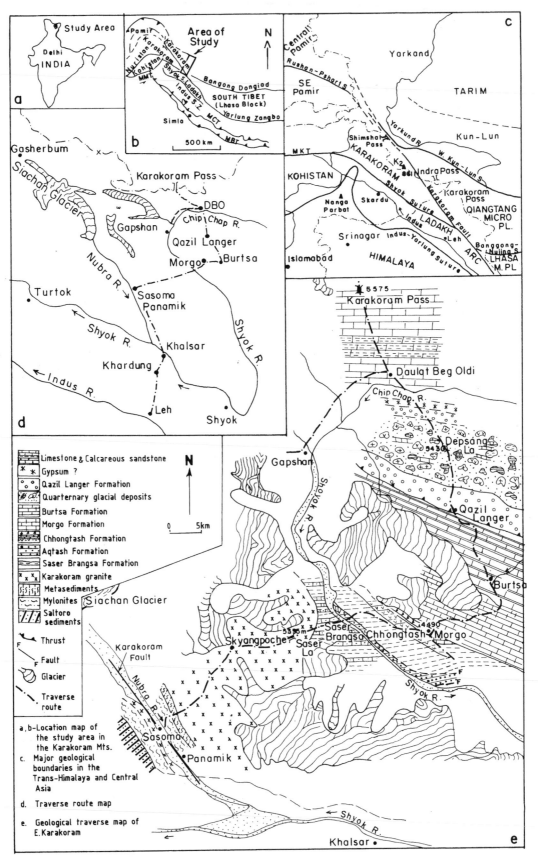

Figure 1. Geological traverse map of the eastern Karakoram. S.Z. = suture zone, MCT = Main Central thrust, M. PL = microplate, MKT = Main Karakoram thrust.

been made to the Main Karakoram mountain and through the Shyok suture zone (Stoliczka, *in* Blanford, 1878; De Fillipi, 1912; De Terra, 1932; Dainelli, 1932; Visser, 1934; Wyss, 1940; Norin, 1946; Desio, 1964, 1974, 1979, 1980). The pioneer workers described the geology of the expedition routes mainly on the northwest extension of the Main Karakoram mountain. However, Norin (1946) provided a monograph with a compiled map of western Tibet. In recent years data have been generated on different aspects of the northwest Karakoram region in northern Pakistan (e.g., Desio, 1974, 1980; Desio and Zanettin, 1970; Gaetani et al., 1990a, 1990b, 1995; Rex et al., 1988; Searle, 1991; Caporali, 1993; Tongiorgi et al., 1994). However, geological information describing different aspects of the eastern Karakoram region is still in an initial stage. Gergan and Pant's expeditional research in 1980 in some areas of eastern Karakoram was followed by that of Bagati et al. (1994). Our expedition to the Karakoram region was, however, a first attempt to cover extensively the entire transect from Ladakh collision zone as far as the Karakoram Pass point (5,575 m), the end of Indian territory (Figs. 1, b and c, and 2). The results of the earlier two expeditions were incorporated in Gergan and Pant (1983), Bagati et al. (1994), and Rai (1995). There are gaps in the stratigraphic column and information is needed to explain the structure and evolution of the Karakoram. For the first time a rich plant fossil horizon has been discovered. A rich mineralized zone of gypsum has also been found before the Karakoram Pass zone. We attempt in this chapter to cover these aspects present in a less-accessible region of Karakoram.

REGIONAL GEOLOGICAL SETTING

The 2,500-km-long Indus-Tsangpo suture has been recognized as one of the best examples of a suture zone (Figs. 1c and 2); it came into existence as a result of subduction followed by continental collision (55–60 Ma) between the Indian and Eurasian plates (Dewey et al., 1988; Frank et al., 1977; Gaetani and Garzanti, 1991; Sinha, 1989, 1997; Sinha and Upadhyay, 1993, 1994a, 1994b, 1997; Searle, 1991; Thakur, 1992; Beck et al., 1995). Recent work in central Asia and Tibet has revealed the presence of several parallel ophiolitic belts north of the Indus-Tsangpo suture (Fig. 1c) (Gaetani et al., 1990a, 1990b; Searle, 1991; Sengör, 1984, 1987; Srimal, 1986; Srimal et al., 1987; Matte et al., 1996). It has been proposed that these ophiolitic belts mark the sites of late Paleozoic and Mesozoic collisions between fragments of Gondwana and the Siberian shield (Allegre et al., 1984; Bassoullet et al., 1980; Gaetani et al., 1990a, 1990b, Srimal, 1986; Sinha, 1997; Sinha and Upadhyay, 1997). Similarly, the Karakoram mountain region has been considered as one among such fragments. It has been observed that south to north, the eastern extension of the Karakoram is between two recognized sutures, the Shyok suture or Main Karakoram thrust, which separates the Kohistan arc from the Karakoram (Coward et al., 1986; Gaetani et al., 1990b; Searle, 1991), and the west Kun-Lun suture (Gaetani et al., 1990a; Sinha, 1997; Sinha and Upadhyay, 1997) (Figs.1, b and c). The western extension of the Main Karakoram mountain is between the Main Karakoram thrust and the Rushan-Pshart suture zone (Fig. 1c), which divides the southeast Pamir from the central Pamir (Shvolman, 1981; Ruzhentsev and Shvolman, 1981). However, on the basis of Permian and Triassic stratigraphy, the significance of the Rushan-Pshart as a true suture or its east projection has been argued by Leven (1995). In recent years it has been observed in several paleogeographic reconstructions that the Rushan-Pshart suture is parallel to the Bangong-Nujiang suture in Tibet (Fig. 1c). Therefore, the north Karakoram should be equivalent to the Lhasa block (Gaetani et al., 1990b). Similarly, the Farah Rud block and/or the Helmand

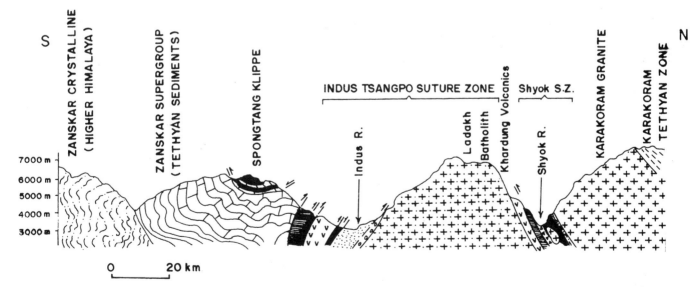

Figure 2. Geological cross section between Zanskar Himalayan ranges and Karakoram mountain (modified after Thakur, 1981).

block in central Afghanistan can be compared to Karakoram (Tapponnier et al., 1981; Boulin, 1981; Sengör, 1984; Montenat et al., 1986; Gaetani et al., 1990b).

SOUTH TO NORTH GEOLOGICAL TRAVERSE IN THE NORTHEAST KARAKORAM REGION

On the basis of field evidence across the 150-km-long south-north traverse from near Sasoma in the Nubra valley to Karakoram Pass in the eastern Karakoram mountain (Figs. 1, d and e), two major tectonic divisions have been recognized (Figs. 1, 2, 3, 4, 5, and 6): (1) the Karakoram Plutonic-Metamorphic Complex and (2) the Karakoram Tethyan zone. The rocks of the Karakoram Tethyan zone are further subdivided into six major lithostratigraphic and tectonostratigraphic subdivisions (Figs. 1e, 3, 4, 5, and 6), ranging in age from Carboniferous-Permian to Late Cretaceous and even early Paleogene (Fig. 3). Along the south-north traverse section, these subdivisions are: Saser Brangsa Formation, Aqtash Formation, Chhongtash Formation, Morgo Formation, Burtsa Formation, Qazil Langer Formation, and sedimentary sequences between the Depsang Plain and Karakoram Pass region.

Following are the preliminary descriptions of these individual tectonostratigraphic subdivisions.

KARAKORAM PLUTONIC- METAMORPHIC COMPLEX

Exposures of this complex are along the left bank of the Nubra river, which flows downstream from north-northwest toward south-southeast for a considerable distance (Figs. 1e, and 4). The Karakoram Plutonic-Metamorphic Complex is almost parallel to the sediments of the Saltoro range. The sediments of the Saltoro range are part of the Shyok suture zone (Figs.1e and 4). The sharp contact between the rocks of the Shyok suture zone and Karakoram Plutonic-Metamorphic Complex is defined by a northwest-southeast–trending fault zone. This fault zone is dotted with hot springs in the region. This alignment coincides with the alignment of the Karakoram fault zone. The metamorphic rocks of the Karakoram Plutonic-Metamorphic Complex are defined by a mylonitic zone that includes slices of strongly foliated carbonatitic slates, marbles, metaconglomerates, micaschists, and gneisses. The maximum width of these metamorphic rocks, seen in a newly constructed road section, appears to be ~50 m. The peaks of Karakoram plutonic complex are sometimes capped by these metamorphic rocks.

The granites of the Karakoram plutonic complex are two-mica varieties having large xenoliths of metasedimentary and mafic rocks. This granitic batholith intruded the Carboniferous-Permian sequence of the Karakoram Tethyan zone (Figs. 3 and 4) to the north. The most abundant rock types are weakly deformed and relatively well preserved granites, granodiorites, and tonalites. The granites are mostly coarse-grained, leucocratic, equigranular, and porphyritic to nonporphyritic types. According to Bagati et al. (1994) and Rai (1995), the oldest rock of the

batholith is tonalite and is exposed mostly in the northern part. This rock is intruded by the granite and granodiorite. At some places it occurs as a cap rock forming a thin sheet over the granites. Due to color contrast (tonalite being darker than granite or granodiorite), the tonalite could easily be distinguishable. A dike swarm mesh-work has also been encountered within the Karakoram plutonic complex. Swarms of aplite, pegmatite dikes and veins, fine-grained quartz, and felspathic veins and dikes are common in addition to the dikes of intermediate composition (Bagati et al., 1994, and our own observations). Tonalite is hornblende-biotite bearing, massive, and equigranular. These rock types show zoned plagioclase, K-feldspar, partly chloritized brown biotite, and muscovite. Apart from perthitic intergrowth, large euhedral laths of plagioclase show original albite twinning.

Geochemistry

We analyzed 18 representative granite samples to obtain major element data. The analyses were performed by the X-ray fluorescence spectrometer (Siemens SRS 3000) at the geochemical laboratory of the Wadia Institute of Himalayan Geology at Dehradun. The results are presented in Table 1. The values of major elements have been recalculated to determine the Cross, Iddings, Persson and Washington norms. The observed chemical compositions have been compared with the available standard values for the granitic rocks. Apart from sample SB-4(a) and SB-4(b), most of the samples represent a corundum-normative value (Table 1). However, the An-Ab-Or plots of Barker and Arth (1976) suggests the presence of granodiorite, quartz-monzonite, and granite in the region (Fig. 7). Similarly, the differentiation trends of the Karakoram granites could be represented by the AFM triangular diagram (Fig. 8). The differentiation trend obtained from the AFM triangular diagram represents a calc-alkaline trend (Fig. 8). Furthermore, if we follow the classification scheme of Chappel and White (1974) and plot our data, it could be envisaged that the Karakoram granites could be classified both as I- and S-type (Fig. 9). The southern S-type leucogranites have a higher molecular $Al_2O_3/Na_2O + K_2O + CaO$ ratio that ranges from 1.05 to 1.23 (The aluminium saturation index [ASI] of Zen, 1986). Therefore, the S-type Karakoram granites represent aluminium-saturated peraluminous character. Almost all the samples are in the S-type field except the tonalitic samples (SLSM 4/95, SLSM 4a/95) and pink granite of the Saser Brangsa (SB-1, SB-4a, SB-4b) region. The tonalitic samples and the pink granites of the Saser Brangsa region represent a diopside normative I-type granite with an ASI ratio generally less than 1.05 (Table 1).

The analyzed Karakoram granite samples show a considerable spread in the major element content. SiO_2 ranges between 61% and 72.95%. However, the tonalite samples represent the lowest SiO_2 content; i.e., 61% have higher TiO_2 and P_2O_5. There is a systematic decrease in all elements with the increasing SiO_2 except K_2O and Na_2O, which may indicate that the fractional crystallization played a major role for the Karakoram granite.

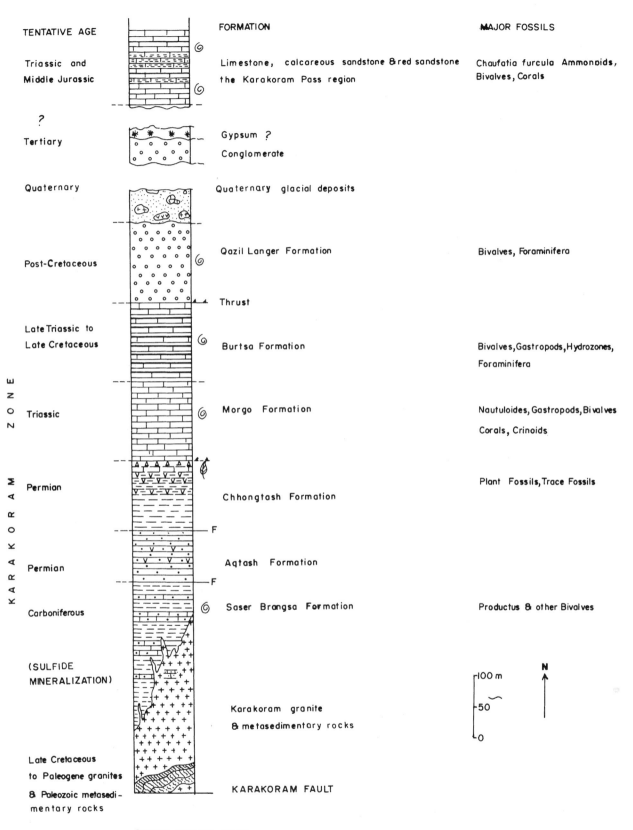

Figure 3. Schematic tectonostratigraphic traverse column of eastern Karakoram.

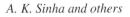

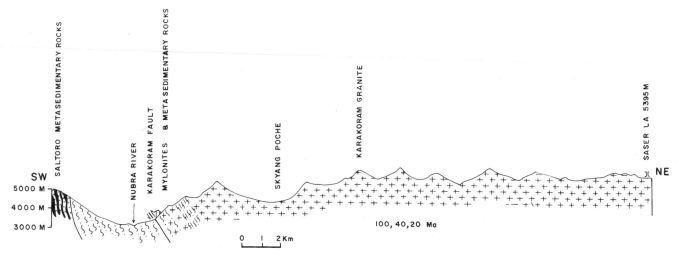

Figure 4. Geological cross section from Sasoma to Saser La.

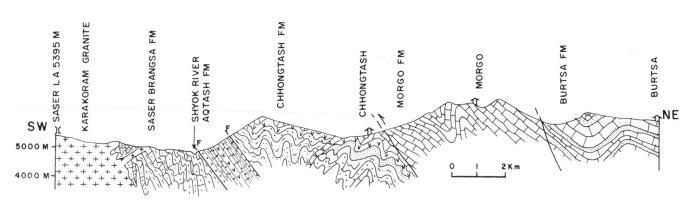

Figure 5. Geological cross section from Saser La to Burtsa Yagma.

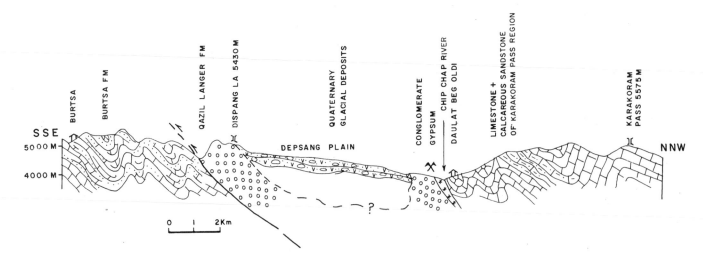

Figure 6. Schematic cross section from Burtsa to Karakoram (K.K.) Pass region. S.S.T = sandstone.

TABLE 1. REPRESENTATIVE MAJOR ELEMENT ANALYSIS OF KARAKORAM GRANITE

	1 KSG-1	2 KSG-2	3 SLSM-18	4 SLSM-18a	5 SLSM-10a	6 SLSM-9	7 SLSM-6a	8 SLSM-4	9 SLSM-4a
Major Oxides wt%									
SiO_2	72.11	72.95	70.22	69.93	69.45	72.57	68.49	61.2	61.22
TiO_2	0.23	0.16	0.29	0.29	0.37	0.2	0.33	0.75	0.76
Al_2O_3	15.13	14.99	15.72	15.63	15.88	14.77	16.46	16.39	16.76
$Fe_2O_3^{(t)}$	1.87	1.53	2.29	2.35	2.29	1.51	2.36	6.1	6.11
MnO	0.03	0.03	0.04	0.04	0.04	0.04	0.03	0.09	0.09
MgO	0.49	0.31	0.55	0.62	0.69	0.35	0.64	3.07	3.12
CaO	1.91	1.37	1.92	2.02	2.31	1.14	2.17	3.83	3.87
Na_2O	4.47	4.11	4.25	4.3	4.22	4.28	4.3	2.69	2.76
K_2O	3.3	4.06	3.5	3.52	3.16	4.74	3.99	4.7	4.74
P_2O_5	0.07	0.06	0.08	0.08	0.11	0.1	0.1	0.31	0.32
LOI	0.8	0.6	1.2	0.8	0.72	1.37	0.7	0.62	0.62
Total	100.41	100.17	100.06	99.58	99.24	101.07	99.57	99.75	100.37
A/CNK	1.05	1.1	1.1	1.09	1.09	1.04	1.07	0.99	1
CIPW Norm.									
Q	28.16	29.68	26.58	25.25	26.36	26.29	22.04	13.4	12.74
Or	19.5	23.99	20.68	20.8	18.67	28.01	23.58	27.78	28.01
Ab	37.82	34.78	35.96	36.39	35.71	36.22	36.39	22.76	23.35
An	9.02	6.4	9	9.5	10.74	5	10.11	16.98	17.11
C	0.9	1.49	1.64	1.57	1.58	0.77	1.36	0.68	0.73
Di	....	....	....	....	....	....	....	....	....
Hy	2.74	2.07	3.21	3.45	3.43	2.11	3.46	12.8	12.69
Mt	0.72	0.6	0.9	0.92	0.88	0.58	0.87	2.32	2.38
Il	0.44	0.3	0.55	0.55	0.7	0.38	0.63	1.42	1.44
Ap	0.18	0.14	0.19	0.19	0.25	0.23	0.23	0.72	0.74
Plagioclase	An19	An16	An20	An21	An23	An12	An22	An43	An42

	10 SLSM-3	11 SLSM-3a	12 SLSM-3b	13 SB-1	14 SB-4a	15 SB-4b	16 MGr-3	17 MGr-7	18 MGr-7a
Major Oxides wt%									
SiO_2	69.98	68.1	70.47	66.4	64.67	64.7	67.49	66.34	68.33
TiO_2	0.34	0.45	0.33	0.5	0.62	0.63	0.45	0.49	0.5
Al_2O_3	15.78	15.46	15.56	15.41	15.55	15.75	15.47	15.97	15.96
$Fe_2O_3^{(t)}$	2.47	3.22	2.4	4.3	4.9	4.95	3.6	3.83	3.89
MnO	0.04	0.05	0.04	0.08	0.08	0.09	0.06	0.08	0.08
MgO	0.71	1.11	0.66	1.9	2.66	2.62	1.57	1.72	1.82
CaO	2.06	2.53	2.07	3.5	4.21	4.32	3.04	2.28	2.29
Na_2O	3.76	3.56	3.8	3.14	2.89	2.98	3.2	2.9	2.9
K_2O	3.79	3.56	3.76	3.56	3.4	3.42	3.2	3.75	3.75
P_2O_5	0.11	0.15	0.11	0.15	0.19	0.19	0.15	0.15	0.15
LOI	1.2	1.04	1.2	1.8	1.7	1.7	1.7	2	2
Total	100.24	99.23	100.4	100.74	100.87	101.35	99.93	99.51	99.67
A/CNK	1.12	1.08	1.1	1	0.97	0.96	1.09	1.23	1.23
CIPW Norm.									
Q	27.59	25.95	28.01	22.99	20.66	19.98	26.88	26.68	26.48
Or	22.4	21.04	22.22	21.04	20.09	20.21	18.91	22.16	22.16
Ab	31.82	30.12	32.15	26.57	24.45	25.22	27.08	24.54	24.54
An	9.5	11.57	9.55	16.38	19.42	19.5	14.1	10.33	10.38
C	2.01	1.51	1.74	0.39	....	....	1.57	3.35	3.33
Di	....	....	....	....	0.19	0.58	....	....	....
Hy	3.63	5.33	3.53	8.27	10.46	10.25	6.81	7.38	7.67
Mt	0.87	1.18	0.94	1.68	1.91	1.93	1.41	1.49	1.52
Il	0.65	0.85	0.63	0.95	1.18	1.2	0.85	0.93	0.95
Ap	0.25	0.35	0.25	0.35	0.44	0.44	0.35	0.35	0.35
Plagioclase	An23	An28	An23	An38	An44	An44	An34	An30	An30

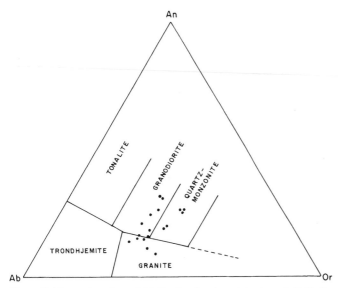

Figure 7. Normative plots of Ab-Or-An showing plutonic rock fields for Karakoram granite (diagram adapted after Barker and Arth, 1976).

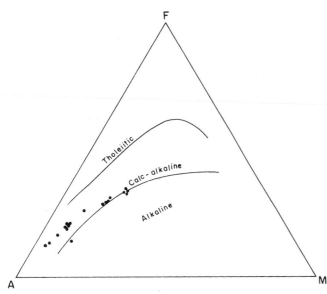

Figure 8. AFM plots showing calc-alkaline differentiation trend for Karakoram granite (diagram adapted after Barker and Arth, 1976).

No age data have been recorded from these granites in the Indian Karakoram sector, although the samples are being analyzed in geochronological laboratories in India and abroad. However, on the basis of oxygen isotope analyses of whole-rock and coexisting mineral separates, Srimal et al. (1987) proposed the existence of two contrasting granitoid suites within the Karakoram granites. The earlier Jurassic–Early Cretaceous granitic phase represents a continental margin arc magmatism (I-type), formed as a result of subduction along the North Saltoro–Bangong–Nujiang zone. The later Miocene S-type granites represent crustal anataxis in the Miocene due to intracontinental thrusting along the rejuvenated North Saltoro suture following the India-

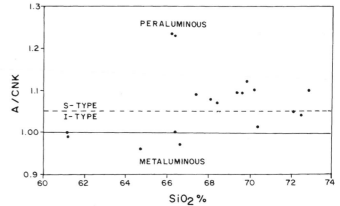

Figure 9. A/CNK diagram shows the presence of both S-type and I-type granite in the Karakoram region (diagram adapted after Chappel and White 1974).

Asia collision (Srimal et al., 1987). However, granitic rocks farther east show a range of 90–200 Ma (Bally et al., 1980). In contrast, granitic rocks from the western extension of the Karakoram belt in Kohistan have yielded mostly Eocene or younger ages (Desio, 1979). However, Debon et al. (1987) reported three major intrusive stages from the western Karakoram axial batholith and northern Kohistan. These stages are: (1) around mid-Cretaceous time (ca. 110–95 Ma); (2) during the Paleogene, to 43 Ma; and (3) during the late Miocene (ca. 9 Ma). In addition, a conspicuous network of aplite-pegmatite dikes was emplaced into the Hunza area, possibly from Eocene to the late Cenozoic time, the maximum during the middle Miocene (ca. 15 Ma) (Debon et al., 1987).

KARAKORAM TETHYAN ZONE

The rocks of the Karakoram Tethyan zone are subdivided into six lithostratigraphic and tectonostratigraphic subdivisions (Figs. 1e, 3, 4, 5, and 6) ranging in age from Carboniferous-Permian to Late Cretaceous and even early Paleogene. The Karakoram plutonic complex intruded the Carboniferous-Permian sedimentary sequence of the Karakoram Tethyan zone (Figs.3 and 10). The Carboniferous-Early Permian sequence of the Karakoram Tethyan facies could be depicted by a thick sedimentary pile (1,000 m) named the Saser Brangsa Formation. The Saser Brangsa Formation consists of thinly bedded yellow-brown shale, black shale, dark siltstone, fine-grained sandstone, recrystallized cherty limestone, and thin- to medium-bedded gray fossiliferous limestone (Fig. 10) containing marl intercalations. Huge chunks of recrystallized limestone sometimes cherty in nature have been intruded by the granite batholith of the Karakoram plutonic complex. Near the contact there is a thick horizon (30 m) that has undergone sulfide mineralization. Near the contact the sulfide mineralization is extreme, whereas disseminated mineralization is revealed by the black shale, dark siltstone, and dark gray limestone, as one moves away from the contact. On the basis of preliminary identification, the major mineralization is

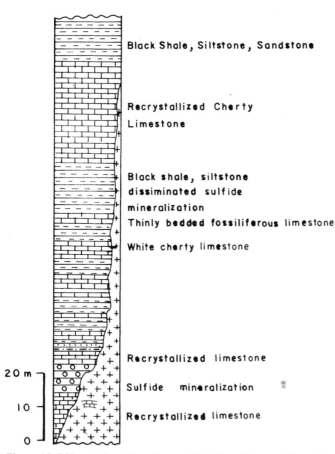

Figure 10. Lithostratigraphic column of the Saser Brangsa Formation near Saser Brangsa.

and 12) is a thick (1,000–1,200 m) sedimentary unit consisting mainly of thin- to medium-bedded black shales, slates, siltstones, dark gray conglomerates, and pillow lava (Fig. 12). This sedimentary sequence is highly folded and faulted. This formation is intruded at several places by volcanic sills and dikes. On the basis of field investigations, the sedimentary asssociation of Chhongtash Formation is consistent with the turbidites having been deposited in a relatively deeper marine environment. The major sedimentary structures discernible at outcrops are parallel lamination, wavy lamination, graded bedding, load casts, and ripple marks (Fig. 12). The middle and upper-middle parts of the Chhongtash Formation contain thoroughly deformed trace fossils. These trace fossils are very large at several places. Some of these trace fossils are similar to the *Domichnia* burrows in the Permian Gircha Formation, Chapursan valley, northern Karakoram (Gaetani et al., 1995). On the basis of occurrences of *Parafusulina, Pseudofusulina,* and *Schwagerina,* Gergan and Pant (1983) assigned a Permian age to the Chhogtash Formation. On the basis of similar fossil assemblages, Juyal and Mathur (1996) assigned a Late Permian age to the Chhongtash Formation. However, on the basis of occurrences of *Fusulinid*-bearing limestone and shales, we assigned a Late Permian age to the middle-upper level of the Chhongtash Formation. Matte et al. (1996) recorded similar *Fusulinid*-bearing limestones and shales from the Mawang Kangri mountains in western Tibet. According to them, this sequence belongs to

pyrite, chalcopyrite, malachite, magnetite, and pyrrhotite. Some of the outcrops of this horizonn have extreme sulfide mineralization. However, our collection of *Productid* brachiopods and unidentifiable bivalves from the dark green to black siltstone horizon reveals, and further confirms, a Carboniferous age for the sediments of the Saser Brangsa Formation. The thinly bedded bioclastic and fossiliferous limestone of this formation has yielded crinoids, algae, and other as-yet unidentified fossils.

Farther northward, the Saser Brangsa Formation is overlain by the Aqtash Formation. The Aqtash Formation is a 500-m-thick tectonically bounded zone of polygenetic conglomerate, purple and green shale, medium-bedded gray-yellow limestone sometimes massive in nature, chert, and volcanics. The sediments of Aqtash Formation do not contain any megafossils; therefore, no precise age could be assigned to this formation. Gergan and Pant (1983), however, assigned a Triassic age to the Aqtash Formation. On the basis of the microfossil assemblages, Juyal and Mathur (1996) assigned a tentative Early Permian age to the Aqtash Formation. However, on the basis of tectonostratigraphy, a Permian age could be assigned to the Aqtash Formation (Figs. 3 and 11). The northern fringe of the Aqtash Formation is in tectonic contact with the Chhongtash Formation (Figs. 1e, 3, and 12). The Chhongtash Formation (Figs. 1e, 3,

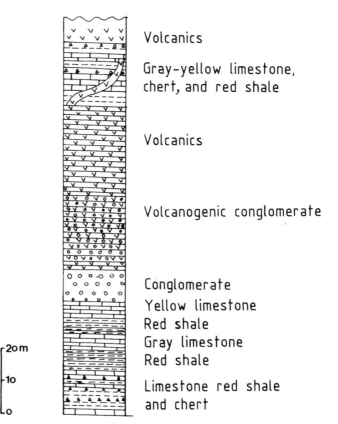

Figure 11. Lithostratigraphic column of the Aqtash Formation.

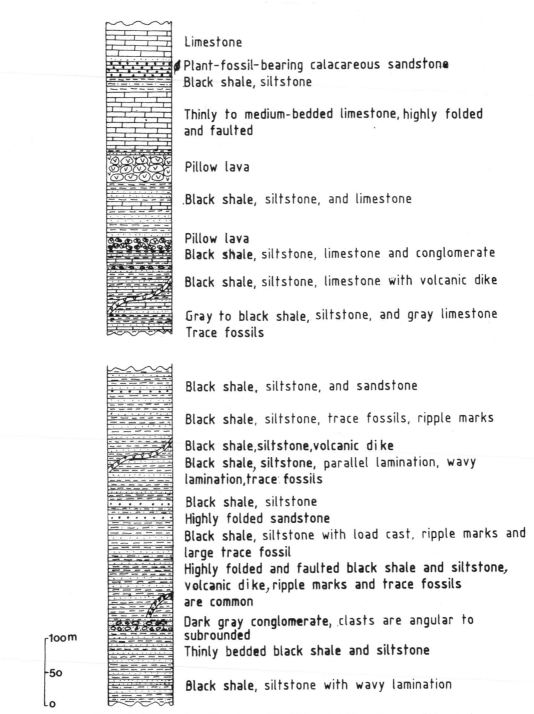

Limestone
Plant-fossil-bearing calacareous sandstone
Black shale, siltstone

Thinly to medium-bedded limestone, highly folded and faulted

Pillow lava

Black shale, siltstone, and limestone

Pillow lava
Black shale, siltstone, limestone and conglomerate

Black shale, siltstone, limestone with volcanic dike

Gray to black shale, siltstone, and gray limestone
Trace fossils

Black shale, siltstone, and sandstone

Black shale, siltstone, trace fossils, ripple marks

Black shale, siltstone, volcanic dike
Black shale, siltstone, parallel lamination, wavy lamination, trace fossils

Black shale, siltstone
Highly folded sandstone
Black shale, siltstone with load cast, ripple marks and large trace fossil
Highly folded and faulted black shale and siltstone, volcanic dike, ripple marks and trace fossils are common
Dark gray conglomerate, clasts are angular to subrounded
Thinly bedded black shale and siltstone

Black shale, siltstone with wavy lamination

100 m

50

0

Figure 12. Lithostratigraphic column of the Chhongtash Formation near Chhongtash.

the western Qiangtang block. Therefore, at this stage we could tentatively correlate the Permian Chhongtash Formation with the Permian sequences of the Mawang Kangri in western Tibet.

The lower and middle parts of the Chhongtash Formation are mostly medium- to fine-grained graywacke, and thus represent a possible deeper marine turbiditic environment of deposition. Pillow lava in the middle and upper-middle portion of the

Chhongtash Formation could be related to the intrabasinal rift volcanism during the Permian. However, the pillow lava is overlain by a thin succession of highly folded and faulted pelagic shale and siltstone, followed by a thick succession of thin- to medium-bedded limestone, highly folded and faulted in nature. The upper portion of the Chhongtash Formation is represented by an important plant-fossils-bearing horizon that is overlain by a thick succession of limestone (Fig. 12). These fragmentary plant fossils are preserved in a gray-brown sandstone that is sometimes calcareous in nature. Preliminary examination of some of the fragmentary plant remains indicates the presence of *Equisetalean* stem fragments. Similar occurrences of *Equisetalean* stem fragments were recorded by Norin (1946) from the southern side of Mawang Kangri in western Tibet. The presence of *Equisetalean* fragments both from the Mawang Kangri and Chhongtash region further suggests geological similarities in these regions. If this is true, the presence of the Qiangtang element is possible in the eastern Karakoram region. However, we recorded reworked marine palynomorphs from the collected samples, which may indicate a possible Carboniferous to Triassic age (B. S. Venkatachala, 1997, personal commun.). Therefore, an upper age limit to the sediments of the Chhongtash Formation could be given at a later stage. The overall geometry of these sediments records a deeper marine environment gradually shallowing toward the north.

The sedimentary sequence of the Chhongtash Formation evolves into a huge, very massive and thick horizon of gray-white-pink shallow-water limestone and dolomite unit named the Morgo Formation (Figs. 1e and 3). The medium- to thick-bedded platform limestone of the Morgo Formation is highly folded and faulted. The formation also contains intercalations of gray and red shale and chert. The upper-middle portion of the Morgo Formation represents a thick horizon of brecciated limestone. The rocks of the Morgo Formation have yielded a very rich fossil assemblage including gastropods, cephalopods, corals, bryozoans, bivalves, and crinoids. Therefore, on the basis of the presence of *Nautiloid*, gastropods, corals, bryozoans, and crinoids, the sediments of the Morgo Formation may be Triassic in age.

Farther north the Morgo Formation is succeeded by a thick succession of thin- to medium-bedded gray-pink limestone, dolomite, chert, cherty limestone, shale, siltstone, and thin bands of gypsum. This sedimentary succession is known as the Burtsa Formation (Figs.1e and 3). The Burtsa Formation is highly folded and faulted, and forms a large intrabasinal synformal structure in the region; the presence of cherty limestone indicates deepening. The microfacies of some of the studied samples are dominated by sponge spicules and foraminifera, and represent the pelagic facies within the Burtsa Formation. We collected *Megadolontid* bivalve, gastropods, brachiopods, bryozoans, hydrozoans, and foraminifers from the Burtsa Formation. On the basis of the reported fauna, a Late Triassic and Late Cretaceous age could be assigned to the lower and upper levels of the Burtsa Formation. However, detailed identification work on different fossils would ascertain the stratigraphic break within and tectonic implications of this long interval.

Farther north, the Burtsa Formation is followed by an intermontane foreland basin consisting mainly of conglomerates. This sedimentary sequence is named the Qazil Langer Formation (Figs.1e, 3, and 6). The lower Qazil Langer Formation is marked by red-yellow conglomerates, whereas the upper part consists of red-yellow mudstone and medium- to coarse-grained sandstone. The rocks of the Qazil Langer Formation are in thrust contact with the underlying Burtsa Formation. The conglomerate of the Qazil Langer Formation is polymictic, containing clasts ranging from pebble to boulder size, fairly rounded and often poorly sorted, embedded in a red-yellow matrix; they are more calcareous-ferrugenous in composition and there is little siliceous cement. The majority of these clasts are of fossiliferous limestone, cherty limestone, and dolomite; some are sandstone. De Terra (1932), Dainelli (1933), and Norin (1946) suggested a Triassic age for the Qazil Langer Formation. Gergan and Pant (1983) assigned a Cretaceous age on the basis of the occurrence of *Globigerinoides* and *Textularia*. Juyal and Mathur (1996) recorded a Maastrichtian *Cymopolia tibetica* algal taxon from a limestone pebble of the Qazil Langer Formation. Therefore, on the basis of similarity in the fossiliferous clasts of limestone and cherty limestone, it could be envisaged that the majority of these clasts were derived from the adjacent Burtsa Formation. Therefore, the age of the Qazil Langer Formation would be post-Late Cretaceous because the age of Burtsa Formation is Late Triassic to Late Cretaceous. Gaetani et al. (1993) correlated the Qazil Langer Formation with the Cretaceous Urdok conglomerate of the Shaksgam valley in northwest Karakoram. However, the Urdok conglomerate is polygenetic in origin containing lesser amounts or no amounts of limestone clasts, whereas the Qazil Langer Formation represents a polymictic conglomerate containing abundant calcareous clasts. Similar conglomeratic sequences were reported from the adjoining Lingzhi-thang region of western Tibet (Norin, 1946). This may indicate that the geological formations of the eastern Karakoram region extend toward western Tibet. Kumar and Rai (1998) proposed that the sediments of the Qazil Langer Formation represent stratigraphic coarsening- and fining-upward sequences deposited by debris flows and braided streams. The facies associations, body geometry, and paleoflow pattern indicate a northward-prograding alluvial fan in a humid warm climate.

Farther north, the rocks of the Qazil Langer Formation are unconformably overlain by the Depsang Plain (Figs. 1e, 3, and 6). The Depsang Plain is a very wide (30–40 km) flat area 5,000–6,000 m in elevation surrounded by high snow-covered peaks. The Depsang Plain is locally dissolved into isolated, usually rounded, although sometimes flat-topped, plateau-like hills. Isolated, smoothly molded low hills resembling roches moutonne are also scattered over the plain. The geological formations of the Depsang Plain are reduced to low ridges and are largely covered with Quarternary-Holocene sediments. On the basis of similar geological structure and geomorphological character, the Depsang Plain could be correlated with the adjoining plains of Lingzi-thang and Sumtsi-ling of western Tibet. Similarly, on the basis of similarity in geological structure, Norin (1946) indicated the presence of Aghil Ranges in the Depsang Plain region.

Farther north the geological formations of the Depsang

Plain region are succeeded by an interesting and important sedimentary unit, tentatively named the sedimentary rocks of the Karakoram Pass region (Figs. 1e, 3, and 6). The limestone, calcareous sandstone, and red-purple-gray-yellow sandstone of this formation are highly folded and at several places faulted. The fold style of this formation is different from that of the rest of the Karakoram Tethyan zone. The strongly folded rocks of this region form sharp, parallel ridges with jagged crests and are perhaps similar to the fan-shaped Loqzung ranges of western Tibet. The limestone of this formation is thin to medium bedded. Near the Karakoram Pass the dark gray limestones are oolitic in nature, and sometimes yield corals; therefore, they represent a shallow-water origin. A significant Middle Jurassic ammonoid-bearing horizon is discernible around 16–17 km southeast of the Karakoram Pass. The red-gray-yellow calcareous sandstone of this formation has yielded ammonoids and some bivalves. Preliminary identification of these ammonoids by Jaikrishna reveals the presence of Middle Jurassic (Bathonian-Bajocian) *Chaufatia furcula* sp. Similar ammonoids were collected from a marly limestone horizon near the Rimo glacier region by Dainelli (1932). De Terra (1932) collected similar ammonoids from a locality near Daulet Beg Oldi. This ammonoid locality may be consistent with our collection. Norin (1946) also reported the presence of Middle Jurassic ammonoids from a locality near Sarig Kol in western Tibet. These fossil occurrences further strengthen our correlating and further extending the geological sequences of the eastern Karakoram region to western Tibet.

The thick sequence of red-purple-gray-yellow sandstone within the Jurassic Formation of the Karakoram Pass region is significant. On the basis of preliminary investigations by and recent work of Gaetani et al. (1990a) in the Sinkiang province of China, a possible correlation of this sandstone with those of the Jurassic Marpo sandstone of Shaksgam cannot be ruled out. If this is true, the Jurassic Formation of the Karakoram Pass region could be related to the Kun-Lun orogen and may be a part of the Qiangtang microplate (Leeder et al., 1988; Gaetani et al., 1990a).

On the basis of these preliminary investigations, it could be envisaged that the sediments of the Karakoram Tethyan zone are more or less similar to the adjoining Permian-Cretaceous Shaksgam sedimentary belt (Gaetani et al., 1990a) of the northwest Karakoram in Sinkiang province, China, and adjoining geological sequences of western Tibet. If we compare our preliminary results with the geological formations of western Tibet described by Matte et al. (1996) and Norin (1946), it could be suggested that there is a close similarity between the western Qiangtang block of Matte et al. (1996) and the eastern Karakoram region.

This chapter is a part of detailed studies of the eastern Karakoram currently conducted by the Wadia Institute of Himalayan Geology, Dehradun, under the Department of Science and Technology, Government of India research project, to elucidate the evolution of the Karakoram in the heart of the Central Asian highlands, which are tectonically active.

ACKNOWLEDGMENTS

We are grateful to the Department of Science and Technology, Government of India, New Delhi, for providing financial assistance under the sponsored project no. ESS/CA/A9-32/93 and partial funding for presentation of this paper. We thank authorities at the Wadia Institute of Himalayan Geology for execution of the project. We thank the Ministry of Defence, Government of India, Indian Army, and Indo-Tibetan Border Police personnel for extending their valuable help during the expedition. Sinha is grateful to organizers of the 11th Himalayan-Karakoram-Tibet workshop (April 28th–May 1st, 1996), Flagstaff, University of Arizona. We also thank N. K. Saini and Shri Chandra Shaker of the Wadia Institute of Himalayan Geology, X-ray flourescence spectrometer lab for analyzing the granite samples and the generation of other geochemical data.

REFERENCES CITED

Allegre, C. J., Courtillot, V., Tapponnier, P., Hirn, A., Mattauer, M., Coulon, C., Jaeger, J. J., Achache, J., Scharer, U., Marcoux, J., Burg, J. P., Girardeau, J., Armijo, R., Gariepy, C., Gopel, C., Li Tindong, Xuchang, X., Chenfa, C., Li Guangqin, Baoyu, L., Jiwen, T., Naiwen, W., Guoming, C., Tonglin, H., Xibin, W., Wanming, D., Huaibin, S., Yougong, C., Zhou Ji, Hongrong, Q., Peisheng, B., Songchan, W., Bixiang, W., Yaoxiu, Z., and Ronghua Xu, 1984, Structure and evolution of the Himalaya-Tibet orogenic belt: Nature, v. 307, p. 17–22.

Bagati, T. N., Rai, H., Kumar, R., and Juyal, K. P., 1994, Expedition report on the geology of eastern Krakoram, India: Journal of Himalayan Geology, v. 5, p. 65–92.

Bally, A. W., Allen, C. R., Geyer, R. B., Hamilton, W. B., Hopson, C. A., Molnar, P. H., Oliver, J. E., Opdyke, N. D., Plafker, G., and Wu, F. T., 1980, Notes on the geology of Tibet and adjacent areas-Report of the America Plate Tectonics delegation to the People's Republic of China: U.S. Geological Survey Open-File Report 80-501, 100 p.

Barker, F., 1979, Trondhjemite: Definition, environment and hypotheses of oirgin, in Barker, F., ed., Trondhjemite, dacite and related rocks in petrology: Armsterdam, Elsevier, v. 6, p. 1–12.

Barker, F., and Arth, J. G., 1976, Generation of trondhjemite-tonalitic liquids and Archean bimodal trondhjemite-basalt suites: Geology, v. 4, p. 596–600.

Bassoullet, J. P., Boulin, J., Colchen, M., Marcoux, J., Mascle, G., and Montenant, C., 1980, L'evolution des domaines tethysiens au pourtour du Carbonifere au Cretace, in Auboin, J., Debelmas, J., and Latreille, M., eds., Geology of the Alpine chains born of the Tethys: Memoires du Bureau de Recherches Geologiques et Minieres de France, v. 115, p. 180–188.

Beck, R. A., Burbank, D. W., Sercombe, W. J., Riley, G. W., Barndt, J. K., Berry, J. R., Afzal, J., Khan, A. M., Jurgen, H., Metje, J., Cheema, A., Shafique, N. A., Lawrence, R. D., and Khan, M. A., 1995, Stratigraphic evidence for early collision between Northwest India and Asia: Nature, v. 373, p. 55–58.

Blandford, W. T., 1878, "Scientific results of the second year and mission": Geology based upon the collection and notes of the late Ferdinand Stoliczka, Memoirs of the Geological Survey of India, Calcutta, v. 17, n.p.

Boulin, J., 1981, Afghanistan structure, Greater India concept and eastern Tethys evolution: Tectonophysics, v. 72, p. 261–287.

Caporali, A., 1993, Recent gravity measurements in the Karakoram, in Treloar, P. J. and Searle, M. P., eds., Himalayan tectonics : Geological Society of London Special Publication, 74, p. 9–20.

Chappel, B. W., and White, A. J. R., 1974, Two contrasting granite types: Pacific Geology, v. 8, p.173–174.

Coward, M. P., Windley, B. F., Broughton, R., Luff, I. W., Petterson, M. G., Pudsey, C., Rex, D., and Khan, M. A., 1986, Collision tectonics in the NW Himalayas, in Coward, M.P., and Ries, A., eds., Collision tectonics: Geological Society of London Special Publication 19, p. 203–219.

Dainelli, G., 1932, My expedition in the Eastern Karakoram 1930: Himalayan Journal, v. IV, p. 46–54.

Dainelli, G., 1933, La Serie dei terreni, in Relazioni Scientifiche della Spedizione Italiana De Filippi nell Himalaia, Caracorume Turchestan Cinese (1913–1914), II, Volume 2: Bologna, Zanichelli, p. 458–542.

Debon, F., Le Fort, P., Dautel, D., Sonet, J., and Zimmermann, J. L., 1987, Granites of western Karakoram and northern Kohistan (Pakistan): A composite Mid-Cretaceous to Upper Cenozoic magmatism: Lithos, v. 20, p. 19–40.

De Fillipi, F., 1912, La Spedizione nel Karakorum e nall imalaia occidentiale 1909 with appendix by Novarese, volume on the Geology of Bologna: Bologna, Zanichelli, 541 p.

Desio, A., 1964, Geological tentative map of the western Karakoram: Milan, Italy, Milano University Institute of Geology, scale 1: 500,000.

Desio, A., 1974, Karakoram Mountains: Geological Society of London Special Publication 4, p. 255–266.

Desio, A., 1979, Geological evolution of the Karakoram, in Farah, A., and DeJong, K. A., eds., Geodynamics of Pakistan: Quetta, Geological Survey of Pakistan, p. 111–124

Desio, A., 1980, Geology of the Upper Shaksgam valley, North-East Karakoram, Xizang (Sinkiang), Italian Expedition to the Karakoram (K2) and Hindu Kush, (Prof. Ardito Desio Leader), Scientific Reports, v. III, no. 4: Leiden, E. Brill, 196 p.

Desio, A., and Zanettin, B., 1970, Geology of the Baltoro Basin in Desio, A., and Zanettin, B., eds., Scientific reports of Italian expedition to Karakoram (K2) and Hindukush, Volume III— Geology-Petrology 2: Leiden, E. Brill, p. 1–308.

De Terra, H., 1932, Geologische Forschungen in west lischen Kun-Lun and Karakoram Himalaya Lwissensch Ergenbn, d, Dr. Trinklerschen Zentralasien Expedition, Volume 2: Berlin, Dietrich Reimer/Ernst Vohsen, 196 p

Dewey, J. F., Shackleton, R. M., Chang Cheng Fa, and Sun Yiyin, 1988, The tectonic evolution of the Tibetan Plateau: Royal Society of London Philosophical Transactions, ser. A, v. 327, p. 379–413.

Frank, W., Gansser, A., and Trommsdorff, V., 1977, Geological observations in the Ladakh area (Himalaya): Schweizerische Mineralogische. und Petrographische Mitteilungen, v. 57, p. 89–113.

Gaetani, M., and Garzanti, E., 1991, Multicyclic history of the northern Indian continental margin (north-western Himalaya): American Association of Petroleum Geologists Bulletin, v. 75, p. 1427–1446.

Gaetani, M., Gosso, G., and Pognante, U., 1990a, A geological transect from Kun-Lun to Karakorum (Sinkiang, China): The western termination of the Tibetan Plateau. Preliminary note: Terra Nova, v. 2, p. 23–30.

Gaetani, M., Jadoul, F., Nicora, A., Tintori, A., Pasini, M., and Kanwar, S. A. K., 1990b, The north Karakoram side of the Central Asia geopuzzle: Geological Society of America Bulletin, v. 102, p. 54–62.

Gaetani, M., Jadoul, F., Erba, E., and Garzanti, E., 1993, Jurassic and Cretaceous orogenic events in the North Karakoram; age constraints from sedimentary rocks, in Treloar, P. J., and Searle, M. P., eds., Himalayan tectonics: Geological Society of London Special Publication 74, p. 39–52.

Gaetani, M., Angiolini, L., Garzanti, E., Jadoul, F., Leven, Y. E., Nicora, A., and Sciunnach, D., 1995, Permian stratigraphy in the northern Karakorum, Pakistan: Rivista Italiana di Paleontologia e Stratigrafia, v. 101, p. 107–152.

Gergan, J. T., and Pant, P. C., 1983, Geology and stratigraphy of Eastern Karakoram, Ladakh, in Thakur, V. C., and Sharma, K. K., eds., Geology of Indus Suture Zone of Ladakh: Dehra Dun, Wadia Institute of Himalayan Geology, p. 99–106.

Juyal, K. P., and Mathur, N. S., 1996, Stratigraphic status and age of the Tethyan sedimentary sequence of the eastern Karakoram, in Pandey, J., Azmi, R. J., Bhandari, A., and Dave, A., eds., Contributions to the XV Indian Colloquium on Micropaleontology and Stratigraphy: Dehradun, K. D. Malaviya Institute of Petroleum Exploration and Wadia Institute of

Himalayan Geology, p. 765–775.

Kumar, R., and Rai, H., 1998, Post-Cretaceous molasse deposits of the intermontane foreland basin in eastern Karakoram, India: Tertiary Research (in press).

Leeder, M. R., Smith, A. B., and Yin Jixiang, 1988, Sedimentology, paleoecology and palaeoenvironmental evolution of the 1985 Lhasa to Golmud geotraverse, in Chang Chenfa, Shackleton, R. M., Dewey, J. F., and Jixiang, Y., eds., The Geological Evolution of Tibet, Royal Society Academica Sinica Geotraverse of the Qinghai-Xizang Plateau: Royal Society of London Philosophical Transactions, ser. A, v. 237, p. 107–143.

Leven, E. Y., 1995, Permian and Triassic of the Rushan-Pshart Zone (Pamir): Rivista Italiana di Paleontologia e Straatigrafia, v. 101, p. 3–16.

Matte, P., Tapponnier, P., Arnaud, N., Bourjot, L., Avouac, J. P., Vidal, P., Qing Liu, Yuaheng Pan, and Wang Yi, 1996, Tectonics of western Tibet the Tarim and Indus: Earth and Planetary Science Letters, v. 142, p. 311–330.

Montenat, C., Girardeau, J., and Marcoux, J., 1986, La ceinture ophiolitique Neo-Cimmerienne au Tibet, dans les Pamirs et an Afghanistan: Evolution geodynamique comparative: Sciences de la Terre Mémoires, v. 47, p. 229–252.

Norin, E., 1946, Geological exploration in western Tibet: Report on Sino-Swedish Expedition 29: Stockholm, Sweden, Aktiebolaget Thule, 214 p.

Rai, H., 1995, Geology of eastern Karakoram, Ladakh district, India: Nepal Geological Society Journal, v. 10, p. 11–20.

Rex, A. J., Searle, M. P., Tirrul, R., Crawford, M. B., Prior, D. J., Rex, D. C., and Barnicoat, A., 1988, The geochemical and tectonic evolution of the central Karakoram, North Pakistan: Royal Society of London Philosophical Transactions, v. 326, p. 229–255.

Ruzhentsev, S. V., and Shvolman, V. A., 1981, Tectonic zoning of the Pamirs and Afghanistan, in Sinha, A. K., ed., Contemporary geoscientific researches in Himalaya: Dehradun Bishan Singh, Mahendra Pal Singh Publishers, v. 1, p. 53–59.

Searle, M. P., 1991, Geology and tectonics of the Karakoram Mountains: Chichester, John Wiley and Sons Ltd., 358 p.

Sengör, A. M. C., 1984, The Cimmeride orogenic system and the tectonics of Eurasia: Geological Society of America Special Paper, 195, 82 p.

Sengör, A. M. C., 1987, Tectonics of the Tethysides: Orogenic collage development in a collisional setting: Annual Review of Earth and Planetary Sciences, v. 15, p. 213–244.

Shvolman, V. A., 1981, Relicts of the Mesotethys in the Pamirs: Himalayan Geology, v. 8, p. 369–378.

Sinha, A. K., 1989, Geology of the Higher Central Himalaya: Chichester, John Wiley and Sons, 219 p.

Sinha, A. K., 1997, The concept of terrane and its application in Himalayan and adjoining region, in Sinha, A. K., Sassi, F. P., and Papanikolaou, D., eds., Geodynamic domains in Alpine Himalayan Tethys: Oxford and New Delhi, India Book House Publication Company, Rotterdam, A.A. Balkema, p. 1–44.

Sinha, A. K., and Upadhyay, R., 1993, Mesozoic Neo-Tethyan pre-orogenic deep marine sediments along the Indus-Yarlung Suture: Terra Nova, v. 5, p. 271–281.

Sinha, A. K., and Upadhyay, R., 1994a, Tectonic setting and pre-orogenic sedimentation along the Indus-Tsangpo (Yarlung) Suture Zone of Ladakh Himalaya, India: Journal of South East Asian Earth Sciences, v. 9, p. 435–450.

Sinha, A. K., and Upadhyay, R., 1994b, Flysch: A historical perspective and the Himalayas: Earth Science Reviews, v. 36, p. 47–58.

Sinha, A. K., and Upadhyay, R., 1997, Tectonics and sedimentation in the passive margin, trench, forearc and backarc areas of the Indus Suture Zone in Ladakh and Karakoram: A review: Geodynimica Acta, v. 10, p. 1–12.

Srimal, N., 1986, India-Asia collision: Implication from the geology of the eastern Karakoram: Geology, v. 14, p. 523–527.

Srimal, N., Basu, A. R., and Kyser, K. Y., 1987, Tectonics inferences from oxygen isotopes in volcano-plutonic complexes of the India-Asia collision zone, NW India: Tectonics, v. 6, p. 261–273.

Tapponnier, P., Mattauer, M., Proust, F., and Cassa, I. C., 1981, Mesozoic ophiolites, sutures and large scale tectonic movements in Afghanistan: Earth and Planetary Science Letters, v. 52, p. 355–371.

Thakur, V. C., 1981, Regional framework and geodynamic evolution of the Indus-Tsangpo Suture Zone in the Ladakh Himalayas: Royal Society of Edinburgh Transactions, v. 72, p. 89–97.

Thakur, V. C., 1992, Geology of Western Himalaya: Oxford, U.K., Pergamon, 1–366 p.

Tongiorgi, M., Di Milla, A., Le Fort, P., and Gaetani, M., 1994, Palynological dating (Arening) of the sedimentary sequence overlying the Ishkarwaz granite (Upper Yarkhun valley, Chitral, Pakistan): Terra Nova, v. 6, p. 595–607.

Visser, P. C., 1934, The Karakoram and Turkistan Expedition of 1929–30: Geographical Journal, v. 84, p. 281–295.

Wyss, R., 1940, Geologie, in Visser, C., and Visser-Hooft, J., eds., Wissenschaftliche Ergebnisse der Niedarlandis chen expedition in den Karakoram, 1922, 1925, 1929–30, 1nd 1935, usw, Bed III, 2: Leiden, E. Brill, 548 p

Zen, E-an, 1986, Aluminum enrichment in silicate melts by fractional crystallization: Some mineralogic and petrographic constraints: Journal of Petrology, v. 27, p. 1095–1117.

MANUSCRIPT ACCEPTED BY THE SOCIETY FEBRUARY 3, 1998.

Geological Society of America
Special Paper 328
1999

Rb-Sr isotopic study of the Chilas Igneous Complex, Kohistan, northern Pakistan

Masumi U. Mikoshiba
Geochemistry Department, Geological Survey of Japan, 1-1-3 Higashi, Tsukuba 305, Japan
Yutaka Takahashi
Geology Department, Geological Survey of Japan, 1-1-3 Higashi, Tsukuba 305, Japan
Yuhei Takahashi
Geological Survey of Japan, Hokkaido Branch, Kita-8, Nishi-2, Kita-ku, Sapporo 060, Japan
Allah Bakhsh Kausar and Tahseenullah Khan
Geoscience Laboratory, Geological Survey of Pakistan, Chak Shahzad, P.O. Box 1461, Islamabad, Pakistan
Kazuya Kubo
Geology Department, Geological Survey of Japan, 1-1-3 Higashi, Tsukuba 305, Japan
Teruo Shirahase
International Geology Office, Geological Survey of Japan, 1-1-3 Higashi, Tsukuba 305, Japan

ABSTRACT

The Chilas Igneous Complex is one of the major geologic units in the Kohistan terrane of the Himalaya of northern Pakistan. The Kohistan terrane is regarded as a tilted island-arc sequence. The Chilas Complex is a 300-km-long, 40-km-wide plutonic body that intrudes the Kamila Amphibolite. The Main facies rocks of the Chilas Complex consist of gabbronorite, diorite, and quartz diorite. Small bodies of ultramafic-mafic association composed mainly of peridotitic-gabbroic cumulates, and a layered gabbronorite body, are also present, probably as xenoliths. A few samples are considered to have been contaminated as a result of assimilation of xenolithic materials and country rocks: Excluding them, 14 whole-rock samples of the Main facies have an Rb-Sr age of 111 ± 24 Ma and an initial $^{87}Sr/^{86}Sr$ ratio of 0.70403 ± 0.00006. Gabbroic rocks from the ultramafic-mafic association, from the layered gabbronorite body, and from mafic dikes, have $^{87}Sr/^{86}Sr$ ratios between 0.7039 and 0.7044, interpreted to be close to the $^{87}Sr/^{86}Sr$ ratios at the time of their generation. The whole-rock isochron age for the Main facies is regarded as the age of intrusion. The initial $^{87}Sr/^{86}Sr$ ratio for the Main facies is within the range of typical arc magmas, suggesting that the igneous activity occurred within an island arc or orogenic belt close to a continental margin. The age of intrusion of the Chilas Complex is similar to that of the earliest magmatism in the Kohistan batholith and to the Cretaceous plutonism in Ladakh and Karakorum, indicating large-scale generation of subduction-related magmas in the western Himalayan region and Karakorum during the mid-Cretaceous.

Mikoshiba, M. U., Takahashi, Y., Takahashi, Y., Kausar, A. B., Khan, T., Kubo, K., and Shirahase, T., 1999, Rb-Sr isotopic study of the Chilas Igneous Complex, Kohistan, northern Pakistan, *in* Macfarlane, A., Sorkhabi, R. B., and Quade, J., eds., Himalaya and Tibet: Mountain Roots to Mountain Tops: Boulder, Colorado, Geological Society of America Special Paper 328.

INTRODUCTION

The Kohistan terrane, which is located in the Himalaya of northern Pakistan, is considered to be an island-arc sequence sandwiched between the Asian and Indian continental crusts (Tahirkheli et al., 1979). Deep crustal members are now exposed over a wide region in Kohistan, which makes it an ideal area to study the genesis and evolution of subduction-related crustal structures and rocks.

The Chilas Igneous Complex, a large mafic-intermediate plutonic body, is one of the major geologic units in Kohistan. Rocks of the Chilas Complex are petrographically and compositionally similar to plutonic xenoliths found in island arcs (Khan et al., 1989). Previous isotopic studies for the Chilas Complex are limited only to K-Ar and ^{40}Ar-^{39}Ar dating (Treloar et al., 1989).

Rb-Sr isotopic data for the Chilas Complex reported here help to determine its age of emplacement and evolutional history with respect to the Kohistan region. The results are compared with mafic-intermediate complexes studied in some other crustal sections.

GEOLOGIC FRAMEWORK OF KOHISTAN

The Kohistan and Ladakh terranes are sandwiched between the Asian and Indian continental crusts. The Kohistan terrane is bounded by the Northern suture in the north and the Main Mantle thrust in the south (Fig. 1; Tahirkheli et al., 1979; Pudsey, 1986). Because the rocks within the Kohistan terrane have been tilted northward, a north to south profile forms a section that extends stratigraphically and structurally downward (Coward et al., 1982). The Chalt Volcanics and overlying Yasin Group, which are Lower Cretaceous volcanics and sedimentary rocks, are exposed just south of the Northern suture (Coward et al., 1986). Sedimentary rocks from the Yasin Group are dated as Aptian-Albian (Pudsey, 1986; 119–97 Ma). The Kohistan batholith is composed of gabbroic to granitic plutons of Cretaceous to Tertiary age (Petterson and Windley, 1985), which intrude the Chalt and Yasin Groups in the north, and intrude metasedimentary and metavolcanic rocks (Jaglot Group in Khan et al., 1996) in the east-central part of the Kohistan terrane. The Chilas Complex is a 300-km-long, 40-km-wide plutonic body (Jan et al., 1984) that extends parallel to the general trend of the Kohistan terrane. The Kamila Amphibolite, a highly deformed sequence of arc-type metavolcanic and metaplutonic rocks (Jan, 1988; Khan et al., 1993) that may contain ocean-floor relics (Coward et al., 1986; Treloar et al., 1996), is south of the Chilas Complex. K-Ar and ^{40}Ar-^{39}Ar ages of hornblende from the Chilas Complex and the Kamila Amphibolite were obtained by Jan and Kempe (1973), Zeitler (1985), Jan (1988), and Treloar et al. (1989). Treloar et al. (1989) considered that the Chilas Complex and the Kamila Amphibolite cooled to below 500 °C by 80 Ma. In the southern part of the Kohistan terrane, garnet-bearing granulite and peridotite of the Jijal Complex are exposed; the Jijal Complex underwent high-pressure metamorphism (670–790°C, 12–14 kbar; Jan and Howie, 1981; 700–950 °C, 10–17 kbar; Yamamoto, 1993). Along the Main Mantle thrust, there is a tectonic wedge (maximum width 10–15 km) that contains high-pres-

sure metamorphic rocks such as glaucophane schist and piedmontite schist (Shams et al., 1980; Coward et al., 1982).

It has been proposed in several studies that northward subduction of the Neo-Tethyan oceanic plate led to the development of the Kohistan-Ladakh terrane (e.g., Tahirkheli et al., 1979; Honegger et al., 1982; Bard, 1983). The collision between the Asian continent and Kohistan was inferred to have taken place between 102 and 75 Ma on the basis of Rb-Sr and K-Ar ages of syncollisional leucogranites and postcollisional basic dikes close to the Northern suture (Petterson and Windley, 1985). The main collision between the Asian-Kohistan block and the Indian continent was initiated during ca. 66–50 Ma (Patriat and Achache, 1984; Beck et al., 1995), during which time the Kohistan block was obducted onto the Indian continent and was juxtaposed along the Main Mantle thrust.

CHILAS IGNEOUS COMPLEX

There have been several studies of the geology and petrography of the Chilas Complex (Jan and Kempe, 1973; Jan, 1979; Jan et al., 1984; Khan et al., 1985, 1989, 1993). The Chilas Complex is well exposed along the Indus and Swat Rivers and mainly consists of gabbronorite, diorite, and quartz diorite (Fig. 1). These rocks compose the Main facies, which was termed the gabbronorite association by Khan et al. (1989). There are also small bodies of ultramafic-mafic association, which were previously termed the ultramafic-mafic-anorthosite association (Khan et al., 1989). In this chapter, we use ultramafic-mafic association,

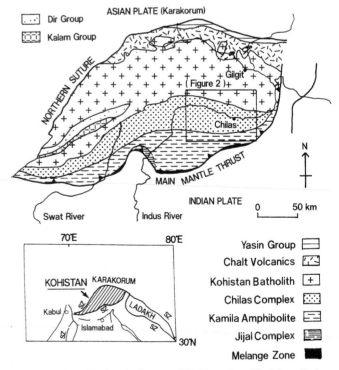

Figure 1. A simplified geologic map of Kohistan (modified form Treloar et al., 1990; Honneger et al., 1982). SZ = suture zone.

because anorthosite is restricted to a small part of layered rocks. According to Jan and Howie (1980), some of the rocks of the Chilas Complex were reequilibrated under granulite facies conditions at 750–850 °C and 6–8 kbar.

The geology and petrography of the eastern part of the Chilas Complex are described in the following (Figs. 1 and 2).

The Kamila Amphibolite is present in the south of the Chilas Complex. In the upper part of the Thor River area, a tributary of the Indus River (Fig. 2), the Chilas Complex intrudes the Kamila Amphibolite and contains amphibolite xenoliths (Takahashi et al., 1993). The same genetic relationship is recognized in the Swat Valley (Fig. 1), on the southern margin of the Chilas Complex (Kubo et al., 1992). Microscope studies of thin sections revealed that the Kamila Amphibolite has a thermally metamorphosed texture and the gabbronorite has an igneous texture without any evidence of recrystallization. A part of the contact between the Chilas Complex and the Kamila Amphibolite is sheared, as in the upper part of the Thak River area (Fig. 2, the Jal shear zone; Khan and Coward, 1990). On the north side of the Chilas Complex, tonalite and quartz diorite of the Kohistan batholith are present, and are probably younger than the Chilas Complex (Fig. 2). In the upper part of the Khanbari River area, amphibolitic rocks, which appear to be thermally metamorphosed plutonic rocks, are intruded by gabbronorite of the Chilas Complex and by the tonalite (Fig. 2; Takahashi et al., 1996). A similar relationship is present in the upper part of the Kiner River area (Fig. 2).

The Main facies rocks are generally homogeneous and consist mainly of gabbronorite, pyroxene diorite, and pyroxene quartz diorite. Pyroxene quartz diorite is present in the areas of the Khanbari and Kiner Rivers, near the junction of the Indus and Hoda Rivers, and in the upper part of the Thor River area. Gabbronorite grades into diorite and quartz diorite without a distinct contact. The Main facies rocks contain plagioclase, orthopyroxene, and clinopyroxene, and small amounts of magnetite and ilmenite. Small amounts of hornblende and biotite are commonly present. Some of the diorite and quartz diorite contain biotite or K-feldspar as well as quartz. The rocks have a granoblastic texture. Locally, some rocks contain a large amount of amphibole, due to retrogressive greenschist metamorphism.

The bodies of ultramafic-mafic association are located mainly in the eastern part of the Chilas Complex. One of them, the Thak body just to the east of Chilas, shows excellent outcrops (Fig. 2). The

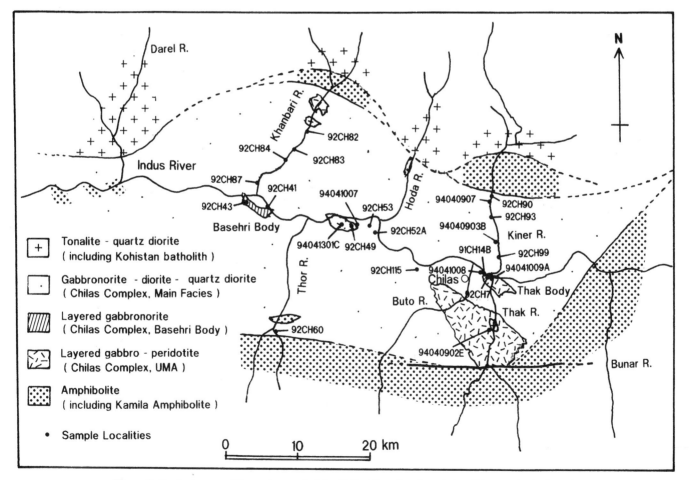

Figure 2. Geologic map of the eastern part of the Chilas Complex. Sample localities are also indicated. R = river, UMA = ultramafic-mafic association.

Thak body is a layered cumulate body, 5 km in width, and is intruded irregularly by gabbronorite probably derived from the Main facies. The cumulate consists mainly of olivine, plagioclase, clinopyroxene, and orthopyroxene, and varies from dunite to anorthosite. Some rocks contain hornblende or a small amount of spinel.

In addition to the ultramafic-mafic association, a layered gabbroic body (the Basehri body) is at the junction of the Indus and Khanbari Rivers, and is characterized by well-developed rhythmic layering. Most of the layers are overturned (Kubo et al., 1996). The Basehri body is composed of gabbronorite similar to that of the Main facies except for its layered structure, coarser grain size, and more Mg-rich composition of pyroxene. This body is intruded by the Main facies rocks. Amphibolite xenoliths are in the Chilas Complex, possibly of the Kamila Amphibolite, and they are thermally recrystallized. Thin dikes of hornblende gabbro are present mainly in the ultramafic-mafic association and partly in the Main facies rocks.

In the northern part of the Kiner River area, many leucocratic layers consisting of quartz, biotite, and garnet are present locally. Some of them appear to have a hybrid origin. The leucocratic layers are probably deformed xenoliths of metasedimentary rocks.

GEOCHEMISTRY

Previous geochemical studies of the Chilas Complex were done by Jan and Kempe (1973) and Khan et al. (1989, 1993). The rocks of the Chilas Complex (the Main facies) have a calc-alkaline nature, and they have more affinity with a mature calc-alkaline arc than with a primitive tholeiitic island arc (Khan et al., 1989). The rocks of the ultramafic-mafic association contain unusually high abundances of compatible elements reflecting the predominantly cumulate character, and they have rare earth element (REE) abundances distinctively lower than the main gabbronorites (Khan et al., 1993).

In this study, major and trace elements were determined by X-ray fluorescence spectrometry (XRF) using a RIGAKU 3370E in the Geoscience Laboratory at the Geological Survey of Pakistan. Some of the trace element data were obtained by XRF using a PW1404 at the Geological Survey of Japan. The chemical compositions of the rock samples are presented in Table 1.

Figure 3 shows the variations in chemical composition of the Main facies rocks. The silica content ranges from 49 to 60 wt% in almost all samples, except for one peculiar gabbronorite located at the northern edge of the Chilas Complex (92CH90, not presented in Fig. 3) that has a very low silica content (40 wt%), and is characterized by very large amounts of opaque minerals (about 10 vol%). The Main facies rocks have relatively linear continuous trends that suggest a comagmatic genesis for the rocks (Fig. 3). This chemical variation may be as a result of crystallization of a single evolving magma, or solidification of magmas from a common source. Sr concentration in most rocks of the Main facies is between 300 and 500 ppm, and does not change with silica content. Rb concentration, however, varies with silica content. Some rocks having more than 54 wt% silica

are rich in Rb. Concentrations of Rb and K are positively correlative with each other, and they are also correlative with the amounts of biotite and K-feldspar.

Gabbroic cumulates of the ultramafic-mafic association are relatively depleted in silica compared to the Main facies rocks, and are characterized by low contents of incompatible elements. Some of the cumulate rocks have high CaO and Al_2O_3 contents and low FeO contents, reflecting accumulation of plagioclase (e.g., 92CH7). Hornblende gabbro from the dikes is relatively depleted in silica.

RB-SR ISOTOPIC STUDY

Analytical techniques and measured samples

$^{87}Sr/^{86}Sr$ ratios were determined by VG Sector 54 and VG Micromass 30 54R mass spectrometers at the Geological Survey of Japan, and by a Finnigan MAT 262Q mass spectrometer at the University of Tsukuba. All $^{87}Sr/^{86}Sr$ ratios were normalized to a $^{86}Sr/^{88}Sr$ value of 0.1194. During the period of this analysis, the $^{87}Sr/^{86}Sr$ ratios of NBS 987 standard were 0.710257 ± 0.000004 (1σ) for the Sector 54, 0.710261 ± 0.000017 for the Micromass 30 54R, and 0.710237 ± 0.000005 for the MAT 262Q. Thus, $^{87}Sr/^{86}Sr$ data measured by the Micromass 30 54R and the MAT 262Q were normalized by adding –0.000004 and +0.000020, respectively, to the ratios by the VG Sector 54. Rb and Sr concentrations were determined by isotope dilution method using the Micromass 30 54R mass spectrometer and by XRF. Calculation of the Rb-Sr isochron follows the method of York (1966), taking into account uncertainties of ±0.010% (1σ) for $^{87}Sr/^{86}Sr$ ratios and ±3% (1σ) for $^{87}Rb/^{86}Sr$ ratios (or ±5% when Rb content is less than 5 ppm). The uncertainty of ages and the initial $^{87}Sr/^{86}Sr$ ratios are shown by 2σ. The decay constant of ^{87}Rb used for calculations is $\lambda = 1.42 \times 10^{-11}$/yr.

Localities of the analyzed samples are shown in Figure 2. In addition, two samples were collected from the Swat Valley. The descriptions of the samples are presented in Table 2. Samples were collected from outcrops without xenoliths to avoid contamination. They are generally fresh except for one sample (92CH82) from the Khanbari River site. Most samples are gabbronorite, diorite, and quartz diorite from the Main facies. Plagioclase-rich cumulate of the Thak body (the ultramafic-mafic association), gabbronorite of the Basehri body, and hornblende gabbro from dikes were also analyzed. A sample from a leucocratic layer at the Kiner River site was also analyzed. Peridotites were not analyzed in this study.

Analytical results

The analytical results are presented in Table 3. Sr concentrations in samples from the Main facies are less than 500 ppm, except for one sample (92CH90) having an 800 ppm Sr content (Table 3). Rb concentrations in the Main facies samples are

TABLE 1. MAJOR AND TRACE ELEMENT DATA
FOR THE ROCKS FROM THE CHLAS COMPLEX*

Unit	Main facies					Thak body	Basehri body	Dike
Sample	92CH41	92CH84	92CH87	92CH60	92CH99	92CH7	92CH43	94041301C
(wt.%)								
SiO_2	50.63	53.99	55.05	58.76	58.14	44.95	53.51	46.03
TiO_2	1.02	0.70	0.88	0.92	0.93	0.04	0.37	1.27
Al_2O_3	18.37	19.54	17.31	15.95	16.28	27.97	18.98	19.29
Fe_2O_3[†]	10.11	7.56	8.82	7.23	7.72	4.06	7.38	10.67
MnO	0.16	0.13	0.14	0.11	0.12	0.06	0.12	0.14
MgO	5.83	4.24	4.86	4.32	4.33	6.43	6.33	8.76
CaO	10.49	8.79	8.51	6.88	7.29	15.86	9.41	11.21
Na_2O	2.96	3.98	3.23	3.47	3.32	0.63	3.33	2.17
K_2O	0.30	0.78	1.06	1.88	1.43	0.02	0.53	0.44
P_2O_5	0.15	0.15	0.14	0.18	0.20	<0.01	0.04	0.02
(ppm)								
V	228	159	171	206	171	27	117	299
Cr	126	85	105	159	157	222	159	121
Co	38	30	30	28	26	22	37	n.d.
Ni	46	27	42	59	38	102	83	118
Cu	42	37	78	116	91	n.d.	19	215
Zn	75	66	69	63	64	98	56	76
Rb	1.34[§]	5.80[§]	14.53[§]	68.68[§]	33.66[§]	0.13[§]	4.16[§]	1.2
Sr	344.9[§]	452.2	333.7[§]	279.2[§]	362.1[§]	406.1	363.1	394.1
Y	17	19	21	26	23	3.2	9	24
Zr	34	58	95	127	163	29	33	38
Nb	2	4	4	6	5	<1	1	2
Ba	156	337	263	300	331	21	120	46

*Sample localities are shown in Figure 2. Sample description are given in Table 2. Samples were analyzed on dry basis.
[†]Total iron is represented as Fe_2O_3.
[§]Determined by isotope dilution method.
n.d.: No data.

between 0.7 and 69 ppm. The samples that have relatively high ratios of $^{87}Rb/^{86}Sr$ (>0.1) show scattered distribution in the areas of the Indus, Kiner, Thor, Khanbari, and Swat Rivers.

The results of the isotopic analyses of the Main facies samples are presented in the $^{87}Sr/^{86}Sr$ versus $^{87}Rb/^{86}Sr$ plot (Fig. 4). The samples from the northern part of the Kiner River (92CH90, 94040907, 92CH93) and the altered sample (92CH82) have higher $^{87}Sr/^{86}Sr$ ratios than the other samples at a given $^{87}Rb/^{86}Sr$ ratio (Fig. 4). Leucocratic layers are developed in the northern part of the Kiner River area, and one sample analyzed from the leucocratic layer has a considerably high $^{87}Sr/^{86}Sr$ ratio (Table 3). Sample 92CH90 has a unique chemical and modal composition. Thus, the samples from the northern part of the Kiner River area were probably contaminated by assimilation of country rocks before their solidification, even though these rocks are homogeneous. Therefore, these samples, indicated by solid triangles in Figure 4, are excluded from the following discussions.

The rest of the data have a positive correlation in Figure 4, indicating that most of the Main facies rocks were previously homogenized with regard to Sr isotope ratio. If the sample with the highest

$^{87}Rb/^{86}Sr$ ratio (92CH60) is included in the calculation, we obtain an age of 87 ± 19 Ma with an initial $^{87}Sr/^{86}Sr$ ratio of 0.70407 ± 0.00006, indicated by a broken line in Figure 4. However, sample 92CH60, which is by far the richest in Rb of all analyzed samples, was obtained about 1 km from the southern margin of the Chilas Complex. The pyroxene quartz diorite, which contains a large amount of biotite and/or K-feldspar, like sample 92CH60, is present only near the southern margin of the Chilas Complex along the Thor River. Inclusions of amphibolites are observed in the outcrop close to the contact, as described earlier. Near the contact, quartz-rich veins or pegmatitic veins are abundant in the Kamila Amphibolite, and they are also in the Chilas Complex. Moreover, other samples that have moderately high $^{87}Rb/^{86}Sr$ ratios are plotted above the calculated broken line in Figure 4. Therefore, we propose that sample 92CH60 has a Rb-Sr isotope composition different from other samples. This sample may have been contaminated by the wall rock or possibly by some fluid-rich component that interacted with the wall rock before solidification of the magma. Alternatively, it may have a thermal history different from other rocks of the Main facies. Excluding sample 92CH60, 14 whole-rock samples have a Rb-Sr

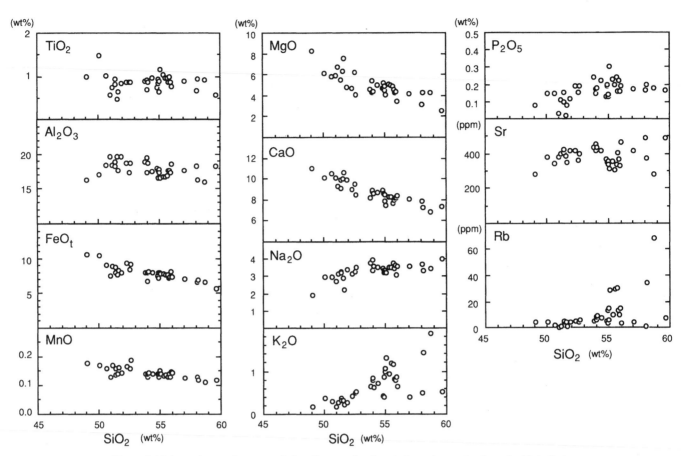

Figure 3. Major and trace element variation diagrams for the whole-rock samples from the Main facies of the Chilas Complex.

age of 111 ± 24 Ma and an initial $^{87}Sr/^{86}Sr$ ratio of 0.70403 ± 0.00006, shown as the solid line in Figure 4. This line is considered to be the best isochron for the Main facies rocks.

The five gabbroic rocks other than the Main facies have $^{87}Rb/^{86}Sr$ ratios <0.05, reflecting their low concentration of Rb (Fig. 5). The $^{87}Sr/^{86}Sr$ ratios of the plagioclase-rich cumulate from the Thak body are 0.70392 and 0.70434. The $^{87}Sr/^{86}Sr$ ratio of the gabbronorite from the Basehri body is 0.70407. The $^{87}Sr/^{86}Sr$ ratios of the hornblende gabbro dikes are 0.70401 and 0.70407. The number of samples may not be sufficient to identify any systematic variation of the isotopic compositions according to locality or rock units. The $^{87}Sr/^{86}Sr$ ratios of these five samples at the time of their generation are close to their present $^{87}Sr/^{86}Sr$ ratios, because of their low $^{87}Rb/^{86}Sr$ ratios. For example, the $^{87}Sr/^{86}Sr$ ratios of the five samples at 111 Ma are calculated to be between 0.70391 and 0.70434, very close to their present ratios, which overlap the initial $^{87}Sr/^{86}Sr$ ratio of the Main facies rocks.

DISCUSSION

The Rb-Sr isotopic data for the Main facies rocks of the Chilas Complex (excluding the contaminated samples) define a Cretaceous age. The samples that have relatively high $^{87}Rb/^{86}Sr$ ratios

occur as homogeneous rocks in outcrops, not as veins or pegmatitic dikes. The variation of the $^{87}Rb/^{86}Sr$ ratio in the Main facies rocks, as supported by whole-rock chemical variation, is a consequence of the generation or evolution processes of the magma, and is not due to secondary mobilization of Sr and/or Rb by metamorphic processes. The Rb-Sr whole-rock age is regarded to represent the age of intrusion of the Main facies, and the constituent magma had a homogeneous Sr isotopic composition at that time. The results lead to the following two possibilities: (1) the Main facies may represent a crystallization sequence from a single parental magma; and (2) the Main facies may be composed of several intrusive units derived from a common source over a short period of time. In both cases, a large amount of magma was supplied to the deep part of the crust.

The Rb-Sr whole-rock isochron age of 111 ± 24 Ma for the Main facies rocks obtained in this study is consistent with $^{40}Ar-^{39}Ar$ ages of 82 ± 5 Ma and 82 ± 3 Ma from hornblende in the Chilas Complex, which may date cooling through 500 °C (Treloar et al., 1989). Several researchers have presumed the intrusive age to be Cretaceous (Jan et al., 1984; Khan et al., 1993). Our study provides quantitative data and supports this proposal.

The initial $^{87}Sr/^{86}Sr$ ratio for the Main facies, 0.70403 ±

TABLE 2. DESCRIPTIONS OF THE SAMPLES FOR THE Rb-Sr ISOTOPIC ANALYSIS

Sample	Locality (River)	Rock name*	Features
Main facies			
92CH41	Indus	Hb-opx-cpx gabbronorite	
92CH49	Thurli	Bi bg. hb-cpx-opx gabbronorite	
94041008	Indus	Hb-cpx-opx gabbronorite	
92CH84	Khanbari	Hb-bi-cpx-opx diorite	Weakly lineated
92CH115	Indus	Bi-cpx-opx gabbronorite	
91CH14B	Indus	Hb-bi-cpx diorite	
92CH87	Khanbari	Hb bg. bi-cpx-opx diorite	Weakly lineated
92CH83	Khanbari	Bi-cpx-opx-hb quartz diorite	
92CH52A	Indus	Bi-opx-cpx diorite	
92CH53	Indus	Hb bg. bi-cpx-opx quartz diorite	Weakly lineated
94041007	Indus	Bi-cpx-opx quartz diorite	
92CH99	Kiner	Bi-opx-cpx quartz diorite	
92CH60	Thor	Hb-opx-cpx-bi quartz diorite	
90CH51	Swat	Hb-opx-cpx-bi quartz diorite	
90CH52	Swat	Hb-cpx-bi-opx quartz diorite	
92CH90	Kiner	Hb-opx-cpx gabbronorite	Abundant in opaque minerals
94040907	Kiner	Hb-bi-cpx-opx quartz diorite	
92CH93	Kiner	Bi-cpx-opx quartz diorite	Hetrogeneous distribution of biotite
92CH82	Khanbari	Bi bg. cpx-opx-hb tonalite	Weathered
Thak body			
92CH7	Indus	Ol-spi-hb-opx-cpx gabbronorite	Layered, pl-cpx-opx cumulate
94041009A	Indus	Cpx-hb gabbro	Plagioclase-rich cumulate
Basehri body			
92CH43	Indus	Hb-bi-cpx-opx gabbronorite	Layered
Dike			
94041301C	Indus	Bi-opx bg. hb gabbro	1 – 5 cm wide dike, fine-grained
94040902E	Thak	Opx-hb gabbro	5 – 20 cm wide dike, fine-grained
Leucocratic layer†			
94040903B	Kiner	Grp-spi-sil-gt-bi gneiss	Foliated, including porphyroblasts of garnet

*Rock names are after IUGS Subcomission, 1973. Abbreviations: hb = hornblende; opx = orthopyroxene; cpx = clinopyroxene; bi = biotite; bg. = bearing; ol = olivine; spi = spinel; gt = garnet; sil = sillimanite; grp = graphite.
†Sample is probably deformed xenolith of metasedimentary rock.

0.00006, is apparently higher than the ^{87}Sr/^{86}Sr ratios for mid-ocean ridge basalt (MORB) (0.7024–0.7030 for normal MORB, 0.7030–0.7035 for plume MORB; Wilson, 1989), but it is an appropriate value for subduction-related magmas, and is especially typical for island-arc magmas (Faure, 1986). This radiogenic isotope result indicates that the Main facies rocks formed from subduction-related magma that originated at a typical arc or continental margin orogenic belt. Any contribution of the magmas derived directly from depleted source mantle such as ocean-floor basalt is negligible. This result is in agreement with the calc-alkaline arc-type geochemical characteristics of the Main facies. The Main facies intruded the arc-type mafic-intermediate rocks (the Kamila Amphibolite), and there is no evidence for the existence of a previous continental crust in Kohistan. Therefore, we propose that the generation of the Chilas Complex (the Main facies) is regarded as a result of subduction-related magmatic activity along the Kohistan arc, possibly near the continental margin of Asia.

Several researchers have suggested that the Chilas Complex represents magmatic activity during the initial stages of intra-arc splitting (Khan et al., 1993) or during an episode of back-arc rifting (Khan et al., 1996). Cenozoic back-arc basalts have ^{87}Sr/^{86}Sr ratios (0.7024–0.7039; Saunders and Tarney, 1984) transitional between MORB and arc basalts. The initial ^{87}Sr/^{86}Sr ratio of the Main facies of the Chilas Complex corresponds to the upper limit of that range, and is not contradictory to these suggestions.

The calculated ^{87}Sr/^{86}Sr ratios at 111 Ma for the plagioclase-rich cumulate of the Thak body (the ultramafic-mafic association), for the gabbronorite of the Basehri body, and for the hornblende gabbro dikes, are not distinguishable from one another, and these ratios are similar to the initial ^{87}Sr/^{86}Sr ratio

**TABLE 3. Rb-Sr ISOTOPIC DATA FOR THE CHILAS COMPLEX
AND ASSOCIATED ROCK**

Sample	Sr (ppm)	Rb (ppm)	^{87}Rb/^{86}Sr	^{87}Sr/^{86}Sr
Main facies				
92CH41	344.9*	1.34	0.0113	0.704148
92CH49	349.2*	1.09	0.0090	0.704126
94041008	400.6*	0.76	0.0055	0.703976
92CH84	452.2*	5.80	0.0371	0.704072
92CH115	416.1	8.52	0.0592	0.704034
91CH14B	355.4*	5.78	0.0471	0.704021
92CH87	333.7	14.53	0.1260	0.704276
92CH83	466.5*	3.08	0.0191	0.704086
92CH52A	356.0	9.68	0.0786	0.704130
92CH53	305.9	29.05	0.2747	0.704615
94041007	335.6	30.38	0.2619	0.704405
92CH99	362.1	33.66	0.2689	0.704371
92CH60	279.2	68.68	0.7115	0.704806
90CH51	350.4	43.59	0.3598	0.704550
90CH52	446.7	38.68	0.2504	0.704466
92CH90	800.5*	5.80*	0.0210	0.704534
94040907	433.3*	5.06*	0.0338	0.704224
92CH93	331.7	14.79	0.1290	0.704560
92CH82	489.6*	0.75*	0.0044	0.704128
Thak body				
92CH7	406.1*	0.13	0.0009	0.703915
94041009A	400.5*	0.83*	0.0060	0.704344
Basehri body				
92CH43	363.1*	4.16	0.0332	0.704065
Dike				
94041301C	394.1*	1.18*	0.0087	0.704066
94040902E	247.5*	0.52	0.0061	0.704007
Leucocratic layer†				
94040903B	320.8*	148.1*	1.336	0.712700

*Determined by X-ray fluorescence.
†Sample is probably deformed xenolith of metasedimentary rock.

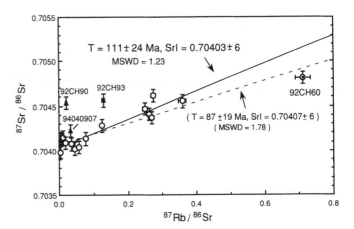

Figure 4. ^{87}Sr/^{86}Sr versus ^{87}Rb/^{86}Sr diagram for the whole-rock samples from the Main facies of the Chilas Complex. Solid triangles indicate one weathered sample (92CH82) and three samples from the northern part of the Kiner River probably contaminated by assimilation of the country rocks. The solid and broken lines indicate the age and initial ^{87}Sr/^{86}Sr ratio calculated for 14 samples (open circles) excluding sample 92CH60, and for 15 samples including 92CH60, respectively. SrI = initial ^{87}Sr/^{86}Sr ratio, MSWD = mean square weighted deviation, T = time.

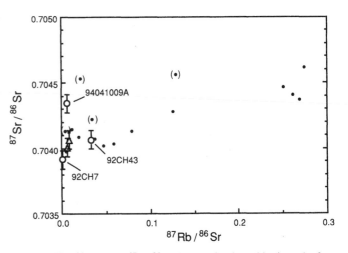

Figure 5. ^{87}Sr/^{86}Sr versus ^{87}Rb/^{86}Sr diagram for the gabbroic rocks from the Thak and Basehri bodies (open circles) and from dikes (open triangles) of the Chilas Complex. The Main facies rocks that have ^{87}Rb/^{86}Sr ratios <0.3 are also plotted for comparison (dots). The Main facies rocks that were weathered or probably contaminated are expressed by dots in parentheses.

of the Main facies rocks. This suggests that all these rocks may have been derived from the source materials similar to those of the Main facies rocks.

Figure 6 shows the Rb-Sr isotope data from this study and those from the Kohistan batholith (Petterson and Windley, 1985; Debon et al., 1987). The whole-rock age and the initial ^{87}Sr/^{86}Sr ratio of the Main facies are similar to those of the oldest pluton in the Kohistan batholith (Matum Das pluton, 102 ± 12 Ma, initial ^{87}Sr/^{86}Sr = 0.7039 ± 0.0001; Petterson and Windley, 1985). Thus, there may be a correspondence in the timing of intrusion of the Chilas Complex and the first magmatism of the Kohistan batholith. Nevertheless, a direct genetic relationship between the Chilas Complex and the Matum Das pluton is doubtful because of the differences in their chemical trends and in their REE compositions (see Petterson and Windley, 1985, 1991; Khan et al., 1993). In the Kohistan terrane, the Yasin Group is dated as Aptian-Albian (Pudsey, 1986). The timing of magmatism of the Chilas Complex may overlap with the period of formation of the Yasin Group and/or underlying Chalt Volcanics.

Mid-Cretaceous plutonic rocks are also found in Ladakh (Kargil intrusive complex, 103 ± 3 Ma, Honegger et al., 1982; 101 ± 2 Ma, Schärer et al., 1984; both determined by U-Pb zircon method), and in Karakorum (Darkot Pass plutonic unit, 109 ± 4 Ma or 111 ± 6 Ma; Hunza plutonic unit, 97 ± 17 Ma; both determined by Rb-Sr whole-rock isochron by Debon et al., 1987), indicating that intensive igneous activity occurred over a wide region including Kohistan, Karakorum, and Ladakh around 90–110 Ma, probably related to the subduction of the Tethyan

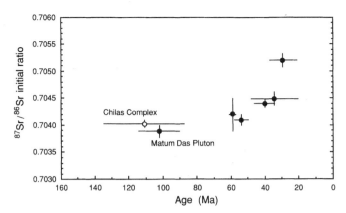

Figure 6. Rb-Sr whole-rock isochron ages and initial ^{87}Sr/^{86}Sr ratios for plutonic units of Kohistan. The open circle with the crossed bars represents the value for the Main facies of the Chilas Complex defined by the 14 samples in this study. The solid circles with the crossed bars represent the values for the Kohistan batholith (Petterson and Windley, 1985; Debon et al., 1987).

oceanic plate. The Ladakh intrusives have initial ^{87}Sr/^{86}Sr ratios between 0.7034 and 0.7048 (Honegger et al., 1982).

Isotopic compositions of the Chilas Complex are comparable to similar Cretaceous mafic-intermediate complexes in other orogenic belts. The Western Fiordland Orthogneiss in New Zealand mostly has a diorite-monzodiorite composition, a Rb-Sr whole-rock isochron of 120 ± 15 Ma, and a primitive initial ^{87}Sr/^{86}Sr ratio of 0.70391 ± 0.00004 (McCulloch et al., 1987), similar to isotopic characteristics of the Main facies of the Chilas Complex. The original magma of the Western Fiordland Orthogneiss intruded the Paleozoic metasedimentary rocks and plutons, probably in the southeastern margin of Gondwana (McCulloch et al., 1987), whereas the Chilas Complex intruded arc-type mafic-intermediate rocks of Kohistan. Evidence from both complexes suggests that the intrusion of mafic-intermediate magma having the Sr isotopic composition typical for arc magmas played an important role in a growth of the middle to deep crust in island arcs or continental margins in the Cretaceous.

Khan et al. (1989) pointed out the petrographic and compositional similarity between the Chilas Complex and the Mafic Complex in the Ivrea zone of northern Italy. Voshage et al. (1990) demonstrated genetic relationships between Hercynian granitoids and the hybrid magmas of the Ivrea Mafic Complex, based on their similar isotopic compositions. The Main facies rocks of the Chilas Complex are younger, and they had lower ^{87}Sr/^{86}Sr ratios at solidification than most of the hybrid mafic-intermediate rocks in the Ivrea zone. However, the correspondence of initial Sr isotope ratios and ages between the gabbro-diorite complex (Chilas Complex) and granitic plutons (the Kohistan batholith) is also observed in the Kohistan terrane. Further studies of the Chilas Complex and the Kohistan batholith may be able to clarify their petrogenetic relationships and improve our knowledge of the evolution of plutonic rocks.

CONCLUSIONS

The Main facies rocks of the Chilas Complex consist of gabbronorite, diorite, and quartz diorite. Small bodies of ultramafic-mafic association composed mainly of peridotitic-gabbroic cumulates, and a layered gabbronorite body, are also present as xenoliths.

A few samples were probably contaminated by assimilation of xenolithic materials and country rocks. If these samples are excluded, 14 whole-rock samples of the Main facies give a Rb-Sr age of 111 ± 24 Ma and an initial ^{87}Sr/^{86}Sr ratio of 0.70403 ± 0.00006. The Main facies rocks were homogenized with regard to their Sr isotopic composition in the Cretaceous, when they intruded and solidified. The initial ^{87}Sr/^{86}Sr ratio for the Main facies rocks is higher than the range found for MORB, but it is an appropriate value for subduction-related magmas, and is especially typical for island-arc magmas. The isotopic and other geochemical characteristics of the Main facies rocks indicate that they formed from subduction-related magma which originated in an island arc or orogenic belt close to a continental margin.

The ^{87}Sr/^{86}Sr ratios of gabbroic rocks from the ultramafic-mafic association (the Thak body), the layered gabbronorite body, and the dikes, are within the range 0.7039 to 0.7044, which can be considered to be close to the ^{87}Sr/^{86}Sr ratios at the time of their solidification, because their ^{87}Rb/^{86}Sr ratios are sufficiently low. Their ^{87}Sr/^{86}Sr ratios are close to the initial ^{87}Sr/^{86}Sr ratio of the Main facies, suggesting that they may have been derived from source materials similar to those of the Main facies.

The Chilas Complex intruded the arc-type calc-alkaline and partially tholeiitic mafic-intermediate rocks (the Kamila Amphibolite), and there is no evidence for a previous continental crust in Kohistan. Therefore, we propose that the generation of the Chilas Complex (the Main facies) is regarded as a subduction-related magmatism along the Kohistan arc, possibly near the continental margin of Asia. The magma of the Main facies raised several cumulate bodies of the ultramafic-mafic association. After solidification, the rocks cooled to below 500 °C by 80 Ma (Treloar et al., 1989).

The magmatism of the Chilas Complex may have been related to the earliest magmatism in the Kohistan batholith (Petterson and Windley, 1985). The Cretaceous plutonic episodes in Ladakh (Honegger et al., 1982; Schärer et al., 1984) and in Karakorum (Debon et al., 1987) are also about the same age, indicating that there was a large-scale generation of subduction-related magmas in the western Himalayan region and Karakorum during the mid-Cretaceous, probably as a result of the northward subduction of the Neo-Tethyan oceanic plate.

The Sr isotopic composition and age characteristics of the Chilas Complex are similar to those of the Western Fiordland Orthogneiss in New Zealand, which was probably generated in the margin of Gondwana (McCulloch et al., 1987). These similarities suggest that emplacement of a large amount of mafic-intermediate magma that had a primitive Sr isotopic composition may have had an important role in the growth of middle to deep crust in island arcs or continental margins in the Cretaceous.

ACKNOWLEDGMENTS

This work was performed as a part of technical transfer program for the Geoscience Laboratory, Geological Survey of Pakistan, by the Japan International Cooperation Agency. We acknowledge S. H. Gauhar, Y. Ikeda, and J. Yajima for their encouragement. We are grateful to Y. Arakawa for some of Sr isotopic analyses, and to A. Aziz, A. Ali, and I. Jabeen for carrying out some of the X-ray fluorescence analyses. We appreciate helpful technical support in the Rb-Sr analysis of H. Kamioka, T. Nakajima, S. Togashi, and N. T. Kita. We thank K. Faure for his helpful comments on earlier version of this paper, and our colleagues at the Geological Survey of Japan and the Geoscience Laboratory for valuable discussions and help. We are grateful to R. B. Sorkhabi for helpful comments and to K. Arita and P. J. Treloar for critical reviews and valuable suggestions.

REFERENCES CITED

Bard, J. P., 1983, Metamorphism of an obducted island arc; example of the Kohistan sequence (Pakistan) in the Himalayan collided range: Earth and Planetary Science Letters, v. 65, p. 133–144.

Beck, R. A., Burbank, D. W., Sercombe, W. J., Riley, G. W., Barndt, J. K., Berry, J. R., Afzal, J., Khan, A. M., Jurgen, H., Metje, J., Cheema, A., Shafique, N. A., Lawrence, R. D., and Khan, M. A., 1995, Stratigraphic evidence for an early collision between northwest India and Asia: Nature, v. 373, p. 55–58.

Coward, M. P., Jan, M. Q., Rex, D., Tarney, J., Thirlwall, M. and Windley, B. F., 1982, Geo-tectonic framework of the Himalaya of N Pakistan: Geological Society of London Journal, v. 139, p. 299–308.

Coward, M. P., Windley, B. F., Broughton, R. D., Luff, I. D., Petterson, M. G., Pudsey, C. J., Rex, D. C., and Khan, M. A., 1986, Collision tectonics in the NW Himalayas, *in* Coward, M. P., and Ries, A. C., eds., Collision tectonics: Geological Society of London Special Publication 19, p. 203–219.

Debon, F., Le Fort, P., Dautel, D., Sonet, J., and Zimmermann, J. L., 1987, Granites of western Karakorum and northern Kohistan (Pakistan): A composite mid-Cretaceous to upper Cenozoic magmatism: Lithos, v. 20, p. 19–40.

Faure, G., 1986, Principles of isotope geology (second edition): New York, John Wiley & Sons, 589 p.

Honegger, K., Dietrich, V., Frank, W., Gansser, A., Thöni, M., and Trommsdorff, V., 1982, Magmatism and metamorphism in the Ladakh Himalayas (the Indus-Tsangpo suture zone): Earth and Planetary Science Letters, v. 60, p. 253–292.

IUGS Subcommission, 1973, Plutonic rocks: Classification and nomenclature recommended by IUGS Subcommission on the systematics of igneous rocks: Geotimes, v. 18, p. 26–30.

Jan, M. Q., 1979, Petrography of pyroxene granulites from northern Swat and Kohistan, *in* Tahirkheli, R. A. K., and Jan, M. Q., eds., Geology of Kohistan, Karakoram Himalaya, northern Pakistan: University of Peshawar Geological Bulletin, Special Issue, v. 11, p. 65–88.

Jan, M. Q., 1988, Geochemistry of amphibolites from the southern part of the Kohistan arc, N. Pakistan: Mineralogical Magazine, v. 52, p. 147–159.

Jan, M. Q., and Howie, R. A., 1980, Ortho- and clinopyroxenes from the pyroxene granulites of Swat Kohistan, northern Pakistan: Mineralogical Magazine, v. 43, p. 715–726.

Jan, M. Q., and Howie, R. A., 1981, The mineralogy and geochemistry of the metamorphosed basic and ultrabasic rocks of the Jijal complex, Kohistan, NW Pakistan: Journal of Petrology, v. 22, p. 85–126.

Jan, M. Q., and Kempe, D. R. C., 1973, The petrology of the basic and intermediate rocks of upper Swat, Pakistan: Geological Magazine, v. 110, p. 285–300.

Jan, M. Q., Khattak, M. U. K., Parvez, M. K., and Windley, B. F., 1984, The Chilas stratiform complex: Field and mineralogical aspects: University of Peshawar Geological Bulletin, v. 17, p. 153–169.

Khan, M. A., and Coward, M. P., 1990, Entrapment of an intra-oceanic island arc in collision tectonics: A review of the structural history of the Kohistan arc, NW Himalaya: Physics and Chemistry of the Earth, v. 17, p. 1–18.

Khan, M. A., Habib, M., and Jan, M. Q., 1985, Ultramafic and mafic rocks of Thurley Gah and their relationship to the Chilas Complex, N. Pakistan: University of Peshawar Geological Bulletin, v. 18, p. 83–102.

Khan, M. A., Jan, M. Q., Windley, B. F., Tarney, J., and Thirlwall, M. F., 1989, The Chilas mafic-ultramafic igneous complex; the root of the Kohistan island arc in the Himalaya of northern Pakistan, *in* Malinconico, L. L., Jr., and Lillie, R. J., eds., Tectonics of the Western Himalayas: Geological Society of America Special Paper 232, p. 75–94.

Khan, M. A., Jan, M. Q., and Weaver, B. L., 1993, Evolution of the lower arc crust in Kohistan, N. Pakistan: Temporal arc magmatism through early, mature and intra-arc rift stages, *in* Treloar, P. J., and Searle, M. P., eds., Himalayan tectonics: Geological Society of London Special Publication 74, p. 123–138.

Khan, T., Khan, M. A., Jan, M. Q., and Naseem, M., 1996, Back-arc basin assemblages in Kohistan, northern Pakistan: Geodinamica Acta, v. 9, p. 30–40.

Kubo, K., Sawada, Y., Takahashi, Yuh., Kausar, A. B., Seki, Y., Khan, I. H., Khan, T., Khan, N. A., and Takahashi, Yut., 1992, The Chilas Complex in the western Himalaya of northern Pakistan: Symposium on Himalayan Geology, Shimane, 1992, Japan, Abstracts, p. 25.

Kubo, K., Sawada, Y., Takahashi, Yuh., Kausar, A. B., Seki, Y., Khan, I. H., Khan, T., Khan, N. A., and Takahashi, Yut., 1996, The Chilas Igneous Complex in the western Himalayas of northern Pakistan: Proceedings of Geoscience Colloquium, Volume 14: Geoscience Laboratory, Geological Survey of Pakistan, p. 63–68.

McCulloch, M. T., Bradshaw, J. Y., and Taylor, S. R., 1987, Sm-Nd and Rb-Sr isotopic and geochemical systematics in Phanerozoic granulites from Fiordland, Southwest New Zealand: Contributions to Mineralogy and Petrology, v. 97, p. 183–195.

Patriat, P., and Achache, J., 1984, India-Eurasia collision chronology has implications for crustal shortening and driving mechanism of plates: Nature, v. 311, p. 615–621.

Petterson, M. G., and Windley, B. F., 1985, Rb-Sr dating of the Kohistan arc-batholith in the Trans-Himalaya of north Pakistan, and tectonic implications: Earth and Planetary Science Letters, v. 74, p. 45–57.

Petterson, M. G., and Windley, B. F., 1991, Changing source regions of magmas and crustal growth in the Trans-Himalayas: Evidence from the Chalt volcanics and Kohistan batholith, Kohistan, northern Pakistan: Earth and Planetary Science Letters, v. 102, p. 326–341.

Pudsey, C. J., 1986, The Northern Suture, Pakistan: Margin of a Cretaceous island arc: Geological Magazine, v. 123, p. 405–423.

Saunders, A. D., and Tarney, J., 1984, Geochemical characteristics of basaltic volcanism within back-arc basins, *in* Kokelaar, B. P., and Howells, M. F., eds., Marginal basin geology: Volcanic and associated sedimentary and tectonic processes in modern and ancient marginal basins: Geological Society of London Special Publication 16, p. 59–76.

Schärer, U., Hamet, J., and Allègre, C. J., 1984, The Transhimalaya (Gangdese) plutonism in the Ladakh region: A U-Pb and Rb-Sr study: Earth and Planetary Science Letters, v. 67, p. 327–339.

Shams, F. A., Jones, G. C., and Kempe, D. R. C., 1980, Blueschists from Topsin, Swat district, NW Pakistan: Mineralogical Magazine, v. 43, p. 941–942.

Tahirkheli, R. A. K., Mattauer, M., Proust, F., and Tapponnier, P., 1979, The India Eurasia suture zone in northern Pakistan: Synthesis and interpretation of recent data at plate scale, *in* Farah, A., and DeJong, K. A., eds., Geodynamics of Pakistan: Quetta, Geological Survey of Pakistan, p. 125–130.

Takahashi, Yuh., Kausar, A. B., Takahashi, Yut. and Khan, T., 1993, Field relationships between the rock units of the Chilas Complex, Chilas, northern Pakistan: Proceedings of Geoscience Colloquium, Volume 4: Geoscience

Laboratory, Geological Survey of Pakistan, p. 41–50.

Takahashi, Yut., Takahashi, Yuh., Kausar, A. B., and Mikoshiba, M. U., 1996, Geology and geochemistry of eastern part of the Chilas Complex, northern Pakistan—Implications for the tectonic development of the Kohistan island arc: Proceedings of Geoscience Colloquium, Volume 14: Geoscience Laboratory, Geological Survey of Pakistan, p. 39–61.

Treloar, P. J., Rex, D. C., Guise, P. G., Coward, M. P., Searle, M. P., Windley, B. F., Petterson, M. G., Jan, M. Q., and Luff, I. W., 1989, K-Ar and Ar-Ar geochronology of the Himalayan collision in NW Pakistan: Constraints on the timing of suturing, deformation, metamorphism and uplift: Tectonics, v. 8, p. 881-909.

Treloar, P. J., Brodie, K. H., Coward, M. P., Jan, M. Q., Khan, M. A., Knipe, R. J., Rex, D. C., and Williams, M. P., 1990, The evolution of the Kamila shear zone, Pakistan, *in* Salisbury, M. H., and Fountain, D. M., eds., Exposed cross-sections of the continental crust: Dordrecht, Kluwer Academic Publishers, p. 175–214.

Treloar, P. J., Petterson, M. G., Jan, M. Q., and Sullivan, M. A., 1996, A re-evaluation of the stratigraphy and evolution of the Kohistan arc sequence, Pakistan Himalaya: Implications for magmatic and tectonic arc-building processes: Geological Society of London Journal, v. 153, p. 681–693.

Voshage, H., Hofmann, A. W., Mazzucchelli, M., Rivalenti, G., Sinigoi, S., Raczek, I., and Demarchi, G., 1990, Isotopic evidence from the Ivrea Zone for a hybrid lower crust formed by magmatic underplating: Nature, v. 347, p. 731–736.

Wilson, M., 1989, Igneous petrogenesis: London, Unwin Hyman, p. 466.

Yamamoto, H., 1993, Contrasting metamorphic P-T-time paths of the Kohistan granulites and tectonics of the western Himalayas: Geological Society of London Journal, v. 150, p. 843–856.

York, D., 1966, Least-squares fitting of a straight line: Canadian Journal of Physics, v. 44, p.1079–1086.

Zeitler, P. K., 1985, Cooling history of the NW Himalaya, Pakistan: Tectonics, v. 4, p. 127–151.

MANUSCRIPT ACCEPTED BY THE SOCIETY FEBRUARY 3, 1998

Geological Society of America
Special Paper 328
1999

Parh Group basalts of northeastern Balochistan, Pakistan: Precursors to the Deccan Traps

Wazir Khan,* George R. McCormick, and Mark K. Reagan
Department of Geology, University of Iowa, Iowa City, Iowa 52242

ABSTRACT

The Late Cretaceous Parh Group basalts of northeastern Balochistan, Pakistan, crop out in a northeast-trending linear belt of more than 300 km, from Kach in the southwest to Waziristan Northwest Frontier Province in the northeast. The base of the Parh Group volcanic rocks generally consists of pillow basalt, grading upward into volcanic agglomerate, breccia, and tuff. Cherty limestone is associated with both the pillow basalts and the agglomerates. The volcanic rocks in the Parh Group are predominantly alkali olivine basalt, and have lesser olivine tholeiite and very minor quartz tholeiite. With the exception of one quartz tholeiite unit, which has a mid-ocean ridge basalt composition, the Parh Group basalts have whole-rock major and trace element compositions similar to those of hotspot-related oceanic-island basalts of the Southern Hemisphere, such as Reunion and Tristan Da Cunha. The compositions of the Parh Group volcanic rocks and their geological setting suggest that the source for the volcanic rocks was oceanic islands on the continental shelf or slope along the boundary between the Indo-Pakistan plate and the Tethys sea, before they were thrust into their present position in the India-Eurasia suture.

The ages of the Parh Group volcanics precede and slightly overlap those of the nearby Deccan Traps, suggesting that they represent the earliest magmas generated from the rising Reunion hotspot plume, which would have been below the Tethyan ocean floor before the main pulse of Deccan volcanism. Therefore, these early Parh Group lavas probably are the northernmost and oldest of the Reunion hotspot trail. The low volume and generally alkaline nature of all of these lava flows suggest that they represent small-degree melts associated with cooler edges of the thermal plume that created the immense Deccan Traps.

INTRODUCTION

The Late Cretaceous Parh Group volcanic rocks of northeastern Balochistan, Pakistan, erupted during a tectonically active time in the geologic history of southwest Asia. Their presence, however, has largely been neglected in the tectono-magmatic models of the late Mesozoic–early Cenozoic collision of the Indian and Eurasian plates (Powell, 1979; Molnar and Tapponier, 1975). During the Late Cretaceous, plates that formed in the Triassic from the breakup of Gondwana began to reassemble into the current configuration. The Indian and African-Arabian plates moved north, closing the Tethys ocean, which was between the Gondwanan continents and Laurasia. By the Late Cretaceous, numerous microcontinents, pieces of Gondwana and/or Laurasia, were located in the Tethys north of the Arabian and Indian plates (Powell, 1979; Tapponier et al., 1981). A subduction zone and an accompanying island arc were located to the south of Laurasia and extended eastward through the Tethys ocean north of the Indian plate (Powell, 1979). In Late Cretaceous to early Tertiary time,

---

*Present address: Geological Survey of Pakistan, Quetta, Pakistan.

Khan, W., McCormick, G. R., and Reagan, M. K., 1999, Parh Group basalts of northeastern Balochistan, Pakistan: Precursors to the Deccan Traps, *in* Macfarlane, A., Sorkhabi, R. B., and Quade, J., eds., Himalaya and Tibet: Mountain Roots to Mountain Tops: Boulder, Colorado, Geological Society of America Special Paper 328.

there were large outpourings of basaltic lava in the Deccan region of the Indian plate, probably associated with the impingement of the upwelling head of a mantle plume with the Indo-Pakistani lithosphere (White and McKenzie, 1989; Richards et al., 1989; and Campbell and Griffiths, 1990). Most of this volcanism occurred over a short interval of time at 65 ± 1 Ma (Basu et al., 1993).

The volcanic rocks of the Parh Group were first described by Vredenburg (1909), who related them to the Deccan Traps of India. The Hunting Survey Corporation (1960) recognized these volcanic rocks in their reconnaissance geological report on West Pakistan as an irregularly interlayered heterogeneous assemblage of volcanic and sedimentary rocks in the upper part of the Cretaceous sequence. They also identified these volcanic rocks as basalt of submarine origin, like those of modern arc systems. Kazmi (1979) and Otsuki et al. (1989) also considered the Parh Group lavas to be island-arc basalts.

McCormick (1985) proposed that the volcanic rocks in the Cretaceous Parh formation of northeast Balochistan represent eruptions from the Reunion hotspot prior to Deccan time and also that the volcanics represent offshore oceanic islands.

This study uses geological mapping, petrography, and whole-rock geochemistry to determine the petrogenetic origin of the Parh Group volcanics and determine their relationship to the Reunion hotspot prior to Deccan continental flood-basalt volcanism.

METHODS OF STUDY

A program of geologic mapping and rock sampling in the study area was carried out during the months of June, July, and August 1991, and reconnaissance geological maps of the volcanic rocks and associated sedimentary rocks were prepared. More than 200 representative samples of volcanic rocks were collected for laboratory work. Appendix 1 contains the geologic maps of this study area on which sample locations are plotted for all samples reported in the present study.

Thin sections of 150 Parh Group samples were made and studied and 58 relatively fresh samples were selected for whole-rock chemistry. X-ray fluorescence (XRF) analyses for major and trace elements were performed at Michigan State University on a Rigaku (S-Max) automated XRF spectrometer. Major element concentrations (Si, Ti, Al, Fe, Mn, Mg, Ca, Na, K, and P) were determined using the Criss matrix absorption parameter (Criss, 1980) from fused glass wafers made according to the method of Hagan (1982); trace elements were determined from pressed powder pellets.

Replicate XRF analyses of standard BHVO-1 produced the following means and standard deviations for major oxides in (wt %), SiO_2 = 49.86 ± 0.02, TiO_2 = 2.64 ± 0.0294, Al_2O_3 = 13.51 ± 0.09, FeO* = 11.0 ± 0.06, MgO = 7.05 ± 0.04, CaO = 11.15 ± 0.049, Na_2O = 2.17 ± 0.02, K_2O = 0.52 ± 0.01, and P_2O_5 = 0.27 ± 0.02; and for trace elements (in ppm), Cr = 297 ± 6, Ni = 127 ± 2, Nb =17.5 ± 2, Zr = 173 ± 2, and Y = 26.4 ± 4.

One analysis was made on each sample for trace and rare elements (Cs, Ba, Th, U, Ce, Ba, Ta, La, Sr, Hf, Nd, Sm, Eu, Tb, Yb, Dy, and Lu) using instrumental neutron activation analysis

(INAA) techniques at the Phoenix Laboratory at the University of Michigan. Estimated 1σ errors for INAA analyses of typical Parh Group samples are: Ba = 7%, La = 8.5%, Nd = 14%, Sm = 8.8%, U = 1%, Yb = 9.5%, Lu = 17%, Cs = 7%, Eu = 5.4%, Hf = 3%, Rb = 1.5%, Ta = 10%, Tb = 12%, and Th = 1.2%.

REGIONAL GEOLOGIC SETTING

The Himalayan mountain system resulted from the continent-continent collision between the Indo-Pakistani plate, Eurasian microcontinent(s), and Laurasia beginning 50–55 Ma (Powell and Conaghan, 1973, 1975; Dewey and Burke, 1973; Auden, 1974; Molnar and Tapponier, 1975; Johnson et al., 1976; Powell, 1979; Reddy et al., 1993). The system bends sharply at the Pamir Mountains and extends into southwestern Pakistan (Balochistan) (Fig. 1). The Cenozoic and Mesozoic sedimentary rocks along the leading edge of the Indo-Pakistani plate have been folded and thrust eastward and southward, forming the Sulaiman and Kirther Ranges in northeastern and southeastern Balochistan, respectively. These ranges are bordered to the west by the left-lateral Chaman transform fault (Lawrence and Yeats, 1979).

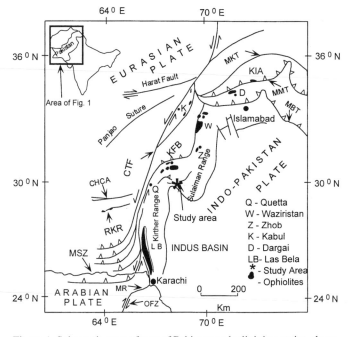

Figure 1. Schematic map of part of Pakistan and adjoining region showing the main tectonic zones. Sulaiman Range (northeast Balochistan) and Kirther Range (southeast Balochistan) are fold and thrust belts. MSZ = Makran subduction zone (southwest Balochistan), CHCA = Chagai calc-alkaline arc, RKR = Ras Koh Range (west Balochistan), CTF = Chaman transform fault (continent-continent boundary between the Indo-Pakistani plate and the Afghan microcontinent(s), KFB = Katawaz flysch basin, MKT = Main Karakorum thrust (between Kohistan island arc and Eurasia), MMT = Main Mantle thrust (between the Indo-Pakistani plate and Kohistan island arc), KIA = Kohistan island arc between MMT and MKT. MBT = Main Boundary thrust (Miogene sediments thrust onto the Indo-Pakistani craton), MR = Murray Ridge, OFZ = Owen Fracture Zone.

A discontinuous zone of ultramafic and gabbroic rocks, sheeted dikes, pillow basalts, and associated melanges (Las Bela, Muslimbagh, and Waziristan) (Hunting Survey Corporation, 1960; Gansser, 1979; Asrarullah et al., 1979; Ahmad and Abbas, 1979; DeJong and Subhani, 1979) were obducted east and southward onto the Indo-Pakistani subcontinent during the Paleocene to early Eocene (Alleman, 1979). South of the Parh Group volcanic rocks is a thick succession of folded and faulted Jurassic and Triassic limestone and shale that the Hunting Survey Corporation (1960) referred to as the Calcareous Zone. Miocene-Pliocene molasse deposits border the fold belt to the east and south in a wide zone and separate the Sulaiman and Kirther fold belts from the Indo-Pakistani shield. Southward-propagating thrusting of the Sulaiman Range since late Oligocene–early Miocene time has progressively reworked the molasse deposits (Banks and Warburton, 1986; Ahmad and Khan, 1990; Waheed and Wells, 1990).

PARH GROUP VOLCANICS

The Parh Group volcanics and associated clastic sediments, limestone, and marl were mapped and sampled in detail from Kach on the west eastward to Spara Ragha–Chinjan and Ghunda Manra (Khan, 1994) (Fig. 2, Appendix 1). Undisturbed volcanic units near Kach are in the upper part of the Parh Group limestone. They are predominantly pillow lavas and flows in the lower part, grading upward to tuff and volcanic ash. The lavas are light gray to brownish- or greenish-gray on fresh surfaces and contain pillows ranging from 6 cm to 2 m in diameter. Nodules of Parh limestone are present between individual pillows. Farther to the east near Ahmadun the volcanic rocks are present as two distinct lithostratigraphic units (Kazmi, 1979). The lower unit consists of massive and amygdaloidal lava flows, pillow lavas, agglomerate, tuff, and ash, whereas the upper unit is composed of volcanic ash, tuff, and volcanic conglomerate. These ash beds exhibit current bedding and contain varying amounts of terrigenous material (Kazmi, 1979). The tuffs are interbedded upward with thick lenses of boulder conglomerate in the upper unit. The conglomerate consists of boulders and pebbles of amygdaloidal, porphyritic, and homogeneous basalt in a brownish-gray ash and glassy matrix that interfingers upward within the upper unit with a sequence of coarse sandstone, argillaceous tuffs, and soft mudstone. The volcanic conglomerate beds here and elsewhere in the Parh Group indicate emerging islands, which also provided material for the volcanogenic terrigenous deposits in the Late Cretaceous.

The Parh Group volcanic rocks in the Spara Ragha–Chinjan area constitute the thickest succession in northeastern Balochistan, and have an average thickness of ~1,500 m. Lava flows are restricted to the lower parts of the volcanic sequence and are commonly found as small isolated outcrops. The flows are basaltic and rarely pillowed. They commonly exhibit spheroidal weathering and are intermixed with agglomerates and volcanic breccia and contain pockets or nodules of fine-grained, hard, white limestone. The major portion of the volcanic sequence in this area consists of agglomerates and volcanic breccia. The pyroclastic units are commonly interbedded with lava flows and Parh limestone.

The best-exposed volcanic rock section is southeast of Ghunda Manra. It consists of stacks of pillow lavas that are tens of meters thick, pyroclastics, and volcanogenic sedimentary rocks that thin to the east. The lower part of the sequence predominately consists of pillow lavas containing minor intercalations of agglomerate and tuff, whereas the upper part contains agglomerate, tuff, ash, volcanic conglomerates, and tuffaceous sandstone. The pillow basalts are amygdaloidal and highly weathered. Amygdules contain zeolites and calcite, and cavities between pillows contain pockets of cream-colored limestone and calcareous shale. Primary hornblende phenocrysts are present in some fragments within the volcanic conglomerate of Gunda Manra (Khan, 1994).

The Parh Group basalts commonly are porphyritic, containing between 1 and 50 vol% phenocrysts and glomeroporphyritic clots of titaniferous ($Ti_{0.03}$ to $Ti_{0.16}$), aluminous ($Al^{iv}_{0.09-0.45}$) and calcic (Wo_{46-53}) augite, forsteritic olivine (Fo_{76-89}), plagioclase (An_{54-89}), and magnetite (Khan, 1994). Kaersutitic hornblende phenocrysts are present in a few relatively differentiated samples. The groundmass of the porphyritic samples is fine grained and consists of augite, olivine, plagioclase, magnetite, ilmenite, and altered glass. Primary plagioclase and olivine phenocrysts and matrix phases commonly are partially to completely altered to calcite, zeolites, serpentine, and chlorite.

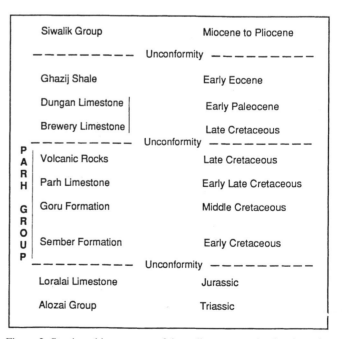

Siwalik Group	Miocene to Pliocene
——————— Unconformity ———————	
Ghazij Shale	Early Eocene
Dungan Limestone	Early Paleocene
Brewery Limestone	Late Cretaceous

P A R H G R O U P	——————— Unconformity ———————	
	Volcanic Rocks	Late Cretaceous
	Parh Limestone	Early Late Cretaceous
	Goru Formation	Middle Cretaceous
	Sember Formation	Early Cretaceous
	——————— Unconformity ———————	
	Loralai Limestone	Jurassic
	Alozai Group	Triassic

Figure 2. Stratigraphic sequence of the sedimentary and volcanic rocks of northeastern Balochistan, Pakistan.

A number of samples in all the volcanic sequences lack phenocrysts and consist of intergrown plagioclase, augite, magnetite, and rarely, olivine and hornblende. Ilmenite and apatite are accessory minerals, and K-feldspar is present in a few homogeneous alkali olivine basalts. The textures are mostly doloritic and intersertal. The rocks are slightly altered and secondary minerals consist of calcite, chlorite, zeolite, serpentine, biotite, and chlorophaeite.

Some porphyritic and non porphyritic basalts contain abundant amygdules filled with zeolite, calcite, and chlorite.

WHOLE-ROCK CHEMISTRY

Major elements

About equal numbers of analyzed samples are alkali olivine basalts (olivine-nepheline normative) and olivine tholeiites (olivine-hypersthene normative), and only a few samples are quartz tholeiites (quartz-hypersthene normative; Fig. 3). Most compositions are in the alkaline and subalkaline fields on a plot of total alkalis vs. silica (Fig. 4). MgO concentrations range from 4 to 19 wt% for the alkali olivine basalts; the majority of samples have 5–8 wt% (Table 1). The olivine tholeiites are somewhat more mafic than the alkali olivine basalts, typically having 6–14 wt% MgO: some have as much as 30 wt% MgO. The quartz tholeiites are more consistently differentiated, 4–8 wt% MgO. All of the rocks with >18 wt% MgO are highly porphyritic, and have high abundances of olivine and augite phenocrysts, high magnesium numbers (molar $Mg^{2+}/Mg^{2+} + Fe^{2+}$ >0.72), and high concentrations of compatible trace elements such as Ni and Cr, in concentrations as high as 1,300 ppm and 2,600 ppm, respectively (Table 2), suggesting that these samples do not represent true liquid compositions, but contain a significant fraction of accumulated olivine and augite (Khan, 1994). TiO_2 concentrations are high in both the alkali olivine basalts (1.5–3.5 wt%) and tholeiites (0.8–3.0 wt%), generally increasing with decreasing MgO.

Trace elements

Like many alkaline and transitional ocean-island basalts (OIB), the Parh Group basalts are enriched in large ion lithophile elements (LILE), light rare earth elements (REE), and high field strength elements (HFSE) with respect to primitive mantle (Table 2; Fig. 5). All the basalts show similar patterns of enrichment in the REEs and a consistent decrease in enrichment toward the heavy REEs. All lack a negative Eu anomaly (Fig. 5). Ratios between HFSEs are typical of the basalts from some Southern Hemisphere oceanic islands such as Tristan Da Cunha and Reunion. For example, these volcanics also have low Zr/Nb ratios (2.2–6), La/Nb ratios <1, Ti/Y ratios >500, Ti/V >30, and Ti/Zr ratios from 50 to 192 (Table 3). The normalized patterns of these volcanic rocks contain positive anomalies for Nb and Ta of about equal intensity (Fig. 6). Ratios involving LILEs are highly variable because zeolite facies metamorphism altered the

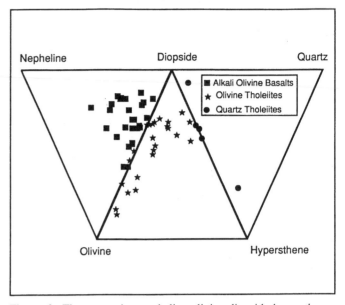

Figure 3. The normative nepheline-olivine-diopside-hypersthene–quartz projection on the basalt tetrahedron from plagioclase showing fields for alkali olivine basalt, olivine tholeiites and quartz tholeiites, of northeastern Balochistan, Pakistan. Modified from Basaltic Volcanism Study Project (1981).

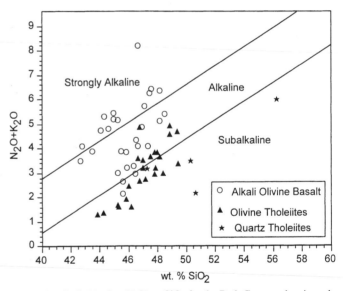

Figure 4. Alkali ($Na_2O + K_2O$) vs. SiO_2 for the Parh Group volcanic rocks of northeastern Balochistan, Pakistan. The field boundaries are after MacDonald and Katsura (1964). Oxides are reported in weight percent.

concentrations of these relatively water-soluble elements. Thus, these ratios are not used here as primary discriminators of tectonic setting. Nevertheless, ratios involving incompatible LILEs such as Ba are like those of OIB for most samples. For example, Ba/Nb ratios are less than 30 for all but 5 samples and Ba/La ratios are less than 17 in about two-thirds of the samples (Table 3).

TABLE 1. MAJOR ELEMENT DATA (WT%) FOR SELECTED VOLCANIC ROCKS OF NORTHEASTERN BALOCHISTAN, PAKISTAN

Basalt Type	AOB	AOB	AOB	AOB	AOB	AOB	AOB	AOB	OT	OT	OT	OT	OT	OT	OT	OT	QT
Sample No.	206	121	85	101	127	236	10	110	77	132	243	27	83	116	5	32	181
SiO_2	44.12	48.22	48.23	45.56	45.96	44.68	45.63	47.00	48.85	45.20	45.83	49.39	49.98	48.76	47.63	50.47	50.74
TiO_2	2.99	2.30	2.79	2.39	2.12	3.79	1.51	2.50	2.22	0.76	1.31	2.34	1.61	1.96	1.18	2.50	1.13
Al_2O_3	15.11	14.28	17.77	13.87	12.53	14.53	9.39	14.97	16.14	6.56	8.23	15.47	13.57	12.75	8.19	16.21	14.72
$FeO*$	12.74	10.95	9.50	11.98	11.45	14.96	11.55	11.52	11.61	11.82	11.86	11.84	10.76	11.31	10.62	11.45	10.30
MnO	0.19	0.19	0.33	0.20	0.19	0.21	0.18	0.19	0.18	0.18	0.18	0.19	0.17	0.18	0.17	0.22	0.20
MgO	7.03	6.87	4.60	9.50	12.70	6.48	18.88	6.63	6.75	31.51	23.42	7.53	12.06	13.78	23.42	4.98	4.82
CaO	12.55	11.88	9.90	12.36	11.59	9.75	10.69	12.08	12.13	5.65	8.50	11.66	11.83	11.50	10.04	11.24	15.90
Na_2O	3.84	2.26	3.92	2.36	2.05	3.78	1.46	1.93	2.52	0.94	1.09	2.36	2.33	1.84	1.12	2.89	1.82
K_2O	0.76	2.74	2.30	1.41	1.04	0.91	0.54	2.80	1.28	0.26	0.45	1.26	0.62	0.87	0.45	1.76	0.22
P_2O_5	0.67	0.31	0.66	0.39	0.36	0.92	0.17	0.38	0.33	0.10	0.17	0.34	0.20	0.28	0.14	0.37	0.16
Total†	93.90	94.67	95.08	96.77	96.86	94.28	96.43	95.02	95.79	96.69	94.87	96.15	96.83	96.94	96.67	95.86	95.61

*FeO is the total iron.
†Total is before normalizing to 100%. Major element data and figures are from 100% normalized values.
AOB = alkali olivine basalts, OT = olivine tholeiite, QT = quartz tholeiite.

DISCUSSION

Tectonic setting

Four possible origins for the Parh Group basalts are considered here. First, these volcanic rocks may represent slivers of island-arc volcanics that formed because of either the southward subduction of the Neo-Tethys oceanic crust under the northwestern margin of the Indo-Pakistani continent (Otsuki et al., 1989), or the northward subduction of the Neo-Tethys oceanic crust under the Eurasian plate (Kazmi, 1984). Second, these basalts may represent small-volume lavas erupted at the periphery of the Deccan continental flood-basalt province. Third, these volcanic rocks may be fragments of the Muslimbagh ophiolite complex, which was once part of the Neo-Tethys ocean floor–back arc basin. Fourth, these volcanic rocks may represent oceanic-island basalts formed on the Neo-Tethyan ocean floor as it passed over the Reunion hotspot (McCormick, 1985).

The Parh Group rocks are exclusively basaltic and largely alkali olivine basalts and olivine tholeiites. They are enriched in REEs and HFSEs relative to chondrites, and have Zr/Nb and La/Nb ratios significantly lower than those for volcanic arc lavas (e.g, Gill, 1981; Morris and Hart, 1983), and Ti/V ratios that are significantly higher (see Shervais, 1982). In addition, these volcanic rocks consistently plot outside the fields of arc basalts on the various published tectonic setting discrimination diagrams (Table 4; Figs. 7 and 8). Thus, it is highly unlikely that the Parh Group lavas erupted in a subduction-related setting.

Studies of continental flood basalts have shown that they vary chemically and isotopically from province to province and that they are often modified before eruption by assimilation of continental crust. There is consensus that flood basalts are triggered by the impingement of the head of a new mantle plume at the base of the continental lithosphere (Richards et al., 1989; White and McKenzie; 1989; Campbell and Griffiths, 1990). The hotspot plume head can be 2,000–2,500 km in diameter when it impinges the lithosphere (Richards et al., 1989; White and McKenzie, 1989; Campbell and Griffiths, 1990). One such example is the Deccan Traps of India, which is linked to the birth of the Reunion hotspot (Morgan, 1981; Duncan, 1990). The Deccan continental flood basalts cover an area of ~500,000 km^2 in India with considerable thicknesses of lava flows. These lava flows lack pillow structures and are not mixed with marine sediments. They are predominantly tholeiites and some alkaline and picritic basalts (Mahoney, 1988). They are enriched in LILEs and light REEs but are depleted in HFSEs. They contain La/Nb ratios from 1.1 to 2.25, Ti/Y ratios from 250 to 530, and Ti/Zr ratios from 77 to 104 (Peng et al., 1994).

The most striking feature of most Deccan flood basalts is the negative Nb and Ta anomalies on the primitive mantle/chondritic normalized patterns (Peng et al., 1994), rather than the positive anomalies found on the patterns of the Parh Group basalts. In addition, spider diagrams of the Deccan flood basalts exhibit negative Eu anomalies, whereas they are absent on the diagrams of

TABLE 2. TRACE ELEMENT DATA (PPM) FOR SELECTED VOLCANIC ROCKS OF NORTHEASTERN BALOCHISTAN, PAKISTAN

Basalt Type	AOB	AOB	AOB	AOB	AOB	AOB	AOB	AOB	OT	OT	OT	OT	OT	OT	OT	OT	QT
Sample No.	206	121	85	101	127	236	10	110	77	132	243	27	83	116	5	32	181
Cs	1.43	nd	0.73	nd	nd	0.8	2.19	nd	nd	0.9	2.29	nd	0.62	nd	nd	nd	nd
Rb	13.20	49	39	37.1	26.1	19.4	13	45	25.1	8	12.5	26.4	10.6	24.2	11.2	34.3	4.6
Ba	722	672	933	571	392	819	237	779	496	345	271	362	719	464	118	480	11
Th	6.1	2.7	6.8	4	2.7	10	1.6	3.4	3.6	nd	1.3	3.3	5.8	2.2	0.9	4.4	0.3
U	1	0.8	nd	0.7	nd	2.3	nd	0.6	0.9	nd	0.3	0.4	0.7	nd	0.2	0.9	nd
Nb	76.1	25.4	69	40.5	35.4	68.3	18.6	29.3	25.8	12.3	19.4	32.2	61.4	25.3	18.2	23.5	7.1
Ta	4.63	2.36	5.42	2.8	2.4	6.1	1.3	2.73	2.3	0.8	1.1	2.4	4.7	1.7	1	2.7	0.3
La	56.7	24.7	53.3	32.8	25.2	79.1	13.7	29.8	31.6	65.3	13.3	28.3	52.1	21.9	11.1	32.3	6.1
Ce	106.7	49.9	105.3	68.3	53.6	156.4	29.5	58.2	62.5	24.5	25.1	57.6	96.4	43.4	26.2	67.7	nd
Sr	631	833	792	620	467	1149	27	961	799	121	231	448	626	403	183	1192	85
Nd	53	40.8	38.4	37.9	25.2	76.7	698	nd	40.4	8.5	8.4	14.3	52.2	24.6	17.8	29.5	nd
Sm	9.7	5.8	8.9	6.51	5.6	14.3	nd	6.7	6.9	1.8	3.3	6.5	10.2	5.4	3.1	7.3	3.3
Zr	208	122	225	168	141	271	3.8	144	147	49	85	153	240	123	72	144	78
Hf	5.3	3.7	5.5	4.6	3.99	9.2	96	4.6	4.7	1.3	2.3	4.6	7.1	3.4	2.1	5.47	2.4
Eu	2.9	2	2.8	2.2	1.87	4.55	2.8	2.2	2.32	0.68	0.9	2.3	3	1.7	1	2.5	1.2
Tb	1.1	0.6	0.9	0.7	0.6	1.8	1.3	0.8	nd	0.5	0.6	0.8	1.2	0.5	0.5	1.1	0.7
Dy	4.8	4.4	6	4.2	3.2	7	0.4	4.5	4.6	1.5	1.7	4.8	4.6	4	3.6	5.6	3.4
Y	23.4	18	24.8	20.9	18.7	32.8	3.3	21	22.5	9.9	13.6	23.9	25.2	18	12.1	24.2	25.3
Yb	1.7	1.6	2	1.3	1.8	2.4	14.4	1.71	1.9	0.8	0.8	2	2	1.3	1.1	1.9	3.1
Lu	0.24	0.2	0.18	0.2	nd	0.3	1	0.2	0.3	0.1	0.1	0.2	0.2	0.2	0.2	0.2	0.3
Cr	15	139	26	438	779	21	0.08	93	68	2627	1553	145	61	852	2132	57	25
Co	48	45	50	56	58	47	1384	42	51	102	88	46	49	67	81	45	32
V	315	302	247	309	247	278	78	307	285	137	184	289	182	264	185	298	268
Zn	151	93	135	206	75	310	230	139	96	103	126	97	182	157	151	221	86
Ni	38	92	67	211	335	17	83	81	68	1297	897	87	27	358	909	63	13

AOB = alkali olivine basalts, OT = olivine tholeiite, QT = quartz tholeiite.

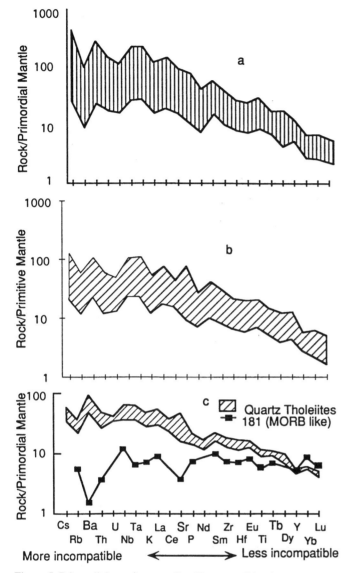

Figure 5. Primordial mantle normalized incompatible element concentrations of Parh Group volcanic rocks. Normalizing values are from Wood (1980). a: alkali olivine basalts, b: olivine tholeiites; and c: quartz tholeiites. Sample 181 is a quartz tholeiite that has a normal-type mid-ocean ridge basalt (MORB) composition. It is quite possible that the sample may be from a fault-bounded sliver of the Muslimbagh ophiolite sequence.

Parh Group lavas (Mahoney, 1988). Thus, the chemical compositions of the Parh Group basalts are different from those of the Deccan or other flood basalts.

Ocean-floor basalts (normal [N]-type mid-ocean ridge basalt [MORB]) are hypersthene normative, are depleted in LILEs and light REEs, and have Zr/Nb ratios >10 (e.g.,Wood et al., 1979; Schilling et al., 1983). All of the Parh Group basalt samples, with the exception of one sample (181), have higher contents of Ti, Zr, Nb, LILEs, and light REEs, and lower Zr/Nb ratios than those for MORB. Sample 181 is a quartz tholeiite that always plots in the N-type MORB field on tectonic discrimination diagrams (Table

TABLE 3. TRACE ELEMENT RATIOS FOR SELECTED VOLCANIC ROCKS OF NORTHEASTERN BALOCHISTAN, PAKISTAN

Basalt Type	AOB	AOB	AOB	AOB	AOB	AOB	AOB	AOB	OT	OT	OT	OT	OT	OT	OT	OT	OT
Sample No.	206	121	85	101	127	236	10	110	77	132	243	27	83	116	5	32	181
Ba/La	13	27	18	17	15	10	17	26	4	53	20	13	14	21	11	15	2
Ba/Nb	10	26	14	14	11	12	13	27	3	28	14	11	12	18	6	20	2
La/Nb	0.8	1	0.8	0.8	0.7	1.2	0.7	1	0.7	0.5	0.7	0.9	0.9	0.9	0.6	1.4	0.9
Ti/V	53.5	43.3	64.3	44.8	49.8	77	38.1	46.4	43.8	31.1	40.1	45.6	49.7	41.8	36	47.3	24.2
Ti/Y	719.9	726.1	640.6	662.6	657.2	653	607.8	679.4	554.2	429.9	542.2	551.8	359.2	612.8	550	582	255.9
Ti/Zr	81	107.1	70.6	82.4	87.2	79	91.2	99.1	84.8	86.9	86.8	86.2	37.7	89.7	92.4	97.8	83
Zr/Nb	2.7	4.8	3.3	4.2	4	4	5.2	4.9	4	4	4.4	4.8	4	5	4	6.1	11

AOB = alkali olivine basalt, OT = olivine tholeiite, QT = quartz tholeiite.

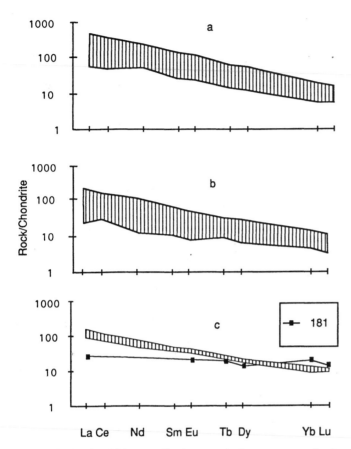

Figure 6. The chondritic normalized rare earth element patterns for the volcanic rocks of northeastern Balochistan, Pakistan. Normalization values are from Sun and McDonough (1989). Elements are arranged in increasing atomic weight from left to right. a: alkali olivine basalt, b: olivine tholeiite and c: quartz tholeiite. Sample 181 is a quartz tholeiite that has a N-type mid-ocean ridge basalt composition. It is possible that the sample may be from a fault-bounded sliver of the Muslimbagh ophiolite sequence.

4; Figs. 7 and 8). Therefore, the Parh Group basalts are not similar to MORB and probably are not a part of the Muslimbagh ophiolites. The Muslimbagh ophiolites, which have been obducted onto the older Mesozoic sediments and volcanics, are pillowed basalts that have MORB characteristics (Munir and Ahmed, 1985).

The compositions of the rocks of northeastern Balochistan are not like those of continental-rift–related volcanic rocks. Most of the Parh Group rocks have very low La/Nb and Ba/Nb, and thus show little evidence of interaction with continental crust or derivation from old lithospheric mantle as some rift–related volcanics do. Furthermore, at the time these volcanics were formed (75.9–67.5 Ma), this part of the Indo-Pakistani plate was under compression rather than extension, and subduction had started on the north within the Neo-Tethys ocean (Powell, 1979).

The chemical characteristics of the Parh Group basalts are similar to those of the Southern Hemisphere OIB. On the various published tectonic setting discrimination diagrams, these basalts consistently plot in the field of within-plate basalts (Figs. 7 and 8; Table 4). Specifically, the Ba/Nb, La/Nb, and other trace element characteristics of the Parh Group basalts are similar to those of OIB, and have Dupal-like trace element signatures (e.g., Reunion, Kerguelen, Tristan Da Cunha, and Gough; Hart, 1984; Weaver et al., 1986).

Special note must be made about the quartz tholeiite sample 181, which has a composition like that of a N-type MORB. It was collected on the northern end of the continuous outcrop at Gunda Manra, just north of a fault which is thought to mark the boundary of the obducted ophiolite sequence with the Mesozoic rocks to the south. Therefore, this sample may be from a fault-bounded sliver of N-type MORB from the Muslimbagh ophiolite sequence.

Geotectonic model

The progressive linear age changes with distance of volcanic chains within ocean basins and continents are generally linked with the relatively fixed upper mantle melting anomalies termed hotspots (Wilson, 1963; Morgan, 1971, 1981, 1983; Duncan, 1990; Mahoney, 1988). Hotspots can be active for tens of millions of years or more and produce magmas geochemically distinct from those erupted at spreading ridges and destructive plate boundaries. The hotspots are initiated as boundary-layer instabilities, although whether the instabilities originate at the core-mantle boundary or at a lower mantle boundary (White, 1992) is debated.

The Reunion hotspot, currently under Reunion Island in the Indian Ocean, is such a hotspot. The arrival of the Reunion plume head at the base of the Indo-Pakistani continental lithosphere is thought to have generated the Deccan Traps (Duncan and Hargraves, 1990; Duncan, 1990; Valdamme and Courtillot, 1990). Continued movement of the Indian plate over this hotspot generated the Chagos Ridge and Maldives-Laccadive Ridge (Fig. 9; Duncan, 1990). With a few exceptions, the age of the volcanic rocks decreases linearly from the Deccan Traps (64–72 Ma) to Reunion Island (0–2 Ma) along the suggested Reunion hotspot trail (Morgan, 1981; Fleitout et al., 1989; Royer et al., 1991). There has been no definite report of a trace of the Reunion hotspot to the north of the Deccan flood basalts. However, Mahoney (1988) speculated that some of the volcanic rocks in southern Pakistan might be related to the Reunion hotspot, and Morgan (1981) suggested that the Reunion hotspot may have been active prior to the main Deccan flood-basalt eruption.

The Parh Group basalts, which are along the northward projection of the Reunion hotspot trail north of the Deccan Traps (Fig. 9), have been dated as 65.7 to 75.9 Ma by the $^{40}Ar/^{39}Ar$ method (R. A. Duncan, 1994, personal communication). When the geochemistry and age of these volcanic rocks are considered along with the paleogeographic position and reconstruction of the Indo-Pakistani continent for Late Cretaceous time (Powell, 1979), it appears that the Parh Group basalts are related to the Reunion hotspot and may represent its earliest and northernmost

TABLE 4. SUMMARY OF THE DISCRIMINATION DIAGRAMS USED TO DETERMINE THE TECTONIC SETTING OF THE PARH GROUP BASALTS

Tectonic setting discrimination diagram	Island Arc	MORB	Within-plate Basalts
Ti-Zr (Pearce, 1983)			*[52]
Th/Yb - Ta/Yb (Pearce, 1983)		N[1]	*[57]
Zr/Y - Zr (Pearce, 1983)		N[1]	*[45]
Th/Y - Nb/Y (Pearce, 1987)		N[1]	*[57]
Ce/Nb - Th/Nb (Saunders and Tarney, 1991)		E[3–4]	*[45]
2xNb - Zr/4 -Y (Meschede, 1986)		N[1]	*[52]
Ti/100 -Zr -Y×3 (Pearce and Cann, 1973)		N[1]	*[52]
Th-Hf/3 -Ta (Wood et al., 1979)		N[1]	*[48]
TiO$_2$ - MnO -P$_2$O$_5$ × 10 (Mullen, 1983)	[5]	N[1]	*[46]
F1 -F$_2$ major element functions (Pearce, 1976)			*[41]
Augite [TiO$_2$ - MnO -Na$_2$O] (Nisbet and Pearce, 1977)		OFB[10]	*[62]

MORB = Mid-ocean ridge basalt, N = N-type basalts, E = E-type basalts, OFB = ocean-floor basalts. Number in brackets is number of samples plotting in the field.
*Majority of the samples.

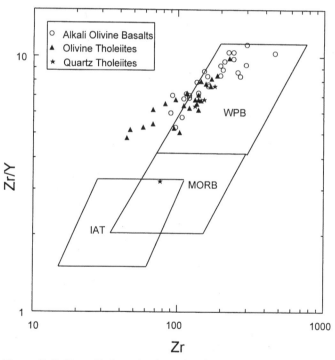

Figure 7. Zr/Y vs. Zr for volcanic rocks of northeastern Balochistan, Pakistan.WPB = within-plate basalts, MORB = mid-ocean ridge basalts, IAT = island-arc tholeiites. The field boundaries are after Pearce (1987).

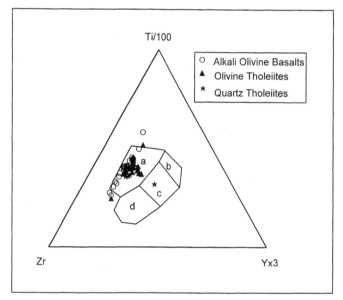

Figure 8. Ti/100-Zr-Y×3 for the volcanic rocks of northeastern Balochistan, Pakistan. a = Within-plate basalts, b = low potassic tholeiites, c = ocean-floor basalts, and d = volcanic-arc basalts. Field boundaries are after Pearce and Cann (1973).

magmatism. A plume head has elevated temperatures and melts extensively, generating magma mainly of tholeiitic composition. The small volume of principally alkaline volcanic rocks in northeastern Balochistan implies that they were not generated by the same mechanism as the Deccan Traps.

The genetic model proposed for the West Greenland basalts by Thompson and Gibson (1991) and Larsen et al. (1992) may best explain the origin of the Parh Group basalts. The volcanism associated with the continental breakup of the

North Atlantic region in the early Tertiary is attributed to the Iceland mantle plume, which was centered beneath East Greenland (White and McKenzie, 1989). This model suggests that the West Greenland basalts were generated when the mantle plume head impinged at the base of the lithosphere. The rate and timing of melt production in the mantle plume were strongly dependent on the thickness of the overlying lithosphere (White and McKenzie, 1989; Watson and McKenzie, 1991). Magma generation began above peripheral parts of the plume because it was able to rise to shallow levels into thinned areas of lithosphere along the continental margin. Magma generation began

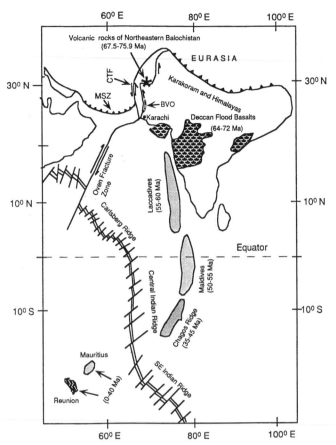

Figure 9. Regional map showing the major tectonic zones, continental flood basalts of the Deccan Traps (India), location of the study area, and present position of the Reunion hotspot. CTF = Chaman transform fault, MSZ = Makran subduction zone, BVO = Bela volcanics and ophiolitic melange.

The Reunion hotspot plume is thought to have been under the Deccan flood-basalt province at 65–69 Ma (Morgan, 1981; Duncan and Pyle, 1988; Courtillot et al., 1988; Fleitout et al., 1989). At about 65 Ma the Reunion hotspot erupted massive volumes of flood basalts (Duncan, 1990; Basu et al., 1993). The Reunion hotspot plume head, which was probably ~2,000 km in diameter when it impinged the continental lithosphere, may have been centered beneath the Deccan province before the main pulse of volcanism (Morgan, 1971, 1981; Fleitout et al., 1989). When the plume head impinged the thick continental lithosphere, it also extended under the Tethys ocean to the north. Material in the periphery of the plume head may have risen to shallower levels, melted by decompression, and erupted earlier than the main Deccan flood-basalt volcanism. This is reflected in the slightly older age of some of the Parh Group basalts compared to those of the Deccan flood basalts. The relatively low temperature along the plume-head periphery (Campbell and Griffiths, 1990) may have been responsible for the small degree of partial melting, which is reflected by the predominant alkaline chemistry and low volume of the basalts in northeastern Balochistan. Shortly after, or during, the late

4–6 m.y. later below the continent interior, where the lithosphere was thicker (Watson and McKenzie, 1991; Thompson and Gibson, 1991; Larsen et al., 1992).

The Indo-Pakistani plate separated from the rest of Gondwana in the Mesozoic and moved more than 5,000 km northward before colliding with the Eurasian continents (Klootwijk, 1979). It separated from Madagascar about 83 Ma (Duncan, 1990; Powell, 1979) and closed the Tethyan ocean as it moved northward. When the volcanism in northeastern Balochistan began, the Tethyan ocean could have been as much as 2,000 km wide east of the proto-Owen Fracture Zone (Fig. 10; Powell, 1979). Plate reconstruction (Fig. 10) shows that the Indo-Pakistani continent was south of the equator from 65 to 70 Ma (Klootwijk, 1979; Klootwijk et al., 1992; Powell, 1979). The association of radiolarian chert nodules and thin-bedded porcelaneous limestone associated with the volcanic rocks indicates that the Parh Group basalts erupted in water that was shallower than the calcite compensation depth, perhaps along the continental shelf or slope at the west to northwest margin of the Indo-Pakistani continent near the southern shore of the Tethyan ocean.

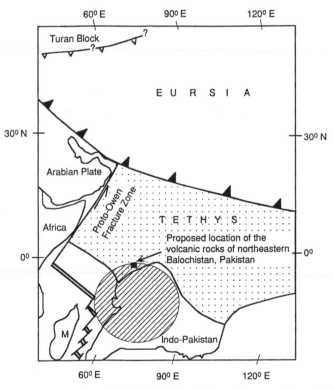

Figure 10. Tectonics of the Indo-Pakistani plate and surroundings at 70 Ma relative to Africa in its present position. The barbed heavy lines represent the convergence zone. The thick double offset lines represent the mid-ocean ridge in the Indian Ocean. The circle shows the suggested plume head extent (modified after Powell, 1979). The plume head diameter (about 2,000 km when it impinged the lithosphere) is after Campbell and Griffiths (1990) and White and McKenzie (1989). M is Madagascar.

stages of the basaltic volcanism in northeastern Balochistan, the center of the high-temperature mantle plume head thinned the continental lithosphere and erupted immense volumes of tholeiitic flood basalts in the Deccan province.

In the north, subduction started within the Tethyan ocean, forming oceanic island arcs (Kohistan and Ladakh). The motion of the Indo-Pakistani plate slowed from 10–12 to 4–6 cm/yr at 50 to 55 Ma, which indicates the first contact and/or collision between the Indo-Pakistani continent and Eurasia (Besse et al., 1984). Crustal shortening began along the collisional boundary between the two continents (Besse and Courtillot, 1988) and ophiolitic melanges including the Muslimbagh ophiolites were emplaced southward onto the Indo-Pakistani continental margin during the late Paleocene to Eocene (Gansser, 1974, 1979; Alleman, 1979). The Parh formation was thrust southward onto the Mesozoic sediments of the Loralai and Alozai Groups in the Sulaiman Range during late Paleocene to Eocene time. These rocks are now collectively found in the melange zone of the ophiolites and immediately to the south of it on the folded Mesozoic platform. From Eocene to Miocene time the indentation of the Indo-Pakistani plate caused many strike-slip faults to develop in the region. As the Indo-Pakistani plate continued to move northward, flysch sedimentation took place in the Katawaz basin and molasse-type sediments were deposited along the southern border of the Mesozoic Sulaiman Range.

CONCLUSIONS

Field and laboratory studies of the volcanic rocks within the Cretaceous Parh Group along the western boundary of the Indo-Pakistani plate demonstrate that they are the northernmost and oldest volcanic rocks related to the Reunion Island hotspot. The principal magmatism associated with the arrival of this hotspot plume below the Indo-Pakistani plate generated the Deccan Traps between 65 and 69 Ma (Morgan, 1981; Duncan and Pyle, 1988; Courtillot et al., 1988; Fleitout et al., 1989), the great bulk of lavas being erupted at 65 ± 1 Ma (Basu et al., 1993). These lavas were dominantly tholeiitic and had trace element signatures reflecting melting or assimilation of the Indo-Pakistani crust or lithospheric mantle.

The ^{40}Ar/^{39}Ar ages of the Parh Group volcanics (65.7–75.9 Ma) are generally older than those of the main Deccan eruptions. Their major and trace element compositions are similar to those of alkali olivine basalts and olivine tholeiites from Southern Hemisphere ocean islands, and they lack the lithospheric signature of the Deccan Traps. The low volume, generally alkaline nature, and trace element signatures of these lavas suggest that they represent small-degree melts that did not interact significantly with continental crust or ancient lithospheric mantle. We propose that the Parh Group volcanics were the first generated from the Reunion Island hotspot plume. They were generated from the northern edge of the plume as it rose beneath the Tethys sea off the north coast of the Indo-Pakistani plate. Northward migration of this plate trapped the Parh Group rocks between the Indo-Pakistani and Eurasian continents beginning at 50 and 55 Ma.

APPENDIX 1

Index map and geologic maps of the study area containing sample locations.

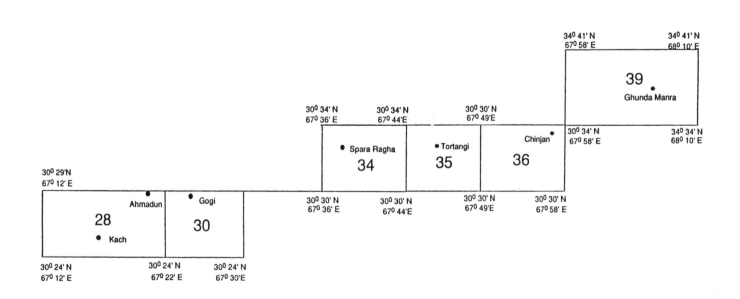

Map 30

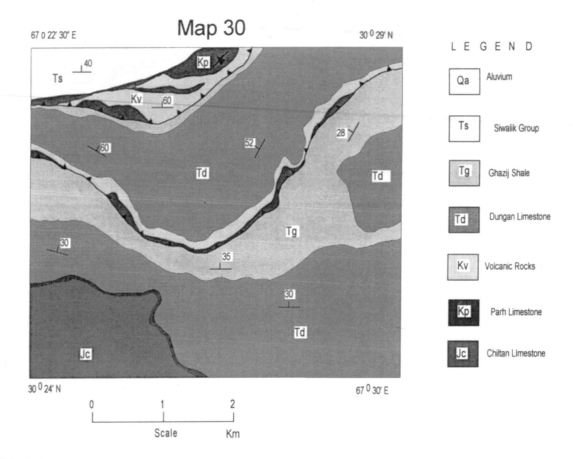

67 0 22' 30" E
30 0 29' N

Ts

40

Kp

Kv   60

60

52

28

Td

Td

30

Tg

35

30

Td

Jc

30 0 24' N
67 0 30' E

LEGEND

Qa   Aluvium

Ts   Siwalik Group

Tg   Ghazij Shale

Td   Dungan Limestone

Kv   Volcanic Rocks

Kp   Parh Limestone

Jc   Chiltan Limestone

0   1   2

Scale   Km

Map 34

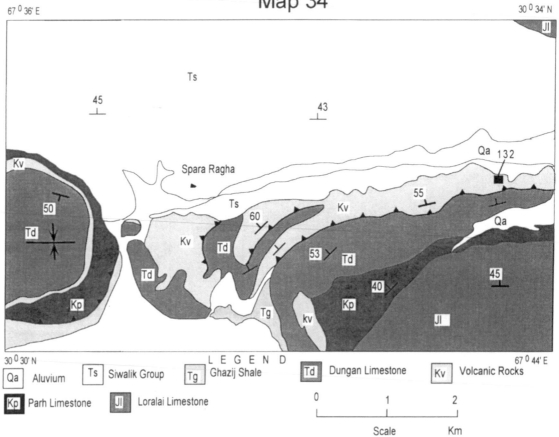

67 0 36' E
30 0 34' N

Jl

Ts

45

43

Kv

Qa   1 3 2

55

50

Spara Ragha

Ts

Qa

Td

Kv

60

Td

Kv

53   Td

Td

40

Tg

Kp

45

Kp

kv

Jl

30 0 30' N
67 0 44' E

LEGEND

Qa   Aluvium   Ts   Siwalik Group   Tg   Ghazij Shale   Td   Dungan Limestone   Kv   Volcanic Rocks

Kp   Parh Limestone   Jl   Loralai Limestone

0   1   2

Scale   Km

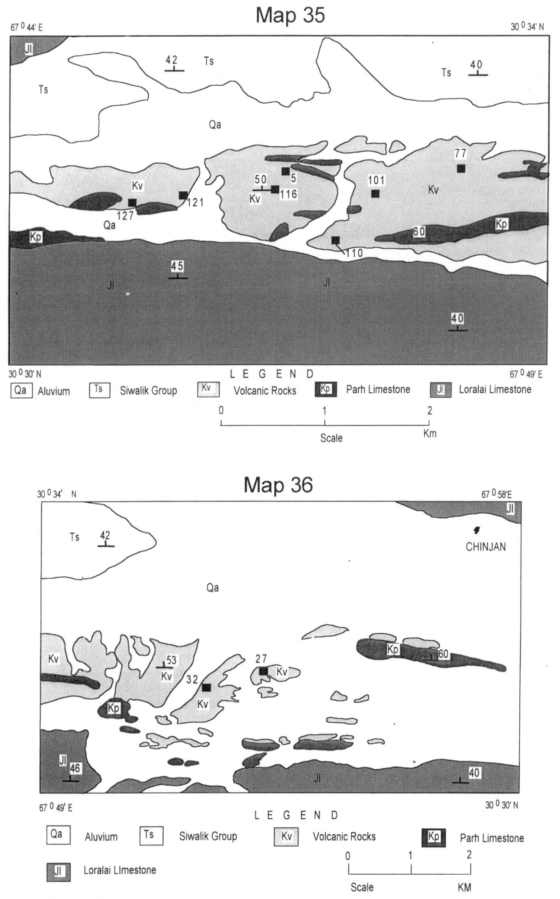

Map 39

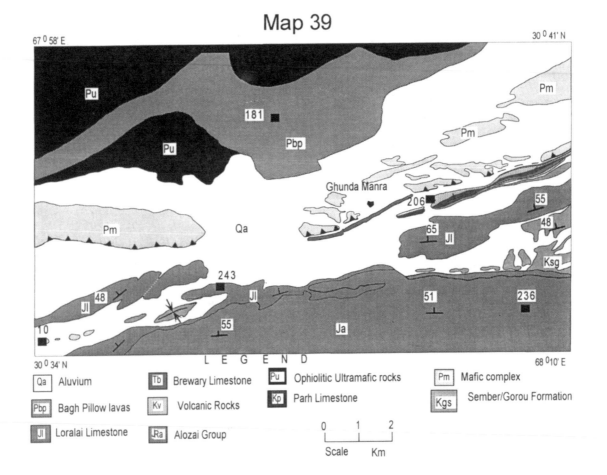

67 ⁰ 58' E   30 ⁰ 41' N

30 ⁰ 34' N   68 ⁰10' E

L E G E N D

Qa	Aluvium	
Pbp	Bagh Pillow lavas	
Jl	Loralai Limestone	
Tb	Brewary Limestone	
Kv	Volcanic Rocks	
Ra	Alozai Group	
Pu	Ophiolitic Ultramafic rocks	
Kp	Parh Limestone	
Pm	Mafic complex	
Kgs	Sember/Gorou Formation	

0   1   2
Scale   Km

ACKNOWLEDGMENTS

We are indebted to N. A. Durrani and Peter Warwick of the U.S. Geological Survey (USGS) in Islamabad, who arranged for USGS to clear and ship the rock samples from the field to Iowa. We thank Tom Vogal of Michigan State University for allowing the use of his laboratory to prepare and analyze rock samples for major and trace elements by X-ray fluorescence. Rare earth and trace element analyses were performed at the University of Michigan. Mineral chemical analyses were performed on the microprobe in the Department of Geological Sciences at the University of Chicago; We thank Ian Steele for his assistance. Robert Duncan of Oregon State University kindly furnished the $^{40}Ar/^{39}Ar$ age dates. The Midwest University Consortium for International Activities is acknowledged for furnishing one round-trip air ticket from the United States to Pakistan to Wazir Khan to enable him to complete his field work.

REFERENCES CITED

Ahmad, W., and Khan, M. J., 1990, Sedimentologic and magnetic-stratigraphic studies of the upper Siwalik Group, Sulaiman Range, Pakistan: Second Pakistan Geologic Congress, Abstracts: Pakistan, Department of Geology, University of Peshawar, p. 33–34.

Ahmad, Z., and Abbas, S. G., 1979, The Muslimbagh ophiolites, in Farah, A., and DeJong, K. A., eds., Geodynamics of Pakistan: Quetta, Pakistan, Geological Survey of Pakistan, p. 243–249.

Alleman, F., 1979, Time of emplacement of the Zhob and Bela ophiolites (preliminary report), in Farah, A. and DeJong, K. A., eds., Geodynamics of Pakistan: Quetta, Pakistan Geological Survey of Pakistan,.p. 215–242.

Asrarullah, Ahmad, Z., and Abbas, S. G, 1979, Ophiolites in Pakistan an introduction, in Farah, A., and DeJong, K. A., eds., Geodynamics of Pakistan: Quetta, Pakistan, Geological Survey of Pakistan, p. 181–192.

Auden, J. B., 1974, Afghanistan-West Pakistan, in Spencer, A. M., ed., Mesozoic-Cenozoic orogenic belts data for orogenic studies: Geological Society of London Special Publication 4, p. 235–253.

Banks, C. J., and Warburton, J., 1986, 'Passive roof' duplex geometry in the frontal structures of the Kirther and Sulaiman mountain belt, Pakistan: Journal of Structural Geology, v. 8, p. 229–237.

Basaltic Volcanism Study Project, 1981, Volcanism on the Terrestrial Planets: New York, Pergamon Press, Inc., 1286 p.

Basu, A. R. Renne, P. R., Das Gupta, D. K., Teichman, Friedrich and Preda, R. J., 1993, Early and late alkalai igneous pulses and a high-^{3}He plume origin for the Deccan flood basalts: Science, v. 261, p. 902–906.

Besse, J., and Courtillot, V., 1988, Paleogeographic maps of the continents bordering the Indian Ocean since Early Jurassic: Journal of Geophysical Research, v. 93, p. 11791–11808.

Besse, J., Courtillot, V., Pozzi, J.P., and Zhu, Y.X., 1984, Paleomagnetic estimates of crustal shortening in the Himalayan thrusts and Zangpo suture: Nature, v. 311, p. 621–626.

Campbell, I. H., and Griffiths, R. W., 1990, Implications of mantle plume structure for the evolution of flood basalts: Earth and Planetary Science Letters, v. 99, p. 79-93.

Courtillot, V., Feraud, G., Maluski, H., Vandamme, D., Moreau, M. G., and Besse, J., 1988, Deccan flood basalts and the Cretaceous /Tertiary bound-

Map 28

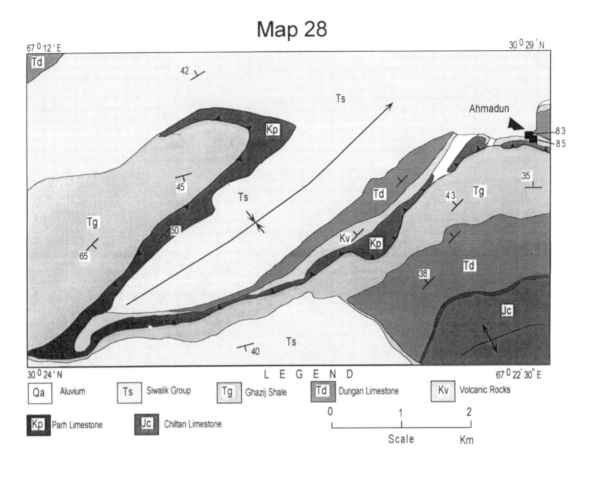

67° 12' E   30° 29' N

42

Td

Ts

Kp   Ahmadun

45   8 3

Ts   8 5

Tg   Ts   Td   43   Tg   35

50

65   Kv   Kp

38   Td

Jc

40   Ts

30° 24' N   L E G E N D   67° 22' 30" E

| Qa | Aluvium | | Ts | Siwalik Group | | Tg | Ghazij Shale | | Td | Dungan Limestone | | Kv | Volcanic Rocks |

| Kp | Parh Limestone | | Jc | Chiltan Limestone |

0   1   2

Scale   Km

ary: Nature, v. 333, p. 843–846.

Criss, J., 1980, Fundamental parameter calculations on a labortory microcomputer: Advanced X-Ray Analysis, v. 23, p. 93–97

De Jong, K. A., and Subhani, A. M., 1979, Note on the Bela ophiolites with special reference to the Kanar area, *in* Farah, A., and De Jong, K. A., eds., Geodynamics of Pakistan: Quetta, Pakistan, Geological Survey of Pakistan, p. 263–269.

Dewey, J. F., and Burke, K. C. A., 1973, Tibetan Variscan and Pre Cambrian basement reactivation products of continental collision: Journal of Geology, v. 81, p. 683–692.

Duncan, R. A., 1990, The volcanic records of the Reunion hotspot: Proceedings of the Ocean Drilling Program, Scientific results, Volume 115: College Station, Texas, Ocean Drilling Program, p. 3–10.

Duncan, R. A., and Hargraves, R. B., 1990, ^{40}Ar/^{39}Ar geochronology of basement rocks from the Mascarene plateau, the Chagos Bank and Maldives: Proceedings of the Ocean Drilling Program, Scientific results, Volume 115: College Station, Texas, Ocean Drilling Program, p. 43–51.

Duncan, R. A. and Pyle, D. G., 1988, Rapid eruption of the Deccan flood basalts at the Cretaceous/Tertiary boundary: Nature, v. 333, p. 841–843.

Fleitout, L., Dalloubex, C., and Moriceau, C., 1989, Small wavelength geoid and topography anomalies in the South Atlantic ocean; a clue to new hotspot tracks and lithospheric deformation: Geophysical Research Letters, v. 16, p. 637–640.

Gansser, A., 1974, The ophiolite melange, a world-wide problem *in* Tethyan examples: Eclogae Geologicae Helvetiae, v. 67, p. 479–507.

Gansser, A., 1979, Reconnaissance visit to the ophiolites in Balochistan and Himalayas, in Farah, A., and DeJong, K. A., eds., Geodynamics of Pakistan: Quetta, Pakistan, Geological Survey of Pakistan, p. 193–214.

Gill, J. B., 1981, Orogenic andesites and plate tectonics: Berlin, Springer-Verlag,

390 p.

Hagan, R. C., 1982, X-ray fluorescence analysis: Major elements in silicate minerals: Los Alamos National Laboratory Report 9400-MS, p. 1–13.

Hart, S. R., 1984, A large scale isotope anomaly in the Southern Hemisphere mantle: Nature, v. 309, p. 753–757.

Hunting Survey Corporation, 1960, Reconnaissance geology of Western Pakistan, a Colombo Plan Cooperative Project: Toronto, Government of Canada, 550 p.

Johnson, B. D., Powell, C. M., and Veevers, J. J., 1976, Spreading history of the eastern Indian Ocean, and the Greater India's northward flight from Antactica and Australia: Geological Society of America Bulletin, v. 87, p. 1560–1566.

Kazmi, A. H., 1979, The Bibai and Gogai nappes *in* the Kach-Ziarat area of Northeastern Baluchistan, in Farah, A., and DeJong, K. A., eds., Geodynamics of Pakistan: Quetta, Pakistan, Geological Survey of Pakistan, p. 333–339.

Kazmi, A. H., 1984, Petrology of the Bibai volcanics, Northeastern Balochistan: University of Peshawar Geological Bulletin, v. 17, p. 43–51.

Khan, W., 1994, The geology, geochemistry and tectonic setting of the volcanic rocks of Chinjan and Ghanda Manra areas, northeastern Balochistan, Pakistan [Ph.D.thesis]: Iowa City, University of Iowa, 257 p.

Klootwijk, C. T., 1979, A review of paleomagnetism data from the Indo-Pakistani fragments of Gondwanaland, *in* Farah, A., and DeJong, K. A., eds., Geodynamics of Pakistan: Quetta, Pakistan, Geological Survey of Pakistan, p. 41–80.

Klootwijk, C. T., Gee, J. S., Peirce, J. W., Smith, G. M. and McFadden, P. L., 1992, An early India Asia contact: Paleomagnetic constraints from Ninety East Ridge: Ocean Drilling Program, Leg 121: Geology, v. .20, p. 395–398.

Larsen, L. M., Pedersen, A. K., Pedersen, G. K., and Piasecki, S., 1992, Timing and duration of early Tertiary volcanism in the North Atlantic: New evidence from West Greenland, *in* Storey, B. C, Alabaster, T., and Pankhurst R. J., eds., Magmatism and the causes of continental break-up: Geological Society of London Special Publication 68, p. 321–333.

Lawrence, R. D., and Yeats, R. S., 1979, Geological reconnaissance of the Chaman fault in Pakistan, *in* Farah, A., and DeJong, K. A., eds., Geodynamics of Pakistan: Quetta, Pakistan, Geological Survey of Pakistan, p. 352–361.

MacDonald, G. A., and Katsura, T., 1964, Chemical composition of Hawaiian lavas: Journal of Petrology, v. 5, p. 83–133.

Mahoney, J. J., 1988, Deccan Traps, *in* Macdougall J.D., ed., Continental flood basalts: Amsterdam, Kluwer Academic Publishers, p. 151–194.

McCormick, G. R., 1985, Preliminary study of the volcanic rocks of the southern Tethyan suture in Balochistan, Pakistan: Acta Mineralogica Pakistanica, v. 1, p. 2–9.

Meschede, M., 1986, A method of discriminating between different types of mid-ocean ridge basalts and continental tholeiites with the Nb-Zr-Y diagram: Chemical Geology, v. 56, p. 207–218.

Molnar, P., and Tapponnier, P., 1975, Cenozoic tectonics of Asia: Effects of a continental collision: Science, v. 189, p. 419-426.

Morgan, W. J.1971, Convection plumes in the lower mantle: Nature, v. 230, p. 42–43.

Morgan, W. J., 1981, Hotspot track and opening of the Atlantic and Indian Oceans, in Emiliani, C., ed., The oceanic lithosphere: The Sea, Volume 7: New York, Wiley, p. 443–487.

Morgan, W. J., 1983, Hotspot tracks and the early rifting of the Atlantic: Tectonophysics, v. 94, p. 123–139.

Morris, J. D., and Hart, S. R., 1983, Isotopic and incompatible element constraints on the genesis of island arc volcanics from Cold Bay and Amak Island, Aleutians, and implications for mantle structure: Geochimica et Cosmochimica Acta, v. 47, p. 2015–2030.

Mullen, E.D., 1983, MnO/TiO_2/P_2O_5: A minor element discriminant for basaltic rocks of oceanic environments and its implications for the petrogenesis: Earth and Planetary Science Letters, v. 62, p. 53–62.

Munir, M., and Ahmed, Z., 1985, Petrochemistry of the contact rocks from the northwestern Jungtorgarh segment of the Zhob Valley ophiolites, Pakistan: Acta Mineralogica Pakistanica, v. 1, p. 38–48.

Nisbet, E. G., and Pearce, J. A., 1977, Clinopyroxene composition in mafic lavas from different tectonic settings: Contributions to Mineralogy and Petrology, v. 63, p. 149–160.

Otsuki, K., Hoshino, K., Anwar, M., Mengal, J. M., Brohi, I. A., Fatmi, A. N, and Yuji, O, 1989, Breakup of Gondwanaland and emplacement of ophiolitic complex in Muslimbagh area of Balochistan, Pakistan: University of Peshawar Geological Bulletin, v. 22, p. 103–126.

Pearce, J. A., 1976, Statistical analysis of major element patterns in basalts: Journal of Petrology, v. 17, p. 15–43.

Pearce, J. A., 1983, Role of the subcontinental lithosphere in magma genesis at active continental margins, *in* Hawksworth, C. J., and Nory, M. J., eds., Continental basalts and mantle xenoliths: Cheshire, Shiva Publishing Co., p. 230–250.

Pearce, J. A., 1987, An expert system for the tectonic characterization of ancient volcanic rocks: Journal of Volcanology and Geothermal Research, v. 32, p. 51–65.

Pearce, J. A., and Cann, J. R., 1973, Tectonic setting of basic volcanic rocks determined using trace element analysis: Earth and Planetary Science Letters, v. 19, p. 290–300.

Peng, Z. X., Mahoney, J. J., Hooper, P., Harris, C., and Beane, J., 1994, A role for lower continental crust in flood basalt genesis? Isotopic and incompatible element study of the lower six formations of the western Deccan Traps: Geochimica et Cosmochimica Acta, v. 58, p. 267–288.

Powell C. M., 1979, A speculative tectonic history of Pakistan and surroundings: Some constraints from the Indian ocean, *in* Farah, A.and DeJong, K. A., eds., Geodynamics of Pakistan: Quetta Pakistan Geological Survey of Pakistan, p. 5–24.

Powell C. M., and Conaghan, P. J., 1973, Plate tectonics and the Himalayas: Earth and Planetary Science Letters, v. 20, p. 1–12.

Powell C. M., and Conaghan, P. J., 1975, Tectonic model for the Tibetan Plateau:Geology, v. 4, p. 727–731.

Reddy, S. M., Searle, M. P., and Massey, J. A., 1993, Structural evolution of the Himalayan gneiss sequence, Lantang Valley, *in* Treloar, J. P., and Searle, M. P., eds., Himalayan tectonics: Geological Society of London Special Publication. 74, p. 375–389.

Richards, M. A., Duncan, R. A., and Courtillot, V. E., 1989, Flood basalts and hot-spot: Plumes heads and tails: Science, v. 246, p. 103–107.

Royer, J. Y., Peirce, W. J., and Weissel, J. K., 1991, Tectonic constraints on hot spot formation of the Ninety East Ridge *in* Proceedings of the Ocean Drilling Program, Scientific results, Volume 121: College Station, Texas, Ocean Drilling Program, p. 763–776.

Saunders, A., and Tarney, J., 1991, Back arc basins, *in* Floyd, P. A., ed., Oceanic Basalts: London, Blackie, p. 219–263.

Schilling, J. G., Meyer, P. S., and Kingsley, R. H., 1983, Evolution of the Iceland hotspot: Nature, v. 296, p. 313–320.

Shervais, J. W., 1982, Ti-V plots and the petrogenesis of modern and ophiolitic lavas: Earth and Planetary Science Letters, v. 57, p. 101–118.

Sun, S. S.and McDonough, W. F., 1989, Chemical and isotopic systematics of oceanic basalts: Implication for mantle composition and processes, *in* Saunders, A. D., and Norry, M. J., eds., Magmatism in ocean basins: Geological Society of London Special Publication 42, p. 313–345.

Tapponier, P., Mattauer, M., Proust, F., and Cassaigneau, C., 1981, Mesozoic ophiolites, sutures and large-scale tectonic movements in Afghanistan: Earth and Planetary Science Letters, v. 52, p. 355–371.

Thompson, R. N., and Gibson, S. A., 1991, Subcontinental mantle plumes, hotspots and preexisting thin spots: Geological Society of London Journal, v. 148, p. 973–977.

Valdamme, D., and Courtillot, V., 1990, Paleomagnetism of Leg 115, basement rocks and latitudinal evolution of the Reunion hotspot *in* Proceedings of the Ocean Drilling Program, Scientific results, Volume 115: College Station, Texas, Ocean Drilling Program p. 111–117.

Vredenburg, E. W., 1909, Report on the geology of Srawan Jhalawan, Makran and the State of Las Bela: Indian Geological Survey Records, v. 38, p. 303–338.

Waheed, A., and Wells, N. A., 1990, Fluvial history of late Cenozoic molasse, Sulaiman Range, Pakistan: Sedimentary Geology, v. 67, p. 237–261.

Watson, S., and McKenzie, D., 1991, Melt generation by plumes: A study of Hawaiian volcanism: Journal of Petrology, v.32, p. 501–537.

Weaver B. L., Wood, D. A., Tarney, J.and Joron, J. L., 1986, Role of subducted sediment in the genesis of ocean-island basalts: geochemical evidence from south Atlantic Ocean islands: Geology, v. 14, p. 275-278.

White, R. S., 1992, Magmatism during and after continental break-up, *in* Storey, B. C., Alabaster, T.and Pankhurst, R. J., eds., Magmatism and the causes of continental break-up: Geological Society of London Special Publication, 68, p. 1–16.

White, R. S., and McKenzie, D. P., 1989, Magmatism at rift zones: The generation of volcanic continental margins and flood basalts: Journal of Geophysical Research, v. 94, p. 7685–7729.

Wilson, J. T., 1963, A possible origin of the Hawaiian islands: Canadian Journal of Physics, v. 41, p. 863–870.

Wood, D. A., 1980, The application of the Th-Hf-Ta diagram to problems of tectonomagmatic classification and establishing the nature of crustal contamination of basaltic lavas of the British Tertiary Volcanic Province: Earth and Planetary Science Letters, v. 50, p. 11–30.

Wood, D. A., Joron, J. L., Treuil, M., and Norry, M., 1979, A reappraisal of the use of trace elements to classify and discriminate between magma genesis erupted in different tectonic settings: Earth and Planetary Science Letters, v. 45, p. 326–336.

MANUSCRIPT ACCEPTED BY THE SOCIETY FEBRUARY 3, 1998

Geological Society of America
Special Paper 328
1999

Jurassic sedimentary facies and paleogeography of the former Indian passive margin in southern Tibet

Guanghua Liu* and Gerhard Einsele
*Institute and Museum of Geology and Paleontology, University of Tübingen, Sigwartstrasse 10,
D-72076 Tübingen, Germany*

ABSTRACT

The Jurassic sedimentary sequence of southern Tibet is dominated by mixed carbonate and siliciclastic rocks in the southern area and by micritic limestones, turbiditic siliciclastic rocks, and radiolarites in the north, close to the Indus-Yarlung suture. Both the sedimentary features and the lithofacies distribution indicate that these areas represented a part of the Indian passive continental margin during the Jurassic.

In the Early Jurassic, southern Tibet was characterized by a ramp-type shelf. Within the southern inner ramp, carbonate shoals formed in the west, whereas a siliciclastic estuarine system developed in the east. Tide-influenced deposition in the inner ramp may result from shallow water depth and gentle slope. Fine-grained clastics and cherts accumulated in the northern outer ramp to oceanic basin.

During the Middle Jurassic, the ramp-type shelf setting was maintained, but the southeastern region evolved into a delta-dominated setting. Increasing sedimentation rate led to aggradation and progradation of the thick shallow-water sediments on the southern shelf. Basaltic sills intruded in the northern deep-water basin, indicating that the Tethyan ocean was in an expanding stage.

The late Callovian and Oxfordian represent transgressive periods, in which the shelf became sediment starved so that ferruginous oolitic and coquina-rich condensed beds were widespread. However, a terrigenous-dominated wedge prograded onto the southern shelf in the Kimmeridgian, when the northern deeper basin still received little sediment. Until the early Tithonian, a carbonate oolite-dominated platform built up in the southwest, whereas the progradation of the terrigenous wedge persisted in the southeast. The late Tithonian was a period of rapid deposition, in which thick, fine clastics accumulated on the southern deepening shelf, and extensive slope-apron and basin-floor fans developed in the northern zone. A short regression occoured in the latest Jurassic and earliest Cretaceous, and led to the development of a barrier-island complex in the southern area and the southward retrograding of the submarine fans in the northern zone.

INTRODUCTION

Our study area spans from about long 86° to 90°E and from lat 28°00′ to 28°4′N in southern Tibet (Fig. 1), a part of the Tethyan Himalayas (Gansser, 1964). Mesozoic sedimentary rocks here are preserved along the strike of the orogen between the Indus-Yarlung suture and the High Himalayan crystalline belt; they document the geological history of the Neotethys and the former India shelf.

In this area, the Neotethys evolved during the early Mesozoic between the Lhasa block and the Indian plate (e.g., Mercier

*e-mail: liu@uni-tuebingen.de

Liu, G., and Einsele, G., 1999, Jurassic sedimentary facies and paleogeography of the former Indian passive margin in southern Tibet, *in* Macfarlane, A., Sorkhabi, R. B., and Quade, J., eds., Himalaya and Tibet: Mountain Roots to Mountain Tops: Boulder, Colorado, Geological Society of America Special Paper 328.

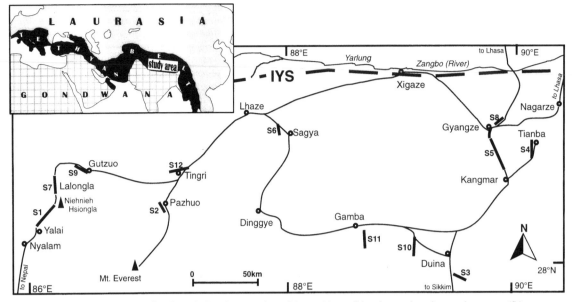

Figure 1. Sketch showing the main locations, roads, and the positions of the observed sections and outcrops (S1 though S12) in the study area. The inset shows the present configuration of the Tethyan belt (in black) and study area (white rectangle) between the Laurasian and Gondwanan continents. IYS: the Indus-Yarlung suture zone.

and Li, 1984; Xiao et al., 1988; Liu, 1992). The passive continental margin of the Indian plate developed during the Jurassic after a Triassic rifting stage. Collision took place between the Indian and the amalgamated Eurasian plates during the latest Cretaceous and earliest Tertiary, giving rise to the Indus-Yarlung suture (Liu, 1992; Willems, 1993; Liu and Einsele, 1994, 1996). After collision, northward indentation by the Indian plate resulted in continental escape, large-scale crustal shortening, and the uplift of the Himalayas (Mercier and Li, 1984; Xiao et al., 1988; Shackleton et al., 1988; Liu, 1992; Ratschbacher et al., 1994).

The purpose of this chapter is to describe the lithofacies distribution and paleogeographic evolution of southern Tibet during the Jurassic. Most results presented here are based on our own observations (Fig. 1) and previous work mainly carried out during the 1980s (e.g., Academia Sinica, 1974, 1981, 1984; Tibet Regional Geological Team [TRGT in following], 1983; Yu et al., 1983; Wang et al., 1983; Liu et al., 1983; Westermann and Wang, 1988; Gradstein et al., 1989). It should be taken into account that the area investigated is very large and the biostratigraphical and sedimentological studies in general have not yet reached the same level as in more accessible countries. For this reason, some of our conclusions are tentative and supported only by relatively sparse field observations and laboratory data. The sea-level fluctuations discussed here are to be regarded as relative changes that do not necessarily correspond to sea-level changes of global extent.

STRATIGRAPHY AND LITHOLOGICAL ASSOCIATION

Jurassic strata are well preserved and exposed in the study area. Detailed chronostratigraphic studies were not carried out until recently, but pioneering work began as early as 1903 in Spiti (Uhlig, 1910) and

in Gamba (Arkell, 1953). Subsequently, Academia Sinica (1974, 1981, 1984), Wang and Zhang (1974), Zhao (1976), TRGT (1983), Yu et al. (1983), Shi (1987), and Westermann and Wang (1988), and others published a series of stratigraphic studies, which led to the establishment of the basic Jurassic stratigraphic system in this region (Fig. 2).

As a result of facies changes from south to north, this region can be divided into two lithological zones. The thicknesses of Jurassic deposits vary from 3,500–4,500 m in the southern zone to 2,000–3,000 m in the northern zone. In the southern zone (between Nyalam-Duina and Tingri-Kangmar), the Jurassic formations consist mainly of bioclastic carbonates and terrigenous clastics. These sediments can be divided into five depositional sequences that record the Jurassic sedimentary history from coastal to outer shelf environments in the southern zone (Fig. 3).

The Jurassic formations of the northern zone (between the Indus-Yarlung suture zone and Tingri-Kangmar) are dominated by calcareous shales, dark shales, and micritic limestones, as well as some volcaniclastic rocks. These sediments have been interpreted as outer shelf to continental rise deposits (Fig. 4).

Farther northward in the Indus-Yarlung suture zone, the Jurassic strata are characterized by dark shales, radiolarites, and basaltic lava, i.e., typical oceanic deposits. Because of the monotonous lithology, rare macrofossils, and strongly tectonic deformation in this area, no detailed stratigraphic division has been achieved.

LITHOFACIES AND PALEOGEOGRAPHY OF THE EARLY JURASSIC

The generalized lithofacies distribution (Fig. 5) and the paleogeographic reconstruction (Fig. 6) indicate that the northern

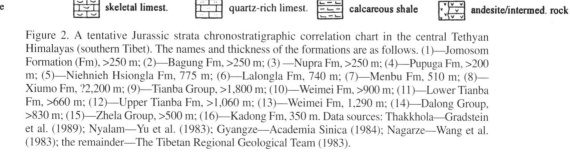

Figure 2. A tentative Jurassic strata chronostratigraphic correlation chart in the central Tethyan Himalayas (southern Tibet). The names and thickness of the formations are as follows. (1)—Jomosom Formation (Fm), >250 m; (2)—Bagung Fm, >250 m; (3) —Nupra Fm, >250 m; (4)—Pupuga Fm, >200 m; (5)—Niehnieh Hsiongla Fm, 775 m; (6)—Lalongla Fm, 740 m; (7)—Menbu Fm, 510 m; (8)— Xiumo Fm, ?2,200 m; (9)—Tianba Group, >1,800 m; (10)—Weimei Fm, >900 m; (11)—Lower Tianba Fm, >660 m; (12)—Upper Tianba Fm, >1,060 m; (13)—Weimei Fm, 1,290 m; (14)—Dalong Group, >830 m; (15)—Zhela Group, >500 m; (16)—Kadong Fm, 350 m. Data sources: Thakkhola—Gradstein et al. (1989); Nyalam—Yu et al. (1983); Gyangze—Academia Sinica (1984); Nagarze—Wang et al. (1983); the remainder—The Tibetan Regional Geological Team (1983).

Lithology						Description	Interpretation			
							Facies	Seq. Str.		Rel. Sea-l.
shale	silt	fs	m	cs						rise — fall
Cret.								LST		
					4500 m	graded, interbedded black shales and grayish green silty shales, intercalated with coarse siltstone, with abundant pyritic concretions.	outer	HST		
34						a bed (1m) of medium-grained quartz sandstone with belemnites at the base.	shelf			
					4000 m	upper: very thin-bedded micritic limestones, with intercalated gray and purple calcareous shales, increasing in bed thickness upward.	fore-slope (mid. shelf)	TST	sequence 5	
33					3500 m	middle: grainstones and packstones with medium calcareous sandstones, showing thinning-upward trend.		SM ST		
						lower: cross-bedded coarse calarenite and sandstone.	carbonate platform			
32					3000 m	upper: strongly bioturbated micritic limestones, with thin silty shale and siltstone beds.	offshore	HST	sequence 4	
						lower: medium-bedded calcareous quartz sandstones, oolites & pelletal grainstones.	ooidal shoal	TST		
							tide channel shoreface	SM ST		
31					2500 m	dark laminated silty shales & silstones with strong bioturbation and abundant pyritic concretions.	middle to outer shelf	HST		
30 29						coquina and red-brown Fe-oolitic layers, passing upward into interbedded black shales & siltstones.	starved shelf	TST	sequence 3	
28 27						thin-bedded dark micrites, with intercalated black shales.	offshore			
26 25					2000 m	upper: bioturbated siltstones, micrites and quartzose oolites; lower: medium- to coarse-grained, well-sorted, sparitic calcarenites & quartz sandstones with oolites.	carbonate shoals	LST		
24							tide channel			
23 22					1500 m	cross-bedded, medium- to coarse-grained calcareous quartz sandstone, quartz-rich calcarenites, oolites and intercalated shales and micrites, with coquina beds and ferruginous limestones in the middle part.	alternating shoreface, offshore, & shoals	HST	sequence 2	
21 20 19								TST		
18								LST		
17 16 15					1000 m	interbedded micrites, oolitic grainstones and coquina beds.	upper offshore	HST	sequence 1	
						missing (600m) due to a thrust belt.	??			
5 3						quartzose packstones & oolitic grainstones, with thin-bedded wackestones, pelmicrites and quartz sandstones.	tidal flats & shoreface	TST		
1					0 m	quartz sandstones, quartz-rich oolites and dolomitic limestones.	tidal channel	LST		

Formation labels (left column, top to bottom): Xiumo Fm. (Tithonian); Menbu Fm. (Call.-Kim.); Lanongla Fm. (Bath.); Niehnieh Hsiongla Fm. (Aal.-Baj.); Pupuga Fm.; Triassic

Indian margin in the study area was a relatively smooth shelf during the Early Jurassic, i.e., a ramp-type margin, that formed as a result of rapid progradation of clastic material during the latest Triassic (Liu, 1992). Sedimentation rates range from 60 m/m.y. in the south (Gamba-Yalai) to about 90 m/m.y. in the north (Kangmar-Gyangze; Liu and Einsele, 1994). From south to north, three lithofacies belts have been recognized: (1) coastal to inner ramp, (2) outer ramp, and (3) ramp toe to abyssal plain.

Coastal to inner ramp lithofacies belt

Sediments of the coastal to inner shelf belt consist of carbonates in the southwestern segment (Yalai-Pazhuo area) and siliciclastic-dominated rocks in the southeastern segment (Dinggye-Gamba-Duina area). They are represented by the Pupuga Formation, which is from 100 to >500 m thick (Fig. 5).

Carbonate-dominated facies association

This association is characterized by skeletal, oolitic grainstones, and packstones and thin intercalations of quartz sandstones. The profiles in both Niehnieh Hsiongla (S1 in Fig. 1), north of Yalai, and Pazhuo (S2 in Fig. 1) provide good examples.

Niehnieh Hsiongla section (S1). The Lower Jurassic Pupuga Formation is exposed along the Lhasa-Nyalam highway through Niehnieh Hsiongla hill near Yalai (S1 in Fig. 1), and is conformably underlain by Triassic sandstones (Academia Sinica, 1974; TRGT, 1983; Yu et al., 1983). Our observed section may represent only the lower part of this formation (units 2 to 5 in Fig. 3), because its upper part has been cut off by a thrust and replaced by the Lower Cretaceous strata (Zhang, 1985). The observed part is characterized by quartz-rich packstone, oolites, and calcarenites, intercalated with wackestones, quartz sandstones, and pelmicrites. These are interpreted as a shoreface-dominated facies association (Fig. 3). A detailed facies study, as an example, has been made on the sediments of the lowermost few meters, in which the following subfacies have been distinguished (Fig. 7).

Tidal channel facies. This facies is represented by a 1.5-m-thick unit of calcarenite at the base. The sequence begins with an erosional surface and a lag layer consisting of quartz pebbles, mud clasts, and shells. The lower sediments are quartz-rich skeletal packstones, in which the quartz fraction may be as much as 30% and pisoids range from 10% to 40%. Large-scale

---

Figure 3. Lithostratigraphic column and sedimentary interpretation of the Jurassic in the southern facies zone. Generalized from profiles (S1, S7, and S9) between Yalai and Gutzuo, along the Lhasa-Kathmandu highway. Stratigraphic divisions and thicknesses are based on Yu et al. (1983); Tibetan Regional Geological Team (1983); Academia Sinica (1984);, Westermann and Wang (1988); and our own observations. See Figures 2 and 4B for legends. LST: lowstand systems tract; TST: transgressive systems tract; HST: highstand systems tract; SMST: shelf-margin systems tract.

trough, tabular, and herringbone cross-bedding (Fig. 8, 1)), as thick as 50 cm, displays variation of grain size and orientation of skeletal fragments. The subsequent subunit is a parallel-bedded, thin layer of skeletal and oolitic grainstone that truncated the underlying packstone. The upper part is a tabular cross-bedded, medium-grained grainstone showing evidence of some bioturbation.

The fining-upward trend, scour surface, and herringbone and tabular cross-bedding indicate the infilling of a tidal channel. The thin intercalation of the parallel-bedded grainstone possibly represents a reworked bed or a so-called higher energy layer (Froude number >1; Reineck and Singh, 1980), perhaps caused by storm or combined storm-tidal currents. The 50-cm-thick cross-bedding sets and the general relationship between ripple height and water depth suggest that the water depth of the channel was perhaps <4 m (Allen, 1968).

Lower shoreface facies. This facies is characterized by medium-grained, low-angle cross-bedded skeletal and oolitic wackestones and subordinate packstones as well as some grainstones. Petrographically, the wackestone consists of 35% skeletal particles derived from foraminifera, mollusks, corals, and other fossils, 20%–40% pisoids, and 30%–40% micritic matrix. The packstone is composed of 50%–60% ooids (Fig. 8, 2), 15%–25% skeletal particles, and lesser amounts of mud intraclasts, which are cemented by sparry calcite. Some ooids have quartz sand nuclei. A lenticular packstone and grainstone bed, as thick as 0.7 m, is in the upper part. This bed shows a fining-upward trend and large cross-beds that have northward (seaward) foresets and graded bedding.

The textural properties reflect a medium- to low-energy environment, possibly within a lower shoreface. The cross-bedded packstone and grainstone lens may represent a minor rip channel caused by storm backflow (Einsele and Seilacher, 1991).

Storm deposits. Two units of storm deposits have been interpreted from quartz sandstone and thin coquina layers. The quartz sandstones are well-sorted, medium-grained, and laterally continuous layers and display hummocky cross-stratification. In thin sections, they show high textural maturity and a composition of ~95% rounded to subrounded quartz and ooids, mainly cemented by sparite. The coquina layers, 10–30 cm thick, are dominated by molluscan shells oriented parallel to the bedding surface and in places supported by a skeletal and siliceous sandy matrix.

The typical hummocky cross-bedded quartz sandstones may represent storm current-generated redeposits, whereas the coquina beds appear to be storm-winnowed and reworked sediments.

Offshore facies. This facies is represented by thinly bedded dark gray to black argillaceous micrites, calcareous shales, and nodular limestones. Parallel lamination and bioturbation are present. These features and the sedimentary context suggest that these sediments were formed mainly in a low-energy setting below the normal wave base.

Oolite shoal (shoreface facies). Rocks of this facies are quartz-rich skeletal and oolitic grainstones having structures ranging from parallel to trough cross-bedding. The skeletal

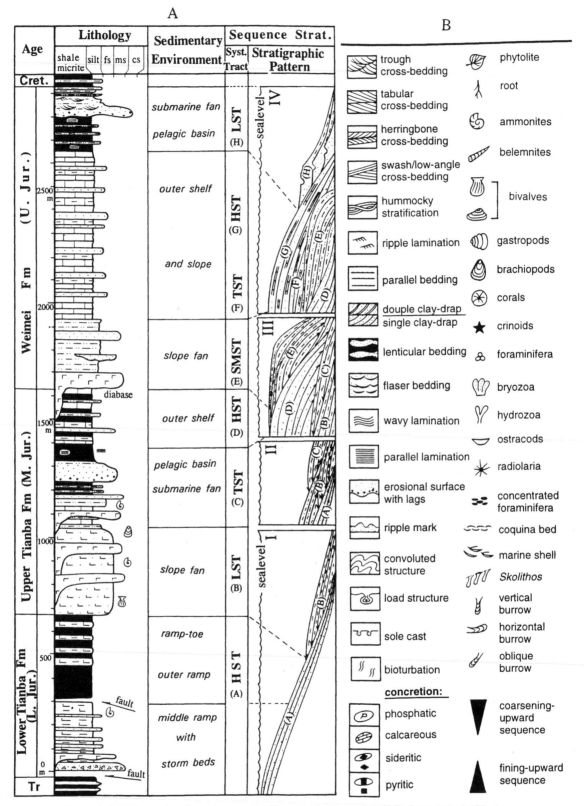

Figure 4. A: Lithostratigraphic column and sedimentary interpretation of the Jurassic in the Tianba section (S4), northeast of Kangmar (partly based on Tibetan Regional Geological Team, 1983). I through IV show the stacking patterns of depositional units based on both this section and the adjacent sections. LST: lowstand systems tract; TST: transgressive systems tract; HST: highstand systems tract; SMST: shelf-margin systems tract. B: General legends for the text figures. See text for discussion and Figure 2 for the lithological explanation.

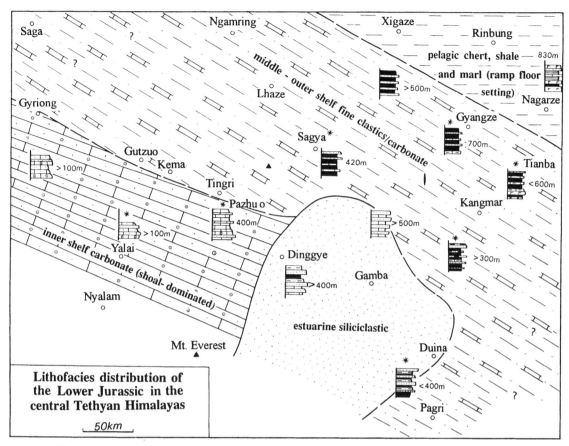

Figure 5. Lithofacies distribution and selected sequences (no scale) of the Lower Jurassic in southern Tibet. The north-south scale of this map has been restored, using balanced sections, to its original state prior to crustal shortening (Liu, 1992). The sequences with asterisks are based on our own field observations; the rest are from the literature. See Figure 2 for lithological explanation.

grainstones are characterized by well-sorted, oriented bioclastic particles and sparitic cements. Fragments of red algae and coccoliths, detrital bivalves, gastropods, and crinoids dominate. The oolitic grainstones are composed of >95% ooids; most have concentric coatings, and some have radial structures. Their nuclei are mainly micritic carbonate grains (pellets and skeletal fragments), but some are detrital quartz.

This suite of features, in particular the bedding style, dominance of grainstones, algal types, and evidence of extensive reworking, suggest high-energy conditions in a carbonate-shoal setting (Sellwood, 1986; Tucker and Wright, 1990).

Pazhuo section (S2). This section is situated on the western side of the main road from Tingri to Mt. Everest, 5 km north of the village of Pazhuo and some 30 km southeast of Tingri (S2 in Fig. 1). Only the lower 200 m of this section has been studied in detail. From bottom to top, the following two facies associations have been distinguished (Fig. 9).

Tide-dominated coastal to inner shelf carbonate facies. These facies are within the lower 50 m of sediments. The underlying Upper Triassic quartz sandstones display bimodal, current-generated herringbone cross-bedding with double- and single-mud drapes and reactivation surfaces (Fig. 8, 3). The

base of the Jurassic is a thin but coarse calcarenite layer with an undulating erosional surface and intraclastic and quartz pebble lags, and it passes into trough and herringbone cross-bedded, quartz-rich, medium-grained packstones. The sediments of this part may represent a high-energy tidal flat environment (i.e., sandy flats or intertidal shoals with small tidal channels).

The middle and upper parts of this unit are irregularly alternating beds of calcareous arenites, micrites, and muddy limestones. The calcarenites display dense vertical tube burrows, such as *Skolithos*, and contain a high proportion of fine-grained matrix, up to 35%. The argillaceous sandstone shows flaser and wavy bedding. The micrites and muddy limestones contain in situ ammonites, brachiopods, and horizontal burrows.

We assume that the calcarenites and sandstones formed in a low- to medium-energy tidal flat setting (Seilacher, 1978; Reineck and Singh, 1980), and the micrites and muddy limestones formed in a subtidal lower energy environment. The lowermost Jurassic appears to represent a slow transgression over the former delta plain of the Upper Triassic (Liu, 1992). A depositional model for this tide-dominated littoral setting is proposed in Figure 9g.

Storm-influenced upper offshore facies. This facies is represented by the middle and upper parts of the sequence and is domi-

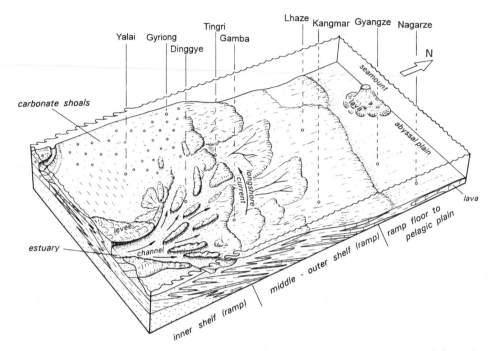

Figure 6. Paleogeographic reconstruction and sedimentary environments of the Lower Jurassic in southern Tibet, chiefly interpreted from Figure 5.

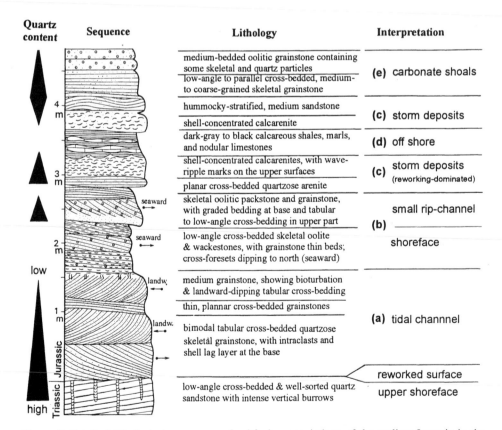

Figure 7. Detailed lithological sequence and subfacies associations of the earliest Jurassic in the Niehnieh Hsiongla section (S1), 5 km north of Yalai. See Figures 2 and 4B for legends.

nated by laminated lime mudstone, wackestone, and argillaceous limestone, and a predominantly planktonic fauna (ammonites and forams) and horizontal burrows. Intercalations of sandstone, skeletal packstone, and grainstone are common. The frequency and the thickness of these beds tend to decrease upward. Most intercalations in the lower part are trough cross-bedded, medium- to coarse-grained quartz sandstones and hummocky cross-strati-fied, quartz-rich calcarenites, often with an erosional base. The intercalations pass upward into thinly bedded, fine-grained cal-carenites and quartzose sandstones. Intraclasts, ripple lamination, and small-scale cross-bedding are common. These features indi-cate that the fine-grained carbonates were deposited in an offshore setting during fairweather conditions, and that the intercalated sandstones and bioclastic carbonates formed during storm periods. The storm beds in the lower part are dominated by proximal types (in the sense of Aigner and Reineck, 1982; Einsele and Seilacher, 1991). Storm-generated channel fills, characterized by a fining-upward sequence and an erosional base, are recognized from the deposits at 62 m (Fig. 9a) and at 105 m (Fig. 9b) of the section. Their storm-generated cross-bedding was strongly bioturbated during a subsequent fairweather period (Fig. 8, 4). The frequent occurrence of the storm channel quartz sandstones may suggest that the depositional processes during that period were dominated by the storm action (Fig. 9e).

Another type of storm sediment is represented by intraclastic limestone beds (10–40 cm thick) between 70 and 95 m above the section base. These beds are composed of subangular intraclasts and lesser amounts of quartz particles and fossil fragments. The intraclasts, ranging in size from 0.1 to 5 cm, are mainly derived from the micrites, which are petrologically similar to the under-lying sediments. No distinct sedimentary structures are noted, but some poorly preserved hummocky cross-bedding is present in the intercalated packstone. These beds may have been produced mainly by storm reworking and winnowing (Fig. 9f).

In the upper part, distal storm beds (fine-grained calcarenite and calcisiltite) dominate. With their host sediments (micrite and shale), the distal storm layers comprise numerous fining- and thinning-upward subcycles, ranging from 1 to 3 m in thickness (Fig. 9c). Indi-vidual beds tend to vary in thickness, from 25 cm to <1 cm. Some meter-scale subcycle sets are assembled in two coarsening-upward cycles, as found between 110 and 170 m of this section. Each cycle is ~30 m in thickness, and consists of gray, medium-bedded micrite and distal storm beds as well as proximal oolites and calcarenites. Both the bed thickness and frequency of the proximal storm intercalations increase upward in the cycles, suggesting a shallowing-upward trend resulting from progradation of a carbonate shoal (Fig. 9d).

Generally, a slight deepening-upward tendency can be observed in this section.

Terrigenous clastic facies association

The siliciclastic-dominated Lower Jurassic is distributed over the southeastern areas (Fig. 5). Detailed and complete bio-stratigraphic and sedimentary records are not available.

According to TRGT (1983), the Lower Jurassic in Dinggye is >400 m thick; it is a fining-upward sequence composed of thickly bedded quartz sandstones and argillaceous limestones in the lower part, thinly bedded sandstones, siltstones, and shales in the middle part, and black shales and siltstones in the upper part, which contains marine bivalves.

Another siliciclastic-dominated sequence crops out 15 km to the north of Gamba. Its lower part is a unit of medium-bedded quartz sandstone and intercalated glauconitic arenites, pebbly sandstones, and mudstones. The measured thickness is 164 m. The overlying sediments, 360 m thick, consist of calcareous lithic arenites and calcarenites and subordinate pebbly arenites and shales. Farther upsection is a 42-m-thick unit of medium-bedded, cross-bedded quartz arenite.

The depositional environments of these areas may be tenta-tively proposed as an estuarine or tidal-dominated delta system for the following reasons.

1. The shallow-marine terrigenous-dominated lithology indi-cates that this area was a coastal to inner shelf setting. On the plan view (Fig. 5), these sediments display a lobate deltaic distribution.

2. Sandstone-dominated sequences and limited thickness are not typical of a fluvial-dominated delta, which is normally char-acterized by coarsening-upward sequences and thick prodelta mudstone (Reineck and Singh, 1980; Pettijohn et al., 1987; Read-ing, 1996; and others). Similarly, the lithic arenite–dominated composition and low mineralogical and textural maturity of the sediments may exclude a wave-dominated delta system (in the sense of Reineck and Singh, 1980; Elliot, 1986).

3. The wide occurrence of the intertidal and subtidal deposits in the adjacent area and the presence of elongated sandbodies, oblique with respect to the regional depositional strike (shore-line), suggest tidal-dominated depositional processes.

Other Lower Jurassic rocks have been observed in the out-crops near Duina (S3 and S10 in Fig. 1). They consist of irregu-larly interstratified thin beds of silty shale and fine-grained sandstone and calcarenite. The silty shale:sandstone ratio in sec-tion S10 tends to decrease upward from about 3:1 to 1:1, showing a coarsening-upward trend. The silty shale is black, moderately bioturbated, and rich in organic matter. The sandstone is rich in carbonate and contains mollusks, brachiopods, and plant frag-ments. Cross-bedding and parallel lamination are common. These sediments may represent a periestuarine offshore setting.

Outer ramp–shelf belt

The Lower Jurassic rocks in this facies zone are largely in the central and northern areas. They mainly consist of dark gray silty shales, shales, and siltstones, and subordinate thin beds of fine-grained sandstone and limestone. The subfacies associations vary slightly from place to place, on the basis of observations made in three sections.

In the Tianba section (S4) northeast of Kangmar, the Lower Jurassic is represented by the Lower Tianba Formation, which is composed of three units (Fig. 4). The lower 140 m is composed

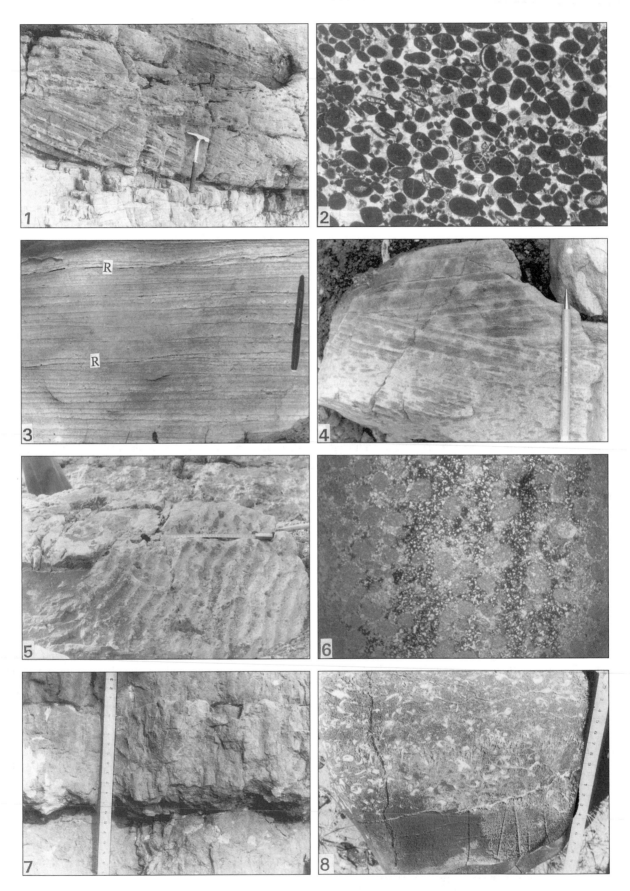

of brown, calcareous chlorite-rich shale and intraformational dia-base, separated from the underlying Triassic by a normal fault and a tectonic breccia. The middle portion, 160 m thick, is dominated by calcareous shale and chloritic slate containing thin layers of fine-grained quartzose sandstone and ammonites, such as *Schlotheimia* sp. The upper unit is composed of about 370 m of dark gray pyrite-rich calcareous mudstone and shale, intercalated with centimeter-scale cross-bedded sandstones.

This Lower Jurassic section is interpreted as a middle to outer ramp facies, representing a highstand systems tract (tract A in inset I of Fig. 4). The intrusion of the diabase indicates the influence of oceanic volcanism.

Another Jurassic section, described by Wang and Zhang (1974) and Academia Sinica (1984), was examined along the Lhasa-Yadong highway ~6–10 km south of Gyangze (S5). The Lower Jurassic Ridang Formation corresponds to the Lower Tianba Formation, is about 300 m thick, and overlies Triassic quartz sandstones (Fig. 10A). The lower 100 m of sediments (unit 1 to 4) consists of thin-bedded limestones, marlstones, and shales with some fine sandstone and diabase intercalations. Bioturbation, wavy and parallel lamination, and concretions of pyrite and siderite are common. The carbonate content tends to decrease upward. The middle part (units 5 and 6) is characterized by thinly bedded dark silty shales and thicker oolitic ironstones, possibly consisting of chamosite. The upper part (unit 7) is composed of gray shales and thin-bedded siltstones containing abundant pyrite and siderite. It shows some bioturbation.

The units 1 to 4 represent a deepening-upward facies association from a barrier island to the middle shelf (Fig. 10B) and possibly reflect a sea-level rise. The oolitic ironstones within units 5 and 6 may indicate slow deposition and slightly anoxic bottom conditions. They formed during relatively sediment-starved periods (see following discussion; Einsele, 1992). The principal environments of these rocks (unit 5 through 7) were probably a middle to outer ramp with relatively slow sedimentation, likely due to relative sea-level rise.

Figure 8. 1. Large-scale herringbone cross-bedding (lower part) and trough cross-bedding (upper part) in the channel sandstone. Lower Jurassic, Niehnieh Hsiongla section, north of Nyalam. 2. Ooids, mud intraclasts, skeletal particles, and sparry calcite cements in the oolitic packstone. Lower Jurassic, Niehnieh Hsiongla section, north of Nyalam. × 31. 3. Mud drapes and reactivation surfaces (R) in a tidal channel sandstone. Lower Jurassic, Puzhou section, south of Tingri. 4. Cross-bedding in the calcarenite, which was strongly bioturbated by burrowing during a poststorm period. Lower Jurassic, Pazhuo section, south of Tingri. 5. Symmetrical wave ripple marks on the top surface of an oolite. Middle Jurassic, Niehnieh Hsiongla section, north of Nyalam. 6. Fecal pellets and micritic matrix in a subtidal limestone. Middle Jurassic, Niehnieh Hsiongla section, north of Nyalam. × 22. 7. Intense, vertical burrows (*Skolithos* sp.) in a muddy sandstone. Middle Jurassic, Niehnieh Hsiongla section, north of Nyalam. 8. Reworked storm deposits showing poorly sorted but oriented bioclasts, intraclasts, quartz pebbles, and ooids. Middle Jurassic, Niehnieh Hsiongla section, north of Nyalam.

In the area 40–50 km southwest of Kangmar, the Lower Jurassic is discontinuously exposed over a distance of 20 km and tends to increase in fine-grained siliciclastics. This section is characterized by interstratified beds of laminated calcareous siltstones, gray bioturbated shales, and marls that have lenses of hummocky cross-bedded, fine-grained quartz sandstones. These sediments may represent a storm-influenced middle shelf facies. The increase in the proportion of siliciclastics may suggest a reactivation of the estuarine system landward.

A similar Lower Jurassic section (S6) is present in outcrops 4 km south of Sagya. The rocks there are 260 m thick, consist of laminated calcareous shale and black shale at the base, and are overlain by interbedded marls and black shales with thinly bedded siltstones, passing up into marl-limestone rhythms. They are capped by ferruginous concretion-rich mudstones, thin siltstones, and fine sandstones (0.05–0.5 m). The depositional features in this section are similar to the upper part of the Gyangze section (S5) and represent an outer shelf setting.

Ramp toe to abyssal-plain facies belt

The rocks in this belt, known as the Dalong Group (Wang et al., 1983), are mainly in the regions of Gyangze and Nagarze. They are characterized by interstratified thin beds of pelagic marls, limestones and shales associated with radiolaria-rich chert and subordinate turbidites, and locally intraformational intrusions of diabase and lava. The Dalong Group is >830 m thick in south of Nagarze.

Compared to the central facies zone, the decrease in the proportion of turbidites and the increase in the proportion of pelagic sediments and volcanic rocks in this section suggest that the sedimentary environment here progressively evolved into a ramp-toe to abyssal-plain setting.

LITHOFACIES AND PALEOGEOGRAPHY OF THE MIDDLE JURASSIC

During the Middle Jurassic, the general lithofacies distribution and paleogeographic framework were similar to the Lower Jurassic (Figs. 11 and 12). However, the thickness of sediments increased to 1,500 m in the southern coastal and inner shelf belts and to >1,200 m in the central outer shelf. Thickness decreased to ~500 m during this period in the northern deep-water zone, as the result of changes in sedimentation rates: 85 m/m.y. in the south, 50 m/m.y. in the center, and 24 m/m.y. in the north (Liu, 1992; Liu and Einsele, 1994). The facies distribution is indicative of a continuous basinward progradation of shallow-water sediments. The persistent development of the terrigenous clastic systems in the southeast and the carbonate systems in the southwest since the Early Jurassic, and the abrupt facies change between both systems, may suggest that a syndepositional strike-slip fault, perhaps transform-related, activated with a right-lateral movement along the facies boundary across the shelf. This right-lateral motion of the pos-

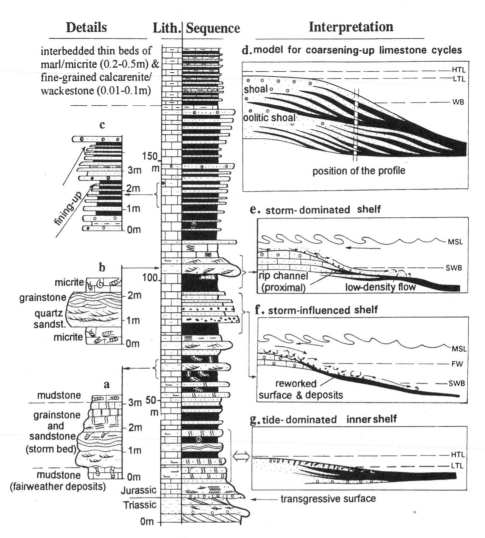

Figure 9. Detailed Lower Jurassic sequences of the Pazhuo section (S2), southern Tingri, and their interpretation (d through g). See Figures 2 and 4B for legends.

sible fault created more accommodation space and a lower sea floor for the sedimentation on the eastern block than that in the western block, which resulted in the continuous development of a terrigenous pathway in the east (Fig. 12).

Inner carbonate ramp

The carbonate ramp in the southwest, initiated in the Early Jurassic, can be divided into two main lithofacies belts, an inner ramp and a middle to outer ramp. The sediments of the inner ramp are represented by the Niehnieh Hsiongla Formation, the Lalongla Formation, and the lower part of the Menbu Formation (Figs. 2 and 3). They are mainly composed of bioclastic calcarenite and oolite, and intercalated thin siliciclastic beds. This belt extends in the northwest-southeast from Pazhuo via Gyriong to the Thakkhola area (Gradstein et al., 1989) and northward gives way to interbedded marl and shales and limestones of middle shelf facies.

Our interpretation is mainly based on observations on the sections between north of Yalai and south of Gutzuo, where the Middle Jurassic is well exposed and complete. These sections can be subdivided into 15 lithological units (Fig. 3, units 15 to 29). Units 15 to 24 are exposed in the Niehnieh Hsiongla section (S1), and units 25 to 29 are in the Lalongla section (S7). Unit 29 represents a condensed horizon at the boundary between the Lalongla Formation (Bathonian) and the Menbu Formation (Callovian-Kimmeridgian), and largely consists of oolitic ironstones and coquinoid limestones. Five facies associations have been recognized from the base to the top of this section.

Facies association 1.
This association is present in units 15 through 18, and is about 180 m thick (Fig. 13). It contains typical Aalenian and Bajocian bivalves and corals.

The lower part of unit 15 consists of thin- to medium-bedded, dark gray to black micrite, containing trace fossils (e.g., *Phycodes pedum*, *Planolites* sp.; Yu and Wang, 1990) on the

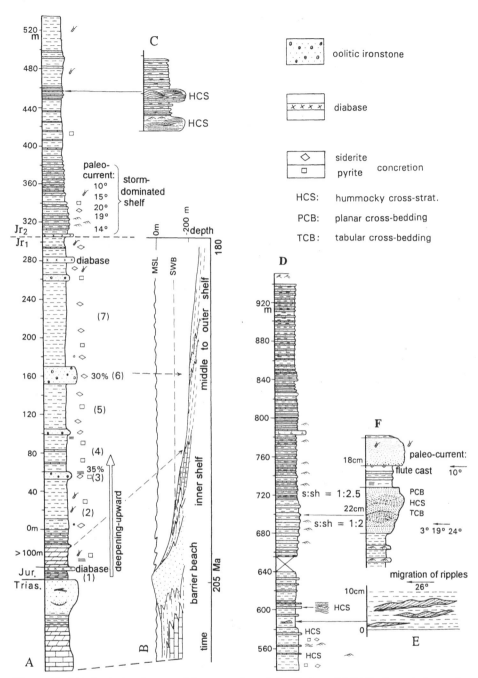

Figure 10. Lithological column and interpretation of the Early and Middle Jurassic in southern Gyangze, along the roadside of the Lhasa-Yadong highway (S5). See text for discussion and Figures 2 and 4B for legends.

upper surface. The proportion of intercalated packstones and grainstones tends to increase upward. This part has been interpreted as a low-energy offshore belt.

The upper part of unit 15 and the unit 16 are oolites, skeletal packstones, and grainstones containing intercalations of well-sorted, medium-bedded quartz arenites. Tabular and trough cross-bedding are common. Small symmetrical wave ripples, 0.05–0.1 m in wavelength, can be seen on bedding sur-

faces (Fig. 8, 5). These sediments may represent an oolitic shoal subfacies.

Unit 17 consists of interstratified beds of ooid-bearing, skeletal wacke and/or packstones and dark to black lime mudstones containing unabraded bivalves. These sediments could have formed in a relatively low energy belt, possibly representing a back shoal lagoon.

Unit 18 is characterized by irregularly interstratified beds

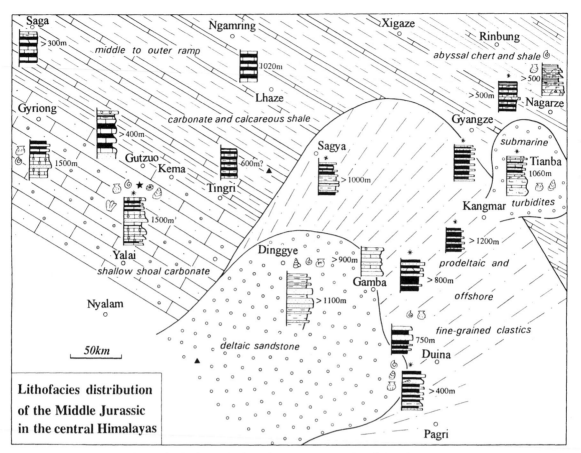

Figure 11. Lithofacies distribution and selected sequences (no scale) of the Middle Jurassic in southern Tibet. The north-south scale of this map has been restored to its original state prior to crustal shortening. The sequences with asterisks are based on our own field observations, and the others are from the literature. See Figures 2 and 4B for explanation.

of thin carbonaceous shale and strongly bioturbated sandstone, associated with lesser amounts of dark nodular argillaceous limestones and coaly shales. The nodular limestones consist of abundant fecal pellets (0.2–0.4 mm) and micritic matrix (Fig. 8, 6), and some unabraded bivalves. Intense vertical burrows (*Skolithos* sp.) and some rootlets occur in the muddy sandstone (Fig. 8, 7). This unit is interpreted to have formed on intertidal flats and in supratidal zones (Fig. 13B).

Facies association 2. This association (unit 19) is about 40 m thick and is composed of several fining-upward cycles. A typical cycle includes a lower part of coarse carbonates consisting of poorly sorted but oriented bioclasts, intraclasts, quartz pebbles, ooids, and calcareous sandy matrix (Fig. 8, 8), a middle part of planar and hummocky cross-stratified, medium- to fine-grained quartz-rich packstones and grainstones (A, B in Fig. 14, 1), and an upper part of strongly bioturbated or ripple-laminated, fine-grained packstones and wackestones with abundant plant fragments (C in Fig. 14, 1).

Each cycle may represent a deepening-upward sequence from upper shoreface via lower shoreface to offshore deposits. The cycles were possibly produced by repeated retrogradation of inner shelf sediments as a result of relative sea-level rise (Fig. 13C).

Facies association 3. This association (units 20 to 22) is composed of six coarsening-upward sequences produced by the progradation of carbonate shoals. The total thickness reaches ~200 m. One of the observed cycles is described here.

The lower part of the cycle is characterized by thinly bedded (0.05–0.2 m) nodular carbonates, which consist of regularly bedded micritic limestones separated by very thin, undulating fine-grained packstone and grainstone layers. The micrites display some oblique and horizontal burrows and unabraded bivalves. The thin intercalated packstones and grainstones (< 0.05 m) are ripple laminated and cross-bedded. This part can be interpreted as deposits of alternating storm and fairweather processes in the upper offshore. The nodular shape of the micritic limestones may have been enhanced by diagenetic and weathering processes, such as differential compaction and pressure solution.

The upper part of the cycle consists of medium- to thick-bedded oolitic wackestone, packstone, oolites, and quartz sandstones containing intercalated coquina beds. The oolitic wackestones and packstones (Fig. 14, 2) are composed of 60%–70% ooids, 20% skeletal sands and other carbonate particles, and about 5% detrital quartz; they display hummocky and

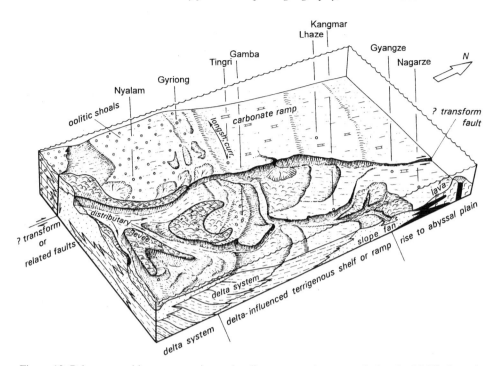

Figure 12. Paleogeographic reconstruction and sedimentary environments during the Middle Jurassic (Bajocian) in southern Tibet, chiefly interpreted from Figure 11.

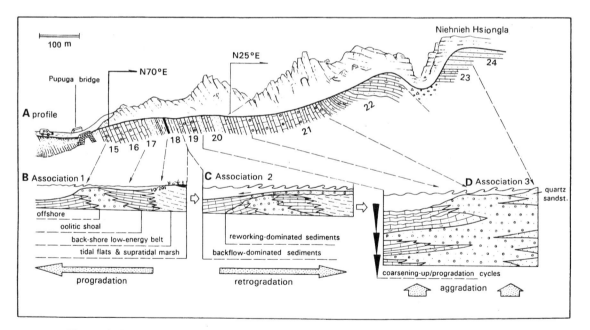

Figure 13. Sketch of the Middle Jurassic in the Niehnieh Hsiongla section (S1) and its depositional interpretation (B to D). See text for discussion and Figures 2 and 4B for legends.

low-angle cross-bedding and bioturbation. Various types of cross-bedding, particularly tabular cross-bedding, as thick as 0.8 m, are also notable in the oolites and quartz sandstones. The ooid content constitutes as much as 90% in the oolites; about one-half have detrital quartz as nuclei. Their fabric is mostly grain supported and cemented by sparry calcite. The quartz content increases from about 5% at the base to about 20% at the top. The oolitic grainstones are normally interbedded with quartz sandstones (Fig. 14, 3). The quartz arenite is coarse grained and consists of well-sorted, rounded quartz particles (0.5–1 mm), and some ooids, peloid and skeletal grains, and sparitic calcite cements. The petrological features and sedimen-

tary structures indicate that this part represents mixed siliciclastic-carbonate shoals. The wackestones and packstones may have formed on the lower shoreface, and the oolitic grainstone, oolites, and quartz sandstones may have been deposited on the upper shoreface of a carbonate shoal. The thick, herringbone cross-bedded, coarse sandstones are regarded as deposits of tidal channels.

The development of six similar cycles indicates that the sedimentation here during the late Bajocian was dominated by lateral migration and aggradation of carbonate shoals (Fig. 13D).

Facies association 4. This association is a coarse sediment-dominated unit (Fig. 15, unit 23), consisting of cross-bedded oolitic grainstones and packstones (lower 20 m) and of two coarsening-upward carbonate cycles (upper 10 m). The sedimentary characteristics (Fig. 15, left) indicate that this unit may represent a barrier-lagoon complex. The lower part can be regarded as a barrier island carbonate sandbody that includes a tidal inlet facies (lower subunit) and a foreshore and backshore facies (upper subunit). The tidal inlet facies exhibits an erosional base and lag deposits incised into underlying offshore lime-mudstone. The tabular cross-bedding (north-dipping foresets) indicates that they were largely produced by seaward migration of sand waves or dunes driven by ebb-tidal currents. The upper subunit consists of oolitic grainstones and intercalated thin storm layers of quartz arenite and coquina beds. It developed directly on top of an inlet fill, as a result of lateral channel migration. The low-angle cross-bedding and well-sorted texture of the oolitic grainstone indicate that it may have formed in a high-energy belt of a barrier island, i.e., on the shoreface, where winnowing and reworking were prominent.

The overlying two minor coarsening-upward cycles may represent spillover or washover fans into a back-barrier lagoon. The intercalated coquina beds may have formed as deposits of wave or storm winnowing. The bioturbated, dark lime-mudstones and thinly bedded marl can be regarded as lagoonal deposits.

Figure 14. 1. Depositional sequence consisting of planar cross-bedding (A) in the lower part, hummocky stratification (B) in the middle part, and strong bioturbation (C) at the top. Middle Jurassic, Niehnieh Hsiongla section, north of Nyalam. 2. Moderately sorted oolitic carbonate. Middle Jurassic, Niehnieh Hsiongla section, north of Nyalam. × 22. 3. Cross-bedded oolitic grainstone (O) with interbedded quartz arenites (Q). Upper Jurassic, Niehnieh Hsiongla section, north of Nyalam. 4. Trace fossils *Paleodictyon* sp. (a) and *Chondrites* sp. (b). Middle Jurassic, about 10 km south of Gyangze. 5. Unsorted bioclastic carbonate. Middle Jurassic, Lalongla section, north of Nyalam. × 62. 6. Bi polar tabular cross-bedding with landward-dipping foresets (a) and seaward-dipping foresets (b) in quartz-rich oolitic and skeletal grainstones; note that the cross-bedding and reactivation surfaces (c) are mainly in the quartz-concentrated layers. Upper Jurassic, Lalongla section, north of Nyalam. 7. Carbonate of platform interior facies. w is wackestone, p is packstone, and i is intraclastic limestion. Upper Jurassic, Lalongla section, north of Nyalam. These are vertical beds; the beds on the left are older than those on the right. The black pen is 14 cm long.

Facies association 5. This association is represented by the Lalongla Formation (Bathonian) and is >700 m thick. The lower portion (unit 24 in Fig. 3), >300 m in thickness, is composed of thick- and medium-bedded quartz sandstones containing intercalations of quartzose grainstones and oolitic, skeletal grainstones. The quartz arenite mainly consists of as much as 90% well-sorted, rounded, coarse- to medium-grained detrital quartz, and lesser amounts of skeletal grains, feldspar, and rock fragments (~10%). The grainstones are characterized by particle-supported textures and sparry calcite cementation. Their structure is dominated by low-angle cross-bedding and hummocky cross-stratification, and locally by trough and bipolar tabular cross-bedding, over which the foresets are draped with thin mud layers.

These features indicate that the lower part of this association was produced under a nearshore, high-energy regime by both wave and tidal processes.

The upper portion of the Lalongla Formation (units 25 to 28 in Fig. 3) is dominated by quartz-bearing oolitic packstones and/or grainstones, wackestones, and some micrites with thin shales, displaying a fining-upward trend. Considerable numbers of ammonites, epifaunal bivalves, some infaunal corals, and thin-shell bivalves have been found (Yu et al., 1983) within them. These sediments may represent an open offshore environment ranging from shoals to low-energy setting below the storm wave base. They may have formed during a transgression.

In summary, the Middle Jurassic depositional facies of the southwestern shelf or ramp were dominated by shoals and barrier-beach complexes, associated with tidal flats, lagoons, and some offshore sediments. Fluctuations of relative sea level may have played an important role in controlling the development of the cyclic sequences and condensed sections (Fig. 3). The topography of the shelf appears to have been relatively smooth during this period.

Middle to outer carbonate ramp

The northern middle and outer ramp facies belts are represented mainly by alternating bioclastic wackestones, gray micrites, and dark calcareous shales. Due to poor biostratigraphic control and a monotonous lithofacies, the exact stratigraphic boundaries and thicknesses of these deposits are unknown. The thicknesses of the sequences in Figure 11 are roughly estimated in accordance with TRGT (1983) and Academia Sinica (1984), as well as personal field investigations. The type sections are discussed as follows.

Gutzuo section (S9). The Middle Jurassic section at Gutzuo, described by Westermann and Wang (1988), has been reexamined. It was divided into three parts.

The lower part consists of >400 m of thin- and medium-bedded, nonfossiliferous limestones and marls, underlain by ~300 m of massive quartzose sandstones. The regional paleogeographic reconstruction and sedimentary features imply that this portion may have formed on a relatively deep shelf or outer ramp.

The middle part constitutes thick-bedded bioclastic carbonates and interbedded marly limestones, containing bivalves, brachiopods, belemnites, and crinoids. The vertical facies association suggests that this unit represents a transitional belt from the lower, low-energy outer ramp to the upper, relatively high-energy inner ramp.

The top part is a unit of 6–8 m of ferruginous oolite associated with coquina layers, in which a lower and middle Callovian fauna (*Grayiceras* assemblage) has been found (Westermann and Wang, 1988). Similar to the Lalongla section, this part represents a condensed section.

This profile seems to be a shallowing-upward sequence produced by the progradation of the ramp carbonate, whereas the condensed section at the top could have formed during the subsequent transgression.

Banqiong section (S8). At Banqiong village, 6 km east of Gyangze, the Middle Jurassic (Gyangze Formation; Academia Sinica, 1984), consists of 300-m-thick rhythmites of gray marls, argillaceous limestones, and calcareous shales (Fig. 16, A and B). Parallel lamination is well developed and characterized by a frequent variation in the ratio of carbonate versus clay fraction. Macrofossils are absent, but some deep-water trace fossils, such as *Chondrites* sp., are present at the top of these layers.

These sediments are thought to have formed under very low-energy conditions of an outer ramp to ramp-toe setting. The rhythms and laminae of the limestone-marl and/or marl-clay reflect periodic changes in suspended sediment supply. The material came either from the delta system in the southeastern segment (fine terrigenous) or from the carbonate shoals in the southwestern segment (lime mud). Seasonal and longer term changes in river influx may have been the principal controls on the formation of the rhythmites and the majority of the laminations (Fig. 16C). During the rainy period, carbonate production may have been diluted by enhanced terrigenous influx.

This resulted in a clay-dominated layer on the outer shelf. In comparison, during dry periods, terrigenous influx was reduced and carbonate production increased, resulting in formation of a carbonate-dominated layer. Siliciclastic laminae are likely to represent major flood events. One laminar couplet may have been formed between days and months. However, diagenesis and weathering may further enhance the difference in the thickness of such layers and laminae (Ricken, 1986; Ricken and Eder, 1991).

The carbonate:clay ratio decreased upward from the Middle Jurassic to the Upper Jurassic. Several cycles displaying an upward increase in clay or shale fraction (Fig. 16B) can be distinguished in the outcrops. These cycles may have formed in response to relatively long-term changes in the terrigenous input and/or carbonate productivity in the shallow sea (Fig. 16C). The duration of such cycles may range from less than 1 k.y. to more than 1 m.y.

Terrigenous clastics-dominated inner shelf

The Middle Jurassic in the southeastern area is dominated by terrigenous clastics. One of the type sections is situated in the southwest of Dinggye and consists of a coarsening-upward sequence >1,100 m thick (TRGT, 1983). The lower section there is made up of black to dark gray shales, intercalated with silty shale and thin beds of fine-grained sandstones and siltstones, ~400 m thick. The middle part of the section is >400 m thick and consists of gray to white massive, fine-grained quartz arenites, sandstones, and lesser amounts of shales and siltstones. Abundant fragments of ammonites and other shallow-marine fossils have been found in the fine-grained sediments. Its upper part is 300 m thick and is represented by mottled silty shale, intercalated with siltstones and sandstones.

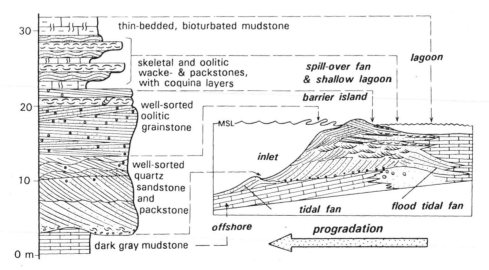

Figure 15. Detailed sequence of the lower part of unit 23 (facies association 4) and facies model for the Niehnieh Hsiongla Formation (Bajocian) at the Niehnieh Hsiongla section (S1), Nyalam. See Figures 2 and 4B for legends.

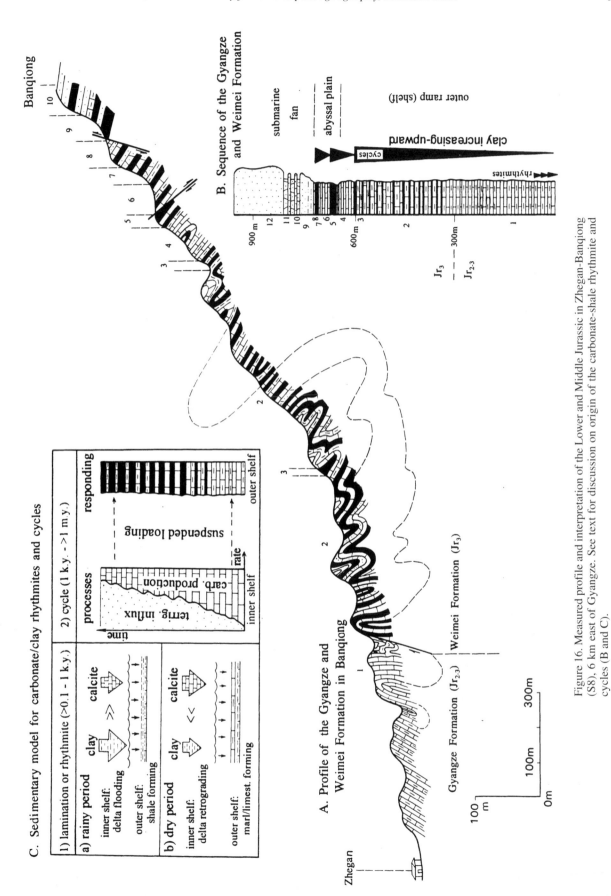

Figure 16. Measured profile and interpretation of the Lower and Middle Jurassic in Zhegan-Banqiong (S8), 6 km east of Gyangze. See text for discussion on origin of the carbonate-shale rhythmite and cycles (B and C).

This coarsening-upward succession is tentatively interpreted as fluvial-dominated prodelta deposits (the lower part), sandstone-dominated delta-front deposits (the middle part), and mottled sandstones and shales of a delta–plain facies (the upper part).

To the southeast, in the Jiulongla section (S10) west of Duina, the Middle Jurassic is characterized by fine-grained clastics >400 m thick. Its lower part consists of dark gray to black massive mudstones containing lenses of siltstone and sandstone (mudstone:siltstone + sandstone = 10:1). This part may represent a prodelta facies, containing some minor channel deposits. The middle part is dominated by well-sorted quartz sandstones and parallel-bedded coquina. These are interpreted as deposits of a distal delta front, where wave and storm processes normally predominate over fluvial processes. The upper part is similar to the lower one, again representing prodelta sediments of a subsequent deltaic cycle.

Another Middle Jurassic section is located at 10 km northeast of Gamba. It also consists of >900 m of sandstone-dominated deltaic deposits (TRGT, 1983).

Middle to outer clastic ramp (shelf)

This facies zone is distributed over the area between Sagya-Gyangze and Dinggye-Gamba-Pagri.

Gamba section (S11). The section (S11) of Gamba has a total thickness >800 m (TRGT, 1983) and consists of the following horizons, from top to base: 90 m of dark laminated siliceous shale; 700 m of alternating dark gray and light gray massive mudstones intercalated with thin-bedded siltstone, shales, and fine sandstones, yielding ammonites and bivalves; and >37 m of thin-bedded and laminated black shale with abundant siderite concretions.

This section appears to reflect changes in relative water depth from deep (outer ramp) to shallow (delta), and then back to deep (outer ramp).

Sagya section (S6). The thickness and stratigraphic boundaries of the Middle Jurassic section near Sagya (S6; Fig. 1) cannot be determined with certainty (TRGT, 1983). The sediments there consist of interstratified thin beds of gray siltstone, silty shale and shale, and intercalated sandstone lenses, as well as marly mudstone. The siltstone interbeds are laminated and ripple cross-bedded. They seem to be middle shelf deposits that originated as a result of storm action. The sandstone lenses may represent minor channel deposits.

A distinct channel sandstone belt is developed in the middle profile. It is 8 m thick and consists of several superimposed sandstone lenses, showing a fining-upward sequence. The lowermost lens is about 3 m thick at the axis and 10 to 20 m wide. The lenses consist of coarse- to medium-grained quartz sandstones, either massive or cross-bedded and poorly sorted, containing lags of angular mud clasts to 1 m long and flute casts on erosional bases. These features indicate strong current scouring and rapid channel filling, possibly due to a major storm event, during which the delta-front sands were transported seaward to the prodelta slope or the peridelta shelf.

The overlying sediments are dark gray shales characterized by abundant pyrite concretions, indicating deeper water and anoxic conditions.

Southern Gyangze section (S5). The Middle Jurassic in southern Gyangze (S5) is dominated by bioturbated dark gray silty shales and shales, parallel-laminated siltstones, and cross-bedded sandstones intercalated with thin-bedded marls (Fig. 10, A and D). The lithologic association, hummocky stratification, ammonites, and deep-water trace fossils *Cosmorhaphe* sp., *Paleodictyon* sp., *Chondrites* sp. (Fig. 14, 4), and *Thalassinoides* sp. indicate that this section represents a storm-influenced shelf environment.

The storm-generated beds are characterized by cross-bedded, fine- to medium-grained quartz sandstones intercalated within shales and siltstones (Fig. 10, C and F). Measurements ($n = 17$) of the cross-bedding of the thin sandstones indicate that the paleocurrents ranged from 3° to 24° (north-northeast, directed basinward). At the top of the black shales, some isolated sandstone lenses with asymmetrical storm current ripple marks can be observed. The mean strike of the ripples is 116°, parallel to the regional paleoshoreline, and their migration direction is N26°E (Fig. 10E), indicating down-slope storm back flows.

In comparison with Sagya, the thickness of individual storm beds here is distinctly thinner and channelized sandstones are absent. All trace fossils mentioned here are in Seilacher's *Zoophycus* and *Nereites* assemblages, which are believed to represent relatively deep water environments from outer shelf to pelagic settings (Seilacher, 1967). This supports our interpretation that this part of the Middle Jurassic represents outer ramp-dominated deposits.

Tianba section (S4). This section is located at Tianba, northeast of Kangmar, and its Middle Jurassic rocks, about 1,000 m thick, are composed of interbedded shale and sandstones. Three sedimentary systems, slope fan, ramp-toe, and outer shelf slope, have been recognized from this section (Fig. 4).

Slope fans. The interpretation of this facies is based on two units between 700 m and 1,050 m and from 1,250 to 1,350 m in the measured section (Fig. 4). The lower unit mainly consists of medium-grained calcareous turbidite sandstones, in which intraformational diabase occurs, indicating oceanic volcanic activity. Slump structures are visible. This unit may have formed on the ramp toe as slope fan (unit B in inset I of Fig. 4).

The upper slope-fan sediments display a fining-upward package ranging from lower thick-bedded, coarse feldspathic quartz arenites to upper interbedded mudstones and sandstones. The sandstones turbidites occur within typical Bouma sequences.

Ramp-toe facies. The ramp-toe facies is represented by fine-grained sediments from 1,050 to 1,350 m and is characterized by distal fine-grained turbidites consisting of thin interbedded siltstones, shales, fine sandstones, and micrites, associated with diabase intrusions. The cross-bedded siltstones and sandstones may have accumulated as deposits of low-density flow, whereas the micrites and shales may represent hemipelagic sediments.

Outer shelf to slope facies. The deposits from 1,350 m to 1,600 m are composed of thin- to medium-bedded, gray to dark gray micritic limestones and shale and quartz sandstone in the lower part, and medium-bedded, light gray micrite and shale and siltstone in the upper part. The lithological association and facies context indicate that this unit may have been produced within a prograding ramp or slope setting. Correlating this unit with the landward inner shelf facies, this interval seems to correspond to the upper part of the Lalongla Formation (units 28 and 27) and the lower part of the Menbu Formation (unit 29, i.e., the beds of the ferruginous oolite of a condensed section).

Abyssal plain

Oceanic sediments of the Middle Jurassic are present in the Nagarze area (Wang et al., 1983). In a section about 60 km east of Nagarze village, the Middle Jurassic was divided into the Binhu Formation, the Xiaxi Formation, and the Bajiutang Formation. This section begins with basalt, tuff, intercalated siliceous limestones, and radiolarian chert lenses, which pass upward into thin- to medium-bedded interlayers of gray micritic limestones, siliceous shales, marls, and calcareous shales. It terminates with grayish green and red thin-bedded cherts, radiolaria-bearing siliceous shales, and siltstones.

The basalt lava and radiolarites indicate that the Middle Jurassic was deposited in an oceanic basin. The siliceous limestones and marls are typical of a pelagic setting, whereas the intercalated sandstone lenses may represent distal turbidites.

LITHOFACIES AND PALEOGEOGRAPHY OF THE LATE JURASSIC

Sediment starvation during the middle Callovian to late Oxfordian in southern Tibet produced extensive condensed sections (Fig. 17). Subsequently, rapid progradation of the shallow-water sediments during the Kimmeridgian led to the transformation of the ramp into a shelf with a relatively steep slope. Until the early Tithonian, a carbonate platform was built up on the western inner shelf, and a siliciclastic barrier-lagoon complex developed on the eastern inner shelf. Meanwhile, mixed fine clastics and carbonates dominated the middle to outer shelf in the central area and submarine and pelagic deposits formed in the northern region. During the late Tithonian the sea transgressed, causing the deep-marine environment to shift landward.

Condensed sections of the Callovian and Oxfordian

Westermann and Wang (1988) argued, on the basis of biostratigraphic evidence from the Gutzuo section, that there is a hiatus between the middle Callovian to the early Kimmeridgian. However, in the Lalongla section (S7; unit 29 in Fig. 3), Yu et al. (1983) found a few specimens of *Reineckia* and *Reineckeites* in ferruginous oolitic beds, which point to a middle to late Callovian age. In addition, late Oxfordian ammonites *Dhosaites, Epi-*

mayaites, and *Mayaites* were also found in the shale immediately overlying the oolitic ironstone. Shi (1987) identified Oxfordian brachiopods (*Argovithyris bauger* and *Mexicaria* sp.) at the same place. This horizon represents a condensed section formed during the middle Callovian through middle Oxfordian. On the basis of several sections in the southern area, the calculated sedimentation rate during this period was only 20 m/m.y., only 25% of previous rates (Liu, 1992; Liu and Einsele, 1994).

Lithologically, the condensed sediments in section S7 largely consist of oolitic ironstones and coquinoid limestones. The oolitic ironstones and associated Fe-oolitic siltstones are structureless; their thicknesses range from 10 m to 20 m. They mainly consist of olive-green to red-brown chamosite (60% to 70%), and ferruginous clay or micritic matrix (30% to 40%) with traces of terrigenous and skeletal grains. The coquina layers contain abundant unabraded and unsorted fossils (Fig. 14, 5) including brachiopods, bivalves, ostracodea, foraminifera, echinoderms, gastropods, belemnites, and ammonites. The brachiopods, such as *Hynchellida*, are dominated by small and thin-shell types (Yu and Wang, 1990). The presence of concentrated biota and a calcisiltite-dominated matrix indicate a relatively deep water, low-energy environment. Winnowing by bottom currents was weak and the overall sedimentation rate was low.

Analogous to modern sediments, the occurrence of chamosite may point to a tropical shelf setting in areas of low detrital input and a water depth ranging from 10 to 170 m (Porrenga, 1967; Johnson and Baldwin, 1986). The present-day formation of chamosite off the Niger and Orinoco deltas may be good examples. Paleomagnetic data suggest that the Indian northern shelf was located at low latitudes during the Middle Jurassic (Gyangze at 23°S; Liu, 1992; Liu and Einsele, 1994). Moreover, Hallam and Bradshaw (1979) discussed the Jurassic oolitic ironstones in northern Europe and emphasized that the mechanical winnowing of seawater plays an important role in the origin of these deposits.

On the shelf in the Nyalam and Gutzuo areas, condensed sediments formed from the Callovian to the Oxfordian, but from the Late Oxfordian through Kimmeridgian, condensation shifted into the northern basin of Nagarze (Fig. 17). Regionally, similar oolitic condensed sections were documented by Jadoul et al. (1985) in Zanskar, Krishna et al. (1983) in Spiti-Niti, and Bordet et al. (1971) and Gradstein et al. (1989) in the Thakkhola area. The diachronous condensed sections and/or hiatuses may be interpreted as follows (Fig. 18). During the late Callovian and Oxfordian, a rapid sea-level rise, indicated by the underlying deepening-upward sequences, took place, leading to coastal onlap and inundation of the former delta system. As a result, sediment supply was cut off and the shelf became sediment starved. During this phase, condensed beds of chamosite-rich ooids and coquina layers formed. Agitated water was pumped into and out these sediments and promoted cementation to form hardground. At the same time, a hiatus developed on the outer ramp or shelf margin, due to submarine erosion. However, sedimentation continued at the ramp toe (Fig. 18A). Thus, the thickness of the condensed sections decreased from 10 to 20 m at the landward Lalongla profile (S7) to only 6 to 8 m in the basinward Gutzuo profile (S12), whereas farther north (Kangmar-Nagarze) turbidites and pelagic sediments were deposited. During the subsequent Kimmeridgian, highstand terrigenous sediments entered the shelf in significant quantities in a prograding delta system (highstand system tracts). Because the sediments were mainly trapped on the deepening shelf, the northern slope and continental rise became sediment starved, especially in the Nagarze area (Fig. 18B).

Lithofacies and paleogeography of the Oxfordian and Kimmeridgian

The Oxfordian and Kimmeridgian deposits, >300 m thick, are represented by the upper part of the Menbu Formation (Yu et al., 1983) or the lower part of the Menkatun Formation (Wang and Zhang, 1974) in the southern zone, and the lower part of the Weimei Formation (TRGT, 1983) in the northern zone. They are dominated by terrigenous clastics and can be interpreted to be depositional systems ranging from delta and siliciclastic shelf to slope fan and oceanic basin (Figs. 19 and 20).

Deltaic depositional systems

The depositional characteristics in the southeastern area, such as the lobate sandbodies, coarsening-upward sequences, and higher deposition rates (70 m/m.y.; Liu and Einsele, 1994) provide evidence for the presence of a fluvial-dominated delta system in the southeastern area (Figs. 19 and 20). As observed in the Lalongla section (S7), these sediments are about 200 m thick. Their lower part (60 m) consists of dark gray, massive silty mudstones containing small siderite concretions and scattered planktonic fossils (e.g., ammonites and belemnites). The massive

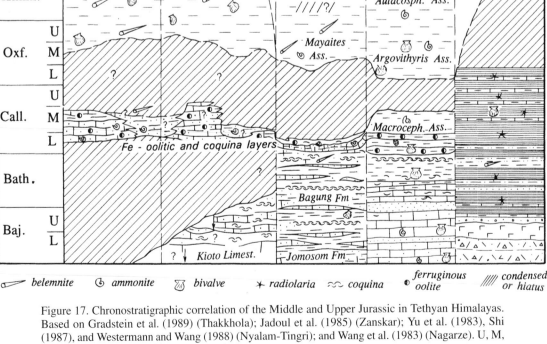

Figure 17. Chronostratigraphic correlation of the Middle and Upper Jurassic in Tethyan Himalayas. Based on Gradstein et al. (1989) (Thakkhola); Jadoul et al. (1985) (Zanskar); Yu et al. (1983), Shi (1987), and Westermann and Wang (1988) (Nyalam-Tingri); and Wang et al. (1983) (Nagarze). U, M, L, are upper, middle, and lower, respectively.

A. Late Callovian to Middle Oxfordian (lowstand and transgression)

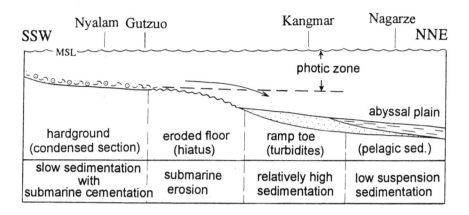

B. Late Oxfordian to Kimmeridgian (stationary sealevel and highstand)

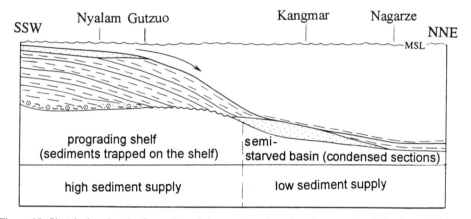

Figure 18. Sketch showing the formation of the condensed sections between the Callovian and Kimmeridgian (see text for discussion).

structure, contrasting with the underlying well-laminated calcareous shales interpreted as open shelf facies, indicates a high deposition rate and limited physical reworking, as known from modern prodelta environments (e.g., Mississippi prodelta; Coleman and Wright, 1975; Elliott, 1986).

The middle section, 60 m thick, is dominated by dark and black siltstones and intercalated muddy siltstones and mudstones. There are many unabraded bivalves, brachiopods, oriented belemnites, ammonites, and lenticular and spherical ferruginous concretions. Wavy and parallel lamination is developed in the siltstones. This part may represent a prodelta to distal delta front facies.

The uppermost 80 m are dominated by medium- to fine-grained quartz sandstones, siltstone, and massive mudstone containing some ammonites and belemnites. Sandstones contain intraclasts and glauconite and display small-scale cross-bedding and wavy lamination. Bioturbation, in particular vertical burrows (*Skolithos* assemblages), is intense in some beds. These sediments may have been formed at a delta front or in a delta-plain setting. The sandstones may represent either mouth-bar sandbodies or distributary channel fills.

The entire sequence is characterized by a coarsening-upward trend, indicating that it was produced by the progradation of delta lobes. The well-developed, thick subaquatic facies (prodelta and delta front) may suggest a relatively great water depth. Sediment supply must have been sufficiently high to overcome the influence of the Oxfordian and late Callovian transgression.

Another, similar section is situated in Jiulongla (S10), west of Duina. Here, the lower Upper Jurassic is dominated by interstratified thin beds of fine-grained quartz sandstones and silt-

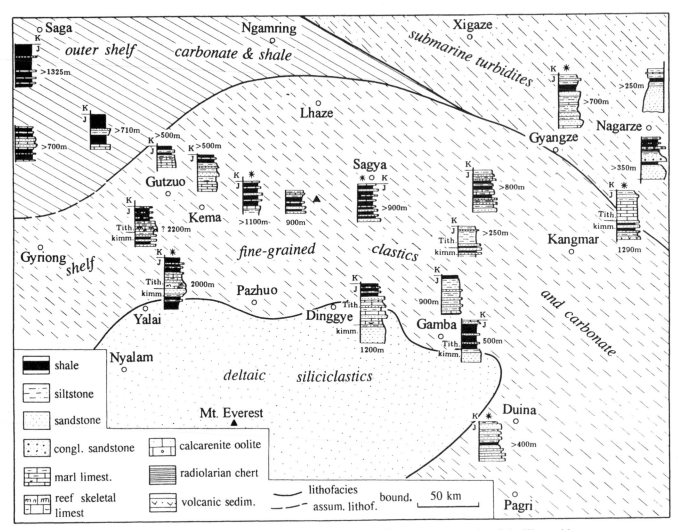

Figure 19. Lithofacies distribution and selected sequences (lower parts, no scale) of the Kimmeridgian in southern Tibet. The north-south scale of this map has been restored, using balanced sections, to its original state prior to crustal shortening. The sequences with asterisks are based on our own field observations. See Figures 2 and 4B for legends.

stones, and intercalated laminated shales. The sandstones show ripple bedding, likely to be both wave and current produced, and contain considerable amounts of fossil fragments. The shale:sandstone ratio decreases upward and is only 1:3 at the top. In combination with the underlying Middle Jurassic mudstones, this part also is a coarsening and/or thickening-upward sequence. However, there are no thick mouth and distributary channel deposits. This section seems to be dominated by the deposits of a distal delta front.

In the Dinggye area, a 400-m-thick unit of massive quartz sandstones and calcareous sandstones has been observed (TRGT, 1983). This sandbody displays a coarsening-upward trend and a lens-like shape (thinning to only 100 m in the Gamba area). Shallow-marine bivalve fragments have been found. The underlying strata are thick siltstones and silty shales. The lens-shaped sandstones probably formed at a delta front with several distributary channels.

Outer shelf to slope deposits

The terrigenous-dominated outer shelf is extensively distributed in front of the deltaic lobes (Figs. 19 and 20). The sediments mainly consist of fine-grained clastics ranging from massive mudstones to laminated shales, and intervals of cross-bedded sandstone. The massive mudstones normally show less bioturbation and contain in situ fossils; they are interpreted as deposits of a prodelta-dominated shelf. For example, the Kimmeridgian deposits 2 km west of Tingri (S11) belong to this facies. The massive gray micaceous silty mudstones and mudstones there are about 300 m thick and contain small calcareous concretions and plant fragments, as well as lenses of fine sandstone. A debris-flow bed (0.8 m thick), consisting of 65% mud clasts (0.3–5 cm in size) and 35% sandy matrix, is within the mudstone.

In contrast, the normal outer shelf facies are strongly bioturbated and/or laminated black shales, calcareous shales, and marls.

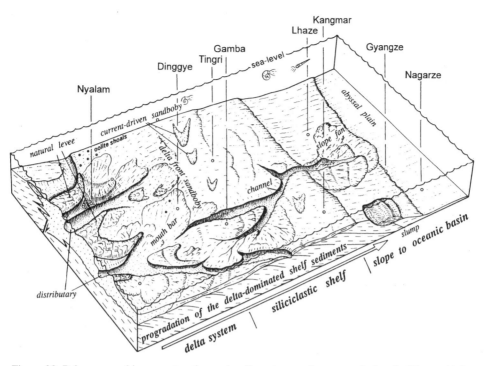

Figure 20. Paleogeographic reconstruction and sedimentary environments during the Kimmeridgian in southern Tibet, chiefly interpreted from Figure 19.

In Sagya (S6), for example, the intercalated black calcareous shales and marls contain well-developed laminations and some trace fossils of the *Zoophycus* facies. The abundant pyrite concretions, some occurring as fillings of burrows, and the black color of the sediments indicate accummulation in anoxic deep water.

The lower part of the Weimei Formation in the Tianba section is interpreted as the facies of a slope apron or slope fan (unit E in inset of Fig. 4). The exposed thickness of this formation is 310 m. It is characterized by lenticular, cross-bedded quartz-rich sandstones and green siltstones. The lenticular quartz-rich sandstones may represent channel fills of a deep-sea fan. The green, massive to rippled siltstones probably are overbank and levee deposits. The occurrence of diabase at the base of this unit indicates submarine volcanic activity.

Lithofacies and paleogeography of the Tithonian

During the Tithonian, a carbonate platform was built up in the southwest, whereas a siliciclastic inner shelf persisted in the southeastern area (Figs. 21 and 22). Lime-mudstone deposition predominated on the outer shelf occupying the central and northern regions. Pelagic sedimentation continued on the slope apron in the northeastern corner of the study area.

Carbonate-dominated shelf

A Tithonian carbonate-dominated shelf can be traced in outcrops from northern Nyalam northward to Gutzuo and Tingri. In these areas, three facies belts range from south to north, from carbonate platform through fore-slope shelf to a basinal setting.

Carbonate platform complex. This facies belt is well represented by the units 32 and 33 (Fig. 3) in the sections of Nyalam-Tingri. Detailed studies have been carried out in the Lalongla section (association 8 in Fig. 23). Three main subfacies can be distinguished.

Platform fore slope. The lower section represents a fore-slope facies and documents the initiation of the platform buildup on the former deltaic deposits. The lower 15 m are dominated by dark to black, strongly bioturbated bioclastic micrites and pelmicrites, in which the pellets consist of dark, homogenous fecal particles, ranging in diameter from 0.05 to 0.2 mm. A cross-bedded layer (2 m thick) consisting of fine-grained quartz sands (~80%) and skeletal grains (20%–30%) derived from crinoids, brachiopods, bivalves, foraminifera, and lesser amounts of ooids, is intercalated. The micrites represent a subtidal low-energy environment, whereas the intercalated sandstone may have formed by storm action.

The following 5 m of deposits consists of two parts: the lower part is characterized by slump structures, and the upper part is dominated by a poorly sorted calcirudite consisting of unoriented and irregular-shaped intraclasts. The latter represents talus derived from skeletal and micritic limestones, as well as terrigenous pebbles to 40 cm in diameter.

Platform front (reef). The upper 10 m in association 8 is characterized by massive structure and an in situ organic framework dominated by Hexacorallia (*Thecosmilia*, *Actinostrea*,

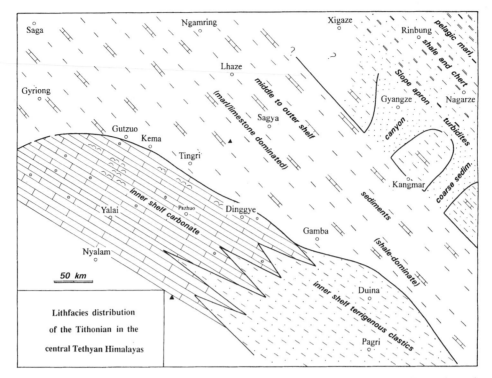

Figure 21. Lithofacies distribution of the Tithonian in the central Tethyan Himalayas. The north-south scale of this map has been restored, using balanced sections, to its original state prior to crustal shortening. See Figure 19 for controlling sequences (upper parts) and explanation.

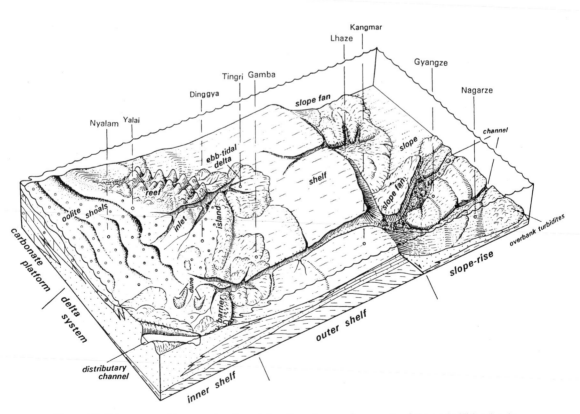

Figure 22. Paleogeographic reconstruction and sedimentary environments of the early Tithonian in southern Tibet, chiefly interpreted from Figure 21.

Antillophyllia), Hydrozoans (*Spongiomorpha*), Chaetetids (*Bauneia* sp.), stromatoporoids (*Actinostromaria* sp.), and foraminifera (Liu et al., 1983). The matrix of the skeletal framework consists of siliciclastics, skeletal fragments of crinoids, brachiopods, bivalves, and gastropods, as well as calcareous algae. The vertical facies evolution and regional facies distribution indicate that this buildup may have developed on the front of a former delta lobe (Fig. 23B). Hence, it can be regarded as a type of fringing reef. A modern analogue exists at the Great Barrier reef of Australia (Maxwell, 1968; Maxwell and Swinchatt, 1970).

Platform interior. The sediments of association 9 (Fig. 23) are dominated by calcarenites and quartz sandstones. They are subdivided into three lithofacies.

Mixed quartz and carbonate subunit. These consist of oolitic grainstones and packstones and interlayers of quartz sandstones (32 m to 82 m in Fig. 23). The most prominent characteristics are various types of large-scale cross-bedding and irregular alternations of thicker carbonates and thinner quartz sandstones (Fig. 14, 6). In modern carbonate environments, oolite and oolitic grainstones are mainly formed in shallow shoals of the platform interior (Reading, 1996). Therefore, this unit is interpreted as deposits of a shoal-dominated inner carbonate shelf that had episodic siliciclastic input.

Siliciclastic-carbonate alternations constitute many cycles in which the interlayers decrease both in quartz contents from >90% to <10% and in thickness from centimeter scale to millimeter scale. Pure quartz sandstones and quartz-rich grainstones are normally present in the lower part of the cycles, whereas pure calcareous arenites are mainly present in the upper part. In thin section, the quartz grains are rounded and well sorted, and are chiefly cemented by sparitic calcite. Most of the quartz sandstones, even a thin bed, can be traced over a considerable distance along the outcrop. Cross-bedding is dominated by a large-scale tabular type to 60 cm in thickness; there is a lesser amount of trough cross-bedding, herringbone cross-bedding, and hummocky and parallel stratification. The overall paleocurrent direction inferred from measurements ($n = 12$) on tabular foresets and reactivation surfaces is toward the north-northwest (seaward), indicating that they reflect ebb tide–dominated or storm rip current–dominated flows. Quartz grains commonly are concentrated on reactivation surfaces and scour surfaces, as well as within foreset laminae of the cross-bedding (Fig. 14, 6C).

The mechanism of the mixing of carbonate and quartz sands may be as follows (Fig. 23C). During fairweather periods, megaripples and dunes of skeletal sands and ooid shoals migrated in tidal flows on the platform flats, resulting in herringbone or tabular cross-bedding (Fig. 23C,a). During storm periods, parts of these waves and shoals were reworked and eroded, leading to scour and reactivation surfaces. Storm back currents or rip currents carried great amounts of siliciclastics from the coast into the carbonate shoals. These formed thin siliciclastic-dominated pavements on the top of the lime sands and reactivation surfaces. The quartz-rich bedforms shifted to form quartz-dominated foresets and quartz sand layers (Fig. 23C,b). Later, normal tidal currents and wave action over-

printed the bedforms and mixed the quartz sand with bioclastic grains and ooids (Fig. 23C,c). The siliciclastic-carbonate cycles may reflect the frequency and strength of the extreme storm events.

Carbonate-dominated subunit. The middle portion (from 83 to 103 m) is made up of wackestones, skeletal packstones, and mudstones, intercalated with thin layers of intraclastic limestones and calcareous arenites (Fig. 14, 7). The wackestones and mudstones are thin to medium bedded and display well-developed ripple cross-lamination and some bioturbation. The calcirudites and the calcarenites are composed of poorly sorted micritic intraclasts. A horizon of micrites that have birdseye structures (or fenestral fabric) is notable at about 90 m in the section.

All these features indicate that most of this subunit was probably deposited in a subtidal setting affected by storms. The occurrence of the birdseye structures suggests the occasional establishment of a supratidal environment. This subtidal zone probably developed on the carbonate platform interior and represents a shallow, channel-like (or bay) setting.

Oolite-dominated subunit. The upper subunit is characterized by cross-bedded oolitic grainstones, packstones, and coquina beds, and very little terrigenous material (<5%). The high proportion of skeletal and ooids may suggest that these carbonate shoals formed close to a barrier reef or offshore carbonate bank (Fig. 23D).

In summary, this section documents sediments from a fore slope via a fringing reef to a platform flat complex. The thick oolites indicate that the platform was characterized by both progradation and aggradation.

Fore-slope shelf. In the Gutzuo-Tingri area, the carbonate platform-dominated facies are replaced by fore slope–dominated facies of alternating mudstones, shales, wackestones, and calcirudites. In the section behind the Gutzuo military station (S9, Fig. 1), the Tithonian strata reflect the transition from platform margin to outer shelf (Fig. 24).

The lower 55 m of this section (unit 1) is composed of coarse skeletal and lithoclast wackestones, intraclastic limestones, as well as thin-bedded calcarenite turbidites consisting of cross-bedded, graded calcarenites having an erosional base, and calcisiltites (Fig. 24, B and D). The intraclasts (to 3 cm in size) are poorly sorted and angular in shape (Fig. 24C). The overlying sediments of lime-mudstones, wackestones, packstones, and marls show slump structures (unit 2 and 3, Fig. 24) and *Zoophycus* and *Chondrites*. Intercalations of matrix-supported calcarenites and calcirudites are found within this unit (Fig. 24, E and F). Unit 4 consists of coarse grainstones and oolitic grainstone-packstones. The grainstones contain ooids, peloids, skeletal and aggregate particles, and intraclasts (Fig. 24G), indicating reworking of the front of a barrier shoal.

The following strata (units 4 through 7) consist of wackestones, mudstones, and calcareous shale-marl rhythmites. No macrofossils have been seen, but there are some trace fossils, mostly horizontal and oblique burrows. These units display a deepening-upward trend and can be regarded as fore-slope to outer shelf facies (Fig. 24A).

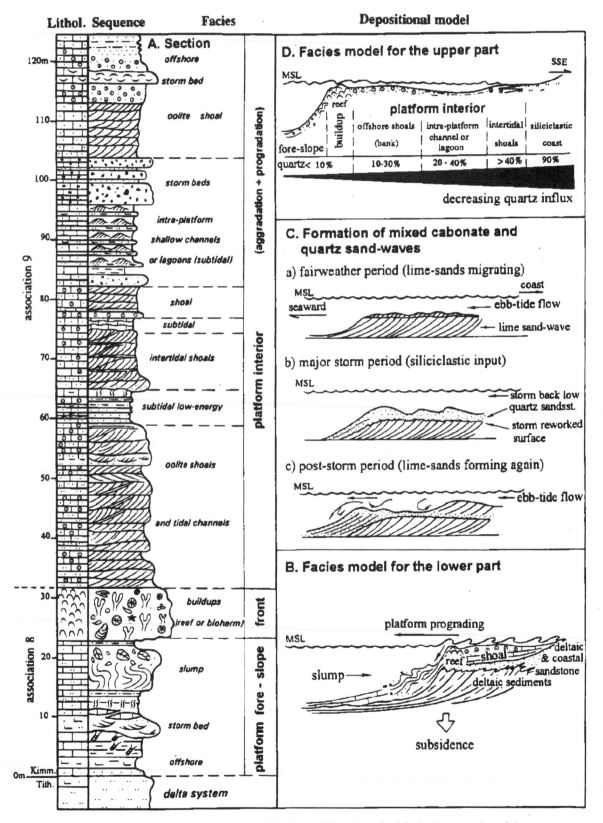

Figure 23. Detailed sedimentary sequences of the lower Tithonian and subfacies interpretation of the carbonate platform of the Lalongla section (lower part of unit 32 in Fig. 3).

The upper section (units 8 and 9) shows a coarsening-upward trend from black shales and siltstones to low-angle, cross-bedded, fine-grained quartz sandstones (Cretaceous). This trend and the high maturity of the sandstone may indicate the presence of a prograding siliciclastic barrier complex (Fig. 24H).

Another example documenting the facies evolution from a platform margin to outer shelf facies is observed in a section across Tingri town (S12, Fig. 1). The Tithonian strata (about 500 m thick) start with interbedded micrite, marl, and shale, overlying the Kimmeridgian massive prodelta mudstone. Individual beds range in thickness from 0.05 to 0.3 m. *Zoophycus*, *Chondrites*, and other types of bioturbation are common. Carbonate contents and the thicknesses of limestones tend to decrease upward. This unit may have accumulated on an outer shelf. In the upper part (the eastern hill of the town), calcareous shales and shales and thin beds of marls or micrites dominate. Distal carbonate turbidites are also noted. They are 10–20 cm thick and mainly represent divisions C, D, and E of Bouma's turbidite sequence. A horizon of slump deposits is within the shales. This part can be regarded as facies of outer shelf to slope toe. A generalized facies cross-section of the stratigraphic pattern and facies association across the Nyalam-Tingri area is shown in Figure 25.

Terrigenous shelf

The southeastern part of the study area, including Duina and Pagri, was a terrigenous shelf, whereas its northern part was a relatively sediment-starved outer shelf and slope setting. Detailed data and evidence to support this interpretation are given in the following.

Julongla section (S10). One of the sections representing a storm-dominated shelf is located in Julongla (S10), west of Duina (Fig. 26). The Lower to Middle Jurassic deposits have been interpreted to be deltaic facies above. The Tithonian rocks (unit 2 in Fig. 26A) are 200 m thick and mainly consist of thin-bedded, fine-grained sandstones, siltstones, and silty shales. The quartz sandstones are partly well sorted and contain a coarse-grained lag sediment at their base, consisting of shells, mud clasts, and small pebbles. The shell lags are dominated by poorly sorted fossils of bivalves and brachiopods, partly reflecting an in situ benthonic community. Parallel and wavy cross-bedding are common and, in places, there is hummocky cross-stratification. One type sequence, showing alternating sandstones and shales and their internal structures, is illustrated in Figure 26, C and D. These features indicate that this section may represent an inner shelf setting. Considering the fact that storm beds are also common in the western carbonate-dominated shelf, it appears that the inner shelf during this period was episodically dominated by storm processes.

Sections in Gamba. The Upper Jurassic of Gamba is composed of laminated black shales and silty shales containing abundant concretions, and thinly bedded, dark, fine-grained sandstones. Ammonites and thin-shelled bivalves are preserved. The most noticeable characteristic of this formation is its abundance of concretions, which are lenticular in shape and range in size from several millimeters to more than 10×20 cm. The concretions are dominated by calcareous, sideritic and/or pyritic, and phosphatic types ($P_2O_5 = 2\%$; TRGT, 1983). Normally, ferruginous and phosphatic concretions reflect a low depositional rate. In addition, volcanic tuff and siliceous shale associated with thinly bedded chert have been noticed in the outcrop east of Gamba. All this evidence points to a deep shelf environment and a low deposition rate.

Tianba section (S4). The Tithonian strata (upper part of the Weimei Formation) can be subdivided into three parts in the Tianba section (from ?2,300 m to 2,930 m in Fig. 4). The lower part (350 m) consists of interbedded layers of marls and/or limestones and calcareous shales and lesser amounts of very thin beds of fine-grained sandstones. This unit is similar to that of Tingri, but contains more fine-grained sandstones. It is interpreted to represent an outer shelf to continental slope facies (tracts G in inset IV of Fig. 4).

The middle part consists of gray to black siltstones and shales and intercalated thin, dark gray fine-grained sandstones showing graded bedding. Several lenses of cross-bedded quartz sandstone have been found within the massive silty mudstone, in which sideritic and phosphatic concretions as well as ammonites are common. This unit can be regarded to represent outer shelf to continental-rise environments. The sandstone lenses may originate in the minor channel fills of slope fans (part of tract H in inset IV, Fig. 4).

The upper part mainly consists of massive, fine- to medium-grained quartzose sandstones, and has an erosional base. Upward, the sandstones pass into alternations of thinly bedded gray shale, calcareous shale, and marl and/or micrite (millimeter scale). The sandstones are of relatively high textural and mineralogical maturity and display crude cross-bedding. The general facies context may indicate that the sandstones represent a shelf-edge relict sandbody formed during a regressive period, or a submarine fan or canyon fill (part of tract H, Fig. 4).

Sections in the Gyangze area. The uppermost Jurassic rocks of Gyangze evolve into quartz-rich sandstones associated with dark shales, siltstones, and tuff (e.g., the top part of the Banqiong section, Fig. 16, A and B). The type section of the Weimei Formation is located at Weimei village, east of Gyangze. Its upper part (Fig. 27A) is dated as Tithonian, on the basis of the assemblage of ammonites (*Haplophylloceras, Berriasella,* and *Himalayites*), and belemnites (*Belemnopsis uhligi,* Academia Sinica, 1984). This section is ~600 m thick and can be interpreted as submarine-fan deposits that include three turbidite cycles (Fig. 27B). Each turbidite cycle is made up of a lower unit of sandstones and an upper unit of dark shales, siltstones, and some marl and/or limestone beds, showing a fining-up tendency. The lower sandstones are characterized by a quartz content of as much as 85%, and are moderately sorted, medium to fine grained, and massive to thick bedded. In places, crude cross-bedding and erosional surfaces that have lag deposits are visible. Laterally, the sandstone unit changes in thickness from 2 m to 60 m.

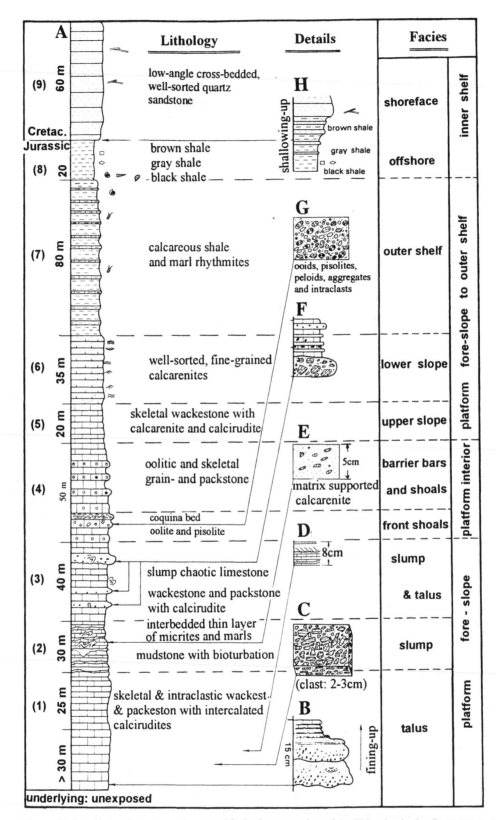

Figure 24. Detailed sedimentary column and facies interpretation of the Tithonian in the Gutzuo section (S9).

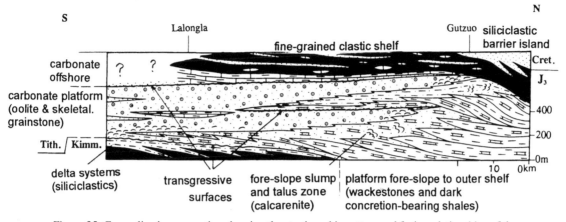

Figure 25. Generalized cross section showing the stratigraphic pattern and facies relationships of the carbonate platform and outer shelf facies zones in the Nyalam-Tingri area during the Late Jurassic, based on the sections by Yu et al. (1983); Tibetan Regional Geological Team (1983); Academia Sinica (1984); and our own observations.

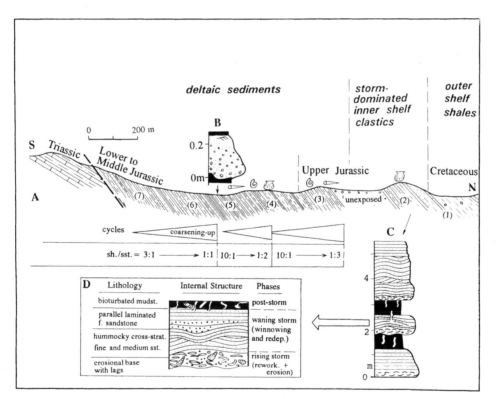

Figure 26. Sedimentary characteristics and facies interpretation of the Jurassic section at Jiulongla (S10), west of Duina. A: Simplified profile. The stratigraphic boundaries are based on data from the Tibetan Regional Geological Team (1983) and our own correlation. The Lower and Middle Jurassic deposits have been discussed in the corresponding text. B: Sequence of a debris flow. C: Sequence with Tithonian-age storm beds. D: Detailed diagram showing the inner structure and interpretation of the storm beds.

The lower sandstones mainly represent channel fills and the upper part of the cycle represents overbank turbidites and hemipelagic deposits. The three cycles, in turn, form a fining- and thinning-upward megacycle, probably caused by landward shift of the slope-fan system during the latest Jurassic and earliest Cretaceous.

Pelagic basin

The regional facies distribution indicates that the Tithonian sediments in the Nagarze area should be abyssal-plain deposits. They are ~130 m in thickness, but only the upper 20 to 30 m contain Tithonian ammonites (Wang et al., 1983). The fossilifer-

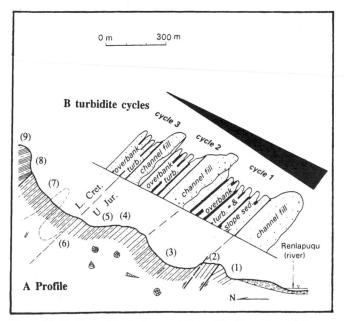

Figure 27. Profile and facies interpretation of the Upper Jurassic (upper part of Weimei Formation) in Weimei, Gyangze. A: Field exposure. B: Fining-upward cycles of turbidites.

ous part consists of interbedded siltstones, silty shales, and shales, and may represent distal fan deposits. The lower unfossiliferous rocks are composed of lava, tuff, grayish-green siliceous shales (?radiolarite), gray shales, and siltstones, possibly representing deposits of an oceanic basin. The underlying rocks are 200 m of very coarse clastics of a submarine fan of unknown age. Wang et al. (1983) assigned these beds to the late Kimmeridgian or earliest Tithonian (cf. Fig. 2), on the basis of regional lithological correlation.

PALEOGEOGRAPHIC EVOLUTION OF THE JURASSIC

Generally, the Jurassic is dominated by shallow-water carbonates and siliciclastics in the south and by deep-water fine-grained terrigenous clastics and pelagic sediments in the north. Both the uniform facies distribution and a stable tectonic setting indicate that the Jurassic Indian shelf in southern Tibet represented a passive margin. Deepening-upward cycles containing condensed beds and repeated progradational packages of shelf sediments in the southern area, as well as extensive abyssal deposits with local basaltic lava in the northern facies zone, reflect continued Tethyan ocean spreading and relative sea-level fluctuations (Fig. 3), in response to thermal subsidence (Liu and Einsele, 1994) and eustasy.

The paleogeographic evolution in southern Tibet during the Jurassic is summarized as follows (Fig. 28). During the Early Jurassic a ramp-type shelf, having a siliciclastic estuarine system in the southeast and carbonate shoal-dominated inner ramp in the southwest, developed in the study area. Perhaps owing to the shallow water depth and gentle slope gradient, the southern coast was

dominated by tidal processes. Pelagic sediments and local basaltic intrusions are in the northern oceanic environment (Fig. 28A).

During the Middle Jurassic, in particular in the Bathonian and Bajocian, the ramp-dominated paleogeographic framework was maintained, but the southeastern region evolved from an estuary-dominated setting into a delta-dominated shelf. Higher sedimentation rates on the ramp led to progradation and aggradation of thick carbonate-dominated sediments in the southern zone. A syndepositional strike-slip fault (?transform) may have developed in the slope and controlled the facies distribution there (Fig. 28B). Thick basaltic lava in the Nagarze area indicates that the Tethyan ocean was in an expanding stage.

Rapid sea-level rise and/or subsidence took place during the late Callovian and Oxfordian. As a result, the southern shelf became sediment starved, so that condensed ferruginous oolitic and coquina beds and local hiatuses formed widely. Turbidites and pelagic sediments of limited thickness accumulated in the northern deep basin (Fig. 28C).

During the Kimmeridgian, a terrigenous-dominated platform prograded rapidly into the southern zone. Meanwhile, the oceanic basin in the northern Gyangze and Nagarze areas still received little sediment. The terrigenous sediments may have been trapped on the deepening inner shelf (Fig. 28D).

Until the early Tithonian, an oolite-dominated shallow platform built up on the subsiding former delta lobes in the southwest. In contrast, the terrigenous shelf continued to prograde in the southeastern area (Fig. 28D). The middle to late Tithonian was a period of faster deposition, in which thick, fine-grained clastics (>1,000 m?) accumulated on the deepening shelf. Extensive slope-apron and basin-floor turbidites were deposited (Fig. 28E).

A short regression occurred in the latest Jurassic and earliest Cretaceous, in which a barrier island complex developed in the southern area, and in the northern zone submarine fans shifted southward.

ACKNOWLEDGMENTS

We acknowledge the German Research Foundation (DFG) for financial support and the Chengdu Research Institute of Geology and Mineral Resources, People's Republic of China, for efficient assistance during the field seasons. We thank our colleagues of the Geological and Palaeontological Institute, University of Tuebingen, and the Chengdu Research Institute, who gave us much support and valuable advice, in particular Liu Baojun, Yu Guangming, Werner Ricken, and Xu Qiang. We also thank Allison M. Macfarlane, Rasoul B. Sorkhobi, and Jay Quade for their encouragement, and Brian S. Currie, J. Quade, and Neil A. Wells for their critical reviews of the manuscript and useful comments.

REFERENCES CITED

Academia Sinica, 1974, Scientific report of investigation in Qomolangma Peak (Mt. Everest) area, geology: Beijing, Science Press, 280 p.
Academia Sinica, 1981, The sedimentary rocks in southern Xizang: Beijing, Science Press, 86 p.

E. Late Tithonian progradation of fine-grained sediments

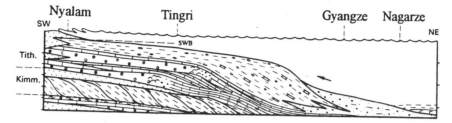

D. Kimmeridgian delta and early Tithonian carbonate platform

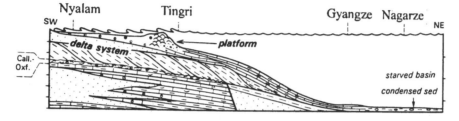

C. Callovian-Oxfordian transgression and semi-starved basin

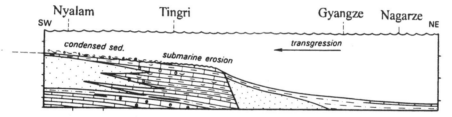

B. Bathonian-Bajocian carbonate and siliciclastic-mixed shelf

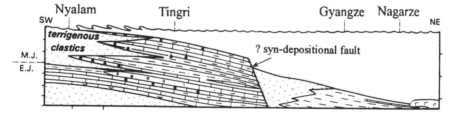

A. Early Jurassic carbonate ramp

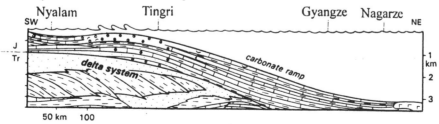

Figure 28. Generalized facies cross sections of the former Indian shelf in southern Tibet illustrating its lithofacies and paleogeographic evolution during the Jurassic (after Liu and Einsele, 1994).

Academia Sinica, 1984, Stratigraphy of Xizang (Tibet) Plateau: Beijing, Science Press, 405 p.

Aigner, T., and Reineck, H. K., 1982, Proximal trends in modern storm sands from the Helegoland Bight (North Sea) and their implication for basin analysis: Senckenbergiana Maritima, v. 14, p. 183–215.

Allen, J. R. L., 1968, Current ripples, their relation to patterns of water and sediment motion: Amsterdam, North-Holland, 433 p.

Arkell, W. L., 1953, Bajocian ammonites collected by Sir Henry Hayden near Kampdazong, Tibet: Geological Magazine, v. 90, p. 331–339.

Bordet, P., Colchen, M., Krummenacher, D., Le Fort, P., Mouterde, R., and Remy, M., 1971, Recherches geologiques dens L'Himalaya du Nepal, region de la Thakkhola: Paris, Edition Centre National Recherches Scientifique, 279 p.

Coleman, J. M., and Wright, L. D., 1975, Modern river deltas: Variability of processes and sandbodies, in Broussard, M. L., ed., Delta models for exploration: Houston, Texas, Houston Geological Society, p. 99–149.

Einsele, G., 1992, Sedimentary basins: Berlin Heidelberg, Springer-Verlag, 628 p.

Einsele, G., and Seilacher, A., 1991, Distinction of tempestites and turbidites, in Einsele, G., Ricken, W., and Seilacher, A., eds., Cycles and events in stratigraphy: Berlin, Heidelberg, New York, Springer-Verlag, p. 377–382.

Elliott, T., 1986, Deltas, in Reading, H. G., ed., Sedimentary environments and facies: Oxford, London, Blackwell Scientific Publications, p. 113–154.

Gansser, A., 1964, Geology of the Himalayas: London, New York, Interscience Publishers, 289 p.

Gradstein, F. M., Gibling, M. R., Jansa, L. F., Kaminski, M. K., Ogg, J. G., Sarti, M., Thurow, J. W., Von Rad, U., and Westermann, G. E. G., 1989, Mesozoic stratigraphy of Thakkhola, central Nepal: Dalhousie University, Centre for Marine Geology, Special Report no. 1, 115 p.

Hallam, A., and Bradshaw, M. J., 1979, Bituminous shales and oolitic ironstones as indicators of transgressions and regressions: Geological Society of London Journal, v. 136, p. 157–164.

Jadoul, F., Fois, E., Tintori, A., and Garzanti, E., 1985, Preliminary results on Jurassic stratigraphy in Zanskar (NW Himalaya): Rendiconti della Società Geologica Italiana, v. 8, p. 9–13.

Johnson, H. D., and Baldwin, C. T., 1986, Shallow siliciclastic seas, in Reading H. G., ed., Sedimentary environments and facies: Oxford, London, Blackwell Science Publication, p. 229–272.

Krishna, J., 1983, Callovian-Albian ammonoid stratigraphy and paleobiogeography in the Indian sub-continent, with special reference to the Tethys Himalaya: Himalaya Geology, v. 11, p. 43–72.

Liu Baojun, Yu Guangmin, Wang Chengshan, and Lan Bolong, 1983, Jurassic sedimentary environment in the Qomolangma Region: Acta Sedimentologica Sinica, v. 1, no. 2, p. 2–16.

Liu Guanghua, 1992, Permian to Eocene sediments and Indian passive margin evolution in the Tibetan Himalayas: Tuebinger Geowissenschaftliche Arbeiten, Reihe A, Nummer 13, 268 p.

Liu Guanghua, and Einsele, G., 1994, Sedimentary history of the Tethyan basin in the Tibetan Himalayas: Geologische Rundschau, v. 82, p. 32–61.

Liu Guanghua, and Einsele, G., 1996, Various types of olitostromes in a closing ocean basin, Tethyan Himalaya (Cretaceous, Tibet): Sedimentary Geology, v. 104, p. 203–226.

Maxwell, W. G. H., 1968, Atlas of the Great Barrier reef: Amsterdam, Elsevier, 258 p.

Maxwell, W. G. H., and Swinchatt, J. P., 1970, Great Barrier reef: Variation in a terrigenous carbonate province: Geological Society of America Bulletin, v. 81, p. 691–724.

Mercier, J. L., and Li Guangcen, 1984, Mission Franco-Chinoise au Tibet, 1980: Paris, Centre National de la Recherche Scientifique, 433 p.

Pettijohn, F. J., Potter, P. E., and Sierer, R., 1987, Sand and sandstone: Berlin, Springer-Verlag, 553 p.

Porrenga, D. H., 1967, Glauconite and chamosite as depth indicators in the marine environments: Marine Geology, v. 5, p. 495–501.

Ratsbacher, L., Frisch, W., Liu Guanghua, and Chen Chenshen, 1994, Distributed deformation in southern and western Tibet during and after the India-Asia collision: Journal of Geophysical Research, v. 9, p. 19917–19945.

Reading, H. G., ed., 1996, Sedimentary environments: processes, facies and stratigraphy: Oxford, London, Blackwell Science Publications, 688 p.

Reineck, H. E., and Singh, I. B., 1980, Depositional sedimentary environments: Berlin, Heidelberg, New York, Springer-Verlag, 549 p.

Ricken, W., 1986, Digenetic bedding: A model for marl-limestone alternations (Lecture Notes in Earth Science, 6): Berlin, Heidelberg, New York, Springer-Kerlag, 210 p.

Ricken, W., and Eder, W., 1991, Digenetic modification of calcareous bed—an overview, in Einsele, G., Ricken, W., and Seilacher, A., eds., Cycles and events in stratigraphy: Berlin, Heidelberg, New York, Springer-Verlag, p. 430-449.

Seilacher, A., 1967, Bathymetry of trace fossils: Marine Geology, v. 5, p. 413–428.

Seilacher, A., 1978, Use of trace fossil assemblages for recognizing depositional environments, in Basan, P., ed., Trace fossil concepts: Society of Economic Paleontologists and Minealogists, Short Course 5, p. 185–201.

Sellwood, B. W., 1986, Shallow marine carbonate environment, in Reading, H. G., ed., Sedimentary environments & facies: Oxford, London, Edinburgh, Blackwell Scientific Publications, p. 283–342.

Shackleton, R. M., Dewey, J. F., and Windley, B. F., eds., 1988, Tectonic evolution of the Himalaya and Tibet: Royal Society of London, 325 p.

Shi Xiaoying, 1987, The Middle Jurassic brachiopods from Nyalam area southern Xizang (Tibet) Plateau: Contribution to the Geology of the Qinghai-Xizang (Tibet), v. 18, p. 44–49.

Tibetan Regional Geological Team (TRGT), 1983, Geological report of 1:1,000,000 mapping in the Xigaze-Yadong areas: Lhasa, Xizang Autonomous Region, Bureau of Geology and Mineral Resources, 568 p.

Tucker, M., and Wright, E., 1990, Carbonate sedimentology: Oxford, London, Blackwell Scientific Publications, 482 p.

Uhlig, V., 1910, Die Fauna der Spiti-Schiefer des Himalaya, ihr geologisches Alter und ihre Weltstellung: Denkschriften der Akademie der Wissenschaften, Wien, v. 85, p. 531–609.

Wang Naiwen, Liu Guifang, and Chen Guoming, 1983, Regional stratigraphy of Yamzho Yumco area, South Xizang (Tibet): Contribution to the Geology of the Qinghai-Xizang (Tibet) Plateau, v. 3, p. 1–17.

Wang Yigang, and Zhang Mingliang, 1974, The stratigraphy of Mt. Qomolangma region: Jurassic, in Academia Sinica, ed., Report of scientific expedition in the Mount Qomolangma region (1966–1968)—Geology: Beijing, Science Press, p. 127–146.

Westermann, G. E. G., and Wang Yigang, 1988, Middle Jurassic ammonites of Tibet and the age of the Lower Spiti shales: Paleontology, v. 31, p. 295–339.

Willems, H., 1993, Sedimentary history of the Tethys Himalaya continental shelf in South Tibet (Gamba, Tingri) during Upper Cretaceous and Lower Tertiary (Xizang Autonomous Region, P. R. China), in Willems, H., ed., Geoscientific investigation in the Tethys Himalayas: Berichte, Fachbereich Geowissenschaften, Universtät Bremen, Nummer 38, p. 49–183.

Xiao Xuchang, Li Tingdong, Li Guangcen, Zhang Chengfa, and Yuan Xuecheng, 1988, Tectonic evolution of the lithosphere of the Himalayas, general principle (Geological Memories, ser. 5, no. 7): Beijing, Geological Publishing House, 236 p.

Yu Guangming and Wang Chengshan, 1990, Sedimentary geology of the Xizang (Tibet) Tethys: Beijing, Geological Publishing House, 185 p.

Yu Guangming, Zhang Qihua, Gou Zonghai, Xu Yulin, Wang Guoren, and Li Xiaochi, 1983, Subdivision and correlation of Jurassic system in the Nyalam area, Xizang (Tibet): Contribution to the Geology of the Qinghai-Xizang (Tibet) Plateau, v. 11, p. 165–177.

Zhang Qihau, 1985, The discovery of Lower Cretaceous ammonites from the Pupuga Formation in the Nyalam area, Xizang (Tibet) and its significance on the stratigraphy: Contribution to Geology of the Qihai-Xizang(Tibet) Plateau, v. 16, p. 166–180.

Zhao Jinke, 1976, Jurassic and Cretaceous ammonites from the Mount Qomolongma region, in Academia Sinica, ed., Report of scientific expedition in the Mount Qomolangma region (1966–1968)—Paleontology: Beijing, Science Press, p. 503–554.

MANUSCRIPT ACCEPTED BY THE SOCIETY FEBRUARY 3, 1998

Geological Society of America
Special Paper 328
1999

Biostratigraphy and biogeography of Himalayan Cambrian trilobites

Nigel C. Hughes
Department of Earth Sciences, University of California, Riverside, California 92521
Peter A. Jell
Queensland Museum, P.O. Box 3300, South Brisbane, Queensland 4101, Australia

ABSTRACT

Revision of type material and new collections of trilobites permit establishment of a Cambrian biostratigraphy for the Himalayan region, and an assessment of faunal affinities with other areas. These data support arguments for a passive northern margin of the Indian subcontinent during Cambrian time, constrain the timing of the latest Cambrian–early Ordovician orogenic event, and increase confidence in current models of Himalayan tectonic evolution. Trilobite faunal diversity within the area is low compared to similar successions from shelf environments. Trilobites of late Early Cambrian age are widespread in the Himalaya, but strata containing middle Middle Cambrian and younger faunas are restricted to the Tethyan Himalayan basins of the Kashmir Valley and the Zanskar-Spiti region. Basal Upper Cambrian taxa are known only in Kashmir. A major unconformity truncates Cambrian deposits in all Himalayan basins. In contrast to previous suggestions, Cambrian trilobite faunas do not suggest major environmental or structural separation between Himalayan basins during the Cambrian. The zonal scheme for the Cambrian of China can be applied to the Himalaya, and many Himalayan taxa are common to other equatorial peri-Gondwanan regions, particularly South and North China, Vietnam, Australia, and Iran.

INTRODUCTION

The Himalaya provides a unique setting for understanding collision tectonics and orogenic processes. The regional geology of the area is particularly important because models of Himalayan evolution can be constrained by improved resolution of field relationships. A basic premise of Himalayan geology is that the northern margin of India was passive from earliest Phanerozoic time until the collision of India with Asia (e.g., Brookfield, 1993). This view permits interpretation of the current disposition of rocks within the Himalaya as the result of one major phase of tectonic activity: the ongoing collision of India with Asia. Indian shield and Himalayan Paleozoic sections are highly incomplete, and only Cambrian and Permian deposits are sufficiently widespread and extensive to permit resolution of regional paleoenvironmental relationships. Hence, Cambrian rocks assume a special

significance for investigations of the early Phanerozoic history of the region. Despite this importance, the Himalayan Cambrian lacks a regional biostratigraphic framework, and understanding of its paleontology rests largely on work published more than 50 years ago. Furthermore, in marked contrast to the passive margin model of northern India, time-equivalent Himalayan Cambrian faunas from different outcrop belts are reported to show striking differences (Reed, 1934; Shah, 1993). In particular, the reported European and North American affinities of trilobites from Spiti (Reed, 1910) suggests the presence of an exotic terrane within the Himalaya because contiguous Kashmiri faunas have an Asian aspect (Reed, 1934). If this is true, it has major implications for models of Himalayan evolution because it refutes the passive margin model for earliest Phanerozoic time. For these reasons a thorough revision of regional trilobite faunas is critical for improved understanding of Himalayan geology.

Hughes, N. C., and Jell, P. A., 1999, Biostratigraphy and biogeography of Himalayan Cambrian trilobites, *in* Macfarlane, A., Sorkhabi, R. B., and Quade, J., eds., Himalaya and Tibet: Mountain Roots to Mountain Tops: Boulder, Colorado, Geological Society of America Special Paper 328.

OUTCROPS AND FAUNAS

Cambrian rocks are exposed in several Himalayan outcrop belts (Fig. 1), and record a general trend from a proximal mixed evaporitic-siliciclastic-carbonate suite in the Salt Range and Krol-Tal Belt, south of the High Himalaya, to distal finer grained clastics and minor carbonates in the Kashmir and Zanskar-Spiti Valleys to the north, collectively known as the Tethyan Himalaya. A variety of body and trace fossils have been used to date these strata (e.g., Bhargava et al., 1982; Bhatt, 1989; Hughes and Droser, 1992; Prasad et al., 1990; Tewari, 1984), but trilobites are the only fossils sufficiently well known to permit correlation at multiple horizons within and among Himalayan basins. Trilobites have been collected from the Salt Range since the nineteenth century (Waagen, 1889), but the first detailed Cambrian biozonation for India was based on the section in Spiti in the Tethyan Himalaya (Hayden, 1904; Reed, 1910). Hayden recognized six discrete horizons bearing trilobites, which were assigned Middle to Late Cambrian ages. The discovery of Middle Cambrian trilobites in Kashmir (Kobayashi, 1934; Wadia, 1934) permitted regional comparisons between these Tethyan basins. Despite Kashmir and Spiti being only 600 km apart, and sharing similar sedimentary facies and ages, no species were found common to both areas (Reed, 1934). The Kashmir fauna, in the west, was

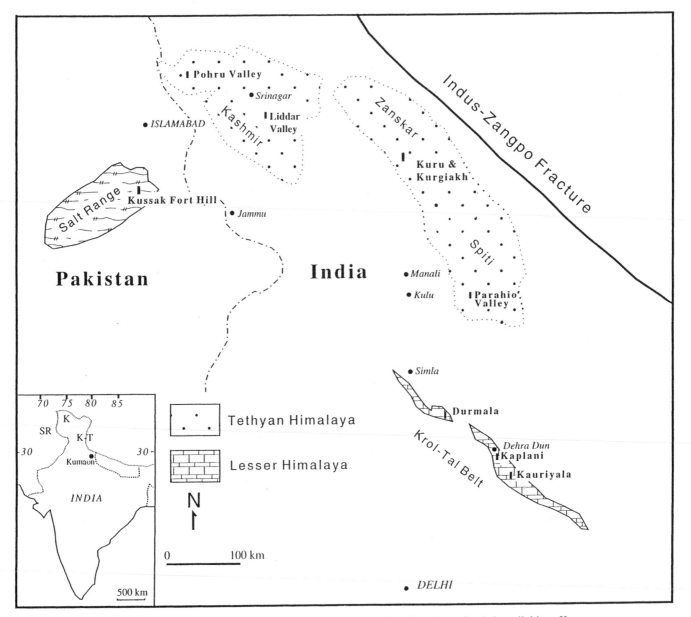

Figure 1. Sketch map of position of outcrops belts containing Himalayan Cambrian trilobites. Key localities are indicated by vertical bars. Inset map shows position of outcrops belts within the Indian subcontinent: SR = Salt Range, K = Kashmir, K-T = Krol-Tal Belt.

considered to be of Indo-Chinese affinity, and the Spiti fauna, in the east, was considered similar to European or North American faunas (Reed, 1910).

In recent years additional Himalayan Cambrian trilobites have been discovered, both within the Tethyan Himalaya and in other regions (e.g., Kumar and Singh, 1983; Mathur and Joshi, 1989; Shah, 1973; Whittington, 1986). In spite of these finds, Reed's interpretation of the biostratigraphy has remained unchallenged. As Kashmiri faunas have become better known, the apparent distinctness of the two areas has been maintained, although approximate correlations between Kashmir and Spiti have been attempted using genera whose biostratigraphic occurrence is known from non-Himalayan areas (e.g., Shah et al., 1991; Shah, 1993). Examples are the genera *Tonkinella*, which occurs in Kashmir, and *Oryctocephalus*, which is found in Spiti. These genera co-occur at certain horizons in North China and Laurentia, and the stratigraphic levels containing these trilobites in the Himalayan sections have been correlated on this basis. The marked difference between contemporary faunas in the two regions may be explained as (1) a consequence of paleogeographic differences related to water depth (Shah, 1993; Wakhaloo and Shah, 1965), or (2) deposition in separate sedimentary basins (Gupta and Suneja, 1977). Paleogeographic reconstructions for the Cambrian place India within the Gondwanan supercontinent (Scotese and McKerrow, 1990; Moores, 1991; Dalziel, 1991; Yang and Tong, 1993) and the fauna of Kashmir is consistent with others characteristic of this part of the peri-Gondwanan shelf (Jell, 1974). However, the Spiti fauna appears irregular for this region because it reportedly (Reed, 1910) contains genera of North American and northern European aspect. These genera are not found within 8,000 km of the Himalaya and raise the possibility that the Zanskar-Spiti basin represents an exotic terrane. The emplacement of terranes following supercontinent breakup is well known (e.g., Murphy and Nance, 1991), and given that Reed's (1910, 1934) interpretations are the basis of current understanding of the Cambrian paleontology of the Himalaya, it is important that they be reevaluated in the light of advances in knowledge of Cambrian faunas, and improved analytical techniques.

APPROACH

Latex replicas were made of all available type material of Himalayan trilobites held in the repository of the Geological Survey of India in Calcutta (including Reed's Kashmir and Spiti material, and those of several more recent studies), and in the Department of Geology, Jammu University. These replicas were combined with new field collections from Kashmir, Spiti, and Zanskar to provide the most complete sample of Himalayan trilobites yet assembled. More than 2,000 specimens were examined during the course of this study. The effects of tectonic deformation on the morphology of fossils were overcome by using a combination of statistical and computer-graphic approaches to isolate and eliminate morphological variations caused by deformation

(Hughes and Jell, 1992). The relationship between lithofacies and trilobite preservation was assessed because preservational artifacts have frequently been mistaken for features of taxonomic significance (Hughes, 1995). Specimens were then assigned to morphotypes on the basis of shared discrete characters; morphometric approaches were employed where specimen numbers permitted. Morphotypes were then assigned to taxa based on comparisons with published literature, or directly with type specimens. A monograph illustrating type specimens of Himalayan Cambrian trilobites and detailing their taxonomy has been published elsewhere (Jell and Hughes, 1997).

RESULTS

Our research has produced the following results: (1) a marked reduction in the faunal diversity of previously described collections due to improved resolution of tectonic deformation and intraspecific variation, including ontogenetic differences; (2) a refined comparison of Himalayan material with specimens from other areas, resulting in improved interregional correlation and faunistic comparison; (3) resolution of a regional biostratigraphy and integration of this biostratigraphy with the zonal scheme of China.

Improved resolution of the effects of tectonic deformation and intraspecific variation on trilobite morphology (Hughes and Jell, 1992) resulted in the synonymy of many previously described taxa into a total of 33 identifiable species belonging to 26 genera and an additional 10 taxa questionably assigned to species or discernible at the generic level only. The diversity of taxa within collections from individual horizons is low compared to collections of similar age from other regions (e.g., Lu et al., 1965; Zhang et al., 1980; Zhang and Jell, 1987), possibly because many of these collections come from deeper water settings, which are commonly characterized by relatively reduced diversity in the Cambrian (e.g., Ludvigsen and Westrop, 1983, Fig. 4). Low intensity of sampling may be another reason for this observation.

On the basis of these revisions, a new Cambrian stratigraphy for the Himalaya is proposed (Fig. 2). Intraregional correlations can be established at three horizons. The lowermost horizon can be correlated among six sections from the Salt Range to the Lesser and Tethyan Himalaya, and is characterized by redlichiide trilobites of late Early Cambrian age. The two other horizons are based on shared species of primitive libristomate trilobites and are of middle-Middle Cambrian age. These two horizons are recognized only within the Tethyan Himalaya.

Of the genera and the identified species, 97% and 48%, respectively, are found outside the Himalaya. These taxa either possess a peri-Gondwanan or worldwide distribution. Himalayan Cambrian trilobite diversity is generally low, and includes several taxa with global distributions (e.g., *Bailiella, Tonkinella, Lejopyge*). Limited diversity limits the applicability of statistical comparisons of faunal similarity in this case. Nevertheless, the Himalayan Cambrian bears the greatest similarity at the species level to faunas from South and North China, with seven and five species in common, respectively. Fewer species in common with

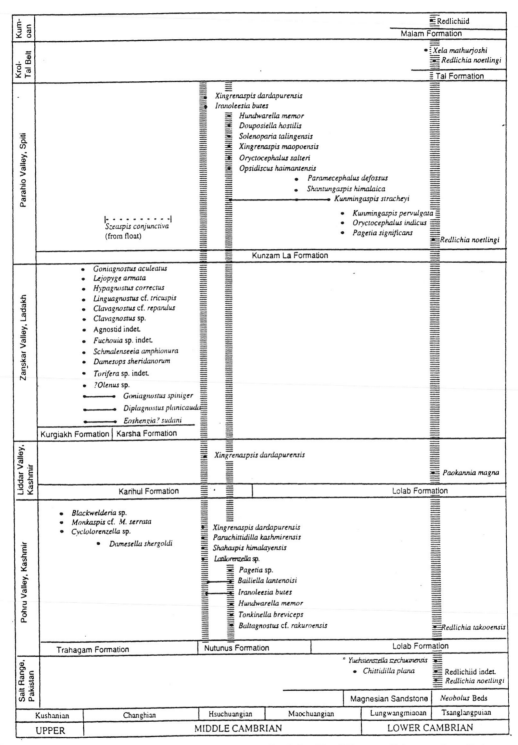

Figure 2. Biostratigraphic scheme for the Himalayan Cambrian. The Chinese stadial system is applied to the faunas of the region. Outcrop belts are ordered from west to east (see Fig. 1). Bullet points and vertical lines above taxon names indicate stratigraphic ranges; horizontal bars indicate correlations among outcrop regions. The names of local lithostratigraphic units are shown to the left of taxonomic ranges.

Australia, Vietnam, and Iran may reflect the fact that fewer trilobites have been described from those areas (Fig. 3). This distribution is concordant with current paleogeographic models for the Cambrian (Scotese and McKerrow, 1990; Yang and Tong, 1993) that place South and North China, Vietnam, Iran, and Australia in close geographic proximity, and at similar equatorial latitudes. Elements of the agnostoid-rich faunas of Ladakh (Fig. 2) are widely distributed across paleolatitudes about the periphery of Gondwana, and also in Kazakhstan (Fig 4). Given the low regional diversity of the Himalayan faunas and its similarity to those of China, the Chinese stadial scheme has been applied directly to the Himalayan Cambrian, rather than erecting a separate Himalayan scheme (Fig. 2).

CONSTRAINTS ON THE EVOLUTION OF THE INDIAN PASSIVE MARGIN DURING CAMBRIAN TIME

The new biostratigraphy permits the following conclusions about the Himalayan Cambrian. (1) The earliest trilobites known from the Himalaya are of late Early Cambrian (Tsanglangpuian) age. (2) Deposits of this age are the most widespread trilobite-bearing deposits of the Himalayan Cambrian. (3) Middle Cambrian (Maochungian-Changian) deposits are restricted to the Tethyan Himalaya and the Salt Range. (4) The top of the Spiti section correlates with the base of the Kashmir section, and hence the supposed discreteness of these faunas is partly the result of biostratigraphic differences between the areas. (5) Faunal differences between contemporary Kashmiri and Spiti faunas are likely the result of biofacies differences. (6) All taxic distributions are consistent with current understanding of Cambrian paleogeography and there are no marked faunal anomalies within the region. (7) Faunal similarity is greatest between areas positioned at similar paleolatitudes. (8) The youngest Cambrian trilobites yet recorded in the region are from northwestern Kashmir and are of early Late Cambrian (Kushanian) age.

The Early Cambrian is marked by a transgressive succession throughout the Himalayan region, but temporal resolution within the Early Cambrian remains disputed. The first Himalayan trilo-

	NTH AMERICA	EUROPE	AUSTRALIA	SIBERIA	NTH CHINA	STH CHINA	VIETNAM	IRAN
Redlichia noetlingi			G	G	G	S	G	S
Redlichia takooensis			S			S		
Xela mathurjoshi			G					
Paokannia magna						S		
Pagetia significans			S		G	G		
Opsidiscus haimantensis		G	G	G				
Baltagnostus rakuroensis	G		G		S			
Oryctocephalus indicus	G		G	G		S		
Oryctocephalus salteri								
Tonkinella breviceps	S			G	G	G	S	
Yuehsienszella szechuanensis						S		
Kunmingaspis pervulgata						G		S
Kunmingaspis stracheyi								
Paramecephalus defossus						G		
Shantungaspis himalaica					G			
Douposiella hostilis		G	G			G		
Xingrenaspis maopoensis						G		
Xingrenaspis dardapurensis						G		
Solenoparia talingensis					S			
Bailiella lantenoisi		G		G	S	S	S	
Chittidilla plana						S		
Parachittidilla kashmirensis					G	G		
Hundwarella memor				G	S	S	G	
Iranoleesia butes					S	G	S	G
Szeaspis conjunctiva					S			
Shahaspis himalayensis								
Latilorenzella sp.					G			

Figure 3. Distribution of Early and Middle Himalayan polymerid trilobites elsewhere. G = same genus; S = same species.

	QLD	KAZAKH	ZHEJIANG	QINLING	TURKEST	SWEDEN
Goniagnostus spiniger	S	G	S	G	G	S
Lejopyge armata	S	S	S	G	G	S
Goniagnostus aculeatus	S	S	S	S	S	G
Diplagnostus planicauda	S		S	S		S
Linguagnostus tricuspis	G		S	G	S	G
Clavagnostus repandus	G	G	G	S	G	S
Hypagnostus correctus	S	S	S	S	G	G
Fuchouia sp.	G		G	G		
Schmalenseeia amphionura						S
Damesops sheridanorum	G	G		G		
Eoshengia? sudani				G		
?Olenus sp.	G		G			G

Figure 4. Distribution of uppermost Middle Cambrian Ladakh agnostoid fauna elsewhere. G = same genus; S = same species.

bites are of late Early Cambrian age, and it is possible that the earliest Cambrian is condensed in the Lesser Himalaya as the first trilobites occur in the Lower Tal Formation, which is characterized by a phosphatic base (Joshi et al., 1989; Rai and Singh, 1983). Middle Cambrian deposits have not been identified in the Lesser Himalaya, but are well developed in the Tethyan Himalaya, where they occur in fine-grained, slope lithofacies. The Lesser Himalaya are characterized by shallower water deposits: Tethyan basins also show transgressive successions with relatively shallow water deposits in Early Cambrian time (Garzanti et al., 1986; Hughes and Droser, 1992).

Biostratigraphic overlap occurs between the top of the Spiti section and the base of the Kashmiri section. Three Middle Cambrian trilobite-bearing horizons in Spiti are older than any known in Kashmir. Of the 19 Middle Cambrian taxa recorded from these basins, 5 belong to intervals unique to one or other area. Of the 14 contemporary taxa, 3 are common to both areas, 7 are unique to Kashmir, and 4 are unique to Spiti. Paleoenvironmental differences may be responsible for differences between contemporary Kashmiri and Spiti faunas, but the sedimentology of both areas is too poorly known to evaluate this further. Despite these differences none of the taxa in either basin is exotic to the equatorial peri-Gondwanan realm. Only one new genus and three new species have been recognized during the study, and these forms all have relatives in the equatorial peri-Gondwana region. The relatively small number of endemic taxa suggests that trilobite-bearing Himalayan Cambrian environments had open access to a broad equatorial peri-Gondwanan faunal realm. Himalayan Middle Cambrian trilobites also belong to slope faunas that tend to have broad geographic distributions (Taylor, 1977; Babcock, 1994). This interpretation is supported by the presence of globally cosmopolitan genera such as *Bailiella, Tonkinella,* and all the agnostoids. The Himalayan Cambrian trilobite fauna is consistent with the passive margin model for the northern margin of India, and with current concepts of regional land mass distributions. The faunal similarity of Himalayan sequences with those of South

China is consistent with similarities in the stratigraphic evolution of the two areas during latest Precambrian–earliest Phanerozoic time (Zhang, 1988), and supports arguments that the South China block was the complimentary passive margin to the Himalaya during the earliest Phanerozoic (Brookfield, 1994).

The lithologic and tectonic histories of the Himalayan Cambrian closely resemble successions in the Middle East and Mediterranean (Wolfart, 1983), but this similarity is not mirrored in the trilobite faunas of the Mediterranean region (cf. Šnajdr, 1958; Lotze and Sdzuy, 1961a, 1961b). Many sectors of the peri-Gondwanan margin apparently had similar geological evolutions; however, their faunas differed regionally. Paleogeographic reconstructions place components of present-day eastern Asia at similar latitudes to the Himalaya during Cambrian time (Scotese and McKerrow, 1990). This suggests that in this case paleolatitude was the principal paleogeographic constraint on faunal distributions.

In the Himalaya, Late Cambrian time is represented only by earliest Late Cambrian trilobites from Kashmir (Jell, 1986), and wherever a stratigraphic (as opposed to tectonic) contact terminates the Cambrian, it is always a marked erosional unconformity (Brookfield, 1993; Garzanti et al., 1986). In the Tethyan Himalaya the Cambrian is overlain by the Ordovician Thaple Formation, a coarse alluvial-fan conglomerate. This deposit, along with ash beds in late Middle Cambrian deposits, mild metamorphism, and widespread intrusions of ca. 500 Ma granites in the Himalaya, suggests a thermal event during the Late Cambrian–Early Ordovician. The presence of extensive Cambrian marine deposits in the Himalaya, each with an overall transgressive succession, suggests a period of passive marginal subsidence following rifting in the Precambrian that was terminated by uplift in latest Cambrian time (Garzanti et al., 1986). Whether this orogeny was related to collision or simply an internal thermal event remains unclear (Brookfield, 1993). The stratigraphic and tectonic history of the Himalayan Cambrian resembles that of Sardinia (Garzanti et al., 1986), suggesting equivalence to the contemporary Sardic orogenic phase that affected some southern parts of the peri-Gondwanan margin. A Late Cambrian orogeny is evident in Bohemia (Snajdr, 1958), but is less clear in middle eastern areas such as Turkey (Dean and Monod, 1990), Iran (Wolfart and Kursten, 1974), and Oman (Fortey, 1994), and other peri-Gondwanan slope settings such as Wales (Cowie et al., 1972). In these areas the presence of Upper Cambrian and Lower Ordovician deposits suggests more continuous deposition. The similarity of the Mediterranean and Himalayan lithologic and tectonic history may be the result of localized tectonic activity around the margin of Gondwana that was associated with supercontinent breakup and tectonic block dispersal (Murphy and Nance, 1991), or with the final stages of the assembly of Gondwana (Dalziel, 1991; Gaetani and Garzanti, 1991).

ACKNOWLEDGMENTS

Funding for research was provided by the Natural Environment Research Council, the Queensland Museum, and the Cincinnati Museum Center, and IGCP grants 303, 320, and 366. Thanks are due to officers of the Geological Survey of India, S. K. Shah and C. S. Sudan of Jammu University, A. Príeur of the Université Claude Bernard, and R. D. White of Yale University for access to collections in their care. We also thank M. Gaetani, Shyamali Khastigir, Dowa Jora, V. K. Mathur, J. L. Pillola, J. Sheridan, R. Sheridan, and J. A. Talent for their practical help with the project. M. L. Droser, C. Dietsch, and G. W. Storrs read the manuscript and offered helpful suggestions. A. R. Palmer, R. A. Robison, and F. A. Sundberg gave insight on trilobite distributions. L. E. Babcock, M. E. Brookfield, and S. R. Westrop provided astute reviews of this paper.

REFERENCES CITED

Babcock, L. E., 1994, Biogeography and biofacies patterns of polymeroid trilobites from North Greenland: Palaeogeographic and palaeo-oceanographic implications: Grønlands Geologiske Undersøgelse Bulletin, v. 169, p. 129–147.

Bhargava, O. N., Kumar, G., and Gupta, S. S., 1982, Cambrian trace fossils from the Spiti Valley Himachal Himalaya: Geological Society of India Journal, v. 23, p. 183–191.

Bhatt, D. K., 1989, Small shelly fossils, Tommotian and Meishucunian stages and the Precambrian-Cambrian boundary—Implications of the recent studies in the Himalayan sequences: Palaeontological Society of India Journal, v. 34, p. 55–68.

Brookfield, M. E., 1993, The Himalayan passive margin from Precambrian to Cretaceous times: Sedimentary Geology, v. 84, p. 1–35.

Brookfield, M. E., 1994, Problems in applying preservation, facies and sequence models to Sinian (Neoproterozoic) glacial sequences in Australia and Asia: Precambrian Research, v. 70, p. 113–143.

Cowie, J. W., Rushton, A. W. A., and Stubblefield, C. J., 1972, A correlation of Cambrian rocks in the British Isles: Geological Society of London Special Report, v. 2, p. 1–42.

Dalziel, I. W. D., 1991, Pacific margins of Laurentia and East Antarctica–Australia as a conjugate rift pair: Evidence and implications for an Eocambrian supercontinent: Geology, v. 19, p. 598–601.

Dean, W. T., and Monod, O., 1990, Revised stratigraphy and relationship of Lower Palaeozoic rocks, eastern Taurus mountains, south central Turkey: Geological Magazine, v. 127, p. 333–347.

Fortey, R. A., 1994, Late Cambrian trilobites from the Sultanate of Oman: Neues Jahrbuch für Paläontologie Abhandlung, v. 194, p. 25–53.

Gaetani, M., and Garzanti, E., 1991, Multicyclic history of the northern India continental margin (northwestern Himalaya): American Association of Petroleum Geologists Bulletin, v. 75, p. 1427–1446.

Garzanti, E., Casnedi, R., and Jadoul, F., 1986, Sedimentary evidence of a Cambro-Ordovician orogenic event in the northwestern Himalaya: Sedimentary Geology, v. 48, p. 237–265.

Gupta, V. J., and Suneja, I. J., 1977, New facts on the Lower Cambrian palaeo-geography of the Himalaya: Science and Culture, v. 43, p. 258.

Hayden, H. H., 1904, The geology of Spiti with parts of Bashahr and Rupshu: Geological Survey of India Memoirs, v. 36, p. 1–121.

Hughes, N. C., 1995, Trilobite taphonomy and taxonomy: A problem and some implications: Palaios, v. 10, p. 283–285.

Hughes, N. C., and Droser, M. L., 1992, Trace fossils from the Phe Formation (Lower Cambrian), Zanskar Valley, northwestern India: Queensland Museum Memoirs, v. 32, p. 139–144.

Hughes, N. C., and Jell, P. A., 1992, A statistical/computer-graphic method for assessing variation in tectonically deformed fossils and its application to Cambrian trilobites from Kashmir: Lethaia, v. 25, p. 317–330.

Jell, P. A., 1974, Faunal provinces and possible planetary reconstruction of the Middle Cambrian: Journal of Geology, v. 82, p. 319–350.

Jell, P. A., 1986, An early Late Cambrian trilobite faunule from Kashmir: Geological Magazine, v. 123, p. 487–492.

Jell, P. A., and Hughes, N. C., 1997, Himalayan Cambrian trilobites: Special Papers in Palaeontology, v. 58, p. 1–113.

Joshi, A., Mathur, V. K., and Bhatt, D. K., 1989, Discovery of redlichid trilobites from the Arenaceous Member of the Tal Formation, Garhwal Syncline, Lesser Himalaya, India: Geological Society of India Journal, v. 33, p. 538–546.

Kobayashi, T., 1934, Middle Cambrian fossils from Kashmir: American Journal of Science, v. 27, p. 295–302.

Kumar, G., and Singh, G., 1983, Middle Cambrian trilobites from Karihul, Liddar Valley, Anantnag District, Kashmir and its significance: Current Science, v. 52, p. 548–549.

Lotze, F., and Sdzuy, K., 1961a, Das Kambrium Spaniens, Teil 2: Trilobiten: Abhandlungen der Mathematisch-Naturwissenschaftlichen Klasse, v. 7, p. 501–594.

Lotze, F., and Sdzuy, K., 1961b, Das Kambrium Spaniens, Teil 2: Trilobiten: Abhandlungen der Mathematisch-Naturwissenschaftlichen Klasse, v. 8, p. 597–693.

Lu, Y. H., Zhang, W. T., Chu, C. L., Chien, Y. Y., and Hsiang, L. W., 1965, Chinese fossils of all groups (Trilobita): Beijing, China, Science Press, 766 p.

Ludvigsen, R., and Westrop, S. R., 1983, Trilobite biofacies of the Cambrian-Ordovician boundary interval in northern North America: Alcheringa, v. 7, p. 301–319.

Mathur, V. K., and Joshi, A., 1989, Record of Redlichiid Trilobite from the Lower Cambrian Tal Formation, Mussoorie Syncline, Lesser Himalaya, India: Geological Society of India Journal, v. 33, p. 268–270.

Moores, E. M., 1991, Southwest U.S.–East Antarctica (SWEAT) connection: A hypothesis: Geology, v. 19, p. 425–428.

Murphy, J. B., and Nance, R. D., 1991, Supercontinent model for the contrasting character of Late Proterozoic orogenic belts: Geology, v. 19, p. 469–472.

Prasad, B., Maithy, P. K., Kumar, G., and Raina, B. K., 1990, Precambrian-Cambrian acritarchs from the Blaini-Krol-Tal sequence of Mussoorie Syncline, Garhwal Lesser Himalaya, India: Geological Society of India Memoirs, v. 16, p. 19–32.

Rai, V., and Singh, I. B., 1983, Discovery of trilobite impression in the Arenaceous Member of Tal Formation, Mussoorie area, India: Palaeontological Society of India Journal, v. 28, p. 114–117.

Reed, F. R. C., 1910, The Cambrian fossils of Spiti: Palaeontologia Indica, ser. 15, v. 7, p. 1–70.

Reed, F. R. C., 1934, Cambrian and Ordovician fossils from Kashmir: Palaeontologia Indica, v. 21, p. 1–38.

Scotese, C. R., and McKerrow, W. S., 1990, Revised world maps and introduction, *in* McKerrow, W. S., and Scotese, C. R., eds., Palaeozoic palaeogeography and biogeography: Geological Society of London Memoir 12, p. 1–21.

Shah, S. K., 1973, New Conocoryphids from the Middle Cambrian of Kashmir: Himalayan Geology, v. 3, p. 83–93.

Shah, S. K., 1993, Cambrian biofacies and faunal provinces of Himalaya: Palaeontological Society of India Journal, v. 38, p. 37–42.

Shah, S. K., Parcha, S. K., and Raina, A. K., 1991, Late Cambrian trilobites from Himalaya: Palaeontological Society of India Journal, v. 36, p. 89–107.

Šnajdr, M., 1958, Trilobiti Českého Středního Kambria: Rozpravy ústředního ústavu geologického, v. 24, p. 1–280.

Taylor, M. E., 1977, Late Cambrian of western North America: Trilobite biofacies, environmental significance, and biostratigraphic implications, *in* Kauffman, E. G., and Hazel, J. E., eds., Concepts and methods of biostratigraphy: Stroudsburg, Pennsylvania, Dowden, Hutchinson and Ross, Inc., p. 397–425.

Tewari, V. C., 1984, Discovery of the Lower Cambrian stromatolites from the Mussorie Tal phosphorite, India: Current Science, v. 53, p. 319–321.

Waagen, W., 1889, Salt Range fossils: Palaeontologia Indica, ser. 13, v. 4, p. 89–242.

Wadia, D. N., 1934, The Cambrian-Trias sequence of north-western Kashmir (parts of Muzaffarabad and Barmula districts): Geological Survey of India Records, v. 67, p. 121–176.

Wakhaloo, S. N., and Shah, S. K., 1965, Cambrian fauna of Kashmir with special reference to palaeogeography: Current Science, v. 34, p. 377–378.

Whittington, H. B., 1986, Late Middle Cambrian trilobites from Zanskar, Ladakh, northern India: Rivista Italiana di Paleontologia e Stratigrafia, v. 92, p. 171–188.

Wolfart, R., 1983, The Cambrian System in the Near and Middle East: Correlation chart and explanatory notes, *in* Shergold, J. H., and Palmer, A. R., eds.: International Union of Geological Sciences Publication 15, p. 1–71.

Wolfart, R., and Kursten, M., 1974, Stratigraphie und Paläogeographie des Kambriums im mittleren Süd-Asien (Iran bis Nord-Indien): Geologisches Jahrbuch, v. 8, p. 185–234.

Yang, J. L., and Tong, J. N., 1993, Early Cambrian paleobiogeography and revision of positions of paleocontinents: Stratigraphy and Paleontology of China, v. 2, p. 223–234.

Zhang, W. T., 1988, The Cambrian System in eastern Asia: Correlation chart and explanatory notes, *in* Shergold, J. H., and Palmer, A. R., eds.: International Union of Geological Sciences Publication 24, p. 1–81.

Zhang, W. T., Lu, Y. H., Chu, C. L., Qian, Y. Y., Lin, H. G., Zhou, Z. Y., Zheng, S. G., and Yuan, J. L., 1980, Cambrian trilobite faunas of southwestern China: Palaeontologica Sinica, ser. B, v. 159, p. 1–497.

Zhang, W., and Jell, P. A., 1987, Cambrian trilobites of North China: Beijing, China, Science Press, 459 p.

MANUSCRIPT ACCEPTED BY THE SOCIETY FEBRUARY 3, 1998

Geological Society of America
Special Paper 328
1999

Contrasting metamorphic and geochronologic evolution
along the Himalayan belt

Stéphane Guillot
CNRS, UMR 5570, Laboratoire de Pétrologie et Tectonique, Villeurbanne 69622, France
Michael Cosca
Institut de Minéralogie, Université de Lausanne, UNIL-BFSH2, CH-1015 Lausanne, Suisse
Pascal Allemand
CNRS, UMR 5570, Laboratoire de Sciences de la Terre, 69384 Lyon 07, France
Patrick Le Fort
CNRS, UPRES-A 5025, Institut Dolomieu, Laboratoire de Géodynamique des Chaînes Alpines,
15 rue Maurice Gignoux, Grenoble 38031, France

ABSTRACT

Systematic different pressure-temperature-time paths are recorded along the internal zone of the Himalayan orogen. High-pressure rocks rapidly exhumed during the Eocene and Oligocene are restricted to the western part of the Himalayan belt. Farther to the east, both in the North Himalayan Crystalline massif sand in the High Himalayan Crystalline slab, there are upper amphibolite facies rocks, which were unroofed during the Miocene. In the High Himalayan Crystalline slab, a systematic decrease in mica $^{40}Ar/^{39}Ar$ cooling ages can be correlated with the degree of low-pressure anatexis to the east. The observed contrasts in both the metamorphic and geochronologic evolution along the Himalayan belt can be related to the counterclockwise rotation of the Indian plate during the India-Asia collision. Such rotation, together with a shallower dip of the intracontinental subduction plane to the east, would explain the delay in nappe stacking, a warmer thickened upper crust, and the observed decrease in ages from west to east.

INTRODUCTION

Contrasting pressure-temperature-time (*P-T-t*) paths and diachronous emplacement of syntectonic granites in the same metamorphic unit, along continuous exposures of a mountain range, can be explained by one or a combination of the following parameters: (1) different initial geometric or thermal conditions (number of units involved, initial depth of burial, variations in the mantle, and crustal heat production); (2) differences in tectonic processes (continuous or discontinuous); (3) differences in unroofing processes (geomorphic erosion or tectonic extension) (England and Thompson, 1984; Mercier et al., 1991).

A compilation of the recent metamorphic and geochrono-

logic studies along the Higher Himalaya provides evidence for such contrasting *P-T-t* paths and differential cooling of leucogranites of Oligocene to Miocene age (Pognante, 1993) (Fig. 1). Eclogites (Pognante and Spencer, 1991; Guillot et al., 1995a) and high-*P* granulites (Pognante et al., 1993) have been reported only in the western part of the Himalayan belt. The contrasting Himalayan metamorphic evolution has been attributed to rapid exhumation of the deepest rocks in the western part of the belt, while in the eastern part slower collision rates favored thermal relaxation of the thickened Indian crust, which promoted pervasive anatexis (Pognante, 1993). While this interpretation can explain the contrasting thermal evolution, the contrasting *P-T-t* evolution and the occurrence of high-*P* rocks

Guillot, S., Cosca, M., Allemand, P., and Le Fort, P., 1999, Contrasting metamorphic and geochronologic evolution along the Himalayan belt, *in* Macfarlane, A., Sorkhabi, R. B., and Quade, J., eds., Himalaya and Tibet: Mountain Roots to Mountain Tops: Boulder, Colorado, Geological Society of America Special Paper 328.

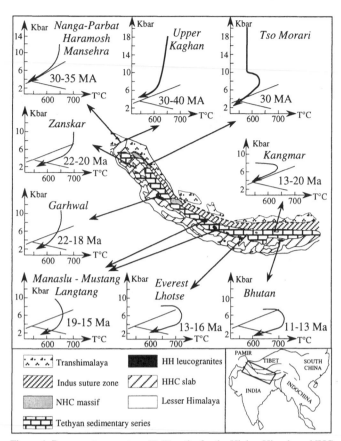

Figure 1. Pressure-temperature (*P-T*) paths for the Higher Himalaya. NHC massif: North Himalayan Crystalline massifs (Upper Kaghan, Tso Morari, and Kangmar); HHC slab: High Himalayan Crystalline slab (Nanga-Parbat Haramosh, Manshera, Zanskar, Garhwal, Manaslu, Mustang, Langtang, Everest-Lhotse, and Bhutan). The ages correspond to $^{40}Ar/^{39}Ar$ micas cooling ages from the High Himalayan (HH) leucogranites in the temperature range 300–400 °C. References are given in Table 1.

solely in the northwestern part can also be related to variations in the dip of the subduction plane and the counterclockwise rotation of the Indian plate. In this chapter we attempt to correlate geometric variations of the continental subduction plane with the counterclockwise rotation of the Indian plate in order to explain (1) the exclusive occurrence of high-*P* rocks in the northwestern part of the belt; (2) the contrasting *P-T* paths all along the Higher Himalaya; and (3) the striking variation in crystallization and cooling ages of metamorphic rocks and High Himalayan leucogranites from west to east. This last point is supported on the basis of new muscovite and biotite $^{40}Ar/^{39}Ar$ age data from two High Himalayan leucogranites (Mugu-Mustang from central Nepal and Kula-Kangri from southern Tibet), together with published ages of other leucogranitic plutons along the Himalaya.

METAMORPHIC EVOLUTION OF THE HIMALAYA

Metamorphic rocks are present along the internal part of the Himalayan belt in three distinctive zones: (1) in the North

Himalayan Crystalline massifs, located between the Indus-Tsangpo suture zone in the north and the Tethyan sedimentary cover to the south; (2) in the High Himalayan Crystalline slab, bounded to the north by the South Tibetan detachment system and to the south by the Main Central thrust; and (3) in the Lesser Himalaya. The North Himalayan Crystalline massifs and the High Himalayan Crystalline slab define the Higher Himalaya investigated in this chapter. Broadly speaking, two main Eocene to Miocene Himalayan metamorphic phases are recognized in the Higher Himalaya (Brunel and Kienast, 1986; Pêcher and Le Fort, 1986; Hodges and Silverberg, 1988; Searle et al., 1987; Pognante et al., 1990): an early Eohimalayan metamorphic phase (M1) that corresponded to the pressure peak and a decompressional Neohimalayan phase (M2) that often corresponds to the temperature peak and is generally associated with migmatization in the High Himalayan Crystalline slab. The available *P-T* estimates on the deepest levels of selected regions of the Higher Himalaya for which there are geochronological data summarized in Table 1. In this contribution, we do not consider the late Pliocene thermal events of the High Himalayan Crystalline slab described in the western Himalaya (Zeitler and Chamberlain, 1991) and in the central Himalaya (Copeland et al., 1990; Harrison et al., 1995).

Early stage M1

In metapelitic and basic lithologies, evidence of high-*P* relics (granulites and eclogites) decreases eastward, from Pakistan to Bhutan. In the Higher Himalaya, high-*P* garnet-bearing granulites and eclogites are common around the termination of the Nanga-Parbat-Haramosh syntaxis (northern Pakistan), south of the Main Mantle thrust (the Pakistani equivalent of the Indus-Tsangpo suture). The garnet-bearing granulites of Pakistan formed at an average pressure of 10 ± 3 kbar and temperature of 650 ± 50 °C (Greco et al., 1989; Treloar et al., 1989a; DiPietro, 1991; Pognante et al., 1993). Locally, in the Upper Kaghan valley, Eocene eclogites formed at higher pressure: 16 ± 2 kbar and 650 ± 50 °C (Pognante and Spencer, 1991). In contrast to the eastern part of the Himalayan belt, it is difficult to distinguish between north Pakistan, the North Himalayan Crystalline massif and the High Himalayan Crystalline slab sensu stricto because the different metamorphic units are invariably stacked within an imbricate thrust pile. However, higher grade rocks are stacked on top of lower grade rocks (Treloar et al., 1989a). In Ladakh, high-*P* rocks are present, and eclogites derived from metabasic and metapelitic rocks have been discovered in the Tso Morari massif south of the Indus-Tsangpo suture zone, referred to as one of the North Himalayan Crystalline massifs (Guillot et al., 1995a). The omphacite-garnet-glaucophane-rutile-quartz assemblage in the basic eclogites and the jadeite-garnet-paragonite-chloritoid-rutile-quartz assemblage in the metapelitic eclogites yield the highest metamorphic pressures recorded in the Himalayan belt, 20 ± 2 kbar at 550 ± 50 °C (de Sigoyer et al., 1997; Guillot et al., 1997). Farther to the east in another North Himalayan Crystalline massif, the Kangmar dome, there is no

TABLE 1. SUMMARY OF P-T-t DATA*

Zones	M1	M2	References[†]
Upper Kaghan	13–18 kbar 600–700 °C 55–43 Ma (Sm/Nd)	8–9 kbar 500–600 °C 40 Ma (U/Pb)	1, 2
North Pakistan	9–13 kbar 650–700 °C 38 Ma (Ar/Ar)	8–6 kbar 550–600 °C 35–30 Ma (Ar/Ar)	3, 4, 5
Tso Morari	18–22 kbar 500–600 °C	11–7 kbar 580–680 °C 30 Ma (Ar/Ar)	6
Kangmar	7–9 kbar 500–550 °C	6–7 kbar 600–650 °C 20–13 Ma (Ar/Ar)	7, 8, 9, 10 Pers. observation
Zanskar	8–10 kbar 650–720 °C 40–30 Ma (Ar/Ar)	5–7 kbar 650–700 °C 26–20 Ma (U-Pb, Ar/Ar)	11, 12, 13, 14, 15, 16, 17
Gahrwal	8–10 kbar 550–700 °C 35 Ma (Ar/Ar)	4–6 kbar 500–600 °C 22–18 Ma (Ar/Ar, Rb/Sr)	18, 19, 20
Central Nepal	8–10 kbar 650–700 °C 37–34 Ma (Rb/Sr, U/Pb, Ar/Ar)	5–7 kbar 650–750 °C 23–15 Ma (U/Pb, Rb/Sr, Ar/Ar)	21, 22, 23, 24 25, 26, 27, 28 29, 30, 31, 32
East Nepal	6–8 kbar 600–650 °C 25 Ma (Ar/Ar)	6–8 kbar/2–4 kbar 700–750 °C 24–21 Ma (Ar/Ar, U-Pb) 17–13 Ma (Ar/Ar, U-Pb)	33, 34, 35 36, 37, 38
Bhutan	6–8 kbar 550–650 °C	6–8 kbar/2–4 kbar 600–700 °C 13–11 Ma (Ar/Ar, U-Pb)	39, 40, 41 42, 43, 44

*Synthesis of P-T conditions of metamorphism of the middle-higher structural levels of the Higher Himalaya and representative ages of the M1 and M2 events.
[†]1 = Pognante and Spencer, 1991; 2 = Tonarini et al., 1993; 3 = Treloar et al., 1989b; 4 = DiPietro, 1991; 5 = Poganante et al., 1993; 6 = de Sigoyer et al, 1996; 7 = Burg et al., 1987; 8 = Debon et al., 1985; 9 = Maluski et al., 1988; 10 = Chen et al., 1990; 11 = Villa and Oddone, 1988; 12 = Pognante et al., 1990; 13 = Searle et al., 1992; 14 = Sorkhabi et al., 1993; 15 = Spring et al., 1993; 16 = Epard et al., 1995; 17 = Noble and Searle, 1995; 18 = Hodges and Silverberg, 1988; 19 = Stern et al., 1989; 20 = Metcalfe, 1993; 21 = Krummenacher, 1971; 22 = Pêcher and Le Fort, 1986; 23 = Deniel et al., 1987; 24 = Copeland et al., 1990; 25 = Inger and Harris, 1992; 26 = Mac Farlane et al., 1992; 27 = Parrish and Hodges, 1992; 28 = Guillot et al, 1994; 29 = Harrison et al., 1995; 30 = Vannay and Hodges, 1996; 31 = Hodges et al., 1996a; 32 = This volume; 33 = Schärer, 1984; Schärer et al., 1986; 34 = Brunel and Kienast, 1986; 35 = Hubbard et al., 1991; 36 = Pognante and Benna, 1993; 37 = Hodges et al., 1994; 38 = Hodges et al., 1996b; 39 = Dietrich and Gansser, 1981; 40 = Ferrara et al., 1983; 41 = Maluski et al., 1988; 42 = Hubbard et al., 1991; 43 = Swapp and Hollister, 1991; 44 = Edwards and Harrison, 1997.

evidence of high-*P* relics. Only upper amphibolite garnet + kyanite + staurolite assemblages have been described, suggesting *P-T* conditions of 8 ± 1 kbar and 550 ± 50 °C (Burg et al., 1987; Chen et al., 1990).

In the High Himalayan Crystalline slab, scattered relics of high-*P* granulites (12 ± 2 kbar and 750 ± 50 °C) have also been described in Zanskar, but were tentatively attributed to pre-Himalayan metamorphic event (e.g., Pognante et al., 1990). In this area, the M1 event took place at 8–10 kbar and 650–720 °C (Pognante et al., 1990). Farther to the east, evidence of high-*P* granulitic conditions during M1 is absent. From Gahrwal to Bhutan, in the vicinity of the Main Central thrust, M1 is characterized by garnet + kyanite + plagioclase + biotite + rutile ± K-feldspar metapelitic assemblages. They give similar metamorphic conditions: *P* = 6–10 kbar and *T* = 600–750 °C (Hodges and Silverberg, 1988; Pêcher and Le Fort, 1986; Swapp and Hollister,

1991; Inger and Harris, 1992; Metcalfe, 1993; Pognante and Benna, 1993).

Decompressional stage M2

In the North Himalayan Crystalline massifs, from northern Pakistan to southern Xizang, metamorphic rocks initially underwent exhumation under isothermal conditions within the kyanite stability field (Burg et al., 1987; Pognante and Spencer; 1991; Pognante et al., 1993; de Sigoyer et al., 1997). In the western part of the High Himalayan Crystalline slab (from Pakistan to Gahrwal), there is scattered evidence of migmatization. The end of the retrogression is solely characterized by low-*T* assemblages with muscovite or biotite ± chlorite ± margarite (Treloar et al., 1989a). In this part of the belt, M2 metamorphism is contemporaneous with a number of large-scale south-verging crustal nappes (Hodges and Silverberg, 1988; Treloar et al., 1989a). Farther to the east, the early granulitic metapelite assemblages were partially to completely transformed during M2 into high-T sillimanite + biotite–bearing assemblages, and the garnet-bearing basic granulites are transformed into high-T amphibolites. Although the P and T vary, the M2 event is generally related to decompression associated with increasing T (to 750 °C) in the 4–8 kbar range (Brunel and Kienast, 1986; Pêcher and Le Fort, 1986; Pognante and Lombardo, 1989; Inger and Harris, 1992). This metamorphic stage was associated with extensive migmatization and formation of leucogranitic melts in the middle crustal levels of the High Himalayan Crystalline slab (e.g., Le Fort et al., 1987). Structural and geochronological studies emphasize that the M2 metamorphic event was contemporaneous with motions along the Main Central thrust and the South Tibetan detachment system (Hodges et al., 1992). In the eastern part of the belt (Everest area and Bhutan), the retrogression continues in high-T conditions with widespread cordierite and andalusite development at the expense of garnet and sillimanite in the middle to upper structural levels of the High Himalayan Crystalline slab, indicating P-T conditions of 3 ± 1 kbar and 650–750 °C (Gansser, 1983; Brunel and Kienast, 1986; Swapp and Hollister, 1991; Pognante and Benna, 1993). This low-P high-T event was contemporaneous with a second migmatization, producing cordierite-bearing leucosomes.

GEOCHRONOLOGICAL EVOLUTION OF THE HIGHER HIMALAYA

Metamorphic ages for the M1 event are not well constrained. U/Pb rutile and zircon ages and a Sm-Nd garnet-clinopyroxene isochron give results of around 44–50 Ma from the Kaghan eclogites (Tonarini et al., 1993; Spencer and Gebauer, 1996). Occasional ^{40}Ar/^{39}Ar hornblende ages and Rb/Sr muscovite ages have been reported, and were tentatively ascribed to the M1 metamorphic event. Treloar et al. (1989b) reported ^{40}Ar/^{39}Ar cooling ages of 38 Ma for the M1 event in the High Himalayan Crystalline slab in north Pakistan, whereas ^{40}Ar/^{39}Ar, Rb/Sr cooling, and U/Pb ages of around 40–30 Ma have been reported in Zanskar (Searle et al., 1992; Sorkhabi et al., 1993; Spring et al., 1993), in Gahrwal (Hodges and Silverberg, 1988), and in central Nepal (Inger and Harris, 1992; Vannay and Hodges, 1996; Hodges et al., 1996a). Moreover, inheritance U/Pb monazite ages between 40 and 30 Ma from the Manaslu granite in central Nepal have been interpreted as representative of an earlier metamorphic event (Harrison et al., 1995). Hodges et al. (1994) reported ^{40}Ar/^{39}Ar hornblende ages of 25 Ma in the Dinggyê area (west of Everest), interpreted as the metamorphic age of the M1 event (Table 1). These data suggest that the M1 phase took place in middle Eocene–early Oligocene time in the western and central Himalaya and in late Oligocene time in the eastern Himalaya.

Geochronological data (^{40}Ar/^{39}Ar and Rb/Sr) around 30–35 Ma, directly related to the M2 metamorphic event, have been reported for north Pakistan by Treloar et al. (1989b) and Tonarini et al. (1993). From Zanskar to Everest, numerous ages between 22 and 15 Ma have been reported using different isotopic systems (^{40}Ar/^{39}Ar , U/Pb, Rb/Sr) related to the M2 event and motion along the Main Central thrust and the South Tibetan detachment system (Hubbard et al., 1991; Inger and Harris, 1992; Metcalfe, 1993; Parrish and Hodges, 1992; Spring et al., 1993; Vannay and Hodges, 1996). In the Kangmar dome, there is also evidence of Miocene ^{40}Ar/^{39}Ar cooling ages around 20–13 Ma, which are assigned to the M2 metamorphic event (Debon et al., 1985; Chen et al., 1990) (Table 1).

HIGH HIMALAYAN LEUCOGRANITES

The High Himalayan leucogranites are chiefly concentrated in the central and eastern Himalaya, from Gahrwal to Bhutan. They are scattered in Zanskar (e.g., Pognante et al., 1990), and are rare or absent in Pakistan, where they usually form dikes (Greco et al., 1989). From Gahrwal to Bhutan the leucogranites form kilometer-sized, lens-shaped synextensional laccoliths, emplaced above or below the South Tibetan detachment system (Gansser, 1983; Le Fort et al., 1987; Guillot et al., 1993). Geochemical studies indicate that the peraluminous Himalayan leucogranites were formed by low degrees of decompressional melting of the metasediments of the High Himalayan Crystalline slab during M2 retrogression during rapid denudation along the South Tibetan detachment system (Le Fort et al., 1987; Harris and Massey, 1994; Hodges et al., 1996a) and/or by rapid transport along an intermediate thrust (Swapp and Hollister, 1991). The present-day rapid exhumation of warm tectonic sheets along a crustal ramp in the Nanga-Parbat-Haramosh syntaxis and associated anatexis may be seen as a possible analogue to Himalayan Miocene evolution (Zeitler and Chamberlain, 1991).

As suggested by Pognante (1993), the leucogranites and the associated anatectic leucosomes have significant mineralogical differences. In Bhutan and eastern Nepal, they are characterized by the abundance of andalusite or sillimanite and cordierite (Ferrara et al., 1983; Gansser, 1983; Lombardo et al., 1993). In central Nepal, they contain solely sillimanite (Le Fort et al., 1987), whereas in Zanskar and north Pakistan the migmatitic leucosomes contain widespread kyanite (Pognante et al., 1990). The depths of emplacement of the High Himalayan leucogranites are similar, 12 ± 2 km (Guillot et al., 1995b), so the mineralogical differences are probably related to different P-T conditions of incongruent melting (e.g., Thompson, 1982). The presence of low-P minerals in the eastern part suggests a shallower depth of melting of the High Himalayan Crystalline slab.

Crystallization ages of the leucogranites

The crystallization ages of the leucogranites have been determined by U-Pb, Rb/Sr, and Ar/Ar dating. These studies show that an important period of leucogranite production occurred between 24 and 18 Ma from Zanskar to Everest. Noble and Searle (1995) reported ages of Zanskar leucogranites between 21 and 19.5 Ma. There are no U/Pb data for Gahrwal; however, the Gangotri granite was dated as 21 Ma by a Rb/Sr mineral isochron (Stern et al., 1989). In central Nepal, the Manaslu leucogranite was intensively studied. Early monazite data indicated a crystallization age of 25 Ma (Deniel et al., 1987). Reexamination by the Ar/Ar method on hornblende mineral yields a 22–23 Ma age (Guillot et al., 1994), consistent with a monazite age (Harrison et al., 1995). Another group of ages around 19–18 Ma for the Manaslu pluton suggest two distinct episodes of melting (Deniel et al., 1987; Guillot and Le Fort, 1995). U/Pb dating of migmatitic leucosomes as 22.5 Ma and 18.5 Ma in the Formation I of the High Himalayan Crystalline slab, south of the Annapurna-Manaslu area, confirms the existence of successive episodes of melting related to successive episodes of extensional deformation along the South Tibetan detachment system (Hodges et al., 1996a). In the Langtang valley, east of the Manaslu, Parrish and Hodges (1992) reported ages of around 21 Ma. To the east the Makalu granite yields U/Pb ages of 24.0 ± 0.4 Ma and 21.9 ± 0.2 Ma (Schärer, 1984). The Rongbuk granite has been investigated extensively, and U-Th-Pb dating suggest crystallization ages between 23 Ma and 19.5 Ma (Copeland et al., 1988; Hodges et al., 1992, 1996b; Harrison et al., 1995). These ages have been interpreted as reflecting inheritance of premagmatic zircon (Copeland et al., 1988). An older, mylonitized granite sill in the Rongbuk area is dated as 16.6 Ma by the U/Pb method (Hodges et al., 1996b). Younger leucogranites are also present, particularly in the eastern part of the High Himalayan Crystalline slab. In the Nyalam and Mount Everest areas, Schärer et al. (1986) reported U/Pb ages of 14.3 ± 0.6 and 16.8 ± 0.6, respectively. Moreover, the Kula-Kangri granite in Bhutan gives U/Pb on monazite ages of 12.5 Ma (Edwards and Harrison, 1997).

^{40}Ar/^{39}Ar cooling ages of the leucogranites

Most of the High Himalayan leucogranites have been dated by the Ar/Ar and K/Ar methods on micas. In Zanskar and Gahrwal, ages are in the range 22 to 18 Ma; in central Nepal, ages are between 19 and 15 Ma; in the Everest area, ages are between 13 and 16 Ma; and in Bhutan, ages are between 11 and 13 Ma (Fig. 1). (Dietrich and Gansser, 1981; Debon et al., 1985; Maluski et al., 1988; Stern et al., 1989; Copeland et al., 1990; Inger and Harris, 1992; Metcalfe, 1993; Sorkhabi et al., 1993, 1996; Guillot et al., 1994; Hodges et al., 1994).

In order to determine the cooling ages of other High Himalayan leucogranites and to discuss the different cooling ages along the belt, we have chosen to study two poorly dated leucogranites: the Mugu granite, located in central Nepal, which crops out 50 km north of the South Tibetan detachment system (Le Fort and France-Lanord, 1994), and the Kula-Kangri granite, located 800 km farther to the east, in the Lhozag region, which intrudes the top of the Higher Himalayan Crystalline slab, just below the detachment system (Pêcher et al., 1994) (Fig. 2).

Methodology. Eight samples were selected (five for Kula-

Kangri and three for Mugu-Mustang). They are typically medium-grained (<1 cm) granites, comprising quartz, plagioclase, K-feldspar, muscovite, biotite ± tourmaline. We obtained 12 populations of pure, unaltered muscovite and biotite after crushing by density contrast and magnetic separation. Standards and samples were irradiated in the U.S. Geological Survey TRIGA reactor at Denver, Colorado (Dalrymple et al., 1981). The standard biotite HD-B1 was used for the ^{40}Ar/^{39}Ar experiments using a refined K/Ar age of 24.21 Ma (Hess and Lippolt, 1994). We performed ^{40}Ar/^{39}Ar analyses using a low blank furnace at the Université de Lausanne on a MAP 215-50 mass spectrometer with an electron multiplier. Typical ^{40}Ar blank values were 4×10^{-15} mol at temperatures below 1000 °C rising to 9×10^{-15} mol at 1600 °C. The raw isotopic data, extrapolated to time zero, were corrected for backgrounds, blank, mass discrimination, radioactive decay, and interfering isotopic reactions. Nine mineral fractions gave satisfactory results. All ages and errors are given at the 2σ level of uncertainty.

Results. The ^{40}Ar/^{39}Ar age spectra of the bulk mica separates show common features with a general apparent age perturbation in the first 10% of ^{39}Ar released, followed by age plateaus or near plateaus at higher temperature extraction steps (Fig. 3). Data plotted on ^{39}Ar/^{40}Ar vs. ^{36}Ar/^{40}Ar isochron diagrams give the following results: Mugu-Mustang muscovite ages are 15.4 ± 0.2 Ma and 15.9 ± 0.2 Ma, and biotites are 16.0 ± 0.8 Ma and 16.7 ± 0.2 Ma; Kula-Kangri muscovites are 10.9 ± 0.4 Ma and 11.0 ± 0.2 Ma and biotites range between 11.0 ± 0.2 Ma and 12.8 ± 0.4 Ma. The ^{40}Ar/^{39}Ar age spectra are consistent with the isochron ages (Table 2). Data steps regressed in

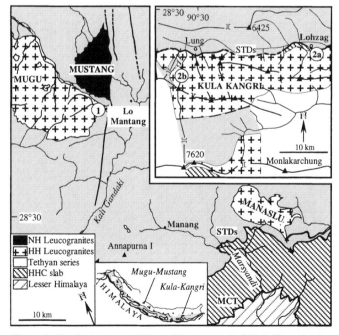

Figure 2. Geologic maps of Mugu-Mustang and of Kula-Kangri (after Guillot et al., 1995b). Sample locations: 1: samples LO93 and LO94; 2a: sample KG23; 2b: samples KG28, KG30 and KG33. NH, North Himalayan; HH, High Himalayan; HHC, High Himalayan crystalline.

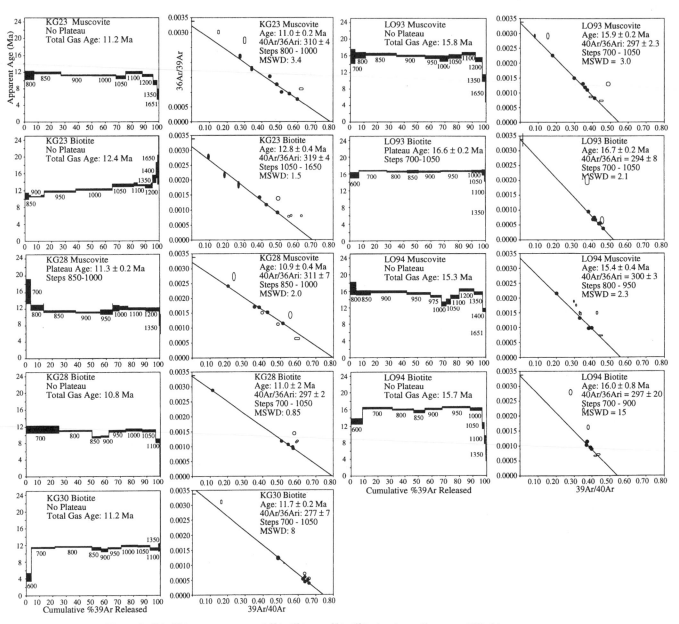

Figure 3. ⁴⁰Ar/³⁹Ar age spectra and ³⁹Ar/⁴⁰Ar vs. ³⁶Ar/⁴⁰Ar isochron diagrams. Filled boxes represent the 2σ error for each temperature step as indicated. Data used for the regression of the isochrons are shown as filled ellipses. MSWD is mean square of weighed deviates. GSA Data Repository item 9889 is available on request from the GSA document secretary at: GSA, P. O. Box 3140, Boulder, CO 80301.

the isochron calculations yield initial ⁴⁰Ar/³⁶Ar intercepts very close to modern atmosphere (295.5). Nonetheless, the biotites, without exception, have slighty older ages than the muscovites from the same sample, indicating that these samples are partially contaminated by excess ⁴⁰Ar. Therefore, the biotite ages should be interpreted as maxima. As exemplified by the Manaslu granite (Copeland et al., 1990; Guillot et al., 1994), both muscovite and biotite cooling ages are nearly identical, indicating very rapid cooling in the range 350–300 °C, the nominal closure temperatures for muscovite and biotite, respectively (McDougall and Harrison, 1988).

The consistency of our muscovite and biotite ages with earlier K/Ar and ⁴⁰Ar/³⁹Ar data from both granites (Krummenacher, 1971; Dietrich and Gansser, 1981; Debon et al., 1985; Maluski et al., 1988) leads us to conclude that the Mustang granite and the Kula-Kangri granite cooled through the 300–350 °C temperature range at 15–17 Ma and 11–13 Ma, respectively. As first pointed out by Villa and Oddone (1988), and on the basis of these new data, together with published data, it appears that cooling ages of High Himalayan leucogranites decrease eastward from 22–18 Ma to 11–13 Ma over a distance of 1,500 km from Zanskar to Bhutan (Fig. 1).

TABLE 2. SUMMARY OF ^{40}Ar/^{39}Ar RESULTS

Sample	Mineral*	Age Spectrum (Ma ± 3σ)†	^{39}Ar$_p$§ (%)	Isochron Age (Ma ± 2σ)**	Regressed Steps	^{39}Ar$_i$‡ (%)	^{40}Ar/^{36}Ar$_i$	MSWD
KG23	Ms	11.2	....	11.0 ± 0.2800–1000	68	310 ± 4	3.4
KG23	Bt	12.4	....	12.8 ± 0.41050–1650	35	319 ± 4	1.5
KG28	Ms	**11.3 ± 0.2**	52	10.9 ± 0.4850–1000	57	311 ± 7	2.0
KG28	Bt	10.8	....	11.0 ± 0.2700–1050	82	297 ± 2	0.9
KG30	Bt	11.2	....	11.7 ± 0.2700–1050	88	277 ± 7	8.0
LO93	Ms	15.8		15.9 ± 0.2700–1050	82	297 ± 2	3.0
LO93	Bt	**16.6 ± 0.2**	72	16.7 ± 0.2700–1050	92	294 ± 8	2.1
LO94	Ms	15.3	....	15.4 ± 0.4800–950	60	300 ± 3	2.3
LO94	Bt	15.7	....	16.0 ± 0.8700–900	59	297 ± 20	15.0

*Ms = muscovite; Bt = biotite.
†Plateau ages given in bold type.
§^{39}Ar$_p$(%) = percentage of total ^{39}Ar evolved from heating steps on the plateau.
**Isochron ages were calculated using fitting algorithms from York, 1969.
‡39Ar$_i$(%) = percentage of total ^{39}Ar evolved from heating steps used for regression.

DISCUSSION

In the western part of the Himalaya (north Pakistan and Ladakh), the *P-T-t* path is relatively well constrained, which indicates middle Eocene High-*P* metamorphism, followed by rapid cooling during late Eocene time. As suggested by Treloar et al. (1989b), the main period of crustal thickening occurred between 50 and 40 Ma, followed by rapid exhumation around 30 Ma. The Zanskar region appears as a transition area with an early High-*P* evolution around 30–40 Ma, followed by a slight temperature decrease during M2 at around 20 Ma. In the central part of the belt (Gahrwal and central Nepal), the late Eocene metamorphic stage underwent advanced reequilibration during the Miocene, with extensive melting between 23 and 18 Ma, followed by regional cooling below 300 °C between 18 and 16 Ma. The eastern part of the belt records two successive evolutions. In its northern part (Kangmar dome), the earlier metamorphic evolution is similar to those observed in Ladakh and north Pakistan, without evidence of high pressure. In contrast, the southern part (Everest-Makalu and Bhutan) records the latest metamorphic and anatectic evolution between 17 and 12 Ma, characterized by low pressures and high temperatures. In summary, the internal zone of the Himalayan belt records a well-defined, contrasting metamorphic and geochronologic evolution from west to east.

Variable dip of the subduction plane

The initial burial conditions of the North Himalayan Crystalline massifs decrease from 60–70 km (Tso Morari and Kaghan) to 30–35 km (Kangmar) from west to east (Fig. 4A). This observation could be interpreted in two ways: (1) the North Himalaya massifs recorded the same burial all along the belt but the indenter geometry of the western part favored eclogite exhumation; or (2) the dip of the intracontinental subduction plane decreased from west

to east during the progressive eastward suturing of the Neo-Tethys. Similarly, from west to east along the High Himalayan Crystalline slab, we observe a decrease of the maximum burial from 40–45 km to 25–30 km (Fig. 4B), indicating the possibility of a variation of the dip of the subduction plane. The following model is based on available metamorphic and geochronologic data presented here and is likely to evolve as more data become available, particularly for the North Himalayan Crystalline massifs. There is a strong correlation between a hypothetical dip variation of the subduction plane

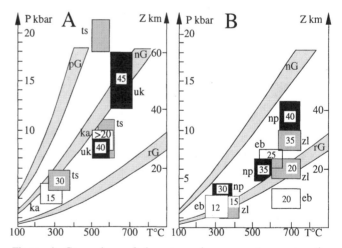

Figure 4. Comparison of the retrograde pressure-temperature-time (*P-T-t*) evolution of the different metamorphic Himalayan zones (z) in a *P-T-z-t* diagram. A: North Himalayan Crystalline massifs. B: High Himalayan Crystalline slab. The representative ages correspond to a synthesis of the available geochronologic data (see Table 1 for references); the uncertainty is ±5 Ma. The evolving geotherms of thickened crust are from Mercier et al. (1991), according to the thermal parameters of England and Thompson (1984). pG: perturbed geotherm; nG: normal geotherm; rG, relaxed geotherm; ts, Tso Morari; uk, Upper Kaghan; ka, Kangmar; np, North Pakistan; zl, Zanskar to Langtang; eb, Everest-Bhutan.

and the simultaneous motion along the Main Central thrust and the South Tibetan detachment system. From Pakistan to Bhutan, the estimate of the total shortening accommodated along the Main Central thrust increases from around 100 km to around 200 km (Pêcher, 1978; Searle et al., 1987; Schelling and Arita, 1991; Epard et al., 1995), whereas the vertical unroofing of the High Himalayan Crystalline slab deduced from the barometric data decreases from around 40 km to 30 km. In the same way, the estimates of displacement along the South Tibetan detachment system decreases to the east. Herren (1987) estimated a displacement of 19 km in Zanskar, Hodges et al. (1992) estimated it as around 6 km in the Everest area, and we estimated a displacement of around 3.5 km in Bhutan (Guillot et al., 1995b). Although we have no direct evidence to reject the first solution mentioned, an eastward decrease in the dip of the paleo-subduction plane remains compatible with the present-day geometry of the Himalayan belt. In the eastern part of the belt, the depth of the top of the Indian continental crust subducted below the Himalaya does not exceed 40 km (Zhao et al., 1993). This is consistent with seismicity (Ten Ji Wen, 1981) and the gravity studies of the southernmost Tibetan plateau, which suggest that flat underthrusting of the Indian upper mantle extends about 200 km north of the suture zone (Molnar, 1988; Makovsky et al., 1996). In the western part of the belt, seismic data are more consistent with a steeper continental subduction plane and a continental subduction of at least 150 km below the Pamir-Hindu Kush (Chatelain et al., 1980; Roecker, 1982; Baranowski et al., 1984) and are directly related to the indenter geometry of the Indian plate (Mattauer, 1986; Treloar and Coward, 1991). Consequently, we interpret the present-day ~100 km width of the belt in the western part and the ~200 km width in the eastern part as being directly related to an eastward decrease in the dip of the subducting plane (Fig. 5).

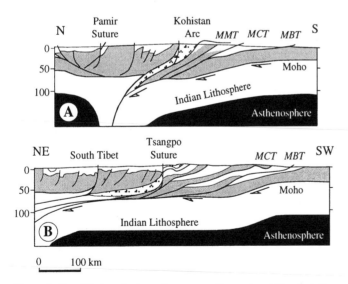

Figure 5. Simplified geologic sections across the western (A) and eastern (B) Himalaya showing the west-east geometric differences in the dip of the continental subduction and of the main thrusts and the width of the belt (modified from Mattauer, 1986). MMT, Main Mantle thrust; MCT, Main Central thrust; MBT, Main Boundary thrust.

Thermal evolution and cooling during exhumation

England and Thompson (1984) and Mercier et al. (1991) showed that the maximum temperature recorded during the exhumation of the metamorphic rocks increases with deeper initial burial conditions. In contrast, along the High Himalayan Crystalline slab, temperatures increased during exhumation in the less-buried rocks. Thus, if a variation in the dip of the paleosubduction plane explains the difference of initial burial conditions from west to east, it cannot explain the temperature increase of the High Himalayan Crystalline slab (Fig. 1) and the younger cooling ages recorded toward the east. Villa and Oddone (1988) suggested both diachronic indentation of the Indian plate and differential exhumation as causes for the decreasing east-west granite cooling age pattern.

As the High Himalayan leucogranite formation and emplacement is related to the motion of the South Tibetan detachment system (Guillot et al., 1993, 1994; Harris and Massey, 1994), the age differences between the Manaslu and the Everest granites have been previously interpreted as a result of diachronous extension along the detachment system (Guillot et al., 1994; Hodges et al., 1994). The compilation of the leucogranite ages from Zanskar (Pognante et al., 1990; Noble and Searle, 1995), Annapurna-Manaslu area (Guillot et al., 1994 ; Harrison et al., 1995; Hodges et al., 1996a) at 23–18 Ma, Rongbuk valley (Hodges et al., 1996b) and Kula-Kangri (Edwards and Harrison, 1997) at 16.6 Ma and 12.5 Ma, respectively, seem to confirm a diachronism all along the South Tibetan detachment system. Moreover, Hodges et al. (1996a) showed that they were also multiple stages of movement of the detachment system in a single transect. Even though the diachronous crystallization and cooling ages of High Himalayan leucogranites could be eventually related to diachronous motion along the South Tibetan detachment system, the younger ages of the M1 metamorphic event and the temperature increase during M2 toward the east should have alternative explanations. We choose to discuss only the *P-T-t* evolution of the High Himalayan Crystalline slab because of the better geochronological constraints. Mercier et al. (1991) suggested two possiblities to explain the contrasting *P-T-t* evolution recorded by metamorphic rocks. Variable numbers of units are involved in the nappe stacking or diachronic nappe stacking. In the Himalayan belt, there is no evidence for a variation in the number of units involved in the nappe piling. The detailed geochronologic studies show, however, that the nappe stacking in the western part of the range started between 50 and 30 Ma and terminated before 20 Ma (Treloar and Rex, 1990). In contrast, east of central Himalaya, nappe stacking took place later, as suggested by absence of ages older than 25 Ma (e.g., Hodges et al., 1994). Other evidence of later thrusting in the eastern part of the belt is given by the timing of slip on the Gangdese thrust (southeastern Tibet), estimated to be 27–23 Ma, suggesting that most Main Central thrust activity was later (Yin et al., 1994), between 24 and 21 Ma. In Everest and Bhutan, the younger U/Pb ages suggest that there was some later tectonic activity along the South Tibetan detachment system (Edward and Harrison, 1997; Hodges et al., 1996b). Thus, we must explain a delay of about 10–20 m.y. from west to east for development of the nappe pile.

Because the variations in the cooling and unroofing histories occur over ~1,500 km, the relative motion of the Indian plate with respect to Eurasia during the Himalayan collision should be considered. The initial India-Asia encounter at around 52 Ma in the northwestern part of the belt was followed by an eastward progressive suturing as young as 41 Ma (e.g., Rowley, 1996). This diachroneity is related to the counterclockwise rotation of India (Patriat and Achache, 1984; Klootwijk et al., 1985) (Fig. 6). The counterclockwise motion was contemporaneous with a dramatic northward deceleration in the relative motion of India between 55+ Ma and 40 Ma from 18 cm/yr to 5 cm/yr (Patriat and Achache, 1984; Klootwijk et al., 1992). Moreover, Patriat and Achache (1984) documented a minimum of 20° continuous counterclockwise rotation of the Indian plate since 45 Ma. We propose that this rotation at the plate tectonic scale during and after the initial India-Asia contact had two consequences: (1) it could have induced the delay of around 10–20 m.y. in the nappe stacking from west to east, and (2) the slower rate of subduction during the eastward progressive suturing could have induced a warmer Indian lithosphere, as shown by Staudigel and King (1992).

Thus, we proposed that the exhumation of the High Himalayan Crystalline slab in the eastern part of the belt that occurred with the increase of temperature is related to a delay in the nappe stacking and by an eastward decrease of the rates of convergence, and the resultant shallowing of the dip of continental subduction plane. Our conclusions are compatible with the observations of Yin et al. (1994), who suggested that no thrust was active before 35 Ma in the eastern part of the Indian continental margin. Thus, it suggests that the main part of the India-Asia convergence was not accommodated before 35 Ma by intracontinental thrusting of the Indian crust in the eastern part, but by other tectonic processes such as crustal shortening along major crustal-scale thrusts farther north of the suture zone (Chang, 1986) or by tectonic extrusion along major strike-slip faults such as the Red River Fault (Tapponnier et al., 1986).

CONCLUSION

A working hypothesis is developed for the contrasting metamorphic and geochronologic evolution of the internal zone of the Himalayan belt, incorporating variations of the dip of the intracontinental subduction plane and delay in nappe stacking. Rapid continental subduction between 50–55 Ma and 35 Ma and the initial indenter geometry of the northwestern Indian margin favored a cold thermal regime and a steep subduction. In contrast, in the eastern part of the belt a lower convergence rate and a later frontal collision favored a warmer lithosphere and a flatter continental subduction, respectively. In the west-

ern domain, exhumation of the metamorphic rocks started immediately after the peak of metamorphism during an earlier nappe stacking and before the thermal relaxation of the thickenned crust. In this case, the steep geometry of the crustal-stacking wedge associated with a rapid convergence rate before 35 Ma could have favored rapid exhumation and reinforced the thermal screen effect. In contrast, in the eastern part, a late tectonic exhumation favored thermal relaxation and induced a temperature rise. Moreover, a shallower geometry of the crustal-stacking wedge, reinforced by the global decrease of the subduction rate after 35 Ma, favored a slower exhumation and a temperature increase during decompression. The later production and cooling of High Himalayan leucogranites at lower pressure and higher temperature toward the east remains compatible with this orogen-scale thermal and geometric evolution.

We propose that this contrasting west-east thermal and mechanical evolution is directly related to the initial India-Asia encounter in the northwestern part of the belt, followed by eastward suturing associated with the counterclockwise rotation of India. As a consequence, the India-Asia convergence was immediately accommodated by Indian intracontinental thrusting in the northwestern part, whereas in the eastern part of the belt deformation was initially accommodated by Asian deformation.

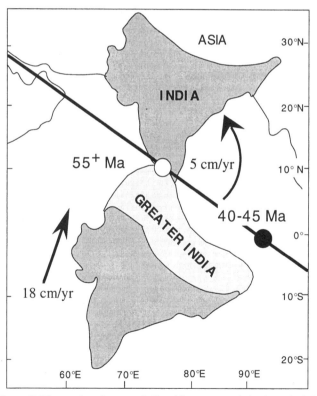

Figure 6. Kinematics of greater India with respect to Asia since the initial India-Asia contact ca. 50–55 Ma in the western indenter and 40–45 Ma in the eastern indenter, showing the northward speed of the Indian plate before and after 55–50 Ma (data from Patriat and Achache, 1984; Klootwijk et al., 1985, 1992; Rowley, 1996). The thicker line indicates the inferred position of the Asian margin prior to the collision (after Tapponnier et al., 1986).

ACKNOWLEDGMENTS

We acknowledge the financial support of the CNRS-INSU by the IDYL-HIMALAYA program and the Swiss National Science Foundation. Discussions on the evolution of the Himalayan belt and on thermal processes with V. Gardien, J. de Sigoyer, A. Pêcher and J. M. Lardeaux were very stimulating. S. Guillot thanks J. Dipietro, K. Hodges, M. Searle, D. Spencer, and A. Whittington for useful comments during the 11th Himalayan-Karakorum-Tibet workshop (Flagstaff, Arizona, 1996). We thank P. Treloar for his constructive review of an earlier draft and F. Senebier for the mineral separations. Kazunori Arita, Kip Hodges, Rasoul Sorkhabi, and Igor Villa provided careful reviews that greatly improved the manuscript.

REFERENCES CITED

Baranowski, J., Armbuster, J., Seeber, L., and Molnar, P., 1984, Focal depths and fault plane solutions of eathquakes and active tectonics of the Himalaya: Journal of Geophysical Research, v. 89, p. 6918–6928.

Brunel, M., and Kienast, J. R., 1986, Etude pétrostructurale des chevauchements ductiles himalayens sur la transversale de l'Everest-Makalu (Népal Oriental): Canadian Journal of Earth Sciences, v. 23, p. 1117–1137.

Burg, J. P., Leyreloup, A., Girardeau, J., and Chen, G. M., 1987, Structure and metamorphism of a tectonically thickened continental crust: The Yalu Tsangpo suture zone (Tibet): Royal Society of London Philosophical Transactions, v. 321, p. 67–86.

Chang, C., 1986, Preliminary conclusions of the Royal Society and Academia Sinica 1985 Geotraverse of Tibet: Nature, v. 323, p. 501–507.

Chatelain, J. L., Roecker, S. W., Hatzfeld, D., and Molnar, P., 1980, Microearthquake seismicity and fault plane solutions in the Hindu-Kush region and their tectonic implications: Journal of Geophysical Research, v. 85, p. 1365–1387.

Chen, Z., Liu, Y., Hodges, K. V., Burchfiel, B. C., Royden, L. H., and Deng, C., 1990, The Kangmar Dome: A metamorphic core complex in southern Xizang (Tibet): Science, v. 250, p. 1552–1556.

Copeland, P., Parrish, R. R., and Harrison, T. M., 1988, Identification of inherited radiogenic Pb in monazite and its applications for U-Pb systematics: Nature, v. 333, p. 760–763.

Copeland, P., Harrison, T. M., and Le Fort, P., 1990, Age and cooling of the Manaslu granite: Implications for Himalayan tectonics: Journal of Volcanology and Geothermal Research, v. 44, p. 33–50.

Dalrymple, G. B., Alexander, E. C. Jr., Lanphere, M. A., and Kraker, G. P., 1981, Irradiation of samples for 40Ar/39Ar dating using the Geological Survey TRIGA reactor: U. S. Geological Survey Professional Paper 1176, 55 p.

Debon, F., Zimmerman, J. L., Liu, J. H., Jin, C. W., and Xu, R. H., 1985, Time relationships between magmatism, tectonics and metamorphism in three plutonic belts in southern Tibet: New K-Ar data: Geologische Rundschau, v. 74, p. 229–236.

Deniel, C., Vidal, A., Fernandez, A., and Le Fort, P., 1987, Isotopic study of the Manaslu granite (Himalaya, Nepal): Inferences on the age and source of Himalayan leucogranites: Contributions to Mineralogy and Petrology, v. 96, p. 78–82.

de Sigoyer J., Guillot, S., Lardeaux, J. M., and Mascle, G., 1996, HP-LT metabasalts and metapelites in the Himalayan belt (Tso Morari, NW Ladakh): 11th Himalaya-Karakoram-Tibet Worshop (Flagstaff, Arizona) Abstract volume: p. 42–43.

de Sigoyer, J., Guillot, S., Lardeaux, J. M., and Mascle, G., 1997, Occurences of glaucophane bearing eclogites in the Tso Morari dome (East-Ladakh, Internal Himalayan belt): European Journal of Mineralogy, v. 9, p. 1073–1083.

Dietrich, V., and Gansser, A., 1981, The leucogranites of the Bhutan Himalaya (crustal anatexis vs mantle melting): Bulletin Suisse de Minéralogie et Pétrographie, v. 61, p. 177–202.

DiPietro, J. A., 1991, Metamorphic pressure-temperature conditions of Indian plate rocks south of the Main Mantle Thrust, Lower Swat, Pakistan: Tectonics, v. 10, p. 742–757.

Edwards, M. A., and Harrison, T. M., 1997, When did the roof collapse? Late Miocene north-south extension in the High Himalaya revealed by Th-Pb monazite dating of the Khula Kangri granite: Geology, v. 25, p. 543–546.

England, P. C., and Thompson, A. B., 1984, Pressure-temperature-time paths of regional metamorphism I. Heat transfer during the evolution of regions of thickened continental crust: Journal of Petrology, v. 25, p. 894–928.

Epard, J. L., Steck, A., Vannay, J. C., and Hunziker, J., 1995, Tertiary Himalayan structures and metamorphism in the Kulu valley (Mandi-Khoksar transect of the Western Himalaya)—Shikar Beh Nappe and Crystalline Nappe: Schweizerische Mineralogische und Petrographische Mitteilungen, v. 75, p. 59–84.

Ferrara, G., Lombardo, B., and Tonarini, S., 1983, Rb/Sr geochronology of granites and gneisses from the Mount Everest region, Nepal Himalaya: Geologische Rundsch, v. 72, p. 119–136.

Gansser, A., 1983, Geology of the Bhutan Himalaya: Basel, Switzerland, Birkhaüser Verlag, 181 p.

Greco, A., Martinotti, G., Papritz, K., Ramsay, G. J., and Rey, R., 1989, The crystalline rocks of the Kaghan Valley (NE-Pakistan): Eclogae Geologicae Helvetiae, v. 82, p. 629–653.

Guillot, S., and Le Fort, P., 1995, Geochemical constraints on the bimodal origin of High Himalayan leucogranites: Lithos, v. 35, p. 221–234.

Guillot, S., Pêcher, A., Rochette, P., and Le Fort, P., 1993, The emplacement of the Manaslu granite (Central Nepal): Field and and magnetic susceptibility constraints, in Treolar, P. J., and Searle, M. P., eds., Himalayan tectonics: Geological Society of London Special Publication 74, p. 413–428.

Guillot, S., Hodges, K. V., Le Fort, P., and Pêcher, A., 1994, New constraints on the age of the Manaslu leucogranite: Evidence for episodic tectonic denudation in the Central Himalayas: Geology, v. 22, p. 559–562.

Guillot, S., Lardeaux, J. M., Mascle, G., and Colchen, M., 1995a, Un nouveau témoin du métamorphisme de haute-pression dans la chaîne himalayenne (Dôme du Tso Morari, Est Ladakh): Paris, Académie des Sciences, Comptes Rendues, v. 320, p. 931–936.

Guillot, S., Pêcher, A. and Le Fort, P., 1995b, Contrôles tectoniques et thermiques de la mise en place des leucogranites himalayens: Paris, Académie des Sciences, Comptes Rendus, v. 320, p. 55–61.

Guillot, S., de Sigoyer, J., Lardeaux, J. M., and Mascle, G., 1997, Eclogitic metasediments from the Tso Morari (Ladakh, Himalaya): Petrological evidence for continental subduction during India-Asia convergence: Contributions to Mineralogy and Petrology, v. 128, p. 197–212.

Harris, N., and Massey, J., 1994, Decompression and anatexis of Himalayan metapelites: Tectonics, v. 13, p. 1537–1546.

Harrison, T. M., Mckeegan, K. D., and Le Fort, P., 1995, Detection of inherited monazite in the Manaslu leucogranite by Pb-208/Th-232 ion microprobe dating: Crystallization age and tectonic implications: Earth and Planetary Science Letters, v. 133, p. 271–282.

Herren, E., 1987, Zanskar shear zone: Northeast-southwest extension within the Higher Himalayas (Ladakh, India): Geology, v. 15, p. 409–413.

Hess, J. C., and Lippolt, H. J., 1994, Compilation of K/Ar measurements on HD-B1 standard biotite 1994 status report: Bulletin of Liaison and Information of IUGS, subcommission of Geochronology, v. 12, p. 119–123.

Hodges, K. V., and Silverberg, D. S., 1988, Thermal evolution of the greater Himalaya, Garhwal, India: Tectonics, v. 73, p. 583–600.

Hodges, K. V., Parrish, R., Housh, T., Lux, D., Burchfiel, B. C., Royden, L., and Chen, Z., 1992, Simultaneous Miocene extension and shortening in the Himalaya orogen: Science, v. 258, p. 1466–1470.

Hodges, K. V., Hames, W. E., Olszewski, W., Burchfiel, B. C., Royden, L. H., and Chen, Z., 1994, Thermobarometric and 40Ar/39Ar geochronologic constraints on Eohimalayan metamorphism in the Dinggyê area, southern Tibet: Contributions to Mineralogy and Petrology, v. 117, p. 151–163.

Hodges, K. V., Parrish, R. R., and Searle, M. P., 1996a, Tectonic evolution of the central Annapurna Range, Nepalese Himalayas: Tectonics, v. 15,

p. 1264–1291.

Hodges, K. V., Bowring, S., Hawkins, D., and Davidek, K., 1996b, The age of the Rongbuk granite and Qomolangma detachment, Mount Everest region, Southern Tibet: 11th Himalaya-Karakorum-Tibet Workshop (Flagstaff, Arizona), Abstract volume: p. 63–64.

Hubbard, M., Royden, L., and Hodges, K., 1991, Constraints on unroofing rates in the High Himalaya, Eastern Nepal: Tectonics, v. 10, p. 287–298.

Inger, S., and Harris, B. W., 1992, Tectonothermal evolution of the High Himalayan Crystalline sequence, Langtang valley, Northern Nepal: Journal of Metamorphic Geology, v. 10, p. 439–452.

Klootwijk, C. T., Conaghan, P. J., and Powell, C. M., 1985, The Himalayan arc: Large-scale continental subduction, oroclinal bending and back-arc spreading: Earth and Planetary Science Letters, v. 75, p. 167–183.

Klootwijk, C. T., Gee, J. S., Peirce, J. W., Smith, G. M., and McFadden, P. L., 1992, An early India-Asia contact: Paleomagnetic constraints from Ninetyeast Ridge, ODP Leg 121: Geology, v. 20, p. 395–398.

Krummenacher, D., 1971, Géochronométrie des roches de l'Himalaya, in Recherches géologiques dans l'Himalaya du Népal, région de la Takkhola: Paris, Edition du Centre Nationale de la Recherche Scientifique, v. 6, p. 187–202.

Le Fort, P., and France-Lanord, C., 1994, Granites from Mustang and surrounding regions, Central Nepal: Nepal Geological Society Journal, v. 10, p. 79–80.

Le Fort, P., Cuney, C., Deniel, C., France-Lanord, C., Sheppard, S. M. F., Upreti, B. N., and Vidal, P., 1987, Crustal generation of the Himalayan leucogranites: Tectonophysics, v. 134, p. 39–57.

Lombardo, B., Pertusati, P., and Borghi, S., 1993, Geology and tectonometamorphic evolution of the eastern Himalaya along the Chomolungma-Makalu transect, in Treloar, P. J., and Searle, M. P., eds., Himalayan tectonics: Geological Society of London Special Publication 74, p. 341–356.

Macfarlane, A., Hodges, K. V., and Lux, D., 1992, A structural analysis of the Main Central thrust zone, Langtang National Park, Central Nepal Himalaya: Geological Society of America Bulletin, v. 104, p. 1389–1402.

Makovsky, Y., Klemperer, S. L., Liyan, H., Deyuan, L., and Team, P. I., 1996, Structural elements of the southern Tethyan Himalaya crust from wide-angle seismic data: Tectonics, v. 15, p. 997–1005.

Maluski, H., Matte, P., and Brunel, M., 1988, Argon39-Argon40 dating of metamorphic and plutonic events in the North and High Himalaya belts (Southern Tibet, China): Tectonics, v. 7, p. 299–326.

Mattauer, M., 1986, Intracontinental subduction, crust mantle décollement and crustal-stacking wedge in the Himalayas and other collision belts, in Coward, M. P., and Ries, A. C., eds., Collisions tectonics: Geological Society of London Special Publication 19, p. 37–50.

McDougall, I., and Harrison, T. M., 1988, Geochronology and thermochronology by the $^{40}Ar/^{39}Ar$ method: New York, Oxford University Press, 212 p.

Mercier, L., Lardeaux, J. M., and Davy, P., 1991, On the tectonic significance of retrograde P-T-t path in eclogites of the French Massif Central: Tectonics, v. 10, p. 131–140.

Metcalfe, R. P., 1993, Pressure, temperature and time constraints on metamorphic across the Main Central Thrust zone and High Himalayan slab in the Garhwal Himalaya, in Treloar, P. J., and Searle, M. P., eds., Himalayan tectonics: Geological Society of London Special Publication 74, p. 485–509.

Molnar, P., 1988, A review of geophysical constraints on the deep structure of the Tibetan Plateau, the Himalaya and the Karakorum, and their tectonic implications: Royal Society of London Philosophical Transactions, ser. A, v. 326, p. 33–38.

Noble, S. R., and Searle, M. P., 1995, Age of crustal melting and leucogranite formation from U-Pb zircon and monazite dating in the western Himalaya, Zanskar, India: Geology, v. 23, p. 1135–1138.

Parrish, R. R., and Hodges, K. V., 1992, Miocene (22 +/– 1 Ma) metamorphism and two stage of thrusting in the Greater Himalayan sequence, Annapurna Sanctuary, Nepal: Geological Society of America Abstracts with Programs, v. 25, no. 6, p. A174.

Patriat, P., and Achache, J., 1984, India-Eurasia collision chronology has implications for crustal shortening and driving mechanisms of plates: Nature, v. 311, p. 615–621.

Pêcher, A., 1978, Déformations et métamorphisme associés à une zone de cisaillement. Exemple du grand chevauchement central himalayen (M.C.T.), transversale des Annapurna et du Manaslu, Népal [thesis]: Grenoble, University of Grenoble, 310 p.

Pêcher, A., Guillot, S., and Le Fort, P., 1994, Geology of the Kula-Kangri (South Tibet): Nepal Geological Society Journal, v. 10, p. 98–100.

Pêcher, A., and Le Fort, P., 1986, The metamorphism in Central Himalaya, its relations with the thrust tectonic, in Le Fort, P., Colchen, M., and Montenat, C., eds., Evolution des domaines orogéniques d'Asie méridionale (de la Turquie à l'Indonésie): Science de la Terre, volume 47: Nancy, Editions de la Fondation Scientifique de la géologie et de ses applications, p. 285–309.

Pognante, U., 1993, Different P-T-t paths and leucogranite occurences along the High Himalayan Crystallines: Implications for subduction and collision along the northern Indian margin: Geodinamica Acta, v. 6, p. 5–17.

Pognante, U., and Benna, P., 1993, Metamorphic zonation, migmatization and leucogranites along the Everest transect of Eastern Nepal and Tibet: Record of an exhumation history, in Treolar, P. J., and Searle, M. P., eds., Himalayan tectonics: Geological Society of London Special Publication 74, p. 323-340.

Pognante, H., and Lombardo, B., 1989, Metamorphic evolution of the High Himalayan Crystallines in SE Zanskar, India: Journal of Metamorphic Geology, v. 7, p. 9–17.

Pognante, U., and Spencer, D. A., 1991, First record of eclogites from the High Himalayan belt, Kaghan valley (northern Pakistan): European Journal of Mineralogy, v. 3, p. 613–618.

Pognante, U., Castelli, D., Benna, P., Genovese, G., Oberli, F., Meir, M., and Tonarini, S., 1990, The crystalline units of High Himalayas in the Lahul-Zanskar region (northwest India): Metamorphic-tectonic history and geochronology of the collided and imbricated Indian plate: Geological Magazine, v. 127, p. 101–116.

Pognante, U., Benna, P., and Le Fort, P., 1993, High-pressure metamorphism in the High Himalayan Crystallines of the Stak valley, northeastern Nanga-Parbat-Haramosh syntaxis, Pakistan Himalaya, in Treolar, P. J., and Searle, M. P., eds., Himalayan tectonics: Geological Society of London Special Publication 74, p. 161–172.

Roecker, S. W., 1982, Velocity structure of the Pamir–Indu Kush region: Possible evidence of subducted crust: Journal of Geophysical Research, v. 87, p. 945–959.

Rowley, D. B., 1996, Age of initiation of collision between India and Asia: A review of stratigraphic data: Earth and Planetary Science Letters, v. 145, p. 1–13.

Schärer, U., 1984, The effect of initial ^{230}Th disequilibrium on young U-Pb ages: The Makalu case, Himalaya: Earth and Planetary Science Letters, v. 67, p. 191–204.

Schärer, U., Xu, R. H., and Allegre, C. J., 1986, U-Th-Pb systematics and age of Himalayan leucogranites, South Tibet: Earth and Planetary Science Letters, v. 77, p. 35–48.

Schelling, D., and Arita, K., 1991, Thrust tectonics, crustal shortening, and the structure of the far-eastern Nepal Himalaya: Tectonics, v. 10, p. 851–862.

Searle, M. P., Windley, B. F., Coward, M. P., Cooper, D. J. W., Rex, A. J., Li, T., Xiao, X., Jan, M. Q., Thakur, V. C., and Kumar, S., 1987, The closing of Tethys and the tectonics of the Himalaya: Geological Society of American Bulletin, v. 98, p. 678–701.

Searle, M. P., Waters, D. J., Rex, D. C., and Wilson, R. N., 1992, Pressure-temperature and time constraints on Himalayan metamorphism from eastern Kashmir and western Zanskar: Geological Society of London Journal, v. 149, p. 753–773.

Sorkhabi, R. B., Jain, A. K., Itaya, T., Nishimura, S., Manickavasagam, R., and Lal, N., 1993, K/Ar cooling ages from Zanskar Himalaya: Implications for the tectonics and exhumation of Higher Himalayan metamorphic complex: Current Science, v. 65, p. 687–693.

Sorkhabi, R. B., Stump, E., Foland, K. A. and Jain, A. K., 1996, Fission-track and $^{40}Ar/^{39}Ar$ evidence for episodic denudation of the Gangotri granites in the Garhwal Higher Himalaya, India: Tectonophysics, v. 260, p. 187–199.

Spencer, D. A., and Gebauer, D., 1996, SHRIMP evidence for a Permian protolith age and a 44 Ma age for the Himalayan eclogites, Upper Kaghan, Pakistan: Implications for the subduction of Tethys and the subdivision terminology of the NW Himalaya: 11th Himalaya-Karakoram-Tibet Workshop (Flagstaff, Arizona), Abstract volume: p. 147–150.

Spring, L., Bussy, F., Vannay, J. C., Huon, S., and Cosca, M., 1993, Early Permian granitic dykes of alkaline affinity in the Indian High Himalayan of Upper Lahul and SE Zanskar: Geochemical characterization and geotectonic implications: *in* Treolar, P. J., and Searle, M. P., eds., Himalayan Tectonics: Geological Society of London Special Publication 74, p. 251–264.

Staudigel, H., and King, S., 1992, Ultrafast subduction: The key to slab recycling efficiency and mantle differenciation: Earth and Planetary Science Letters, v. 109, p. 517–530.

Stern, C. R., Kligfield, R., Schelling, D., Virdi, N. S., Futa, K., Peterman, Z. E., and Amini, H., 1989, The Bhagirathi leucogranite of the High Himalayas (Garhwal, India); age, petrogenesis, and tectonic implications, *in* Malinconico, L. L., and Lillie, R. J., eds., Geological Society of America Special Paper 232, p. 33–46.

Swapp, S. M., and Hollister, L. S., 1991, Inverted metamorphism within the Tibetan slab of Bhutan: Evidence for a tectonically transported heatsource: Canadian Mineralogist, v. 29, p. 1019–1041.

Tapponnier, P., Peltze, G., and Armijo, R., 1986, On the mechanics of the collision between India and Asia: in Coward, M. P., and Riess, A. C., eds., Collision tectonics: Geological Society of London Special Publication 19, p. 115–157.

Ten Ji Wen, 1981, Characteristics of geophysical fields and plate tectonics of the Quinghai-Xigang plateau and its neighbouring regions: Procedures on Symposium on Tibet Plateau: Beijing, Science Press, p. 633–649.

Thompson, A. B., 1982, Dehydratation melting of pelitic rocks and the generation of H_2O-undersaturated granitic liquids: American Journal of Sciences, v. 282, p. 1567–1595.

Tonarini, S., Villa, I., Oberli, M., Meier, F., Spencer, D. A., Pognante, U., and Ramsay, J. G., 1993, Eocene age of eclogite metamorphism in Pakistan Himalaya: Implications for India-Eurasia collision: Terra Nova, v. 5, p. 13–20.

Treolar, P. J., and Coward, M. P., 1991, Indian plate motion and shape: Constraints on the geometry of the Himalaya orogen: Tectonophysics, v. 191, p. 189–198.

Treolar, P. J., and Rex, D. C., 1990, Post-metamorphic cooling history of the Indian plate crystalline thrust stack, Pakistan Himalaya: Geological Society of London Journal, v. 147, p. 735–738.

Treolar, P. J., Coward, M. P., Williams, M. P., and Khan, M. A. 1989a, Basement-cover imbrication south of the Main Mantle Thrust, north Pakistan, *in* Malinconico, L. L., and Lillie, R. J., eds., Geology of Western Himalaya: Geological Society of America Special Papers 232, p. 137–152.

Treolar, P. J., Rex, D. C., Guise, P. G., Coward, M. P., Searle, M. P., Windley, B. F., Petterson, M. G., Jan, M. Q., and Luff, I. W., 1989b, K-Ar and Ar-Ar geochronology of the Himalayan collision in NW Pakistan: constraints on the timing of suturing, deformation, metamorphism and uplift: Tectonics, v. 8, p. 881–909.

Vannay, J. C., and Hodges, K. V., 1996, Tectonometamorphic evolution of the Himalayan metamorphic core between the Annapurna and Dhaulagiri, central Nepal: Journal of Metamorphic Geology, v. 14, p. 635–656.

Villa, I., and Oddone, M., 1988, $^{39}Ar/^{40}Ar$ ages of Himalayan leucogranites decrease eastward: 6th Himalaya-Tibet-Karakorum Workshop (Lausanne, Switzerland), Abstract volume: p. 16.

Yin, A., Harrison, M., Ryerson, F. J., Wenji, C., Kidd, W. S. F., and Copeland, P., 1994, Tertiary structural evolution of the Gangdese thrust system, southeastern Tibet: Journal of Geophysical Research, v. 99, p. 18175–18201.

York, D., 1969, Least squares fitting of a straight line with correlated errors: Earth and Planetary Science Letters, v. 5, p. 320–324.

Zeitler, P. K., and Chamberlain, C. P., 1991, Petrogenic and tectonic significance of young leucogranites from the Northwestern Himalaya, Pakistan: Tectonics, v. 10, p. 729–741.

Zhao, W., Nelson, K. D., and Team, P. I., 1993, Deep seismic reflection evidence for continental underthrusting beneath southern Tibet: Nature, v. 366, p. 557–559.

MANUSCRIPT ACCEPTED BY THE SOCIETY FEBRUARY 3, 1998

Geological Society of America
Special Paper 328
1999

Contrasting anatectic styles at Nanga Parbat, northern Pakistan

Alan G. Whittington
*Laboratoire de Physique des Géomatériaux, Institut de Physique du Globe,
4 place Jussieu, 75252 Paris Cedex 05, France*

Nigel B. W. Harris
Department of Earth Sciences, Open University, Milton Keynes MK7 6AA, United Kingdom

Robert W. H. Butler
Department of Earth Sciences, Leeds University, Leeds LS2 9JT, United Kingdom

ABSTRACT

Tourmaline-bearing two-mica granite plutons and sheets intruding the basement lithologies of the Nanga Parbat–Haramosh massif represent the youngest known occurrence of High Himalayan leucogranite magmatism. Trace-element modeling using Rb, Sr, and Ba indicates an origin by vapor-absent muscovite melting. Accessory phase modeling suggests that anatexis occurred at temperatures of ~720 °C, and therefore depths of 20–25 km. The source of one such intrusion (the Tato pluton) is considered to be metapelitic gneiss similar to that cropping out in the massif, and isotopically distinct from the source of the Miocene Himalayan leucogranites. Initial $^{87}Sr/^{86}Sr$ ratios of ~0.88 for the Tato pluton compare with 0.74–0.78 for Miocene granites intruded into the central Himalayan orogen.

Subsequent to, or coeval with, leucogranite emplacement, small cordierite-bearing leucosomes have been generated in ductile shear zones within the interior of the massif. These are geochemically variable, but are consistently characterized by strong depletion in high field strength elements and other incompatible trace elements. Petrographic and geochemical constraints indicate that at least some seams may be restitic, following localized incongruent melting of biotite in the presence of a fluid yielding a high melt fraction (F ~ 0.5). Other seams may be wholly or partly subsolidus in nature. Thermobarometric data from these seams indicate that channelled fluid migration within the massif occurred at pressures <400 MPa and temperatures of about 630 °C.

Geochemical constraints on contrasting granitic rocks from the interior of the Nanga Parbat–Haramosh massif chart a changing regime from fluid-absent anatexis in the mid-crust (~20 km depth) to fluid infiltration during ductile deformation in the upper crust (~10 km depth). These findings are consistent with the rapid exhumation of the massif with more modest exhumation rates around the margins.

INTRODUCTION

The Nanga Parbat–Haramosh massif in northern Pakistan is the most northerly outcrop of Indian continental crust within the Himalayan orogen (Fig. 1). The massif exhibits unusually young metamorphism, high exhumation rates, and the most recent melting event in the Himalaya, making it ideal to study the interaction between deformation, magmatism, and the thermal state of the crust during active thickening (Zeitler et al., 1993; Zeitler and Chamberlain, 1991; Winslow et al., 1994, 1995; Whittington, 1996; Butler et al., 1997).

Intruding the basement gneisses are a swarm of peraluminous leucogranite sheets and discrete plutons; the most accessible is the Tato pluton, exposed about 6 km southwest of the village of Tato (Fig.

Whittington, A. G., Harris, N. B. W., and Butler, R. W. H., 1999, Contrasting anatectic styles at Nanga Parbat, northern Pakistan, *in* Macfarlane, A., Sorkhabi, R. B., and Quade, J., eds., Himalaya and Tibet: Mountain Roots to Mountain Tops: Boulder, Colorado, Geological Society of America Special Paper 328.

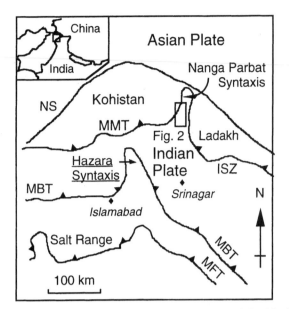

Figure 1. Tectonic sketch map of the western Himalaya. NS = Northern suture, ISZ = Indus suture zone, MMT = Main Mantle thrust, MBT = Main Boundary thrust, MFT = Main Frontal thrust.

In addition to leucogranite formation, there is evidence of recent metamorphism involving biotite breakdown and cordierite growth, and of a leucosome-forming event resulting in leucocratic seams containing cordierite. Cordierite has been described from metapelites in the Himalaya (Brunel and Kienast, 1986; Inger and Harris, 1992), but has only been reported once from granitic rocks (Hodges et al., 1993). This chapter presents a geochemical study of both the leucogranites and cordierite seams found at Nanga Parbat, and specifically addresses the conditions of leucogranite and cordierite seam formation, and the relationship between their petrogenesis and the thermal evolution of the Nanga Parbat-Haramosh massif.

GEOTECTONIC SETTING

Nanga Parbat basement formed the footwall to the collision suture, locally named the Main Mantle thrust, but has been exhumed through the Kohistan-Ladakh arc, which originally was in the hang-

2). Rapid exhumation of as much as several millimeters per year has been reported from the Nanga Parbat-Haramosh massif (Zeitler et al., 1982; Zeitler, 1985; Whittington, 1996), and vapor-absent melting has been suggested as a mechanism for leucogranite formation at Nanga Parbat on the basis of the temporal coincidence of melting and exhumation (Zeitler and Chamberlain, 1991). Vapor-absent melting, also called dehydration melting, occurs when the breakdown of a hydrous phase produces a water-undersaturated melt and anhydrous solid products without the direct participation of a vapor phase.

Leucogranites intruding the massif are of broadly similar geochemical composition to Miocene (ca. 20 Ma) plutons described from the High Himalaya (George et al., 1993; Butler et al., 1997) but isotopic studies indicate zircon ages between 7.0 and 1.0 Ma for the Nanga Parbat-Haramosh massif leucogranites (Zeitler and Chamberlain, 1991; Zeitler et al., 1993). Whereas rapid decompression in the main Himalayan orogen was achieved by extension on the South Tibet detachment system, at Nanga Parbat exhumation is achieved solely by erosion in the absence of extensional structures (Whittington, 1996; Butler et al., 1997).

Various models suggested for Himalayan leucogranite formation include shear heating on the Main Central thrust (Le Fort, 1975; England et al., 1992), contrasting thermal conductivity and internal heat production (Pinet and Jaupart, 1987), pervasive fluid infiltration of the mid-lower crust from dehydrating sediments (Le Fort et al., 1987), and vapor-absent melting due to rapid decompression (Swapp and Hollister, 1991; Harris et al., 1993; Harris and Massey, 1994). Each of these models requires a specific thermal regime, which will control the melt reaction involved in leucogranite formation. By correct interpretation of geochemical signatures, important constraints can be placed on the thermal and tectonic evolution of mountain belts.

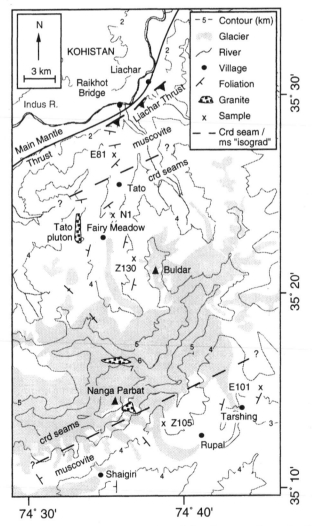

Figure 2. Map showing field area and sample locations; samples are listed in Table 1. Isograds for occurrence of primary muscovite and cordierite seams are shown as dashed lines. Geography is based on the map of Finsterwalder (1936).

ing wall. The Nanga Parbat-Haramosh massif may be broadly described as a north-plunging crustal-scale antiformal structure (Coward et al., 1986; Treloar et al., 1991), although the youngest structures form shear zones along the western margin of the Nanga Parbat massif. The reverse dip-slip Liachar shear zone carries the massif back across the suture onto the Kohistan arc, and locally over Holocene sediments (Butler and Prior, 1988). Farther north the western margin shows a transition from reverse dip slip to oblique dextral reverse faulting over time (Butler et al., 1989; Treloar et al., 1991), and more than 15 km of dextral Quaternary displacement (Madin et al., 1989).

The structurally deepest outcrops are exposed in the central and western parts of the massif, and consist of upper amphibolite grade orthogneisses and paragneisses showing evidence for polymetamorphism (Wheeler et al., 1995). The margins of the Nanga Parbat-Haramosh massif show lower grade muscovite-bearing assemblages, and the term "interior" is used to denote muscovite-absent rocks from south of the Liachar shear zone and north of the Rupal valley (Fig. 2). The true core of the massif is higher than 6,000 m elevation on Nanga Parbat, and currently eludes geological investigation except by the use of binoculars.

PETROGRAPHY AND FIELD DESCRIPTION

Leucogranites

Leucogranite plutons from the Nanga Parbat-Haramosh massif were first reported from a poorly exposed locality at Jutial in the northwest (Butler et al., 1993). We present here a detailed geochemical study of the Tato pluton (Fig. 2), which has sharp contacts discordant to gneissic foliation (Fig. 3A), but no chilled margin. The pluton appears to be compositionally homogeneous and nondeformed throughout its outcrop, both horizontally over at least 3 km, and vertically throughout 500 m.

The pluton is a medium- to coarse-grained leucogranite containing quartz (30% to 35%), perthitic alkali feldspar (30% to 35% by volume), plagioclase feldspar (25% to 30%), biotite (<5%), tourmaline (<5%), and muscovite (<2%) (Table 1). Plagioclase feldspar is commonly zoned, typically from $An_{0.31}$ to $An_{0.06}$, core to rim. Biotite and muscovite are evenly distributed; however, strongly pleochroic and zoned tourmaline grains often occur in small clusters of subhedral crystals. The granite shows an interlocking seriate igneous texture in thin section; late-crystallizing alkali feldspar sometimes contains inclusions of plagioclase and quartz (Fig. 3B).

In thin section, alkali feldspar often shows irregular or deformed twin planes, sometimes with minor alteration to sericite. Quartz shows undulose extinction indicative of strain, and serrated grain boundaries suggesting grain-boundary migration. Despite these indicators of deformation in the pluton, no pervasive fabric that might result from deformation or magmatic flow can be observed in the pluton, either in the field or in thin section.

There are also numerous leucogranitic sheets and dikes associated with the pluton, rarely more than 1 m in width. Some of these disappear into the base of the pluton, and are probably feeder dikes, indicating emplacement through brittle fractures,

driven either by buoyancy or injection pressure (Clemens and Mawer, 1992). In the interior of the massif, both on the Fairy Meadows and Rupal sides of Nanga Parbat, they are usually subhorizontal in orientation, consistent with vertical extension during unroofing of the massif. Several sheets show textures indicative of multiple episodes of magma injection, and tourmaline crystals are often aligned at the margins of successive magma batches, or within single injection horizons. At least one sheet from the Rupal valley shows narrow mylonitic zones in thin section, indicating postcrystallization deformation at high strain.

On the western margin of the massif these leucogranitic dikes are often very coarse grained and pegmatitic, and have been deformed in the Liachar shear zone (Fig. 3C). Boudinaged dikes show syncrystallization deformation fabrics, indicating syntectonic emplacement (Butler et al., 1997). Some sheets are almost entirely quartzofeldspathic, others contain small euhedral inclusion-free garnets, and some pegmatites show tourmaline growth to several centimeters long. Occasional late crosscutting aplites are not deformed by the Liachar shear zone, suggesting that their emplacement was very recent.

Basement gneisses

The basement of the Nanga Parbat massif is composed of Indian plate gneisses metamorphosed under upper amphibolite facies conditions. Compositions range from metapelites and metagraywackes with occasional calc-silicate layers to granitic orthogneisses. Because metapelites are the most likely source material for crustally derived granitic melts (Wyllie, 1977), these lithologies are described in more detail. Lit-par-lit migmatites found in some locations are unlikely to represent the source of the leucogranites, because migmatitic fabrics are crosscut by metabasaltic sheets of probable pre-Himalayan age (Wheeler et al., 1995).

Typical metapelitic assemblages contain quartz, sillimanite, biotite, potassium feldspar, and plagioclase feldspar, and variable occurrences of garnet, cordierite, spinel, and muscovite. Kyanite was not observed from the interior of the massif. Muscovite is found in the Rupal valley and in the Tato valley on the margin of the massif (Fig. 2), but is not a primary phase in the central region of the massif.

Garnets enclose quartz inclusion trails oriented at high angles to external fabrics, indicating that garnet growth predated the latest metamorphism and deformation. In more aluminous lithologies, garnet is often mantled by cordierite. This texture has been observed in metapelites from the central Himalaya (Inger and Harris, 1992), and is indicative of heating and/or decompression. Biotite from pelitic horizons has a ragged appearance, in contrast to its occurrence as the major fabric-forming phase in less-aluminous lithologies, and shows partial breakdown to an ilmenite-bearing assemblage. Cordierite reaction rims separate biotite from fibrolitic sillimanite and from small equant spinel crystals. Similar textures have been recognized in the Wilmington Complex (Srogi et al., 1993) and ascribed to dehydration partial melting of biotite. The significance of these textures is discussed in Whittington et al. (1998).

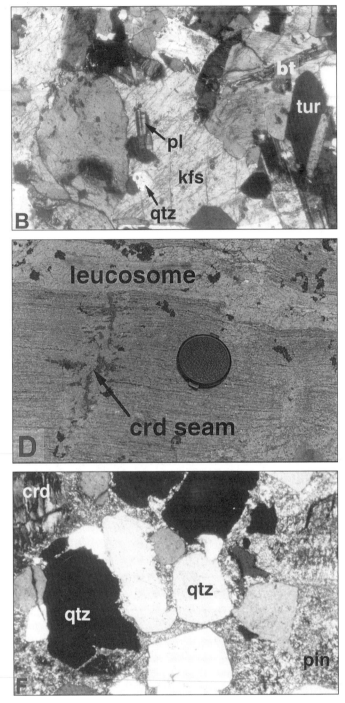

Figure 3 (above and right column). A: Contact of Tato pluton with orthogneiss wall rock. Photo looking west, hammer head is 20 cm across. B: Photomicrograph of Tato pluton sample under crossed polars showing tourmaline (tur), biotite (bi), and potassium feldspar (kfs) with inclusions of plagioclase feldspar (pl) and quartz (qtz). Long dimension is 3 mm. C: Deformed leucogranite sheets in Liachar shear zone showing boudinage with a top-to-north shear sense, looking west. Hammer is 30 cm long. D: Cordierite exhibiting "ghost foliation" after biotite, with a biotite-free rim in pelitic gneiss, apparently truncated by a granitic leucosome (see text for discussion). Lens cap is 6 cm across. Very dark patches are lichen. E: Cordierite seam in shear zone displaying vertical displacement. Photo looking north-west, compass is 8 cm long. F: Photomicrograph of cordierite seam under crossed polars showing rounded restitic quartz set within interstitial cordierite, largely altered to pinite (pin). Long dimension is 3 mm. Mineral abbreviations follow Kretz (1983).

Cordierite seams

Cordierite-bearing seams consist of dark nodular masses in a pale biotite-free host material which has somewhat indistinct boundaries against the surrounding biotite gneiss. The dark cordierite nodules compose about 20% to 30% of the seams, which are rarely more than 50 cm across. These nodules sometimes form thin bands that replicate biotite foliation, indicating that biotite is an essential reactant (Fig. 3D). In addition to quartz, potassium feldspar, and cordierite, which compose more than 90% of the modal mineralogy of seams, small plagioclase crystals and myrmekitic quartz-plagioclase intergrowths can be found near the margins of bleached zones. Relict biotite and more rarely garnet crystals and ilmenite occasionally occur as inclusions within interstitial cordierite (Table 1).

This latest metamorphic event is generally localized in steeply dipping reverse shear zones, but is not offset by them (Fig. 3E). The seams that are not in shear zones are generally subhorizontal; both orientations are consistent with vertical stretching during rapid unroofing (Butler et al., 1997). The seams appear to cross leucogranite sheets, and the sheets are deformed by shear zones containing seams. Cordierite nodules are, however, rarely found where seams cross sheets or leucocratic bands (Fig. 3D), perhaps due to the paucity of biotite in many sheets, which prevents cordierite growth. This can give the impression that sheets crosscut seams, and it may be that formation of the two was coeval during exhumation.

Cordierite seams are found in the Tato valley south of the village, in a variety of biotite-bearing lithologies. They are not found in situ in the Rupal valley to the south of Nanga Parbat (Fig. 2), but occasional boulders containing seams can be found in scree and in moraine deposits, suggesting that seams exist higher up on the Rupal face.

Some cut slabs of these seams were stained with sodium cobaltinitrite solution to identify the distribution of alkali feldspar within hand specimens. Seams were found to contain large quantities of potassium feldspar (locally >80%); some grains occur as inclusions within the dark nodules.

In thin section seams are dominated by coarse subhedral potassium feldspar crystals and interstitial cordierite, both phases enclosing generally rounded quartz grains. These textures range in appearance from a cumulate texture (Fig. 3F) to an interstitial grain-boundary texture, depending on the percentage area filled by cordierite. The proportion of cordierite present decreases toward the margins of seams. In general, cordierite is usually altered around rims, and in places has been completely replaced by a fine-grained white mica aggregate (pinite). Cordierite has different textures in aluminous layers in metapelites and in cordierite seams, and it is therefore argued that these were two separate cordierite-forming events.

Two sample pairs of unaltered gneiss and adjacent cordierite seam were analyzed (Z130a and Z130b) and are discussed in detail.

ANALYTICAL TECHNIQUES

Major and trace element analyses were carried out by wavelength dispersive X-ray fluorescence (XRF) spectrometry at the Open University, United Kingdom. X-rays were generated using a 3 kW Rh anode end-window X-ray tube, and the diffracting crystals used were AX06, PET, Ge111, LiF200, and LiF220. Elemental intensities were corrected for background and known peak overlap interferences. Instrumental intensity drift was taken into account using a drift monitor. Count times for most trace elements were selected to achieve 2σ precision better than 2 ppm or 2% relative at concentrations >100

TABLE 1. SAMPLE MINERALOGY AND LOCATION*

Sample	Location	Type	Qtz	Kfs	Pl	Crd	Bt	Grt	Sil	Tur	Ms	Ilm
E5a/i	Tato pluton	Pluton	✓	✓	✓	–	tr	–	tr	✓	tr	–
E5a/ii	Tato pluton	Pluton	✓	✓	✓	–	tr	–	–	✓	tr	–
Z66a	Tato pluton	Pluton	✓	✓	✓	–	tr	–	–	✓	tr	–
E70a	Tato pluton	Pluton	✓	✓	✓	–	tr	–	–	✓	tr	–
E111	Tato pluton	Pluton	✓	✓	✓	–	tr	–	–	✓	tr	–
Z140	Tato pluton	Pluton	✓	✓	✓	–	tr	–	tr	✓	tr	–
Z141	Tato pluton	Pluton	✓	✓	✓	–	tr	–	–	✓	tr	–
E64	Tato pluton	Dike	✓	✓	✓	–	tr	–	tr	tr	tr	–
E81*	LSZ	Dike	✓	✓	✓	–	tr	–	–	–	tr	–
Z105*	Rupal	Dike	✓	✓	✓	–	tr	–	–	tr	tr	–
X1	Fairy Meadow	Crd seam	✓	✓	✓	✓	tr	tr	tr	–	–	–
X10	Fairy Meadow	Crd seam	✓	✓	tr	✓	tr	–	–	–	–	tr
Z42i	Fairy Meadow	Crd seam	✓	✓	tr	✓	tr	–	–	–	–	tr
Z42iv	Fairy Meadow	Crd seam	✓	✓	tr	✓	tr	–	tr	–	–	–
Z46Ci	Fairy Meadow	Crd seam	✓	✓	tr	✓	tr	–	–	–	–	–
Z46Civ	Fairy Meadow	Crd seam	✓	✓	tr	✓	tr	–	–	–	–	–
Z130a/i*	Buldar	Crd seam	✓	✓	tr	✓	tr	–	tr	–	–	tr
Z130b/i*	Buldar	Crd seam	✓	✓	tr	✓	tr	tr	tr	–	–	tr
Z130a/ii*	Buldar	Peltic gneiss	✓	✓	✓	✓	✓	✓	✓	–	–	tr
Z130b/ii*	Buldar	Peltic gneiss	✓	✓	✓	✓	✓	✓	✓	–	–	tr
N1*	Fairy Meadow	Peltic gneiss	✓	✓	tr	✓	✓	✓	✓	–	–	tr
Z9/i*	Fairy Meadow	Peltic gneiss	✓	✓	✓	✓	✓	✓	✓	–	–	tr
E101*	Tarshing	Peltic gneiss	✓	✓	✓	–	✓	tr	✓	–	✓	–

*Sample locations refer to place names in Figure 2. Samples marked * are labeled individually. ✓ = major phase; tr = minor phase, – = absent. Mineral abbreviations follow Kretz (1983). Crd is cordierite.

ppm. Major element matrix corrections employed the empirical Traill-Lachance procedure; trace element matrix corrections usually involved ratioing with the Compton scattered tube lines.

Instrumental neutron activation analysis (INAA) was used to determine the concentrations of the rare earth elements La, Ce, Nd, Sm, Eu, Tb, Yb, and Lu together with Th, U, Co, Ta, and Hf. The two standards used in each cylinder were an irradiation standard AC-2 (Ailsa Craig microgranite) and a sample from the Whin Sill, which was used as an internal standard. Samples were irradiated in the core tube at the Imperial College Reactor Centre, Ascot, in a thermal neutron flux of 1×10^{12} n cm^2 s^{-1} for 8 hr. The samples were left for a week before analysis to allow short-lived radioactive isotopes to decay; details of counting conditions, peak fitting, calibration, and corrections were described in Potts et al. (1985).

Strontium and neodymium isotopic analyses and preparations were carried out in a clean-air laboratory in which a positive air pressure was maintained. All solutions used in the dissolutions were made up with Teflon-distilled Milli-Q reverse osmosis (RO) purified water. Samples for $^{87}Sr/^{86}Sr$ and $^{143}Nd/^{144}Nd$ ratio measurements were carried out on a Finnegan M80 262 solid-source, multicollector mass spectrometer, interfaced with a Hewlett Packard 9836 computer using software designed by D. W. Wright and P. W. C. van Calsteren. Filaments were outgassed before loading for 5 min at 4.5 A in a vacuum better than 10^{-6} torr. Strontium was loaded in phosphoric acid on single Ta filaments, and the measured $^{87}Sr/^{86}Sr$ ratios were exponentially fractionation corrected within each run to $^{87}Sr/^{86}Sr = 0.1194$. Machine standard NBS 987 was run with each batch of samples and reported analyses have been corrected to a value of NBS 987 of 0.710220. Measurements ($n = 13$) of NBS 987 gave an average $^{87}Sr/^{86}Sr$ ratio of 0.710223 ± 0.000017 (1 σ), and the rock standard NBS 607 gave an $^{87}Sr/^{86}Sr$ ratio of 1.200872 ± 0.000016 (1 σ). Total procedural Sr blanks were <3 ng.

Neodymium was loaded on Ta filaments (a Re ionization filament was used) and run as metal ions. $^{143}Nd/^{144}Nd$ ratios were exponentially fraction corrected to $^{146}Nd/^{144}Nd = 0.72190$. Eight analyses of an internal J M Nd standard over the period of analysis had a mean value of 0.511753 ± 0.000010 (1 σ), and reported ratios have been corrected to a value for J M of 0.511836, corresponding to a value for BCR-1 of 0.512638. Total procedural Nd blanks were <1 ng. $^{87}Rb/^{86}Sr$ and $^{147}Sm/^{144}Nd$ ratios were calculated for each sample from the elemental ratios measured by XRF and INAA.

Mineral compositions were determined by wavelength dispersive microprobe analysis on a Cameca SX 100 at the Open University. Approximately 50 analyses of cores and rims from each phase were undertaken using a 20 nA beam current, 20 kV accelerating potential, and a typical spot size of 20 μm.

GEOCHEMISTRY

Major element geochemistry

Quartz and feldspars compose more than 90% of the modal mineralogy of both the leucogranites and cordierite seams at Nanga Parbat. Hence their petrogenesis is interpreted in part from major element compositions plotted on a quartz (Qtz)-albite (Ab)-orthoclase (Or) diagram (Fig. 4).

Tato leucogranites. Tato leucogranites are peraluminous, and have normative compositions of $Qtz_{33.5-36.1}Ab_{32.0-35.5}Or_{29.1-33.3}$. These compositions are compared with a range of experimental melt compositions from the literature (Fig. 4). Samples ($n = 17$) from the Tato pluton plot close to experimental minimum melts in the haplogranitic system at 200 MPa and a water activity of 0.3 (Johannes and Holtz, 1990). With increasing pressure, experimental minimum melt compositions become less quartz rich, and with increasing water activity the modal percentage of albite increases at the expense of orthoclase. It is unlikely that leucogranite formation occurred at such a low pressure, but some deviation from the haplogranite system may be expected due to the complex chemistry of natural source rocks, particularly the abundance of volatile elements at the magmatic stage (France-Lanord and Le Fort, 1988). To examine the effects of a more complex system, Tato is compared to experimental melts of metapelitic protoliths.

An experimental vapor-present biotite gneiss melt at 750 °C and 0.5 GPa (Holtz and Johannes, 1991) is considerably more quartz rich than Tato compositions, having a modal composition of $Qtz_{50.8}Ab_{26.3}Or_{22.9}$ (7wt% added H$_2$O). For lower percentages of added water, the experimental compositions become slightly less quartz rich.

Experimental melts of a Himalayan muscovite-schist formed at 600 MPa under vapor-absent conditions (Patino Douce, 1996, personal communication) have modal compositions similar to those of the Tato pluton; $Qtz_{33.3}Ab_{35}Or_{31.7}$ at 850 °C, and $Qtz_{39.6}Ab_{32.8}Or_{27.5}$ at 775 °C. Although the melt at 850 °C is the closest match to Tato, we suggest that the elevated temperatures required for melting under experimental conditions and time scales may not necessarily imply that such high temperatures are required under geologically realistic conditions. Whereas normative Tato compositions are more compatible with an origin through vapor-absent muscovite melting, firm conclusions about pressure, water activity, and melting reaction cannot be drawn from these data.

Leucogranite sheets exhibit more varied normative compositions, from $Qtz_{44.1}Ab_{40.5}Or_{5.4}$ to $Qtz_{32.8}Ab_{25.2}Or_{42.0}$, consistent with fluid-melt interaction during crystallization. Analyses ($n = 11$) define a roughly linear trend away from the normative orthoclase apex, passing through the well-defined Tato pluton field, while quartz/albite ratios remain roughly constant.

Cordierite seams. Cordierite seams plot as a widely scattered field at low albite (Ab <30) and high silica (Qtz 30–50) and orthoclase (Or 30–50). Cordierite seams are less albite rich than the Tato pluton, and much more heterogeneous. They are also considerably less albite rich than haplogranite minimum melts of Johannes and Holtz (1990), and experimental vapor-absent muscovite breakdown melts (Patino Douce, 1996, personal communication). The field of cordierite seams overlaps with the experimental vapor-present biotite melts of Holtz and Johannes (1991), particularly for melts produced with little added H$_2$O. The cordierite seams also extend to compositions far more orthoclase rich than experimental melts however, suggesting that some seams cannot be pure melts.

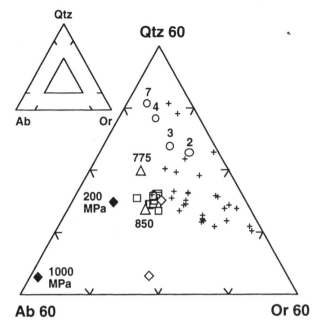

Figure 4. CIPW normative compositions of Tato leucogranites (squares) and cordierite seams (crosses). Inset shows location of main plot in Q-Pl-KF ternary system. Also shown are experimental melts in the haplogranitic system for 200 MPa and 1000 MPa, $a_{H_2O} = 1$ (black diamonds) and $a_{H_2O} = 0.3$ (white diamonds) from Johannes and Holtz (1990); experimental melts of a muscovite-rich pelite under vapor-absent conditions (Patino Douce, 1996, personal communication) at 850 °C and 775 °C at 600 Mpa (white triangles); and experimental melts from a biotite gneiss under vapor-present conditions at 750 °C and 500 MPa (circles) from Holtz and Johannes (1991); numbers refer to added wt% H_2O.

Trace element geochemistry

Tato leucogranites. Trace element concentrations are illustrated on a spidergram (Fig. 5), normalized to the theoretical ocean ridge granite (ORG) composition of Pearce et al. (1984). Tato leucogranites show enrichments in the high field strength elements (HFSE) Nb, Ta, Hf, and Zr and rare earth elements (REE), except Yb, with respect to an average of eight Langtang leucogranites (Inger and Harris, 1993), selected as a typical Miocene High Himalayan leucogranite. The overall pattern is similar, however, with positive Th and Ce anomalies, and strong depletion of Ba with respect to Rb. The distinctive chemistry of the Tato leucogranite is shared by the Jutial intrusion emplaced into the Nanga Parbat-Haramosh massif 70 km to the north (George, 1993; George et al., 1993).

Tato granites all have very similar REE patterns, at the lower abundance limit of the representative Nanga Parbat metapelite field for light REE and Eu (Fig. 6A). Tato light REEs show a negative slope, a pronounced negative Eu anomaly and slight enrichment in heavy REEs, whereas the metapelite field shows a negative slope in both light and heavy REEs. The negative Eu anomaly of the leucogranites may indicate either residual feldspar in the source, production of peritectic feldspar left in the source, fractional crystallization of feldspar, or a negative Eu

anomaly in the source. It is likely that the distribution of other REEs will be controlled largely by the accessory phases monazite, apatite, and zircon (Watt and Harley, 1993).

Analyses (*n* = 17) of the Tato leucogranites define a narrow range of trace element compositions, confirming chemical homogeneity within the pluton. In contrast, trace element patterns are heterogeneous in leucogranite sheets, which also have a more variable mineralogy.

Cordierite seams. In general, the geochemistry of 16 cordierite seams is highly variable, both in element concentration and relative enrichments and depletions (Table 2). This may be in part due to source heterogeneity, because they are localized phenomena. With one exception they are generally more depleted than the Tato leucogranites in most trace elements, but particularly Th, Ta, Nb, and the REEs. Because Rb and Ba have similar concentrations or even enrichment in the seams relative to the leucogranites, depletion in other trace elements may reflect removal or dissolution of trace element–rich accessory phases from seams. Of particular note are pronounced negative Nb and Ba anomalies in some seams.

Metapelites often show negative Eu anomalies and a general decrease in chondrite-normalized abundance from light through heavy REEs (Fig. 6A). The two paired seams from Z130 both show depletion relative to their host metapelites in light and middle REEs, and the heaviest elements (Yb and Lu) have similar concentrations in both metapelites and seams (Fig. 6B). Whereas the metapelites have a negative Eu anomaly, the cordierite seams have a positive anomaly, so that Eu concentrations in both groups are similar.

Isotope Geochemistry

Tato leucogranites. The Tato pluton shows a restricted isotopic range of values, with an average ($^{87}Sr/^{86}Sr$)$_S$ ratio of 0.877 ± 0.011 and ($^{143}Nd/^{144}Nd$)$_S$ ratio of 0.511424 ± 0.000017 (Fig. 7,

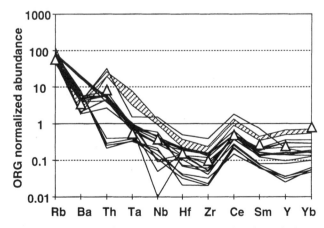

Figure 5. Spidergram of trace elements normalized to theoretical ocean ridge granite (ORG) abundance of Pearce et al. (1984). Average Langtang leucogranite of Inger and Harris (1993) is shown as triangles, 17 Tato leucogranites are shown as striped field, and 16 cordierite seams are shown as solid lines.

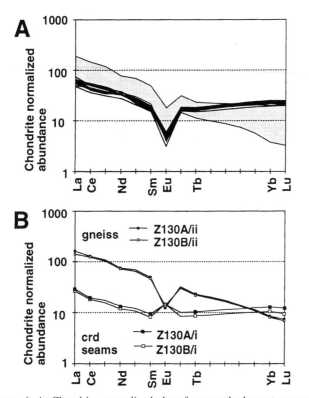

Figure 6. A: Chondrite-normalized plot of rare earth element concentrations in 12 Tato leucogranites and 10 metapelites (shaded field). B: Chondrite-normalized plot of rare earth elements in cordierite seams Z130A/i (large black squares) and Z130B/i (large white squares), and paired gneiss samples Z130A/ii (small black squares) and Z130B/ii (small white squares). Average chondrite composition is from Sun and McDonough (1989).

Table 2). Such low variance suggests either a homogeneous source or thorough mixing prior to crystallization. These initial Sr values are higher than those from other Himalayan leucogranites, which typically range from 0.74 to 0.78 corrected to 20 Ma (Le Fort et al., 1987 and references therein). Values of ε Nd for the Tato pluton (at 5 Ma) are about –23, compared with –13 to –17 for the Miocene Manaslu leucogranite (Le Fort et al., 1987).

Leucogranite sheets show more variable initial Sr ratios, particularly for sheets emplaced syntectonically in the Liachar shear zone, possibly due in part to interaction with fluids. Initial Nd ratios are also more variable in the sheets, perhaps due to fluid involvement, the effect of syntectonic emplacement leading to accessory phase concentrations in boudin necks, or to crystal fractionation.

Cordierite seams. The large range of initial Sr isotopic compositions for basement gneisses (from 0.72 to 1.26) suggests that pervasive fluid influx has not occurred. Cordierite seams show a similarly wide range of compositions, the clusters being due to several seams taken from the same host gneiss outcrop. This indicates that the host gneiss exerts the major control over the Sr isotopic composition of the seams, although there is a small but significant shift between isotopic compositions in host gneiss and cordierite seam. The shift in $(^{87}Sr/^{86}Sr)_5$ is

–0.003 for Z130A and –0.006 for Z130B, the seams having the lower ratio. This suggests either a very limited effect of a fluid of unknown composition, or it is possible that the systematic shifts result from disequilibrium melting where the melt, with a slightly higher $^{87}Sr/^{86}Sr$ ratio than the pelite due to reactant biotite, is extracted before equilibrating with restitic feldspar. However, the range of ratios in both gneisses and seams suggests that seam ratios depend much more on host gneiss than on fluid composition.

Fewer Nd analyses have been undertaken, but available data are consistent with the larger Sr isotope database, with a wide range in composition of both basement rocks and cordierite seams (Fig. 7). The shift in $(^{143}Nd/^{144}Nd)_5$ between gneiss and seam is +0.000065 for both samples Z130A and Z130B; the seams have the higher ratio. Because Nd is immobile in hydrous fluids, this may suggest that the shift in both Sr and Nd ratios may not be due to influx of aqueous fluids.

THERMOBAROMETRY

Sample Z130, taken across the seam-gneiss contact zone, was investigated to determine thermobarometric conditions of seam formation. The seam assemblage consists of cordierite, alkali feldspar, and quartz, and the adjacent gneiss includes garnet rimmed by cordierite coexisting with biotite, sillimanite, alkali feldspar, and quartz.

Thermobarometric calculations were done using version 2.3 of the THERMOCALC program of Powell and Holland (1988) and the internally consistent thermodynamic data set of Holland and Powell (1990). All phases analyzed (see Table 3 for sample rim analyses and Table 4 for end-member activities used in calculations) were used to calculate an average pressure (P) and temperature (T) of 310 ± 40 MPa at 643 ± 43 °C for an assumed water activity of unity. When P and T were tested independently, the best fit was 300 ± 40 MPa at 630 ± 30 °C. For a lower water activity of 0.5 in the presence of CO_2, a lower average (P-T) of 240 ± 40 MPa at 586 ± 37 °C was obtained. The dominant control on the pressure result was the reaction Gnt + Sil + Qtz = Crd, which is observed in thin section. The dominant control on the temperature result was the dehydration reaction Bt + Sil + Qtz = Crd + Kfs + H_2O.

If the cordierite seams are subsolidus in origin, this represents the most likely reaction for seam formation, although the calculated P-T conditions overlap the vapor-present pelitic solidus of Le Breton and Thompson (1988), indicating that fluid influx into the rock would induce anatexis. These conditions also overlap the field of the divariant dehydration-melting reaction Bt + Sil + Pl + Qtz = Crd + Kfs + L for the mineral compositions observed. Alkali feldspar may be a reactant, provided it is present in the protolith. This is the first (and only) biotite dehydration-melting reaction accessible to these rocks, and will produce a melt only slightly undersaturated in H_2O. The amount of melt produced will not be very much greater than the amount of biotite consumed. To discern between the possible melt reactions, trace element modeling is employed below.

TABLE 2. GEOCHEMICAL COMPOSITION OF REPRESENTATIVE SAMPLES*

Type	Tato Lcg	Tato Lcg	Tato Lcg	Tato Lcg	Tato Lcg	Lcg Dike	Crd Seam	Crd Seam	Crd Seam	Crd Seam	Crd Seam	Crd Seam	Pelite	Pelite	Pelite	Pelite	Pelite
Sample	E5a/i	E5a/ii	Z66a	E70a	E111	E64	X1	X10	Z42/i	Z42/iv	Z130a/i	Z130b/i	Z130a/ii	Z130b/ii	E101	N1	Z9/i
(wt.%)																	
SiO_2	73.7	73.36	74.74	73.95	73.83	74.84	73.29	74.05	74.48	74.34	73.97	73.45	73.41	68.94	69.24	51.06	74.00
TiO_2	0.07	0.09	0.08	0.09	0.08	0.06	0.25	0.10	0.04	0.04	0.04	0.05	0.05	0.52	0.66	0.75	0.21
Al_2O_3	14.33	14.30	14.02	14.11	14.23	14.09	13.79	13.92	14.13	14.24	14.27	14.71	14.72	14.91	14.28	25.78	13.88
Fe_2O_3	1.08	1.15	1.04	1.18	1.14	0.90	2.19	2.52	0.56	0.33	0.78	0.66	0.67	4.53	4.58	10.99	2.01
MnO	0.03	0.04	0.03	0.03	0.04	0.05	0.02	0.06	0.01	0.01	0.02	0.02	0.02	0.05	0.06	0.06	0.02
MgO	0.09	0.11	0.06	0.11	0.13	0.07	0.43	0.67	0.10	0.06	0.13	0.09	0.12	1.04	1.24	4.43	0.36
CaO	1.21	1.24	1.18	1.41	1.37	0.87	0.72	0.52	0.57	0.6	1.03	0.98	0.99	1.97	1.49	0.24	0.68
Na_2O	3.43	3.61	3.44	3.48	3.47	3.87	3.24	2.30	2.64	2.63	2.48	2.39	2.53	2.98	3.26	0.52	3.16
K_2O	4.80	4.80	4.92	4.91	4.77	4.55	5.58	4.08	6.82	6.45	6.68	6.86	6.94	4.25	4.64	3.96	4.95
P_2O_5	0.09	0.09	0.05	0.06	0.06	0.07	0.24	0.18	0.31	0.28	0.14	0.12	0.12	0.19	0.11	0.05	0.21
LOI	0.52	0.60	0.14	0.42	0.52	0.49	0.35	1.34	0.54	0.39	0.58	0.65	0.68	0.75	0.74	2.25	0.67
Total	99.35	99.38	99.70	99.75	99.64	99.86	100.10	99.74	100.20	99.36	100.11	99.98	100.25	100.13	100.29	100.08	100.16
(ppm)																	
Rb	453	458	444	395	474	497	391	200	341	316	326	315	258	273	240	233	355
Sr	58.5	60.0	57.6	71.7	67.5	35.7	65.7	66.2	81.5	78.0	168.9	176.7	142.8	155.2	155.0	46.1	58.9
Y	38.8	41.2	46.7	44.6	41.5	40.5	14.8	10.1	1.8	2.5	24.5	21.4	24.2	24.0	35.1	17.5	10.8
Zr	60	62	70	74	78	44	133	41	7	8	18	26	207	199	211	108	102
Nb	11.2	12.1	11.2	11.1	11.7	13.4	15.1	4.4	1.1	1.8	0.1	1	21.7	23.5	13.0	13.5	15.1
Ba	164	166	147	195	182	94	196	210	385	359	884	881	434	463	608	568	184
Pb	77	77	90	89	91	65	30	23	36	34	48	48	28	31	37	14	30
La	18.5	17.9	19.3	22.2	18.9	15.7	26.9	7.9	3.7	4.3	9.5	8.8	53.8	46.3	66.0	54.4	21.0
Ce	38.0	36.0	44.0	44.0	38.1	31.86	62.4	17.5	7.2	8.8	17.1	15.7	112	107	143	104	48
Nd	21.7	20.7	21.5	24.4	20.6	17.4	30.1	7.7	3.0	3.6	8.5	7.5	47.9	46.0	62.9	41.2	22.8
Sm	3.47	3.47	3.93	3.72	3.30	3.12	6.66	1.44	0.60	0.69	1.92	1.65	10.2	9.45	11.50	7.03	4.44
Eu	0.36	0.38	0.36	0.45	0.38	0.24	0.35	0.26	0.42	0.51	1.13	1.14	0.95	1.05	1.02	1.59	0.31
Tb	0.83	0.83	0.95	0.90	0.87	0.82	0.78	0.29	0.10	0.14	0.54	0.45	1.21	1.16	1.23	0.80	0.59
Yb	5.01	5.11	5.48	5.29	4.76	5.65	1.27	1.35	0.45	0.51	2.86	2.29	1.85	1.75	4.67	1.98	1.06
Lu	0.76	0.74	0.85	0.77	0.70	0.82	0.15	0.20	0.06	0.07	0.42	0.32	0.25	0.23	0.69	0.30	0.11
Th	16.4	16.1	20.7	20.9	17.2	16.0	25.4	4.6	0.2	0.2	4.4	3.9	28.8	26.7	37.2	18.1	16.6
U	43.7	40.5	33.0	39.4	33.8	27.0	13.8	6.6	3.2	3.3	9.5	5.1	8.9	6.3	7.1	1.9	11.9
Ta	3.8	4.02	3.4	2.47	2.86	5.5	1.05	0.57	0.26	0.23	0.53	0.60	4.18	3.89	1.52	0.91	1.62
Hf	2.6	2.58	3.1	3.29	3.16	2.1	4.43	1.22	0.29	0.35	1.22	1.27	6.00	6.42	6.65	3.10	3.33
Cs	67.7	68.6	64.5	36.0	70.5	47.3	4.3	6.6	3.9	4.4	11.5	8.4	9.9	11.0	6.4	11.1	11.5
Zn	32	33	30	32.2	29	28	50	26	16	50	12	10	80	74	78	140	57
$^{87}Sr/^{86}Sr$	0.877334	0.873815	0.880225	0.885430	0.873002	0.898255	1.195304	1.034153	1.003039	1.004527	0.846662	0.84759	0.849484	0.853127	0.834933	0.887004	1.261778
$^{143}Nd/^{144}Nd$	0.511402	0.511442	0.511428	0.511418	n.d.	n.d.	0.511702	0.511598	0.511401	n.d.	0.511586	0.511557	0.511521	0.511492	0.511230	0.511147	0.511607

*Major and trace elements determined by X-ray fluorescence analysis at the Open University. Rare earth elements Th, U, Ta, Hf, Cs, and Zn determined by instrumental neutron activation analysis at the Open University.

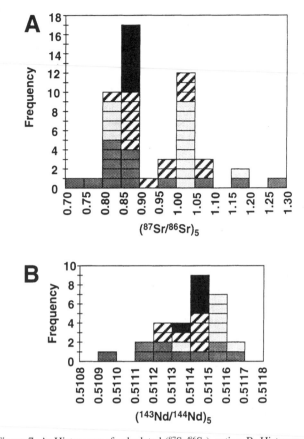

Figure 7. A: Histogram of calculated $(^{87}Sr/^{86}Sr)_5$ ratios. B: Histogram of calculated $(^{143}Nd/^{144}Nd)_5$ ratios. Black boxes are Tato pluton, striped boxes are leucogranite sheets, dark shaded boxes are basement gneisses, and light shaded boxes are cordierite seams. Strontium analyses for eight leucogranite sheets and eight basement gneisses, and Nd analyses for one leucogranite sheet and three basement gneisses are from George (1993).

PETROGENESIS OF GRANITIC ROCKS

Tato leucogranite

The homogeneous nature of the Tato pluton, in both major element composition, which is similar to experimental minimum melts, and in trace element geochemistry, combined with interlocking equigranular igneous textures support the conclusion that Tato leucogranites are crystallized granitic melts. In general tourmaline and two micas coexist in the same assemblages, whereas in Miocene granites from the central Himalaya two distinct facies of tourmaline-muscovite granites and biotite-muscovite granites have been identified (Reddy et al., 1993; Guillot and Le Fort, 1995). It has been suggested that tourmaline is favored over biotite during water-undersaturated melting, independent of source composition (Guillot and Le Fort, 1995), although the presence of boron is also required.

The source of the Tato leucogranite must in any case be different from that of Miocene leucogranites because it displays extremely high initial Sr ratios and low initial Nd ratios compared

to other Himalayan plutons. The source rocks are isotopically similar to metapelitic gneisses outcropping within the Nanga Parbat-Haramosh massif. Hence trace element concentrations in the Tato granite have been normalized against an average metapelitic composition from the massif to investigate possible trace element enrichment trends during anatexis (Fig. 8).

In general, the Tato pluton shows slight enrichment in Rb, Ta, Y, and heavy REEs and slight depletion in Ba, Th, Nb, Hf, Zr, and light REEs relative to a range of metapelitic compositions. An experimental vapor-absent melt from a metapelitic gneiss at 870 °C and 700 MPa (Cavallini et al., 1995) shows a similar pattern of trace element partitioning between protolith and melt, except for the heavy REEs, which mostly reside in accessory phases such as zircon. The release of heavy REEs into the melt will therefore be controlled by dissolution of accessory phases, and equilibrium is unlikely to be reached on experimental time scales.

On geological time scales, however, zirconium and REEs should equilibrate with a coexisting magma, and a temperature of magma formation can be calculated using the techniques of Watson and Harrison (1983) for zircon, and Montel (1993) for monazite.

TABLE 3. SAMPLE RIM ANALYSES OF PHASES USED IN THERMOBAROMETRIC CALCULATIONS

Mineral Number	Biotite 106	Garnet 64	K-feldspar 41	Cordierite 134
(wt.%)				
SiO₂	35.41	36.38	64.82	47.03
TiO₂	4.31	0.01	n.d.	0.01
Al₂O₃	17.54	20.97	18.77	32.50
Cr₂O₃	n.d.	0.04	n.d.	n.d.
FeO	26.47	37.93	0.02	14.98
MnO	0.11	2.37	n.d.	0.31
ZnO	n.d.	0.04	n.d.	n.d.
MgO	3.72	1.51	n.d.	3.47
CaO	0.00	0.65	0.15	0.02
BaO	0.04	n.d.	0.05	n.d.
Na₂O	0.23	n.d.	3.29	0.28
K₂O	8.53	n.d.	11.14	0.02
F	1.03	n.d.	n.d.	0.00
Cl	0.18	n.d.	n.d	0.01
Total	97.56	99.90	98.23	98.62
(ppm)				
Si	5.427	2.978	2.992	4.985
Ti	0.497	0.000	n.d.	0.001
Al	3.168	2.023	1.021	4.061
Cr	n.d.	0.003	n.d.	n.d.
Fe	3.393	2.596	0.001	1.328
Mn	0.014	0.165	n.d.	0.028
Zn	n.d.	0.002	n.d.	n.d.
Mg	0.850	0.184	n.d.	0.548
Ca	0.000	0.057	0.007	0.002
Ba	0.003	n.d.	0.001	n.d.
Na	0.069	n.d.	0.294	0.058
K	1.668	n.d.	0.656	0.003
O = F	-0.432	n.d.	n.d.	0.000
O = Cl	-0.041	n.d.	n.d.	-0.002
Total (cations)	14.616	8.005	4.972	11.012

n.d. = no data.

**TABLE 4. END-MEMBER ACTIVITIES USED IN
THERMOBAROMETRIC CALCULATIONS**

End member	Activity
Biotgite No. 106	
Phlogopite	2.33×10^{-3}
Annite	1.48×10^{-1}
Eastonite	4.93×10^{-3}
Na-phlogopite*	9.65×10^{-5}
Cordierite No. 134	
Mg-cordierite	9.92×10^{-2}
Fe-cordierite	4.49×10^{-1}
Mn-cordierite*	2.18×10^{-4}
Alkali Feldspar No. 41	
Orthoclase	6.85×10^{-1}
Albite	3.07×10^{-1}
Garnet No. 64	
Pyrope	2.30×10^{-4}
Gossular	6.80×10^{-6}
Almandine	6.29×10^{-1}
Spessartine*	1.65×10^{-4}
Sillimanite	1
Quartz	1
H_2O	Variable
CO_2	Variable

*Phases were not used for thermobarometric calculations.

The Tato pluton yields generally consistent results of 710 to 730 °C for both thermometers (Table 5, Fig. 9). Some inheritance of accessory phases not in equilibrium with the melt is anticipated, but this is likely to be a random process, and wide variations in modeled temperatures would be expected within the pluton if a significant proportion of accessory phases was inherited. Discordance between the two thermometers would also be expected if there was disequilibrium between melt and restite due to rapid melt extraction (Ayres et al., 1997). These temperatures of melting are too low for biotite melting under vapor-absent conditions, so either vapor-present melting or vapor-absent muscovite melting is implied. These alternatives can be distinguished by the use of a Rb/Sr vs. Ba diagram.

Rb, Sr, and Ba are the trace elements that reside in the major reactants and products of melting reactions (feldspars and micas). Quantitative modeling is undertaken in three stages. (1) Balanced reactions are obtained from given mineral and melt compositions and variable melt fraction. (2) Restite modes are obtained by mass balance using stoichiometric coefficients and modes for the gneiss protolith (Harris and Inger, 1992). (3) Concentration ratios in the liquid relative to the source (Cl/Co) are calculated from appropriate partition coefficients (Kd) for granitic melts, using a range of values from Blundy and Wood (1991), Harris et al. (1993), and Nash and Crecraft (1985). Simple melts have well-defined Cl/Co ratios for Rb, Sr, and Ba, whether controlled by mineral fractionation or by the partial melting reaction. For example, fluid-absent melting results in high Rb/Sr ratios and depleted Ba relative to their source as seen in the Tato granite (Fig. 10).

Compositions from basement pelites define a large field, but Tato pluton analyses extend well beyond its limits. Harris et al. (1993) reported that Rb/Sr ratios greater than 3.5 cannot be achieved by vapor-present melting. The Tato granite ranges of Rb/Sr are between 5 and 14, defining an array similar to that modeled by Inger and Harris (1993) for vapor-absent muscovite melting. An alternative cause of such a trend is crystal fractionation of alkali feldspar, but petrographic evidence shows alkali feldspar to be a late-crystallizing phase containing both quartz and plagioclase inclusions, and hence this explanation can be discounted.

We conclude that the Tato pluton was formed by vapor-absent muscovite melting of a metapelitic protolith at temperatures of around 720 °C. From the fluid-absent muscovite solidus of Petö (1976), this implies a pressure of 700 to 800 MPa, and hence a depth for the onset of melting between 20 and 25 km.

Cordierite seams

In the following section we investigate whether formation of cordierite seams was a metasomatic process, or if a melt phase was involved. There are four possible origins for the seams.

Seams are metasomatic. The argument for a purely metasomatic origin for the seams rests on the in situ nature of the outcrops (e.g., biotite foliation is undisturbed locally) and their nonmagmatic modal composition (rich in cordierite and alkali feldspar) and textures. A study of apparently similar seams from the Massif Central (Didier and Dupraz, 1985) describes nodules of poikilitic cordierite containing inclusions of quartz surrounded by biotite-free patches; these "nodules" occur along structural discontinuities within a granite. They are ascribed to a metasomatic origin in the absence of geochemical evidence. An infiltrating metasomatic fluid will be either aqueous, i.e., the dominant anion is hydroxyl, or nonaqueous (probably carbonic in the absence of sulfides, phosphates, or halides).

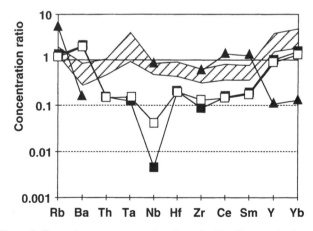

Figure 8. Trace element concentrations in melts. The Tato granite is normalized to a range of five metapelites from the field area (striped field). Two cordierite seams ratioed to their adjacent gneiss pairs are shown, Z130a (black squares) and Z130b (white squares), and data from an experimental pelitic melt at 700 MPa and 870 °C (black triangles) from Cavallini et al. (1995).

TABLE 5. ACCESSORY PHASE THERMOMETRY DATA*

Type Sample	Zr (ppm)	Zircon thermometer (°C)†	ΣLREE (ppm)	Monazite thermometer (°C)§
Tato pluton				
E5a/i	60	713	0.611	725
E5a/ii	62	712	0.584	715
Z66A	70	722	0.664	726
E70A	74	723	0.706	724
E111	76	728	0.605	718
Z140	81	731	0.694	725
Z141	66	717	0.614	719
Lcg sheets				
E64	44	690	0.509	711
E81	25	645	0.182	628
Z105	31	671	0.425	712
Cordierite seams				
Z42/i	7	575	0.108	612
Z42(IV)	8	585	0.130	630
Z45B	29	664	0.287	679
Z46C/i	32	689	0.198	691
Z48C/iv	52	704	0.247	665
Z130a/i	18	629	0.276	667
Z130b/i	26	654	0.251	666
Z130C	14	615	0.207	654
Z130d	18	625	0.271	659

*All calculations assume a magmatic H_2O content of 7 weight percent.
†Using the zircon thermometer of Watson and Harrison (1983). LREE = light rare earth elements.
§Using the monazite thermometer of Montel (1993).

In general, the trace element variations between seams and gneiss are difficult to reconcile with an aqueous fluid causing metasomatism. Aqueous fluids transport the alkalies Rb and Cs, together with Ba and U, much more readily than HFS elements such as Zr, Nb, and Th. Infiltration by a hydrous fluid typically causes a high U/Th ratio. In fact, U appears to be immobile during seam formation, as do alkalies, whereas the strongest depletion is for Nb; Th and other HFS elements are also depleted.

If formation of seams is a subsolidus event occurring at peak metamorphic conditions, then the fluid must be poor in H_2O and F in order to destabilize biotite without forming a melt. A nonaqueous fluid will probably be carbonic, as inferred by Didier and Dupraz (1985). The general reaction inferred from that study requires the generation of an alkali-rich fluid. In the Nanga Parbat seams, however, there is little change in alkali concentrations between gneiss and seam (Fig. 8B).

Seams are melts resulting from equilibrium anatexis. Both field evidence and geochemical parameters preclude simple melt injection; K_2O and MgO concentrations are too high in some seams for a magmatic origin, the positive Eu anomaly in many seams is inconsistent with residual feldspar, and Nb/Ta ratios are anomalously high for a magmatic rock. Textures of subrounded quartz, subhedral alkali feldspar, and interstitial cordierite are nonmagmatic, in that igneous cordierite is likely to form stubby subhedral crystals (Clarke, 1995).

Alternatively, the cordierite may be an entrained peritectic phase generated through a biotite-breakdown melting reaction, which would account for the elevated MgO concentration. Abundant alkali feldspar in the source implies that it would be a reactant, together with plagioclase and quartz. At the pressures and temperatures obtained by thermobarometry of the seam Z130, a melt could only form in response to fluid infiltration, because the assemblage is muscovite-absent. Both the starting assemblage and *P-T* conditions are similar to those used by Holtz and Johannes (1991) for experimental melting; at 750 °C and 500 MPa, granitic melts were formed from a pelitic gneiss with added H_2O (for 4 wt% H_2O, F ~ 0.5). Note that the melt is undersaturated in H_2O despite the fact that water is required for the reaction. In general, Rb-Sr-Ba modeling for melting the metapelitic protolith in this experiment results in modest enrichment (in the melt) of Rb, modest to strong depletion of Sr, and strong depletion of Ba (Fig. 10B). Strontium is sensitive to modal plagioclase and alkali feldspar in the restite, while Rb and Ba are sensitive to modal alkali feldspar (and/or biotite) in the restite. Under equilibrium conditions it is not possible to model enriched Ba without enriching Rb in the melt, thus confirming that the cordierite seams are not simple intrusive melts.

Seams are melts resulting from disequilibrium anatexis. Some evidence for disequilibrium melting comes from calculated accessory phase temperatures from cordierite seams. These form a scattered field, generally displaced toward higher monazite temperatures (Fig. 9), implying either an excess of light REEs, undersaturation of zirconium, or a nonanatectic origin. This could be due to incomplete dissolution of zircon, either due to shielding in restitic phases or lack of time for dissolution of trace elements

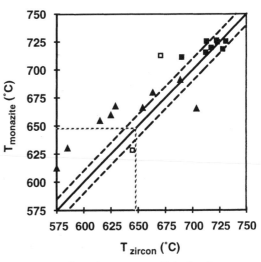

Figure 9. Accessory phase thermometry. Calculated temperatures (*T*) shown use the zirconium thermometer of Watson and Harrison (1983) and the light rare earth element (REE) thermometer of Montel (1993), assuming a magma water content of 7 wt%. Solid line is for *T* (Zr) = *T* (light REE), and dashed lines enclose data within 10 °C of concordance. Thick dotted line shows vapor-present solidus at 500 MPa. Black squares are Tato pluton samples (*n* = 8), white squares are leucogranite dikes (*n* = 2), and black triangles are cordierite seams (*n* = 9).

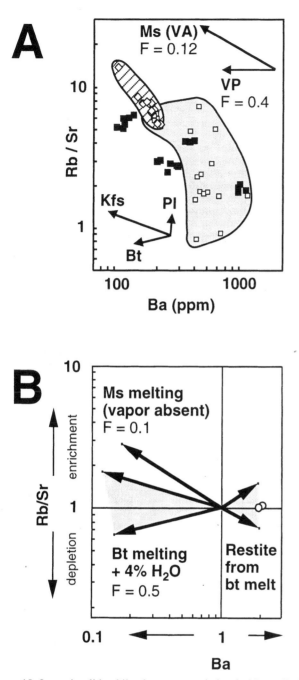

Figure 10. Large ion lithophile element covariation in Nanga Parbat gneisses, leucogranites, and cordierite seams. A: Basement pelites (white squares, shaded field), Tato leucogranite (white diamonds, striped field), and cordierite seams (black squares). Melting vectors indicate the significance of compositional displacement of a melt from its source (Ms [VA]) = vapor-absent muscovite melting, VP = vapor-present melting), and fractional crystallization vectors indicate compositional displacement of a melt that undergoes 10% fractional crystallization of potassium feldspar, plagioclase, and biotite (Kfs, Pl, and Bt). Vectors are from Inger and Harris (1993). B: Modeled evolution vectors for vapor-present biotite melting of Z130 gneisses, F = 0.5. Open circles are seam-gneiss pairs from Z130. Also shown is the evolution vector for a restite associated with melting. Shaded field indicates propagated uncertainties in Kd values for Rb and Sr in biotite. Distribution coefficients are from Henderson (1982) and Nash and Crecraft (1985).

into the melt (disequilibrium melting). Some seams give temperatures below the wet solidus, and it is concluded that calculated temperatures for the seams are meaningless.

Disequilibrium melting can be modeled if the distribution of trace elements between coexisting phases in the protolith is known from ion-probe data. If it is assumed that Ba does not have time to partition between melt and restite phases (i.e., disequilibrium), then enrichment of Ba can be modeled at high melt fractions (F = 0.6–0.7), provided that rapid melting leads to consumption of virtually all alkali feldspar in the source.

There are some problems with this model. (1) Abundant alkali feldspar is observed in seams before and after melting. (2) Both Rb and Sr are also enriched in melt by disequilibrium melting, although Rb/Sr may remain fairly constant. The modeled enrichment in Rb and Sr can only be prevented if diffusion rates for Ba are substantially slower than for the other phases; this is not supported by diffusion data for Sr and Ba in plagioclase (Giletti, 1991), although not all seams show Ba enrichment relative to basement gneisses (Fig. 10). (3) Textures are not indicative of a magmatic origin of any kind. One might expect to observe an aplitic texture for a melt formed and crystallized very rapidly.

Seams are restites following anatexis and melt extraction. Influx of an aqueous fluid along shear zones may have generated a melt along grain boundaries that was extracted leaving a restite with minor melt entrapment. The biotite-alkali feldspar gneiss is similar in composition to a granite (approximate modal composition Qtz 30%, Kfs 35%, Pl 20%, Bt 10%, Sil 5%), so the major element composition is not greatly changed by melt extraction. However, large changes in trace elements are observed. In order to double Ba abundances between protolith and restite, the melt fraction cannot be less than 0.5 (although lower F values are possible if the fluid enriches the seam in Ba). The extraction of higher melt fractions is precluded by the relatively small enrichment of Sr in the seam. We have assumed F = 0.5 for modeling.

From mass balance of major phases, the composition of the melt extracted from Z130 is that of a cordierite granite (Kfs = 0.47, Pl = 0.16, Qtz = 0.29, Crd = 0.05, Sil = 0.02). A balanced melt reaction for such a melt (F = 0.5; 4 wt% H_2O added) is given by:

$$0.11 \text{ Bt} + 0.19 \text{ Pl} + 0.08 \text{ Sil} + 0.22 \text{ Qtz} + 0.44 \text{ Kfs} + 0.07 \text{ } H_2O = L + 0.11 \text{ Crd}.$$

Both plagioclase and biotite must be virtually exhausted by the melt phase in order to generate the observed values of Cr/Co (Rb = 1.2; Sr = 1.1; Ba = 1.9; see Fig. 10B). High Ba and the appropriate modest enrichments in Rb and Sr can be generated for an alkali feldspar–rich restite for F = 0.5. A restite model also accounts for residual quartz textures (Fig. 3F). The textures are suggestive of restitic quartz and alkali feldspar that have peritectic cordierite occupying intergranular areas.

The positive Eu anomaly in the high Ba seams is consistent with a restite origin, generating a liquid with a negative Eu anomaly due to restitic alkali feldspar. Rare earth elements and other trace elements in seams appear to mirror the trends seen in the experimental study of trace element distribution during anatexis of a pelite (Cavallini et al., 1995; Fig. 6). This suggests that in the case of the cordierite seams, the melt was enriched in HFS elements by entrainment of accessory phases rather than dissolution, leaving behind a depleted restite in the seams (Table 2). Zircon (Zr, Hf), monazite (light REEs, Th), and ilmenite (Nb, Ta) would all have been extracted with the melt, released from inclusions in biotite, along grain boundaries or (for ilmenite) as peritectic phases of the melt reaction.

The interstitial texture of cordierite from the seams contrasts with the reactant texture of cordierite seen between biotite and silli-manite in aluminous layers from some anatectic metapelitic gneisses (e.g., N1). This may be because the seams represent restites from melting after a high melt fraction has been extracted (F = 0.5), and the aluminous layers represent in situ melting of much smaller melt fractions in the absence of fluid channeled along shear zones.

In summary, although the restite model fits our detailed analysis of seam Z130, and from petrographic evidence the model should fit many other seams, it is not necessarily a unique explanation. In many cases there may be traces of melt retained in the seams. The melt reaction would yield a melt fraction of about 0.5 for 4 wt% added H_2O. Because most seams are in shear zones, and melting was probably triggered by fluid influx along these zones, it seems reasonable to suggest that the melt also escaped along these channels. Although small in volume, such a large melt fraction could segregate rapidly from the source, espe-cially under conditions of active deformation (Clemens and Mawer, 1992; Rutter and Neumann, 1995).

DISCUSSION

Nanga Parbat leucogranites formed by vapor-undersatu-rated muscovite breakdown synchronous with rapid exhumation (Fig. 11). A zircon age of 1.0 Ma has been obtained from the Tato pluton (Zeitler et al., 1993), and so cooling and exhumation to the surface occurred on time scales shorter than this.

The rate-determining step for melt extraction is critically dependant on both the deviatoric stress and the viscosity of the magma, which in turn depends on its water content and tempera-ture. Applying equation 23 of Rutter and Neumann (1995) to Himalayan leucogranite melts formed under fluid-absent condi-tions at temperatures of 700 to 750 °C, a viscosity in the range 10^7 to 10^9 Pa s is obtained. Under these conditions the rate-deter-mining step is more likely to be flow though the vein network (Fig. 16 of Rutter and Neumann, 1995); extraction of a 10% melt fraction by this process will occur over a period of 1 to 50 k.y.

Rapid transport of melt can be effected by fracture propa-gation, over a time scale <1 k.y. (Clemens and Mawer, 1992; Petford et al., 1993). Magma transport through dikes is sug-gested by the abundance of both sheets and dikes displaying several episodes of magma injection, and feeder dikes connect-ing with the Tato pluton. Some leucogranitic sheets were emplaced syntectonically in the Liachar shear zone, which par-tially accommodates exhumation, whereas in the interior of the massif, sheets are generally found as undeformed subhorizontal

sills, suggesting emplacement in a vertical extensional regime, probably due to rapid unroofing.

A subsequent event led to formation of cordierite-bearing seams, which show a range of textures and geochemistry. Although several models may account for their origin, all involve biotite breakdown, cordierite growth, and require a fluid influx. Trace element modeling of the biotite breakdown reaction allows Ba depletion in magma with a modest depletion in Rb and Sr, provided virtually all plagioclase and biotite are exhausted. Thus the seams could be restites that include some peritectic cordierite and variable proportions of melt. If so, about 4 wt% water is required to generate a melt fraction of about 0.5. Such a melt will be undersaturated in H_2O and be able to rise through the crust prior to crystallization. Although small in volume, the melt could segregate rapidly from the source, especially under conditions of active deformation along the shear zones in which they are found.

New thermobarometric data show the conditions of seam formation to be 300 ± 40 MPa and 630 ± 50 °C, which allows the possibility that some seams formed at subsolidus temperatures (Fig. 11). However, whether seams are restites or a purely meta-somatic feature, fluid influx is required, and hence the seams are indicative of channeled fluid migration within the massif at pres-sures of at least 300 MPa.

These *P-T* calculations on a seam compare with similar cal-culations on an unmelted pelitic gneiss (Whittington, 1996) of 440 ± 60 MPa at 700 ± 60 °C. If the two rocks were exhumed on the same path, i.e., their relative positions have not been tectoni-cally altered since closure to elemental diffusion, then the meta-morphic geotherm shows decompression of about 150 MPa and cooling of about 80 °C. This would indicate some combination of a gentle geothermal gradient at depth, contrasting with the steep near-surface geotherm (Winslow et al., 1994; Whittington, 1996), and rapid exhumation leading to advection of heat faster than heat loss by conduction.

Seams are restricted to the interior of the massif, whereas out-crops of gneisses from the Rupal valley and western margin are characterized by muscovite-bearing subsolidus assemblages. Con-siderations of the likely *P-T-t* path during exhumation of the mas-sif suggests that this mutual exclusivity is no coincidence. Assemblages that have been exhumed very rapidly in the interior of the massif (path 4, Fig. 11) crossed the vapor-absent muscovite solidus before cooling below the wet pelite solidus. Along this path, micaceous assemblages could melt twice; first from mus-covite breakdown during decompression to produce leucogranites, and subsequently during fluid infiltration, resulting in cordierite seams. In contrast, assemblages from the margins of the massif have been exhumed less rapidly, and so cooled earlier during exhumation. Juxtaposition of marginal rocks against the cooler foot wall during thrusting will also lead to earlier cooling, although not necessarily due to slower exhumation, and the *P-T-t* path of mar-ginal zones need not cross the vapor-absent muscovite solidus. In this case cordierite seams will not be formed; by the time these rocks had reached the depths at which focused fluid flow occurred, temperatures were subsolidus relative to the fluid-present reaction.

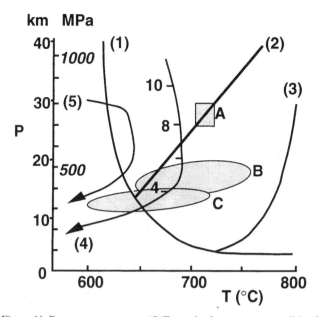

Figure 11. Pressure-temperature (*P-T*) graph of vapor-present solidus for metapelites (1), vapor-absent melting of muscovite (2), and vapor-absent melting of biotite (3). Data are from Le Breton and Thompson (1988) and Petö (1976). Modeled exhumation path for lithologies currently exposed in the core of the massif (4) is from Whittington (1996); (5) is inferred qualitative path of rocks at the massif margin. Numbered ticks indicate time in millions of years. Field of leucogranite formation (A) is determined from accessory phase thermometry. Fields of basement metamorphism (B) and cordierite seam formation (C) are from solid-phase thermobarometry.

Thus the Neogene magmatic history of the Nanga Parbat-Haramosh massif results from the complex interaction between its thermal structure, tectonic evolution, and fluid advection, reflecting both the broad Himalayan affiliation of the massif, and its singular neotectonic activity, which is anomalous within the orogen.

ACKNOWLEDGMENTS

Dave Waters, Mike Searle, Allison Macfarlane, and an anonymous reader provided helpful reviews and constructive criticism. Whittington thanks Mubarik Ali and A. Khwaja for hospitality in Islamabad, Jim Davis for services in the field, John Watson and Pete Webb for assistance with X-ray fluorescence analyses, Nick Rogers for the instrumental neutron activation analyses, Andy Tindle and Phil Potts for assistance with microprobe analyses, Jessica Bartlett, Peter van Calsteren, and Mabs Johnston for help in the isotope lab, and Allison Macfarlane, Jay Quade and Rasoul Sorkhabi for organizing the 11th Himalaya-Karakorum-Tibet Workshop. Whittington was funded by a Natural Environment Research Council (NERC) studentship, and field work for Harris and Butler was funded by NERC grant GR9/1304.

REFERENCES CITED

Ayres, M. W., Harris, N. B. W., and Vance, D., 1997, Possible constraints on anatectic melt residence times from accessory mineral dissolution rates: An example from Himalayan leucogranites: Mineralogical Magazine, v. 61, p. 29–36.

Blundy, J. D., and Wood, B. J., 1991, Crystal-chemical controls on the partitioning of Sr and Ba between plagioclase feldspar, silicate melts, and hydrothermal solutions: Geochimica et Cosmochimica Acta, v. 55, p. 193–209.

Brunel, M., and Kienast, J. R., 1986, Étude petro-structurale des chevauchements ductiles himalayans sur la transversale de l'Everest-Makalu (Nepal oriental): Canadian Journal of Earth Sciences, v. 23, p. 1117–1137.

Butler, R. W. H., and Prior, D. J., 1988, Tectonic controls on the uplift of the Nanga Parbat Massif, Pakistan Himalayas: Nature, v. 333, p. 247–250.

Butler, R. W. H., Prior, D. J., and Knipe, R. J., 1989, Neotectonics of the Nanga Parbat syntaxis, Pakistan, and crustal stacking in the northwest Himalayas: Earth and Planetary Science Letters, v. 94, p. 329–343.

Butler, R. W. H., George, M., Harris, N. B. W., Jones, C., Prior, D. J., Treloar, P. J., and Wheeler, J., 1993, Geology of the northern part of the Nanga Parbat massif, northern Pakistan, and its implications for Himalayan tectonics: Geological Society of London Journal, v. 149, p. 557–567.

Butler, R. W. H., Harris, N. B. W., and Whittington, A. G., 1997, Interactions between deformation, magmatism and hydrothermal activity during active crustal thickening: A field example from Nanga Parbat, Pakistan Himalayas: Mineralogical Magazine, v. 61, p. 37–51.

Cavallini, M., Vielzeuf, D., Bottazzi, P., Mazzuchelli, M., Martin, H., and Ottolini, L., 1995, Direct measurements of rare-earth contents in partial melts from metapelites: European Union of Geosciences, 8th meeting, Strasbourg: Terra Abstracts, v. 7, p. 143.

Clarke, D. B., 1995, Cordierite in felsic igneous rocks: A synthesis: Mineralogical Magazine, v. 59, p. 311–325.

Clemens, J. D., and Mawer, C. K., 1992, Granitic magma transport by fracture propagation: Tectonophysics, v. 204, p. 339–360.

Coward, M. P., Windley, B. F., Broughton, R. D., Luff, I. W., Petterson, M. G., Pudsey, C. J., Rex, D. C., and Khan, M. A., 1986, Collision tectonics in the NW Himalaya, *in* Coward, M. P., and Ries, A. C., eds., Collision tectonics: Geological Society of London Special Publication 19, p. 203–219.

Didier, J., and Dupraz, J., 1985, Magmatic and metasomatic cordierites in the Velay granitic massif (French Massif Central), *in* Wu Liren, Yang Taiming, Yuan Kuirong, Didier, J., Greenberg, J. K., Lowell, G. R., Xia Hongyuan, Yu Shoujun, and Augustithis, S. S., eds., The Crust—The significance of granite gneisses in the lithosphere: Athens, Theophrastus Publications, SA, p. 35–77.

England, P., Le Fort, P., Molnar, P., and Pecher, A., 1992, Heat sources for Tertiary metamorphism and anatexis in the Annapurna-Manaslu region, central Nepal: Journal of Geophysical Research, v. 97, no. B2, p. 2107–2128.

Finsterwalder, R., 1936, Karte der Nanga Parbat-Gruppe: München, Germany, Klein und Volbert, Alpensvereinkarte no. 0/7.

France-Lanord, C., and Le Fort, P., 1988, Crustal melting and granite genesis during the Himalayan collision orogenesis: Royal Society of Edinburgh Transactions, Earth Sciences, v. 79, p. 183–195.

George, M. T., 1993, The magmatic, thermal and exhumation history of the Nanga Parbat-Haramosh Massif, western Himalaya [Ph.D. thesis]: Milton Keynes, United Kingdom, The Open University, 402 p.

George, M. T., Harris, N. B. W., and Butler, R. W. H., 1993, The tectonic implications of contrasting granite magmatism between the Kohistan island arc and the Nanga Parbat-Haramosh Massif, Pakistan Himalaya, *in* Treloar, P. J., and Searle, M. P., eds., Himalayan tectonics: Geological Society of London Special Publication 74, p. 173–191.

Giletti, B. J., 1991, Rb and Sr diffusion in alkali feldspars with implications for the cooling histories of rocks: Geochimica et Cosmochimica Acta, v. 55, p. 1331–1343.

Guillot, S., and Le Fort, P., 1995, Geochemical constraints on the bimodal origin of High Himalayan leucogranites: Lithos, v. 35, p. 221–234.

Harris N. B. W., and Inger, S., 1992, Trace element modelling of pelite-derived granites: Contributions to Mineralogy and Petrology, v. 110, p. 46–56.

Harris, N. B. W., and Massey, J. A., 1994, Decompression and anatexis of Himalayan metapelites: Tectonics, v. 13, p. 1537–1546.

Harris, N. B. W., Inger, S., and Massey, J. A., 1993, The role of fluids in the formation of High Himalayan leucogranites, *in* Treloar, P. J., and Searle, M. P., eds., Himalayan tectonics: Geological Society of London Special Publication 74, p. 391–400.

Henderson, P., 1982, Inorganic geochemistry: Oxford, Pergamon Press, 335 p.

Hodges, K. V., Burchfiel, B. C., Royden, L. H., Chen, Z., and Lieu, Y., 1993, The metamorphic signature of contemporaneous extension and shortening in the central Himalayan orogen: Data from the Nyalam transect, southern Tibet: Journal of Metamorphic Geology, v. 11, p. 721–737.

Holland, T. J. B., and Powell, R., 1990, An enlarged and updated internally consistent thermodynamic dataset with uncertainties and correlations: the system $K_2O-Na_2O-CaO-MgO-MnO-FeO-Fe_2O_3-Al_2O_3-TiO_2-SiO_2-C-H_2-O_2$: Journal of Metamorphic Geology, v. 8, p. 89–124.

Holtz, F., and Johannes, W., 1991, Genesis of peraluminous granites 1. Experimental investigation of melt compositions at 3 and 5 kb and various H_2O activities: Journal of Petrology, v. 32, p. 935–958.

Inger, S., and Harris, N. B. W., 1992, Tectonothermal evolution of the High Himalayan Crystalline sequence, Langtang valley, northern Nepal: Journal of Metamorphic Geology, v. 10, p. 439–452.

Inger, S., and Harris, N. B. W., 1993, Geochemical constraints on leucogranite magmatism in the Langtang valley, Nepal Himalaya: Journal of Petrology, v. 34, p. 345–368.

Johannes, W., and Holtz, F., 1990, Formation and composition of H_2O-undersaturated granitic melts, *in* Ashworth, J. R. and Brown, M., eds., High-temperature metamorphism and crustal anatexis: London, Unwin Hyman, p. 87–101.

Kretz, R., 1983, Symbols for rock-forming minerals: American Mineralogist, v. 68, p. 277–279.

Le Breton, N., and Thompson, A. B., 1988, Fluid-absent (dehydration) melting of biotite in metapelites in the early stages of crustal anatexis: Contributions to Mineralogy and Petrology, v. 99, p. 226–237.

Le Fort, P., 1975, Himalaya: The collided range. Present knowledge of the continental arc: American Journal of Science, v. 275, p. 1–44.

Le Fort, P., Cuney, M., Deniel, C., France-Lanord, C., Sheppard, S. M. F., Upreti, B. N., and Vidal, P., 1987, Crustal generation of the Himalayan leucogranites: Tectonophysics, v. 134, p. 39–57.

Madin, I. P., Lawrence, R. D., and Ur-Rehman, S., 1989, The northwestern Nanga Parbat–Haramosh Massif; evidence for crustal uplift of the northwestern corner of the Indian craton, *in* Malinconico, L. L., and Lillie, R. J., eds., Tectonics of the Western Himalayas: Geological Society of America Special Publication 232, p. 169–182.

Montel, J. M., 1993, A model for monazite/melt equilibrium and applications to the generation of granitic magmas: Chemical Geology, v. 110, p. 127–146.

Nash, W. P., and Crecraft, H. R., 1985, Partition coefficients for trace elements in silicic magmas: Geochimica et Cosmochimica Acta, v. 49, p. 2309–2322.

Pearce, J. A., Harris, N. B. W., and Tindle, A. G., 1984, Trace element discrimination diagrams for the tectonic interpretation of granitic rocks: Journal of Petrology, v. 25, p. 956–983.

Petford, N., Lister, J. R., and Kerr, R. C., 1993, Dike transport of granitoid magmas: Geology, v. 21, p. 845–848.

Petö, P., 1976, An experimental investigation of melting relations involving muscovite and paragonite in the silica-saturated portion of the system $K_2O-Na_2O-Al_2O_3-SiO_2-H_2O$: Progress in Experimental Petrology, v. 3, p. 41–v. 45.

Pinet, C., and Jaupart, C., 1987, A thermal model for the distribution in space and time of the Himalayan granites: Earth and Planetary Science Letters, v. 84, p. 87–99.

Potts, P. J., Williams Thorpe, O., Isaacs, M. C., and Wright, D. W., 1985, High precision instrumental neutron activation analysis of geological samples employing simultaneous counting with both planar and coaxial detectors: Chemical Geology, v. 48, p. 145–155.

Powell, R., and Holland, T. J. B., 1988, An internally consistent dataset with uncertainties and correlations: 3. Applications to geobarometry, worked examples and a computer program: Journal of Metamorphic Geology, v. 6, p. 173–204.

Reddy, S. M., Searle, M. P. and Massey, J. A., 1993, Structural evolution of the High Himalayan Gneiss sequence, Langtang valley, Nepal, *in* Treloar, P. J., and Searle, M. P., eds., Himalayan tectonics: Geological Society of London Special Publication 74, p. 375–389.

Rutter, E. H., and Neumann, D. H. K., 1995, Experimental deformation of partially molten Westerly granite under fluid-absent conditions with implications for the extraction of granitic magmas: Journal of Geophysical Research, v. 100, p. 15697–15715.

Srogi, L., Wagner, M. E. and Lutz, T. M., 1993, Dehydration partial melting and disequilibrium in the granulite-facies Wilmington Complex, Pennsylvania-Delaware Piedmont: American Journal of Science, v. 293, p. 405–462.

Sun, S. S., and McDonough, W. F., 1989, Chemical and isotopic systematics of oceanic basalts: implications for mantle composition and processes, *in* Saunders, A. D., and Norry, M. J., eds., Magmatism in ocean basins: Geological Society of London Special Publication 42, p. 313–345.

Swapp, S. M., and Hollister, L. S., 1991, Inverted metamorphism within the Tibetan Slab of Bhutan: Evidence for a tectonically transported heat source: Canadian Mineralogist, v. 29, p. 1019–1041.

Treloar, P. J., Potts, G. J., Wheeler, J., and Rex, D. C., 1991, Structural evolution and asymmetric uplift of the Nanga Parbat syntaxis, Pakistan Himalaya: Geologische Rundschau, v. 80, p. 411–428.

Watson, E. B., and Harrison, T. M., 1983, Zircon saturation revisited: Temperature and composition effects in a variety of crustal magma types: Earth and Planetary Science Letters, v. 64, p. 295–304.

Watt, G. R., and Harley, S. L., 1993, Accessory phase controls on the geochemistry of crustal melts and restites produced during water-undersaturated partial melting: Contributions to Mineralogy and Petrology, v. 114, p. 550–556.

Wheeler, J., Treloar, P. J., and Potts, G. J., 1995, Structural and metamorphic evolution of the Nanga Parbat syntaxis, Pakistan Himalayas, on the Indus gorge transect: The importance of early events: Geological Journal, v. 30, p. 349–371.

Whittington, A. G., 1996, Exhumation overrated at Nanga Parbat, Northern Pakistan: Tectonophysics , v. 260, p. 215–226.

Whittington, A. G., Harris, N. B. W., and Baker, J. B., 1998, Low-pressure crustal anatexis: The significance of spinel and cordierite from metapelitic assemblages at Nanga Parbat, northern Pakistan, *in* Treloar, P. J., and O'Brien, P., eds., What drives metamorphism and metamorphic reactions?: Geological Society of London Special Publication 138, p. 177–192.

Winslow, D. M., Zeitler, P. K., and Chamberlain, C. P., 1994, Direct evidence for a steepened geotherm under conditions of rapid denudation, Pakistan Himalayas: Geology, v. 22, p. 1075–1078.

Winslow, D. M., Chamberlain, C. P., and Zeitler, P. K., 1995, Metamorphism and melting of the lithosphere due to rapid denudation, Nanga Parbat Massif Himalaya: Journal of Geology, v. 103, p. 395–409.

Wyllie, P. J., 1977, Crustal anatexis: An experimental review: Tectonophysics, v. 43, p. 41–71.

Zeitler, P. K., 1985, Cooling history of the NW Himalaya, Pakistan: Tectonics, v. 4, p. 127–151.

Zeitler, P. K., and Chamberlain, C. P., 1991, Petrogenetic and tectonic significance of young leucogranites from the northwestern Himalaya, Pakistan: Tectonics, v. 10, p. 729–741.

Zeitler, P. K., Tahirkheli, R. A. K., Naeser, C. W., and Johnson, N. M., 1982, Unroofing history of a suture zone in the Himalaya of Pakistan by means of fission-track annealing ages: Earth and Planetary Science Letters, v. 57, p. 227–240.

Zeitler, P. K., Chamberlain, C. P., and Smith, H. A., 1993, Synchronous anatexis, metamorphism, and rapid denudation at Nanga Parbat (Pakistan Himalaya): Geology, v. 21, p. 347–350.

MANUSCRIPT ACCEPTED BY THE SOCIETY FEBRUARY 3, 1998

Geological Society of America
Special Paper 328
1999

Late Miocene tectonic evolution of the Karakorum–Nanga Parbat contact zone (northern Pakistan)

Arnaud Pêcher and Patrick Le Fort

CNRS, UPRES-A 5025, Institut Dolomieu, Laboratoire de Géodynamique des Chaînes Alpines,
15 rue Maurice Gignoux, 38031 Grenoble, France

ABSTRACT

In northern Pakistan, the northwestern syntaxis of the Himalaya is marked by the spur of the Nanga Parbat–Haramosh massif, bounded by the Arc formations of Ladakh and Kohistan, and located south of the Karakorum range. The three units are separated by two major tectonic features, corresponding to late reactivation of the southern Indus-Tsangpo suture and northern Shyok suture. Field mapping in the as-yet poorly known Nanga Parbat-Haramosh massif–Karakorum contact zone, together with structural, metamorphic, and geochronological data, has led to new constraints on the interpretation of this key zone, viz.: (1) the backarc belt continues without interruption from Ladakh to Kohistan; (2) the southern Karakorum, the Arc, and the northernmost part of the Nanga Parbat-Haramosh massif display the same recumbent isoclinal folds and related metamorphic schistosity as the major structural event; (3) ductile deformation ended after 6 or 7 Ma; (4) in front of the Nanga Parbat spur, there is no evidence of normal-type faulting, or of Karakorum indentation, either considering the lithological boundaries or the metamorphic fabric; (5) on both sides of the spur, the right-lateral and left-lateral cartographic displacements mainly reflect the late doming of the initial arc-massif contact, a south-directed shear zone. Thus, the three units, east of the Raikot fault, define an east-west–trending broad zone that has thermally and tectonically behaved as a single crustal piece. The northern part of the Nanga Parbat-Haramosh massif can be considered to be a large dome in the westward extension of the Karakorum domes, a line of domes that developed east of the Raikot fault and possibly initiated as a crustal-scale fold system, induced by broad and diffuse northwest-southeast dextral shearing in a transpressive regime.

INTRODUCTION

The northwest syntaxis of the Himalaya is dominated by the spur of the Nanga Parbat-Haramosh massif, bounded by the arc formations of Ladakh and Kohistan, and is located south of the Karakorum range (Fig. 1). To the north, the contact between the Himalayan and the Karakorum units has been poorly documented; the few observations (e.g., maps of Desio, 1964; Desio et al., 1985) are being complemented by detailed structural or petrographic analyses. Tectonic contacts between the three units have been assumed to represent the former sutures (Tahirkheli

et al., 1979; Coward et al., 1986); the Nanga Parbat-Haramosh massif is the westernmost protrusion of the rigid Himalayan indenter (Molnar and Tapponnier, 1975; Tapponnier et al., 1986), and the island arc was squeezed out at the contact with the Karakorum. The latter unit was strongly deformed during the hypercollision (Mattauer, 1986) of the Indian mass with the Eurasian continent following the early Eocene collision (Coward et al., 1986).

From 1991 to 1995, during five field campaigns, we were able to map at a 1:150 000 scale, and locally at a 1:50 000 scale, the Kohistan-Ladakh-Karakorum units north of the Nanga

Pêcher, A., and Le Fort, P., 1999, Late Miocene tectonic evolution of the Karakorum–Nanga-Parbat contact zone (northern Pakistan), *in* Macfarlane, A., Sorkhabi, R. B., and Quade, J., eds., Himalaya and Tibet: Mountain Roots to Mountain Tops: Boulder, Colorado, Geological Society of America Special Paper 328.

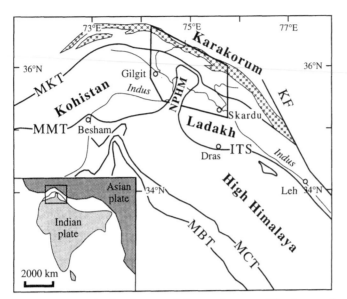

Figure 1. Tectonic sketch map of the northwestern Himalaya and Karakorum, redrawn from Rolfo et al. (1997), showing the regional setting of the investigated area. Inset shows the location of the sketch map in the Himalayan range. The extent of our geological mapping shown in Figure 2 is underlined. ITS = Indus-Tsangpo suture; KF = Karakorum fault; MBT = Main Boundary thrust; MCT = Main Central thrust; MKT = Main Karakorum thrust; MMT = Main Mantle thrust; NPHM = Nanga Parbat-Haramosh massif.

Parbat-Haramosh massif and to study the tectono-metamorphic evolution of the zone. Preliminary reports have been published (Pognante et al., 1993; Rolfo, 1994; Le Fort et al., 1995; Lemennicier, 1996; Lemennicier et al., 1996; Villa et al., 1996a, 1996b; Rolfo et al., 1997). In this chapter we present the results of tectonic analysis, and show that the pattern of the Nanga Parbat–Karakorum contact zone results from the same young (late Miocene) tectonics dominated by a strong flattening followed by domal structure. We propose that this doming phase observed and mapped east of the Raikot fault, in Himalaya as well as in Ladakh and south Karakorum, accounts for the protruding shape of the Nanga Parbat-Haramosh massif.

GEOLOGICAL FRAMEWORK

Three units separated by two major tectonic features compose the Himalaya-Karakorum boundary in the vicinity of the western Himalayan syntaxis (Fig. 1). They are the basement gneiss of the High Himalaya, the paleo-island arc of Kohistan-Ladakh, and the metamorphic and plutonic formations of southern Karakorum. The two tectonic features usually referred to as the Indus-Tsangpo (Main Mantle thrust) suture and the Northern (Shyok) suture reworked along the Main Karakorum thrust are discussed later.

The Himalayan gneisses form the conspicuous high relief Nanga Parbat–Haramosh spur, which has the shape of an indenter in the heart of the Himalayan western syntaxis. This "half-

window of Indian crust" (Zeitler et al., 1993) is made up of Proterozoic to Paleozoic gneiss dominated by orthogneiss, the Iskere gneiss of Madin et al. (1989). The gneisses are metamorphosed to amphibolite facies and partly migmatized. Locally, metabasic dikes record high-pressure garnet-granulite metamorphism of probable early Himalayan age (Pognante et al., 1993). These gneisses have also undergone very recent Pliocene-Pleistocene metamorphism and anatexis associated with high denudation rates (Zeitler et al., 1993; Craw et al., 1994; Winslow et al., 1994; Chamberlain and Zeitler, 1996). The general antiformal structure of the massif described by Coward (1985), Coward et al. (1986), Madin et al. (1989), and Butler et al. (1992) is clearly superimposed on previous isoclinal folds (Coward et al., 1986, Fig. 9), observed from outcrop to cartographic scale.

The Kohistan-Ladakh island arc (Tahirkheli et al., 1979; Bard et al., 1980; Bard, 1983) consists of Cretaceous to Eocene plutonic and volcanic material and some sedimentary rock (shale, marble, and minor quartzite). The arc sequence was first interpreted as a simple cross section in a tilted island arc, but it was later shown to be deformed by kilometer-scale tight folds (Coward et al., 1982a, 1982b) and truncated by steep shear zones (e.g., Khan, 1994). Only the southern part represents the crust of the island arc; the northern part, discussed here, developed in a backarc environment (Khan, 1994; Khan et al., 1996). It has been deformed and metamorphosed to various degrees, roughly from granulite (Jan, 1977; Yamamoto, 1993) to greenschist facies along a south to north section. In the area that we have mapped, two subunits can be distinguished: the Askore amphibolites to the south, and the Greenstone complex to the north (cf. Rolfo et al., 1997). They are separated by a discontinuous screen of serpentinite and pyroxenite that can be traced in Ladakh (lower Turmik valley, Rolfo, 1994) as in Kohistan (Bilchar-Dobani), on both sides of the Nanga Parbat gneiss (Fig. 2). The thickness of the lenticular ultramafics is as much as 1 km. The northern subunit, mainly made up of basaltic and andesitic volcanics and volcanosedimentary formations, is paralleled by marble horizons such as the Pakora marble to the east that can be traced westward through Malubiting up to the Darchan area. This northern subunit passes from the Ladakh to the Kohistan arc on the southern bank of the Chogo Lungma glacier, where we have mapped it (Fig. 2). It is a backarc complex metamorphosed at greenschist facies (the Greenstone complex of Ivanac et al., 1965). The southern subunit, in the area here concerned, is made up of amphibolites and a few marble horizons, intruded by numerous granitic to dioritic plutons, partly described by Petterson and Windley (1985) and Hanson (1986). This subunit corresponds to an island-arc complex metamorphosed in the amphibolite facies. We have observed similar amphibolite folded together with felsic mylonitic Himalayan gneiss, especially in the vicinity of the eastern margin of the Nanga Parbat massif, around the Stak-Indus junction. They may indicate isoclinal refolding of the Himalaya-Arc contact.

The Karakorum crustal unit is usually divided into three subunits, from south to north, these are the Karakorum metamorphic complex, the axial batholith, and the northern sedimentary series. We have mainly mapped the southern fringe of the batholith and the Karakorum metamorphic complex. The Karakorum metamorphic complex represents the northern margin of the Neotethys ocean. It is composed of orthogneiss and metasedimentary formations, and very minor metavolcanic rocks, which have undergone at least two main tectonometamorphic events in upper amphibolite facies. According to Allen and Chamberlain (1991), the metamorphic pattern results mainly from an old evolution; a first phase of metamorphism is linked to the initial thickening of the Asian plate, later followed by a decompressional metamorphism, as southward-directed nappes were emplaced onto Ladakh during the collision. For Lemennicier et al. (1996), the main structures result from a postcollisional, two-stage, tectono-metamorphic evolution; a first phase of south-vergent isoclinal folding, corresponding to peak metamorphic conditions, is followed by a second phase of doming associated to decompressional metamorphism.

Lithological mapping of the Karakorum metamorphic complex has revealed continuity of the different rock formations, clearly marked by limestones beds that can be followed continuously from the Hunza to Shigar valleys for more than 100 km (Fig. 2), despite the two main phases of folding and intense tectonism of the region. Not only is the continuity remarkable, but the rectilinear pattern of the Karakorum metamorphic complex is unique. The protruding mass of the Nanga Parbat spur, in the heart of the western Himalayan syntaxis, south of the arcuate Karakorum range, has had no or little influence on the shape of the Karakorum formations; although it has the geometry of an indenter, it has not indented the Karakorum structure, as often postulated (see Tapponnier et al., 1986, Fig. 13).

DEFORMATION IN THE THREE UNITS

Southern Karakorum

The predominant deformational fabric in the southern Karakorum is the metamorphic foliation, which is the axial surface of isoclinal folds at various scales, folding together both metasediments and large lenses of granitoid rocks (Fig. 3).

Foliation and domal structures. South of the Karakorum axial zone, the metamorphic imprint is strong, i.e., there are staurolite-garnet-kyanite or sillimanite assemblages (Lemennicier et al., 1996). Nevertheless, at landscape scale, the lithological contacts are still the most obvious surfaces. For example, one can easily follow across the mapped area, for nearly 150 km from the Basha valley to the Bar valley, the interleaving of white limestone, brownish metapelites, and black metabasalts. At outcrop scale, the main deformational fabric is the metamorphic foliation and related lineations (mineral lineation, intersection lineation, and the less-obvious

stretching lineation). In some places, the deformational fabric is a shearing fabric, with c/s almonds indicating top-to-the-south movement. We have never been able to follow laterally such shear zones more than a few hundred meters, nor have we been able to demonstrate nappe structures at cartographic scale. Tight to isoclinal folds are the only structures traceable for several kilometers.

On the basis of systematic measurement of the foliation (Figs. 4 and 5), two structural domains can be distinguished.

From Bar to Arandu and the higher Biafo glacier, the foliation is very regularly oriented at N115°E, its average dip increasing from ~45°N close to the Karakorum axial zone to nearly vertical close to the South Karakorum fault (Figs. 4 and 5). This fabric vanishes to the north in the axial zone, but clearly affects the southern part of the axial granites: the 95 Ma Hunza granodiorite (Le Fort et al., 1983), in the Hunza valley, and the 21 Ma Baltoro granite (Parrish and Tirrul, 1989), in the Biafo glacier area.

Southeast of Arandu, the cleavage pattern indicates several typical domal ellipsoidal structures, usually cored by orthogneissic rocks (e.g., the Dassu gneissic dome, Bertrand et al., 1988; Fig. 5). They are as long as 20 km, and trending northwest-southeast; they have steep limbs and an altogether conical geometry, and a steep to nearly vertical cone axis (cf. Lemennicier et al., 1996). These domes, as indicated by the main foliation, are in places associated with a down-dip stretching lineation, along which peak metamorphic minerals recrystallized (e.g., Arandu area, where the strong vertical stretching lineation is marked by sillimanite and biotite, or sometimes kyanite; cf. Lemennicier et al., 1996), thus, the domes appear to have formed before complete cooling of the metamorphic pile.

In the Basha valley, the Hemasil dome (Fig. 5) is an important chrono-tectonic marker. In this small body of syenitic rocks, the domal pattern can be seen in the metamorphic fabric of the surrounding metasediments, in the subsolidus fabric of the external zones of the syenite massif, as well as in the preserved magmatic fabric of the core of the syenite. It implies that dome formation is contemporaneous with syenitic plutonism, which occurred around 9 Ma (^{40}Ar/^{39}Ar hornblende age of 7.0 to 7.7 Ma and biotite age around 4 Ma; Villa et al., 1996a). Those ages and other young ages (Fig. 6) previously found for other late tectonic small granitoids suggest that the main metamorphic fabric in Karakorum is younger than suggested previously (e.g., Searle, 1991, 1996). It was probably acquired between 21 Ma (21.0 ± 0.5 Ma, age of the Baltoro granite; Parrish and Tirrul, 1989) and 7 Ma. The young U-Pb monazite ages (6.8 ± 0.2 Ma and 6.7 ± 0.5 Ma) obtained by Smith et al. (1992) on two samples of schist east of the Dassu dome, would not be so "unrealistic" (Chamberlain and Zeitler, 1996), but would represent the age of the latest peak of amphibolite-grade metamorphism. These data lead us to question the significance of the data from the Mango Gusar granite, a granite body located east of the Dassu dome, dated as 37.0 ± 0.8 (U/Pb on

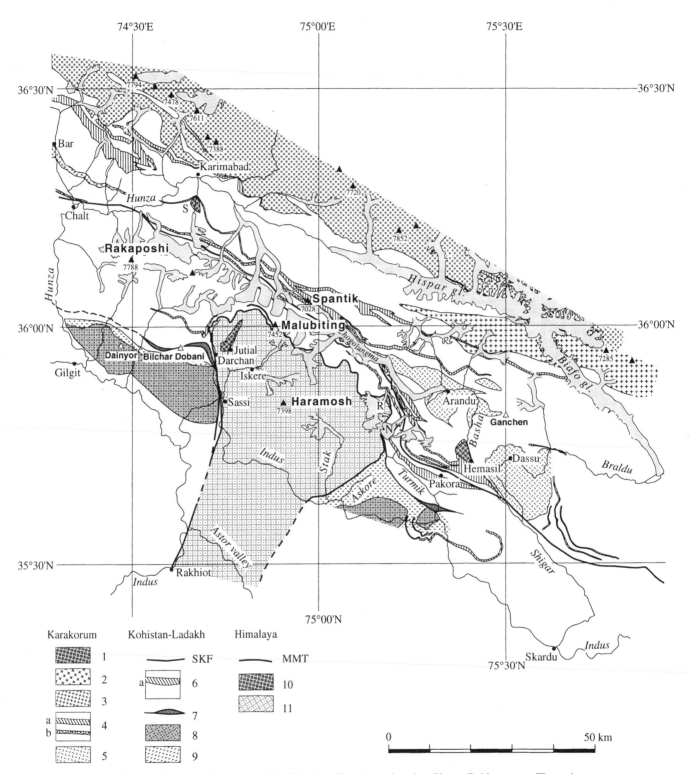

Figure 2. Structural sketch map of the Himalaya-Karakorum junction, Hunza-Baltistan area. The main lithological units are as follows. In Karakorum, (1) the late Miocene granitoids (S, Sumayar), (2) the early Miocene Baltoro granite, (3) the Cretaceous Hunza granodiorite, (4) the South Karakorum metamorphic complex (a: main marbles levels, b: conglomerates), (5) the orthogneiss. In Kohistan-Ladakh, (6) the Greenstone Complex (a: limestones), (7) the serpentinites and pyroxenites, (8) the diorites and granodiorites, (9) the Askore amphibolites. In Himalaya, (10) the Miocene Jutial granite, (11) the gneiss. N is Niamur glacier. R is Miocene Remendok trondjhemite, crosscutting the Main Mantle thrust (MMT). SKF, South Karakorum fault. Black triangles are peaks higher than 7000 m.

Figure 3. Hectometer-scale fold in the upper Chogo Lungma area. A: East-looking photo AP-93-8-13, left bank of the Morraine valley, upper Chogo Lungma area, showing the core of Hunza-type granitoid in an isoclinal antiform (north at the left side of the photo). B: Photo AP-93-6-34, Serac glacier, showing folds with steeply plunging axes, folding limestone (light color), metapelitic gneiss, and amphibolite (north at the right side of the photo).

zircons, Parrish, *in* Rex et al., 1988). This granite-granodiorite, described as crosscutting the metamorphic fabric in the text (Searle, 1991), is mapped in fault contact with the surrounding rocks (Searle et al., 1989, 1996). Because of these discrepancies, the age of the Mango Gusar granite does not adequately fix the relative metamorphic chronology or put a bound on the tectonic evolution of the region.

Folds. Despite the regular map-scale pattern of the various lithological units, outcrop-scale synmetamorphic folds are common. They are marked either by dissected but still-recognizable fold hinges, or, more often, by the bedding-cleavage intersection lineation. Due to deep valley cuts and scarcity of vegetation, hectometer- to kilometer-scale isoclinal folds are also clearly recognizable in many places, for example in the Bar valley (north of Chalt), in the Chogo Lungma north bank tributary glaciers (Serac, Moraine, and Bolocho glaciers, Fig. 3), in the Arandu area, and in the Ganchen area (cf. Desio et al., 1985).

Thus some of the stratigraphic-like alternations of limestone and metapelite actually correspond to the same refolded levels, as suggested by the cartographic pattern.

These folds clearly affect both the sediments and the orthogneisses (Fig. 3A). On the basis of geochemical comparisons, the orthogneisses, mainly present in the eastern domes-rich domain, appear to be derived from plutonic rocks analogous to those of the axial batholith (Lemennicier, 1996). Although not yet confirmed by age dating, it can be inferred that the plutonism of the "axial batholith" is not limited to the axial zone, but extends southward, where it has been overprinted by the young metamorphism and deformation.

Except in the eastern zone, where axes have been reoriented by late doming (Fig. 4, stereograms 4 and 5), most small- and large-scale synmetamorphic fold axes and/or intersection lineations are scattered in the average northwest-southeast–trending foliation plane (Fig. 4, stereograms 1 to 3). In the western part (Hunza area), folds gently plunge to the west, but in the central part, close to the South Karakorum fault (Chogo Lungma area), they usually plunge steeply to vertically (Figs. 3B and 4). Such steeply plunging folds could indicate strike-slip movement in a strike-slip ductile zone, parallel to the South Karakorum fault. Dextral shearing and associated folding in the Hunza area was described by Coward et al. (1986), and interpreted as movement on the northern margin of the Indian indenter, postdating the collision. The dispersion of the axes (curved axes) also suggests that the synmetamorphic folds accommodate local strong flattening by vertical extrusion of the deforming rock.

Ladakh-Kohistan arcs

When crossing the South Karakorum fault, there is no change in the style and orientation of the deformational fabric. On both sides of the Nanga Parbat spur, the Arc formations present the same synmetamorphic isoclinal folds. As in the southern Karakorum, the fold axes, scattered in the foliation plane, usually plunge steeply (cf. Fig. 4, stereograms 6 to 8). Such a pattern probably indicates shearing parallel to the South Karakorum fault in an overall dominant flattening regime.

In the strip of Greenstone complex, north of the Nanga Parbat spur, shear criteria are rare, but generally consistent with an upward movement of the northeastern compartment. No unambiguous criteria of normal-type ductile shearing or brittle faulting have been found. Two samples from the northern strip of Greenstone complex have yielded $^{40}Ar/^{39}Ar$ amphibole ages of 14.3 ± 1.9 Ma and 8.8 ± 2.6 Ma, and biotite plateau ages of 7.9 ± 0.1 and 6.3 ± 0.1 Ma (Villa et al., 1996b). On the eastern side of the Nanga Parbat spur, south of the domes zone recognized in the Karakorum area, the regular pattern of the foliation is also deformed by a large domal structure that we have mapped around the Turmik-Indus confluence (Fig. 4, stereogram 9). However, none of the four samples of Askore formation from the Indus valley, dated by $^{40}Ar/^{39}Ar$ on amphibole

(Villa et al., 1996b), have shown any evidence of Miocene metamorphic episode or overprint.

The screen of ultramafics that divide Kohistan and Ladakh in two subunits is a good marker of the overall deformation of the Arc (Fig. 2). Parallel to the general structural trend, away from the Nanga Parbat-Haramosh massif, it is bent on both sides approaching the contact with the Himalayan gneisses. To the east, the bending of the lower Turmik screen marks and supports the right-lateral shear sense, also found in the Greenstone complex. To the west, the curvature of the Bilchar-Dobani screen indicates right-lateral movement, which seems to contradict the movement deduced from the observation of the mylonitic Himalayan gneiss of the upper Darchan valley (Fig. 7).

Himalayan basement

The Nanga Parbat-Haramosh massif has the general shape of a large dome, but inside the massif, the foliation pattern outlines several typical second-order domal structures. Two of them, described by Gansser (1980) and later by Madin et al. (1989), are cut by the Indus valley (Fig. 4, stereograms 11 and 12). The domes deform earlier isoclinal folds. The relationship between these folds and the metamorphism is not always clear. In the same area (e.g., Stak confluence, east of Shengus) it is sometimes possible to observe isoclinal folds that have similar orientations, either deforming a metamorphic foliation, or having the metamorphic minerals (biotite and kyanite in particular) clearly developed on the axial plane. The Himalayan orthogneiss is often overprinted, especially close to the contact, by a strong mylonitic fabric with ribbon quartz, and c/s structures. The mylonitic structure of the gneiss gives a banded appearance to the outcrops (cf. the Layered Unit of Butler et al., 1992). Toward the border zone, the ductile mylonitic fabric is linked to the suture shearing, postdating magmatic activity in the Kohistan arc. The mylonitic fabric is deformed by the synmetamorphic to late metamorphic folds.

The conditions and the timing of the deformation and metamorphism of the Nanga Parbat-Haramosh massif gneiss are not yet completely known. It is either considered to be dominated by precollisional deformation in large parts of the core of the massif (Butler et al., 1992; Treloar et al., 1991; Wheeler et al., 1995), or to be syncollisional (Chamberlain and Zeitler, 1996). According to Chamberlain and Zeitler (1996), postmetamorphic cooling (and retrogression of the granulitic assemblage into an amphibolitic one as described by Pognante et al., 1993) occurred at a relatively slow rate from 45 to 25 Ma, and at a much higher rate from 25 to 16 Ma. They interpreted the high rate of cooling to be a result of tectonic denudation, as Kohistan moved northward along normal faults. We have found no evidence of normal faulting, either in the massif or in the surrounding Arc rocks. On the contrary, Miocene ^{40}Ar/^{39}Ar cooling ages on two muscovites from the mylonitic banded gneiss of the upper Darchan valley

Figure 4 (opposite page). Orientation of the structural markers in southern Karakorum (stereograms and area labeled 1 to 5), in the northern Kohistan-Ladakh series (stereograms 6 to 9), and in the Himalayan Nanga Parbat-Haramosh massif spur (stereograms 10 to 13). Geological formations: symbols as in Figure 2. Stereograms: equiangular Wulff nets, lower hemisphere. Symbols are common to all stereograms. Cross: metamorphic foliation; plain circles: axis of synmetamorphic fold and bedding-foliation intersection lineation (B lineation); black circles: stretching lineation; circles with a dot at center: axis of postmetamorphic fold. Thick cross: calculated best plane for the foliation; gray circle: pole of the calculated best great circle, for a girdle type distribution of values, or pole of the best small circle, for a small circle (conical) type distribution. Plain line circle: best great (or small) circle calculated using the foliation data (evidence of late- or postmetamorphic refolding). Dotted circles: best great (or small) circle calculated using the synmetamorphic folds axes and intersection lineations (surface of synmetamorphic scattering of the axis). Best axis and best great circle are deduced from the orientation matrix, best small circle is calculated by an iterative process. Orientations are given by plunge (or dip) direction, and plunge (or dip) value (e.g., a line 26-56 means a line plunging 56° in a 26°E direction). Stereograms 1 to 3 illustrate the typical pattern seen in southern Karakorum, away from the eastern domes area. The foliations are regularly oriented, but the lineations, often with steep plunges, are scattered along a plane (a great circle), close to the foliation best value. Best great circles and best foliation planes are oriented 26-56 and 24-72 (stereogram 1), 46-64 and 38-79 (stereogram 2), and 29-68 and 35-78 (stereogram 3), respectively. Stereograms 4 and 5 correspond to the northwestern ending of the Arandu and Dassu orthogneissic domes. The foliation is deformed by the doming process and irregularly scattered. Scattering is best fitted either using a small circle (conical fold, stereogram 4) or by a great circle (cylindrical fold, stereogram 5). In both cases, the axis plunges to the northwest (viz. 341-63 and 317-27). The former lineation is rotated toward the dome axis. In the Arendu dome, a strong ductile stretching lineation is observed, with a direction close to the dome axis. It is underlined by metamorphic minerals, and indicates that the doming occurred before the metamorphic cooling. Stereograms 6 to 8 illustrate the pattern observed in the Kohistan-Ladakh Greenstone complex, very similar to the one observed in South Karakorum (stereograms 1 to 3). B lineations are still scattered in the foliation plane, and usually have a steep plunge (stereogram 6, best great circle at 196-84, and best foliation plane at 185-84). In areas 7 and 8 (Ladakh formations in zone unaffected by late doming), lineations are again steeply plunging (thin great circle: cyclographic trace of the calculated best foliation planes, 33-67 and 36-70, respectively, for stereograms 7 and 8). Stereogram 9 illustrates a domal structure observed in Ladakh formations, along the Indus valley, south of the Turmik valley. The foliation is very irregularly scattered, in highly noncylindrical or nonconical structure. Stereograms 10 to 12 show the domal structures observed in the Himalaya. The bulk shape of the northern termination of the Nanga Parbat-Haramosh massif spur corresponds to a large dome. It is made of the juxtaposition of several smaller domes and/or folds, two of which are cut by the Indus road, west and east of Shengus village (canvas 11 and 12). In the Rakhan pass area (stereogram 10), foliation at the northwest end of the main dome is bent, and draws an approximately conical fold, with an axis at 346-76. In a similar way, the former lineations are dispersed along a small circle, centered at 91-16. In the Indus valley (stereograms 11 and 12), the section of the domes draw two roughly cylindrical folds, of similar orientation but opposite sense of plunge (viz. 216-42 and 25-13). Stereogram 13 displays measurement in the Main Mantle thrust zone, southeast border of the Haramosh dome (stak area). Late- or postmetamorphic folding, visible at outcrop scale, scatters the foliation (fold-axis direction deduced from the best great circle: 46-35). Late folds are parallel to the MMT local direction, and have also the same orientation as synmetamorphic folds. It indicates that doming took place in continuity with the synmetamorphic folding.

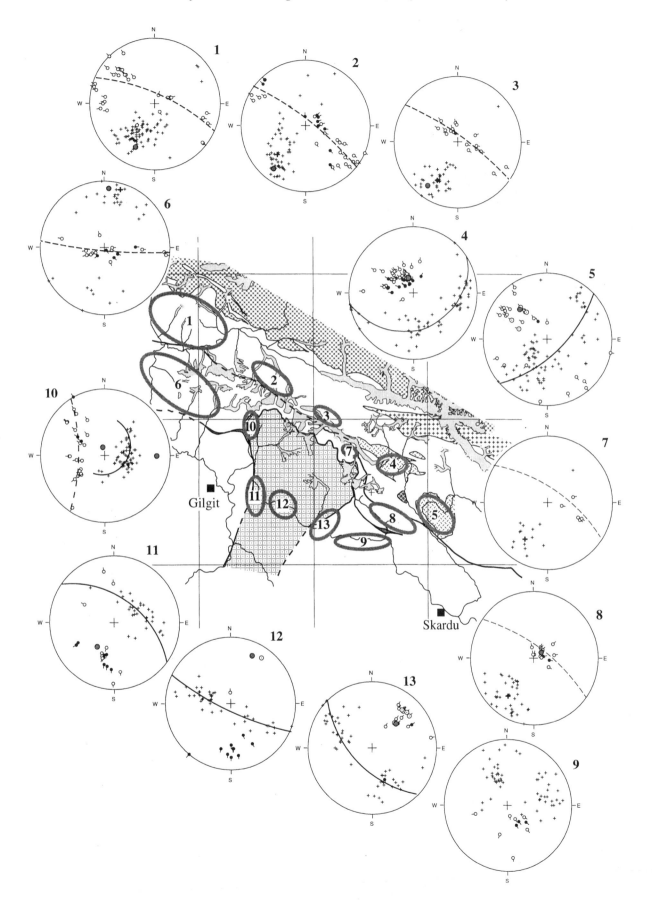

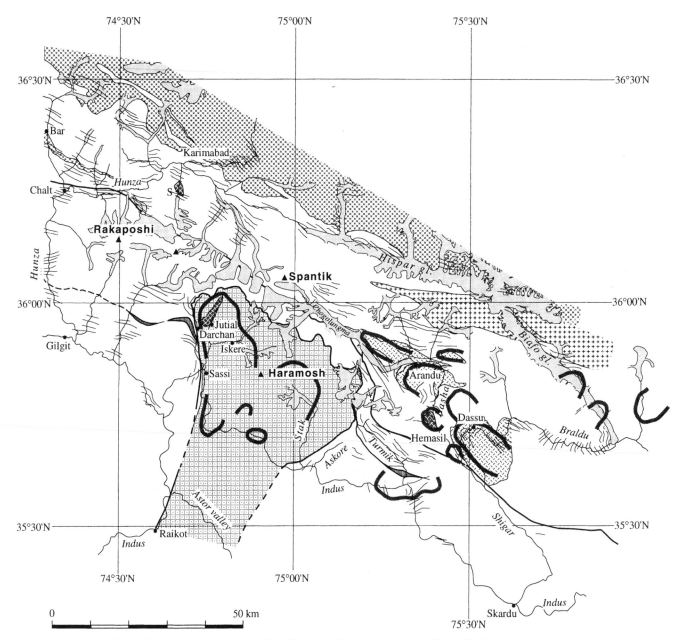

Figure 5. Structural sketch map of the Himalaya-Karakorum junction, Hunza-Baltistan area, showing the pattern of the foliation, deformed by late Miocene domal structures. Symbols as in Figure 2. The trace of the main foliation was drawn from field data by P. Le Fort (1987, 1992, 1993, 1994, 1995, 1996), Y. Lemennicier (1993), A. Pêcher (1988, 1992, 1993, 1994, 1995, 1996), P. Pertusati (1993), and F. Rolfo (1993). Domes are rimmed by a thick gray line.

(14.6 ± 0.2 and 13.3 ± 0.3 Ma; George et al., 1995) and folding of Himalayan mylonites in synmetamorphic to late metamorphic folds attest to a postcollisional compressive deformation stage. One cannot avoid the implication that some deformation relates to the very young metamorphic activity, illustrated by pervasive late Himalayan crustal melts (Zeitler and Chamberlain, 1991; Smith et al., 1992; Zeitler et al., 1993).

THE TWO MAJOR CONTACTS

Arc-Karakorum contact

The Arc-Karakorum contact, sometimes called the Northern megashear (Tahirkheli, 1979) or the Main Karakorum thrust (Bard et al., 1980), corresponds to the reactivation of the Shyok suture by the thrust. It is marked by sporadic pods of serpenti-

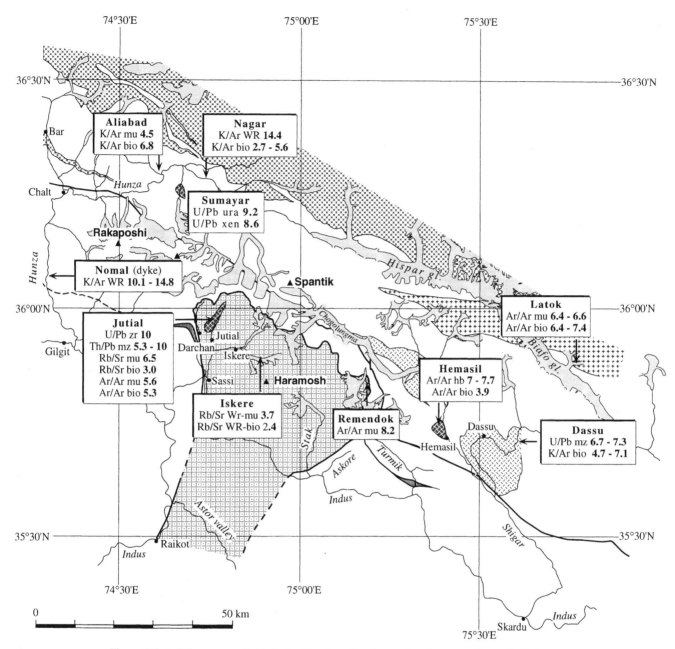

Figure 6. Late Miocene granitoids in the Himalaya-Karakorum junction zone, Hunza-Baltistan area. Symbols as in Figure 2. Data are from Le Fort et al. (1983) (Aliabad); Debon et al. (1987) (Nagar); George et al. (1993) (Jutial, for Rb/Sr and Ar/Ar ages); Schneider et al. (1997) (Jutial, for Th/Pb and U/Pb ages); Villa et al. (1996a) (Remendok and Hemasil); Smith et al. (1992) and Smith (1993) (Dassu gneissic dome); Schärer et al. (1990) (Latok, southern part of the Baltoro granite); Fraser et al. (1009) (Sumayar leucogranite).

nite. Between Chalt and the upper Shigar valley, map and field data show that the contact is not a thrust, but a steep to vertical brittle fault crosscutting the earlier fold pattern at a low angle (Fig. 2 around Niamur), as well as the latest metamorphic fabric. We would rather refer to it as the South Karakorum fault. We have mapped it between Chalt and the Shigar valley, the two areas where it was already defined. Its rectilinear pattern, slightly bent in the Niamur region, strongly contrasts with the Nanga Parbat–Haramosh massif–Arc contact. This very late fault reworks the original northern suture zone, the trace of which is poorly distinguishable, as it has been folded during the main metamorphic episode. For example, in the upper Niamur glacier valley, west of Arandu, there are kilometer-scale folds of the contact between the greenschists from Ladakh and lime-

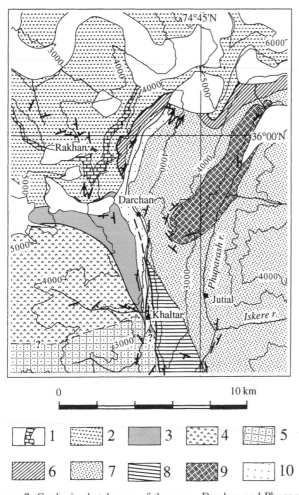

Figure 7. Geologic sketch map of the upper Darchan and Phuparash (Jutial) valleys. Symbols 1 to 5 refer to Kohistan formations, and 6 to 9 refer to Himalayan formations. (1) Main Kohistan dolomitic-limestone level, (2) greenstones, (3) serpentinites and pyroxenites, (4) amphibolites with some minor metasediments, (5) diorite and granodiorite, (6) blastomylonitized Himalayan orthogneiss, (7) Iskere orthogneiss, (8) heterogeneous gneiss, mainly metapelites, minor marbles, quartzites, and amphibolites (possibly of Kohistan origin) (9) Miocene Jutial tourmaline-rich granite, (10) Quaternary deposits. Orientation symbols are for the magmatic orientation in the Jutial granite or the metamorphic foliation elsewhere.

stones from the Karakorum units. Similarly, a narrow band of polygenic conglomerate and greenschist lie in most of the area to the north of the South Karakorum fault, locally oblique to the structural trend (Le Fort and Pêcher, 1995). These rocks probably represent synclinal inliers of arc material folded within the Karakorum metamorphic complex.

Himalaya-Arc contact

The Himalaya-Arc contact, sometimes named Main Mantle thrust (Tahirkheli et al., 1979) corresponds to the Indus-Tsangpo suture zone. It is generally marked by a strong contrast of lithology, between the dioritic arc formations and the granitic

Himalayan gneiss, although here it is not identified by glaucophane- and serpentinite-bearing lenticular bodies, as it is farther southwest and southeast of the Nanga Parbat-Haramosh massif. The nature and characteristics of the contact vary considerably on the three sides of the massif.

On the western side, the Himalaya-Kohistan contact is a brittle east-dipping reverse fault, the Raikot fault (Figs. 2 and 7), also known as the Liachar thrust in the southwest, which carries the Himalayan gneiss over the arc sequence (Lawrence and Ghauri, 1983; Butler and Prior, 1988; Madin et al., 1989). However, this brittle deformation is superimposed on older mylonitic fabric, as in the lower Astor and Raikot valleys, as well as on previous synmetamorphic isoclinal folds as along the Indus, south of Sassi. Actually, the trace of the fault is not always simple, and slices of Kohistan appear within the Himalayan gneiss (Indus road, south of Sassi, Fig. 2). North of the Indus, the contact is relatively simple, and corresponds to a major fault, dipping around 70°E, that has a 2–3-m-thick gouge zone. More to the north, this fault dies out in the upper Darchan valley (Fig. 7), and does not join the northwest-southeast strip of the Greenstone complex. North of Darchan, the old Arc-Himalaya contact is still well preserved. There is no tectonic slicing as shown by Butler et al. (1992, Fig. 2), but instead, hectometer-scale isoclinal folds, folding the Kohistan dolomitic limestone (south of the trail to the Rakhan Gali pass), or refolding Himalayan gneiss and Kohistan-type rock together (bottom of the upper Darchan valley). The activity on the fault is recorded by $^{40}Ar/^{39}Ar$ and fission-track cooling ages that show that the Nanga Parbat gneisses have had a rapid denudation history during the past 10 m.y. (Zeitler, 1985; Zeitler et al., 1989; Treloar et al., 1991).

To the east, the Himalaya-Ladakh contact is well exposed in the upper Turmik valley (Fig. 2) and is marked by a ductile shear zone with right-lateral strike-slip movement, indicated by rotation at map scale of the synmetamorphic structures (Pognante et al., 1993). This shear zone is superimposed by pervasive crenulation folds that indicate a similar right-lateral movement (Arc formations to the south), accompanied by retrograde metamorphism (Le Fort et al., 1995). The shear zone vanishes in the northwest-southeast Greenstone complex strip. Farther south, where it crosses the Indus, the Himalaya-Ladakh contact is difficult to locate accurately. There, Treloar et al. (1991) described interleaving units derived from the Kohistan and Indian continents. On a section more than 6 km west of the Askore valley, numerous folds at various scale (cf. Fig. 4, stereogram 13) lead to the intercalation of amphibolitic Arc-like and granitic Himalaya-like formations, which are sometimes blastomylonitic. Lenticular bodies of serpentinized peridotites and garnet-bearing pyroxenites, retrograded from eclogitic facies, have also been found in the Arc-type material; the pressure-temperature estimates (13 ± 1 kbar, 610 ± 30 °C) is typical of low- to intermediate-temperature eclogites (Le Fort et al., 1997). In addition, the entire zone has been reworked by numerous brittle faults mapped by Verplank (1986).

On the northern side (Fig. 2), the juxtaposition of the elevated Haramosh spur, which has high-grade metamorphic rocks, and the lower and less-metamorphosed domain north of it, suggests a normal fault boundary between the two. However, along the south bank of the Chogo Lungma glacier, most of the local synmetamorphic rotational deformation criteria indicate a top-to-the-south thrust sense of motion. In some places, normal and reverse senses of shearing are both present, indicating a flattening (pure shear) bulk deformation. However, nowhere has clear field evidence of normal faulting been found. Locally, in the Remendok valley, the northern contact is overprinted by a slightly deformed leucotrondhjemitic body (Fig. 2). The muscovite-bearing leucotrondhjemite, about 1 km wide, intrudes both the Arc and the Himalayan units with crosscutting aplitic and pegmatitic dikes that are as much as several hundred of meters from the pluton. Dating of one muscovite by $^{40}Ar/^{39}Ar$ (Villa et al., 1996a) has yielded an age of 8.37 ± 0.07 that represents a lower limit to the thrusting movement along the northern side of the Himalaya.

Wherever we have been able to observe a nonfaulted contact between the Himalayan gneisses and the Arc formations, the deformational pattern remains the same on both sides. In particular, the orientation of the foliation and the orientation of the synmetamorphic and postmetamorphic folds do not change (Fig. 4, stereogram 13). Our observations north of the Nanga Parbat spur (south of the Chogo Lungma glacier, where the Arc formation forms a continuous but very narrow strip) confirm that the Ladakh-Kohistan Arc–Himalaya contact is a broad ductile zone, with a regime of top-to-the-south rotational deformation. We have made similar observations on the northwestern and northeastern sides of the Nanga Parbat-Haramosh massif; however, there the late doming of the Himalayan gneisses and subsequent verticalization of the thrust contact have led to an apparent along-strike shearing, left lateral to the west, and right lateral to the east.

At several localities close to the contact, Himalayan-type felsic gneisses are isoclinally folded together with Arc-type amphibolitic gneisses and marbles. At three places (upper Darchan valley, Stak confluence, lower Astor valley), the Himalayan-type gneisses include the blasto-mylonitic suture-related gneisses.

The continuity and similarity of the fabric from the South Karakorum metamorphic complex to the northern part of the Himalayan gneisses suggest that the complex relates to the same main Karakorum deformation episode, rather than to the older mylonitic shearing. The interleaving of the different units would be due to south-vergent synmetamorphic refolding of the former shear zone, rather than to suture tectonics, a hypothesis to be confirmed by more detailed cartography of the zone.

NORTHERN NANGA-PARBAT STRUCTURE: A DOME-DOMINATED STRUCTURE?

Our geologic mapping of the South Karakorum–North Himalaya transition zone brings some additional constraints to the tectonic interpretation of the Nanga Parbat-Haramosh massif. These constraints are twofold; a first group concerns the continuity of the lithology, the metamorphism, and the tectonic evolution; and a second group concerns the significance of the structural pattern. The continuity constraints in the region are the following:

The island-arc belt, made up of the Greenstone complex to the north and the Askore amphibolite to the south, continues without interruption from Ladakh to Kohistan, along a narrow strip that separates Karakorum from Himalaya.

The main structural imprint, the isoclinal synmetamorphic folding followed by doming, corresponds to two main deformation stages that occurred during the decompressive path of the metamorphism. Uncertainties remain as to the timing of the synmetamorphic folding, as well as to the possible lateral diachronism, but it seems younger than usually accepted: younger than the Baltoro granite in Karakorum and younger than the Main Mantle thrust–related mylonitic fabric in Himalaya. Doming, around 10 Ma or later, follows isoclinal folding with no metamorphic or structural gap.

When considering the postcollisional evolution and young synmetamorphic to late metamorphic structures, there is a clear structural continuity from southern Karakorum to Kohistan-Ladakh and from Kohistan-Ladakh to Himalaya.

The ordering of the structural patterns around the Nanga Parbat-Haramosh massif is as follows:

North of the massif, the pattern of structures is very regular and remains almost unaffected in front of the spur. The main deformation results in strong flattening plus top-to-the-south shearing. The steep plunge of fold axis suggests a strike-slip shearing component.

On both sides of the massif, extension of the lateral strike-slip shear zones does not cut through the arc strip or through the southern Karakorum. The lateral contacts are not true strike-slip zones, but south-vergent structures that have been brought to vertical.

The right-lateral pattern shown by the Ladakh-Kohistan ultramafic screen on both sides of the massif could relate to the early collisional evolution of the region, around the time of collision. The Raikot fault has inherited its location, if not its kinematics, from this major structure.

Nowhere around the massif it has been possible to find evidence of northward sliding of the Kohistan arc along normal faults, or to observe systematic extensional structures. About 100 km south-southwest of the region discussed here, Hubbard et al. (1995), and Vince and Treloar (1996) emphasized the role of postmetamorphic west-southwest– and north-directed extensional shear in the exhumation of the Nanga Parbat massif and Himalayan gneiss. Hubbard et al. (1995) bracketed the age of this extensional movement between 40–56 and around 20 Ma, and Vince and Treloar (1996) estimated its age from the comparison of the local cooling histories of Kohistan and the Himalaya at around 18 ± 2 Ma. Because there is no evidence of such extensional tectonics in the northern part of the massif, one may hypothesize on the existence, south of the study area (south of the Nanga-Parbat peak?), of a decoupling feature, possibly equivalent to the "Shontargali thrust" described by Tahirkheli (1987).

These observations indicate that during the hypercollision stages, the southern Karakorum metamorphic complex, the northern Nanga Parbat-Haramosh massif Himalaya, and the intermediate arc strip defined a northwest-southeast–trending broad corridor that has behaved thermally and tectonically as a single crustal piece, in a regime of predominantly southward-directed shearing, including minor diffuse strike-slip shearing. The linearity of the main structures of southern Karakorum cannot be explained without a significantly more extensive Himalayan basement that is not restricted to the Nanga Parbat spur, but also underlies Ladakh and Kohistan.

In the southern Karakorum units, from the lower Chogo Lungma glacier to the Biafo glacier, the synmetamorphic fabric is folded by domal structures. The northern termination of the Nanga Parbat-Haramosh massif appears to be a double-dome shaped structure. Timing of the domal deformation in Nanga-Parbat is poorly constrained, but as in the Karakorum, doming is a late- to postmetamorphic event, bracketed between the Remendok granite emplacement (9 Ma) and the Quaternary brittle reactivation of its western limb along the Raikot fault.

Our mapping shows that the Karakorum and northern Nanga Parbat-Haramosh massif domes are part of a single corridor of domes trending east-west (Fig. 5), oblique to the average trend of the synmetamorphic fabric. Such a pattern suggests that the domes were initiated as a crustal-scale fold system, induced by broad and diffuse northwest-southeast dextral shearing in a transpressive regime. This interpretation is akin to that of Coward et al. (1986) for the formation of the Nanga Parbat syntaxis as a fold at crustal scale, by rotation and sticking of the Himalayan thrust sheets against a pinning point, possibly the tip of the Raikot fault. The abrupt ending of the dome corridor against the Raikot fault shows that this fault may have reactivated an important north-south thermal and rheological boundary of the Himalayan crust, already present at the beginning of the dome formation.

Nanga Parbat, from this perspective, corresponds to a large late Miocene gneiss dome, similar to the other Ladakh or Karakorum domes, but singular in its position at the junction of two crustal-scale lineaments, the north-south South Karakorum fault and the northwest-southeast Raikot fault.

ACKNOWLEDGMENTS

Field work over several years has been supported by European Economic Community contract CT1*CT 90/0852 from 1991 to 1993 (Gaetani, principal investigator), by a U.S. National Science Foundation contract in 1995 ("Crustal shortening during orogeny," Zeitler, principal investigator), and by the Foreign Affairs Ministry of France through the French Embassy in Islamabad. Laboratory work has been supported by the Laboratoire de géodynamique des chaînes alpines in Grenoble (UPRES-A 5025, Centre National de la Recherche Scientifique). Sincere thanks are due to our Italian and French field companions Piera Benna, Yves Lemennicier, Bruno Lombardo, Piero Pertusati, Ugo Pognante, and Franco Rolfo. We are very grateful to Allison Macfarlane, C. J. Northrup, and an anonymous reviewer for their detailed comments and corrections on the first version of the manuscript.

REFERENCES CITED

Allen, P., and Chamberlain, C. P., 1991, Metamorphic evidence for an inverted crustal section, with constraints on the Main Karakorum Thrust, Baltistan, northern Pakistan: Metamorphic Geology, v. 9, p. 403–418.

Bard J. P., 1983, Metamorphism of an obducted island arc: Example of the Kohistan sequence (Pakistan) in the Himalayan collided range: Earth and Planetary Science Letters, v. 65, p. 133–144.

Bard, J. P., Maluski, H., Matte, P., and Proust, F., 1980, The Kohistan sequence: Crust and mantle of an obducted island arc: University of Peshawar Geological Bulletin, v. 13, p. 87–93.

Bertrand, J. M., Kienast, J. R., and Pinardon, J. L., 1988, Structure and metamorphism of the Karakorum gneisses in the Braldu-Baltoro Valley (North Pakistan): Geodinamica Acta, v. 2, p. 135–150.

Butler, R. W. H., and Prior, D. J., 1988, Anatomy of a continental subduction zone; the Main Mantle Thrust in northern Pakistan: Geologische Rundschau, v. 77, p. 239–255.

Butler, R. W. H., George, M., Harris, N. B. W., Jones, C., Prior, D. J., Treloar, P. J., and Wheeler, J., 1992, Geology of the northern part of the Nanga Parbat massif, northern Pakistan, and its implications for Himalayan tectonics: Geological Society of London Journal, v. 149, p. 557–567.

Chamberlain, C. P., and Zeitler, P. K., 1996, Assembly of the crystalline terranes of northwestern Himalaya and Karakoram, northwestern Pakistan, in An Yin, and Harrison, T. M., eds., The tectonic evolution of Asia: Cambridge, United Kingdom, Cambridge University Press, p. 138–149.

Coward, M. P., 1985, A section through the Nanga Parbat syntaxis, Indus valley, Kohistan: University Peshawar Geological Bulletin, v. 18, p. 147–152.

Coward, M. P., Jan, M. Q., Rex, D., Tarney, J., Thirlwall, M., and Windley, B. F., 1982a, Geo-tectonic framework of the Himalaya of N Pakistan: Geological Society of London Journal, v. 139, p. 299–308.

Coward, M. P., Jan, M. Q., Rex, D., Tarney, J., Thirlwall, M., and Windley, B. F., 1982b, Structural evolution of a crustal section in the western Himalaya: Nature, v. 295, p. 22–24.

Coward, M. P., Windley, B. F., Broughton, R. D., Luff, I. W., Petterson, M. G., Pudsey, C. J., Rex, D. C., and Khan, M. A., 1986, Collision tectonics in the NW Himalayas, in Coward, M. P., and Ries, A. C., eds., Collision tectonics: Geological Society of London Special Publication 19, p. 203–219.

Craw, D., Koons, P. O., Winslow, D., Chamberlain, C. P., and Zeitler, P., 1994, Boiling fluids in a region of rapid uplift, Nanga Parbat Massif, Pakistan: Earth and Planetary Science Letters, v. 128, p. 169–182.

Crawford, M. B., and Searle, M. P., 1993, Field relationships and geochemistry of pre-collisional (India-Asia) granitoid magmatism in the Central Karakoram, North Pakistan, in Treloar, P. J., and Searle, M. P., eds., Himalayan tectonics: Geological Society of London Special Publication 74, p. 53–68.

Debon, F., Le Fort, P., Dautel, D., Sonet, J., and Zimmermann, J. L., 1987, Granites of western Karakorum and northern Kohistan (Pakistan): A composite Mid-Cretaceous to Upper Cenozoic magmatism: Lithos, v. 20, p. 19–40.

Desio, A., 1964, Geological tentative map of the western Karakorum: Milano, Istituto Geologia, 1 sheet, scale 1:500,000.

Desio, A., Martina, E., Spadea, P., and Notarpietro, A., 1985, Geology of the

Chogo Lungma-Biafo-Hispar area, Karakorum (NW Pakistan): Atti Della Accademia Nazionale dei Lincei Memorie, v. 18, p. 1–53.

Fraser, J., Searle, M., Parrish, R., Noble, S., and Thimm, K., 1998, U-Pb geochronology on the timing of metamorphism and magmatism in the Hunza Karakoram, *in* Abstract volume 13th Himalaya-Karakoram-Tibet workshop, Peshawar, 1998, University of Peshawar Geological Bulletin, Special Issue 31, p. 66-67.

Gansser, A., 1980, The division between Himalaya and Karakorum, *in* Proceedings, International Committee on Geodynamics, Peshawar, November 1979: University of Peshawar Geological Bulletin, Special Issue 13, p. 9–22.

George, M. T., Harris, N. B. W., and Butler, R. W. H., 1993, The tectonic implications of contrasting granite magmatism between the Kohistan arc and the Nanga Parbat-Haramosh massif, Pakistan Himalaya, *in* Treloar, P. J., and Searle, M. P., eds., Himalayan tectonics: Geological Society of London Special Publication 74, p. 173–191.

George, M. T., Reddy, S., and Harris, N. B. W., 1995, Isotopic constraints on the cooling history of the Nanga Parbat-Haramosh Massif and Kohistan arc, western Himalaya: Tectonics, v. 14, p. 237–252.

Hanson, C. R., 1986, Bedrock geology of the Shigar valley area, Skardu, northern Pakistan [Ph.D. thesis]: Dartmouth, New Hampshire, Dartmouth College, 124 p.

Hubbard, M. S., Spencer, D. A., and West, D. P., 1995, Tectonic exhumation of the Nanga Parbat massif, northern Pakistan: Earth and Planetary Science Letters, v. 133, p. 213–225.

Ivanac, J. F., Traves, D. M., and King, D., 1965, The geology of the north-west region of Gilgit Agency: Geological Survey of Pakistan Record, v. 3, no. 2, p. 3–27.

Jan, M. Q., 1977, The Kohistan basic sequence. A summary based on recent petrological research: University of Peshawar Geological Bulletin, v. 9-10, p. 36–42.

Khan, T., 1994, Evolution of the upper and middle crust in Kohistan island-arc, northern Pakistan [Ph.D. thesis]: Peshawar, Pakistan, Peshawar University, 225 p.

Khan, T., Khan, M. A., Jan, M. Q., and Naseem, M., 1996, Back-arc basin assemblages in Kohistan, northern Pakistan: Geodinamica Acta, v. 9, p. 30–40.

Lawrence, R. D., and Ghauri, A. A. K., 1983, Evidence for active faulting in Chilas District, N Pakistan: University of Peshawar Geological Bulletin, v. 10, p. 185–186.

Le Fort, P., and Pêcher, A., 1995, The Scar of the Shyok Suture between Kohistan-Ladakh and Karakorum from Hunza to Baltistan (Pakistan): 10th Himalaya-Karakorum-Tibet Workshop, Ascona, 1995, Abstract volume: Zürich, ETH, p. 3.

Le Fort, P., Michard, A., Sonet, J., and Zimmermann, J. L., 1983, Petrography, geochemistry and geochronology of some samples from the Karakorum axial batholith (northern Pakistan), *in* Shams, F. A., ed., Granites of Himalayas, Karakorum and Hindu-Kush: Lahore, Pakistan, Institute of Geology of Punjab University, p. 377–387.

Le Fort, P., Lemennicier, Y., Lombardo, B., Pêcher, A., Pertusati, P., Pognante, U., and Rolfo, F., 1995, Preliminary geological map and description of the Himalaya-Karakorum junction in Chogo Lungma to Turmik area (Baltistan, northern Pakistan): Nepal Geological Society Journal, v. 11, p. 17–38.

Le Fort, P., Guillot, S., and Pêcher, A., 1997, Discovery of retrogressed eclogites in the Indus suture, east of Nanga Parbat-Haramosh massif (northern Pakistan): European Union of Geoscientists no. 9, Terra Nova, v. 8, abstract supplement 1, p. 56.

Lemennicier, Y., 1996, Le complexe métamorphique du Sud-Karakorum dans le secteur du Chogo Lungma (Baltistan-Nord-Pakistan). Étude structurale, métamorphique, géochimique et radiochronologique [Ph.D. thesis]: Grenoble, France, Université Joseph Fourier, 239 p.

Lemennicier, Y., Le Fort, P., Lombardo, B., Pêcher, A., and Rolfo, F., 1996, Tectonometamorphic evolution of the central Karakorum (Baltistan, northern Pakistan): Tectonophysics, v. 260, p. 119–143.

Madin, I. P., Lawrence, R. D., and Ur-Rehman, S., 1989, The northwestern Nanga Parbat-Haramosh massif; evidence for crustal uplift at the northwestern corner of the Indian craton, *in* Malinconico, L. L., Jr., and Lillie, R. S., eds., Tectonics of the western Himalayas: Geological Society of America Special Paper 232, p. 169–182.

Mattauer, M., 1986, Intracontinental subduction, crust-mantle décollement and crustal-stacking wedge in the Himalayas and other collision belts, *in* Coward, M. P., and Ries, A. C., eds., Collision tectonics: Geological Society of London Special Publication 19, p. 37–50.

Molnar, P., and Tapponnier, P., 1975, Cenozoic tectonics of Asia: effects of a continental collision: Science, v. 189, p. 419–426.

Parrish, R. P., and Tirrul, R., 1989, U-Pb ages of the Baltoro granite, northwest Himalaya, and implications for zircon inheritance and monazite U-Pb systematics: Geology, v. 17, p. 1076–1079.

Petterson, M. G., and Windley, B. F., 1985, Rb-Sr dating of the Kohistan arc-batholith in the Trans-Himalaya of north Pakistan, and tectonic implications: Earth and Planetary Science Letters, v. 74, p. 45–57.

Pognante, U., Benna, P., and Le Fort, P., 1993, High-pressure metamorphism in the High Himalayan Crystallines of the Stak valley, northeastern Nanga Parbat-Haramosh syntaxis, Pakistan Himalaya, *in* Treloar, P. J., and Searle, M. P., eds., Himalayan tectonics: Geological Society of London Special Publication 74, p. 161–172.

Rex, A. J., Searle, M. P., Tirrul, R., Crawford, M. B., Prior, D. J., Rex, D. C., and Barnicoat, A., 1988, The geochemical and tectonic evolution of the central Karakoram, N. Pakistan: Philosophic Transactions Royal Society of London, ser. A, v. 326, p. 229–255.

Rolfo, F., 1994, Studio geologico-petrografico dei terreni compresi tra Himalaya e Karakorum nelle regione ad est della sintassi Haramosh-Nanga Parbat (Baltistan, Pakistan settentrionale) [tesi di laurea]: Torino, Università degli studi, 130 p.

Rolfo, F., Lombardo, B., Compagnoni, R., Le Fort, P., Lemennicier, Y., and Pêcher, A., 1997, Ladakh terrain and Shyok suture zone in the Chogo Lungma–Turmik area (northern Pakistan): Geodinamica Acta, v. 10, p. 251–270.

Schärer, U., Copeland, P., Harrison, T. M., and Searle, M. P., 1990, Age, cooling history, and origin of post-collisional leucogranites in the Karakorum batholith; a multi-system isotope study: Journal of Geology, v. 98, p. 233–251.

Schneider, D. A., Zeitler, P. K., Edwards, M. A., and Kidd, W. S. F., 1997, Geochronological constraints on the geometry and timing of anatexis and exhumation at Nanga-Parbat: A progress report [abs.]: Eos (Transactions, American Geophysical Union), v. 78, p. S111.

Searle, M. P., 1991, Geology and tectonics of the Karakoram mountains: Chichester, United Kingdom, John Wiley & sons Ltd, 358 p.

Searle, M. P., 1996, Cooling history, erosion, exhumation, and kinematics of the Himalaya-Karakoram-Tibet orogenic belt, *in* An Yin, and Harrison, T. M., eds., The tectonic evolution of Asia: Cambridge, United Kingdom, Cambridge University Press, p. 110–137.

Searle, M. P., Rex, A. J., Tirrul, R., Rex, D. C., Barnicoat, A., and Windley, B. F., 1989, Metamorphic, magmatic, and tectonic evolution of the central Karakoram in the Biafo-Baltoro-Hushe regions of northern Pakistan, *in* Malinconico, L. L., Jr., and Lillie, R. J., eds., Tectonics of the western Himalayas: Geological Society of America Special Paper 232, p. 47–74.

Searle, M. P., Khan, M. A., Jan, M. Q., Di Pietro, J. A., Pogue, K. R., Pivnik, D. A., Sercombe, W. J., Izatt, C. N., Blisniuk, P. M., Treloar, P. J., Gaetani, M., and Zanchi, A., 1996, Geological map of the north Pakistan and adjacent areas of northern Ladakh and western Tibet (western Himalaya, Salt Ranges, Kohistan, Karakoram, Hindu Kush): scale 1:650,000, 1 sheet.

Smith, H. A., 1993, Characterisation and timing of metamorphism within the Indo-Asian suture zone, Himalayas, northern Pakistan [Ph.D. thesis]: Dartmouth, New Hampshire, Dartmouth College, 196 p.

Smith, H. A., Chamberlain, C. P., and Zeitler, P. K., 1992, Documentation of Neogene regional metamorphism in the Himalayas of Pakistan using

U-Pb in monazite: Earth and Planetary Science Letters, v. 113, p. 93–105.

Tahirkheli, R. A. K., 1979, Geotectonic evolution of Kohistan: University Peshawar Geological Bulletin, v. 11, p. 113–130.

Tahirkheli, R. A. K., 1987, Shontargali thrust: an analogue of the Main Central Thrust (MCT) in the NW Himalaya in Pakistan: University of Peshawar Geological Bulletin, v. 20, p. 131–140.

Tahirkheli, R. A. K., Mattauer, M., Proust, F., and Tapponnier, P., 1979, The India-Eurasia suture zone in northern Pakistan: Synthesis and interpretation of recent data at plate scale, in Farah, A., and De Jong, K. A., eds., Geodynamics of Pakistan: Quetta, Geological Survey of Pakistan, p. 125–130.

Tapponnier, P., Peltzer, G., and Armijo, R., 1986, On the mechanics of the collision between India and Asia, in Coward, M. P., and Ries, A. C., eds., Collision tectonics: Geological Society of London Special Publication 19, p. 115–157.

Treloar, P. J., Potts, G. J., Wheeler, J., and Rex, D. C., 1991, Structural evolution and asymmetric uplift of the Nanga Parbat syntaxis, Pakistan Himalaya: Geologische Rundschau, v. 80, p. 411–428.

Verplanck, P. L., 1986, A field and geochemical study of the boundary between the Nanga Parbat-Haramosh massif and the Ladakh arc terrane, northern Pakistan [M.Sc. thesis]: Corvallis, Oregon State University, 135 p.

Villa, I., Le Fort, P., and Lemennicier, Y., 1996a, Late Miocene to early Pliocene tectonometamorphism and cooling in south central Karakorum and Indus-Tsangpo suture, Chomo Lungma area (NE Pakistan): Tectonophysics, v. 260, p. 201–214.

Villa, I., Ruffini, R., Rolfo, F., and Lombardo, B., 1996b, Diachronous metamorphism of the Ladakh terrain et the Karakorum-Nanga Parbat-Haramosh junction (NW Baltistan, Pakistan): Bulletin Suisse de Pétrographie et Minéralogie, v. 76, p. 245–264.

Vince, K. J., and Treloar, P. J., 1996, Miocene, north-vergent extensional displacements along the Main Mantle Thrust, NW Himalaya, Pakistan: Geological Society of London Journal, v. 153, p. 677–680.

Wheeler, J., Treloar, P. J., and Potts, G. J., 1995, Structural and metamorphic evolution of the Nanga Parbat syntaxis, Pakistan Himalayas, on the Indus gorge transect: The importance of early events: Geological Journal, v. 30, p. 349–371.

Winslow, D. M., Zeitler, P. K., Chamberlain, C. P., and Hollister, L. S., 1994, Direct evidence for a steep geotherm under conditions of rapid denudation, Western Himalaya, Pakistan: Geology, v. 22, p. 1075–1078.

Yamamoto, H., 1993, Contrasting metamorphic P-T-time paths of the Kohistan granulites and tectonics of the western Himalayas: Geological Society of London Journal, v. 150, p. 843–856.

Zeitler, P. K., 1985, Cooling history of the NW Himalaya, Pakistan: Tectonics, v. 4, p. 127–151.

Zeitler, P. K., and Chamberlain, C. P., 1991, Petrogenetic and tectonic significance of young leucogranites from the northwestern Himalaya, Pakistan: Tectonics, v. 10, p. 729–741.

Zeitler, P. K., Sutter, J. F., Williams, I. S., Zartman, R., and Tahirkheli, R. A. K., 1989, Geochronology and temperature history of the Nanga-Parbat-Haramosh massif, Pakistan, in Malinconico, L. L., Jr., and Lillie, R. J., eds., Tectonics of the western Himalayas: Geological Society of America Special Paper 232, p. 1–22.

Zeitler, P. K., Chamberlain, C. P., and Smith, H. A., 1993, Synchronous anatexis, metamorphism, and rapid denudation at Nanga Parbat (Pakistan Himalaya): Geology, v. 21, p. 347–350.

MANUSCRIPT ACCEPTED BY THE SOCIETY FEBRUARY 3, 1998

Geological Society of America
Special Paper 328
1999

Geologic map of the Indus syntaxis and surrounding area, northwest Himalaya, Pakistan

Joseph A. DiPietro
Department of Geology, University of Southern Indiana, 8600 University Boulevard, Evansville, Indiana 47712
Kevin R. Pogue
Department of Geology, Whitman College, Walla Walla, Washington 97331
Ahmad Hussain*
Geological Survey of Pakistan, P.O. Box 1355, Shami Road, Peshawar, Pakistan
Irshad Ahmad
National Centre of Excellence in Geology, University of Peshawar, Peshawar, Pakistan

ABSTRACT

The stratigraphy, structure, and metamorphism of the hinterland area of the Indian plate in northwestern Pakistan is described in relation to a geologic map. We conclude that this is one of the few areas in the Himalaya where amphibolite facies rock can be traced southward from the Indus-Tsangpo suture zone to low-grade fossiliferous rock without crossing a major fault. The absence of a major fault provides an opportunity to constrain the depositional ages of the metamorphic stratigraphy by direct correlation with fossiliferous rock in conjunction with isotopic dating of intrusive rock. The stratigraphy is divided into the following age groups, each bounded by an unconformity: Early Proterozoic, Late Proterozoic; early-middle Paleozoic, late Paleozoic-Triassic, and Mesozoic. Within this stratigraphy there is evidence for plutonism in the Early Proterozoic, Late Proterozoic, early Paleozoic, late Paleozoic, and Cenozoic; deformation in the Early Proterozoic and late Paleozoic; and volcanism in the late Paleozoic-Triassic. All of the rocks record deformation and greenschist to amphibolite facies metamorphism in the Late Cretaceous–Cenozoic as a result of the obduction of Indus melange onto the Indian plate along the Main Mantle thrust and the ensuing collision, thrusting, and final emplacement of the Kohistan arc complex along the Kohistan fault.

The Main Mantle thrust is a premetamorphic or synmetamorphic fault that dates the time of obduction as pre-late Eocene and possibly as early as Late Cretaceous. Obduction along the Main Mantle thrust is associated with west-southwest–vergent folds on the Indian plate. Exhumation and cooling of the Indian plate following peak metamorphism may have begun by the late Paleocene or early Eocene in the Indus syntaxis, and by the middle Eocene in the Loe Sar dome. Cooling and exhumation are associated with the development of large-scale, north-south–trending folds that fold the Main Mantle thrust. The time of initial collision of Kohistan with the Indian plate is unconstrained in the field area, but brittle-ductile fabrics along the Kohistan fault indi-

*Present address: Geological Survey of Pakistan, 65B, Upper Chattar, Muzaffarabad, Pakistan.

DiPietro, J. A., Pogue, K. R., Hussain, A., and Ahmad, I., 1999, Geologic map of the Indus syntaxis and surrounding area, northwest Himalaya, Pakistan, *in* Macfarlane, A., Sorkhabi, R. B., and Quade, J., eds., Himalaya and Tibet: Mountain Roots to Mountain Tops: Boulder, Colorado, Geological Society of America Special Paper 328.

cate that final emplacement occurred during retrograde metamorphism, probably in the late Oligocene. Final emplacement of Kohistan is associated with the initial development of south-vergent folds on the Indian plate. Neogene and younger deformation is present in the Indus syntaxis area, in contrast to the Loe Sar dome area, where deformation largely ended in the early Miocene. There is no conclusive evidence for pre-Cenozoic amphibolite facies metamorphism in rock as old as Early Proterozoic.

INTRODUCTION

The Himalayan orogenic belt extends for more than 2,500 km across India, Nepal, and Tibet in an arc that is convex to the south. At its western margin in Pakistan the arc bends sharply around a series of syntaxes that include the Nanga Parbat–Haramosh syntaxis, the Hazara-Kashmir syntaxis, and the Indus syntaxis (Fig. 1; Wadia, 1931; Calkins et al., 1975; Lawrence and Ghauri, 1983).

In this chapter, we present a geologic map of the Indus syntaxis area and the adjacent area to the west that includes the Loe Sar dome and the northern Peshawar basin (Plate 1; DiPietro, 1990; Hussain et al., 1991; Ahmad, 1991; Pogue, 1994). The map covers ~16 15′ quadrangles that encompass the area from the Panjal-Khairabad fault on the Indian plate in the south to the Kohistan arc in the north. The area is in the Swat and Hazara regions of Pakistan, between 34°00′N and 35°12′N and 72°15′E and 73°7.5′E. The geologic map is based on systematic off-road traverses using topographic base maps (1:50,000) and global positioning. Although we acknowledge previous mapping, the geology of the Indian plate and the Indus melange shown in Plate 1 is based on our own field observations, with the exception of the area east of 73°00′E and south of 34°45′N, which is based on Calkins et al. (1975). The mapping has resulted in the reevaluation of existing formations, the description of new formations, and a more detailed understanding of the geologic and tectonic history. One important conclusion is the recognition of a metamorphosed Early Proterozoic to Mesozoic stratigraphy that can be traced, without disruption by major faults, from low-grade fossiliferous rock near the Panjal-Khairabad fault, to amphibolite facies rock near the Indus-Tsangpo suture zone. We also recognize strong Late Cretaceous–Paleogene metamorphism in the Besham area of the Indus syntaxis, which previously was interpreted as Early Proterozoic (Treloar and Rex, 1990; Baig, 1990). We have gained a more complete understanding of the pre-Cenozoic geologic history, including the recognition that the Karora and Gandaf Formations are Early Proterozoic and that these formations probably correlate with the Salkhala Formation of Hazara, Kaghan, and Kashmir. We conclude with a tectonic interpretation of the India-Kohistan collision that is consistent with field observations and with the geologic map.

Rocks of the Indian plate record a complex history of deformation, igneous intrusion, and metamorphism that extends to the Early Proterozoic. Establishing a stratigraphy in these rocks is complicated by structural disruptions, a general lack of fossils, and amphibolite facies metamorphism. In the course of geologic mapping, we have avoided lumping together unfossilif-

erous rocks that cannot be traced laterally into each other; rocks that cannot be shown to be stratigraphically equivalent; or rocks that are lithologically distinctive. This procedure will preserve the stratigraphic order that is present in the area regardless of how future workers correlate the rocks.

The Swat area, including the Loe Sar dome, was originally mapped by Martin et al. (1962) and by King (1964), who recognized the general stratigraphy and structure. Parts of Swat and the northern Peshawar basin were remapped by Siddiqui et al. (1968), Tahirkheli (1970, 1971), Yeats and Hussain (1987), Hylland et al., (1988); Hussain et al. (1990, 1995), DiPietro (1990), Ahmad (1991), Riaz et al. (1991), Ahmad and Lawrence (1992), Pogue (1994), Khan and Khan (1994), R. N. Khan et al. (1995), and S. R. Khan et al. (1995). Calkins et al. (1975) mapped part of the Hazara area to the east of the Indus River as well as the southern margin of the Indus syntaxis surrounding Tarbela Lake. They recognized the northward bending of structures and the anticlinal nature of the syntaxis, which they referred to as the Indus reentrant. We follow Lawrence and Ghauri (1983) and Baig (1990) and use the term Indus syntaxis because it more accurately describes the structure. Ashraf et al. (1980), Fletcher et al. (1986), Williams (1989), LaFortune (1989), and Baig (1990) mapped the northern part of the Indus syntaxis surrounding Besham and Thakot. The intervening area between ~34°25′ and 34°45′N and 72°30′ and 73°00′E was previously unmapped or was mapped only on a reconnaissance basis (Middlemiss, 1896; Jan and Tahirkheli, 1969; Tahirkheli, 1970, 1979a, 1979b, 1982; Jan et al., 1981; Lawrence et al., 1989; Williams, 1989; Baig, 1990).

Previous maps lumped together rocks of very different origin and age, such as metasedimentary and granitic rock within the same formation (Calkins et al., 1975). Other workers, in some instances, assigned names of regional significance, such as the Salkhala, Hazara, or Dogra, without proving lateral continuity with their respective type sections, or without proving similar stratigraphic position (Ashraf et al., 1980). In addition, lithologic contacts that we have mapped in detail cut across some of the formation boundaries that are shown on earlier maps. For these reasons and because of confusion in the literature regarding the age, origin, and extent of some of the Precambrian rock, we have abandoned some previously assigned formation names such as Thakot, Pazang, and Salkhala, and have revised other formation names, such as Karora and Besham, in order to retain consistency with the field data. In addition, we have assigned new formation names, such as Kotla, Black Mountain, Duma, and Gandaf, to lithologically distinctive rock units found in previously unmapped areas. The revised stratigraphy is shown in Plate 1 and Figure 2 and compared with previous work in Figures 3 and 4.

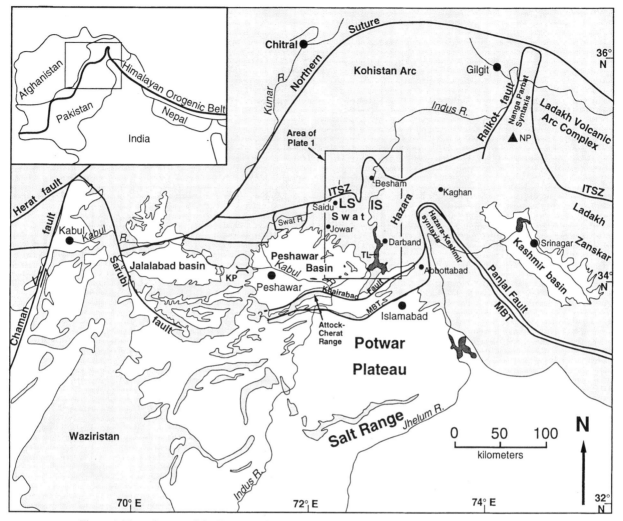

Figure 1. Tectonic map of the Western Himalayan syntaxis in northwestern Pakistan showing the Swat and Hazara areas and the location of Plate I. Inset shows the regional location and the general trend of the Himalayan orogenic belt. Heavy dark lines represent faults. Shaded areas represent pre-Quaternary rock. ITSZ—Indus-Tsangpo suture zone; IS—Indus syntaxis; KP—Kyber Pass; LS—Loe Sar dome; MBT—Main Boundary thrust; NP—Nanga Parbat; TL—Tarbela Lake.

GEOLOGIC SETTING

In the mountains surrounding the Peshawar basin, Indian plate rock that underwent Late Cretaceous–Paleogene metamorphism and plutonism is restricted to the hanging-wall block of the south-southeast–vergent Khairabad fault (Fig. 1). This fault is presumed to be the western continuation of the Panjal fault as mapped by Calkins et al. (1975) and represents the boundary between deformed foreland to the south and deformed and metamorphosed hinterland to the north (Pogue et al., 1996). An Early Proterozoic to Mesozoic stratigraphy including abundant intrusive rock, and Late Cretaceous–Paleogene greenschist to amphibolite facies metamorphism, can be traced northward from the Khairabad fault without significant stratigraphic, structural, or metamorphic discordance for ~100 km to where the rocks are overthrust by melange of the Indus-Tsangpo suture zone (hereafter referred to as Indus melange). The Indus-Tsangpo suture zone is a regional structure that separates the Indian plate from the Asian plate across the Himalaya (Gansser, 1980). In northwestern Pakistan, the southern margin of the Asian plate is represented by the Kohistan arc, which is interpreted as an island-arc complex that developed in the Cretaceous in response to northward subduction of Indian oceanic lithosphere prior to continental collision (Tahirkheli, 1979a, 1979b; Tahirkheli et al., 1979). The basal fault or series of faults that carry the Indus melange in its hanging-wall block is referred to as the Main Mantle thrust (Tahirkheli et al., 1979). The Indus melange is bounded on its north side by the Kohistan fault, which is the basal fault, or series of faults, that carries the Kohistan arc in its hanging-wall block (Kazmi et al., 1984). The metamorphic fabric of the Indian plate developed in the Late Cretaceous and Paleogene as a result of Late Cretaceous (≤95 Ma) obduction of the

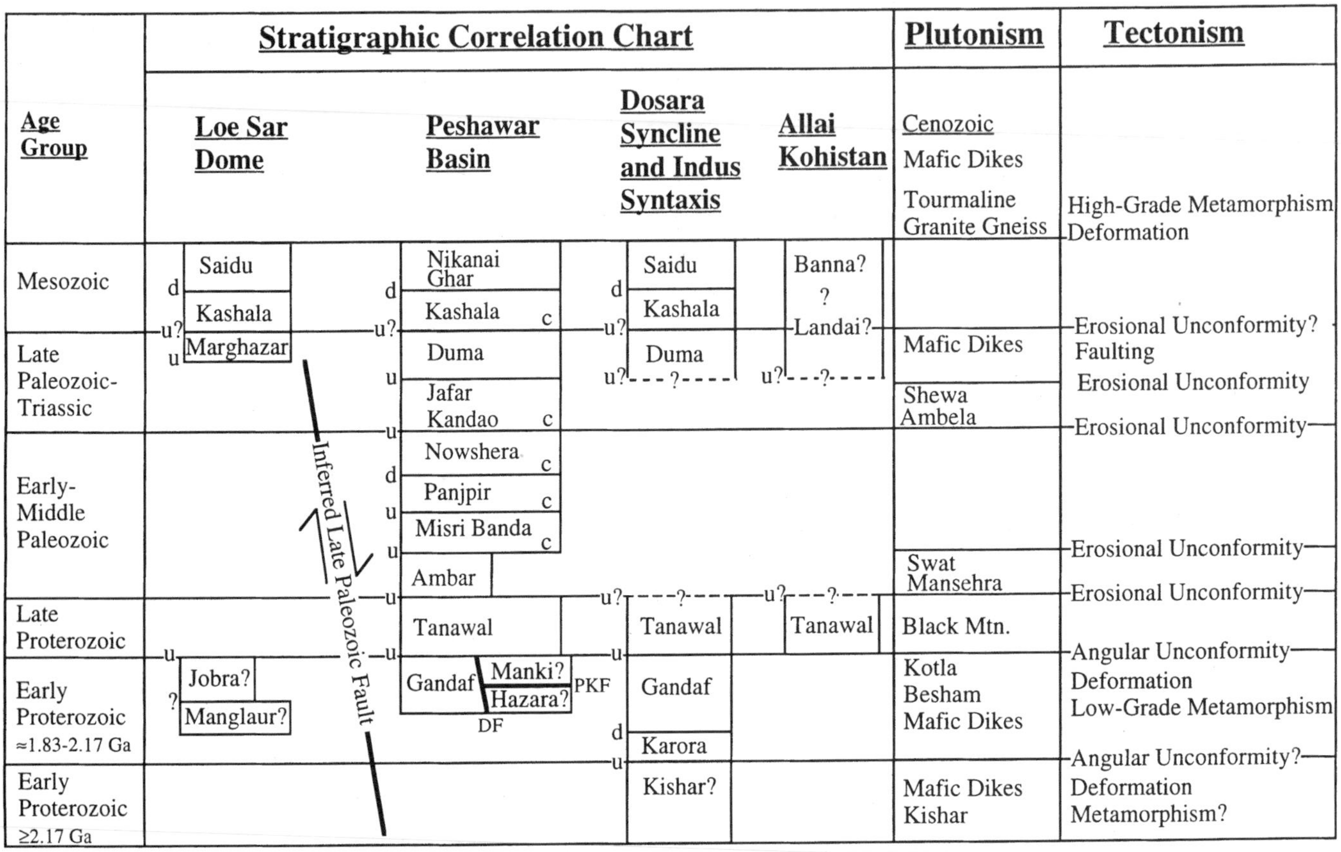

Age Group	Stratigraphic Correlation Chart				Plutonism	Tectonism
	Loe Sar Dome	Peshawar Basin	Dosara Syncline and Indus Syntaxis	Allai Kohistan	Cenozoic Mafic Dikes Tourmaline Granite Gneiss	High-Grade Metamorphism Deformation
Mesozoic	d Saidu u? Kashala u Marghazar	d Nikanai Ghar Kashala c Duma	d Saidu u? Kashala Duma	Banna? ? Landai?	Mafic Dikes	Erosional Unconformity? Faulting Erosional Unconformity
Late Paleozoic-Triassic		u Jafar Kandao c	u?---?----	u?---?----	Shewa Ambela	Erosional Unconformity
Early-Middle Paleozoic		d Nowshera c u Panjpir c u Misri Banda c Ambar			Swat Mansehra	Erosional Unconformity
Late Proterozoic	u Tanawal	u Tanawal	u? Tanawal	u? Tanawal	Black Mtn.	Erosional Unconformity Angular Unconformity
Early Proterozoic ≈1.83-2.17 Ga	u Jobra? ? Manglaur?	Gandaf Manki? PKF Hazara? DF	Gandaf d Karora		Kotla Besham Mafic Dikes	Deformation Low-Grade Metamorphism Angular Unconformity?
Early Proterozoic ≥2.17 Ga			u Kishar?		Mafic Dikes Kishar	Deformation Metamorphism?

(Inferred Late Paleozoic Fault shown diagonally across Loe Sar Dome / Peshawar Basin columns)

Figure 2. Stratigraphic correlation chart with associated plutonism and tectonism. The Manki Formation is separated from the Gandaf Formation by the Darband fault (DF) and from the Hazara Formation by the Panjal-Khairabad fault (PKF). Additional abbreviations are: c—conodont age; d—conformable contact; u—unconformity; ?—uncertain contact or stratigraphic age.

Indus melange onto the Indian plate (DiPietro and Lawrence, 1991; Beck et al., 1996; Isachsen and DiPietro, 1997). Accretion of the Kohistan arc to the Asian mainland along the Northern suture is thought to have occurred in the Late Cretaceous between about 100 and 85 Ma (Coward et al., 1987; Treloar et al., 1989b) at about the same time, or slightly earlier than, the obduction event on the Indian plate. The collision of the Indian plate with Kohistan probably began in the Paleocene between about 66 and 56 Ma (Beck et al., 1996). The lack of Paleogene metamorphism in Kohistan and the abundance of brittle fabrics developed along the Kohistan fault suggests that the arc was cold prior to final emplacement against the Indian plate, probably in the late Oligocene (DiPietro and Lawrence, 1991).

INDUS MELANGE

The Indus melange extends as a belt along the northern margin of the Indian plate. The melange is cut out by the Kohistan fault in the Indus syntaxis area but reappears along the eastern margin of the syntaxis (Plate 1). The dominant rock throughout the Indus melange is greenstone. Blueschist, in association with greenstone, is present in the Shin Kamar–Shergarh Sar area on the east side of the Indus syntaxis (Majid and Shah, 1985, Baig, 1989), and in road cuts in the Topsin area west of Alpurai where Shams (1980) referred to them as Shangla blueschist. Serpentinite forms large bodies in the Alpurai area (Arif and Moon, 1994) and smaller bodies elsewhere. Dark gray and green phyllite are widespread and act as a matrix to blocks of greenstone, blueschist, and serpentinite. A wide variety of additional rock is present, including talc-carbonate schist, which is host to emerald deposits in the Loe Sar dome area (Kazmi et al., 1984; Lawrence et al., 1989); Middle Jurassic to Late Cretaceous fossiliferous limestone, which is present in the Loe Sar dome area (Kazmer, 1986); tectonic slivers of Saidu graphitic schist that are common across the area; tectonic slivers of Kashala marble and Marghazar(?) amphibolite that are uncommon but occur in the Alpurai area; and tectonic slivers of Kohistan (Kamila) amphibolite that are present particularly in the Banna area.

KOHISTAN ARC

With the exception of a few traverses along its southern margin we have not mapped in the Kohistan arc. The geology shown in Plate 1 is based on previous work (Tahirkheli and Jan, 1979;

	Ashraf et al., 1980	Fletcher et al., 1986	Williams, 1989	Baig, 1990	This Study
Paleozoic		Karora	Karora	Tanawal	Tanawal
Precambrian	Tanawal Sirban Dogra Hazara	Pazang	Tanawal	Karora	*Black Mtn. Kotla Besham*
	Lahor Thakot	*Besham*	*Besham*	*Besham* Pazang Thakot	*Gandaf Karora* *Kishar*

Figure 3. Stratigraphic nomenclature for Precambrian rock in the Besham area of the Indus syntaxis. Italics represent intrusive rock.

Jan, 1979a; Miller et al., 1991; Yamamoto, 1993) and on unpublished Geological Survey of Pakistan maps.

Rocks of the dominantly Cretaceous Kohistan arc extend across the northern part of the map area on the north side of the Kohistan fault, where they are divided into three intrusive complexes: the Kamila Amphibolite Belt; the Jijal Complex; and the Chilas Complex (Plate 1). The Kamila Amphibolite Belt consists of amphibolite and subordinate hornblendite, diorite, and plagiogranite (Jan, 1979b; Khan et al., 1993). The Chilas Complex is dominated by gabbronorite that intrudes the Kamila Amphibolite Belt (Khan et al., 1993). The Jijal Complex is divided into a southern part composed of ultramafic rock and a northern part dominated by garnet granulite (Jan, 1979a). All three complexes are interpreted to represent a section of the middle to lower part of the Kohistan arc (Tahirkheli, 1979a; Khan et al., 1993). Miller et al. (1991) indicated that the northern boundary of the Jijal Complex is a fault. Limited mapping could not confirm this fault; therefore, we show the contact as uncertain.

METAMORPHIC AND STRUCTURAL FRAMEWORK OF THE INDIAN PLATE

Rocks on the Indian plate are divided into six age groups, each of which are associated with tectonism and are bounded by an unconformity (Fig. 2; Plate 1). The rocks record plutonism in the Early Proterozoic, Late Proterozoic, early Paleozoic, late Paleozoic, and Cenozoic; deformation in the Early Proterozoic and late Paleozoic; volcanism in the late Paleozoic-Triassic, and strong metamorphism and deformation in the Late Cretaceous–Cenozoic.

The effect of regional Late Cretaceous–Paleogene metamorphism on the Indian plate increases gradually from south to north. Rocks along the northern margin of the Peshawar basin are in the greenschist facies and have recognizable sedimentary structures and fossils. Garnet appears sporadically between the latitudes of Darband and Jowar in Precambrian pelitic schist (Gandaf, Tanawal) and in Mesozoic calcareous schist (Kashala). The transition from greenschist to amphibolite facies, as seen in Late Paleozoic-Triassic metavolcanic rock (Karapa), also occurs within this zone. Precambrian and Paleozoic rocks are in the amphibolite facies in the Loe Sar dome and Indus syntaxis, where hornblende, plagioclase, and garnet are ubiquitous in mafic rock, and kyanite and sillimanite occur sporadically in

	Martin et al., 1962	Kazmi et al., 1984	DiPietro, 1990	Pogue et al., 1992a	This Study
C	*Swat* Swabi Chamla		*Tourmaline gneiss*		*Tourmaline gneiss*
Late Paleozoic-Mesozoic	Lower Swat-Buner Schistose Group	Saidu Alpurai	Alpurai Group: Saidu, Nikanai Ghar, Kashala, Marghazar	Nikanai Ghar, Kashala, Karapa, *Ambela/Shewa*, Jafar Kandao	Alpurai Group: Saidu, Nikanai Ghar, Kashala, Marghazar, Duma, *Ambela/Shewa*, Jafar Kandao — Banna?, Landai?
Early-Middle Paleozoic			Jobra?	Nowshera, Panjpir, Misri Banda	Nowshera, Panjpir, Misri Banda
		Swat	*Swat*	Ambar	*Swat/Mansehra*, Ambar
pЄ	Manglaur	Manglaur	Manglaur	Tanawal	Tanawal —?— Jobra?, Manglaur?

Figure 4. Stratigraphic nomenclature for Phanerozoic rock. The Duma Formation includes the Karapa Member in its upper part and the Malandrai Member in its lower part. Lines marked with u represent unconformities. C—Cenozoic; ?—uncertain contact or stratigraphic position. Italics represent intrusive rock.

pelitic (Gandaf, Manglaur, Tanawal) and granitic rock (Black Mountains, Mansehra, Swat). Metamorphism decreases in the overlying Mesozoic rock and into the Indus melange where greenstone and blueschist are present. The transition from amphibolite to greenschist facies extends through the Kashala and Saidu Formations, where rare kyanite, staurolite, or chloritoid are present with garnet, and across the ductile shear zone of the Main Mantle thrust. The absence of a metamorphic break across the thrust suggests that it is a synmetamorphic fault and that the rocks in the immediate hanging wall of the Main Mantle thrust were metamorphosed in the Late Cretaceous–Paleogene with the Indian plate. Maluski and Matte (1984) obtained a $^{40}Ar/^{39}Ar$ age of 83.5 ± 2 Ma on phengite from a blueschist block from the Indus melange, and Isachsen and DiPietro (1997) report a concordant U-Pb zircon age of 88 Ma from the Kishar Formation on the Indian plate. These ages could represent the approximate age for the beginning of metamorphism on the Indian plate. The Indus melange is bordered on the north side by brittle and ductile shear zones of the Kohistan fault. Postmetamorphic thrust and strike-slip displacement along the Kohistan fault has juxtaposed amphibolite and ultramafic rock of the Kohistan arc against the Indus melange (Plate 1). The Kohistan fault cuts out the Indus melange in the Indus syntaxis area and places ultramafic rock of the Jijal Complex directly against the Indian plate (Plate 1).

Peak metamorphic conditions in the Precambrian and Paleozoic rock of the Loe Sar dome average between ~600 and 700 °C and 9–11 kbar (DiPietro, 1991). Farther south, in the Peshawar basin, the color alteration index of conodonts from Paleozoic and Mesozoic rock is between 5.0 and 7.0, suggesting peak metamorphic temperatures above 300 °C (Epstein et al., 1977; Pogue et al., 1992a). Metamorphic conditions along the eastern flank of the Indus syntaxis and farther eastward in Hazara average between 565 and 665 °C and 6.3 and 8.3 kbar in the area approximately north of the latitude of Oghi and between 490 and 590 °C and 5.4 and 7.4 kbar in the southern area approximately as far south as the latitude of Darband (Treloar et al., 1989a). South of Darband, Calkins et al. (1975) mapped a biotite-chlorite isograd, suggesting a further southward decrease in the metamorphism. K/Ar and $^{40}Ar/^{39}Ar$ cooling ages from hornblende in the Loe Sar dome and the Indus syntaxis vary from 67 to 31 Ma (L. Snee, *in* Palmer-Rosenberg, 1985; Treloar et al., 1989b; Treloar and Rex, 1990; Baig, 1990). This suggests a Late Cretaceous–early Paleogene peak metamorphism.

Prograde metamorphism is associated with the development of early isoclinal fold generations and a composite, dominantly layer-parallel, foliation that forms the regional foliation in the area (DiPietro and Lawrence, 1991). The folds are developed primarily at the scale of the outcrop and are restricted generally to rocks north of the latitude of Darband. However, map-scale early folds are recognized in the Loe Sar dome area where they trend north-northwest–south-southeast and are overturned to the west (Plate 1). The folds are interpreted as developing before peak metamorphism during obduction of the Indus melange onto the

Indian plate along the Main Mantle thrust (DiPietro and Lawrence, 1991).

The most prominent folds on the Indian plate are late-metamorphic, north-south–trending, upright folds that deform the regional foliation and the Main Mantle thrust. Map-scale folds include the Loe Sar dome, the Dosara-Budal syncline, and the Indus River anticline, which is a major structure in the Indus syntaxis (Plate 1). The folds are locally associated with an axial-plane foliation but, more commonly, are associated with a strong crenulation of the regional foliation. DiPietro and Lawrence (1991) and DiPietro (1991) interpreted the folds as developing during cooling and exhumation following peak metamorphism. The folds die out or bend to east-west trends near the Khairabad fault, where additional east-west–trending folds are prominent. East-west–trending folds are also present in the Loe Sar dome where they are superimposed on the earlier north-south–trending folds. DiPietro and Lawrence (1991) interpreted the east-west–trending folds as developing during retrograde metamorphism during final emplacement of Kohistan against the Indian plate. The folds are associated with a weak crenulation of the regional foliation.

The Indus River anticline, and the region near Tarbela Lake, are cut by north-south–striking, high-angle faults of limited displacement (<10 km; Plate 1). The faults generally die out along strike, and displacement is transferred to other faults and to folds. Major faults in this system include the Puran, Chakesar, and Darband faults. The faults show postmetamorphic, brittle deformation that is characterized by graphitic gauge zones as wide as 15 m and by fracture zones that, in some areas such as along the Puran and Chakesar faults, are more than 1 km wide (Plate 1). The cross section (Plate 1) suggests that the major faults in the northern part of the Indus syntaxis are up on the east side; however, horizontal slickenlines are developed along most of the fault zones, suggesting that the last movement was strike slip. Vertical displacement along the fault system may have begun in the late Oligocene following the development of the Indus River anticline. Subsequently, the faults may have acted as minor strike-slip tear faults associated with south-vergent displacement along the foreland-hinterland transition. The timing of faulting appears to coincide with the development of east-west–trending folds in the Loe Sar dome area.

The fault system is restricted generally to Early Proterozoic rock. The Puran fault, in particular, is deflected along the contact with the Swat granitic gneiss (Plate 1). This relationship suggests that the faults have reactivated preexisting anisotropies in the Early Proterozoic rock succession. Proterozoic (pre-Tanawal Formation) displacement along the Darband fault has been suggested to explain lithologic and metamorphic differences present in the Gandaf and Manki Formations, both of which unconformably underlie the Tanawal Formation (Plate 1; Pogue et al., this volume).

Treloar and Rex (1990) and Baig (1990) previously considered the postmetamorphic faults to be major bounding faults that separated rock in the Indus syntaxis, having an Early Proterozoic amphibolite facies metamorphism and a low-grade Paleogene metamorphic overprint, from adjacent younger rock in Swat and Hazara, having regional Paleogene amphibolite facies metamorphism. Baig (1990) considered the bounding faults to be the Puran fault on the west side and the Thakot fault on the east. The field relationships and map patterns shown in Plate 1 suggest that stratigraphy can be correlated across the postmetamorphic faults and that none of the faults mark a distinct break in the metamorphic fabric. The Puran fault is prominent in Plate 1, but it appears to have minor displacement that dies out to the north and south. The Thakot fault is exposed in a roadcut north of Thakot. We found rocks of similar lithology and metamorphic grade on both sides of the fault and could find no field evidence to support its continuation either to the north or south (Plate 1). Rather than being a major fault, it appears to die out into a series of shear zones and faults that are well displayed in the Korara and Gandaf Formations east of Thakot (Plate 1).

The Karora and Gandaf Formations are Early Proterozoic, on the basis of U-Pb zircon ages of 1858 ± 17 and 1836 ± 1 Ma from orthogneiss within the Besham and Kotla Complexes, which intrude the Karora and Gandaf Formations, and a U-Pb zircon age of 2175 ± 7 Ma from the Kishar Formation, which unconformably underlies the Karora Formation (DiPietro and Isachsen, 1997; Isachsen and DiPietro, 1997). As described earlier, the Late Cretaceous–Paleogene amphibolite facies metamorphism that affects Mesozoic rock decreases southward to greenschist facies in the Peshawar basin. A similar decrease in metamorphic grade is observed in the garnet schist of the Gandaf Formation. The rock is highly garnetiferous in the north, but becomes nongarnetiferous in the south. Other Proterozoic rocks in the south, such as the Manki and Hazara Formations, are only weakly metamorphosed. We conclude that metamorphism across the area is the same age and, because it affects Mesozoic rock, is Late Cretaceous–Paleogene. This does not exclude the possibility of Early Proterozoic amphibolite facies metamorphism, however; the extent of this metamorphism would have to parallel the Late Cretaceous–Paleogene metamorphism such that it would be strong in the northern part of the Indus syntaxis but die out to the south. We have found no conclusive field or thin-section evidence to support this interpretation.

Treloar and Rex (1990), and Baig (1990) based the existence of an Early Proterozoic amphibolite facies metamorphism on ca. 1900 Ma $^{40}Ar/^{39}Ar$ and K/Ar ages obtained from hornblende in mafic dikes within the Besham Complex and on the presence of an unconformity between rock mapped as part of the Besham Complex and an overlying metaconglomerate in the Karora Formation. The assumption was that the ca. 1900 Ma ages recorded high-grade metamorphism and deformation in the Besham Complex prior to deposition of the Karora Formation. Our mapping indicates that the Besham Complex intrudes the Karora Formation and that the rock that unconformably underlies the Karora Formation is of very limited extent. On this basis, we have separated this rock from the Besham Complex and mapped it as a separate rock unit that we name the Kishar Formation (Plate 1).

Rather than dating metamorphism, we interpret the Early Pro-

terozoic argon ages as dating the approximate time of intrusion of mafic dikes into the Besham Complex. The Early Proterozoic intrusive ages are preserved within gabbroic and dioritic rock despite later amphibolite facies regional metamorphism in the Late Cretaceous–Paleogene. Such a situation, where older $^{40}Ar/^{39}Ar$ ages are preserved despite later metamorphism, is not unprecedented. For example, Lanphere and Albee (1974) show that coarse-grained muscovites from northern Vermont preserve an older Taconic metamorphism, whereas fine-grained micas from the same rock preserve a younger Acadian metamorphism. Chamberlain et al. (1991) described an amphibolite from the Indian plate in the Babusar Pass area of northern Pakistan that preserves a Precambrian $^{40}Ar/^{39}Ar$ age despite later Paleogene amphibolite facies metamorphism. We conclude that both the Karora and Gandaf Formations are older than the Besham Complex and that the Early Proterozoic thermal event is plutonic and probably associated with regional low-grade metamorphism (as discussed later), but not necessarily associated with regional amphibolite facies metamorphism for which there is no conclusive evidence.

STRATIGRAPHY OF THE INDIAN PLATE

Early Proterozoic (≥2175 Ma) Rock

Kishar Formation. The Kishar Formation is a new formation used for rock, originally considered to be part of the Besham Complex, that unconformably underlies the Karora Formation. The Kishar Formation is known to occur at only two small, isolated areas. The first is the well-known roadcut along the Besham-Karora road ~5 km west of Besham. The second is a less-well-known roadcut along the Karakoram highway ~6 km north of Besham (Plate 1). In both areas, the Kishar Formation is unconformably overlain by the Amlo Metaconglomerate Member of the Karora Formation. Along the Besham-Karora road the Amlo metaconglomerate is overlain by a thick succession of undifferentiated Karora Formation, providing the impression that the unconformity is regional and that the Kishar Formation is characteristic of the Besham Complex. The roadcut along the Karakoram highway, by contrast, is isolated, structurally overturned, and surrounded by intrusive rock of the Besham Complex.

The Kishar Formation, in both areas, is characterized by two lithologies of unknown protolith. The first is a dark gray, very fine grained, nonschistose, biotite-quartz-plagioclase rock without obvious foliation that, in thin section, shows pervasive alteration of plagioclase to sericite and calcite. The second is a dark gray, granular, fine- to medium-grained biotite-bearing, quartz–plagioclase–K-feldspar rock with weak foliation. Zircons from the Kishar Formation yield a U-Pb age of 2175 ± 7 Ma (Isachsen and DiPietro, 1997).

Proterozoic metasedimentary rock

In addition to the Kishar Formation, rocks of known Early Proterozoic age include the Karora Formation and the overlying

Gandaf Formation. The base of the Karora Formation is exposed in the Besham area, where it unconformably overlies the Kishar Formation. The top of the Gandaf Formation is exposed in the Tarbela Lake region, where it unconformably underlies the Late Proterozoic Tanawal Formation. The contact between the Karora and Gandaf Formations appears to be depositional. On a regional basis, the rocks display lithologic and stratigraphic characteristics that are similar to those of the Salkhala Formation in Hazara, Kaghan, and Kashmir (Wadia, 1931, 1934; Calkins et al., 1975; Greco et al., 1989; Greco and Spencer, 1993). U-Pb zircon ages bracket deposition of the Karora and Gandaf Formations to be between about 1858 and 2175 Ma (Isachsen and DiPietro, 1997).

The age of the Manki, Hazara, and Manglaur Formations, in the study area, is unconstrained between the Early and Late Proterozoic. A direct correlation of these rocks with the Karora or Gandaf Formations is not possible because they are separated either by faults, or by areas of younger rock. The Manki Formation is separated from the Gandaf Formation by the Darband fault and from the Hazara Formation by the Panjal-Khairabad fault. The Manki and Hazara Formations are placed in the Early Proterozoic succession because, like the Gandaf Formation, both unconformably underlie the Tanawal Formation. There are lithologic and metamorphic differences between the Gandaf and Manki Formations across the Darband fault. These differences are not seen in the overlying Tanawal Formation, suggesting pre-Tanawal displacement along the Darband fault (Pogue et al., this volume). The Manglaur Formation is placed with the Early Proterozoic succession because it displays lithologic similarities with the Gandaf Formation.

Karora Formation. The Karora Formation name was first applied to rock in the Besham area by Fletcher et al. (1986) and used later by workers including Treloar et al. (1989a), and Baig (1990). The Karora Formation mapped in this report generally follows that of earlier workers, but we have extended the formation into previously unmapped areas and refined the contacts. The Karora Formation occurs as an inner belt within the Besham Complex and as an outer belt that surrounds the Besham Complex (Plate 1). The formation is characterized by thick layers of very fine grained, dark, quartz-rich, graphite-muscovite-plagioclase-quartz schist with or without accessory biotite (hereafter referred to as graphitic schist) that is associated with thick layers of calcite, dolomite, and tremolite marble. Also present are subordinate layers of dark, fine-grained, nonschistose, muscovite-biotite-plagioclase-quartz metapsammite. Rare quartzite and intraformational metaconglomerate are also present. Intrusive contacts with the largely underlying granitic gneiss of the Besham Complex are present along the inner belt of the Karora Formation east of Shang, and in many areas along the outer belt, especially on the eastern limb of the Indus River anticline. Intrusive contacts are characterized by interlayered granitic gneiss and schist; by the presence of small plutons in the Karora Formation; by dikes that crosscut schist and marble; and by xenoliths of graphitic schist and marble in the Besham Complex.

The Amlo Metaconglomerate Member (Baig, 1990) is at the base of the inner belt of Karora Formation where it unconformably overlies the Kishar Formation. The metaconglomerate contains pebble- to boulder-size clasts of granitic gneiss, leucogneiss, leucogranite, amphibolite, metapsammite, quartzite, and quartz-sericite rock, within a dark, graphite-bearing psammitic matrix that grades upward into graphitic schist of undifferentiated Karora Formation.

Gandaf Formation. The Gandaf Formation was first applied to Precambrian rock in the Tarbela area by Pogue et al. (1995; this volume). We have extended the Gandaf Formation northward along the Indus River to the Besham area. Rocks in this formation were previously unmapped except in the Besham area, where they were mapped, in part, as the Besham Group, Karora Group, Manglaur Formation, or Tanawal Formation (Calkins et al., 1975; Williams, 1989; Baig, 1990). We use the name Gandaf Formation for these rocks because they are continuous with the Gandaf Formation as defined by Pogue et al. (this volume) and because none of the previously used names fit the stratigraphic location, description, or age of the rocks. At its type locality, near the village of Gandaf in the Tarbela Lake area, the formation consists of dark schists interlayered with graphitic slate, phyllite, schist and marble, calcareous phyllite and schist, and nongraphitic marble. The base of the formation is not exposed at its type locality.

The Gandaf Formation can be traced northward to the area just southwest of Darband, where garnet appears in the dark schist. North of Darband, the formation is characterized by thick layers of dark, garnet-biotite-muscovite-plagioclase-quartz schist typically with quartz veins (hereafter referred to as garnet schist). The garnet schist is used as a marker unit that can be traced along the eastern and western limbs of the Indus River anticline, where it occurs at more than one stratigraphic horizon. The repetition of the garnet schist is believed to be an original sedimentary feature complicated by folding. Associated with the garnet schist are thick layers of fine-grained, nonschistose, plagioclase-biotite-quartz metapsammite. The metapsammite is similar to metapsammite in the Karora Formation but is typically lighter in color and more variable, grading either to a quartzite or becoming more schistose and grading to a medium-grained, quartzo-feldspathic schist. In addition to garnet schist and metapsammite, the Gandaf Formation contains thick layers of graphitic schist, and subordinate dark muscovite schist, calcite marble, tremolite marble, and quartzite. The abundance of garnet schist and nongraphitic rock distinguishes the Gandaf Formation from the more graphitic and calcareous Karora Formation.

The base of the Gandaf Formation is well exposed along the eastern limb of the Indus River anticline east of Bar Kabulgram and locally along the western limb west of Chakesar. The contact appears to be depositional (transitional) over a few meters; graphitic schist of the Karora Formation grades into lighter colored metapsammite and garnet schist of the Gandaf Formation. The contact along the eastern limb of the Indus River anticline near Thakot is difficult to place due to intrusions of granitic gneiss.

Swat and Mansehra granitic gneisses intrude the Gandaf Formation along its upper contact (Plate 1). North of ~34°45′N, schist and metapsammite are interlayered with concordant sheets of augen gneiss. Contacts in this area are locally sheared along both brittle and ductile faults. South of ~34°45′N, the contact is discordant, and there are abundant xenoliths of schist and metapsammite within augen gneiss. A discordant relationship is particularly evident in the Black Mountains, where compositional layers in the Gandaf Formation are truncated by Mansehra granitic gneiss.

There are abundant intrusive rocks in the Gandaf Formation. These include biotite orthogneiss and mafic rock of the Kotla Complex, and a pegmatite-mafic dike and sill sequence correlated with the Besham Complex (Plate 1). Numerous additional bodies of granite, granitic gneiss, pegmatite, and mafic rock are also present but are too small to separate from the Gandaf Formation at the scale of the map. The smaller intrusions are particularly abundant in the northern part of the formation north of 34°30′N. Presumably these intrusions represent part of the Kotla and Besham Complexes.

Part of the Gandaf Formation along the eastern limb of the Indus River anticline near Thakot was previously mapped as Tanawal Formation (Ashraf et al., 1980; Williams, 1989; Baig, 1990). These rocks are included as part of the Gandaf Formation on the basis of interlayers of graphitic rock, marble, and orthogneiss (including the Kotla Complex) that are typical of the Gandaf Formation and not typical of the Tanawal Formation.

Manki Formation. Tahirkheli (1970) applied the name Manki slate to rocks in the Attock-Cherat Range and later (Tahirkheli, 1971) correlated them with lithologically similar and laterally equivalent rock in the adjacent Gandghar Range. Hylland et al. (1988) applied the name Manki Formation to the rocks in the Gandghar Range, consistent with current usage by the Geological Survey of Pakistan. Rocks in the Gandghar Range were mapped as Hazara Formation by Calkins et al. (1975), but Pogue et al. (this volume) point out differences between these rocks and those mapped as Hazara Formation south of the Panjal fault. We therefore follow the current usage of the Geological Survey of Pakistan and map the rocks north of the Panjal fault in the Gandghar Range as Manki Formation and those south of the fault as Hazara Formation.

The Manki Formation is characterized by interlayered gray, black, or brown argillite, slate, phyllite, and metasiltstone, and subordinate metapsammite, marble, calcareous phyllite, and quartzite. A thin layer of graphitic rock is present at the base of the exposed section along the Baghdarra fault, which Pogue et al. (1995) mapped as part of the Gandaf Formation. In this report, the graphitic rock is mapped as part of the Manki Formation because of its uncertain correlation with the Gandaf Formation. As much as 500 m of thin-bedded to massive dolomitic marble are present in discontinuous layers above the Manki Formation and along faults where it is interlayered with subordinate quartzite and argillite. The marbles are part of the Sobrah, Shekhai, and Shahkot Formations of Riaz et al. (1991) and Pogue et al. (1995). They unconformably underlie the Tanawal Formation and therefore are considered to be part of the Early Proterozoic succession.

They are included with the Manki Formation in Plate 1 due to their limited abundance.

Hazara Formation. The Hazara Formation as mapped by Calkins et al. (1975) crops out in the southeast corner of Plate 1, south of the Panjal-Khairabad fault, where it consists of unmetamorphosed to weakly metamorphosed slate, argillite, and graywacke, and minor limestone in its upper part.

Manglaur Formation. The Manglaur Formation (DiPietro, 1990; DiPietro et al., 1993) is restricted to the Loe Sar dome area, where it is surrounded and intruded by Swat granitic gneiss. It consists of garnet-biotite-plagioclase-quartz-muscovite schist, garnet-quartz-muscovite schist, and micaceous quartzite. Thick interlayers of quartzite, feldspathic quartzite, and tremolite marble are particularly abundant near the top of the formation. Subordinate layers of graphitic schist are also present.

Previous workers have correlated the Manglaur Formation with the Tanawal Formation and assigned the Manglaur Formation a Late Proterozoic age (Kazmi et al., 1984; DiPietro et al., 1993). This correlation may be correct; however, it cannot be proven due to the isolated occurrence of the Manglaur Formation. Several lines of evidence suggest that the Manglaur Formation is entirely or, at least in part, Early Proterozoic. The evidence includes the abundance of marble near the top of the formation and the presence of graphitic schist, both of which are typical of rocks that unconformably underlie the Tanawal Formation. The base of the Manglaur Formation is not exposed but the lower part, in the vicinity of Jambil, contains an abundance of granitic gneiss, leucogneiss, and mafic intrusions that do not appear elsewhere in the Loe Sar dome and do not appear to be correlative with the Swat gneiss. The intrusions may be comagmatic with Early Proterozoic intrusions in the Indus syntaxis, suggesting that at least part of the Manglaur Formation is Early Proterozoic. Because we find no evidence of an unconformity within this formation, we tentatively suggest that it is Early Proterozoic in age. The stratigraphic position of the Manglaur Formation depicted in the cross section (Plate 1) suggests a correlation with the Gandaf Formation.

Late Proterozoic metasedimentary rock

Tanawal Formation. Calkins et al. (1975) mapped the Tanawal Formation along the eastern margin of the area shown in Plate 1, where it is extensively intruded by the Mansehra granitic gneiss. The Tanawal Formation was also mapped in the area surrounding the southern part of Tarbela Lake where it unconformably overlies the Gandaf and Manki Formations (Riaz et al., 1991; S. R. Khan et al., 1995; Pogue, 1994; Pogue et al., 1995). We have extended the formation to include lithologically similar rock along the eastern and southern limbs of the Dosara-Budal syncline (Plate 1). A Late Proterozoic age is inferred for the Tanawal Formation on the basis of its unconformable relationship with the underlying Early Proterozoic rock; the presence of Cambrian rock units unconformably above the Tanawal Formation; and a whole-rock Rb/Sr isotopic age of 516 ± 16 Ma from the Mansehra augen granitic gneiss, which intrudes Tanawal Formation (Le Fort et al., 1980).

In the low-grade areas south of 34°30′N, the Tanawal Formation is characterized by an abundance of quartzite and quartz-rich schist and lesser argillite and muscovite schist. Quartzite beds display asymmetric ripple marks and crossbedding. North of 34°30′N the formation is characterized by an abundance of soft, friable, mica-rich, garnet-biotite-plagioclase-quartz-muscovite schist and subordinate quartzite, quartz schist, biotite schist, and rare schistose marble.

In the southern Tarbela Lake area, quartzite of the Tanawal Formation unconformably overlies dark schist and phyllite of the Gandaf Formation north of the Darband fault, and unconformably overlies argillite and slate of the Manki Formation south of the Darband fault. The contacts are sharp except locally where a conglomerate provides evidence for the unconformity. Northward, the Gandaf-Tanawal contact disappears beneath the discordant Swat and Mansehra granitic gneisses (Plate 1). The location of the contact in this area is complicated by intrusion of granitic gneiss and by similarities between garnet schist and quartz-rich metapsammite that are present in both the Tanawal and Gandaf Formations. The contact is placed above interlayers of marble and graphitic schist that are characteristic of the Gandaf Formation and that are virtually absent in the Tanawal Formation. Clear evidence for an unconformity is lacking in this area.

Paleozoic and Mesozoic metasedimentary rock

The stratigraphy and depositional history of Paleozoic and Mesozoic rock in the Loe Sar dome and Peshawar basin has been discussed in detail elsewhere (Pogue and Hussain, 1986; DiPietro, 1990; Hussain et al., 1991; Pogue et al., 1992a, 1992b; DiPietro et al., 1993). In this chapter we extend the stratigraphy into the Dosara-Budal syncline, which had not previously been mapped in detail. The stratigraphy is unchanged from our previous work with the exception of the following revisions. The first revision is the stratigraphic position of the Jobra Formation, which has been revised from Devonian(?) to Cambrian or older in order to reflect evidence that it is intruded by the Swat granitic gneiss. The second is the Karapa greenschist, which previously was considered to be a single stratigraphic horizon directly below the Kashala Formation. Additional mapping in the Peshawar basin north of Rustam indicates that the Karapa greenschist is present as upper and lower stratigraphic layers that enclose a succession of marble that previously was mapped as part of the Kashala Formation. In this chapter the upper and lower greenschist, along with the intervening marble, are grouped together as the Duma Formation (Plate 1). We have restricted the Karapa name to the upper greenschist layer and given it member status in the Duma Formation. The lower layer of greenschist is redefined as the Malandrai Member of the Duma Formation. This revision is consistent with our earlier work, which placed the Karapa greenschist directly below the Kashala Formation (Fig. 4). The end result of the stratigraphic revision is the insertion of the Duma Formation between the Jafar

Kandao and Kashala Formations (Figs. 2 and 4). The Duma Formation, including the Karapa Member, can be traced across the Dosara-Budal syncline, where the Karapa Member becomes intraformational and pinches out (Plate 1). The Malandrai Member extends eastward a short distance where it disappears below a minor shear zone along the north side of the Ambela Complex northeast of Rustam (Plate 1).

The Paleozoic and Mesozoic rock units are divided into three age groups: an early-middle Paleozoic (Cambrian to Devonian) shelf sequence, a late Paleozoic–Triassic (Carboniferous to Permian or Triassic?) rift clastic-metabasalt sequence, and a Mesozoic (Triassic to Jurassic or younger) shelf-slope-rise sequence (Fig. 2; Plate 1). The early-middle Paleozoic shelf sequence contains erosional unconformities and is absent in the Loe Sar dome area. The Mesozoic rocks, by contrast, are continuous across the area (Plate 1). In order to account for the missing early-middle Paleozoic shelf sequence in the Loe Sar dome area, DiPietro (1990) and Pogue et al. (1992b) inferred the existence of a late Paleozoic fault below the Nikanai Ghar Formation that separates rock in the Loe Sar dome area from the more complete early-middle Paleozoic rock sequence in the Peshawar basin. In this chapter we suggest that this fault, or a related fault, extends in a north-northeast direction below the Kashala Formation along the eastern limb of the Dosara syncline where it separates the stratigraphy on the eastern limb of the Dosara-Budal syncline from the stratigraphy in the Loe Sar dome (Plate 1 cross section). The inferred fault corresponds roughly with the trend of the Main Mantle thrust along the western margin of the Indus syntaxis.

Early-middle Paleozoic shelf sequence. Rocks of known early-middle Paleozoic age are restricted to the area surrounding the Peshawar basin. The succession consists of Cambrian Ambar Formation (sandy dolomite), Ordovician Misri Banda Quartzite (feldspathic quartzite), Silurian Panjpir Formation (argillite), and Devonian Nowshera Formation (dolomite; Pogue and Hussain, 1986; Hussain et al., 1991; Pogue et al., 1992a). The age assignments are based on conodont fossils that are present in the Misri Banda, Panjpir, and Nowshera Formations (Pogue et al., 1992a). The rocks unconformably overlie the Tanawal Formation. Locally, a basal conglomerate in the Ambar Formation marks the unconformity. Additional unconformities are present below the Misri Banda Quartzite and Panjpir Formation. In some areas the Ambar Formation is missing and the Misri Banda Quartzite is directly above the Tanawal Formation. All of the unconformities appear to be erosional. Rocks provisionally correlated with the Ambar Formation and with the Misri Banda Quartzite are in the Sherwan syncline east of Tarbela Lake (Plate 1).

Late Paleozoic–Triassic Rift clastic-metabasalt sequence. Late Paleozoic–Triassic rocks are mapped in the Peshawar basin, the Loe Sar dome, and in the Dosara-Budal syncline, where they are represented by the Jafar Kandao, Marghazar, and Duma Formations. The Jafar Kandao Formation of Pogue and Hussain (1986) is restricted to the Peshawar basin where it unconformably overlies the Nowshera Formation (Plate 1; Fig. 2). The Jafar Kandao Formation is composed of argillite and limestone and subordinate calcareous quartzite and intraformational conglomerate. Conodonts in the limestone indicate a latest Devonian to Late Carboniferous age (Pogue et al., 1992a). Intraformational conglomerate layers contain clasts of granitic leucogneiss that are similar to leucogneiss in the Besham Complex. This suggests that a highland underlain by Precambrian rock was exposed to the north during the Carboniferous (Pogue et al., 1992b).

The Duma Formation was originally defined in the Dosara-Budal syncline (DiPietro et al., 1995). In this chapter we redefine the formation to include the Karapa and Malandrai Members and extend the formation into the Peshawar basin. In the Peshawar basin, the Malandrai Member overlies the Jafar Kandao Formation at an erosional unconformity. Both the Malandrai and Karapa Members, in this area, consist of greenschist interlayered with minor argillite, phyllite, calcite marble, dolomitic marble, and graphitic phyllite. The intervening undifferentiated Duma Formation consists of thick layers of poorly foliated, dark gray to white calcite and dolomite marble that resembles marble in the Kashala Formation. Fossils are present in the Duma Formation, but they have not yet been conclusively identified. The age of the Duma Formation in the Peshawar basin area, is constrained by its stratigraphic position above Late Carboniferous rock of the Jafar Kandao Formation and below Late Triassic rock of the Kashala Formation (Pogue et al., 1992a).

The Duma Formation extends along the eastern and southern limbs of the Dosara-Budal syncline where it overlies the Tanawal Formation and underlies the Kashala Formation (Plate 1). In this area, it consists of interlayered marble and amphibolite. White, gray, and banded calcite marble containing minor phlogopite are most common, but phlogopite marble, tremolite marble, and dolomitic marble are also locally abundant. Garnetiferous schistose marble is rare but is present locally in the upper part of the formation. Massive, white to brown dolomitic marble is particularly abundant along the southern limb of the Budal syncline. The Karapa Member is separated from undifferentiated Duma Formation on the basis of abundant amphibolite, greenschist (in the southern part), biotite schist, and quartzite, and only minor marble. The Karapa Member is mapped as a lithostratigraphic rock unit that directly underlies the Kashala Formation in the south but becomes intraformational and pinches out in the north. The Malandrai Member is absent in the Dosara-Budal syncline.

The lower contact with the Tanawal Formation is well exposed along the entire length of the Duma Formation and is transitional with phlogopite-rich marble of the Duma Formation interlayered with, or gradational into, biotite schist of the Tanawal Formation. Conglomerate or other obvious evidence for an unconformity is absent. Although we suspect a Late Carboniferous–Triassic age for the Duma Formation on the basis of its stratigraphic position in the Peshawar basin, the lack of an obvious unconformity with the Tanawal Formation in the Dosara-Budal area suggests that it may extend to the Cambrian and may contain numerous, as-yet unrecognized, intraformational unconformities.

The upper contact between the Karapa Member and the Kashala Formation is typically sharp. Where the Karapa Member is absent, the contact between undifferentiated Duma Formation and Kashala Formation is placed where white marble, banded marble, dolomitic marble, or phlogopite marble of the Duma Formation is in contact with garnetiferous marble or dark gray calcite marble of the Kashala Formation. The contact varies from sharp to interlayered and is locally gradational over several hundred meters. The contact is consistently near the stratigraphically highest appearance of amphibolite in the stratigraphic section. Excellent exposures of the Duma Formation are found in roadcuts south of Tangora and east of Alpurai, and along the ridge north of Rustam. We consider these areas to be type sections.

The Marghazar Formation of DiPietro (1990) and DiPietro et al. (1993) is restricted to the Loe Sar dome area where it unconformably overlies the Late Cambrian Swat granitic gneiss and the Early(?) Proterozoic Manglaur and Jobra Formations. The Marghazar Formation is characterized by an abundance of hornblende schist and amphibolite interlayered with biotite schist, psammitic schist, phlogopite-bearing calcite marble, and minor garnet schist. A layer of amphibolite, typically less than 20 m thick, is present everywhere at the top of the Marghazar Formation except in the area west of Dosara. The contact between the Swat granitic gneiss and Marghazar Formation is interpreted as an uncomformity because there is no clear evidence for intrusion. Where exposed, the contact is sharp and without interlaying. In many areas, the contact is obscured by intrusion of younger tourmaline granite gneiss. The Marghazar and Manglaur Formations are in contact only along the southeastern margin of the Loe Sar dome (Plate 1): here the contact is sharp but folded with psammitic schist, marble, and amphibolite of the Marghazar Formation in contact with garnetiferous quartz schist of the Manglaur Formation. Conglomerate is absent but locally the Marghazar Formation contains pebbles of granitic rock. The contact between the Marghazar and Jobra Formations southwest of Pacha appears to be an angular unconformity (DiPietro, 1990). A correlation of the Marghazar Formation with the Karapa Member is suggested by their similar lithology and stratigraphic position below the Kashala Formation. This constrains the age of the Marghazar Formation to between Late Carboniferous and Late Triassic. Pogue et al. (1992b) and DiPietro et al. (1993) suggested that the Karapa, Malandrai, and Marghazar Formations represent volcanic flows and related volcaniclastic and carbonate rock that correlate with the Panjal volcanic rocks of Wadia (1931, 1934), Calkins et al. (1975), and Greco and Spencer (1993).

Mesozoic shelf-slope rise. Rocks of known Mesozoic age crop out in the Loe Sar dome area and in the Dosara syncline, where they are represented by the Kashala, Nikanai Ghar, and Saidu Formations (Plate 1). These three formations, along with the Marghazar Formation, represent the Alpurai Group (Fig. 4; DiPietro, 1990). The Kashala Formation overlies both the Karapa Member and the Marghazar Formation; the contact is sharp and may represent an erosional unconformity. In low-grade rock north of Rustam, the Kashala Formation consists of dark gray to white calcite and dolomitic marble, and calcareous phyllite. Garnet appears in the calcareous phyllite in the vicinity of Jowar and along the southern limb of the Budal syncline. Farther north, in the Dosara-Budal syncline and in the area surrounding the Loe Sar dome, the Kashala Formation consists of garnetiferous calcareous schist, schistose marble, dark gray calcite marble, and subordinate gray to white crystalline calcite marble. Greenschist and amphibolite are absent.

Along the southern margin of the Loe Sar dome, the Kashala Formation is overlain by massive, dark gray to white calcite marble and dolomitic marble of the Nikanai Ghar Formation. This is in contrast to the northern part of the dome where the Kashala Formation is overlain by graphitic phyllite and subordinate dark gray marble of the Saidu Formation. Near Jowar, the Kashala Formation locally overlies the Saidu Formation and appears to grade laterally into the Nikanai Ghar Formation (Plate 1). In addition, some of the Kashala Formation in the core of the Budal syncline resembles the Nikanai Ghar Formation. The relationships suggest that the Kashala, Saidu, and Nikanai Ghar Formations are partly stratigraphically equivalent and therefore of similar age (Plate 1; DiPietro, 1990). In general, Kashala schistose marble is common near the base, Nikanai Ghar calcite and dolomite marble is typical of the upper part in the south, and Saidu graphitic phyllite is typical of the upper part in the north directly below the Indus melange. Conodonts indicate a Late Triassic age for the Kashala Formation (Pogue et al., 1992a). The upper age limit of the Kashala, Nikanai Ghar, and Saidu Formations is not known, but poorly preserved fossils in the Nikanai Ghar Formation suggest that it may extend at least into the Jurassic (Pogue et al., 1992a).

Metasedimentary rock of unknown age

Jobra Formation. The Jobra Formation of DiPietro (1990) is a rare discontinuous rock unit characterized by wollastonite-bearing calc-silicate rock interlayered with tremolite marble, garnet-biotite schist, quartzite, and amphibolite. It is restricted to the Loe Sar dome area west of Pacha, where it overlies with sharp contact the Swat granitic gneiss and is unconformably below the Marghazar Formation (Plate 1). The Jobra Formation is not in contact with the Manglaur Formation but overlies Swat gneiss structurally above the Manglaur Formation. The Jobra Formation was originally considered to be Devonian in age (Pogue et al., 1992b; DiPietro et al., 1993), but a calc-silicate marble lithologically similar to the Jobra Formation occurs as a xenolith within the Swat gneiss in the area northeast of Saidu (Plate 1). This xenolith, first described by Shams (1963), probably correlates with the Jobra Formation, which would imply that the Jobra Formation is Cambrian or older. The Jobra Formation may correlate with sandy dolomite of the Cambrian Ambar Formation. Alternatively, if the Manglaur Formation is Early Proterozoic, then the Jobra Formation may also be as old as Early Proterozoic.

Banna and Landai Formations. The Banna Formation was named by Tahirkheli (1979a) for rocks along the east side of the Indus syntaxis in the Allai Kohistan area (Plate 1). The formation is in a small syncline; Indus melange is on the north side,

Mansehra augen granite gneiss and Landai Formation are on the west side, and a thin layer of garnet schist and feldspathic quartzite, mapped as the Tanawal Formation, is on the south side. The eastern extension of the formation is uncertain. The Banna Formation consists entirely of graphitic schist and phyllite with interlayered calcite marble that is typically dark gray and varies from massive to well foliated. The Landai Formation is a new name that is used for a small lens of rock that is between the Mansehra augen granite gneiss, the Indus melange, and the Banna Formation (Plate 1). The Landai Formation consists of amphibolite, garnetiferous schistose marble, and white to light gray calcite marble, none of which are present in the Banna Formation. Graphitic schist, which characterizes the Banna Formation, is largely absent in the Landai Formation.

The nature of the contacts surrounding the Banna and Landai Formations is uncertain. The contact between Banna graphitic schist and Mansehra augen granitic gneiss is sharp, and there is no clear evidence for intrusion or faulting. The contact becomes horizontal southwest of Kharg, suggesting that the contact is not a late, high-angle brittle fault. The contact between Banna graphitic schist and Tanawal quartzite and schist is sharp, and there is no clear evidence for an unconformity or a fault. Schistose marble and amphibolite are present locally at the contact. These rocks, which are too thin to show in Plate 1, may correlate with the Landai Formation. The contact between white marble and amphibolite of the Landai Formation and the Mansehra augen granitic gneiss is also sharp, and there is no clear evidence for a fault. Thin layers of pegmatite are present in the marble at the contact, suggesting an intrusive relationship; alternatively, this could be the result of later deformation. The map pattern is consistent with the possibility that both formations are bounded by faults. The absence of brittle fabrics along the contacts suggests that the faults (if present) are synmetamorphic imbricates associated with the obduction and thrusting of the Indus melange.

The Banna Formation is lithologically similar to the Karora Formation and to the Saidu Formation. It has been correlated with the Salkhala Formation, implying a Precambrian age (Ashraf et al., 1980), and with the Alpurai Group, implying a late Paleozoic–Mesozoic age (Treloar et al., 1989c). The position of the Banna Formation below the Indus melange and the absence of mafic intrusions favors a correlation with the Triassic or younger Saidu Formation (Fig. 4). The Landai Formation is lithologically similar to the Kashala and Duma Formations, suggesting a late Paleozoic–Triassic age. The age assignments, which should be viewed as tentative, imply either an unconformity or a synmetamorphic fault contact with the underlying Tanawal Formation and Mansehra granitic gneiss.

Early Proterozoic intrusive rock

Besham Complex. Rocks mapped in this report as the Besham Complex were first described by Jan and Tahirkheli (1969) and later referred to as the Besham granitic gneisses by

Jan et al. (1981). Ashraf et al. (1980) referred to the rocks as Lahor granite (Fig. 3).

Two major intrusive rock types characterize the Besham Complex. The first is the Shang granodiorite gneiss of Jan and Tahirkheli (1969), which is a large, relatively homogeneous, pluton; the boundaries of the pluton have not been precisely located, but it makes up a large part of the southern half of the Besham Complex west and north of Thakot. The rock is a medium- to coarse-grained, white to gray, hornblende-biotite granodiorite gneiss that typically has well-developed foliation. The Indus·River makes a sharp bend around the intrusion, suggesting that the river was deflected eastward by the rising granitic massif (Plate 1). Large boulders and a few isolated outcrops of Shang granodiorite gneiss are present along the Karakoram highway ~2 km east of Shang village. The second rock is an unfoliated, coarse-grained to pegmatitic, leucogranite that contains accessory biotite, muscovite, tourmaline, or magnetite. The leucogranite is ubiquitous throughout the Besham Complex and is well exposed along roadcuts surrounding Besham. The rock surrounds the Shang granodiorite gneiss, suggesting that the two are related. A wide variety of additional intrusive rock is present in the Besham Complex. These include a fine-grained, poorly foliated, dark gray, biotite-quartz-plagioclase orthogneiss; mafic dikes that have ca. 1900 Ma $^{40}Ar/^{39}Ar$ ages (Baig, 1990); whitish, fine-grained, granitic gneiss with or without biotite; and a muscovite-biotite-quartz-plagioclase orthogneiss with small feldspar augen that resembles orthogneiss in the Kotla Complex. All of the rocks intrude the Karora Formation, including the Shang granodiorite gneiss and the leucogranite. Other crosscutting relationships indicate that the leucogranite and the mafic dikes intrude the biotite orthogneiss, and that the leucogranite intrudes the mafic dikes. With the exception of leucogranite, the main body of Shang granodiorite gneiss is generally devoid of other intrusive rock. This suggests that the Shang, along with the leucogranite, represents the youngest of the major intrusive bodies in the Besham Complex. A few small serpentinite bodies in the Besham Complex were interpreted by Baig (1990) to represent slivers of Indus melange carried southward along brittle faults. Because not all serpentinite bodies observed by us are associated with brittle faults, we suggest that they represent Early Proterozoic ultramafic rock associated with the Besham Complex. The stratigraphically highest occurrence of Besham Complex is on the western limb of the Indus River anticline, where a leucogranite-mafic dike and sill sequence intrudes the Gandaf Formation (Plate 1).

We consider the rock in the Besham Complex to be Early Proterozoic on the basis of a U-Pb zircon age of 1858 ± 17 Ma from the Shang granodiorite gneiss (Isachsen and DiPietro, 1997) and published $^{40}Ar/^{39}Ar$ and K/Ar ages on hornblende from mafic dikes and sills that range from 1862 to 2160 Ma (Treloar et al., 1989b; Treloar and Rex, 1990; Baig, 1990). We cannot, however, rule out the possibility that some of the rock is younger. Unrecognized Kishar Formation may also be present in the Besham Complex.

Kotla Complex. The Kotla Complex is a newly defined intrusive rock unit first recognized by DiPietro et al. (1996) that is present in a previously unmapped area of the Indus syntaxis (Plate 1). In the southern Tarbela Lake region, Calkins et al. (1975) mapped part of the Kotla Complex as Salkhala Formation. The Kotla Complex forms sill-like bodies that intrude within and near the top of the Gandaf Formation. The principal rock is a strongly foliated to mylonitic, muscovite-biotite-quartz-plagioclase orthogneiss that typically contains small (<0.5 cm) feldspar augen (hereafter referred to as biotite orthogneiss). Leucogneiss, pegmatite, and mafic dikes are interlayered with the biotite orthogneiss producing, in many areas, a strong banding to the outcrop. Although similar rocks are found in the Besham Complex, the Kotla Complex is mapped as a separate rock unit because it cannot be traced laterally into the Besham Complex and because most of the rock in the Besham Complex, including the Shang granodiorite gneiss, is not observed in the Kotla Complex. Schist and metapsammitic rock correlated with the Gandaf Formation are present within the Kotla Complex, especially along the westernmost belt near Choga. Contacts between the Kotla Complex and Gandaf Formation are either sharp, interlayered, or are cut by late brittle faults. Where interlayered, the contact appears to be intrusive. A U-Pb zircon age of 1836 ± 1 Ma from the Kotla biotite orthogneiss indicates an Early Proterozoic intrusive age (Isachsen and DiPietro, 1997).

Granitic gneiss in the Kotla Complex locally preserves a foliation that is crosscut by interlayered amphibolite. The relationship suggests that a foliation was present in the Kotla Complex prior to Late Cretaceous–Paleogene metamorphism. The foliation could be interpreted either as the result of an earlier (Early Proterozoic?) amphibolite facies metamorphism or as a primary fabric that developed under a stress regime during intrusion. The latter interpretation is preferred on the basis of field relationships south of Darband, where gneissic rock of the Kotla Complex is in contact with low-grade rock of the Gandaf Formation. The lack of amphibolite facies metamorphism in this part of the Gandaf Formation suggests that the younger Kotla Complex also was not strongly metamorphosed.

Late Proterozoic intrusive rock

Black Mountain Complex. The Black Mountain Complex is a newly defined intrusive rock unit first recognized by DiPietro et al. (1996) that is present in a previously unmapped area along the crest of the Black Mountains, where it is completely surrounded and intruded by Late Cambrian Mansehra granitic gneiss (Plate 1). The Black Mountain Complex structurally and topographically overlies the Gandaf Formation. The most characteristic rock is a dark, equigranular, medium- to fine-grained, biotite–K-feldspar–quartz– plagioclase orthogneiss. Although typically well foliated, the rock varies from massive to migmatitic and locally grades to a lighter colored biotite orthogneiss with garnet in leucocratic zones. Other subordinate rock types include biotite- and/or garnet-bearing gneiss, pegmatite, and mafic rock. Metasedimentary rock is rare but xenoliths of metapsammite were found in one area near the southwest margin of the intrusion. Locally, the rock contains small augen and is similar in appearance to the Kotla biotite orthogneiss. Xenoliths of Black Mountain gneiss are abundant in the Mansehra granitic gneiss in the Machai Sar area. A Late Proterozoic age is inferred for the Black Mountain Complex on the basis of a preliminary U-Pb zircon age of ca. 800 Ma (Isachsen and DiPietro, 1997).

Early Paleozoic intrusive rock

Swat and Mansehra augen granitic gneiss. Augen and flaser granitic gneisses crop out extensively across the map area. West of the Indus River these rocks are referred to as the Swat granitic gneiss (Martin et al., 1962). East of the river they are referred to as Mansehra granitic gneiss (Shams, 1961). The rocks on either side of the river are identical, but the names are retained for geographic location purposes and because this nomenclature has been followed by all previous workers. The rocks, in general, are biotite and muscovite bearing and range in texture and composition from a coarse-grained, light colored granite gneiss having characteristic flaser texture and scattered K-feldspar augen, to a dark colored fine-grained granodiorite gneiss characterized by abundant augen of K-feldspar and plagioclase. Included in the Swat granitic gneiss is a coarse-grained, equigranular, weakly foliated, biotite granite that is common in the S-shaped bend of the Indus River north of Manjakot. This rock is either a variant of the augen and flaser gneiss or is a younger intrusion. Late Paleozoic and younger tourmaline granite, alkali granite, biotite granite, pegmatite, amphibolite, metagabbro, and diabase dikes intrude the augen gneisses.

The Swat and Mansehra granitic gneisses occur as sill-like layers that intrude the Gandaf, Tanawal, and Manglaur Formations and the Kotla and Black Mountain Complexes. Along most of its trace, the Gandaf-Tanawal Formation contact is obscured by intrusion of the Swat and Mansehra granitic gneiss (Plate 1). The intrusion between the Gandaf and Tanawal Formations is well exposed in the Black Mountains and is discordant, such that the Tanawal Formation emerges from below the Mansehra gneiss (Plate 1).

Augen granite and gneiss in the Dand Sar area south of the Budal syncline were previously considered to be part of the Ambela Complex. These rocks, which include rocks mapped as the Chingalai gneiss by Siddiqui et al. (1968), are texturally and compositionally similar to the Swat gneiss and are therefore mapped as part of the Swat gneiss. The rocks are considered to be Late Cambrian on the basis of a whole-rock Rb/Sr age of 516 ± 16 Ma from the Mansehra gneiss (Le Fort et al., 1980). In this interpretation, the rocks are contemporaneous with a belt of Cambrian to Lower Ordovician augen granitic gneiss that extends across the Lesser Himalaya (Le Fort et al., 1983).

Late Paleozoic intrusive rock

Ambela Complex and Shewa Complex. The Ambela Complex consists dominantly of aegirene-augite–, amphibole- and biotite-bearing syenite, nepheline syenite, and alkali granite with subordinate biotite- and muscovite-bearing granite, all of which are intruded by mafic dikes (Shams, 1983; Rafiq, 1987; Rafiq and Jan, 1988). The biotite granite also contains xenoliths of mafic dikes. Lenses of Paleogene(?) carbonatite (Siddiqui, 1967) and tourmaline granite, and pre-late Paleozoic(?) granitic gneiss are also present. Siddiqui et al. (1968) mapped part of the Ambela Complex as the Koga and Babaji syenites and granites. Compositionally similar alkaline microgranite and porphyry are present in the Shewa Complex (Kempe and Jan, 1970; Kempe, 1983, 1986; Ahmad et al., 1990; Pogue et al., 1992b). The major intrusive bodies are considered to be late Paleozoic on the basis of whole-rock Rb/Sr ages of 297 ± 4 and 315 ± 15 Ma from the Koga syenite (Le Bas et al., 1987), and intrusive contacts with Carboniferous rock of the Jafar Kandao Formation.

Paleogene intrusive rock

Tourmaline granite gneiss. The largest Paleogene intrusion is a tourmaline-bearing granite gneiss that occurs as small lenses throughout the area but primarily in or near the Swat and Mansehra granitic gneisses. Large bodies of tourmaline granite gneiss are in the Loe Sar dome area where they intrude the unconformity between the Swat gneiss and Marghazar Formation (Plate 1). The rock is a leucocratic, equigranular, tourmaline- and muscovite-bearing granite gneiss typically without biotite. Associated rock includes fine-grained biotite-muscovite–bearing leucogneiss, and unfoliated tourmaline-bearing aplite and pegmatite that cuts across foliation in the Swat gneiss. DiPietro (1990) considered the tourmaline granite to be Paleogene on the basis of the crosscutting relationships. Other intrusions of possible Paleogene age include diabase dikes in the Indus syntaxis and Ambela Complex and carbonatite in the Loe Sar dome and Ambela Complex (DiPietro, 1990).

Mafic rock of multiple age

Dikes, sills, and flows of diabase, metagabbro, metadiorite, and/or amphibolite, are present in all of the formations and igneous complexes in the map area with the exception of the Kashala, Saidu, Nikanai Ghar, and Banna Formations, and the tourmaline granite gneiss. The rocks are considered to be of at least three ages, Early Proterozoic, late Paleozoic–Triassic, and Cenozoic. Early Proterozoic mafic dikes and sills are in the northern part of the Indus syntaxis surrounding Besham, as indicated by ca. 1900 Ma $^{40}Ar/^{39}Ar$ and K/Ar isotopic ages obtained from hornblende (Treloar et al., 1989b; Treloar and Rex, 1990; Baig, 1990). Mafic dikes, sills, and flows of late Paleozoic–Triassic age are present in Precambrian and Paleozoic rock across the area (Baig, 1990; Pogue et al., 1992b). In the Indus syntaxis region, these rocks are not easily distinguished from the Early Proterozoic mafic rock because both are composed dominantly of hornblende and plagioclase. An exception to this are mafic dikes that are intruded by leucogranite of the Besham Complex.

These dikes are inferred to be Early Proterozoic and, in general, tend to be coarse grained relative to late Paleozoic–Triassic mafic rock, which is typically very fine grained. Unmetamorphosed diabase dikes are present in the Indus syntaxis area where they crosscut both foliation and late folds that deform foliation. The crosscutting relationships suggest a Cenozoic age for these rocks. Additional diabase dikes are present in low-grade rock surrounding the Peshawar basin. These have generally been considered to be late Paleozoic (Rafiq, 1987; Pogue et al., 1992b), but Cenozoic intrusions may also be present.

SUMMARY OF PRE-CENOZOIC TECTONIC HISTORY OF THE INDIAN PLATE

The pre-Cenozoic tectonic history is summarized here and in Figure 2. A more detailed account of the Phanerozoic history was given in Pogue et al. (1992a, 1992b) and DiPietro et al. (1993).

The Early Proterozoic (≥2,175 Ma) tectonic history preserved in the Kishar Formation is not well constrained because of the limited extent of the formation and its questionable protolith. Abundant granitic and metamorphic clasts in the unconformably overlying Amlo Metaconglomerate Member of the Karora Formation suggests plutonism, deformation, and metamorphism before deposition of the metaconglomerate.

Following the deposition of the Karora and Gandaf Formations, the Early Proterozoic tectonic history appears to be dominated by plutonism, including the intrusion of the Besham and Kotla Complexes ca. 1,850 Ma. We infer deformation to be associated with plutonism in order to explain the appearance of both the Gandaf Formation and Kotla Complex at the top of the Early Proterozoic rock sequence along the eastern limb of the Dosara syncline near Choga (Plate 1). The relationship suggests that the Gandaf Formation was intruded by the Kotla Complex and subsequently deformed, uplifted, and eroded, such that both the Kotla Complex and the Gandaf Formation were exposed at the surface. The rocks were then unconformably overlain by the Tanawal Formation and the unconformity was subsequently intruded by the Swat granitic gneiss. The truncation of the Kotla Complex along the intruded unconformity is shown in the cross section (Plate 1). Early Proterozoic deformation may also be responsible for the development of north-south–oriented anisotropies that were later reactivated to produce the Chakesar, Darband, and related faults in the Indus syntaxis.

Although there is no conclusive evidence for amphibolite facies metamorphism in the Early Proterozoic succession, there is evidence for low-grade metamorphism. South of the Khairabad-Panjal fault and just east of the southeast corner of the map area near the village of Tanakki, Latif (1970) and Baig and Lawrence (1987) and Baig et al. (1988) described an unconformity between the Hazara Formation and the overlying Cambrian rock units. A conglomerate at the base of the unmetamorphosed Cambrian section contains clasts of low-grade phyllite derived from the Hazara Formation (Baig, 1990). The relationships imply a low-grade Precambrian metamorphism although the age of this metamorphism is uncertain. Baig and Lawrence (1987) and Baig et al. (1988) infer that the metamorphism is Late Proterozoic, and they referred to it as the Hazaran orogeny. Alternatively, the metamorphism could be Early Proterozoic. The Late Proterozoic Tanawal Formation is missing at this location; however, in areas where the Tanawal Formation is present, there is no obvious change in metamorphic grade between the Tanawal Formation and the unconformably overlying early Paleozoic rock. This suggests that the low-grade metamorphism preserved in the Hazara Formation at Tanakki occurred before deposition of the Tanawal Formation. On this basis, we suggest that the metamorphism is pre-Tanawal and possibly Early Proterozoic. The timing of intrusion of the Late Proterozoic Black Mountain Complex relative to low-grade metamorphism and to deposition of the Tanawal Formation is unknown.

Late Proterozoic tectonism that postdates deposition of the Tanawal Formation appears to be minor. In the northern Peshawar basin the Tanawal Formation is unconformably overlain by the Cambrian Ambar Formation. The unconformity is marked locally by conglomerate, but there does not appear to be an angular relationship across the contact. The field relationships suggest only minor uplift and the development of an erosional unconformity prior to deposition of the early-middle Paleozoic shelf sequence.

The early-middle Paleozoic shelf sequence was deposited in an epicontinental, shallow-marine environment (Pogue et al., 1992b). Late Cambrian intrusion of the Swat and Mansehra granitic gneiss into the underlying Precambrian rocks resulted in emergence of the shelf sequence and the partial removal of the Ambar Formation. There is no evidence in Precambrian or Cambrian rock to suggest that strong deformation or regional metamorphism was associated with this intrusion. Shallow-marine sedimentation resumed in the Ordovician and continued with minor interruptions until the close of the Devonian (Fig. 2).

Evidence for late Paleozoic tectonism is widespread; it began in the latest Devonian or Early Carboniferous. An erosional unconformity marks an abrupt change from shallow-marine deposition of the Nowshera Formation, to the clastic-dominated deposition of the Jafar Kandao Formation (Fig. 2; Pogue et al., 1992b). Continued tectonism throughout the late Paleozoic and possibly into the Triassic is indicated by additional erosional unconformities in the Jafar Kandao and possibly the Marghazar and Duma Formations; by intrusion of the Late Carboniferous Ambela and Shewa Complexes; by intrusion of mafic dikes; by deposition of basaltic lava and volcaniclastic rock of the Marghazar and Duma Formations; and by the development of pre-Late Triassic faults that resulted in the removal of the early-middle Paleozoic shelf sequence from the Loe Sar dome area (cross section in Plate 1; Pogue et al., 1992b; DiPietro et al., 1993). The late Paleozoic tectonism is associated with opening of the Neo-Tethys sea along the northern edge of the Indian plate (Sengör, 1984).

Shelf conditions were reestablished by the Late Triassic with deposition of the Kashala and Nikanai Ghar Formations. The

Saidu Formation represents slope-rise deposits that were subsequently overridden by the advancing Indus melange at the onset of the Himalayan orogeny, probably in the Late Cretaceous. It is significant that there is no conclusive evidence for regional, pre-Late Cretaceous, amphibolite facies metamorphism in the post-Kishar rock succession (Fig. 2).

SUMMARY OF CENOZOIC TECTONIC HISTORY

The interpretive summary of the Himalayan orogeny presented in this section is consistent with the field observations described herein and with previous work in the area. The Himalayan orogeny, as outlined in Figure 5, began with Late Cretaceous (≤95 Ma) obduction of the Indus melange onto the Indian plate along the Main Mantle thrust. The obduction was associated with the development of map-scale west-southwest–vergent folds, prograde metamorphism, foliation development, and faulting in the Attock-Cherat Range (Yeats and Hussain,

1987; DiPietro and Lawrence, 1991). The west-southwest vergence of map-scale folds on the Indian plate suggests that obduction of the Indus melange may have been from the east-northeast rather than from the north (DiPietro and Lawrence, 1991). The possibility that Indus melange was obducted from the east seems unlikely given the current configuration of the Indian plate. However, the configuration of the Indian plate would have been different in the Late Cretaceous before most of the deformation on the Indian plate, including the telescoping of rock along foreland thrust faults, had occurred.

Following obduction, and during possible imbrication of the Indus melange, rock on the Indian plate reached peak metamorphic conditions and subsequently began to cool, presumably as a result of exhumation (DiPietro, 1991). Shallow-marine and evaporate deposition prevailed in the foreland during exhumation (Fig. 5; Bossart and Ottiger, 1989; Pivnik and Wells, 1996). A rough estimate for the timing of cooling following peak metamorphism is obtained by comparing and averaging published

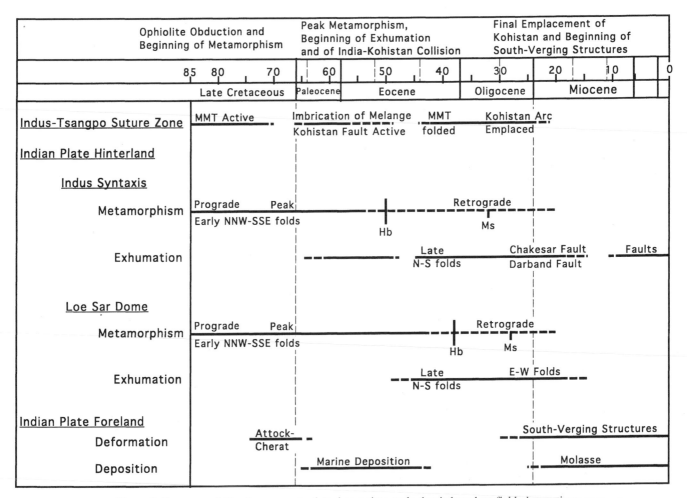

Figure 5. Summary of Himalayan events plotted on a time scale that is based on field observations and argon cooling ages. Top row shows the major tectonic events affecting the Indian plate. Hb—average argon cooling age of hornblende. Ms—average argon cooling age of muscovite. MMT—Main Mantle thrust. Indian plate foreland based on Yeats and Hussain (1987), Bossart and Ottiger (1989), and Pivnik and Wells (1996).

[40]Ar/[39]Ar and K/Ar ages for hornblende and muscovite in the Loe Sar dome and Indus syntaxis, respectively. Hornblende cools through the argon-closure temperature between ~480 and 525 °C (Harrison, 1981; van der Pluijm and Marshak, 1997), and therefore dates the time of cooling to ~100 to 150 °C below peak metamorphism. Muscovite cools through the argon-closure temperature between ~320 and 350 °C (Snee, 1982; van der Pluijm and Marshak, 1997), and therefore dates a stage of retrograde metamorphism. The following averages ignore the high and low extremes in each data set. An average of six hornblende samples and seven muscovite samples from the Loe Sar dome yielded 37.8 ± 4.8 Ma for hornblende and 28.1 ± 1.9 Ma for muscovite (Maluski and Matte, 1984; L. Snee, *in* Palmer-Rosenberg, 1985; Treloar et al., 1989b; Treloar and Rex, 1990; Baig, 1990). An average of five hornblende samples and four muscovite samples from the Indus syntaxis yielded 49.2 ± 1.7 Ma for hornblende and 31.8 ± 2.5 Ma for muscovite (Treloar et al., 1989b; Treloar and Rex, 1990; Baig, 1990). This suggests that metamorphism, as defined by hornblende cooling ages, ended ~10 m.y. earlier in the Indus syntaxis than in the Loe Sar dome. If the cooling ages are related to exhumation, then exhumation may have already begun by the late Paleocene or early Eocene in the Indus syntaxis, and by the middle Eocene in the Loe Sar dome (Fig. 5). Microstructural evidence, including the recrystallization of hornblende in the axes of north-south–trending microfolds in the Loe Sar dome, led DiPietro and Lawrence (1991) to suggest that the folds developed after the peak metamorphism and close to the closure temperature of argon in hornblende. This implies that initial development of the Loe Sar dome, the Dosara-Budal syncline, the Indus River anticline, and the folding of the Main Mantle thrust began before 38 Ma (Fig. 5).

Although the Indus syntaxis reached the closure temperature in hornblende ~10 m.y. before the Loe Sar dome, both areas remained above the argon-closure temperature of muscovite until, statistically, about the same time, roughly 30 Ma. The convergence of muscovite ages may relate to flexure of the Indian lithosphere and accelerated exhumation just prior to final emplacement of Kohistan along the brittle Kohistan fault (Fig. 5). The final emplacement of Kohistan against the Indian plate in the late Oligocene led to the development of east-west–trending folds and continued doming in the Loe Sar dome as well as north-south–striking faults in the Indus syntaxis; the initiation of south-verging structures in the foreland; and the beginning of molasse deposition (Fig. 5). Final emplacement appears to have been oblique with a component of right-lateral strike-slip motion (DiPietro and Lawrence, 1991). Thus, the Kohistan arc may have collided from the northwest.

Development of a deep soil horizon in the early or middle Miocene (Lawrence and Shroder, 1985) suggests that deformation may have ceased in the hinterland following final emplacement of Kohistan. In the Loe Sar dome area, deformation was apparently transferred permanently to the foreland (Fig. 5). The Indus syntaxis, by contrast, has continued to evolve. Late Miocene to Quaternary activity in the Indus syn-taxis is indicated by active seismicity, uplifted river terraces, and tilted and faulted Quaternary sediments (Armbruster et al., 1978; Yeats and Hussain, 1989; Baig, 1990, 1991). The Indus River is antecedent to uplift and cuts a 2,500 m gorge through the core of the Indus River anticline. Quaternary activity may also extend to the Dosara-Budal syncline, where a N66°E striking fault offsets stream gravel in a roadcut ~3.5 km west of Budal. The fault appears to be part of a conjugate fracture and fault system developed primarily in the Dosara-Budal syncline and the Indus syntaxis that includes other minor N65°E and N65°W striking brittle faults. The N65°W orientation is parallel with the trend of the Indus-Kohistan seismic zone as defined by Armbruster et al. (1978). This suggests that the faults may be related to seismicity. Late or postmetamorphic normal faults are present locally in the Indus melange, but these appear to be of very minor displacement and are probably related either to the development of east-west folds or to transtension associated with strike-slip displacement along the Kohistan fault.

The Indus syntaxis shows many of the same features as the Nanga Parbat-Haramosh syntaxis. For example, both are anticlinal flexures that have exposed Precambrian Indian plate rock in their cores. In addition, both are active zones of uplift that are characterized by recent faulting and present-day seismicity. In both cases, the Indus River cuts a deep gorge through the area. These relationships suggest that the style of development of the Indus syntaxis may parallel an early development stage of the Nanga Parbat-Haramosh syntaxis.

NOTE ADDED IN PROOF

Additional field work after this chapter was written suggests a correlation between the Kishar Formation and the lead-zinc stratiform deposits of the Sulphide Formation of the Pazang Group as described by Fletcher et al. (1986). Lead isotope model ages on galena from the Sulphide Formation give average ages of 2120 ± 34 Ma and 2199 ± 35 Ma (Shah et al., 1992). These ages correlate well with the U-Pb zircon age of 2175 ± 7 Ma for the Kishar Formation. Rocks within the Sulphide Formation include quartzite and calc-silicate marble in addition to rock types that are similar to those in the Kishar Formation. The mineralized zones are shown as part of the Kishar Formation in Plate 1. An x is located within or next to each of these zones to indicate mineralization. Note in Plate 1 that discontinuous bodies of Kishar and Karora Formation extend northward from the inner belt of the Karora Formation near Shang to the Lahor-Kishar area. It is possible that the discontinuous bodies turn eastward along a tributary river and connect with the unmapped northern extension of the inner belt of Karora Formation near Gandorai. We suggest that the unmapped area along the tributary river contains additional mineralized zones of Kishar Formation.

Anczkiewicz et al. (1998) obtained a U-Pb zircon age of 268 +7/–3 Ma on Swat augenflaser granitic gneiss near Manglaur and a U-Pb zircon age of 468 ±5 Ma on Swat gneiss a few kilometers east of Alpurai. This implies that the Swat-Mansehra augen-flaser granitic gneisses are at least two distinct ages: Late Cambrian–Middle Ordovician and Early Permian. If an Early Permian age is characteristic of a large part of the Swat gneiss near Manglaur (i.e., characteristic of the Ilam gneiss of DiPietro, 1990; DiPietro et al., 1993), it suggests a Late Permian or Triassic age for the Marghazar Formation and a Devonian(?) or older age for the Jobra Formation.

ACKNOWLEDGMENTS

This research is funded by National Science Foundation grant EAR-9316021. The people of Swat, particularly Sohrob and Regimen, are thanked for gracious hospitality and field assistance. We thank Douglas Burbank and John Dilles for commenting on an early version of this paper. We have also benefited from discussions with R. A. K. Tahirkheli, M. Qasim Jan, John Dilles, M. Shahid Baig, Waliullah Khattak, Rab Nawaz Khan, Bob Lawrence, and Bob Yeats. The final version of this paper was significantly improved by critical reading and constructive comments from David Pivnik, Rasoul Sorkhabi, and an anonymous reviewer. Drafting assistance was provided by Micky Davis, Darcy Clark, and Dawn Ison.

REFERENCES CITED

Ahmad, I., 1991, Structure and metamorphism of the Chakdarra area northwest of the Swat River, Pakistan [M.S. thesis]: Corvallis, Oregon State University, 111 p.

Ahmad, I., and Lawrence, R. D., 1992, Structure and metamorphism of the Chakdara area NW of Swat River, Pakistan: University of Peshawar Geological Bulletin, v. 25, p. 95–112.

Ahmad, I., Hamidullah, S., and Jehan, N., 1990, Petrology of the Shewa-Shabazgarhi Complex, Mardan, North Pakistan: University of Peshawar Geological Bulletin, v. 23, p. 135–159.

Anczkiewicz, R., Oberli, F., Burg, J. P., Meier, M., Dawood, H., and Hussain, S., 1998, Magmatism south of the Indus suture, Lower Swat, Pakistan [abs.], in Proceedings, 13th Himalaya-Karakoram-Tibet Workshop, Peshawar, Pakistan: University of Peshawar Geological Bulletin, v. 31, p. 7–9.

Arif, M., and Moon, C. J., 1994, Occurrence, chemistry and genesis of the nickel-rich phases in the ultramafic rocks from Swat, northwestern Pakistan: University of Peshawar Geological Bulletin, v. 27, p. 29–41.

Armbruster, J., Seeber, L., and Jacob, K. H., 1978, The northwestern termination of the Himalayan mountain front: Active tectonics from microearthquakes: Journal of Geophysical Research, v. 83, p. 269–282.

Ashraf, M., Chaudhry, M. N., and Hussain, S. S., 1980, General geology and economic significance of the Lahor granite and rocks of the southern ophiolite belt in Allai-Kohistan area: University of Peshawar Geological Bulletin, v. 13, p. 207–213.

Baig, M. S., 1989, New occurrences of blueschist from Shin-Kamer and Marin areas of Allai-Kohistan, Northwest Himalaya, Pakistan: Kashmir Journal of Geology, v. 6 and 7, p. 103–108.

Baig, M. S., 1990, Structure and geochronology of pre-Himalayan and Himalayan orogenic events in the northwest Himalaya, Pakistan, with special reference to the Besham area [Ph.D. thesis]: Corvallis, Oregon State University, 300 p.

Baig, M. S., 1991, Geochronology of Pre-Himalayan and Himalayan tectonic events, northwest Himalaya, Pakistan: Kashmir Journal of Geology, v. 8 and 9, p. 197.

Baig, M. S., and Lawrence, R. D., 1987, Precambrian to early Paleozoic orogenesis in the Himalaya: Kashmir Journal of Geology, v. 5, p. 1–22.

Baig, M. S., and Lawrence, R. D., and Snee, L. W., 1988, Evidence for late Precambrian to Early Cambrian orogeny in northwest Himalaya, Pakistan: Geological Magazine, v. 125, p. 83–86.

Beck, R. A., Burbank, D. W., Sercombe, W. J., Khan, A. S., and Lawrence, R. D., 1996, Late Cretaceous ophiolite obduction and Paleocene India-Asia collision in the westernmost Himalaya: Geodinamica Acta, v. 9, p. 114–144.

Bossart, P., and Ottiger, R., 1989, Rocks of the Murree Formation in northern Pakistan: Indicators of a descending foreland basin of late Paleocene to middle Eocene age: Eclogae Geologicae Helvetiae, v. 82, p. 133–165.

Calkins, J. A., Offield, T. W., Abdullah, S. K. M., and Tayyab A. S., 1975, Geology of the southern Himalaya in Hazara, Pakistan, and adjacent areas: U.S. Geological Survey Professional Paper 716-C, 29 p.

Chamberlain, C. P., Zeitler, P. K., and Erickson, E., 1991, Constraints on the tectonic evolution of the northwestern Himalaya from geochronologic and petrologic studies of Babusar Pass, Pakistan: Journal of Geology, v. 99, p. 829–849.

Coward, M. P., Butler, R. W. H., Asif Khan, M., and Knipe, R. J., 1987, The tectonic history of Kohistan and its implications for Himalayan structure: Geological Society of London Journal, v. 144, p. 377–391.

DiPietro, J. A., 1990, Stratigraphy, structure and metamorphism near Saidu Sharif, Lower Swat, Pakistan [Ph.D. thesis]: Corvallis, Oregon State University, 182 p.

DiPietro, J. A., 1991, Metamorphic pressure-temperature conditions of Indian plate rocks south of the Main Mantle thrust, Lower Swat, Pakistan: Tectonics, v. 10, p. 742–757.

DiPietro, J. A., and Isachsen, C. E., 1997, An early Proterozoic age for Precambium rock units in the Indus syntaxis, NW Himalaya, Pakistan [abs.]: 12th Himalaya-Karakoram-Tibet Workshop, Rome, Italy: Milan, Italy, p. 137–138.

DiPietro, J. A., and Lawrence, R. D., 1991, Himalayan structure and metamorphism south of the Main Mantle thrust, Lower Swat, Pakistan: Journal of Metamorphic Geology, v. 9, p. 481–495.

DiPietro, J. A., Pogue K. R., Lawrence, R. D., Baig, M. S., Hussain, A., and Ahmad, I., 1993, Stratigraphy south of the Main Mantle thrust, Lower Swat, Pakistan, in Treloar, P. J., and Searle, M. P., eds., Himalayan Tectonics: Geological Society of London Special Publication 74, p. 207–220.

DiPietro, J. A., Baig, M. S., Pogue, K. R., Hussain, A., and Ahmad, I., 1995, Preliminary geologic map of the Indus syntaxis, Pakistan: 10th Himalaya-Karakoram-Tibet Workshop [abs.]: Mitteilungen aus dem Geologischen Institut, ETH Zurich, Neue Folge, no. 298, p. 203–206.

DiPietro, J. A., Pogue, K. R., Hussain, A., and Ahmad, I., 1996, Precambrian rock of the Black Mountains, NW Himalaya, Pakistan [abs.]: 11th Himalaya-Karakoram-Tibet Workshop, Flagstaff, Arizona: Flagstaff, Northern Arizona University, p. 44–45.

Epstein, A. G., Epstein, J. B., and Harris, L. D., 1977, Conodont color alteration—An index to organic metamorphism: U.S. Geological Survey Professional Paper 915, 27 p.

Fletcher, C. J. N., Leak, R. C., and Haslam, H. W., 1986, Tectonic setting, mineralogy and chemistry of metamorphosed stratiform base metal deposits within the Himalaya of Pakistan: Geological Society of London Journal, v. 143, p. 521–536.

Gansser, A., 1980, The significance of the Himalayan suture zone: Tectonophysics, v. 62, p. 37–52.

Greco, A., and Spencer, D. A., 1993, A section through the Indian plate, Kaghan valley, NW Himalaya, Pakistan, in Treloar, P. J., and Searle, M. P., eds., Himalayan tectonics: Geological Society of London Special Publication 74, p. 221–236.

Greco, A., Martinotti, G., Papritz, K., Ramsay, J. G., and Rey, R., 1989, The crystalline rocks of the Kaghan Valley (NE-Pakistan): Eclogae Geologicae Helvetiae, v. 82, p. 629–653.

Harrison, T. M., 1981, Diffusion of ^{40}Ar in hornblende: Contributions to Mineralogy and Petrology, v. 70, p. 324–331.

Hussain, A., Yeats, R. S., and Pogue, K. R., 1990, Geologic map of Attock-Cherat Range and adjoining areas, N.W.F.P. and Punjab, Pakistan: Geological Survey of Pakistan Geological Map Series, scale 1:100 000.

Hussain, A., Pogue, K. R., Khan, S. R., and Ahmad, I., 1991, Paleozoic stratigraphy of the Peshawar Basin, Pakistan: University of Peshwar Geological Bulletin, v. 24, p. 85–97.

Hussain, A., DiPietro, J. A., and Ihtesham-ul-Haq, 1995, Regional geological map of the Choga quadrangle, Swat district, NWFP, Pakistan: Geological Survey of Pakistan Geological Map Series, v. 3, no. 72, scale 1:50 000.

Hylland, M. D., Riaz, M., and Ahmad, S., 1988, Stratigraphy and structures of the Southern Gandghar Range, Pakistan: University of Peshawar Geological Bulletin, v. 21, p. 1–14.

Isachsen, C. E., and DiPietro, J. A., 1997, U-Pb age constraints on Proterozoic deposition and intrusion and Late Cretaceous metamorphism of rocks in the Indus syntaxis, Northwest Himalaya, Pakistan: American Geophysical Union Abstract volume, v. 48, p. F177.

Jan, M. Q., 1979a, Petrography of the Jijal Complex, Kohistan: University of Peshawar Geological Bulletin, v. 11, p. 31–50.

Jan, M. Q., 1979b, Petrography of the amphibolites of Swat and Kohistan: University of Peshawar Geological Bulletin, v. 11, p. 51–64.

Jan, M. Q., and Tahirkheli, T., 1969, The geology of the lower part of Indus Kohistan (Swat), West Pakistan: University of Peshawar Geological Bulletin, v. 4, p. 1–13.

Jan, M. Q., Asif, M., Tahirkheli, T., and Kamal, M., 1981, Tectonic subdivision of granitic rocks of north Pakistan: University of Peshawar Geological Bulletin, v. 14, p. 159–182.

Kazmer, C., 1986, The Main Mantle Thrust Zone at Jowan pass area: Swat, Pakistan [M.S. thesis]: Cincinnati, Ohio, University of Cincinnati, 79 p.

Kazmi, A. H., Lawrence, R. D., Dawood, H., Snee, L. W., and Hussain, S., 1984, Geology of the Indus suture zone in the Mingora-Shangla area of Swat, N. Pakistan: University of Peshawar Geological Bulletin, v. 17, p. 127–144.

Kempe, D. R. C., 1983, Alkaline granites, syenites, and associated rocks of the Peshawar plain alkaline igneous province, NW Pakistan, *in* Shams, F. A., ed., Granites of the Himalayas Karakoram and Hindu Kush: Lahore, Institute of Geology, Punjab University, p. 143–181.

Kempe, D. R. C., 1986, A note on the ages of the alkaline rocks of the Peshawar plain alkaline igneous province, NW Pakistan: University of Peshawar Geological Bulletin, v. 19, p. 113–119.

Kempe, D. R. C., and Jan, M. Q., 1970, An alkaline igneous province in the North-West Frontier Province, West Pakistan: Geological Magazine, v. 107, p. 395–398.

Khan, M. A., Jan, M. Q., and Weaver, B. L., 1993, Evolution of the lower arc crust in Kohistan, N. Pakistan: Temporal arc magmatism through early, mature and intra-arc rift stages, *in* Treloar, P. J., and Searle, M. P., eds., Himalayan tectonics: Geological Society of London Special Publication 74, p. 123–138.

Khan, R. N., Iqbal, S., Khan, S., and Aslam, M., 1995, Regional geological map of the Marghuzar quadrangle, Swat and Buner districts, NWFP, Pakistan: Geological Survey of Pakistan Geological Map Series, v. 3, no. 71, scale 1:50 000.

Khan, S. R., and Khan M. A., 1994, Late Proterozoic stratigraphy of the Swabi area, NWFP, N. Pakistan: University of Peshwar Geologic Bulletin, v. 27, p. 57–68.

Khan, S. R., Pogue, K. R., Hussain, A., Saeed, G., and Babar, F., 1995, Geological map of the Topi quadrangle, NWFP, Pakistan: Geological Survey of Pakistan Geological Map Series, v. 3, no. 95, scale 1:50 000.

King, B. H., 1964, The structure and petrology of part of Lower Swat, West Pakistan, with special reference to the origin of the granitic gneisses [Ph.D. thesis]: London, University of London, 130 p.

LaFortune, J. R., 1989, Geology and geochemistry of Indian plate rocks south of the Indus Suture zone, Besham area, northern Pakistan [M.S. thesis]: Corvallis, Oregon State University, 70 p.

Lanphere, M. A., and Albee, A. L., 1974, $^{40}Ar/^{39}Ar$ age measurements in the Worcester Mountains: Evidence of Ordovician and Devonian metamorphic events in northern Vermont: American Journal of Science, v. 274, p. 545–555.

Latif, M. A., 1970, Lower Carboniferous rocks near Nowshera, West Pakistan: Geological Society of America Bulletin, v. 81, p. 1585–1588.

Lawrence, R. D., and Ghauri, A. A. K., 1983, Observations on the structure of the Main Mantle thrust at Jijal, Kohistan, Pakistan: University of Peshawar Geological Bulletin, v. 16, p. 1–10.

Lawrence, R. D., and Shroder, J. F., 1985, Tectonic geomorphology between Thakot and Mansehra, Northern Pakistan: University of Peshawar Geological Bulletin, v. 18, p. 153–161.

Lawrence, R. D., Kazmi, A. H., and Snee, L. W., 1989, Geological setting of the emerald deposits, *in* Kazmi, A. H., and Snee, L. W., eds., Emeralds of Pakistan: Geology, gemology, and genesis: New York, Van Nostrand

Reinhold, p. 13–38.

Le Bas, M. J., Mian, I., and Rex, D. C., 1987, Age and nature of carbonatite emplacement in north Pakistan: Geologische Rundschau, v. 76, p. 317–323.

Le Fort, P., Debon, F., and Sonet, J., 1980, The "Lesser Himalayan" cordierite granite belt, typology and age of the pluton of Manserah, Pakistan: University of Peshawar Geological Bulletin, v. 13, p. 51–62.

Le Fort, P., Debon, F., and Sonet, J., 1983, The Lower Paleozoic "Lesser Himalayan" granite belt: Emphasis on the Simchar pluton of central Nepal, *in* Shams, F. A., ed., Granites of the Himalayas Karakoram and Hindu Kush: Lahore, Institute of Geology, Punjab University, p. 235–256.

Majid, M., and Shah, M. T., 1985, Mineralogy of the blueschist facies metagreywacke from the Shergarh Sar area, Allai Kohistan, N. Pakistan: University of Peshawar Geological Bulletin, v. 18, p. 41–52.

Maluski, H., and Matte, P., 1984, Ages of Alpine tectono-metamorphic events in the northwestern Himalaya (northern Pakistan) by $^{39}Ar/^{40}Ar$ methods: Tectonics, v. 3, p. 1–18.

Martin, N. R., Siddiqui, S. F. A., and King, B. H., 1962, A geological reconnaissance of the region between the lower Swat and Indus Rivers of Pakistan: Punjab University Geological Bulletin, v. 2, p. 1–14.

Middlemiss, C. S., 1896, The geology of Hazara and the Black Mountains: Geological Survey of India Memoir, v. 26, 302 p.

Miller, D. J., Loucks, R. R., and Ashraf, M., 1991, Platinum-group element mineralization in the Jijal layered ultramafic-mafic complex, Pakistani Himalayas: Economic Geology, v. 86, p. 1093–1102.

Palmer-Rosenberg, P. S., 1985, Himalayan deformation and metamorphism of rocks south of the Main Mantle thrust zone, Karakar Pass area, southern Swat, Pakistan [M.S. thesis]: Corvallis, Oregon State University, 68 p.

Pivnik, D. A., and Wells, N. A., 1996, The transition from the Tethys to the Himalaya as recorded in northwest Pakistan: Geological Society of America Bulletin, v. 108, p. 1295–1313.

Pogue, K. R., 1994, Stratigraphic and stuctural framework of Himalayan foothills, northern Pakistan [Ph.D. thesis]: Corvallis, Oregon State University, 148 p.

Pogue, K. R., and Hussain, A., 1986, New light on the stratigraphy of the Nowshera area and the discovery of Early to Middle Orodvician trace fossils in NWFP, Pakistan: Geological Survey of Pakistan Information Release no. 135, 15 p.

Pogue, K. R., Wardlaw, B., Harris, A., and Hussain, A., 1992a, Paleozoic and Mesozoic stratigraphy of the Peshawar Basin, Pakistan: Correlations and implications: Geological Society of America Bulletin, v. 104, p. 915–927.

Pogue, K. R., DiPietro, J. A., Hughes, S. S., Dilles, J. A., Rahim, S., and Lawrence, R. D., 1992b, Late Paleozoic rifting in Northern Pakistan: Tectonics, v. 11, p. 871–883.

Pogue, K. R., Sak, P. B., and Khattak, W. U., 1995, A geologic reconnaissance of the Indus syntaxis, Northern Pakistan: 10th Himalaya-Karakoram-Tibet Workshop [abs.], Mitteilungen aus dem Geologischen Institut, ETH Zurich, Neue Folge, no. 298, p. 114–115.

Pogue, K. R., DiPietro, J. A., and Khattak, W. U., 1996, Precambrian stratigraphy and the foreland-hinterland transition in the Himalayan thrust belt of northern Pakistan [abs.]: 11th Himalaya-Karakoram-Tibet Workshop, Flagstaff, Arizona: Flagstaff, Northern Arizona University, p. 118–119.

Rafiq, M., 1987, Petrology and geochemistry of the Ambela granitic complex, N.W.F.P., Pakistan [Ph.D. thesis]: University of Peshawar, 272 p.

Rafiq, M., and Jan, M.Q., 1988, Petrography of the Ambela granitic complex, NW Pakistan: University of Peshwar Geological Bulletin, v. 21, p. 27–48.

Riaz, M., Hylland, M. D., Ahmad, S., and Ghauri, A. A. K., 1991, Structure and stratigraphy of the Northern Gandghar Range, Hazara, Pakistan: University of Peshwar Geological Bulletin, v. 24, p. 71–84.

Sengör, A. M. C., 1984, The Cimmeride orogenic system and the tectonics of Eurasia: Geological Society of America Special Paper 195, 82 p.

Shah, M. T., Thorpe, R. I., and Siddique, S. A., 1992, Lead isotope signature of the Proterozoic sediment-hosted base metal deposits at the margin of the Indian plate in Besham area, northern Pakistan: University of Peshawar Geological Bulletin, v. 25, p. 59–65.

Shams, F. A., 1961, A preliminary account of the Mansehra area, Hazara district, West Pakistan: Punjab University Geological Bulletin, v. 1, p. 57–62.

Shams, F. A., 1963, Reactions in and around a calcareous xenolith lying within the granite-gneiss of Manglaur, Swat State, West Pakistan: Punjab University Geological Bulletin, v. 3, p. 7–18.

Shams, F. A., 1980, Origin of the Shangla blueschists, Swat Himalaya, Pakistan: University of Peshwar Geological Bulletin, v. 13, p. 67–70.

Shams, F. A., 1983, Granites of the NW Himalayas in Pakistan, *in* Shams, F. A., ed., Granites of the Himalayas Karakoram and Hindu Kush: Lahore, Institute of Geology, Punjab University, p. 341–354.

Siddiqui, S. F. A., 1967, Note on the discovery of carbonatite rocks in the Chamla area, Swat state, West Pakistan: Punjab University Geological Bulletin, v. 6, p. 85–88.

Siddiqui, S. F. A., Chaudhry, M. N., and Shakoor, A., 1968, Geology and petrology of the feldspathoidal syenites and associated rocks of the Koga area, Chamla Valley, Swat, West Pakistan: Punjab University Geological Bulletin, v. 7, p. 1–30.

Snee, L. W., 1982, Emplacement and cooling of the Pioneer Batholith, southwestern Montana [Ph.D. thesis]: Columbus, Ohio State University, 320 p.

Tahirkheli, R. A. K., 1970, The geology of the Attock-Cherot Range, West Pakistan: University of Peshawar Geological Bulletin, v. 5, p. 1–26.

Tahirkheli, R. A. K., 1971, The geology of the Gandghar Range, Distt. Hazara, N. W. F. P.: University of Peshawar Geological Bulletin, v. 6, p. 33–42.

Tahirkheli, R. A. K., 1979a, Geology of Kohistan and adjoining Eurasian Indo-Pakistan continents, Pakistan: University of Peshawar Geological Bulletin, v. 11, p. 1–30.

Tahirkheli, R. A. K., 1979b, Geotectonic evolution of Kohistan: University of Peshawar Geological Bulletin, v. 11, p. 113–130.

Tahirkheli, R. A. K., 1982, Geology of the Himalaya, Karakoram and Hindu Kush in Pakistan: University of Peshawar Geological Bulletin, v. 15, p. 1–51.

Tahirkheli, R. A. K., and Jan, M. Q., 1979, A preliminary geological map of Kohistan and the adjoining areas, N. Pakistan: University of Peshawar Geological Bulletin, v. 11, scale 1:1 000 000.

Tahirkheli, R. A. K., Mattauer, M., Proust, F., and Tapponier, P., 1979, The India-Eurasia suture zone in northern Pakistan; synthesis and interpretation of recent data at plate scale, *in* Farah, A., and De Jong, K. A., eds., Geodynamics of Pakistan: Quetta, Geological Survey of Pakistan, p. 125–130.

Treloar, P. J., and Rex, D. C., 1990, Cooling and uplift histories of the crystalline thrust stack of the Indian plate internal zones west of Nanga Parbat, Pakistan Himalaya: Tectonophysics, v. 180, p. 323–349.

Treloar, P. J., Broughton, R. D., Williams, M. P., Coward, M. P., and Windley, B. F., 1989a, Deformation, metamorphism and imbrication of the Indian plate, south of the Main Mantle thrust, north Pakistan: Journal of Metamorphic Geology, v. 7, p. 111–125.

Treloar, P. J., Rex, D. C., Guise, P. G., Coward, M. P., Searle, M. P., Windley, B. F., Petterson, M. G., Jan, M. Q., and Luff, I. A., 1989b, K-Ar and Ar-Ar geochronology of the Himalayan collision in NW Pakistan: Constraints on the timing of suturing, deformation, metamorphism and uplift: Tectonics, v. 8, p. 881–909.

Treloar, P. J., Williams, M. P., and Coward, M. P., 1989c, Metamorphism and crustal stacking in the north Indian plate, North Pakistan: Tectonophysics, v. 165, p. 167–184.

van der Pluijm, B. A., and Marshak, S., 1997, Earth Structure: An introduction to structural geology and tectonics: United States, WCB/McGraw-Hill, 495 p.

Wadia, D. N., 1931, The syntaxis of the northwest Himalaya: Its rocks, tectonics and orogeny: Geological Survey of India Records, v. 65, p. 189–220.

Wadia, D. N., 1934, The Cambrian-Trias sequence of northwest Kashmir (parts of the Mazaffarabad and Baramula District): Geological Survey of India Records, v. 68, p. 121–146.

Williams, M. P., 1989, The geology of the Besham area, north Pakistan: Deformation and imbrication in the footwall of the Main Mantle thrust: University of Peshawar Geological Bulletin, v. 22, p. 65–82.

Yamamoto, H., 1993, Contrasting metamorphic P-T-time paths of the Kohistangranulites and tectonics of the western Himalayas: Geological Society of London Journal, v. 150, p. 843–856.

Yeats, R. S., and Hussain, A., 1987, Timing of structural events in the Himalayanfoothills of northwest Pakistan: Geological Society of America Bulletin, v. 99, p. 161–176.

Yeats, R. S., and Hussain, A., 1989, Zone of late Quaternary deformation in thesouthern Peshawar Basin, Pakistan, *in* Malinconico, L. L., and Lillie, R. J., eds., Tectonics of the western Himalayas: Geological Society of America Special Paper 232, p. 265–274.

Manuscript Accepted by the Society February 3, 1998

Geological Society of America
Special Paper 328
1999

Metamorphic evolution of the northwest Himalaya, India: Pressure-temperature data, inverted metamorphism, and exhumation in the Kashmir, Himachal, and Garhwal Himalayas

R. M. Manickavasagam, Arvind K. Jain, Sandeep Singh, and A. Asokan
Department of Earth Sciences, University of Roorkee, Roorkee 247 667, India

ABSTRACT

The Higher Himalayan Crystallines belt in southeast Kashmir, the Sutlej valley (Himachal), and the Bhagirathi valley (Garhwal) of the northwestern Himalaya (India) are demarcated by the Main Central thrust at the base, and discontinuously by the Zanskar shear zone or Martoli fault along its upper boundary with the Tethyan sedimentary zone. Within this predominantly metamorphic belt, metamorphism is characterized by staurolite-kyanite grade at the base of the Main Central thrust hanging wall to sillimanite–K-feldspar grade in the higher structural level of the Padar-Zanskar region in southeast Kashmir. Textural and inclusion thermobarometric analyses indicate that the entire Higher Himalayan Crystallines belt underwent prograde M2 metamorphism during the tectonic subsidence to about 25 to 35 km due to intracontinental subduction of the leading edge of the Indian plate, when the metamorphic pile recorded ~550 °C and ~8.5 kbar in staurolite-kyanite to ~780 °C and ~10 kbar in sillimanite–K-feldspar grade. This event was followed by intense ductile shearing, exhumation, and late M2 metamorphism, during which the entire Higher Himalayan Crystallines belt was displaced southwestward along ubiquitously developed C-shear foliation in the 15–20-km-thick Higher Himalayan shear zone, thus causing an apparent inverted metamorphism during a pre-Main Central thrust phase. It is well documented in southeast Kashmir, where the rim thermobarometric data record a uniform temperature of about 650° C in all the metamorphic grades and decompression from 8.5 kbar in staurolite-kyanite grade to a minimum of ~4 kbar in sillimanite–K-feldspar grade. This suggests a faster exhumation of the higher grades, compared to the base of the Main Central thrust hanging wall. This resulted in the decompression and cooling of the higher grades with heating of the basal parts of the Main Central thrust hanging wall by conduction. On the contrary, core and rim thermobarometric and garnet zoning data from the Higher Himalayan Crystallines belt along the Sutlej and Bhagirathi valleys exhibit only a prograde M2 metamorphism; there is no evidence for the later cooling and exhumation paths. In these sections, the Crystallines belt appears to have undergone decompression at a comparatively faster rate. Textural and petrographic analyses also indicate that the Main Central thrust postdates these metamorphic events, and has caused truncation, concealment, and repetition of the metamorphic isograds.

Manickavasagam, R. M., Jain, A. K., Singh, S., and Asokan, A., 1999, Metamorphic evolution of the northwest Himalaya, India: Pressure-temperature data, inverted metamorphism, and exhumation in the Kashmir, Himachal, and Garhwal Himalayas, *in* Macfarlane, A., Sorkhabi, R. B., and Quade, J., eds., Himalaya and Tibet: Mountain Roots to Mountain Tops: Boulder, Colorado, Geological Society of America Special Paper 328.

INTRODUCTION

The continent to continent collision between India and Asia during the Cenozoic deformed and remobilized the Proterozoic Indian crust, which is dismembered by numerous thrusts such as the Main Central thrust, the Vaikrita thrust, the Main Boundary thrust, and the Main Frontal thrust (Fig. 1; Gansser, 1964; Le Fort, 1975; Valdiya, 1980a; Thakur, 1993). The Main Central thrust separates the Higher Himalayan Crystallines from the Lesser Himalayan Proterozoic sedimentary sequence. The Higher Himalayan Crystallines belt forms a thick metamorphic pile, which is either overlain unconformably by the Paleozoic-Mesozoic Tethyan sedimentary zone or separated from it by a normal fault (Burg et al., 1984), called the South Tibetan detachment zone (Burchfiel et al., 1992) or the Zanskar shear zone (Herren, 1987; Patel et al., 1993) or Trans-Himadri fault (Valdiya, 1989) along its northern margin.

Several investigations of the Himalayan metamorphic belt have revealed the presence of inverted metamorphism, both in the Lesser Himalaya and the Higher Himalayan Crystallines belt of the northwest Himalaya, Nepal, and Sikkim (Pilgrim and West, 1928; Auden, 1935; Le Fort, 1975; Thakur, 1977; Sinha-Roy, 1982; Arita, 1983; Brunel and Kienast, 1986; Hodges and Silverberg, 1988; Mohan et al., 1989; Searle and Rex, 1989; Stäubli, 1989; Pêcher, 1989; Pognante et al., 1989a; Treloar et al., 1989a). The inverted metamorphism has been explained by different models either independently or in combination; e.g., recumbent folding and thrust imbrication, frictional shear heating along the Main Central thrust, or downward transfer of heat from the hot Higher Himalayan Crystallines or granitic bodies to the cold Lesser Himalaya (Von Loczy, 1907; Pilgrim and West, 1928; Le Fort, 1975; Sinha-Roy, 1982; Frank et al., 1977; Brunel and Kiensat, 1986; Treloar et al., 1989a; for reviews see Windley, 1983; Hodges et al., 1988).

In the northwest Himalaya, inverted metamorphism within the Higher Himalayan Crystallines belt has been reported from southeast Kashmir, the Beas, the Parbati, and the Sutlej valleys in Himachal, and the Bhagirathi and Alaknanda valleys in the Garhwal Himalaya (Frank et al., 1977; Thöni, 1977; Hodges and Silverberg, 1988; Searle and Rex, 1989; Stäubli, 1989; Jain and Manickavasagam, 1993; Metcalfe, 1993). In the southeast Kashmir, the inverted metamorphism has been explained by overthrusting and recumbent folding (Stäubli, 1989; Searle and Rex, 1989). The telescoping of metamorphic isograds at the base and at the top of the Higher Himalayan Crystallines belt has been explained by thrusting along the Main Central thrust at the base and normal faulting at the top (Searle et al., 1992). Along the Beas valley in Himachal, the inverted metamorphism has been explained by recumbent folding for the southern parts and "synmetamorphic shear folding" for the inner parts of the Crystallines belt (Frank et al., 1977; Thöni, 1977). Downward heat conduction from the upper parts of the Higher Himalayan Crystallines belt and its superposition on the Main Central thrust zone have been postulated for the Bhagirathi valley of Garhwal (Metcalfe, 1993).

In this chapter, we present detailed textural, petrological and thermobarometric data from three sections across the Higher Himalayan Crystallines belt in the northwest Himalaya: southeast Kashmir, the Sutlej-Baspa valleys of Himachal Pradesh, and the Bhagirathi valley of Garhwal (Fig. 1). We suggest that the inverted metamorphism within the Higher Himalayan Crys-

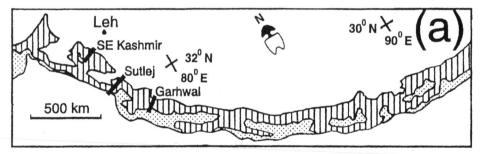

Figure 1 (this and opposite page). **a:** Himalayan metamorphic belt of the Lesser and Higher Himalayan Crystallines (vertical lines), indicating its relationship with the underlying Lesser Himalayan sedimentary zone (dots). Locations of main sections across southeast Kashmir, Sutlej valley in Himachal Pradesh, and Bhagirathi valley in Garhwal are shown by thick lines. **b:** Simplified tectonic framework of the western Himalaya. 1: Eurasian plate margin–Karakoram batholith complex (KBC). 2: Indian plate subduction zone—(a) Shyok suture zone (SSZ), (b) Ladakh batholith complex (LBC), (c) Indus Tsangpo suture zone (ITSZ). 3: Himalayan collision zone—(a) Tso-Morari Crystallines (TMC), (b) Tethyan sedimentary zone (TSZ), (c) Himalayan Metamorphic Belt (HMB) of the Proterozoic remobilized basement and the Lesser Himalayan ca. 500 Ma granitoid belt (c1) and mid-Cenozoic anatectic leucogranite (c2), (d) Lesser Himalayan (LH) Proterozoic sedimentary sequence, (e) Sub-Himalayan (SH) Cenozoic sedimentary foreland. Other abbreviations: MBT—Main Boundary thrust. MCT—Main Central thrust; JT—Jutogh thrust; MF—Martoli fault; ZSZ—Zanskar shear zone; K—Karchham; Ki—Kishtwar; M—Mandi; Sa—Sangla; S—Shimla; UK—Uttarkashi; G—Gangotri; DD—Dehradun. Locations of traverses covered in this work: Atholi-Padam section, southeast Kashmir (Fig. 2); Sutlej valley (Jhakhri-Akpa) and Baspa valley (Karchham-Sangla), Himachal (Fig. 3); and Bhagirathi valley (Uttarkashi-Gangotri), Garhwal (Fig. 4).

tallines belt was caused by southwestward-verging ductile shearing and ensuing exhumation, and that it predated the Main Central thrust movement.

GEOLOGICAL FRAMEWORK

Section A: Southeast Kashmir

In the Padar-Zanskar region of southeast Kashmir, the Higher Himalayan Crystallines belt is thrust over the Lesser Himalayan Kishtwar window along the Main Central thrust along the Chenab and Bhot Nala (River) traverses (Fig. 2) (Vohra et al., 1982; Sandhu, 1985). The northeastern margin of the Crystalline belt is separated from the overlying Paleozoic-Mesozoic Tethyan sedimentary zone by the Zanskar shear

zone (Fig. 2; Herren, 1987; Searle and Rex, 1989; Patel et al., 1993). However, the Crystallines belt, incorporating a part of the Kashmir nappe, is conformably overlain by the Paleozoic-Mesozoic sequence of the Kashmir-Bhadarwah basin in its southwestern and western parts.

The Kishtwar window contains black carbonaceous phyllite, quartzite, sericite schist, metavolcanics, and granitic gneiss. The overthrusted Crystallines belt incorporates largely pelites and a few bands of marble, calc-silicate, and quartzite and occasional amphibolite-greenschist bands. The pelites include garnetiferous mica schist, staurolite-kyanite schist and/or gneiss, and sillimanite schist and/or gneiss. Migmatite and two-mica-bearing leucogranite are associated with the highest-grade metamorphic rocks. The Crystallines belt is also intruded by older granitoids, (probably of Cambrian-Ordovician age), that are now exposed as

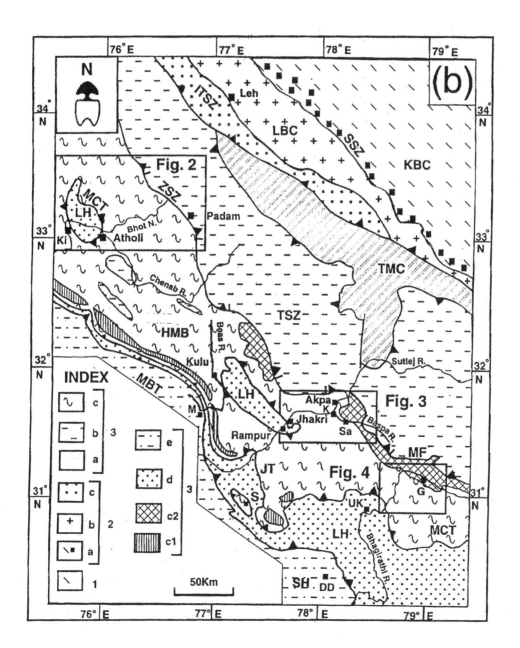

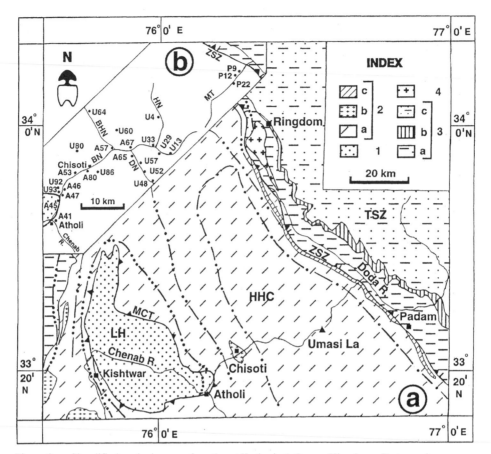

Figure 2. **a:** Simplified geologic map of southeast Kashmir. 1: Lesser Himalayan Proterozoic sequence (quartzite, phyllite, limestone, metavolcanics, granite gneiss; Kishtwar window). 2: Higher Himalayan Crystallines—(a) schist, gneiss, amphibolite, calc-silicate; (b) Proterozoic–early Paleozoic granitoid; (c) Cenozoic leucogranite. 3: Tethyan sedimentary zone—(TSZ) (a) Haimanta-Karsha Group; (b) Phe Volcanics; (c) Lilang Group. 4: Lower Paleozoic granitoid. Metamorphic isograd boundaries are shown by thick dot-dash lines: one dot = sillimanite-K-feldspar, two dots = sillimanite-muscovite, three dots = staurolite-kyanite, four dots = garnet isograd. Large parts of the LH and TSZ are within biotite grade. Insert **b** is the location map of samples, used for thermobarometric calculations, along Atholi–Umasi La–Padam section. Abbreviations: MCT—Main Central thrust; ZSZ—Zanskar shear zone; BN—Bhot Nala; DN—Dharlang Nadi; BHN—Bhujan Nadi; HN—Hangshu Nadi; MT—Mulung Tokpo. Compiled after Srikantia et al. (1978), Vohra et al. (1982), Honeggar et al. (1982), Sandhu (1985), Searle and Fryer (1986), Kundig (1989), Stäubli (1989), and our own observations.

large doubly-plunging domes such as Sankoo, Shafat, Chisoti, and Bhuzun (Honegger et al., 1982; Kündig, 1989).

Section B: Himachal

In the Beas, the Parbati, and the Sutlej valleys of Himachal, the Crystallines belt is thrust southwestward over the Kulu-Rampur window of the Lesser Himalaya along the folded Main Central thrust–Jutogh thrust and its splays (Figs. 1 and 3). The Kulu-Rampur window is a northwest-southeast–trending linear belt of the Rampur Volcanics, Manikaran Quartzite, carbonaceous phyllite, and concordant 1,800 Ma Bandal granitoid, all of which belong to the Rampur Group (Sharma, 1977). The window is overridden by a thin sheet of the dismembered Kulu-Bajura

nappe (Frank et al., 1977) of highly mylonitized augen gneiss between the Ravi and the Sutlej valleys. In the Sutlej valley, the basal and middle parts of the Crystallines belt incorporate pelites and psammites containing amphibolite, and deformed 1,800 to 2,000 Ma Wangtu granite gneiss, respectively (Singh, 1993). This sequence is overridden by garnetiferous mica schist, staurolite-kyanite schist and/or gneiss, sillimanite schist and/or gneiss, and leucogranite along the Vaikrita thrust.

Section C: Garhwal

In the Garhwal Himalaya, the Main Central thrust separates the Lesser Himalayan sequence from the overridden Crystallines belt, which is split into two distinct packages due to an upper splay of the thrust, called the Vaikrita thrust (Fig. 4). To the north, this belt is separated from the Tethyan sedimentary zone by the Martoli fault or the Trans-Himadri fault (Valdiya, 1989). In the lower parts, the Crystallines belt consists of quartzite, amphibolite, calc-silicate, garnet-biotite schist, and augen gneiss immediately on the hanging wall of the Main Central thrust, whereas staurolite-kyanite and sillimanite-bearing schist and/or gneiss, biotite granite gneiss, and Gangotri granite dominate the overlying sequence above the Vaikrita thrust (Valdiya, 1980b).

DEFORMATION HISTORY

Our observations from the western Himalaya of India indicate that the Crystallines belt rocks have undergone at least four phases of recognizable deformation (D1–D4). During the D1, isolated, tight and appressed "flame" folds (F1) were developed on lithological banding and/or metamorphic layering (S0; Fig. 5a). The axial-plane foliation S1 of the F1 folds parallels this layering. During this deformation, most of the minerals crystallizing along the S1 foliation are chlorite, biotite, and quartz; hence the

Crystallines belt appears to have been subjected to lower green-schist facies M1 metamorphism.

D2 was the most widespread phase and produced a penetrative foliation (S2) that parallels the axial surfaces of close to isoclinal, reclined to recumbent F2 folds, developed on S1 foliation or lithological and/or metamorphic layering (Fig. 5b). S2 foliation is essentially a ductile shear fabric, having regional dips between 20° and 40° NE. In schist the foliation is composed of S surfaces that are progressively deflected and become subparallel to the ductile C foliation of high strain on a scale of millimeters (Jain and Manickavasagam, 1993). In various deformed granitoids, this typically resembles the S-C mylonitic foliation (Fig. 5c). Throughout the Crystallines belt, it ubiquitously records a top-to-southwest sense of ductile shearing, also evidenced by asymmetric quartz and feldspar augen, pressure shadows, and rotational fabric within porphyroblasts.

A prominent stretching mineral lineation (L2), coaxial to the F2 folds, plunges northeast or southwest almost down-dip, and was developed on composite S1-S2 and/or C foliation due to preferred orientation of mica, chlorite, tourmaline, amphibole, staurolite, kyanite, sillimanite, quartz, and feldspar (Fig. 5d). Many of

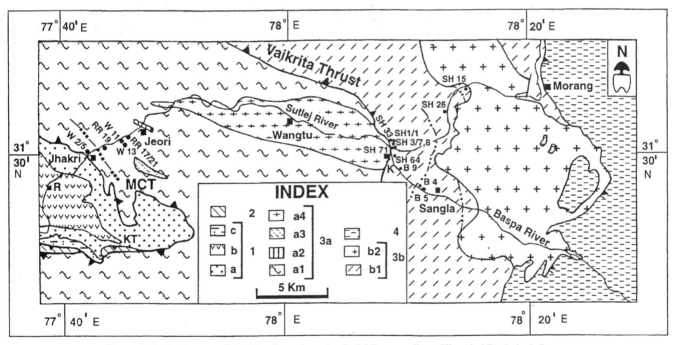

Figure 3. Geologic map of the Himalaya along the Sutlej-Baspa valleys, Himachal Pradesh. 1: Lesser Himalayan Rampur Group—(a) Manikaran Quartzite; (b) Rampur Volcanics; (c) carbonaceous phyllite. 2: Kulu–Bajura nappe–augen mylonite. 3: Higher Himalayan Crystallines—(a) Jeori Group—staurolite and/or garnetiferous schist, banded biotite gneiss, augen gneiss (a1), amphibolite (a2), quartz mica schist (a3), and Wangtu granite gneiss and/or granite (a4); (b) Karchham Group—garnet or staurolite or kyanite or sillimanite schist and/or gneiss, calc-silicate, augen gneiss, and migmatite (b1), Akpa leucogranite (b2). 4: Tethyan sedimentary zone. Abbreviations: KT—Kulu thrust, MCT—Main Central thrust; R—Rampur; K—Karchham. Metamorphic isograd boundaries: two dots = sillimanite-muscovite grade; three dots = staurolite-kyanite grade. MCT hanging wall is in garnet–staurolite-kyanite transition zone. The Lesser Himalayan and Tethys Himalayan sediments are within biotite grade. Locations of samples used for pressure-temperature data are also indicated. Compiled after Tewari et al. (1978), Singh (1993), and our own observations.

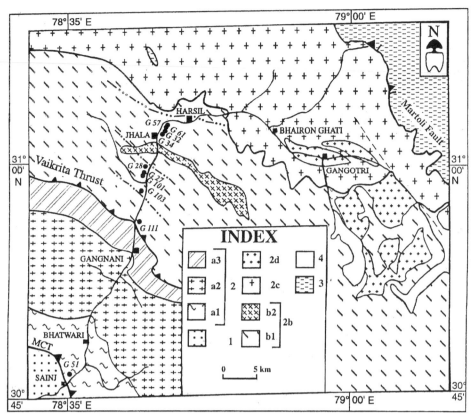

Figure 4. Geologic map of the Himalaya along the Bhagirathi valley, western Garhwal. 1: Lesser
Himalayan Proterozoic sequence. 2: Higher Himalayan Crystallines—(a) Bhatwari Group—porphyro-
clastic granite gneiss, garnetiferous mica schist, amphibolite (a1), mylonitized augen gneiss, mica
schist, amphibolite (a2), phyllonite, schist (a3); (b) Harsil Group—sillimanite or kyanite or staurolite or
garnetiferous schist and/or gneiss and migmatite (b1) and augen gneiss (b2); (c) Bhaironghati granite;
(d) Gangotri leucogranite. 3: Tethyan sedimentary zone (Martoli Group). 4: Glaciers and debris. MCT
is Main Central thrust. Metamorphic isograd boundaries are the same as in Figure 2. Largely based on
our observations; eastern parts of the map compiled after Pêcher and Scaillet (1989). Locations of samples used for pressure-temperature determinations are indicated. MCT hanging wall is in garnet grade;
basal parts of the Vaikrita thrust hanging wall are in staurolite-kyanite grade. The Lesser Himalayan and
Tethyan sediments are in biotite grade.

these minerals grew along S and C surfaces during the M2 metamorphic event, and were rotated due to the D2 ductile phase.
Some of these minerals continued their growths on syntectonically grown mineral phases or developed separately over the foliation in the final stages of the M2 metamorphism in the late to
post-D2 deformation phase.

D3 produced isoclinal to tight F3a and superposed F3b folds
that plunge gently either northwest or southeast. The F3b folds
are open to closed, and are inclined. Development of chlorite at
the expense of garnet and biotite, and D3-related foliation have
been observed during this deformation. Discrete kinks, tensional
gashes, and brittle shear zones represent the youngest D4 deformation event.

Another group of structures, revealing extensional tectonics
and ensuing exhumation of the Crystallines belt, has been
observed throughout this belt, and was produced during the D2
and subsequent deformation phases. These are more penetra-

tively developed toward the Crystallines belt's northern and
upper boundary with the Tethyan sedimentary zone. These are
commonly associated with numerous melt-enhanced leucogranite veinlets in migmatite of the higher grades.

TEXTURES AND INDEX MINERALS

The pelites and psammites in the garnet through staurolite-kyanite grades are schistose and gneissose, having porphyroblastic growth of garnet, staurolite, and kyanite. Muscovite,
biotite, quartz, and/or chlorite and chloritoid define the main foliation. Staurolite is subordinate in the middle structural levels in
southeast Kashmir and western Garhwal, possibly either due to
restricted bulk composition or increased temperature. Chlorite is
occasionally retrograde after garnet, staurolite, and biotite in staurolite-kyanite schist. Minor zircon, apatite, and ilmenite are present in the matrix, and as inclusions in biotite and garnet. The

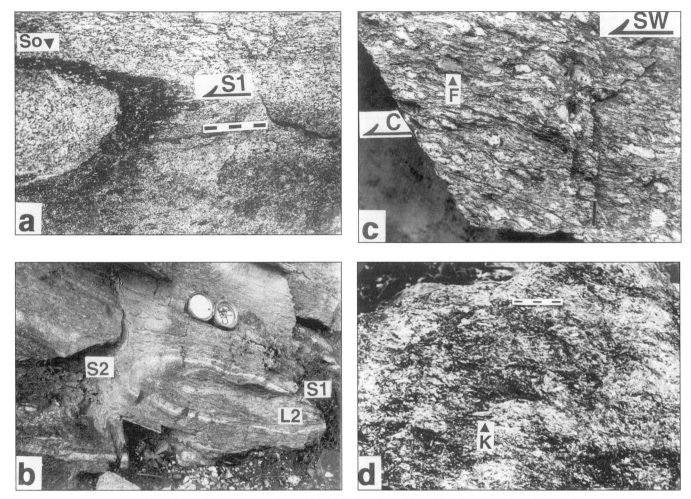

Figure 5. Deformational structures from the Higher Himalayan Crystallines in western Himalaya. a: F1 'flame-type' isoclinal fold having penetrative axial plane foliation S1 on lithological-metamorphic banding S0 in schist and gneiss. Location: Parkachik along the Suru valley, western Zanskar. Scale is 5 cm. b: Reclined isoclinal F2 fold on S1 foliation in alternating schist and gneiss having rounded hinge zone and axial plane foliation S2. Note coaxial L2 mineral lineation on limbs. Location: About 5 km southeast from Sangla along the Baspa valley. c: S-C foliation in augen gneiss, having asymmetric σ-type feldspar megacrysts (F) with top-to-southwest vergence. Location is near Karchham, Sutlej valley, Himachal. Scale is 2 cm. d: Northeast-plunging L2 mineral lineation of long slender kyanite (K) blades in staurolite-kyanite schist. Location: Kundel along the Bhot Nala, southeast Kashmir. Scale is 5 cm.

mineral assemblages include the following: Garnet grade, chlorite-biotite-muscovite-chloritoid-garnet-plagioclase-quartz; and staurolite-kyanite grade, biotite-muscovite-garnet-kyanite-quartz± plagioclase±K-feldspar±staurolite±chlorite.

Sillimanite-muscovite and sillimanite–K-feldspar grades contain medium- to coarse-grained schist and gneiss. Garnet poikiloblasts are subidioblastic, locally broken, and have corroded rims. Sillimanite needles are common, and fibrous sillimanite grows epitaxially in muscovite and biotite. Sillimanite and kyanite polymorphs are noticeable in sillimanite-muscovite grade rocks in southeast Kashmir and the Sutlej valley. Sillimanite–K-feldspar grade is restricted only to southeast Kashmir, where it shows significant migmatization and leucogranite generation. The percentage of K-feldspar varies significantly, and is

generally more than plagioclase; a few samples contain cordierite and secondary muscovite, even as coronas at kyanite rims. The mineral assemblages are as follows. Sillimanite-muscovite grade, garnet-biotite-muscovite-kyanite-sillimanite±plagioclase-K-feldspar-quartz; and Sillimanite–K-feldspar grade, garnet-biotite-sillimanite–K-feldspar-plagioclase-quartz±cordierite.

Garnet. Syntectonic garnet is very common in the Crystallines belt; although growth of small posttectonic garnet seems to be restricted to southeast Kashmir. Syntectonic garnet is subidioblastic to xenoblastic, and sometimes occurs as elongate clusters parallel to the foliation. It is poikiloblastic, having numerous inclusions of quartz, biotite, muscovite, carbon, ilmenite, rutile, plagioclase, kyanite, staurolite, and sillimanite in decreasing order of abundance. Some garnet is overgrown by an inclusion-free rim that may be posttectonic with respect to the main foliation (Fig. 6a). Most of the syntectonic garnet deforms the main foliation, and is characterized by rotational fabric, indicated by numerous inclusions and asymmetrical pressure shadows (Fig. 6a); this suggests that it grew during the main metamorphism M2 and D2 deformation. In the higher metamorphic grades, garnet is irregularly corroded and, in places, surrounded by retrograde biotite and fibrolite. Garnet is generally almandine rich, having varying spessartite, pyrope, and grossular components.

Staurolite. Syntectonic staurolite poikiloblasts contain elongate quartz, and opaque and mica inclusions, that are either rotated like garnet or reveal typical sieve texture with S_i ll S_e (Fig.

6b). A few small subidioblastic staurolite grains, devoid of inclusions, are present in some samples, indicating their growth during late D2 deformation.

Aluminosilicates. In the staurolite-kyanite grade, kyanite poikiloblasts grew mainly parallel to both S and C foliations, and contain quartz inclusions having S_i ll S_e relationships (Fig. 6c). Kyanite porphyroblasts also lack mineral inclusions in this grade. In higher grades, relict kyanite has reaction rims of fibrolite and/or cordierite. Some kyanite was folded by D3 deformation. Sillimanite commonly occurs along the main foliation and C-shear foliation (Fig. 6d), suggesting growth even during the intense ductile shearing of the D2 deformation.

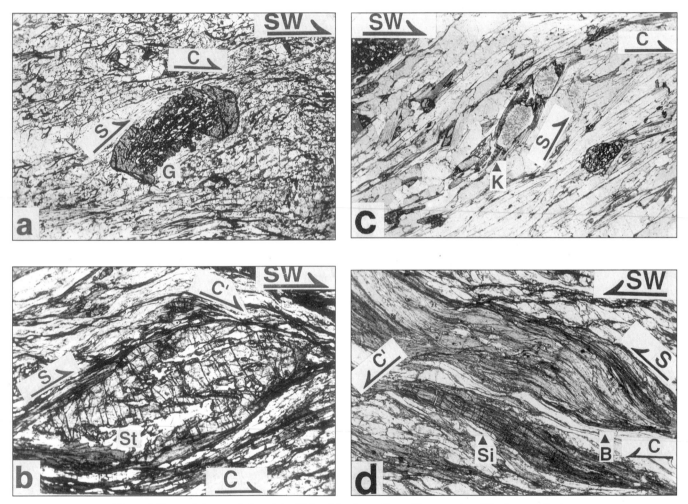

Figure 6. Textural characteristics of the Higher Himalayan Crystallines, western Himalaya. a: Syntectonic garnet (G), riddled with quartz and biotite inclusions, incorporated during its growth in M2 metamorphic episode along the S-C fabric. Inclusion-free rim of subidioblastic garnet represents exhumation history of the rock. Location is about 5 km south of Kishtwar, southeast Kashmir. b: Syntectonic staurolite (St) porphyroblast, having quartz-biotite inclusions, grows during the M2 along the S-C foliation. Note distinct shear band C′ affecting staurolite tail and quartz-mica groundmass. Location: Junkal Gompa in the vicinity of the Zanskar shear zone. c: S-C shear fabric controlling porphyroblastic kyanite(K)-biotite. Location is near Masu, southeast Kashmir. d: Epitiaxally grown sillimanite (Si) over biotite (B) along top-to-southwest S-C fabric in sillimanite-biotite schist near the Zanskar shear zone along the Mulung Tokpo. Note opposite and southwest-dipping extensional shear band C′. All photographs are 9.5 mm in width.

Fibrolite and/or sillimanite replaced biotite, muscovite, and kyanite during this deformation.

Feldspar. K-feldspar and plagioclase occur mostly as subidioblastic grains, having inclusions of quartz and rarely kyanite. Perthite is common in the higher grades. Plagioclase is more albitic (X_{An} = 0.12–0.29), but a few samples show an enriched anorthite content.

Chlorite. Chlorite occurs both in garnet and staurolite-kyanite grades; in the latter grade, chlorite is Mg rich (Mg/Mg + Fe = >0.5), and is associated with staurolite close to the hanging wall of the Vaikrita thrust n the Sutlej valley.

GARNET ZONING

In the Sutlej and the Bhagirathi valleys, garnet from the Crystallines belt rocks in the staurolite-kyanite grade exhibits normal growth zoning (Fig. 7, a, b and c), and bell-shaped Mn and Ca profiles (cf. Tracy, 1982). In the Bhagirathi valley, the staurolite-kyanite grade reveals normal growth zoning and a more relaxed bell-shaped Mn and Ca profiles (Fig. 7, b and c). In these valleys, garnet does not reveal any other pattern, unlike in southeast Kashmir, and appears to have grown much more rapidly, so as to arrest either homogenization or diffusion processes.

Like garnet from the Crystallines belt sequence of the Sutlej and Bhagirathi valleys, the carbonaceous schist of the Lesser Himalayan Kishtwar window exhibits normal growth zoning (Fig. 7d). However, garnet in the staurolite-kyanite grade from the Bhot Nala section (in southeast Kashmir) reveals flat zoning (Fig. 7e), which is similar to the observations made from the Main Central thrust zone in the eastern Garhwal by Hodges and Silverberg (1988) and from the central Nepal by Inger and Harris (1992). Hodges and Silverberg (1988) interpreted such flat zoning pattern to be due to rapid growth rather than diffusive reequilibration. Nevertheless, simulated isobaric heating and cooling models on garnet growth postulate pronounced modifications in X_{alm} and X_{sp} by diffusion, which causes homogenization in grains < 2 mm at about 620 °C with a heating rate of 2-5 °C/m.y. (Florence and Spear, 1991). In the section through southeast Kashmir, garnet growth takes place at elevated temperatures, by about 100 °C from its core to rim at 650 °C (see Table 1). Garnet in most of the staurolite-kyanite grade is <2 mm in size; however, its flat profile appears to be due to rapid growth rather than by diffusion, as suggested by Hodges and Silverberg (1988) for the eastern Garhwal. This is supported possibly by the limited time available for the Himalayan metamorphism, and also from the composition of biotite inclusions (X_{Fe}= 0.513–0.537) and matrix (X_{Fe}= 0.401–0.482). If garnet became homogenized due to diffusion, biotite inclusions should have also reequilibrated with garnet, because interdiffusion in biotite is much more rapid than in garnet at elevated temperatures (Tracy, 1982). That the composition of inclusion biotite is different from matrix biotite probably demonstrates that (1) biotite has not undergone reequilibration during garnet homogenization, and (2) garnet

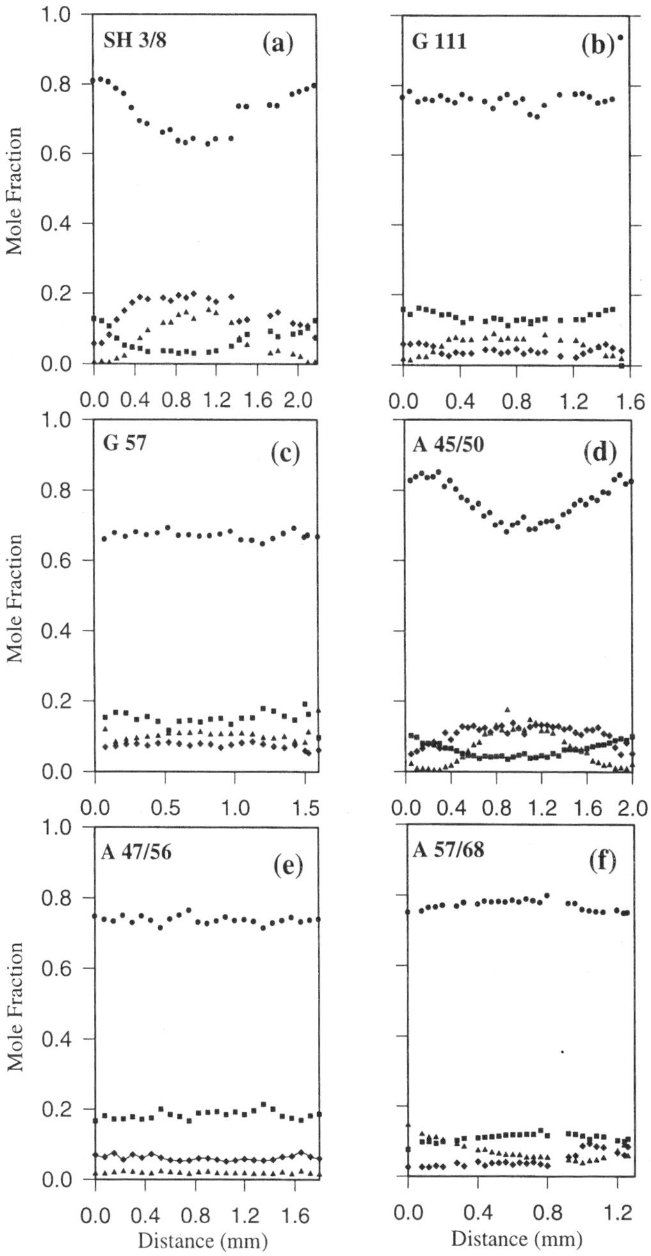

Figure 7. Garnet zoning. a: Staurolite-kyanite grade at the base of the Vaikrita thrust hanging wall near Karchham, Sutlej valley, Himachal. b: Staurolite-kyanite grade at the base of the Vaikrita thrust hanging wall near Dabrani, Bhagirathi valley, Garhwal. c: Staurolite-kyanite grade near the upper structural levels of the Higher Himalayan Crystallines between Jhala and Harsil along the Bhagirathi valley, Garhwal. d: Lesser Himalaya garnet grade within the Kishtwar window near Atholi, southeast Kashmir. e: Staurolite-kyanite grade at the base of the HHC near Masu along the Bhot Nala section, southeast Kashmir. f: Sillimanite-K-feldspar grade at middle structural levels of the HHC near Machel along the Bhot Nala section, southeast Kashmir. Symbols: Dots are almandine, squares are pyrope, triangles are spessartite, and diamonds are grossularite.

has grown relatively rapidly during prograde conditions and produced flattened profiles.

Garnet from sillimanite-muscovite and sillimanite–K-feldspar grades from southeast Kashmir shows reverse zoning (Fig. 7f). Its composition is generally uniform at the core, while Fe and Mg are depleted near the rim with Mn enrichment. Higher temperatures (700 to 780 °C) recorded in garnet cores suggest that volume diffusion and homogenization in garnet took place during its growth (Tracy et al., 1976; Woodsworth, 1977; Tracy, 1982). Subsequent to homogenization in garnet, diffusive requilibration at its rim probably produced the reverse zoning during exhumation of the Crystallines belt, as is evidenced by enrichment of X_{Sp} and X_{Fe} at the rim (Cygan and Lasaga, 1982; Tracy, 1982; St-Onge, 1987; Spear, 1989; Spear et al., 1991).

THERMOBAROMETRIC RESULTS

Methodology and calibrations

Microprobe analyses were performed using an automated JEOL JXA-8600M EPMA (electron probe microanalyzer) with a 15 kv accelerating voltage and 2×10^{-8} amp sample current having a beam size of 1 μm for garnet and staurolite and 10 μm for biotite, muscovite, K-feldspar, and plagioclase. Natural mineral standards (SPI standards, Canada) were used for the analysis. ZAF (atomic number–absorbence-fluorescence) correction was applied to the data that were used for the pressure-temperature (*P-T*) determinations. In each sample, three to four sets of coexisting mineral phases were analyzed; each phase had four to five points for the average mineral composition. The composition of minerals is within 2σ error limit.

The pelites allowed simultaneous solutions of garnet-biotite (GB) exchange thermometer and garnet- plagioclase-Al_2SiO_3-quartz (GPAQ) and garnet-plagioclase-muscovite-biotite (GPMB) barometers in the Crystallines belt. Temperature has been estimated using the ideal Fe-Mg exchange thermometer of Ferry and Spear (1978), and the nonideal mixing model of Hodges and Spear (1982). Mineral mole fraction and *P-T* data, based on the Hodges and Spear (1982) calibrations, are available from the authors upon request. Pressure was obtained by applying calibrations of Newton and Haselton (1981) for GPAQ, and modified calibrations by Hodges and Crowley (1985) for GPMB. Errors in *P-T* estimations were calculated by the method given by Hodges and McKenna (1987). Other calibrations were used for *P-T* calculations; however, these either overestimate or underestimate both the temperature and pressure, and therefore are not presented here.

P-T data for garnet (core as well as rim) were determined using compositions of garnet core and inclusions of biotite, plagioclase, and muscovite (St-Onge, 1987) and the compositions of garnet rims with matrix minerals. In the higher grade rocks, the near-rim compositions of coexisting phases have been used for

the rim *P-T* determinations to avoid the effects of retrogression (Spear, 1989). Samples from the Sutlej and Bhagirathi valleys lack plagioclase in their mineral assemblages, even after careful and close sampling, and hence, pressure determination for these rocks has become difficult. Therefore, only a few pressure data could be determined from these valleys.

Results

The *T-P* calculated by simultaneous solution are given for all the three sections and presented in *P-T*, distance-*T*, and distance-*P* data plots (Tables 1–3; Figs. 8–10).

In southeast Kashmir, the Lesser Himalayan garnet grade within ~500 m of the Main Central thrust footwall zone records rim *T* of 550 °C and pressure 6.5 kbar (Table 1). On the hanging wall of the Main Central thrust, core thermobarometric results from the staurolite-kyanite grade record 500 to 550 °C and 8.5 kbar (Table 1). Sillimanite-muscovite grade shows an increase in core *T* of about 170 °C from the lower grade, but no significant change in *P* (Table 1; Fig. 8a). Sillimanite–K-feldspar grade reveals a further increase in core *T* of about 40 to 80 °C; peak *T* and *P* are 780 °C and 10 kbar (Fig. 8, b and c). Rim data from staurolite-kyanite grade indicate *T* of 600 to 650 °C and *P* of 8 to 9 kbar; there is a nearly 100 °C rise in *T* (Fig. 8b), and no significant change in *P* from the core (Fig. 8c). However, for sillimanite-muscovite and sillimanite–K-feldspar grades, the rim data reveal a reduction of about 50 °C and 1 to 2 kbar, and 100 °C and 4 to 6 kbar from core data (Fig. 8, a–c). However, in the migmatite-leucogranite zone sillimanite-bearing assemblages give much reduced *T-P* values (Table 1), possibly due to effects of anatexis and melting; garnet is broken and shows resorbed margins. The Crystallines belt along the Padar-Zanskar section records a nearly uniform rim *T* for all the metamorphic grades and significant reduction in *P* from lower to higher grade rocks (Fig. 8, b and c).

Along the Sutlej valley, core data could not be obtained from the Crystallines belt due to lack of suitable mineral inclusions in garnet. Rim data record 490 to 500 °C for the garnet to staurolite-kyanite transition zone, and 570 to 590 °C and ~8 kbar for staurolite-kyanite grade, exposed between Jhakri and Wangtu in the lower structural levels above the Main Central thrust (Table 2; Fig. 9, a–c). However, from the Vaikrita thrust to the Tethyan sedimentary zone, the Crystallines belt records a *T* of 575 to 620 °C and *P* of ~7 kbar in staurolite-kyanite grade, whereas sillimanite-muscovite grade exhibits 740 to 800 °C and ~9 kbar (Fig. 9, b and c). *P-T* data from staurolite-kyanite grade of the northern margin could not be determined due to lack of suitable mineral assemblage.

In the Crystallines belt along the Bhagirathi valley, above the Vaikrita thrust, garnet cores record a *T* of 500 to 545 °C for staurolite-kyanite grade, and ~750 °C for sillimanite-muscovite grade (Table 3; Fig. 10, a–c). However, rim thermobarometric results show ~550 °C and ~5.75 kbar for the garnet grade on the hanging wall of the Main Central thrust, and 600 to 650 °C and

TABLE 1. P-T DATA FROM THE HIGHER HIMALAYAN CRYSTALLINES, PADAR–ZANSKAR SECTION, SOUTHEAST KASHMIR

Sample number	Temperature			Pressure	
	Core* (°C)	Rim* (°C)	Core† (°C)	Rim§ (kbar)	Rim† (kbar)
1. A45/50	n.d.	558 ± 18	n.d.	6.94 ± 0.18	n.d.
2. A41/48	n.d.	671 ± 19	n.d.	n.d.	9.55 ± 0.53
3. A46/51	507 ± 5	619 ± 11	n.d.	n.d.	8.28 ± 0.24
4. A47/54	n.d.	686 ± 15	n.d.	n.d.	10.74 ± 0.38
5. A47/55	568 ± 11	655 ± 14	8.74 ± 0.25	n.d.	9.22 ± 0.79
6. A47/56	n.d.	591 ± 11	n.d.	7.45 ± 0.21	7.39 ± 0.36
7. U92/110	n.d.	588 ± 8	n.d.	8.55 ± 0.18	10.02 ± 0.55
8. U93/111A	531 ± 7	559 ± 18	n.d.	7.90 ± 0.42	8.63 ± 0.38
9. U93/111C	n.d.	593 ± 5	n.d.	8.85 ± 0.11	9.68 ± 0.20
10. A53/62	n.d.	639 ± 25	n.d.	5.44 ± 0.17	5.92 ± 0.21
11. U86/103	n.d.	649 ± 32	n.d.	5.09 ± 0.23	5.44 ± 0.40
12. U80/96	702 ± 39	654 ± 27	n.d.	7.20 ± 0.41	8.35 ± 0.23
13. A80/111	n.d.	617 ± 20	n.d.	7.98 ± 0.55	7.94 ± 0.63
14. A57/68	736 ± 9	611 ± 14	7.97 ± 0.28	n.d.	8.16 ± 0.25
15. U64/67	n.d.	643 ± 23	n.d.	n.d.	5.04 ± 0.49
16. U60/63	n.d.	665 ± 22	n.d.	n.d.	6.50 ± 0.30
17. A65/78	778 ± 31	663 ± 19	9.30 ± 0.62	n.d.	6.49 ± 0.37
18. A67/86	837 ± 20	636 ± 19	10.92 ± 0.45	n.d.	7.14 ± 0.27
19. U57/60	n.d.	650 ± 26	n.d.	n.d.	5.23 ± 0.22
20. U33/35	n.d.	575 ± 17	n.d.	n.d.	5.08 ± 0.43
21. U52/55	n.d.	601 ± 14	n.d.	n.d.	4.55 ± 0.52
22. U29/31	n.d.	634 ± 21	n.d.	n.d.	5.63 ± 0.57
23. U48/51	688 ± 16	608 ± 18	n.d.	n.d.	6.71 ± 0.38
24. U13/13	705 ± 14	520 ± 27	n.d.	n.d.	3.77 ± 0.21
25. U4/4	n.d.	694 ± 16	n.d.	n.d.	5.68 ± 0.38
26. P22/86	n.d.	649 ± 6	n.d.	n.d.	5.81 ± 0.15
27. P12/20	n.d.	676 ± 8	n.d.	n.d.	7.73 ± 0.15
28. P9/50	n.d.	521 ± 17	n.d.	6.91 ± 0.29	6.91 ± 0.29
29. P9/46	n.d.	567 ± 13	n.d.	n.d.	6.00 ± 0.43

*Ferry and Spear, 1978.
†Newton and Haselton, 1981.
§Hodges and Crowley, 1985.
n.d. = no data.

8 to 9 kbar for the staurolite-kyanite grade; and ~700 °C and 9 to 11 kbar for the sillimanite-muscovite grade on the hanging wall of the Vaikrita thrust (Fig. 10, b and c). Our rim *P-T* data correspond to those of Metcalfe (1993), reported from the same section.

INTERPRETATION

M1 metamorphism (pre-Himalayan)

Tight folds having "flame-type" hinges developed during the D1 deformation on metamorphic layering indicate that this deformation and the associated metamorphism was pre-Himalayan; we believe it to be M1 metamorphism and possibly Proterozoic in age, because ca. 500 Ma granitoids intrude the metamorphic rocks, which have undergone D1 deformation.

M2 metamorphism (Himalayan)

Syntectonic mineral porphyroblasts grew both along the S1-S2 foliation and ductile shear C foliation, at medium to high *T* and high *P* during the pre-Main Central thrust main M2 metamorphism. These minerals grew during initial prograde regional Barrovian metamorphism, and continued to grow during the formation of southward-verging ductile shear zones, affecting the Crystallines belt in the northwest Himalaya (Jain and Manickavasagam, 1993). This is evident from the mineral assemblages, garnet zoning, and core and/or rim thermobarometric results from garnet through sillimanite–K-feldspar grades, exposed from lower to higher structural levels. In southeast Kashmir, the Crystallines belt records an increasing garnet core temperature (Fig. 8b), and flat to reverse garnet zoning (Fig. 7, e and f). In comparison, the Crystallines belt rocks from the Sutlej and Bhagirathi valleys record increasing garnet rim *T* and *P* (Figs. 9a and 10a)

TABLE 2. P–T DATA FROM THE
HIGHER HIMALAYAN CRYSTALLINES,
SUTLEJ–BASPA VALLEYS, HIMALCHAL PRADESH

Sample Number	Temperature Rim* (°C)	Pressure Rim† (kbar)	Pressure Rim§\ (kbar)
1. W2/5	519 ± 19	n.d.	n.d.
2. R19	564 ± 07	n.d.	n.d.
3. W11	570 ± 15	6.06 ± 0.07	n.d.
4. W13	650 ± 15	7.98 ± 0.18	n.d.
5. RR17/21	666 ± 23	9.92 ± 0.43	n.d.
6. SH1/1	620 ± 44	n.d.	6.62 ± 0.58
7. SH3/7	605 ± 1	n.d.	n.d.
8. SH3/8	591 ± 31	n.d.	n.d.
9. SH33/57	605 ± 17	n.d.	n.d.
10. SH64/95	583 ± 24	n.d.	n.d.
11. SH71/101	575 ± 19	n.d.	n.d.
12. B9	552 ± 22	n.d.	7.03 ± 0.69
13. SH26/50	740 ± 31	8.72 ± 0.86	n.d.
14. B5	727 ± 23	n.d.	9.09 ± 0.53
15. B4	802 ± 40	n.d.	n.d.
16. SH15/28	606 ± 32	n.d.	n.d.

*Ferry and Spear, 1978.
†Newton and Haselton, 1981.
§Hodges and Crowley, 1985.
n.d. = no data.

TABLE 3. P–T DATA FROM THE
HIGHER HIMALAYAN CRYSTALLINES
FROM THE BHAGIRATHI VALLEY, GARHWAL

Sample Number	Temperature Core* (°C)	Temperature Rim† (°C)	Pressure Rim§\ (Kbar)
1. G-51	n.d.	546 ± 1	575 ± 0.35
2. G-111	504 ± 11	656 ± 12	9.93 ± 0.57
3. G-103	n.d.	642 ± 13	8.73 ± 0.05
4. G-101	n.d.	700 ± 10	n.d.
5. G-28	757 ± 8	640 ± 1	10.71 ± 0.32
6. G-27	n.d.	693 ± 10	8.85 ± 0.23
7. G-34	480 ± 31	538 ± 5	6.37 ± 0.14
8. G-32	517 ± 17	604 ± 10	n.d.
9. G-61	n.d.	600 ± 5	n.d.
10. G-57	505 ± 21	599 ± 16	8.00 ± 0.8

*Ferry and Spear, 1978.
†Newton and Haselton, 1981.
§Hodges and Crowley, 1985.
n.d. = no data.

els. However, Hodges and Silverberg (1988), Stäubli (1989), Pognante et al. (1990), Inger and Harris (1992), and Searle et al. (1992) postulated a pre-Main Central thrust–related M1 metamorphism (our M2 event) during the early stages of collision by tectonic burial or crustal thickening for the kyanite-bearing assemblages only that occur close to the Main Central thrust.

Sillimanite-bearing assemblages at higher structural levels of the Crystallines belt from southeast Kashmir, eastern Garhwal, and Nepal has been attributed to the M2 metamorphism by (1) anatectic melting of the Higher Himalayan sequence, accompanied by movement along a blind thrust (Hodges and Silverberg, 1988); (2) folding and thrusting of the Crystallines belt at the base along the Main Central thrust and normal faulting at the top of the belt along the Zanskar shear zone (Searle and Rex, 1989); (3) break-back thrusting on the hanging wall of the previous

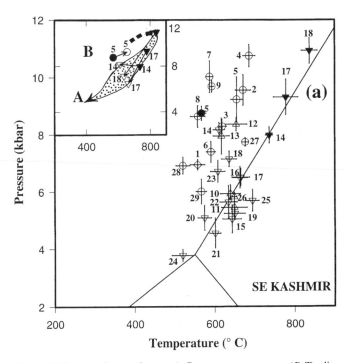

Figure 8 (above and opposite page). Pressure-temperature (P-T), distance-temperature (D-T), and distance-pressure (D-P) plots for the Lesser Himalaya and the Higher Himalayan Crystallines from near the Main Central thrust (MCT) to the Zanskar shear zone, southeast Kashmir and western Zanskar. a: P-T plot of the HHC. Also plotted are garnet rim data for the Lesser Himalaya (diamond). Inset shows the P-T paths derived from garnet core and rim data from sillimanite-muscovite and sillimanite–K-feldspar grades (cooling path—arrow A), and staurolite-kyanite grade (heating path—arrow B) Aluminosilicate triple point is drawn after Holdaway (1971). b: D-T and c: D-P plots of garnet core and rim data for different metamorphic grades. For convenience, serial numbers of samples are indicated in this figure. Symbols: Diamond—garnet zone; squares—garnet–staurolite-kyanite transition zone; circles—staurolite-kyanite isograd; triangles—sillimanite-muscovite zone; inverted triangles—sillimanite–K-feldspar zone. Solid and open symbols are garnet core and rim data, respectively. Distances are measured perpendicular to the trace of the MCT (see Table 1 for the analytical data; Fig. 2 for the sample locations).

and normal to relaxed normal growth zoning (Fig. 7, a to c). The rim P-T data for all the metamorphic grades from the studied sections plot largely in the kyanite stability field; a few higher grade samples, however, plot close to the kyanite-sillimanite univariant line (Figs. 8a, 9a, and 10a), thus confirming the notion that the Crystallines belt rocks in these grades were formed at deeper lev-

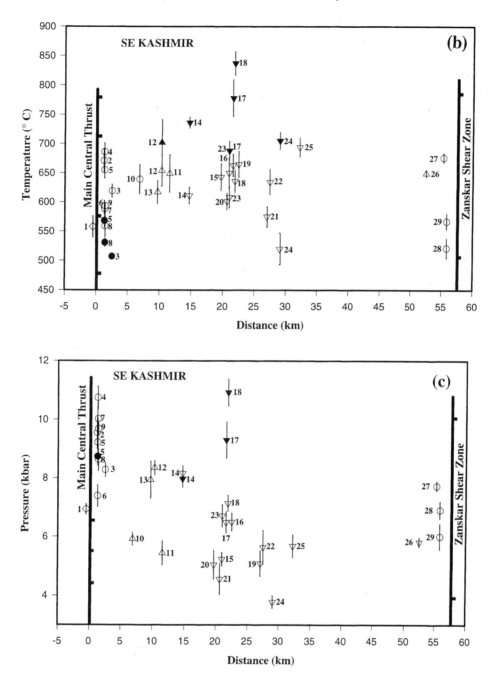

thrust (Searle et al., 1992); and (4) normal faulting at the northern contact of heated Crystallines belt rocks with the Tethyan sedimentary zone cover of low thermal conductivity (Brunal and Kienast, 1986; Inger and Harris, 1992). However, sillimanite growth, both along the main foliation and shear-controlled foliation, supported by core-rim thermobarometric results from the higher grades of the southeast Kashmir and the Sutlej valley, clearly suggests that sillimanite also developed during the M2 metamorphic stage, predating the Main Central thrust and its various splays, such as the Vaikrita thrust. This textural relationship in the higher grades is true for kyanite, staurolite, and mica that

developed along the S-C foliation at relatively lower metamorphic grades. Hence, we postulate that development of sillimanite-bearing assemblages also belonged to the M2 episode in a ductile shear regime.

Only in southeast Kashmir does the Crystallines belt show a uniform rim *T* in all the metamorphic grades, and a significant *P* reduction from middle and higher structural levels, covering the sillimanite-muscovite and sillimanite–K-feldspar grades. When core and rim *P-T* data are compared for the entire Crystallines belt along this section, sillimanite-bearing rocks show decreasing rim *P-T*, whereas the staurolite-kyanite grade records an increase in the rim *T* and no change in *P* (Fig. 8b). Prior to the nappe translation along the Main Central thrust, it appears that the Crystallines belt at the higher structural levels (sillimanite–K-feldspar and sillimanite-muscovite grades) was exhumed initially, resulting in decompression and cooling of the higher grades. During this period, the basal part of the Crystallines belt (staurolite-kyanite grade) seemed to have been affected by apparent heating with no decompression; thus the entire belt attained near-isothermal conditions. The cooling with decompression is supported by reverse garnet zoning with Mg and Fe-rich cores and Mn- and Fe/Fe + Mg-rich rim, fibrolite growth, relict kyanite with reactions rims of cordierite and muscovite, and myrmekitization along feldspar grain boundaries in the higher metamorphic grades. The heating of the lower parts is also evident from flat garnet zoning, development of sillimanite around syntectonic garnet, growth of superposed subidioblastic garnet having ~650 °C *T* over S-C fabric, and relict staurolite in the lower metamorphic grade.

Unlike in southeast Kashmir, the Crystallines belt rocks from the Sutlej and Bhagirathi valleys yield different rim *P-T* conditions. In the absence of garnet core *P-T* data from the Sutlej valley and low garnet core temperatures from the Bhagirathi valley, garnet rim *P-T* data and zoning patterns (Fig. 7, b and c) suggest that garnet and other porphyroblasts, irrespective of the metamorphic grades, grew only during the prograde M2 metamorphism at great paleodepths. The absence of fibrolite and very rare posttectonic garnet or any other porphyroblastic growth over shear-controlled foliation, and the presence of normal growth zoning in garnet from all the metamorphic grades support this postulation. *P-T* data from these valleys record signatures of thermal relaxation and exhumation or decompression path of higher grades nor the heating of the lower grades within the Crystallines belt. Therefore, it is likely that the Crystallines belt was exhumed much faster in this part of the northwest Himalaya.

HIMALAYAN METAMORPHISM AND THE MCT

The Lesser Himalayan belt mostly remains in chlorite to biotite grade in the northwest Himalaya, except for a maximum garnet grade on the northeastern flank of the Kishtwar window in the immediate vicinity of the Main Central thrust footwall (Fig. 2). Garnet from the Kishtwar window shows a prograde growth from core to rim, where the rim *T* is 100 °C less than the rim *T* of the Crystallines belt rocks of the adjoining Main Central thrust hanging wall. Garnet in the footwall has normal bell-shaped Mn and Ca profiles distinctly different from the flat zoning of the Mn and Ca profiles in the hanging wall.

On the northeastern flank of the Kishtwar window in the immediate vicinity of the Main Central thrust, the Crystallines belt is metamorphosed to staurolite-kyanite grade and attains peak sillimanite–K-feldspar grade toward the upper structural levels. Here, it has undergone extensive anatexis, migmatization, and leucogranite development during exhumation and attendant decompression. This is also evident from the resorbed garnet,

reaction rims of cordierite and fibrolite on kyanite, and biotite restites. Farther northeast in the Zanskar region, metamorphism gradually decreases to garnet grade near the Zanskar shear zone. Our data clearly demonstrate that the metamorphic isograds in the Crystallines belt are truncated obliquely by the Main Central thrust and the Zanskar shear zone at different places rather than telescoped on either of its margins (cf. Herren, 1987; Searle and Rex; 1989, Stäubli, 1989).

In the Sutlej and Bhagirathi valleys, the Lesser Himalayan Kulu-Rampur window is metamorphosed to chlorite to biotite grades in the Main Central thrust footwall. The Crystallines belt in these sections is composed of two prograde metamorphic packages that are separated by the Vaikrita thrust at a middle structural level. However, close to the Main Central thrust along the Sutlej valley, the belt records 550 to 600 °C within the garnet to staurolite-kyanite transition zone, and an increase to staurolite-kyanite grade toward the Vaikrita thrust to the northeast along the Sutlej valley (Singh, 1993). The lower parts of the Crystallines belt (i.e., the footwall rocks of the Vaikrita thrust along the Bhagirathi valley), however, remain within the garnet grade. In the basal parts of the hanging wall of the Vaikrita thrust, the Crystallines belt is metamorphosed to staurolite-kyanite grade in both the Sutlej and Bhagirathi valleys, and the metamorphism

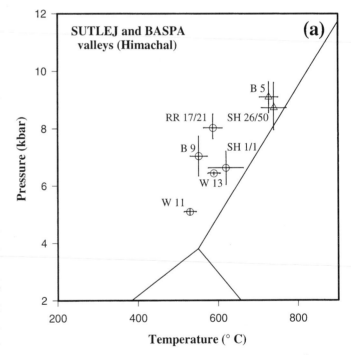

Figure 9 (this and opposite page). Pressure-temperature (*P-T*), distance-temperature (*D-T*) and distance-pressure (*D-P*) plots for the Higher Himalayan Crystallines between the Main Central thrust (MCT) and the Tethyan sedimentary zone along the Sutlej-Baspa valleys, Himachal Pradesh. a: *P-T* plot of garnet rim (open circles) data. b: *D-T* and c: *D-P* plots of garnet rim data for different metamorphic grades. Symbols are as in Figure 8. Distances are measured perpendicular to the traces of the Main Central thrust and the Vaikrita thrust (see Table 2 for the analytical data, and Fig. 3 for the sample location).

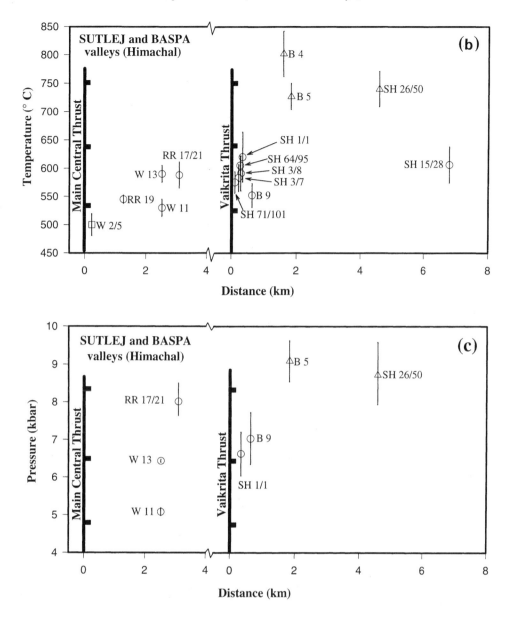

increases to sillimanite-muscovite grade at higher structural levels. Toward the contact with the Tethyan sedimentary zone, the metamorphism decreases to staurolite-kyanite, garnet, and biotite grades. It is noteworthy that (1) along the Sutlej valley, metamorphic isograds are repeated due to the Vaikrita thrust, where the high-*T* staurolite-kyanite grade rocks is overlain by low-temperature staurolite-kyanite grade (Table 2; Fig. 9b); (2) along the Bhagirathi valley, garnet grade rocks are overlain by high-*T* staurolite-kyanite grade rocks (Table 3; Fig. 10b); and (3) an increase of *T* in the lower grade Crystallines belt rocks due to heat conduction from high grades is not recorded in garnet rim data. Metamorphic grades within the Crystallines belt are, therefore, discontinuous, and have undergone truncation, concealment, and repetition only after M2 metamorphism due to passive movements along the Main Central thrust and its splays, such as the Vaikrita thrust.

INVERTED METAMORPHISM

Mineralogical and thermobarometric data from the northwest Himalayan Crystallines belt indicate the presence of inverted metamorphism like other parts of the Himalaya. Some of the possible mechanisms to explain the inverted metamorphism in the Himalaya are summarized in the following.

The hot-iron model postulates heating of relatively colder basal part of the Crystallines belt and the Lesser Himalayan rocks due to emplacement of the hot higher sequence of the belt, prior to the nappe translation along the Main Central thrust (Le Fort, 1975). In southeast Kashmir, no thermal effects of heating have been recorded by the garnet grade Lesser Himalayan footwall of the Main Central thrust. Apparent heating of the basal part of the Crystallines belt to the staurolite-kyanite grade was caused by heat conduction from the higher grades, prior to the juxtaposition

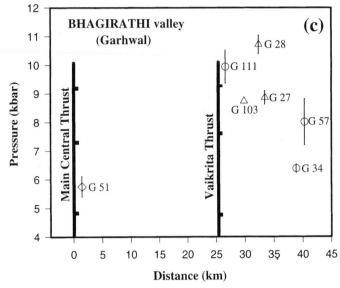

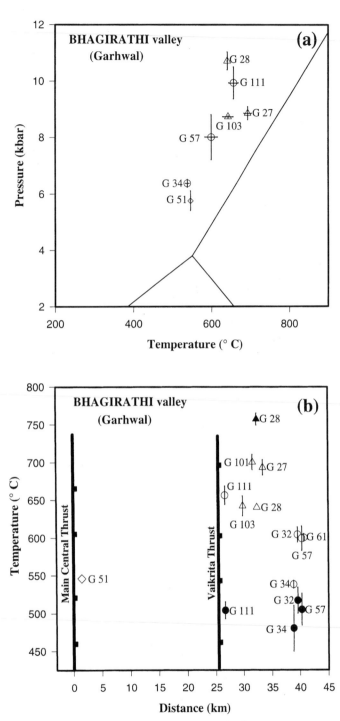

Figure 10 (above). Pressure-temperature (*P-T*), distance-temperature (*D-T*) and distance-pressure (*D-P*) plots for the Higher Himalayan Crystallines between the Main Central thrust and the Martoli fault along the Bhagirathi valley, western Garhwal. a: *P-T* plot of garnet rim (open circle) data. b: *D-T* and c: *D-P* plots of garnet rim (open circles) data for different metamorphic grades. Symbols are as in Figure 8. Distances are measured perpendicular to the traces of the thrust (see Table 3 for the analytical data and Fig. 4 for the sample location).

of the Crystallines belt over the Lesser Himalayan footwall by the movements along the Main Central thrust. Even in southeast Kashmir, an almost uniform rim temperature of around 600 to 650 °C was recorded from staurolite-kyanite to sillimanite–K-feldspar grades. In the Sutlej and Bhagirathi valleys, no evidence for heating of either the basal parts of the Crystallines belt or the Lesser Himalaya–Main Central thrust footwall is recorded. It is therefore evident that the inverted metamorphism in the north-west Himalaya is not related to this model, as is also suggested by thermal modeling (Grasemann, 1993), and mechanical finite element modeling (Jamieson et al., 1996).

Shear heating along the Main Central thrust or the Vaikrita thrust is another possible mechanism for inverting metamor-phism. In this case, however, temperature would have increased on either walls of major thrust in narrow zones (Scholtz, 1980; Sinha-Roy, 1982; Vidal et al., 1982; Arita, 1983; Searle and Fryer, 1986; Searle and Rex, 1989; Molnar and England, 1990). This would have resulted in restricted occurrence of the highest grades only close to the Main Central thrust and not farther away from the thrust. Field and petrological observations of the west-ern Himalaya do not support this model.

Leucogranite emplacement at the highest structural levels in the Crystallines belt might have also caused inverted metamor-phism (Pilgrim and West, 1928; Auden, 1935; Hodges and Sil-verberg, 1988; Pêcher, 1989; Searle and Rex, 1989). In southeast Kashmir and the Sutlej-Bhagirathi valleys (Himachal Pradesh), small leucogranite bodies are confined to the highest structural levels. Thermal effects of such limited bodies would be highly restricted and therefore unlikely to produce large-scale metamor-phic inversion in the northwest Himalaya. In many cases, for example along the Bhagirathi valley, the leucogranite body is located about 10–15 km farther from highest sillimanite-mus-covite grade, and is exposed within biotite schist with extremely narrow contact aureole.

Postmetamorphic folds, F3 in our terminology, are likely to have caused inverted metamorphism (see Von Loczy, 1907; Heim and Gansser, 1939), as locally observed in western Himachal by Frank et al., (1977) and in Zanskar by Searle et al. (1992). Thakur (1977) also recorded divergent isograds in certain sections of the western Himalaya due to decrease in metamorphism on either side of the sillimanite isograd. However, such a regional model for the Crystallines belt would require large-scale overturned and/or recumbent folds, causing stratigraphic inversion and systematic repetition of various isograds that is almost absent from most of the sections through the belt, including the sections studied in this chapter.

Thrust imbrications along metamorphic isograd boundaries to produce inverted metamorphism are also ruled out, as suggested by Treloar et al. (1989a) for the north Pakistan Himalaya, and by Mohan et al. (1989) for the Darjeeling-Sikkim Hills. In the northwest Himalaya in India, mineral paragenesis reveals continuous variation from one metamorphic grade to another within the Crystallines belt, except the Vaikrita thrust, that has caused repetition, truncation, and concealment of metamorphic isograds, but not their inversion. We do not see evidence for thrusts marking the metamorphic isograds in the sections we discuss here.

Frank et al. (1977) and Thöni (1977) proposed a "synmetamorphic shear-folding'" model in which systematic shearing of discordant isograds to main foliation may cause inverted metamorphism in a "metamorphic fold" without causing any inversion of stratigraphic sequence. Such a fold model essentially causes changes in shear sense across the fold hinge, and differs fundamentally from ductile shear zones. The model visualizes differential southward shearing within the lower structural levels and northward shearing at the higher levels to develop large-scale shear folds. Such a shear pattern is not recorded in the Crystallines belt, which has undergone essentially southward-verging shearing along the C foliation in a broad ductile shear zone.

Keeping the various limitations in the models of inverted metamorphism in mind, we proposed a new model to explain the inverted metamorphism, based on limited textural, mineral growth, and thermobarometric data from southeast Kashmir (Jain and Manickavasagam, 1993). In this chapter we elaborate on this model in the light of new metamorphic and structural data presented here. Prograde regional metamorphism was initiated at a considerable depth due to tectonic subsidence of an ~10-km-thick Proterozoic sedimentary pile of the Himalayan metamorphic belt to a maximum depth of 25–35 km during the intracontinental subduction of the leading edge of the Indian plate. During this process, the Crystallines belt attained maximum T and P of 550 to 800 °C and 8 to 10 kbar. This is evident from syntectonic porphyroblastic garnet and its core P-T data from southeast Kashmir and rim data from the Sutlej and Bhagirathi valleys. Garnet, staurolite, kyanite, and sillimanite grew synkinematically along the main foliation during the D2 deformation. All these minerals continued their growth during peak metamorphism at depth along the C foliation also, which is

superposed upon an earlier foliation in a noncoaxial intracontinental ductile shear zone as a consequence of continued continental collision (Fig. 11). During this process, millimeter-spaced C foliation sigmoidally bent the S foliations on a small scale, toward the southwest, the direction of ductile tectonic transport (Jain and Manickavasagam, 1993). This model postulates that isograd boundaries also underwent small-scale displacements along C foliations in the distributed ductile shear zone (Fig. 11, a and b). Observable displacements along such millimeter-spaced C foliations are from 4 to 6 mm. It is therefore likely that the 20-km-thick ductile-type Higher Himalayan shear zone may have been affected by ~80 to 120 km penetrative displacement along the C-foliation planes. Considering the dip of the shear zone as 30° and the average angle between shear fabric and isograd boundaries as 15°, one can calculate the displacement in a 20-km-thick shear zone as 112 km, and the shear strain as 5.6 (see Ramsay and Huber, 1983; Herren, 1987; Hubbard, 1996). Present-day distribution of individual isograd boundaries in different parts of the northwest Himalaya is largely controlled by interaction of various factors, such as (1) dip of the ductile shear zone, (2) displacement within subsidiary and locally developed ductile zones due to high shear strain, (3) interaction between exhumation and ductile shearing, (4) later superposed folds, (5) the level of present-day erosion, and (6) mutual relationships between large dislocations and/or thrusts, and isograd boundaries (Fig. 11b).

Although the ductile shearing seems to have caused inverted metamorphism in the northwest Himalaya and elsewhere (Jain and Manickavasagam, 1993, 1994; Hubbard, 1966; Jamieson et al., 1996), exhumation rates appeared to have been different in all these areas. Relatively slower exhumation of the Crystallines belt in southeast Kashmir possibly resulted in thermal relaxation and decompression, which cooled the higher grade belt rocks at upper structural levels and simultaneously heated the lower grade belt rocks in the basal parts. However, the Crystallines belt in the Sutlej and Bhagirathi valleys appears to have been exhumed at a much faster rate, and thus did not record any thermal relaxation and decompression in their P-T paths.

CONCLUSIONS

Detailed mapping, petrography, and thermobarometric analyses of the Higher Himalayan Crystallines belt in the western parts of the Himalaya constrain the evolution of inverted metamorphism in southeast Kashmir and the Sutlej and Bhagirathi valleys. An early metamorphism (M1—possibly pre-Himalayan) is superposed by main prograde Himalayan M2 metamorphism across the entire Crystallines belt in the northwest Himalaya in a ductile tectonic regime. The Crystallines belt underwent tectonic subsidence to a maximum paleodepth of 25 to 35 km due to an intracontinental subduction of the Indian plate. The M2 event, a product of continued continental collision, in turn resulted in a main metamorphic pile, that has been affected by southwest-verging ubiquitous C-shear foliation in a distributed

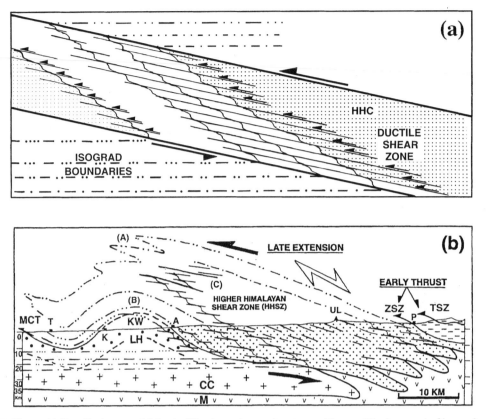

Figure 11. Ductile shear model for the Himalayan inverted metamorphism. **a:** Displacement of isograd boundaries in a distributed ductile shear zone, causing the inverted metamorphism. Numerous subsidiary ductile shear zones of high strain, characterized by S-C fabric, will systematically displace isograd surfaces in an overthrust (top-upward) sense. Sinuous isograd surfaces within ductile shear zone represent effects of high strain. **b:** Distributed ductile shear model for the Higher Himalayan shear zone across southeast Kashmir showing southward-verging C foliation and its effect on the isograde boundaries within the Higher Himalayan Crystallines (HHC). Possible superposed effects of postmetamorphic overturned and/or recumbent folding (A), and thrusting like the Main Central thrust (MCT) (B) and zones of ductile high strains (C) on isograds, causing inverted metamorphism within the HHC are also indicated. See text for details. Double thick arrows represent early ductile shearing. Single arrows represent discrete thrusts. Double open arrow represents late extension. Crustal depths are approximated from the pressure-temperature data of southeast Kashmir. LH—Late Proterozoic sedimentary sequence in the Kishtwar window (KW). TSZ—Tethyan sedimentary zone. CC—Continental crust of the Indian plate; M—upper mantle; T—Thatri; K—Kishtwar; A—Atholi; UL—Umasi La; P— Padam. Metamorphic isograd boundaries (dash-dot lines) are as in Figure 2.

ductile shear zone—hence the inversion of metamorphic isograds during the shearing and exhumation of the Crystallines belt. As a consequence, high-grade metamorphic rocks in the middle to upper structural levels of the Crystallines belt, appeared to have exhumed at a slower rate, but relatively faster than the medium to lower grade metamorphic rocks in the basal parts of the belt, that were heated due to heat conduction from the high-grade belt rocks in the southeast Kashmir section. In the Sutlej and Bhagirathi valleys (Himachal and Garhwal), such a phenomenon of heat conduction is not recorded, possibly due to lack of chemical reequilibration and much faster exhumation. This study also demonstrates that main Himalayan metamorphism predates the Main Central thrust and its splays, such as the Vaikrita thrust, that have insignificant roles in the overall tectonometamorphic evolu-

tion of these belts in this part of the Himalaya, except for truncation, concealment, and repetition of the isograd boundaries.

Distributed ductile shearing appears to be an equally efficient alternative mechanism of inverted metamorphism, and may be a logically expected phenomenon in many other collisional belts.

ACKNOWLEDGMENTS

This work constitutes the main parts of two major research projects, both funded generously by the Department of Science and Technology, New Delhi, through which the microprobe facility was set up at the University of Roorkee (Project 1760/2788-14-21/44/61).

We are grateful to Kailash Chandra for his untiring backup

on EPMA, K. R. Gupta for unending enthusiasm and V. K. S. Dave, R. C. Patel, Kamesh Gupta, and many other friends for their overwhelming encouragement during this work and various field trips to Zanskar. Manickavasagam, Jain, and Singh thank the organizers of the 11th HKT workshop for partial funding of the visit to Arizona, made feasible after receiving additional funds from All India Council of Technical Education, University of Roorkee, Indian National Science Academy, and the Department of Science and Technology. We benefitted from discussions with Kip Hodges; we thank Kazunori Arita, Gautam Mitra, Bernhard Grasemann, and Rasoul Sorkhabi for the reviews of the paper, and for their comments to improve it.

REFERENCES CITED

Arita, K., 1983, Origin of the inverted metamorphism of the Lower Himalayas Central Nepal: Tectonophysics, v. 95, p. 43–60.

Auden, J. B., 1935, Traverses in the Himalaya: India, Geological Survey of India Records, v. 69, p. 123–164.

Brunel, M., and Kienast, J. R., 1986, Etude petro-structurale des chevauchements ductiles himalayans sur la transversale de l'Everest-Makalu (Nepal oriental): Canadian Journal of Earth Sciences, v. 23, p. 1117–1137.

Burchfiel, B. C., Chen Zhiliang, Hodges, K. V., Liu Yuping, Royden, L. H., Deng Changrong, and Xue Jiene, 1992, The South Tibetan detachment system, Himalayan orogen: Extension contemporaneous with and parallel to shortening in a collisional mountain belt: Geological Society of America Special Paper 269, 41 p.

Burg., J. P., Guivaud, M., Chen, G. M., and Li, G. C., 1984, Himalayan metamorphism and deformation in the north Himalayan belt (Southern Tibet, China): Earth and Planetary Science letters, v. 69 p. 391–400.

Cygan, R. T., and Lasaga, A. C., 1982, Crystal growth and the formation of chemical zoning in garnets: Contributions to Mineralogy and Petrology, v. 79, p. 189–200.

Ferry, J. M., and Spear, F.S., 1978, Experimental calibration of the partitioning of Fe and Mg between biotite and garnet: Contributions to Mineralogy and Petrology, v. 66, p. 113–117.

Florence, F. P., and Spear, F.S., 1991, Effects of diffusional modification of garnet growth zoning on *P-T* path calculations: Contributions to Mineralogy and Petrology, v. 107, p. 487–500.

Frank, W., Thöni, M., and Purtscheller, F., 1977, Geology and petrography of Kulu-South Lahaul area, Écologie et Géologie de l'Himalaya: Colloques internationaux du Centre National de la Recherche Scientifique, no. 268, p. 147–172.

Gansser, A., 1964, Geology of the Himalayas: London Interscience Publishers, John Wiley and Sons, 289 p.

Grasemann, B., 1993, Numerical modelling of the thermal history of the northwest Himalayas, Kullu valley, India, *in* Treolar, P. J., and Searle, M. P., eds., Himalayan tectonics: Geological Society of London Special Publication 74, p. 475–484.

Heim, A., and Gansser, A., 1939, Central Himalaya, geological observations of the Swiss Expeditions 1936: Helvetica Science Society Momoirs, v. 73, 245 p.

Herren, E., 1987, The Zanskar shear zone: Northeast-southwest extension within the Higher Himalaya (Ladakh, India): Geology, v. 15, p. 409–413.

Hodges, K. V., and Crowley, P. D., 1985, Error estimation and empirical geothermobarometry for pelitic system: American Mineralogist, v. 70, p. 702–709.

Hodges, K. V., and McKenna, L. W., 1987, Realistic propagation of uncertainties in geologic thermometry: American Mineralogist, v. 72, p. 671–680.

Hodges, K. V., and Silverberg, D. S., 1988, Thermal evolution of the greater Himalaya, Garhwal, India: Tectonics, v. 7, p. 583–600.

Hodges, K. V., and Spear, F. S., 1982, Geothermometry, geobarometry and

Al2SiO5 triple point at Moosilauke, New Hampshire: American Mineralogist, v. 70, p. 1118–1134.

Hodges, K. V., Hubbard, M. S., and Silverberg, D. S., 1988, Metamorphic constraints on the thermal evolution of the central Himalayan Orogen: Royal Society of London Philosophical Transactions, ser. A, v. 326, p. 257–280.

Holdaway, M. J., 1971, Stability of andalusite and the aluminum silicate phase diagram: American Journal of Science, v. 271, p. 97–131.

Honegger, K., Dietrich, V., Frank, W., Gansser, A., Thöni, M., and Trommsdorff, V., 1982, Magmatism and metamorphism in the Ladakh Himalayas (the Indus-Tsangpo Suture zone): Earth and Planetary Science Letters, v. 60, p. 253–292.

Hubbard, M., 1996, Ductile shear as a cause of inverted metamorphism: Example from the Nepal Himalaya: Journal of Geology, v. 104, p. 493–499.

Inger, S., and Harris, N. B. W., 1992, Tectonothermal evolution of the High Himalayan Crystalline sequence, Langtang valley, northern Nepal: Journal of Metamorphic Geology, v. 10, p. 439–452.

Jain, A. K., and Manickavasagam, R. M., 1993, Inverted metamorphism in the intracontinental ductile shear zone during Himalayan collision tectonics: Geology, v. 21, p. 407–410.

Jain, A. K., and Manickavasagam, R. M., 1994, Inverted metamorphism in the intracontinental ductile shear zone during Himalayan collision tectonics: Reply: Geology, v. 22, p. 90–92.

Jamieson, R. A., Beaumont, C., Hamilton, J., and Fullsack, P., 1996, Tectonic assembly of inverted metamorphic sequences: Geology, v. 24, p. 839–842.

Kundig, R., 1989, Domal structures and high-grade metamorphism in the Higher Himalayan Crystalline, Zanskar region, north-west Himalaya, India: Journal of Metamorphic Geology, v. 7, p. 43–55.

Le Fort, P., 1975, Himalaya: the collided range. Present knowledge of the continental arc: American Journal of Science, v. 275-A, p. 1–44.

Metcalfe, R. P., 1993, Pressure, temperature and time constraints on metamorphism across the Main Central thrust one and High Himalayan Slab in the Garhwal Himalaya, *in* Treolar, P. J., and Searle, M. P., eds., Himalayan tectonics: Geological Society of London Special Publication 74, p. 485–510.

Mohan, A., Windley, B. F., and Searle, M. P., 1989, Geothermobarometry and development of inverted metamorphism in the Darjeeling-Sikkim region of the eastern Himalaya: Journal of Metamorphic Geology, v. 7, p. 95–110.

Molnar, P., and England, P. C., 1990, Temperatures, heat flux, and frictional stress near major thrust faults: Journal of Geophysical Research, v. 95, p. 4833–4856.

Newton, R. C., and Haselton, H. T., 1981, Thermodynamics of the garnet-plagioclase-Al_2SiO_5-quartz geobarometer, *in* Newton, R. C., Navrotsky, A., and Wood, B. J., eds., Thermodynamics of minerals and melts: New York, Springer-Verlag, p. 131–147.

Patel, R. C., Sandeep, S., Asokan, A., Manickavasagam, R. M., and Jain, A. K., 1993, Extensional tectonics in the Himalayan orogen Zanskar, NW India, *in* Treolar, P. J., and Searle, M. P., eds., Himalayan tectonics: Geological Society of London Special Publication 74, p. 445–459.

Pêcher, A., 1989, The metamorphism in the Central Himalaya: Journal of Metamorphic Geology, v. 7, p. 31–41.

Pêcher, A., and Scaillet, B., 1989, La structure du haut Himalaya au Garhwal (Indes): Eclogae Geologicael Helvetiae, v. 82, p. 655–668.

Pilgrim, G. E., and West, W. D., 1928, Structure and correlation of Simla Rocks: Geological Survey of India Memoirs, v. 53, 139 p.

Pognante, U., Castelli, D., Benna, P., Genovese, G., Oberli, F., Meier, M., and Tonarinz, S., 1990, The crystalline units of the High Himalayas in the Lahaul-Zanskar region (northwest India): Metamorphic tectonic history and geochronology of the collided and imbricated Indian plate: Geological Magazine, v. 127, p. 101–116.

Ramsay, J. G., and Huber, M. I., 1983, The techniques of modern structural geology—volume 1: Strain analysis: London, Academic Press, 307 p.

Sandhu, C. S., 1985, Deformation and Barrovian metamorphism of Kishtwar area—An example from Lower Himalayan terrain, India, *in* Gupta, V. J., ed., Geology of Western Himalaya (Contribution to Himalayan Geology, Volume 3): New Delhi, Hindustan Publishing Corporation, v. 3, p. 121–149.

Scholtz, C. H., 1980, shear heating and the state of stress on faults: Journal of Geophysical Research, v. 85, p. 6174–6184.

Searle, M. P., and Fryer, B. J., 1986, Garnet, tourmaline and muscovite-bearing leucogranites, gneisses and migmatites of the Higher Himalayas from Zanskar, Kulu, Lahoul and Kashmir, *in* Coward, M. P. and Ries, A. C., eds., Collision tectonics: Geological Society of London Special Publication 19, p. 185–201.

Searle, M. P., and Rex, A. J., 1989, Thermal model for the Zanskar Himalaya: Journal of Metamorphic Geology, v. 7, p. 127–134.

Searle, M. P., Waters, D. J., Rex, D. C., and Wilson, R. N., 1992, Pressure, temperature and time constraints on Himalayan metamorphism from eastern Kashmir and western Zanskar: Geological Society of London Journal, v. 149, p. 753–773.

Sharma, V. P., 1977, The stratigraphy and structure of parts of the Simla Himalaya: Geological Survey of India Memoirs, v. 106, P. 237–407.

Singh, S., 1993, Collision tectonics: Metamorphics and geochronological constraints from parts of Himachal Pradesh, northwest Himalaya [Ph.D. thesis]: Roorkee, India, University of Roorkee, 289 p.

Sinha-Roy, S., 1982, Himalayan Main Central thrust and its implications for Himalayan inverted metamorphism: Tectonophysics, v. 84, p. 197–224.

Spear, F. S., 1989, Petrologic determination of metamorphic pressure-temperature-time paths, *in* Spear, F. S., and Peacock, S. M., eds., Metamorphic pressure-temperature-time paths: American Geophysical Union Short Course in Geology, v. 7, p. 1–55.

Spear, F. S., Kohn, M., and Florence, F. P., 1991, A model for garnet and plagioclase growth in pelitic schists: Implications for thermobarometry and *P-T* path determinations: Journal of Metamorphic Petrology, v. 8, p. 683–696.

Srikantia, S. V., Ganesan, T. M., Rao, P. M., Sinha, P. K., and Tirkey, B., 1978, Geology of the Zanskar area, Ladakh Himalaya: Himalayan Geology, v. 8, p. 1009–1033.

Stäubli, A., 1989, Polyphase metamorphism and the development of the Main Central thrust: Journal of Metamorphic Geology, v. 7, p. 73–93.

St-Onge, M. R., 1987, zoned poikiloblastic garnets: *P-T* path and synmetamorphic uplift through 30 km of structural depth, Wopmay Orogen, Canada: Journal of Petrology, v. 28, p. 1–27.

Tewari, A. P., Gaur, R. K., and Ameta, S. S., 1978, A note on the geology of a part of Kinnaur District, Himachal Pradesh: Himalayan Geology, v. 8, p. 574–582.

Thakur, V. C., 1977, Divergent isograds of metamorphism in some parts of Higher Himalayan zone: Écologie et Géologie de l'Himalaya: Colloques internationaux du Centre National de la Recherche Scientifique, no. 268 p. 433–441.

Thakur, V. C., 1993, Geology of the western Himalaya: London, Pergamon Press, 355 p.

Thöni, M. 1977, Geology, structural evolution and metamorphic zoning in the Kulu valley (Himachal Himalayas, India) with special reference to the reversed metamorphism Mitteilungen der Gessellschaft der geologie und Bergbanstundentan in Oesterreichs, v. 24, p. 125–187.

Tracy, R. J., 1982, Compositional zoning and inclusions in minerals, *in* Ferry, J. M., ed., Characterization of metamorphism through mineral equilibria: Mineralogical Society of America Reviews in Mineralogy, v. 10, p. 355–397.

Tracy, R. J., Robinson, P., and Thompson, A. B., 1976, Garnet composition and zoning in the determination of temperature and pressure of metamorphism, central Massachusetts: American Mineralogist, v. 61, p. 762–775.

Treloar, P. J., and Rex, D. C., 1990, Cooling and uplift histories of the crystalline thrust stack of the Indian plate internal zones west of Nanga Parbat, Pakistan Himalaya: Tectonophysics, v. 180, p. 323–349.

Treloar, P. J., Broughton, R. D., Williams, M. P., Coward, M. P., and Windley, B. F., 1989a, Deformation, metamorphism and imbrication of the Indian plate, south of the Main Mantle thrust, north Pakistan: Journal of Metamorphic Geology, v. 7, p. 111–125.

Treloar, P. J., Coward, M. P., Williams, M. P., and Khan, M. A., 1989b, Basement-cover imbrication south of the Main Mantle thrust, north Pakistan, *in* Malinconico, L. L., and Lillie, R. J., eds., Tectonics of the Western Himalayas: Geological Society of America Special Paper 232, p. 137–152.

Valdiya, K. S., 1980a, The two intracrustal boundary thrust of the Himalaya: Tectonophysics, v. 66, p. 323–348.

Valdiya, K. S., 1980b, Geology of Kumaun Lesser Himalaya : Dehradun, Wadia Institute of Himalayan Geology, 289 p.

Valdiya, K. S., 1989, Trans-Himadri intracrustal fault and basement upwarps south of Indus-Tsangpo suture zone, *in* Malinconico, L. L., and Lillie, R. J., Tectonics of the Western Himalayas: Geological Society of America Special Paper 232, p. 153–168.

Vidal, P., Cocherie, A., and Le Fort, P., 1982, Geochemical investigations of the origin of the Manaslu leucogranite (Himalaya, Nepal): Geochimica et Cosmochimica Acta, v. 64, p. 2274–2292.

Vohra, C. P., Jangpangi, B. S., Mehrotra, P. C., Puri, V. M. K., Kaul, M. K., and Mehta, P., 1982, Geology of the Warwan-Nun Kun area, 'J & K state, *in* Himalayan Geology Seminar 1976, Section IB: Geology, Stratigraphy and Palaeontology: Geological Survey of India Miscellaneous Publication 41, p. 56–63.

Von Loczy, L., 1907, Beobachtungen in östlichen Himalaya (vom 8. bis 28. Febr., 1878): Földtani Közlony, v. 35, p. 1–24.

Windley, B. K., 1983, Metamorphism and tectonics of the Himalaya: Geological Society of London Journal, v. 140, p. 849–865.

Woodsworth, G. S., 1977, Homogenization of zoned garnets from pelitic schists: Canadian Mineralogist, v. 15, p. 230–242.

MANUSCRIPT ACCEPTED BY THE SOCIETY FEBRUARY 3, 1998

Geological Society of America
Special Paper 328
1999

High strain zone in the hanging wall of the Annapurna detachment, central Nepal Himalaya

Laurent Godin and Richard L. Brown
Department of Earth Sciences, Carleton University and Ottawa-Carleton Geoscience Centre, Ottawa, ON, Canada K1S 5B6

Simon Hanmer
Geological Survey of Canada, 601 Booth St., Ottawa, ON, Canada K1A 0E8

ABSTRACT

The Annapurna detachment is part of the orogen-parallel extensional South Tibetan detachment system, which extends along most of the length of the Himalaya. It crops out in the Kali Gandaki area of central Nepal, where it juxtaposes the Tethyan sedimentary sequence in the hanging wall with rocks of the Greater Himalayan metamorphic sequence in the footwall.

A five-stage structural evolution for the Tethyan sedimentary sequence is proposed. The first stage is characterized by southwest-verging isoclinal folds (D_1). The second stage is represented by northeast-verging megascopic tight folds (D_2). These first two stages are transposed in a 1,500-m-thick high strain zone (D_t) affecting the lowermost part of the Tethyan sedimentary sequence and the uppermost part of the Greater Himalayan metamorphic sequence. The high strain fabrics are associated with down-to-the-northeast normal shear-sense indicators, which we link to initial ductile shearing along the Annapurna detachment. The fourth stage is postmetamorphic and marks a return to southwest-vergent thrusting and folding (D_3). During this stage, parts of the high strain zone were reactivated as localized thrusts. The fifth stage is a brittle event associated with east-west extension along the Thakkhola graben structures. Late top-to-the-northeast brittle normal faults also disrupt rocks within the high strain zone during this stage and could mark the southern termination of the Thakkhola graben.

The D_2 northeast-verging folds, classically interpreted to be the result of gravitational sliding along the South Tibetan detachment system, clearly predate ductile extensional faulting. This folding phase, which thickened the Tethyan sedimentary sequence, is probably related to an older compressional event. The Annapurna detachment represents a zone of superposed shearing; both normal and thrust shear-sense indicators are preserved.

INTRODUCTION

The past decade has seen a considerable increase in the recognition of orogen-parallel normal fault systems in active high-elevation orogenic fronts and accompanying coeval thrusting at lower structural levels. The Cordillera Blanca in the Andes of Peru (Dalmayrac and Molnar, 1981) and the Himalayan range south of the Tibetan plateau (Caby et al., 1983; Burg and Chen,

1984; Burg et al., 1984; Burchfiel and Royden, 1985; Burchfiel et al., 1992; Brown and Nazarchuk, 1993) are among the more intensely studied areas that have extensional fault systems. In the Himalaya, down-to-the-northeast movement on detachment faults (the South Tibetan detachment system of Burchfiel et al., 1992) occurred in Miocene time, coeval with structurally lower southwest-vergent thrusting on the Main Central thrust (Hubbard, 1989; Hubbard and Harrison, 1989; Hodges et al., 1992). The

Godin, L., Brown, R. L., and Hanmer, S., 1999, High strain zone in the hanging wall of the Annapurna detachment, central Nepal Himalaya, *in* Macfarlane, A., Sorkhabi, R.B., and Quade, J., eds., Himalaya and Tibet: Mountain Roots to Mountain Tops: Boulder, Colorado, Geological Society of America Special Paper 328.

South Tibetan detachment system consists of a series of normal faults extending for at least 600 km along strike (Burchfiel and Royden, 1985), and regional correlations suggest that the system may be as long as 2,000 km (Burchfiel et al., 1992). This normal fault system is commonly localized at the contact between the Greater Himalayan metamorphic sequence and the Tethyan sedimentary sequence (Fig. 1).

The kinematic history of the South Tibetan detachment system varies considerably along its strike length. Although it is clear that the system represents a major structural break, its kinematic history is still poorly understood. Thrusting, normal faulting, and dextral shearing have all been proposed to explain field observations in certain localities along its contact (Pêcher, 1991; Burchfiel et al., 1992; Vannay and Steck, 1995); however, the relationships between these proposed deformation episodes have not been clearly assessed.

In this chapter, we present results of detailed mapping and structural fabric analyses from the upper Kali Gandaki valley in central Nepal. Our data show the presence of a 1,500-m-thick high strain zone located at the base of the Tethyan sedimentary sequence, characterized by an intense transposition fabric. We attribute this zone to normal-sense distributed ductile shearing associated with movement across the Annapurna detachment. Parts of this zone were later reactivated by southwest-vergent mesoscopic folding and related shearing, and the zone was subsequently locally affected by brittle normal faults.

GEOLOGICAL SETTING

The area investigated is in the Kali Gandaki valley of central Nepal (Fig. 1). From south to north, this valley transects three important tectonostratigraphic units of the central Himalaya: (1) the Lesser Himalayan sedimentary sequence, composed of Precambrian to Mesozoic low-grade metasediments; (2) the Greater Himalayan metamorphic sequence, composed of highly sheared kyanite- and sillimanite-grade gneisses intruded by variably deformed Miocene leucogranites; and (3) the Tethyan sedimentary sequence, a nearly continuous 10-km-thick early Paleozoic to early Tertiary sedimentary sequence representing the continental margin of the Tethys ocean (Bodenhausen and Egeler, 1971; Bordet et al., 1971; Colchen et al., 1981; Gradstein et al., 1992).

Two main tectonic boundaries have been identified in this valley by previous workers: (1) the Main Central thrust, which is a Miocene crustal-scale plastic-brittle shear zone that juxtaposes the Greater Himalayan metamorphic sequence southward over the Lesser Himalayan sedimentary sequence (Bouchez and Pêcher, 1976; Pêcher, 1977); and (2) the Annapurna detachment, which is defined as a plastic-brittle normal fault juxtaposing the Tethyan sedimentary sequence in the hanging wall with the Greater Himalayan metamorphic sequence in the footwall (Caby et al., 1983; Brown and Nazarchuk, 1993). The Annapurna detachment has been correlated by Brown and Nazarchuk (1993) with the South Tibetan detachment system described by Burchfiel et al.

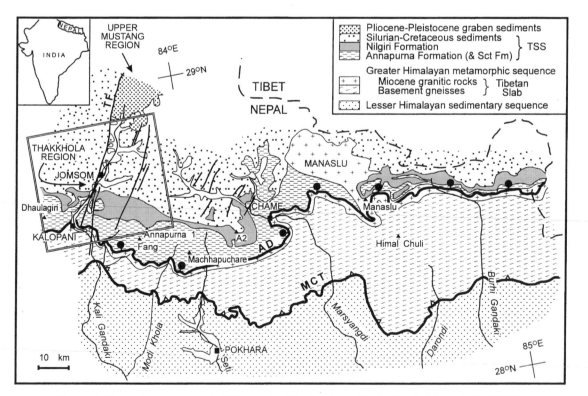

Figure 1. Geologic map of central Nepal, simplified and modified after Colchen et al. (1981): AD, Annapurna detachment; MCT, Main Central thrust; Sct Fm, Sanctuary Formation; TF, Thakkhola fault; TSS, Tethyan sedimentary sequence; box locates the study area.

(1992). Both the Main Central thrust and the Annapurna detachment are well exposed in the vicinity of the Kali Gandaki valley.

Some of the most spectacular structural features affecting the Tethyan sedimentary sequence of central Nepal are northeast-verging megascopic folds. In the Annapurna sector, these folds are well exposed, especially on the west face of the Nilgiris, where Ordovician limestones are folded in a kilometer-scale overturned antiform (Bordet et al., 1971). Most workers relate the formation of these folds to gravitational collapse and associate them with normal movement along the South Tibetan detachment system (Burchfiel et al., 1992, and references therein). However, it has been suggested that they could be the result of an older shortening event associated with crustal thickening (Brown and Nazarchuk, 1993). This study is part of an ongoing research program to further document the kinematic history of the Annapurna detachment and to focus on the kinematic and temporal relationships between these megascopic folds and detachment-related structures.

TETHYAN SEDIMENTARY SEQUENCE

A well-preserved Tethyan stratigraphy is superbly exposed in the Kali Gandaki valley. From Kalopani to Kagbeni, a nearly continuous 10-km-thick section is visible, ranging from Cambrian(?)-Ordovician calcareous schist of the Annapurna Formation to Early Cretaceous detrital sediments of the Chukh Group (Figs. 2, A and B, and 3).

The Paleozoic section is characterized by a calcareous series, mainly comprising massive limestone and calcareous shale and local dolomitic and quartzitic horizons. The lowest part of this section is the Annapurna Formation (also known as the Yellow Formation or the Larjung series), visible just north of Kalopani (Bordet et al., 1971; Colchen et al., 1981). Although there are no direct chronological data, this unit has been interpreted as Cambrian in age, because it is stratigraphically under the Ordovician Nilgiri Formation (Bordet et al., 1971). The Annapurna Formation is composed of calcareous biotite-grade psammitic and semipelitic schist and phyllite. The overlying Nilgiri Formation is composed of gray micritic limestone, grading upward into pink dolomitic sandstone, calcareous shale, and siltstone. The Ordovician series is capped by a 400-m-thick calcareous arkose and siltstone unit (the North face quartzite of Bodenhausen et al., 1964). The upper portion of the Paleozoic is composed of alternating gritty dolomite, black shale, and limestone of the Sombre Formation (Silurian-Devonian), correlative with the Dark Band Formation of the Dolpo area, northwest of the Thakkhola region (Fuchs, 1977). The Permian-Carboniferous units consist of a turbidite sequence dominated by calcareous shales with a minor siliciclastic contribution (Bordet et al., 1971).

The Mesozoic stratigraphy is essentially composed of Permian-Carboniferous calcareous shales (Thini and Thini Chu formations), grading upward to Jurassic fossiliferous limestones and black shales (Jomsom, Bagung, and Lupra formations), which are capped by the detrital units (conglomerates, sandstones) of the

Early Cretaceous Chuckh Group. Complete detailed descriptions of the Mesozoic stratigraphy were given in Gradstein et al. (1992) and complementary observations can be found in Bordet et al. (1971). Pliocene to Pleistocene red alluvial sandstone and conglomerate (molasse) of continental provenance fill the north-northeast–south-southwest–oriented Thakkhola graben, in the upper Kali Gandaki valley (Bordet et al., 1971).

Regional deformation

Four main deformational events have been recognized in the Tethyan sedimentary sequence. The first three events are dominated by folding of differing styles and vergence. Vergence reversals produced an intricate fold pattern, which is further complicated by late faulting associated with the Thakkhola graben.

The oldest structures (D_1) are represented by a schistosity (S_1) parallel to compositional layering defined by the preferred orientation of biotite and muscovite or by flattened detrital grains; locally, this schistosity is axial planar to rootless F_1 isoclinal fold closures. In some localities, a strong transposition of bedding planes is associated with this phase. Crustal-scale F_1 closures are visible near the summit of Fang in the Annapurna massif, where an isoclinal closure is folded in the D_2 Nilgiri structure (Colchen et al., 1981). This F_1 isoclinal nappe originated as a southwest-verging anticline (Colchen et al., 1986; Brown and Nazarchuk, 1993). This vergence is apparent after unfolding and rotating the overturned limb of the Nilgiri F_2 structure (Fig. 3). The complementary F_1 syncline has been cut out by the Annapurna detachment.

The D_2 phase forms the most noticeable structures in the Kali Gandaki. S_2 is a penetrative schistosity oblique to bedding. It is defined by the preferred orientation of biotite, muscovite, and elongate quartz grains in pelitic layers or by a spaced cleavage in more competent layers. Locally, a well-developed crenulation cleavage is preserved, coplanar with F_2 axial surfaces. F_2 folds are macroscopic to megascopic, tight to open, and verge to the northeast. They generally constitute structures parasitic to crustal-scale northeast-verging folds visible on the west face of the Nilgiris (Bordet et al., 1971). Macroscale examples of parasitic folds of the Nilgiri anticline include the Marpha anticline and the Jomsom syncline (Fig. 3). These structures are part of a major fold train that extends at least to the upper reaches of the Kali Gandaki in the upper Mustang–Lo Manthang area 50 km north of Kagbeni. They have also been observed in the upper Dolpo northwest of the Thakkhola region. Throughout the Kali Gandaki valley, the S_2 schistosity dips moderately to the southwest, but south of Khanti, it progressively rotates through the horizontal, then dips northeast, parallel to the Annapurna detachment.

D_3 structures are characterized throughout the valley by a postmetamorphic crenulation cleavage (S_3). This cleavage dips systematically to the northeast and is axial planar to microscopic to mesoscopic kink folds, which consistently verge to the southwest. Lower in the section, in the Annapurna Formation, D_3 is associated

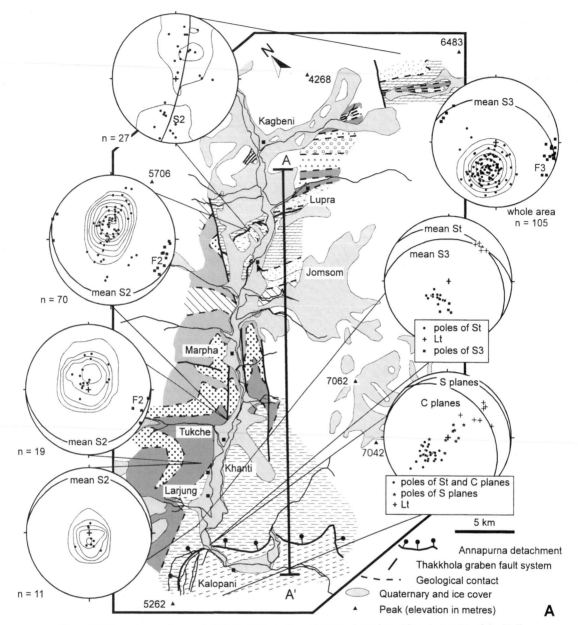

Figure 2 (this and opposite page). Detailed lithologic map (A) and stratigraphic column (B) of the Kali Gandaki valley. Stereonets show the regional orientation of structural features (equal-area, lower hemisphere stereographic plots). The S₂ progressively rotates into parallelism with the high strain zone fabric (St). Regionally, the S₃ remains constant and is superposed on the high strain zone and earlier fabrics. The Cretaceous Dzong unit and the Neogene Thakkhola Formation shown in the stratigraphic column crop out in the vicinity of the mapped area. The geology is adapted from Bordet et al. (1971) and Colchen et al. (1981); the stratigraphy is modified from Bodenhausen and Egeler (1971), Bordet et al. (1971), Colchen et al. (1981), and Gradstein et al. (1992). A-A′ locates the section line of Figure 3.

with boudinage of a suite of tourmaline-bearing quartz-feldspar dikes oriented subparallel to the axial surfaces of F₃ folds and to the S₃ cleavage (Fig. 4, A and B). In the area of Kalopani, D₃ is also associated with localized top-to-the-southwest shear zones. These shear zones are as thick as 10 m and are visible in both the lowermost part of the Tethyan sedimentary sequence and the uppermost part of the Greater Himalayan metamorphic sequence.

D₄ structures consist of brittle fractures and faults related to the Thakkhola graben, which strikes northeast-southwest. These structures typically are associated with calcite veins and fault breccias. The Dangardzong fault (Hagen, 1959; Bodenhausen and Egeler, 1971), also named the Thakkhola fault (Bordet et al., 1971), bounds the western extent of the graben and has ~4,000 m of vertical displace-

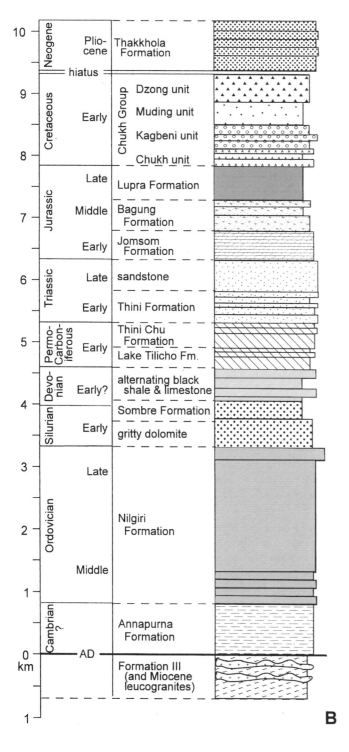

B

ment (Colchen et al., 1986). Hydrothermal muscovite extracted from a calcite vein crosscutting the Annapurna Formation and associated with the Thakkhola fault system yielded a $^{40}Ar/^{39}Ar$ age of ca. 14 Ma (Coleman and Hodges, 1995). Coleman and Hodges interpreted this as a minimum age for the onset of east-west extension within the Thakkhola fault system.

HIGH STRAIN ZONE AND THE ANNAPURNA DETACHMENT

The contact between the Annapurna Formation and the Greater Himalayan metamorphic sequence is visible in a stream gully just northwest of the village of Kalopani and corresponds to the Annapurna detachment (Fig. 2A). Gansser (1964) noted that although this contact appears conformable, it delineates a clear boundary between two domains of contrasting structural style. Many workers followed Gansser, and although some speculated or proposed a faulted contact (Bodenhausen and Egeler, 1971; Bordet et al., 1971; Caby et al., 1983; Colchen et al., 1986; Pêcher, 1991), the Annapurna detachment was not clearly documented until the 1990s (Brown and Nazarchuk, 1993). Our mapping and structural analysis reveal the presence of a 1,500-m-thick high strain zone localized in the lowermost part of the Tethyan sedimentary sequence and the uppermost part of the Greater Himalayan metamorphic sequence, which we link kinematically with normal-sense ductile shearing associated with the Annapurna detachment. This high strain zone straddles the Annapurna detachment and affects rocks from both the hanging wall and the footwall. The high strain zone affects the lowermost section of the Nilgiri Formation, the entire Annapurna Formation, and the uppermost 100 m of Formation III within the Greater Himalayan metamorphic sequence.

It has been shown in the previous section that the Tethyan sedimentary sequence has been affected by three phases of folding with contrasting vergence. North of Khanti, the angular relationships between S_1, S_2, and S_3 are well preserved. South of Khanti, the D_1 and D_2 structures are progressively rotated and transposed into near parallelism. Near Larjung, 1,500 m structurally above the base of the Tethyan sedimentary sequence, the primary stratigraphy and the D_1 and D_2 structures are completely transposed into a broad high strain zone, and only one penetrative fabric (S_t) having an associated down-dip mineral lineation (L_t) is generally preserved. Locally, clear crosscutting relationships are observed between S_2 and S_t, implying that the northeast-verging folds predate the penetrative fabric associated with the high strain zone.

Transposition fabrics

In the biotite calcareous schist and psammite of the Annapurna Formation, the high strain transposition fabric (S_t) is characterized by a continuous schistosity with a northwest strike and a 30° dip. There is an associated downdip mineral-elongation lineation outlined by biotite aggregates and muscovite blades. In thin section, the Annapurna Formation is highly schistose, quartz grains are strained and flattened, and the biotite-muscovite schistosity is continuous and pervasive (Fig. 5A). Locally, recrystallization of fine-grained quartz-calcite matrix has also produced incipient coarse-grained quartz ribbons associated with coarse-grained calcite (Fig. 5B). Post-transposition anneal-

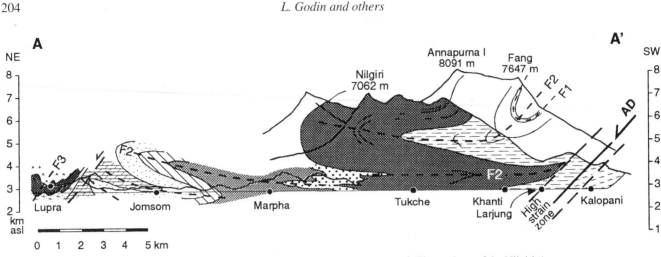

Figure 3. Northeast-southwest cross section from Lupra to Kalopani. The geology of the Nilgiri-Anna-purna-Fang mountains is adapted from Colchen et al. (1981): AD, Annapurna detachment.

ing, outlined by polygonal quartz grains and recrystallized cal-cite, is pervasive throughout this zone and has obliterated part of the transposition fabric.

In the area of Kalopani, rocks from the Greater Himalayan metamorphic sequence (Formation III) within the high strain zone are composed of laminated sillimanite-biotite-garnet pelitic schist, garnet-diopside-hornblende calc-silicate schist, and kyanite-silli-manite-bearing leucosomes, interlayered with garnet-tourmaline two-mica leucogranitic sheets as thick as 100 m. As in the Anna-purna Formation, these metasediments contain a penetrative fabric defined by a continuous biotite (± muscovite) schistosity as well as an associated downdip mineral-elongation lineation. This fabric can be followed through the upper part of the Greater Himalayan metamorphic sequence into the base of the Tethyan sedimentary sequence. On the basis of this continuity, we suggest that the pen-etrative fabric affecting the uppermost part of the Greater Himalayan metamorphic sequence is correlative with S_t observed in the lowermost part of the Tethyan sedimentary sequence.

The leucogranitic sheets found in the upper part of the Greater Himalayan metamorphic sequence are generally concor-dant to S_t. They locally have intrusive contacts with transposed layering and carry an internal fabric parallel to S_t in the sur-rounding metamorphic rocks. These leucogranitic sheets exhibit a wide range of deformation states. In some localities, leucogran-ites contain the penetrative S_t biotite-muscovite foliation, whereas in other places they are very weakly deformed, an incipient undu-lose foliation outlining coarse feldspar grains. Overall, the leucogranite sheets and associated dikes exhibit the behavior of synkinematic intrusions within the high strain zone associated with the Annapurna detachment.

Shear-sense indicators

Several mesoscale shear-sense indicators associated with the high strain zone are readily visible, especially near the contact between the Tethyan sedimentary sequence and the Greater Himalayan metamorphic sequence in the vicinity of Kalopani. Shear-sense indicators include systematic asymmetric isoclinal folds (Fig. 6, A and B), extensional shear bands (Fig. 6, C and D), and S-C fabrics, which consistently indicate down-to-the-northeast normal shearing across the high strain zone. Other shear-sense indicators include pegmatite dike arrays that have been extended or shortened according to their orientation with respect to the shear plane (Fig. 6, E and F).

Quartz crystallographic preferred orientations were measured in the hanging-wall rocks of the Annapurna Formation at three different localities. Quartz c-axis measurements were done on partly annealed quartz ribbons and on flattened quartz grains using thin sections cut perpendicular to the foliation and parallel to the lineation (XZ plane of the finite ellipsoid of deformation). Annealing was important in these thin sections and may have diluted the petrofabric, producing a relatively diffuse asymmetric pattern. Nevertheless, the petrofabric measurements reveal asym-metric quartz c-axis fabrics compatible with normal top-to-the-northeast shearing (Fig. 7). This suggests that the last increments of finite strain recorded by the quartz petrofabrics in the Anna-purna Formation before the annealing phase reflect the same kinematic framework as the mesoscale shear-sense indicators visible in the immediate footwall, as well as the D_2 transposition in the hanging wall.

The transposition resulting from shearing along the Anna-purna detachment is also visible at the crustal scale. The regional S_2 and the axial surface traces of the F_2 folds show a conspicuous rotation approaching the high strain zone. This is readily observed in the cross section and stereonets (Figs. 2, A and B, and 3). The sense of curvature of both foliations and of F_2 axial surface traces is compatible with top-to-the-northeast sense of shear. These data indicate that the distributed ductile shearing within the high strain zone is late- to post-D_2.

Quartz-feldspar-tourmaline pegmatite veins intruding the Annapurna Formation make a systematic 15°–20° clockwise angle with the S_t foliation. These veins are interpreted as having

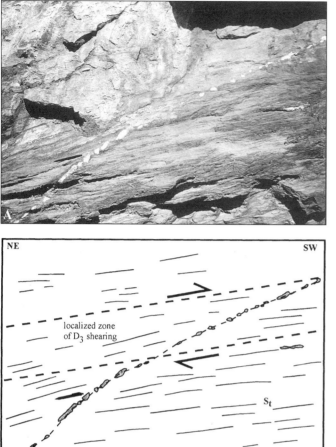

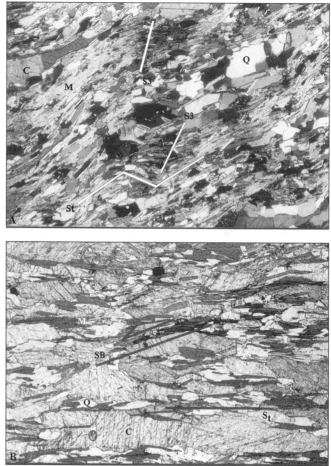

Figure 4. Outcrop photo (A) and line drawing (B) of the Annapurna Formation displaying localized thrust reactivation of the high strain zone; the extended (boudinaged) dike, in which the line connecting the centers of the boudins rotates toward the flow plane, is compatible with top-to-the-southwest thrust motion (Hanmer and Passchier, 1991). S_t is indicated. View is to the southeast. Pen in lower left is for scale.

Figure 5. Microstructures of the Annapurna Formation within the high strain zone, as observed in vertical plane with view to the southeast. A: Partly annealed quartz ribbons used to measure crystallographic preferred orientations, affected by a late postmetamorphic southwest-verging D_3 kink. B: Normal-sense extensional shear band and calcite "ribbon" texture. Crossed-polars, field of view is 0.5 cm: C, calcite; M, micas (muscovite and/or biotite); Q, quartz; SB, extensional shear band. St is indicated.

been injected along tension fractures, perpendicular to the main extensional direction. Accordingly, the systematic obliquity of this vein array is compatible with the other normal top-to-the-northeast shear-sense indicators.

Thermal overprinting of the high strain zone

Metamorphic assemblages at the base of the Tethyan sedimentary sequence typically contain biotite + muscovite ± albite ± tremolite ± chlorite, which are indicative of upper greenschist facies metamorphism. The biotite-in isograd occurs 1,500 m structurally above the Annapurna detachment, coinciding with the upper boundary of the high strain zone. This assemblage overgrows part of the high strain zone fabric, as evidenced by the coarsening of micas and quartz and by the presence of polygonal strain-free quartz grains, but is clearly deformed by postmetamorphic southwest-verging D_3 kinks (Fig. 5A).

Recent studies of the Tethyan sedimentary sequence of central Nepal have locally established a metamorphic gradient. The highest metamorphic temperatures are attained at the deepest structural level in the Cambrian limestones (Garzanti et al., 1994; Schneider and Masch, 1993). In the Marsyangdi valley 60 km east of the Kali Gandaki, Schneider and Masch (1993) estimated temperatures to 530 °C (±30) at the deepest structural level near the detachment fault in the Nilgiri Formation, as calculated by calcite-dolomite solvus geothermometry. They also showed a constant decrease in temperature toward structurally higher levels, as low as 350–390 °C in the Devonian strata. Similarly, in the Kali Gandaki valley, illite and chlorite crystallinity, vitrinite reflectance, and conodont color alteration index studies indicate average temperatures of 380 °C within the Upper Devonian pelites (Garzanti et al., 1994).

The generation of leucogranites in the footwall of the detachment appears to be coeval with shearing in the high

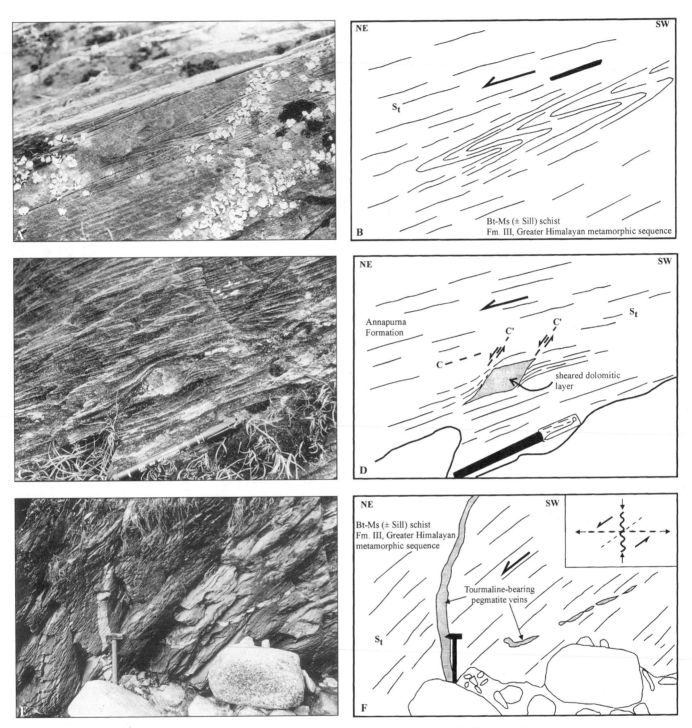

Figure 6. Shear-sense indicators associated with the high strain zone. A, B: Photo and line drawing of asymmetric isoclinal folds within biotite-muscovite (± sillimanite) schist of the Greater Himalayan metamorphic sequence (Fm III), pen is for scale. C, D: Photo and line drawing of extensional shear bands affecting a dolomitic horizon within the Annapurna Formation; pen is for scale. E, F: Photo and line drawing of extended and shortened pegmatite dikes in the Greater Himalayan metamorphic sequence (Fm III); hammer is for scale. Orientation with respect to the shear plane indicates top-to-the-northeast normal shearing. Their systematic orientation and behavior throughout the outcrop area precludes progressive pure shear. S_t is indicated. Views for all photographs are to the southeast.

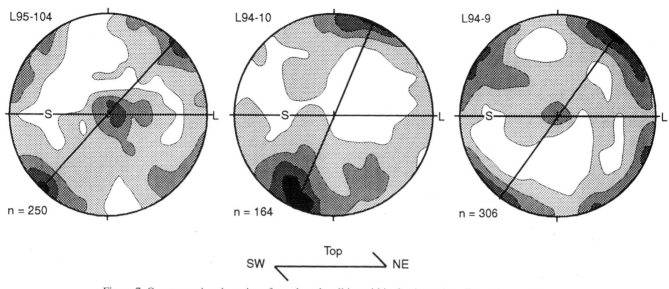

Figure 7. Quartz *c*-axis orientations from three localities within the Annapurna Formation; point maxima define asymmetry (Law, 1990). S marks the trace of the high strain zone fabric (S_t) and L is the mineral-elongation lineation (L_t). These sections correspond to the XZ plane of the finite ellipsoid of deformation. Contours represent 4%, 6%, 8%, and 10% of total data.

strain zone, and therefore synextensional. Although the leucogranitic sheets and associated leucosomes have not been dated in the area of Kalopani, a similar deformed leucosome within the calc-silicate gneiss of the Greater Himalayan metamorphic sequence, about 1.5 km structurally below the Annapurna detachment, has an interpreted crystallization age of 22.5 ± 0.1 Ma (Nazarchuk, 1993). This age, along with regional data on the crystallization age of other leucogranitic bodies (Schärer et al., 1986; Deniel et al., 1987; Hodges et al., 1992), suggests that the leucosomes and leucogranitic sheets in the area of Kalopani are Miocene in age. The presence of leucogranites, kyanite-sillimanite leucosomes, and sillimanite-bearing pelites within the immediate footwall reflects melt conditions above 650° C within the Greater Himalayan metamorphic sequence. The heat from the Greater Himalayan metamorphic sequence could have been in part responsible for rheological weakening of the immediate hanging-wall rocks and localization of the high strain zone. This heating event outlasted ductile normal faulting on the high strain zone, as evidenced by annealing, followed by cooling prior to development of D_3 and associated thrusting.

High strain zone reactivation

Several lines of evidence indicate that the high strain zone was affected by subsequent localized southwest-verging deformation, which we attribute to the D_3 event. It is clear that the S_3 spaced cleavage observed higher in the section is superimposed on the high strain zone within the Tethyan sedimentary sequence and is not affected by the rotational component that reoriented S_1 and S_2. Furthermore, top-to-the-southwest shear-sense indicators,

including oblique boudinaged calcite veins (Fig. 4, A and B), are locally associated with systematic southwest-verging D_3 kinks.

Late discrete brittle fault zones as thick as 3 m within the leucogranitic sheets cut S_t. The faults trend parallel to the main S_t foliation (320/40NE) and show normal sense of movement. The magnitude of displacement on these faults cannot be determined because they are confined to leucogranitic sheets and do not cut across stratigraphy. Their brittle nature and their crosscutting relationship with all penetrative fabrics indicate that they are post-D_3. The link between these late brittle orogen-parallel faults and the orogen-perpendicular Thakkhola graben structures remains unclear, although geographically, the graben faults do not extend south of the leucogranitic sheets. It is possible that these orogen-parallel discrete brittle fault zones represent the southern termination of the Thakkhola graben system.

DISCUSSION

Figure 8 summarizes the structural evolution of the Tethyan sedimentary sequence in the Kali Gandaki area. The transposition zone of the Annapurna detachment, characterized by a penetrative biotite-muscovite foliation (S_t) and associated downdip mineral-elongation lineation, is present in both the uppermost part of the Greater Himalayan metamorphic sequence and the lowermost units of the Tethyan sedimentary sequence. This high strain zone is more than 1,500 m thick, is associated with normal top-to-the-northeast shear-sense indicators, and is therefore an extensional shear zone. It separates two domains of contrasting structural style, distinguished by the presence of northeast-verging folds within the Tethyan sedimentary sequence which have no equivalent in the Greater Himalayan metamorphic sequence.

208   L. Godin and others

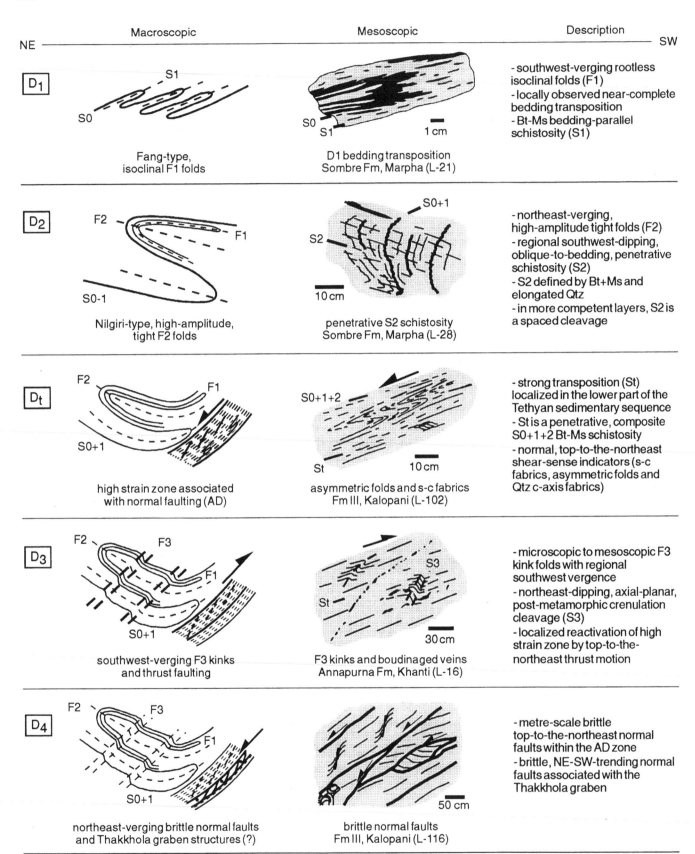

Figure 8. Structural evolution of the Tethyan sedimentary sequence in the Kali Gandaki valley.

It is clear from our study that the reorientation of both S_2 and the axial surface traces of northeast-verging F_2 folds in the high strain zone is compatible with normal faulting. Furthermore, these data indicate that the ductile shearing is late- or even post-D_2. Subsequent southwest-verging D_3 thrust motion was superimposed on the high strain zone. From their synkinematic nature, the leucogranite sheets appear to have been intruded during ductile normal faulting (D_t) along the Annapurna detachment.

The Annapurna detachment extends east into the Annapurna Sanctuary as the Deurali detachment (Hodges et al., 1995), and farther east in the Marsyangdi valley as the Chame detachment (Coleman, 1994). Due to the difficult access within the Annapurna Sanctuary, the hanging-wall rocks of the Deurali detachment have not been studied in detail, and a high strain zone has not been recognized there. In the Marsyangdi valley, extensional deformation is localized in two mylonite zones and one brittle normal fault zone, which step structurally higher with time (Coleman, 1994). The relatively thick high strain zone in the Kali Gandaki is thus distinct in character compared to its lateral equivalents. This might suggest that the deformation was distributed through a wider zone, compared to the narrower mylonitic zones of the Marsyangdi.

Although direct age constraints on the Annapurna detachment are not available for the Kali Gandaki area, it is possible to speculate on its history on the basis of regional correlations. In the Marsyangdi valley, the Chame detachment juxtaposes the same units as in the Kali Gandaki valley along a west-directed normal-sense shear zone (Coleman, 1994). At the top of the Greater Himalayan metamorphic sequence, two deformed leucogranitic dikes intruding a 35 Ma granite (Parrish and Hodges, 1993) yielded reversely discordant monazite ages between 24 and 34 Ma (Coleman, 1995). Coleman interpreted the 34 Ma age as inheritance from the 35 Ma granite and the 24 Ma age as a maximum age for the ductile movement along the Chame detachment. Farther to the east in the Dudh Khola, near Manaslu, two undeformed leucogranites yielded monazite and zircon ages of 18–19 Ma (Coleman, 1995). Furthermore, muscovite extracted from the mylonitic foliation of the Chame detachment yielded a $^{40}Ar/^{39}Ar$ plateau age of ca. 17 Ma (Coleman and Hodges, 1995). In the Marsyangdi valley it is thus possible to envisage ductile normal-sense shearing occurring between 19 and 24 Ma and cooling through the Ar closure temperature of muscovite (~350° C) at ca. 17 Ma.

An important question remains. What is the origin of the northeast-verging D_2 folds? Burchfiel et al. (1992, and references therein) have suggested that they are the result of a continuous, progressive extensional deformation event. However, the northern extent of these folds would necessitate a regional-scale decrease in dip and northern continuation of the detachment, requiring a mechanism capable of producing a crustal-scale asymmetric fold train on an extensive "flat." Furthermore, the Tethyan sedimentary sequence has clearly been thickened and shortened by the D_2 folds, rather than thinned and extended. These observations suggest that the D_2 folds were produced during a compressional event, subsequently overprinted by the extensional Annapurna detachment. Further work is required to clarify their origin.

CONCLUSIONS

1. In the Kali Gandaki area, the immediate hanging wall of the Annapurna detachment is characterized by a 1500-m-thick extensional shear zone (D_t).

2. This high strain zone transposes southwest-verging D_1 phase structures, which are defined by rootless isoclinal folds that have associated foliation parallel to compositional layering, and D_2 phase structures, characterized by spectacular northeast-verging megascopic folds and regional southwest-dipping axial planar schistosity.

3. Greenschist facies thermal overprinting outlasted D_t and resulted in partly annealed extensional fabrics.

4. Reactivation of the high strain zone occurred during the southwest-verging, postmetamorphic D_3 phase of deformation, which is associated with kink folds, regionally northeast-dipping crenulation cleavages, and localized top-to-the-southwest shear zones.

5. Late brittle top-to-the-northeast normal faults (D_4) affecting the high strain zone and the Annapurna detachment could be coeval with the Thakkhola graben faults and, as such, may represent the southern termination of the graben system.

ACKNOWLEDGMENTS

We thank Pasang Tamang, Pemba Tamang, Komar Tamang, and Chamare Tamang and members of the Sherpa Society for their friendly and dedicated assistance. Field work was made easy and pleasant due to the assistance of Annick Chouinard. B. N. Upreti (Tribhuvan University) and Ashok Kumar Duvadi (Department of Mines and Geology of Nepal) are thanked for their assistance. Lengthy discussions with J. Harvey were greatly appreciated. The final draft of this paper has benefited from constructive reviews by G. J. Axen, M. Coleman, and A. M. Macfarlane. We are indebted to L. Hardy for assistance in manuscript preparation and production of figures. Godin benefited from a graduate scholarship from the Natural Sciences and Engineering Research Council of Canada. This research has been funded by Research Grants OGPIN008 and OGP0001897 from the Natural Sciences and Engineering Research Council of Canada to Brown and Hanmer, respectively.

REFERENCES CITED

Bodenhausen, J. W. A., and Egeler, C. G., 1971, On the geology of the upper Kali Gandaki valley, Nepalese Himalayas, I: Akademic van Wetenschappen Proceedings, v. 74, p. 526–538.

Bodenhausen, J. W. A., de Booy, T., Egeler, C. G., and Nijhuis, H. J., 1964, On the geology of central west Nepal: A preliminary note: International Geological Congress, Report of the twenty-second session, India, part XI, 101 p.

Bordet, P., Colchen, M., Krummenacher, D., Le Fort, P., Mouterde, R., and Remy, M., 1971, Recherches géologiques dans l'Himalaya du Népal: région de la Thakkhola: Paris, France, Éditions du Centre National de la Recherche Scientifique, 279 p.

Bouchez, J.-L., and Pêcher, A., 1976, Plasticité du quartz et sens de cisaillement dans les quartzites du Grand Chevauchement Central Himalayen: Bulletin de la Société Géologique de France, v. 18, p. 1377–1385.

Brown, R. L., and Nazarchuk, J. H., 1993, Annapurna detachment fault in the Greater Himalaya of central Nepal, in Treloar, P. J., and Searle, M. P., eds., Himalayan tectonics: Geological Society of London Special Publication 74, p. 461–473.

Burchfiel, B. C., and Royden, L. H., 1985, North-south extension within the convergent Himalayan region: Geology, v. 13, p. 679–682.

Burchfiel, B. C., Chen Zhiliang, Hodges, K. V., Liu Yuping, Royden, L. H., Deng Changrong, and Xu Jiene, 1992, The South Tibetan detachment system, Himalaya orogen: Extension contemporaneous with and parallel to shortening in a collisional mountain belt: Geological Society of America Special Paper 269, 41 p.

Burg, J.-P., and Chen, G. M., 1984, Tectonics and structural zonation of southern Tibet, China: Nature, v. 311, p. 219–223.

Burg, J. P., Brunel, M., Gapais, D., Chen, G. M., and Liu, G. H., 1984, Deformation of leucogranites of the crystalline Main Central Sheet in southern Tibet (China): Journal of Structural Geology, v. 6, p. 535–542.

Caby, R., Pêcher, A., and Le Fort, P., 1983, Le grand chevauchement central himalayen: nouvelles données sur le métamorphisme inverse à la base de la Dalle du Tibet: Revue de Géologie Dynamique et de Géographie Physique, v. 24, p. 89–100.

Colchen, M., Le Fort, P., and Pêcher, A., 1981, Geological map of Annapurnas-Manaslu-Ganesh Himalaya of Nepal, in Gupta, H. K., and Delany, F. M., eds., Zagros-Hindu Kush-Himalaya geodynamic evolution: Washington, D.C., American Geophysical Union, scale 1:200,000.

Colchen, M., Le Fort, P., and Pêcher, A., 1986, Recherches géologiques dans l'Himalaya du Népal: Annapurna-Manaslu-Ganesh Himal: Paris, Éditions du Centre National de la Recherche Scientifique, 136 p.

Coleman, M. E., 1994, West-directed extensional deformation in the north Marsyangdi River region, west-central Nepal Himalaya: Nepal Geological Society Journal, v. 10, p. 24–25.

Coleman, M. E., 1995, Constraints on Miocene high-temperature deformation and anatexis within the Greater Himalaya from U-Pb geochronology [abs.]: Eos (Transactions, American Geophysical Union), v. 76, p. 708.

Coleman, M. E., and Hodges, K., 1995, Evidence for Tibetan plateau uplift before 14 Myr ago from a new minimum age for east-west extension: Nature, v. 374, p. 49–52.

Dalmayrac, B., and Molnar, P., 1981, Parallel thrust and normal faulting in Peru and constraints on the state of stress: Earth and Planetary Science Letters, v. 55, p. 473–481.

Deniel, C., Vidal, P., Fernandez, A., Le Fort, P., and Peucat, J. J., 1987, Isotopic study of the Manaslu granite (Himalaya, Nepal): Inferences on the age and source of Himalayan leucogranites: Contributions to Mineralogy and Petrology, v. 96, p. 78–92.

Fuchs, G., 1977, The geology of the Karnali and Dolpo regions, western Nepal: Jahrbuch der Geologischen Bundesanstalt, Wien, v. 120, p. 165–217.

Gansser, A., 1964, Geology of the Himalayas: London, John Wiley and Sons, 289 p.

Garzanti, E., Gorza, M., Martellini, L., and Nicora, A., 1994, Transition from diagenesis to metamorphism in the Paleozoic to Mesozoic succession of the Dolpo-Manang Synclinorium and Thakkhola graben (Nepal Tethys Himalaya): Eclogae Geologicae Helveticae, v. 87, p. 613–632.

Gradstein, F. M., von Rad, U., Gibling, M. R., Jansa, L. F., Kaminski, M. A., Kristiansen, I.-L., Ogg, J. G., Rohl, U., Sarti, M., Thorow, J. W., Westermann, G. E. G., and Wiedmann, J., 1992, The Mesozoic continental margin of central Nepal: Geologisches Jahrbuch, v. 77, p. 3–141.

Hagen, T., 1959, Geologie des Thakkhola (Nepal): Eclogae Geologicae Helveticae, v. 52, p. 709–720.

Hanmer, S., and Passchier, C., 1991, Shear-sense indicators: A review: Geological Survey of Canada Paper 90-17, 72 p.

Hodges, K. V., Parrish, R. R., Housh, T. B., Lux, D. R., Burchfiel, B. C., Royden, L. H., and Chen, Z., 1992, Simultaneous Miocene extension and shortening in the Himalayan orogen: Science, v. 258, p. 1466–1470.

Hodges, K. V., Parrish, R. R., and Searle, M. P., 1995, Structural evolution of the Annapurna Sanctuary region, central Nepal [abs.], in Spencer, D. A., Burg, J.-P., and Spencer-Cervato, C., eds., 10th Himalaya-Karakoram-Tibet Workshop Abstract volume: ETH-Zürich, Switzerland, p. 89-90.

Hubbard, M. S., 1989, Thermobarometric constraints on the thermal history of the Main Central Thrust Zone and the Tibetan Slab, eastern Nepal Himalaya: Journal of Metamorphic Geology, v. 7, p. 19–30.

Hubbard, M. S., and Harrison, T. M., 1989, $^{40}Ar/^{39}Ar$ age constraints on deformation and metamorphism in the Main Central Thrust Zone and Tibetan Slab, eastern Nepal Himalaya: Tectonics, v. 8, p. 865–880.

Law, R. D., 1990, Crystallographic fabrics: A selective review of their application to research in structural geology, in Knipe, R. J., and Rutter, E. H., eds., Deformation mechanisms, rheology and tectonics: Geological Society of London Special Publication 54, p. 335–352.

Nazarchuk, J. H., 1993, Structure and geochronology of the Greater Himalaya, Kali Gandaki region, west-central Nepal [Master's thesis]: Ottawa, Carleton University, 157 p.

Parrish, R. R., and Hodges, K. V., 1993, Miocene (22 ± 1 Ma) metamorphism and two-stage thrusting in the Greater Himalaya sequence, Annapurna Sanctuary, Nepal: Geological Society of America Abstracts with Programs, v. 25, no. 6, p. A174.

Pêcher, A., 1977, Geology of the Nepal Himalaya: Deformation and petrography in the Main Central Thrust zone: in Himalaya-Sciences de la Terre, Colloques Internationaux du Centre National de la Recherche Scientifique no. 268, p. 301–318.

Pêcher, A., 1991, The contact between the Higher Himalaya crystallines and the Tibetan sedimentary series: Miocene large-scale dextral shearing: Tectonics, v. 10, p. 587–598.

Schärer, U., Xu, R.-H., and Allègre, C. J., 1986, U-(Th)-Pb systematics and ages of Himalayan leucogranites, South Tibet: Earth and Planetary Science Letters, v. 77, p. 35–48.

Schneider, C., and Masch, L., 1993, The metamorphism of the Tibetan Series from the Manang area, Marsyandi valley, central Nepal, in Treloar, P. J., and Searle, M. P., eds., Himalayan tectonics: Geological Society of London Special Publication 74, p. 357–374.

Vannay, J.-C., and Steck, A., 1995, Tectonic evolution of the High Himalaya in Upper Lahul (NW Himalaya, India): Tectonics, v. 14, p. 253–263.

MANUSCRIPT ACCEPTED BY THE SOCIETY FEBRUARY 3, 1998

Geological Society of America
Special Paper 328
1999

Extensional tectonics in the higher Himalayan crystallines of Khumbu Himal, eastern Nepal

R. Carosi, G. Musumeci, and P. C. Pertusati
Dipartimento di Scienze della Terra, via S. Maria 53, Pisa 56126, Italy

ABSTRACT

Two systems of folds that affect the high-grade schistosity have been recognized in the Higher Himalayan Crystallines of the Khumbu Himal: a northwest-southeast– to east-west–trending system (F2a) and a transversal northeast-southwest–trending system (F2b), causing kilometer-scale upright antiforms and synforms. The limbs of these upright folds are affected by F3 collapse folds that have shallowly dipping axial planes and scattered vergences.

Mesoscopic, in places megascopic, reverse and recumbent F3 folds, subhorizontal boudinage in two directions, buckling of leucogranite dikes, and southward- and southeastward extensional shear zones, affecting leucogranite dikes as well as host rocks, indicate the presence of predominantly extensional tectonics in the Higher Himalayan Crystallines in the Khumbu region.

Extension accompanied anatexis and leucogranite emplacement in the Higher Himalayan Crystallines. This deformation is considered to have been linked with upper crustal extension affecting the boundary between the crystallines and the Tibetan allochthon along the South Tibetan detachment system. Extensional deformation was partitioned: mainly coaxial deformation predominated in the upper part of the Higher Himalayan Crystallines, whereas noncoaxial strain concentrated in the South Tibetan detachment system.

INTRODUCTION

The discovery of extensional tectonics contemporaneous with compression in collisional mountain belts has given new insights and has greatly improved our understanding of ancient and modern mountain belts in the past 15 years. The South Tibetan detachment system; (Burg et al., 1984; Burchfiel et al., 1992) is one of the major extensional structures in the Alpine-Himalayan belt, and separates the high-grade metamorphic rocks of the Higher Himalayan Crystallines from the overlying low-grade Tibetan Sedimentary Sequence. The attention of researchers has been focused mainly on this first-order extensional structure and on the consequences for the evolution of the chain (Burchfiel et al., 1992; Hodges et al., 1993).

The purpose of this chapter is to document the presence of 5–6

km extensional structures into the footwall of the South Tibetan detachment system, i.e., inside the middle-upper part of the Higher Himalayan Crystallines, and to assess the influence of the previous compressional structures on the development of the extensional ones. Field work was conducted in eastern Nepal (Fig. 1) along the following transects: Dudh Kosi from Lukla to the south face of Cho-Oyu, and Imja Kola from the Porthse to the south face of Lhotse and Khumbu valley (Khumbu Himal) (Fig. 2). In the investigated area, the Lesser Himalayan and the Higher Himalayan Crystallines, the base of the Tibetan Sedimentary Sequence, and Miocene leucogranite intrusions crop out.

Our research focused on the examination of late tectonic structures and their relationship to Miocene intrusions, which crop out in a zone extending from Makalu in the east to the Ngozupma valley in the west and are bounded by the South

Carosi, R., Musumeci, G., and Pertusati, P. C., 1999, Extensional tectonics in the higher Himalayan crystallines of Khumbu Himal, eastern Nepal, *in* Macfarlane, A., Sorkhabi, R. B., and Quade, J., eds., Himalaya and Tibet: Mountain Roots to Mountain Tops: Boulder, Colorado, Geological Society of America Special Paper 328.

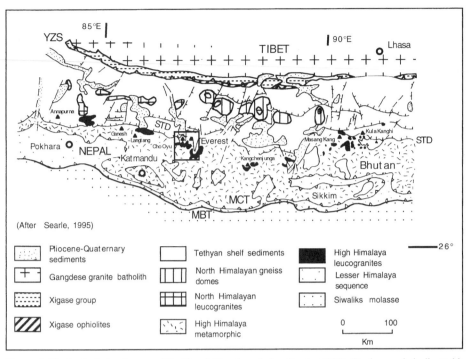

Figure 1. Geological sketch map of the Nepal Himalaya (after Searle, 1995). Study area is indicated by box. STD is South Tibetan detachment; MCT is Main Central thrust; MBT is Main Boundary thrust; YZS is Yarlung-Zangpo suture zone.

Tibetan detachment system to the north and by the Main Central thrust to the south (Fig. 2).

GEOLOGICAL SETTING

North of the Main Central thrust the high peaks of the Higher Himalayan Crystallines are made up of a high-grade metamorphic sequence (Tibetan slab of Bordet, 1961) that is overlain by the Tibetan Sedimentary Sequence (Figs. 3 and 4). Miocene leucogranitic plutons and dike or sill networks are emplaced in the upper part of the Higher Himalayan Crystallines close to the boundary between the metamorphic and sedimentary sequences; the boundary is marked by the north-dipping, low-angle normal fault (Burg et al., 1984), that crosscuts the top of Mt. Everest (Academia Sinica, 1979).

The Higher Himalayan Crystallines are a gneiss sequence nearly 10 km thick (Fig. 4); at the base (Fig. 3) an upper amphibolite facies gneiss (Barun Gneiss; Bordet, 1961), is associated with large bodies of granitic orthogneiss (Namche Migmatite Orthogneiss; Bordet, 1961), which are derived from early Paleozoic granite, possibly of Cambrian age (Kai, 1981; Ferrara et al., 1983). In the study area, the thickness of migmatite orthogneiss decreases from the Dudh Kosi valley in the west toward the Barun valley in the east, where it constitutes a sheet of a few hundred meters thick.

The upper part of the crystallines host a dike network and lens-shaped subconcordant bodies of Miocene leucogranite, and consists of: (1) biotite- and sillimanite-bearing paragneiss

and micaschist at the base (Black Gneiss; Bordet, 1961), (2) biotite and muscovite gneiss, and local cordierite and fibrolite (Rongbuk Formation; Yin and Kuo, 1978), at the top of the sequence (Figs. 3 and 4). The Black Gneiss is derived from a sedimentary sequence with conglomerate and quartzite layers that could represent the sedimentary cover of the underlying Namche Migmatite Orthogneiss (Bortolami et al., 1976).

An extensional ductile fault belonging to the South Tibetan detachment system separates the metamorphic rocks from the overlying low-grade Tibetan Sedimentary Sequence of the North Col Formation (Lombardo et al., 1993). This sequence is made up of biotite-chlorite phyllite, biotite-calcite metagraywacke, and impure quartzite with some crystalline limestone layers (Yellow Band). The North Col Formation is transformed by contact metamorphism to banded biotite-epidote hornfels and calc-silicate rocks. The age of this formation is inferred to be Cambrian-Sinian by analogy with other formations that crop out at the top of the Higher Himalayan Crystallines (Yin and Kuo, 1978).

The North Col Formation is overlain by limestone and crystalline limestone belonging to the Mt. Jolmo Lungma Formation of Ordovician (possibly Arenig-Llanvirn) age, overlain by Silurian and Devonian silty marly sediments. The contact between the North Col Formation and the overlying limestone is apparently stratigraphic near Mt. Everest. Northward, however, the Yellow Band is absent in most outcrops. This omission is due to a tectonic contact by a north-dipping low-angle normal fault (Burg et al., 1984).

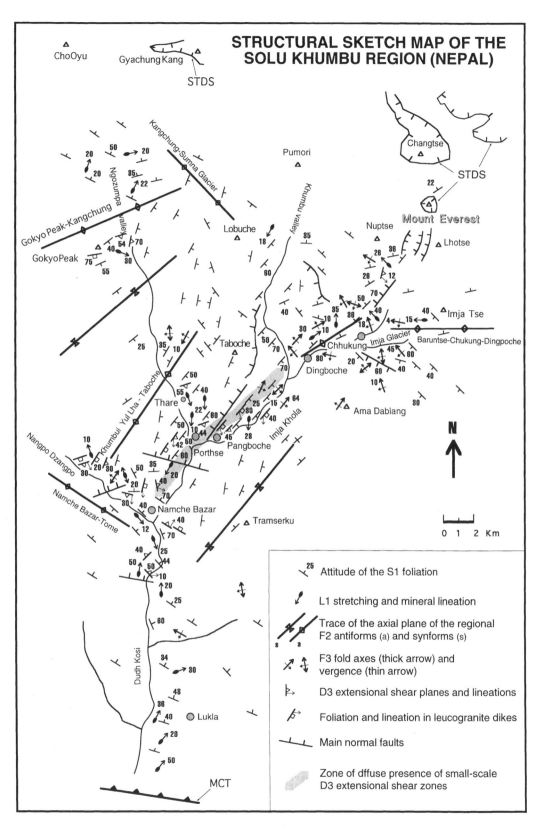

Figure 2. Structural sketch map of the Solu Khumbu region (eastern Nepal). MCT is Main Central thrust; STDS is South Tibetan detachment system.

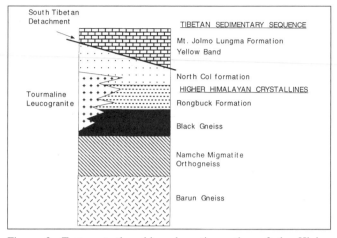

Figure 3. Tectonostratigraphic schematic section of the Higher Himalayan Crystallines and lower part of the Tibetan Sedimentary Sequence. Not to scale.

METAMORPHIC EVOLUTION

In the Everest area, the Higher Himalayan Crystallines are affected by amphibolite facies metamorphism. The metamorphic grade increases upward toward the middle-upper portion of the section and then decreases in the uppermost portion. A polyphase metamorphic evolution, marked by two main metamorphic events, has been recognized (Brunel and Kienast, 1986; Pognante and Benna, 1993). An early Barrovian event of relatively high pressure (6–10 kbar) developed during the subduction-collision stage. The kyanite- and biotite-bearing parageneses belonging to this event are well preserved at the base of crystallines in the lower portion of the Barun Gneiss, and in the Rongbuck Formation (Pognante and Benna, 1993). This event was followed by nearly isothermal decompression responsible for the late high-temperature event, which

occurred at lower pressure (4-7 kbar) during Oligocene-Miocene exhumation (Pognante, 1993). Formation of garnet-sillimanite-biotite and cordierite assemblages, associated with migmatization and formation of anatectic leucosomes as well as leucogranitic melts, occurred during the second event. Furthermore, anatexis and leucogranite melt production continued during a third retrograde event, developed at lower pressure (2–4 kbar; Pognante and Benna, 1993).

In the study area, the metamorphic rocks are widely characterized by sillimanite-garnet-biotite ± cordierite assemblages, joined with diffuse leucosomes, which are in the Barun Gneiss and Namche Migmatite Orthogneiss along the lower Dudh Kosi valley and Imja Khola valley (Tonarini et al., 1994). These parageneses are indicative of extensive development of high-temperature metamorphism in this area, during the exhumation of the chain, following the earlier Barrovian event. Relict kyanite enclosed within plagioclase and biotite are found only in the Barun Gneiss south of Lukla village, close to the Main Central thrust, as also reported by Brunel (1983) and Brunel and Kienast (1986). Furthermore, the recognized cordierite and fibrolitic sillimanite south of the Cho Oyu massif, in the uppermost portion of the sequence, might be related to the lower pressure retrograde metamorphic event affecting the uppermost part of the Higher Himalayan Crystallines (Pognante and Benna, 1993).

LEUCOGRANITE INTRUSIONS

The upper sequence of the Higher Himalayan Crystallines (Black Gneiss, Rongbuck Formation, and North Col Formation) below the South Tibetan detachment system is widely intruded on by Miocene tourmaline and two-mica–bearing leucogranite bodies. They form wide subconcordant, lens-shaped and/or sheet-like intrusions, well exposed in the Makalu, Nuptse, and Cho-Oyu peaks, which reach a maximum thickness of 1–2 km

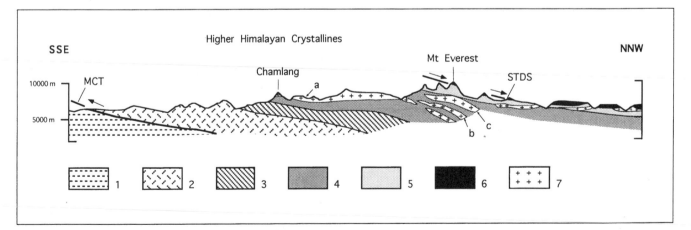

Figure 4. Schematic cross section of Khumbu Himal and southern Tibet (modified from Lombardo et al., 1993). 1, Lesser Himalaya; 2, Barun Gneiss; 3, Namche Migmatite Orthogneiss; 4, Rongbuk Formation and Black Gneiss; 5, North Col Formation; 6, Mt. Jolmo Lungma Formation and Yellow Band; 7, Miocene tourmaline leucogranite; a, Tramserku pluton; b, Baruntse pluton; c, Nuptse pluton. MCT is Main Central thrust; STDS is South Tibetan detachment system.

and dip gently to the north. In a north-south cross section, the lower intrusion is represented by the Tramserku pluton, which is overlain by the Baruntse and Nuptse plutons (Fig. 4). Several dike systems, made up of aplitic and pegmatitic leucogranites, are also associated with the main intrusions. They have concordant and/or discordant relations with the metamorphic host rocks and are often deformed with them (see following section).

The Himalayan leucogranites are characterized by physical inhomogeneity and strong compositional homogeneity close to the minimum melt composition (Pitcher, 1993). They were derived from a crustal source. Water-assisted partial melting of the base of the Tibetan slab was proposed for the Manaslu intrusion by Le Fort (1981).

In the Everest area, "in situ" anatexis via dehydration melting of muscovite-bearing metapelites of the Black Gneiss, without external water influx, was envisaged by Lombardo et al. (1993) and Tonarini et al. (1994). These water-undersaturated melts, characterized by a limited ascent through the crust, collected in the upper part of the Higher Himalayan Crystallines to give rise to sheet-like multipulse intrusions such as the Makalu and Nuptse plutons (Lombardo et al., 1993). Their emplacement and cooling occurred between 24 and 15 Ma and the radiometric ages suggest rapid cooling of leucogranites and metamorphic rocks (Lombardo et al., 1993, and references therein; Searle, 1995). Moreover, Pognante (1993), emphasizing the presence of leucogranite magmas in central and eastern Nepal, pointed out their genetic relationships with the tectono-metamorphic history of this part of the chain (Hodges et al., 1993).

TECTONICS

Observations in the study area led to the recognition of several structures, mainly folds, foliations, stretching lineations, shear zones, and faults. Mutual relations among these structural elements, at the outcrop and microscopic scale, indicate the occurrence of four tectonic phases (D1, D2, D3, and D4).

D1 phase

In the Imja Khola, Khumbu, and Ngozumpa valleys, the foliation (S1) is a composite schistosity, associated with tight to isoclinal folds (Brunel, 1986). The S1 schistosity shows a prominent stretching lineation (L1) marked by sillimanite, sillimanite nodules, elongated quartz grains, and biotite. Two main structural trends were recognized.

1. South of Namche village, the S1 schistosity strikes northwest-southeast and dips moderately toward the northeast (Figs. 2 and 5A), parallel to the Main Central thrust. The L1 stretching lineation trends north-northeast–south-southwest and plunges moderately toward the north-northeast (Fig. 2).

2. North of Namche village, the S1 schistosity strikes northeast-southwest and dips toward the northwest and the southeast (Hubbard, 1989) (Figs. 2 and 5B). The L1 stretching lineation mainly trends north-northeast–south-southwest and

gently plunges toward the south-southwest and north-northeast (Figs. 2 and 5B).

From the Main Central thrust to Porthse village (Fig. 2), meter-size shear zones and mylonites are developed nearly parallel to the S1 schistosity. They strike northwest-southeast and gently dip toward the northeast. The S-C fabrics, σ- and δ-type porphyroclasts (Passchier and Simpson, 1984), quarter folds, and quartz-preferred orientation indicate a top-to-the-south-southwest sense of shear.

D2 phase

The S1 schistosity is folded by large-scale upright F2 folds that have subvertical axial planes (Fig. 2). Two systems of fold were recognized and attributed to the D2 phase (F2a and F2b).

1. The F2a folds are represented by three main structures: (1) Baruntse-Chukung-Dingpoche, (2) Namche Bazar-Tome, and (3) Kangchung-Sumna glacier (Fig. 2). Their axes trend 090°–130° (Fig. 2). The wavelength is nearly 10 km, and longitudinal continuity is 6–8 km. These folds progressively die out toward the north until the S1 schistosity reaches a generalized east-west trend (Fig. 2).

2. The F2b folds are the most evident in the study area. F2b fold axes trend northeast-southwest. North of Namche the S1 schistosity is folded around a calculated F2b axis of 03°, 041° (Fig. 5B). An axial-plane crenulation cleavage developed in the hinge zone of F2b folds. The two main F2b antiforms are: (1) Khumbui Yul Lha–Taboche and (2) Gokyo Peak–Kangchung (Figs. 2 and 6). The F2b fold wavelength ranges from 4 to 6 km and longitudinal continuity is 8–10 km. They have large interlimb angles (90°–120°). This fold system also dies out toward the north.

The interference between the F2a and F2b folds produces large elongated domes and basins. No clear relations are provided to ascertain the relative chronology between the two fold systems in the field.

D3 phase

Folds. Meter- to hectometer-scale F3 folds are present on the limbs of the upright F2 folds. They range from open to tight to isoclinal, and can be assigned to classes 1C and 2 of Ramsay (1967). F3 folds are characterized by asymmetric to symmetric profiles. They fold the S1 schistosity and the S2 crenulation cleavage and show a poorly developed axial-plane, millimeter-spaced, crenulation cleavage (S3). F3 axial planes, subhorizontal to moderately dipping (Fig. 7A), are not parallel to F2 folds axial planes. Furthermore, F3 fold axes are subhorizontal and scattered; the trend maximum is 020°–030°, as shown in the streogram of Figure 7B. The F3 fold vergence is mainly toward the southeast, but vergences toward the south, southwest, and northwest are also represented (Fig. 2). Moreover, the vergence is always in the direction of the dip of the folded foliation (Fig. 2) and it is away from the hinge lines of the F2 antiforms.

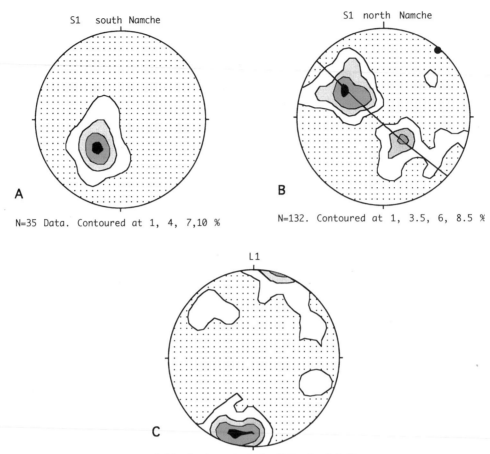

Figure 5. A: Poles to the S1 schistosity, south of Namche Bazar. B: Poles to the S1 schistosity, north of Namche Bazar; black dot: best pole 03, N043. C: L1 stretching lineation, north of Namche Bazar. Lower hemisphere, equal-area projection (Mancktelow, 1995, program Stereoplot v. 3).

A centimeter-scale type 3 interference pattern (Ramsay, 1967) between F3 and F2 folds has been observed in outcrops in the vicinity of Dingboche village. On the southeastern limb of the Khumbui Yul Lha–Taboche antiform, F3 folds are associated with meter-size shear zones (see following) and the asymmetric profile of F3 folds suggests a top-to-the-south and southeast sense of shear.

Miocene leucogranite dikes are also involved in F3 folds, as recognized northwest of Thare village (Ngozumpa valley; Fig. 2), where northwest-verging F3 folds deform meter-scale leucogranite dikes that show a spaced, subhorizontal, axial-plane foliation. Furthermore, in outcrops near the southwest side of the Barun glacier, centimeter- to meter-size leucogranite dikes are also emplaced along the axial planes of southwest-verging mesoscopic F3 folds. Folded dikes, showing symmetric and asymmetric shapes, are shortened in a subvertical direction and are extended in a subhorizontal direction, the latter lying at a low-angle to the S1 schistosity. In well-exposed outcrops near Pangboche village, leucogranite dikes and sills are stretched in two directions (chocolate tablet structure) at low angles to the S1 schistosity. Folded leucogranite dikes are in turn crosscut by later less-deformed and/or undeformed dikes (Fig. 8).

Shear zones. South of the Lhotse-Nuptse massif, in the Imja Khola and Khumbu valleys (Fig. 2), the schistosity (S1) is crosscut by low-angle shear and fault zones, trending east-west and northeast-southwest, gently to moderately dipping toward south and southeast, with down-dip and oblique L3 stretching lineations and slickenside striae (Fig. 9, A and B).

D3 shear zones that clearly postdate the main metamorphic foliation, are mainly concentrated along the southern flank of the Khumbui Yul Lha–Taboche antiform. Moreover, some east-west–trending shear zones are in the lower Bhote Kosi valley and in the upper Dudh Kosi valley along the eastern flank of the Gokyo Peak. These structures are decimeter to meter size in thickness and have an anastomosing pattern. A major zone of diffuse shear zones has been recognized along the Imja Kola valley, in the vicinity of Porthse village (Fig. 2), where they are intruded by concordant fine- and medium-grained biotite and tourmaline-bearing leucogranite dikes, ranging from 1 cm to 1 m in thickness and similar in composition to the large Miocene intrusions. A cooling age of 13.7 Ma (Rb/Sr whole-rock biotite isochron) has been obtained on a leucogranite dike emplaced within shear zones near Porthse village.

Figure 6. Large-scale F2b upright antiform, trending northeast-southwest. Mt. Kangchung (6,100 m), view from Ngozumpa valley is roughly in the direction of the fold axis. The exposed face of Mt. Kangchung is ~1,000 m high.

The dikes underwent shear deformation and now exhibit foliated fabrics, asymmetric boudinage, and folds (Figs. 10 and 11, A and B). The preferred orientation of biotite and tourmaline grains defines magmatic foliations overprinted by high-temperature solid-state deformation (Fig. 11, C and D) shown by subgrain boundaries, ductile deformation of feldspars, and core-mantle texture around K-feldspars. These fabrics show heterogeneous development at the outcrop scale, indicated by the occurrence of a weakly foliated portion wrapped by strongly foliated layers that are characterized by ductile deformation and extensive growth of sillimanite fibers (Figs. 11 and 12A). In the outer portions of larger dikes near Pangboche village (Fig. 2), the magmatic foliation is also crosscut by northeast-southwest–trending shear planes and/or bands that dip moderately to steeply southeast. The foliation in the dikes strikes northeast-southwest and dips gently to moderately (20°–45°) toward the south and the southeast, parallel to the shear-zone boundaries. These foliations contain north-south– and north-northwest–trending mineral lineations (Fig. 9C), marked by alignment of tourmaline grains and/or fibrous sillimanite that plunge toward the south or south-southeast (nearly parallel to the L3 stretching lineation) (Figs. 9 and 11).

The concordant relationships in the field between shear zones and magmatic dikes as well as their deformation features suggest synkinematic emplacement of the dikes into the shear zones. Moreover, the asymmetric boudinage of dikes and the following recognized kinematic indicators (Fig. 12, B, C, and D) indicate a southward extensional movement for the shear zones.

Outcrop-scale S-C fabrics due to deflection of magmatic foliation toward shear planes are marked by abundant fibrolite growth.

There is oblique orientation of magmatic minerals with respect to sillimanite-bearing foliated layers.

There are centimeter- or millimeter-scale southward-facing asymmetric folds in the foliated layers. Furthermore, a dextral strike-slip component is also shown by oblique stretching lineations.

Extensional crenulation cleavages. The folded S1 schistosity is crosscut at low angles by gently south- or southeast-dipping extensional crenulation cleavage and shear bands, often filled by leucosomes and leucogranite veins (Fig. 13). These structures are widely diffuse within the investigated area and are mainly recognized in the Ngozumpa valley from Porthse village to Gokyo Peak (Fig. 2). They show a prevailing top-to-the-south sense of shear and are regarded as coeval with the extensional shear zones and peraluminous magmatism.

D4 phase

Low-angle and high-angle normal faults affected the shear zones as well as the metamorphic rocks during the final brittle stages of extension. One of the most obvious low-angle normal faults is located on the southwest flank of Nuptse, in the Khumbu

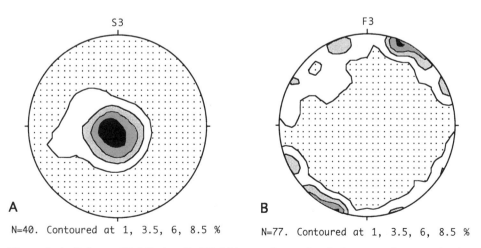

Figure 7. A: Poles to S3 foliation. B: F3 fold axes. Lower hemisphere, equal-area projection (Mancktelow, 1995, program Stereoplot v. 3).

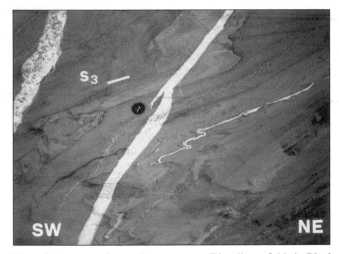

Figure 8. Asymmetric, southwest-vergent F3 collapse folds in Black Gneiss. Early emplaced leucogranite dikes underwent the greatest strain and were cut by later ones that were flattened to a lesser degree and crosscut by undeformed dikes. Chukhung glacier, higher Imja Khola valley; lens cap (5.2 cm) is for scale.

valley; the faults trend northeast-southwest and dip shallowly dipping toward the northwest (Fig. 2).

Two main systems of moderate- to high-angle normal faults have been recognized: They strike west-northwest–east-southeast and northeast-southwest (Fig. 14). North-northeast–striking, high-angle normal faults affect large leucogranite sills in the north face of Gyachung Kang and the North Col Formation in the south face of Nuptse-Lhotse. In the south face of Lhotse, the faults are exposed for 1500–2000 m. They dip steeply toward the west and are connected to a system of east-dipping faults. The two main faults have vertical displacements of ~100 and 160 m on the south face of Lhotse (Fig. 15).

DISCUSSION

The study area of the Higher Himalayan Crystallines of the Himalayan belt is affected by D1 tectonic structures produced by northeast-southwest shortening during the collisional stage between India and Asia. Field work in the Khumbu Himal suggests a more complex compressive tectonic setting than yet

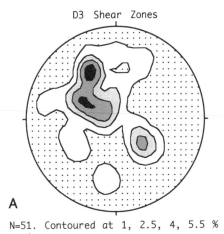

N=51. Contoured at 1, 2.5, 4, 5.5 %

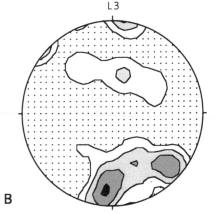

N=28. Contoured at 1, 2.5, 4, 5.5 %

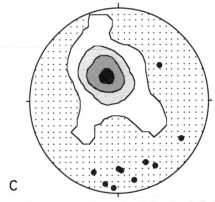

N=16. Contoured at 1, 3.5, 6, 8.5 %

Figure 9. A: Poles to D3 extensional planes. B: L3 extensional stretching lineations. C: Poles to D3 foliation and L3 mineral and stretching lineation (black dots) in small leucogranite dikes involved in D3 shear zones. Southeastern limb of Khumbui Yul Lha–Taboche antiform. Lower hemisphere, equal-area stereographic projection (Mancktelow, 1995, program Stereoplot v. 3).

Figure 10. Meter-size, southeast-verging F3 collapse folds in gneiss and subhorizontal stretched leucogranite dike (γ) in the vicinity of Pangboche village. Width of view is about 30 m.

described (Bortolami et al., 1976), and highlighted the presence of extensional structures in the crystallines. The compressive structures played an important role in the development of the later extensional ones.

The two recognized large-scale fold systems, F2a and F2b, indicate north-northeast–south-southwest and northwest-southeast compression, respectively, and no clear relations are provided by field data to ascertain relative chronology. The F2a fold system could be related to the D3 deformation phase described by Meier and Hiltner (1993) in the adjacent Arun tectonic window. In this suggestion, the F2a folds might relate to shortening connected to the Main Boundary thrust activity. The F2b folds are related to a northwest-southeast direction of shortening. Furthermore, similar transverse regional antiforms, the so-called Transhimalayan antiforms (Hagen, 1969) have been described west, south, and east of the Khumbu Himal. They correspond to the Okhaldunga, Arun, Tamur, and Darjeeling tectonic windows (Brunel, 1983; Meier and Hiltner, 1993). The presence of these

Figure 11 (right column). Photographs and thin-section photographs of fabrics in the leucogranite dikes. Sections are perpendicular to the foliation and parallel to the stretching lineation; large black arrows indicate a top-to-the-southeast sense of shear. A: Poorly foliated leucogranite with strongly foliated portion (lower half of the photo) marked by thin shear planes (Sp) of sillimanite fibers. Scale bar is 0.5 cm. B: Foliated leucogranite centimeter-size dike. Well-developed foliation marked by biotite trails and black tourmaline grains is crosscut by anastomosing shear planes (Sp) with extensive sillimanite growth. Scale bar is 0.5 cm. C: Thin-section photograph of foliated dike. Magmatic fabric is overprinted by ductile deformation (lower half of the photo) with development of thin and fine-grained foliated layers wrapping strained quartz and feldspar elongated grains. Plane-polarized light; scale bar is 0.5 cm. D: Thin-section photograph of well-developed ductile foliation in biotite and tourmaline-bearing dike. Foliation is crosscut at a low angle by thin and discontinuous sillimanite-bearing shear planes (Sp). Cross-polarized light; scale bar is 0.3 cm.

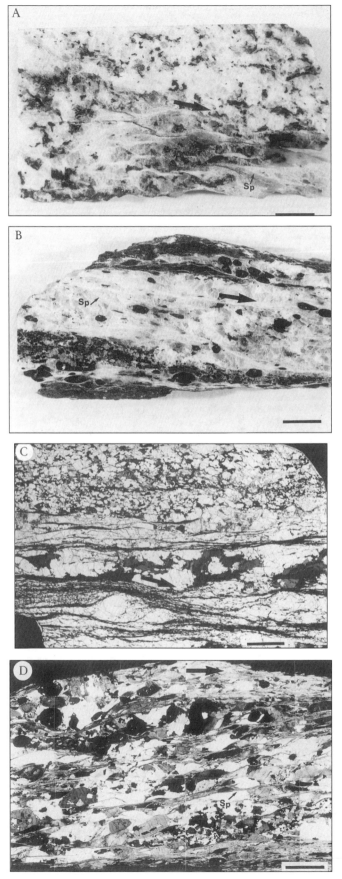

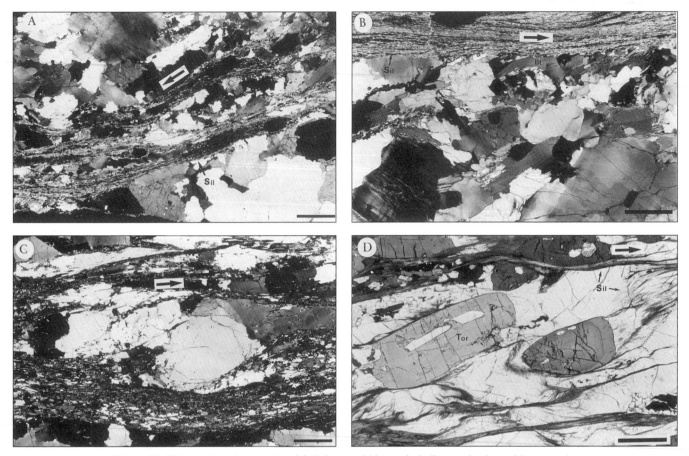

Figure 12. Thin-section photographs of foliations and kinematic indicators in sheared leucogranite dikes. Sections are perpendicular to the foliation and parallel to the stretching lineation; large black arrows indicate top-to-southeast sense of shear. A: Poorly deformed magmatic fabric discordantly crosscut by shear band characterized by grain-size reduction, ductile deformation, and sillimanite growth (Sil). Cross-polarized light; scale bar is 1 mm. B: Magmatic foliation, weakly overprinted by ductile deformation (subgrain boundaries), is crosscut by shear plane marked by finer grain size and growth of new sillimanite (Sil) and quartz grains. Bt is biotite. Cross-polarized light; scale bar is 1 mm. C: S-C texture shown by oblique orientation of strained elongated quartz grains with respect to shear plane marked by growth of sillimanite and fine-grained quartz. Cross-polarized light; scale bar is 1.2 mm. D: Detail of Figure 11D, showing S-C relations between foliation marked by alignment of tourmaline grains (Tor) and the anastomosing shear planes of sillimanite fibers (Sil). In the upper right, sillimanite fibers growing onto the foliation and crosscutting grain boundaries are parallel to shear plane. Plane-polarized light; scale bar is 0.6 mm.

transverse antiforms indicates that the northwest-southeast compression affected the Himalayan belt for at least 300 km.

A dextral shear between the Higher Himalayan Crystallines and the Tibetan Sedimentary Series was proposed by Pêcher et al. (1991), on the basis of clockwise rotation of mineral lineations in central Nepal, from the northeast-southwest close to the Main Central thrust, to the east-west, at the contact with the Tibetan Sedimentary Series. We are not able to confirm a similar rotation of the L1 stretching lineation in the study area because our field observations ended a few kilometers below the contact between the Higher Himalayan Crystallines and the Tibetan Sedimentary Series. However, the axial directions of the F2b folds are compatible with the shortening direction of an overall east-west dextral

shear and, consequently, the F2b fold system might be regarded as a system of en echelon folds.

The reverse to recumbent F3 folds, southward extensional shear zones joined with diffuse extensional crenulation cleavages, as well as the low-angle and high-angle normal faults, suggest extensional tectonics within the Higher Himalayan Crystallines that postdate the previous collisional structures.

The widespread presence of extensional structures indicates that extension was not limited to localized deformation, but affected a large portion of the Higher Himalayan Crystallines (at least 5 km of structural thickness), even though the high concentration of F3 folds, shear zones, and synkinematic dikes on the southern flank of Khumbui Yul La–Taboche antiform indicate a

Figure 13. Granitic melt localized in top-to-the-south-southeast small-scale shear zones of Namche Orthogneiss, Nangpo Tsangpo valley. Lens cap (5.2 cm) is for scale.

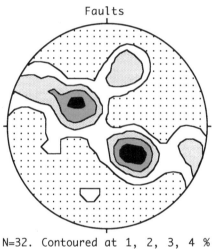

Figure 14. Poles to D4 normal-fault planes. Lower hemisphere, equal-area projection (Mancktelow, 1995, program Stereoplot v. 3).

major zone of extension. In this scenario, the development of extensional structures seems to have been controlled to some extent by the attitudes of the previous F2 folds. The nucleation and amplification of F3 recumbent folds as well as their scattered vergence are influenced by the dip of the S1 schistosity and the axial trend of the F2 folds. The steeply to moderately dipping limbs of the F2 folds were in a favorable position to accommodate vertical shortening. The F3 folds, produced by ductile crustal stretching, are regarded as collapse folds in the same sense as suggested by Spencer (1996) for the Upper Kaghan (Pakistan), and by Froitzheim (1992) for the D2 folds in the Austroalpine nappe of Switzerland.

The presence of leucogranite dikes and sills stretched in two directions (chocolate tablet structure), at a low angle to the S1 schistosity, indicates that the strain can be modeled as oblate strain ellipsoids ($X \geq Y \geq Z$) with a nearly subvertical Z axes.

The geometry of the D3 structures and the opposite vergence

of F3 folds are compatible with an overall coaxial deformation regime in the middle-upper part of the Higher Himalayan Crystallines during extensional tectonics. Most deformation has been partitioned in D3 extensional shear zones, dominated by non-coaxial strain, with prevailing southward extension.

The age of extension, clearly postdating collisional structures, can be constrained by the 13.7 Ma cooling age of synkinematic dikes, emplaced in the shear zones, that crop out near Porthse village. Such an age could be regarded as the lower limit for extensional shear deformation. Moreover, Tonarini et al. (1994) reported a cooling age of 15.9 Ma for anatectic leucosomes in the Namche migmatite orthogneiss, which crops out near Namche. Because the composition of such leucosomes is similar to those filling the extensional crenulation cleavage, we infer a middle Miocene age for extensional structures within the Higher Himalayan Crystallines in the Khumbu region.

All these features allow us to suggest that in the Khumbu region a middle Miocene extensional deformation affected the Higher Himalayan Crystallines, with a prevailing southward movement, when magma emplacement and anatectic processes were still active. The deformation within the shear zones was enhanced by injection of leucogranite melts, as proposed by Hollister and Crawford (1986), and deformation served to mobilize melts in a mutually complementary process.

The recognized extensional tectonics in the Higher Himalayan Crystallines of the Khumbu region show substantial differences with respect to the extension along the South Tibetan detachment system recognized in the Rongbuck valley north of Mt. Everest. The differences can be summarized as follows.

Southward extension is confined within the middle-upper portion of the Higher Himalayan Crystallines, whereas northward extension along the South Tibetan detachment system affected the uppermost portion of the crystallines.

The attributed middle Miocene age is comparatively younger than the lower Miocene age of the South Tibetan detachment system, which is intruded by the unfoliated Rongbuck granite, dated as 20.6 Ma (Hodges et al., 1996).

Diffuse deformation and local concentration of extensional structures contrast with the sharp localized deformation of the South Tibetan detachment system. Some similarities with the system are coeval magmatism and metamorphism, suggesting that in the Higher Himalayan Crystallines both these processes lasted together through the middle Miocene.

Field data do not allow the estimation of the amount of extension during the D3 phase. D3 shear zones do not bring into contact strongly different metamorphic rocks as in the South Tibetan detachment system, where low-grade metamorphic rocks overlie sillimanite-bearing gneiss. However, near Pangboche (Fig. 2), marbles and calc-silicates rocks belonging to the Rongbuk Formation directly overlie the Namche migmatite orthogneiss, with the partial omission of the Black Gneiss. This suggests a vertical displacement of about 100 m accommodated by the D3 shear zones in the Imja Khola valley.

Extensional deformation continued with the formation of

Figure 15. Southwest face of Mt. Lhotse. The height of the exposed face (west-east) is ~2,000 m. In the lower part, Miocene tourmaline leucogranite (L) and Rongbuk Formation (RF) crop out; they are overlain by the North Col Formation (NC), which is marked by light colored, banded calc-silicate rocks. North-northeast–trending normal faults are highlighted by displacements of calc-silicate rocks. The nearly vertical fault has a vertical displacement of ~100 m, whereas the east-dipping fault has a vertical displacement of ~160m.

low-angle and high-angle normal faults, which are the most recent tectonic structures in the Higher Himalayan Crystallines. West-dipping and east-dipping, north-northeast–south-southwest–striking high-angle normal faults, exposed in the south face of Nuptse-Lhotse, indicate west-northwest–east-southeast extension in the Higher Himalayan Crystallines and in the Tibetan Sedimentary Sequence, crosscutting all the previous structures. North-northeast–trending high-angle normal faults are probably linked to the development of Pliocene-Quaternary north-south–trending grabens in southern Tibet.

CONCLUSIONS

Structural investigations in the Higher Himalayan Crystallines of Khumbu Himal us to recognize the presence of extensional structures. The relations among F3 collapse folds, D3 shear zones, and leucogranite dikes suggest that, although most of Miocene extension was accommodated by the South Tibetan detachment systems, deformation was partitioned and thinning also occurred in the footwall of the system, that is, in the middle-upper part (5–6 km) of the High Himalayan Crystallines. Radiometric data indicate that the age of such extension in the footwall is younger (5–6 Ma) than the early Miocene age of the South Tibetan detachment system (Burchfiel et al., 1992). F3 collapse folds testify that the folding in the footwall happened in the Higher Himalayan Crystallines, and the large-scale F2 folds strongly influenced the geometry of the extensional structures. The overall geometries of the recognized F3 collapse folds and D3 shear zones cannot be achieved by the activity of a single shear zone, but they are compatible with a predominant coaxial deformation.

The activity of the South Tibetan detachment system caused nearly isothermal decompression in the Higher Himalayan Crystallines and production of melts that enhanced deformation (Burchfiel et al., 1992; Hodges et al., 1993; Pognante, 1993) and localization of extensional shear zones. Southward extension is coeval with the late stages of exhumation of the Higher Himalayan Crystallines. Although more data are needed to formulate the reliable evolutionary history of such an extension, we propose that it might be related to isostatic reequilibration within the footwall of South Tibetan detachment system. In this scenario, tectonic unloading and uplift gave rise to isostatic instabilities within the uplifted footwall (Higher Himalayan Crystallines), which reequilibrate through internal extensional structures and were coeval with magmatic and metamorphic processes still active during the middle Miocene along the Mt. Everest transect. Our investigation in the Higher Himalayan Crystallines indicates that crustal-scale extension also affects the footwall of the first-order extensional shear zones, such as the South Tibetan detachment system. The footwall is not only uplifted, but it is deformed by collapse folds and shear zones.

ACKNOWLEDGMENTS

This work has been financially supported by CNR (Centro di Studio per la Geologia Strutturale e Dinamica dell'Appennino—Pisa, and Everest-K2 Project). We thank A. Macfarlane, D. Applegate, and an anonymous reviewer for the helpful comments and careful reviews of the earlier version of the manuscript.

REFERENCES CITED

Academia Sinica, 1979, Geological map of Lhasa-Nyalam area, Xizang (Tibet), The People's Republic of China, Compiled by the Geological Division of the Comprehensive Scientific Expedition of the Xizang (Tibet)–Qingai Plateau, Academia Sinica, in: A scientific guidebook to South Xizang (Tibet): Beijing, Academia Sinica, scale 1:1500000.

Bordet, P., 1961, Recherches geologiques dans l'Himalaya du Népal, région du Makalu: Paris, Edition du Centre National de la Recherche Scientifique, 275 p.

Bortolami, G., Lombardo, B., and Polino, R., 1976, The Higher Himalya and the Tibetan Series in the Lhotse area (Eastern Nepal): Bollettino Società Geologica Italiana, v. 95, p. 489–499.

Brunel, M., 1983, Etude pétro-structurale des chevauchements ductiles en Himalaya (Népal oriental et Himalaya du Nord-Ouest) [Ph.D. thesis]: Université Paris VII, 395 p.

Brunel, M., 1986, Ductile thrusting in the Himalayas: Shear sense criteria and stretching lineations: Tectonics, v. 5, p. 247–265.

Brunel, M., and Kienast, J. R., 1986, Etude pétro-structurale des chevauchements ductiles himalayens sur la transversale del l'Everest-Makalu (Népal oriental): Canadian Journal of Earth Sciences, v. 23, p. 1117–1137.

Burchfiel, B. C., Chen, Z., Hodges, K. V., Liu, Y., Royden, L. H., Changrong, D., and Xu, L., 1992, The South Tibetan Detachment System, Himalayan orogen: Extension contemporaneous with and parallel to shortening in a collisional mountain belt: Geological Society of America Special Paper 269, 41 p.

Burg, J. P., Brunel, M., Gapais, D., Chen, G. M., and Liu, G. H., 1984, Deformation of leucogranites of the crystalline main central thrust sheet in southern Tibet (China): Journal of Structural Geology, v. 6, p. 535–542.

Ferrara, G., Lombardo, B., and Tonarini, S., 1983, Rb/Sr geochronology of granites and gneisses from the Mount Everest region, Nepal Himalaya: Geologische Rundschau, v. 72, p. 119–136.

Froitzheim, N., 1992, Formation of recumbent folds during synorogenic crustal extension (Austroalpine nappes, Switzerland), Geology, v. 20, p. 923–926.

Hagen, T., 1969, Reports on geological survey of Nepal: Denkschrift Schweizerische Naturforschen Gesellschaft, v. 1, 185 p.

Hodges, K. V., Burchfiel, B. C., Royden, L. H., Chen, Z., and Liu, Y., 1993, The metamorphic signature of contemporaneous extension and shortening in the central Himalayan orogen: Data from the Nyalam transect, southern Tibet: Journal of Metamorphic Geology, v. 11, p. 721–737.

Hodges, K. V., Bowring, S., Hawkins, D., and Davidek, K., 1996, The age of the Rongbuck granite and Qomolangma detachment, Mount Everest region, southern Tibet: 11th Himalaya-Karakorum-Tibet Workshop, Flagstaff, Arizona, Abstracts, p. 63–64.

Hollister, L. S., and Crawford, M. L., 1986, Melt-enhanced deformation: A major tectonic process: Geology, v. 14, p. 558–561.

Hubbard, M. S., 1989, Thermobarometric constraints on the thermal history of the Main Central Thrust Zone and Tibetan Slab, eastern Nepal Himalaya: Journal of Metamorphic Geology, v. 7, p. 19–30

Kai, K., 1981, Rb/Sr geochronology of the rocks of the Himalayas, Eastern Nepal. Part I. The metamorphic age of the Himalayan Gneiss: Memoirs of the Faculty of Science, Kyoto University, Series of Geology and Mineralogy, v. 47, p. 135–148.

Le Fort, P., 1981, Manaslu granite: A collision signature of the Himalaya. A model for its genesis and emplacement: Journal of Geophysical Research, v. 86, p. 10545–10568.

Lombardo, B., Pertusati, P. C., and Borghi, S., 1993, Geology and tectonomagmatic evolution of the eastern Himalaya along Chomolungma-Makalu tansect, *in* Treloar, P. J., and Searle, M. P., eds., Himalayan tectonics: Geological Society of London Special Publication 74, p. 341–355.

Mancktelow, N., 1995, Stereoplot version 3: Geologisches Institut ETH-Zentrum, Zürich.

Meier, K., and Hiltner, E., 1993, Deformation and metamorphism within the Main Central Thrust zone, Arun Tectonic Window, eastern Nepal, *in* Treloar, P. J., and Searle, M. P., eds., Himalayan tectonics: Geological Society of London Special Publications 74, p. 511–523.

Passchier, W. C., and Simpson, C., 1984, Porphyroclast system as kinematic indicators: Journal of Structural Geology, v. 16, p. 733–741.

Pêcher, A., Bouchez, J. L., and Le Fort, P., 1991, Miocene dextral shearing between Himalaya and Tibet: Geology, v. 19, p. 683–685.

Pitcher, W. S., 1993, The nature and origin of granite: London, Chapman and Hall, 321 p.

Pognante, U., 1993, Different P-T-t paths and leucogranite occurrences along the High Himalayan Crystallines: Implications for subduction and collision along the northern Indian margin: Geodinamica Acta, v. 6, p. 5–17.

Pognante, U., and Benna, P., 1993, Metamorphic zonation, migmatization, and leucogranites along the Everest transect of Eastern Nepal and Tibet: Record of an exhumation history, *in* Treloar, P. J., and Searle, M. P., eds., Himalayan tectonics: Geological Society of London Special Publication 74, p. 328–340.

Ramsay, J. G., 1967, Folding and fracturing of rocks: New York, McGraw-Hill, 568 p.

Searle, M. P., 1995, The timing of metamorphism, magmatism, and cooling in the Zanskar, Garhwal, and Nepal Himalaya: Nepal Geological Society Journal, v. 11, p. 103–120.

Spencer, D. A., 1996, "Collapse folding" as a mechanism of explaining the early ductile extension along the Indus Suture and the subsequent exhumation of the Himalayan eclogites (Upper Kaghan, Pakistan): 11th Himalaya-Karakorum-Tibet Workshop, Flagstaff, Arizona, Abstracts, p. 141–142.

Tonarini, S., Lombardo, B., Ferrara, G., and Marcassa, P., 1994, Partial melting in the Namche Migmatite of Khumbu Himal (Nepal Himalaya): Mineralogica Petrografica Acta, v. 37, p. 277–294.

Yin, C. H., and Kuo, S. T., 1978, Stratigraphy of the Mount Jolmo Lungma and its north slope: Scientia Sinica, v. 21, p. 629–644.

MANUSCRIPT ACCEPTED BY THE SOCIETY FEBRUARY 3, 1998

Geological Society of America
Special Paper 328
1999

Lesser Himalayan crystalline nappes of Nepal: Problems of their origin

Bishal Nath Upreti
Department of Geology, Tri-Chandra Campus, Tribhuvan University, Ghantaghar, Kathmandu, Nepal
Patrick Le Fort
*CNRS, UPRES-A 5025, Institut Dolomieu, Laboratoire de Géodynamique des Chaînes Alpines,
15 rue Maurice Gignoux, 38031 Grenoble, France*

ABSTRACT

Lesser Himalayan crystalline nappes consisting of low- to medium-grade metamorphic rocks are present in Nepal. In the southern part of Kathmandu, in the Jajarkot and Dadeldhura nappes, the rocks are unconformably(?) overlain by lower Paleozoic rocks of Higher Himalayan affinity. In these nappes there is a normal upward-decreasing metamorphic grade. The Karnali nappe in western Nepal, however, consists of kyanite-sillimanite–bearing schists and gneisses, and is different from the other crystalline nappes.

The Higher Himalayan Crystallines, normally considered to be the root zone of the Lesser Himalayan nappes, represent a thick pile of high-grade metamorphic rocks of amphibolite facies essentially consisting of coarse-grained kyanite- and sillimanite-bearing garnet-muscovite-biotite gneisses, orthogneisses, and schists. The Main Central thrust zone, broadly equivalent to the high-strain inverted metamorphic zone below the thrust, is also regarded by some as the root zone of the nappes. On the basis of a variety of evidence, this zone cannot be regarded as the root of the nappes. The Karnali nappe is an exception that is clearly rooted in the Higher Himalayan Crystallines.

It is therefore suggested that most of the Lesser Himalayan crystalline nappes (except the central part of the Kathmandu nappe) have no exposed roots and thus represent exotic slices in the Lesser Himalaya. The rocks of the nappes may represent deposits at the northern edge of the continental marginal sea at an intermediate position between the Lesser Himalayan sediments of the south and the Higher Himalayan facies in the north. They evolved with a different geologic history than that of their northern and southern counterparts. During the Himalayan orogeny, the Main Central thrust brought the Higher Himalayan Crystallines over these rocks, and they in turn were thrust over the Lesser Himalayan sediments along the Mahabharat thrust. The entire thrust stacks were later folded, and after erosion the Lesser Himalayan nappe rocks were preserved in synclinal cores. In most places the thrust tectonics and erosion have not allowed the root zones of these nappes to be preserved.

Upreti, B. N., and Le Fort, P., 1999, Lesser Himalayan crystalline nappes of Nepal: Problems of their origin, *in* Macfarlane, A., Sorkhabi, R. B., and Quade, J., eds., Himalaya and Tibet: Mountain Roots to Mountain Tops: Boulder, Colorado, Geological Society of America Special Paper 328.

INTRODUCTION

The Main Central thrust extends for nearly 2500 km along the Himalayan arc, and is one of the largest intracontinental thrusts on Earth. It brings high-grade metamorphic rocks, including the basement rocks of the Indian shield (Higher Himalayan Crystallines), over low-grade Lesser Himalayan metasediments. There is a great deal of controversy and confusion about the definition, nature, and position of the thrust and the associated thermal history and deformation. The tectonic evolution of the Main Central thrust has a direct bearing on the understanding of the amount of north-south crustal shortening and the upheaval and exhumation history of the Himalaya. Some authors, following Heim and Gansser (1939), who recognized it in Garhwal, recognize another thrust (Valdiya, 1980a, 1980b; Arita, 1983; Fuchs and Frank, 1970; Srivastava and Mitra, 1994) not far below the Main Central thrust, variously named as the Main Central thrust I in Nepal and the Munsiary thrust in Kumaon. Many others, however, do not recognize this thrust (Le Fort, 1975; Stöcklin, 1980; Pêcher and Le Fort, 1986; United Nations Economic and Social Commission for Asia and the Pacific Cooperation Department of Mines and Geology [U.N. ESCAP/DMG], 1993), or point out that it is a secondary thrust and does not mark the boundary between the Lesser and the Higher Himalaya (Valdiya, 1980b, 1981).

Le Fort (1975), and Pêcher and Le Fort (1986) regarded the higher grade of metamorphism shown by the package of rocks of the Main Central thrust zone as the thermal effect associated with the thrusting of the hot Higher Himalayan Crystalline slab over the cold Lesser Himalaya. The role of shear heating produced by movements along the thrust has also been stressed by such workers as Arita (1983), Maruo and Kizaki (1983), Brunel and Kienast (1986), and England et al. (1992). Differing views in the interpretation of the Main Central thrust in the north has also created problems in the interpretation of the origin of the Lesser Himalayan crystalline nappes in the south. This chapter mainly focuses on the problem of the origin of these Lesser Himalayan crystalline nappes in Nepal and proposes an alternative interpretation for their origin.

DISTRIBUTION AND NATURE OF THE NAPPES

Ever since the recognition of the Crystalline nappes in the Kumaon Himalaya, India (e.g., Auden, 1935; Heim and Gansser, 1939), a number of such nappes and crystalline thrust sheets have been mapped throughout the Himalaya (Gansser, 1964; Hagen, 1969; Valdiya, 1980a, 1986; Fuchs, 1981). Well-known crystalline nappes in Nepal are the Kathmandu nappe (Gansser, 1964; Hagen, 1969; Stöcklin, 1980), the Jajarkot nappe (Hagen, 1969; Fuchs and Frank, 1970; Arita et al., 1984), the Bajhang nappe (Bashyal, 1986; Amatya and Jnawali, 1996), and the Dadeldhura nappe (Gansser, 1964; Fuchs, 1981; Arita et al., 1984; Bashyal 1986; Upreti, 1990) (Fig. 1). In addition, there is a crystalline nappe in western Nepal named the Karnali

nappe or the Chakhure-Mabu Crystalline klippe (Kizaki, 1994; Arita et al., 1984). An extensive gently northward-dipping crystalline thrust sheet in the Lesser Himalaya in eastern Nepal has a few tectonic windows such as Okhaldhunga, Arun, and Taplejung, where the underlying low-grade metamorphic units of the Lesser Himalayan zone are exposed (Bordet, 1961) (Fig. 1).

Kathmandu nappe

The Kathmandu nappe was first recognized by Hagen (1969) and later mapped in detail by Arita et al. (1973) and a team of geologists from the Mineral Exploration Project, Department of Mines and Geology, Nepal (Stöcklin and Bhattarai, 1980, Stöcklin, 1980). Hashimoto (1959) traversed from Kathmandu to the Manaslu area and described the Sheopuri granitic gneiss unit (Fig. 2). The front part of Kathmandu nappe almost reaches the Main Boundary thrust in the south, and a very narrow zone of the Lesser Himalayan metasediments separates the crystalline rocks of the nappe from the Siwaliks. A narrow arm of this nappe forms the Mahabharat Range and joins the crystalline thrust sheets of Gosainkund to that of eastern Nepal, 70 km apart (Fig. 1). The thrust separating the crystalline rocks of the nappe from the underlying metasediments of the Lesser Himalaya is called the Mahabharat thrust in the south around Kathmandu (Stöcklin, 1980), and has been interpreted as a direct continuation of the Main Central thrust (Stöcklin, 1980; Fuchs, 1981; Pêcher and Le Fort, 1986; Pandey et al., 1995) (Fig. 2).

The rocks of the southern part of Kathmandu nappe are grouped as the Kathmandu Complex, which is subdivided into the lower Bhimpedi Group (about 10.5 km thick; late Precambrian age rocks) and the unconformably(?) overlying fossiliferous sedimentary sequence of the Phulchauki Group (3.5–4 km thick; lower Paleozoic rocks) (Stöcklin, 1980) (Fig. 3C). An Upper Silurian marine fauna, trilobites and brachiopods in particular, was described by Bordet et al. (1959, 1960). This fauna fits reasonably well with other faunas of typical old Gondwana passive continental margin sequences (Talent et al., 1988). Bordet et al. (1960) suggested that the topmost Godavari sandy dolomite (Fig. 3C) is an equivalent of the Devonian Muth quartzite described in western Himalaya and Kashmir; there are similar detrital dolomites in the Devonian Tilicho Pass formation of north-central Nepal (Colchen et al., 1986). In the south and southwestern parts of the Kathmandu Valley, the Bhimpedi Group is represented by garnet-schist, marble, quartzite, and metabasic rock. A number of granite bodies of various size have been mapped within the Kathmandu nappe (Fig. 1).

Jajarkot nappe

Crystalline rocks similar to the Bhimpedi Group of the Kathmandu nappe do not exist in most parts of the central Nepal. They occur only northeast of Piuthan and form a long and narrow body (~175 km × 25 km) named the Jajarkot nappe

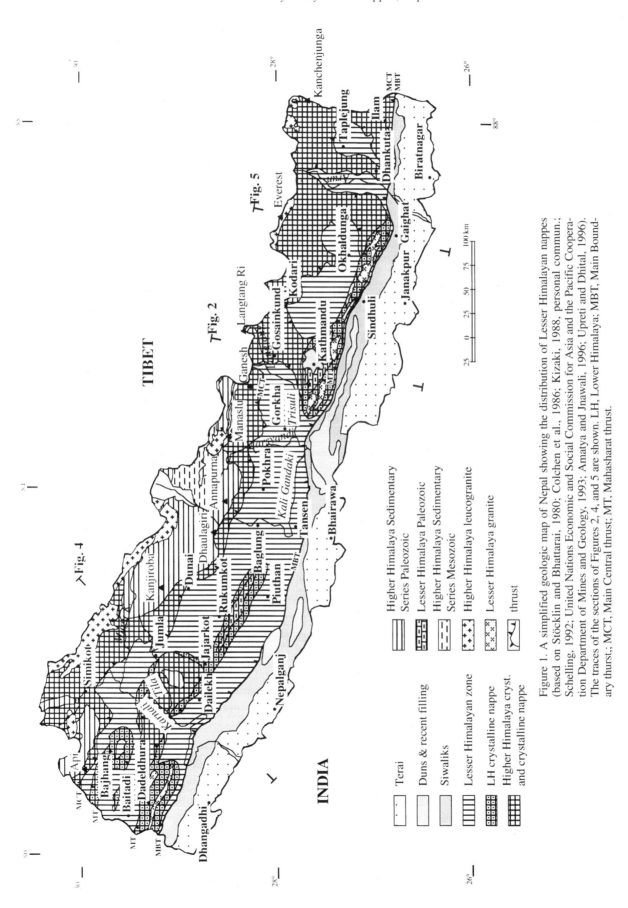

Figure 1. A simplified geologic map of Nepal showing the distribution of Lesser Himalayan nappes (based on Stöcklin and Bhattarai, 1980; Colchen et al., 1986; Kizaki, 1988, personal commun.; Schelling, 1992; United Nations Economic and Social Commission for Asia and the Pacific Cooperation Department of Mines and Geology, 1993; Amatya and Jnawali, 1996; Upreti and Dhital, 1996). The traces of the sections of Figures 2, 4, and 5 are shown. LH, Lower Himalaya; MBT, Main Boundary thrust;; MCT, Main Central thrust; MT, Mahasharat thrust.

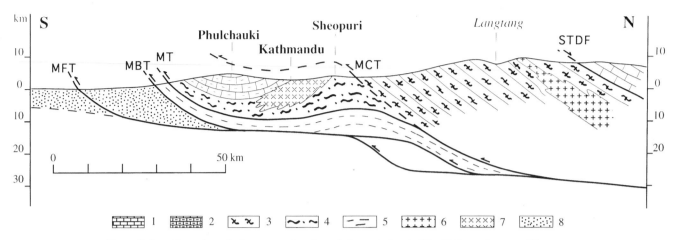

Figure 2. A north-south geologic cross section through the central part of the Kathmandu nappe. The trace of the section is shown in Figure 1. Note the exotic nature of the nappe, which has no exposed root in the north. 1. Tibetan Sedimentary Series of the Higher Himalaya. 2. Sedimentary Series (Paleozoic) of the Lesser Himalayan nappes (Phulchauki group). 3. Higher Himalayan Crystallines. 4. Crystalline rocks of the Lesser Himalayan nappes (Bhimpedi group). 5. Lesser Himalayan metasediments. 6. Tertiary Himalayan granites. 7. Cambrian-Ordovician granites. 8. Siwalik sediments. MBT, Main Boundary thrust; MCT, Main Central thrust; MFT, Main Frontal thrust; MT, Mahabharat thrust; STDF, South Tibetan detachment fault.

(Fig. 1); the crystallines here are capped by carbonate rocks similar to the Phulchauki Group of the Kathmandu nappe. For Fuchs and Frank (1970), this Jaljala limestone resembles both the Chandragiri limestone of the Phulchauki Group and the Annapurna (Dhaulagiri) limestone of the Tibetan Sedimentary Series (Fig. 3, C and D); the crinoids found in the Jaljala limestone strengthen the correlation with other Cambrian(?)-Ordovician limestones. The lower rock units of the nappe, the Chaurjhari Formation (Sharma et al., 1984; Sharma and Kizaki, 1989), consist of muscovite-biotite schist and garnet-biotite-muscovite schist and subordinate micaceous quartzite, garnetiferous graphitic schist, feldspathic schist, and augen gneiss. They also contain granitoid bodies. The metamorphism decreases upward in the sequence, giving way to the carbonate rocks.

Karnali nappe

The Karnali nappe is best developed along the Karnali River and its tributary, the Tila River, in far western Nepal (Fig. 1). It is about 100 km along the east-west and 50 km along north-south directions. This unit consists of kyanite-sillimanite–bearing gneiss, calc-silicate gneiss, migmatitic gneiss, and augen gneiss (Hayashi et al., 1984). Calc-silicate gneiss forms thick interbeds within the garnet-biotite gneiss in the southern part of the nappe. Migmatitic gneiss and augen gneiss form the upper part of the sequence. Le Fort (1975) proposed a three-fold classification of the Higher Himalayan Crystallines in the Marsyandi and the Kali Gandaki sections; Formation I pelitic and graywacke alternations are at the base, Formation II calcitic gneiss and marble are above, and augen gneiss of Formation III is at the top (Fig. 3D). This lithostratigraphic division also fits the Karnali nappe. The Baregaon For-

mation consists of a 1500-m-thick carbonate sequence; it occupies the core of the synform and marks the top of the Karnali nappe (Hayashi et al., 1984). It is composed of calcareous biotite schist and psammitic and pelitic schist, and shows typical brick-red weathering products as commonly seen in the Annapurna (Dhaulagiri) limestone of the Tibetan Sedimentary Series. No fossils are reported, but the lithology and its tectonic position suggest the affinity of this formation with the Tibetan Sedimentary Series.

The boundary between the high-grade gneisses of the Karnali nappe and the underlying medium-grade metamorphic rocks belonging to the Main Central thrust zone of Arita et al. (1984) or the Lower Crystalline nappe of Fuchs and Frank (1970) is marked by a thrust (Kizaki, 1994; Arita, 1983; Hayashi et al., 1984), which is the southward extension of the Main Central thrust. The schistose unit below the Karnali nappe consists of garnet-biotite schist and biotite schist intercalated with lenses of quartzite and quartzose schist. These rocks tectonically overlie low-grade Lesser Himalayan metasediments; this thrust is an equivalent of the Mahabharat thrust (Fig. 4). The eastern continuation of this schistose unit joins with the Jajarkot nappe. More detailed mapping is required to precisely delineate these two thrust packages in the Karnali region. A cross section shown in Figure 4 should be considered tentative.

To the north, near Jumla, a very narrow zone of the Lesser Himalayan metasedimentary rocks separates the very similar rocks of the Karnali nappe from the root zone. It leaves no doubt that the rocks of the Karnali nappe are actually the southward extension of the Higher Himalayan Crystallines or the Higher Himalayan Crystallines brought southward by thrusting along the Main Central thrust.

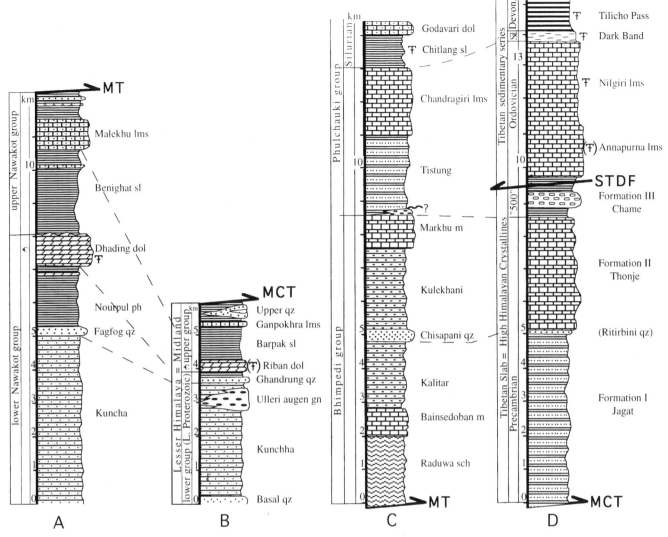

Figure 3. Four lithostratigraphic sections corresponding to the major units defined in the text. A: Section of the Lesser Himalaya below the Kathmandu nappe of section C (after Stöcklin, 1980). Within the Nawakot group, very early Paleozoic algae, probably Early Cambrian, associated with stromatolites and echinoderms, have been found in the Dhading dolomite (dol). The limit between the lower and the upper group has been chosen at the top of the Dhading dolomite because of an erosional unconformity with traces of lateritisation. lms, limestone; sl, slate; ph, phyllite; qz, quartzite. B: Section of the Lesser Himalaya below the Higher Himalaya Crystallines of central Nepal, in the region of the Marsyandi valley (after Colchen et al., 1986). The base of the section is not known. The section compares well with that of the Nawakot Group (A), but with thicknesses reduced by half, in good agreement with the higher metamorphic grade and higher strain of the rocks. The most important difference is the presence here of the Ulleri augen gneiss (gn) toward the top of the Kunchha formation. A pegmatite cutting the Kunchha formation has yielded a Rb-Sr muscovite whole-rock age of 1744 ± 84 Ma (Deniel, 1985), and the Ulleri formation is probably part of the widespread 1900 ± 100 Ma magmatic event (Le Fort, 1989). Brunel et al. (1985) found Cambrian paleoba-sidiospores from magnesite beds of the Upper Midland Group in the Okhaldunga window. Thus, the Lower and Upper Midland Groups respectively correspond to a volcanic-detrital accumulation of lower Proterozoic age, and an epicontinental, mainly marine, shelf sedimentation of lower Paleozoic age. Comparisons with other sections of the Lesser Himalaya can be found in Valdiya (1986) and Le Fort (1989). C: Section of the Kathmandu Complex, the southern part of the Kathmandu nappe (after Stöcklin, 1980). The base tectonically overlies (Mahabharat thrust, MT) the Lesser Himalaya Nawakot Group (A). The Bhimpedi Group is intruded by the Lesser Himalayan cordierite-bearing granite dated as 486 ± 21 Ma and 509 ± 56 Ma by Rb-Sr whole-rock isochrons, and 470 ± 4 Ma by U-Pb on zircon and monazite (see Le Fort et al., 1986a, for complete references). The lower Paleozoic Phulchauki Group overlies the Precambrian Bhimpedi Group; the contact may be slightly unconformable (Stöcklin, 1980), and we have found a discontinuous augen gneiss formation around this limit. Fossils have only been found in the upper three formations, and dated in the Silurian Chithang formation (Bordet et al., 1959; Talent et al., 1988); m, marble; sch, shizt. D: Section of the High Himalayan Crystallines and sedimentary series (after Colchen et al., 1986); only the base of the 10–14-km-thick sedimentary series is represented here. The base of the section tectonically overlies (Main Central thrust, MCT) the Lesser Himalaya Midland Group (B). In the Higher Himalayan Crystallines, the augen gneisses of Formation III have been dated as 513 ± 30 Ma (Le Fort et al., 1986a). The South Tibetan detachment fault separates the Tibetan Sedimentary Series from the Higher Himalayan Crystallines. The section has many similarities to the Kathmandu Complex (C). Both sections have a comparable overall thickness and include Cambrian-Ordovician plutonism, which is not represented in the Lesser Himalaya. Differences include the more varied lithological succession of the Kathmandu Complex, and the lesser importance of the marble-bearing formations in the Katmandu Complex. However, the thickness of Formation II varies greatly; e.g., in the Burhi Gandaki valley, 50 km east of the Marsyandi, Formation II is reduced to a few hundred meters. The Tibetan Sedimentary Series is dominated by calcareous formations of epicontinental marine origin. Fossils belong to a similar paleogeographic province in the Silurian of both domains, the only stage well characterized paleontologically in the Phulchauki Group (Bordet et al., 1959, 1960; Talent et al., 1988).

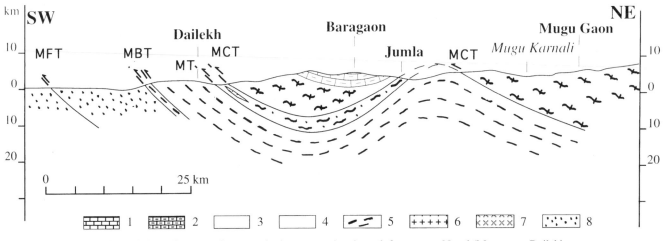

Figure 4. A northeast-southwest geologic cross section through far western Nepal (Mugugaon-Dailekh section) showing the relationship between the Karnali nappe of High Himalayan affinity and the underlying Lesser Himalayan Jajarkot nappe. The trace of the section is shown in Figure 1. This section is tentative. 1. Tibetan Sedimentary Series of the Higher Himalaya. 2. Sedimentary Series (Paleozoic) of the Lesser Himalayan nappes (not represented in this section). 3. Higher Himalayan Crystallines (Higher Himalayan Crystallines and Karnali nappe). 4. Metamorphic rocks of the Lesser Himalayan nappes (Bhimpedi Group of the Jajarkot nappe). 5. Lesser Himalayan metasediments. 6. Tertiary Himalayan granites. 7. Cambrian-Ordovician granite and orthogneiss. 8. Siwalik sediments. MBT, Main Boundary thrust; MCT, Main Central thrust; MFT, Main Frontal thrust; MT, Mahabharat thrust.

Dadeldhura and Bajhang nappes

The Dadeldhura nappe, which forms a large synformal crystalline nappe in far western Nepal, is the direct eastward continuation of the Almora nappe or klippe of Kumaon (Gansser, 1964; Fuchs, 1981; Valdiya, 1981; Arita et al., 1984). The basal part of the nappe consists of the Gaira Formation, which is exposed on both sides of the synform (Bashyal, 1986; Upreti, 1990), and is composed of garnet-mica schist, carbonaceous schist, quartzite, metabasic rock, and granitic gneiss. The granitic gneiss covers most of the Dadeldhura nappe to the south. A 4–5-km-wide granitic body, the Dadeldhura granite, dated as 470.0 ± 5.6 Ma (Einfalt et al., 1993), is bounded marginally by granitic orthogneiss. The core of the Dadeldhura synform is occupied by lead-gray to black carbonaceous phyllite containing minor quartzite beds, sometimes traversed by coarse pegmatitic veins. A small outcrop of sedimentary rock that has a Tibetan Sedimentary Series affinity has been reported in the northern part of the nappe, northwest of Dipayal (Amatya and Jnawali, 1996; U.N. ESCAP/DMG, 1993).

The Bajhang nappe is to the north of the Dadeldhura nappe; the two are separated by an ~100-km-wide zone of Lesser Himalayan rocks. It is the direct eastward extension of the Chiplakot or Munsiari nappe of Kumaon (Valdiya, 1980a; Arita, 1983), and consists of phyllite, quartzite, and gneiss. A small crystalline body, the Parchauni crystalline klippe (Bashyal, 1986; Upreti, 1990), is also between the Dadeldhura nappe and the Bajhang nappe (Fig. 1). It is ~25 km by 50 km and is made up of garnetiferous schist and gneiss.

COMMON CHARACTERISTICS OF THE LESSER HIMALAYAN CRYSTALLINE NAPPES

The crystalline nappes just described (except the crystalline thrust sheets of the eastern Nepal and the Karnali nappe) are primarily composed of medium-grade (containing biotite and garnet and rarely kyanite) metasedimentary rock and metavolcanic rock and gneiss of granitic origin. It is named the Bhimpedi Group in the southern part of the Kathmandu nappe. It may be appropriate that the name Bhimpedi Group be extended to the similar assemblage of rocks throughout the Lesser Himalaya (as proposed UN-ESCAP/DMG, 1993; Amatya and Jnawali, 1996). In three areas (Kathmandu, Jajarkot, and Dadeldhura nappes) these metamorphic sequences are unconformably(?) succeeded by little-metamorphosed to nonmetamorphosed fossiliferous rock sequences of Tibetan Sedimentary Series affinity. Invariably cordierite-bearing two-mica granites intrude the Bhimpedi Group and the younger sedimentary rocks. The granites in these crystalline nappes of the Lesser Himalayan granitic belt (Le Fort et al., 1983, 1986a) are Cambrian-Ordovician age, dated as 470.0 ± 5.6 Ma (Dadeldhura granite; Einfalt et al., 1993), 470 ± 4 Ma (Palung granite of Kathmandu nappe; Schärer and Allègre, 1983), or 493 ± 11 Ma (Simchar-Palung granite; Le Fort et al., 1983). The smaller bodies of granite, and the rims of the larger ones, are normally highly sheared and foliated and converted into granitic gneisses.

The grade of metamorphism in the Lesser Himalayan nappes does not normally exceed the albite-epidote-almandine subfacies of the greenschist facies of regional metamorphism. Metamorphic grade in the lower part is most often marked by chlorite-biotite or biotite-garnet assemblages showing a gradual decrease in grade toward the upper part. In most cases these crystalline nappes have clear thrust contacts having a sharp metamorphic break with the underlying less-metamorphosed to nonmetamorphosed rocks of the Lesser Himalaya.

Very few data are available on the nature of deformation, metamorphism, cooling ages of minerals, and the thermobarometry of the rocks of the Lesser Himalayan crystalline nappes. Morrison and Oliver (1993) studied the index minerals and illite crystallinity and tried to evaluate the grade of metamorphism of different rocks in the Kathmandu nappe and Main Central thrust zone. They found that the regional metamorphism within the anticlinal Lesser Himalayan formations underlying the crystalline rocks of the Kathmandu nappe varied between the epidote-chlorite and garnet zone, the highest grades being in the core of the structure. They also found that the grade of metamorphism is lowest at the core of the Kathmandu synclinorium (epidote-chlorite zone) and highest on the north and south limbs (garnet zone). Metamorphism in the Kathmandu nappe is believed by Stöcklin (1980) to predate the emplacement of the Cambrian-Ordovician granites. Many xenoliths in the granites have metamorphic rocks that have random foliations with respect to the granite foliation, and thus predate the granite. However, the granites are strongly deformed and metamorphosed together with the surrounding formations. Along the rim, they are transformed to orthogneiss with recrystallization of biotite, muscovite, and sometimes garnet that underlie the foliation and the strong mineral lineation trending N20°E, the regional Himalayan stretching lineation (Le Fort et al., 1983). Geothermometric data (garnet-biotite method) from texturally slightly zoned garnets from kyanite-grade rocks (northwestern part of the Kathmandu nappe) indicate a temperature of 660 to 686 °C (Johnson and Rogers, 1995), and, according to Rai et al. (1997), a temperature of 550 to 700 °C for a pressure of 7 to 9 kbar. In their study of the metamorphic and thermal evolution of the Kathmandu nappe, Rai et al. (1997) found a normal metamorphic gradient in the nappe and a thermal peak close to the base of the nappe; similar results were obtained by Sharma and Kizaki (1989) on the Jajarkot nappe.

CHARACTERISTICS OF THE SUPPOSED ROOT ZONES

Higher Himalayan Crystallines

The crystalline formations of the Higher Himalaya form a continuous belt throughout the Himalaya. Variously named the Central Crystallines (Heim and Gansser, 1939; Gansser, 1964) and the Vaikrita Group (Valdiya, 1980a) in Kumaon, and the Tibetan Slab (Le Fort, 1975), the Himalayan Gneiss zone (Hashimoto et al., 1973; Arita, 1983), the Upper Crystalline nappe (Fuchs and Frank, 1970) and Higher Himalayan Crys-

tallines in Nepal, these rock units constitute a very thick pile (more than 12 km in western Nepal) of amphibolite facies high-grade metamorphic rocks consisting of very coarse-grained kyanite- and sillimanite-bearing garnet-muscovite-biotite psammitic gneiss and schist. In Nepal these rocks have been divided, from bottom to top, into Formation I, alternating metapelites and metagraywackes; Formation II, characteristically composed of calcic gneisses and marbles; and Formation III, which has thick horizons of coarse augen gneiss (Le Fort, 1975). Formation III (from a few hundred meters to about 1.5 km exposed thickness) is the augen gneiss member that may correspond to the lower Paleozoic deformed granitic bodies, intruded at 517 Ma (Le Fort et al., 1983, 1986a). Kyanite, which is normally abundant in the Higher Himalayan Crystallines, is often a good marker of the base of the unit, although it is present in places in the Lesser Himalaya beneath the Main Central thrust (Colchen et al., 1986; Pêcher and Le Fort, 1986). Sillimanite is abundant in the upper part of the section, especially where the total thickness of the rock sequence is higher, but is also linked to a high-grade metamorphic episode accompanied by partial melting.

The Higher Himalayan Crystallines have undergone two main phases of metamorphism: an early eo-Himalayan Barrovian-type metamorphism (M1) caused by subduction and crustal thickening during India-Eurasia collision, followed by the Himalayan metamorphism (M2) linked to movement on the Main Central thrust and characterized by an inverted metamorphic pattern in the thrust zone (Le Fort, 1989). The metamorphic pressure-temperature (*P-T*) conditions of the M2 metamorphism in the Higher Himalayan Crystallines formations of central Nepal have been estimated by garnet-biotite-plagioclase geothermobarometers as *T* = 600–690 °C and *P* = 7–8 kbar (Modi Khola section, Pêcher and Le Fort, 1986) and *T* = 620–740 °C and *P* = 5.5–8 kbar (Kali Gandaki section, Le Fort et al., 1986b). In the Annapurna region, where the Higher Himalayan Crystallines thickness is about 3 km, the estimated temperature at the base of the crystallines is 700 °C, and the estimated pressure is 8.5 kbar. In the Manaslu region, where the Higher Himalayan Crystallines thickness is about 12 km, the estimated temperature is 750 °C, and the estimated pressure is 10 kbar (Pêcher and Le Fort, 1986). North of Kathmandu, in the Gosainkund region, where the crystallines thickness is about 10 km, the temperature is estimated between 550 and 750 °C, and the pressure has a normal gradient from 6 to 9 kbar; a retrograde biotite-sillimanite assemblage (M3) corresponds to a drop in pressure and temperature of 1 kbar and 60 °C (Rai et al., 1997). In eastern Nepal the values are *T* = 640–720 °C and *P* = 6–9 kbar (Maruo and Kizaki, 1983). In the Everest area Pognante and Benna (1993) estimated the pressure and temperature of the three phases of metamorphism as: M1, *T* = 550–680 °C and *P* = 8–10 kbar; M2, *T* = 650–750 °C and *P* = 4–7 kbar; and M3, *T* = 600–700 °C and *P* = 2–4 kbar.

Main Central thrust zone

The group of rocks belonging to the Main Central thrust zone has been variously interpreted as a separate tectonic unit bounded on both sides by thrusts (Fuchs and Frank, 1970; Valdiya, 1980a, 1980b; Arita, 1983; Arita et al., 1984) or as belonging to the upper part of the Lesser Himalayan sequence overridden at the top by the Higher Himalayan Crystallines along the thrust (Le Fort, 1975). This zone has higher grade metamorphic rocks than those of the lower sections of the Lesser Himalaya. The grade of metamorphism gradually increases from the lower to the upper section of the Lesser Himalaya as it approaches the Main Central thrust. This is the well-known inverted metamorphic grade in the Himalaya. The rocks in this zone are characterized by the development of large rotated garnets, and reaches kyanite grade below the thrust in several locations (e.g., in the Darondi Khola section, central Nepal). Primarily because of the similarity in the metamorphic grades between the Lesser Himalayan crystalline nappes and the Main Central thrust zone, some regard this unit as the root zone of some Lesser Himalayan nappes (e.g., Jajarkot nappe, Arita et al., 1984). In some places, such as the Langtang valley of central Nepal, the thrust zone is regarded as a package of slices of different rocks of both Higher Himalayan crystallines and the Lesser Himalayan metasediments juxtaposed by a number of brittle faults (Macfarlane, 1992).

While considering the root zones of the Lesser Himalayan nappes it is logical to evaluate the lithologic and stratigraphic similarities, metamorphism, magmatism, and the deformational history of the rock sequences between the supposed root zones and the nappes: the problems of the root zones of the Lesser Himalayan nappes are discussed in the following.

Kathmandu nappe

It is widely believed that the Kathmandu nappe is a large folded thrust sheet of the Higher Himalayan Crystallines, its leading edge reaching the Main Boundary thrust in the south. Hagen (1969) considered the Gosainkund area to the north of Kathmandu as the tectonic bridge between the nappe and the root zone in the Langtang Himal. However, the metamorphism found within the rocks of the southern part of the Kathmandu nappe and the Higher Himalayan Crystallines in the north shows a marked difference. The Higher Himalayan crystalline rocks of the Gosainkund and Langtang areas to the north of Kathmandu are metamorphosed generally at a moderate pressure and high temperature ($T = 560–660$ °C and $P = 4–8$ kbar) (Macfarlane, 1995), minerals like kyanite and sillimanite develop. It is in sharp contrast to the low- to medium-grade rocks (containing biotite and garnet) in the southern part of the Kathmandu nappe. The ca. 500 Ma cordierite-bearing two-mica granites that are so abundant in the nappes are not represented in the Higher Himalayan Crystallines, except the augen gneisses of Formation III, possibly representing the deformed granites. Another striking difference is in the stratigraphy and lithology between the rocks of Kathmandu Complex and the supposed root zone. A comparison between the stratigraphy and lithology of the Kathmandu Complex and the Higher

Himalayan Crystallines shows that, whereas the Higher Himalayan Crystallines can be subdivided only into three broad lithological units (Le Fort, 1975), the Kathmandu nappe has a rock sequence of more varied lithology (Stöcklin, 1980) (Fig. 3, C and D) and differs significantly in detail from the Higher Himalayan Crystallines. Even the Phulchauki Group, supposedly the representative of the Tibetan Sedimentary Series within the nappe, has strong differences when compared to its root zone, including reduced thicknesses, sedimentation lacunae, and hardgrounds such as that represented by the hematitic fossiliferous level of the Phulchauki section (Bordet et al., 1959, 1960).

On the basis of stratigraphy, lithology, and metamorphism, the main body of the Kathmandu nappe (Fig. 1) can be divided into northern and southern parts. Earlier workers expressed this idea in their geologic maps (Hashimoto et al., 1973; Brunel, 1975; Lombardo et al., 1993, Fig. 2). Hagen (1969) always separated the Kathmandu nappe from the overlying Khumbu nappe, thus recognizing two units of different lithology and metamorphic grades. To us the boundary between these two parts is marked by the Main Central thrust, which may pass through the north of the Kathmandu Valley (Figs. 1 and 2). Thus the Main Central thrust does not extend south of the Kathmandu Valley, as normally interpreted (Hagen, 1969; Stöcklin, 1980; Pandey et al., 1995).

A zone of granite, granitic gneiss, and augen gneiss containing a profuse development of pegmatites is to the north of the Kathmandu valley and forms the Sheopuri range (Fig. 2). It separates two lithologically and metamorphically different domains: high-grade Higher Himalayan Crystallines to the north, from lower-grade varied Bhimpedi Group to the south (Fig. 3, C and D). The gneisses and granites of this range are sometimes interpreted as an independent unit bounded on both sides by vertical faults named the Sheopuri injection gneiss zone (Arita et al., 1973; Hashimoto et al., 1973), or sometimes considered as the southward continuation of the Higher Himalayan Crystallines (Hagen, 1969; Stöcklin, 1980). The northern boundary of this granite-gneiss zone with the Higher Himalayan Crystallines that marks the Main Central thrust is not well studied. In many transects this boundary seems to be vague and indistinct due to the lithologic similarities of rocks on both sides. This may be why there is so much variation in the interpretation of the geology of the northern part of the Kathmandu area. However, careful observation reveals that the Sheopuri Gneiss zone is characterized by granites and granitic gneisses containing profuse coarse pegmatites that intrude low-grade metasediments such as sandstones and shales of the Phulchauki Group and that do not contain high-grade minerals such as kyanite and sillimanite typical of the Higher Himalayan Crystallines. On the contrary, farther north, after crossing the Main Central thrust, these rocks give way to a coherent sequence of the typical high-grade gneisses of the Higher Himalayan Crystallines.

The lower Paleozoic Phulchauki Group of the southern

part of the Kathmandu nappe unconformably overlies the medium-grade rocks of the Bhimpedi Group. This is in contrast to the Tibetan Sedimentary Series zone in the north, where sedimentary rocks overlie the Higher Himalayan Crystalline rocks along the north-dipping South Tibetan detachment fault (Pêcher, 1991; Burchfiel et al., 1992; Brown and Nazarchuk, 1993).

No detailed study on the age and the structural and metamorphic history of the granites and gneisses in the Sheopuri area has been carried out. Therefore, although at this stage a comparison between these rock units with the others (500 Ma Lesser Himalayan granites and gneisses) may not be definitive, an affinity with the Cambrian-Ordovician Lesser Himalayan granites cannot be ruled out. Some of these rocks also resemble the Formation III augen gneiss of the Higher Himalayan Crystallines, that crop out in the Langtang Valley, and has been dated as 482 Ma (Le Fort et al., 1986a). These old granites and gneisses of the Sheopuri zone must have undergone pronounced metamorphism and deformation related to the thrusting of the hot Higher Himalayan Crystallines along the Main Central thrust. The widespread development of pegmatitic bodies that crosscut most of the preexisting rock fabrics seems to be the result of this late-stage remobilization of the granite and granitic gneisses.

In eastern Nepal the narrow arm of the Kathmandu nappe forming an east-west–extending synform that was investigated in some detail by Ishida (1969), Brunel (1975), Stöcklin and Bhattarai (1977), Maruo and Kizaki (1983) and Schelling (1992). The north-south cross sections by Brunel (1975) and Schelling (1992) show kyanite-sillimanite–bearing gneiss overlying the low-grade Lesser Himalayan metasediments with a

thrust contact (equivalent to the Main Central thrust). However, a more detailed geologic map of this area (Stöcklin and Bhattarai, 1977) shows almost the entire area covered by the Bhimpedi Group, in addition to granite intrusions similar to the south-central part of the Kathmandu nappe. This map also shows some small kyanite-bearing gneiss outcrops within the area. These rocks units rest on metasediments of the Lesser Himalaya along the Mahabharat thrust (shown as the southward extension of the Main Central thrust). Maruo and Kizaki (1983), however, recognized two thrusts within the crystalline nappe. The Bhimpedi Group, which overlies the Lesser Himalayan metasediments along the Phaplu thrust (equivalent to the Main Central thrust I of Arita, 1983), is in turn overthrust by high-grade kyanite-sillimanite–bearing gneiss and schist along their Sarung thrust (equivalent to the Main Central thrust). Farther east, north of Gaighat, Dangol et al. (1993, Fig. 1) recognized a narrow zone of the Bhimpedi Group between the Lesser Himalayan sediments and the kyanite-bearing high-grade gneiss and schist belonging to the Higher Himalayan Crystallines thrust sheet. We agree with the interpretation of the tectonics of Mahabharat syncline of Maruo and Kizaki (1983), but because of the complete dissimilarity of the lithology, we do not think that the rock unit bounded by the Phaplu and the Sarung thrusts has its roots in the Main Central thrust zone.

These observations indicate that the Kathmandu nappe is not a single body extending from its supposed root zone in the Langtang Himal in the north to the Main Boundary thrust in the south. It consists of two separate tectonic units. The Main Central thrust, passing through the north of the Kathmandu Valley, separates the nappe into the northern and southern parts

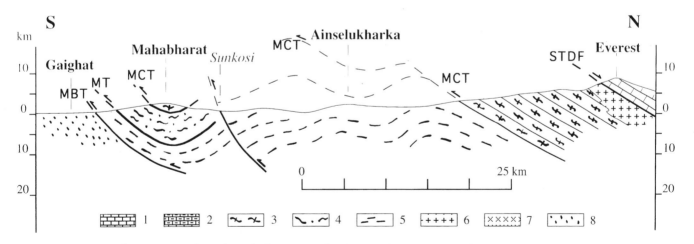

Figure 5. A north-south geologic cross section through the eastern part of the Kathmandu nappe (Everest-Gaighat section) (modified after Maruo and Kizaki, 1983; Schelling, 1992). Trace of the section is shown in Figure 1. 1. Tibetan Sedimentary Series of the Higher Himalaya. 2. Sedimentary Series (Paleozoic) of the Lesser Himalayan nappes (Phulchauki Group). 3. Higher Himalayan Crystallines. 4. Metamorphic rocks of the Lesser Himalayan nappes (Bhimpedi Group). 5. Lesser Himalayan metasediments and sediments. 6. Tertiary Himalayan granites. 7. Cambrian-Ordovician granites. 8. Siwalik sediments. MBT, Main Boundary thrust; MCT, Main Central thrust; MT, Mahabharat thrust; STDF, South Tibetan detachment fault.

(Figs. 1 and 2). North of the Main Central thrust, the high-grade crystalline rocks through Gosainkund continue to their root zone in the Langtang Himal. The southern part of the nappe, consisting of the Bhimpedi and Phulchauki Groups and intruded by the Cambrian-Ordovician granites, overlies the metasediments of the Lesser Himalaya along the Mahabharat thrust, and does not show any affinity to the high-grade crystallines of the northern part. Following Stöcklin and Bhattarai (1977), the rock units of the southern part of the Kathmandu nappe (Bhimpedi Group) extend eastward along the eastern arm of this nappe. However, the kyanite-sillimanite gneiss and schist in this eastern extension of the nappe may represent small tectonic outliers of the Higher Himalayan Crystallines that overlie the Bhimpedi Group with a thrust contact (Fig. 5). The position of the Main Central thrust shown in Figure 5 is only suggestive.

Nappes of western Nepal

In western Nepal the Jajarkot nappe, consisting of the low- to medium-grade metamorphic rocks (Bhimpedi Group) and lower Paleozoic sedimentary (Phulchauki Group) cover, can be compared with the Kathmandu nappe. Earlier workers placed the root zone of this nappe either in the Main Central thrust zone (Arita et al., 1984) or in the Higher Himalayan Crystallines (Fuchs and Frank, 1970). The lithology and the metamorphic grade clearly do not support the affinity of this nappe to the Higher Himalayan Crystallines. Although the rocks of the Main Central thrust zone may show a comparable metamorphic grade, they cannot be considered the root zone of the nappe. The difference in the stratigraphy and lithology, the presence of normal metamorphic sequence in the nappe in contrast to the Main Central thrust zone and the presence of lower Paleozoic cover in the nappe do not support the Main Central thrust zone constituting the root zone of the nappe. Therefore, the Jajarkot nappe exists as an exotic slice overlying the Lesser Himalayan metasediments without a root in the north. In the west the Karnali nappe tectonically overlies the Jajarkot nappe (Fig. 4).

The Dadeldhura nappe, which has many similarities to the Kathmandu nappe, has no clearly defined root zone in the north. Neither the Main Central thrust zone (the Munsiari Formation of Valdiya, 1980a) nor the Higher Himalayan Crystallines can be regarded as its root zone because of the lithological and metamorphic differences. The eastern part of the Dadeldhura nappe is overthrust by the Karnali nappe. However, detailed mapping is required to precisely outline the thrust contact of the Karnali nappe with the underlying Jajarkot and the Dadeldhura nappes. On the basis of lithology and mapping, the Jajarkot and the Dadeldhura nappes may represent a single continuous thrust body separated by the Karnali nappe. The Bajhang nappe is poorly mapped and therefore it is not known whether the nappe is composed of only rocks similar to the Bhimpedi Group or it is a higher nappe rooted in the Higher Himalayan Crystallines and thrust over it.

ORIGIN OF THE NAPPES

Because of the difficulty in accepting the Higher Himalayan Crystallines or the Main Central thrust zone as the root zone of the Lesser Himalayan crystalline nappes, we believe that the root zone of the just-listed crystalline nappes (except the Karnali nappe) are not exposed anywhere in the north and their rock assemblages, including the lower Paleozoic cover, have no comparable counterparts. This implies that all these nappes form exotic slices in the Lesser Himalaya. Wherever the Higher Himalayan Crystallines are thrust to the south and preserved as thrust sheets and nappes, they are easily recognized and their roots are easily traced. In such cases, the broad stratigraphy, lithology, and metamorphic grade between the nappes and the root zones are also comparable. In eastern Nepal, even in the frontal part of the considerably thinned thrust sheets that have traveled nearly 100 km to the south, the rocks can be traced back to the Higher Himalaya. As pointed out here, the root of the Karnali nappe can be traced easily to the Higher Himalayan Crystallines. Even the small tectonic outliers preserved over the Lesser Himalayan crystalline nappes (eastern arm of the Kathmandu nappe) can be identified and their affinity to the Higher Himalayan Crystallines can be recognized. On the contrary, wherever the Kathmandu, Jajarkot, or Dadeldhura nappes consisting of rocks of the Bhimpedi and Phulchauki Groups are present, their root zones cannot be established with certainty. Therefore we have tried to present an alternative tectonic interpretation to explain the origin of these Lesser Himalayan nappes.

The study of the lithology, stratigraphy, and the metamorphic, deformational, and magmatic history of the rocks belonging to the Lesser Himalayan sediments, the Lesser Himalayan crystalline nappes, and the Higher Himalayan Crystallines leads to the conclusion that these different rock groups were deposited in three different environments in widely separated areas. The reconstruction of the paleogeography of the basin is shown in Figure 6A. A similar idea was also proposed by Hagen (1969, p. 141, Fig. 113). The rocks of the Lesser Himalayan nappes consisting of the Precambrian Bhimpedi Group that are succeeded unconformably(?) upward by the lower Paleozoic rocks of Tibetan Sedimentary Series affinity may have been deposited on the northern edge of the Indian continental marginal sea at an intermediate position between the Lesser Himalayan sediments of the south and the more northern facies (Fig. 6A). Therefore, the rock units of all the three zones characterized by their own specific lithology and stratigraphy evolved under different metamorphic and magmatic conditions.

It seems that uninterrupted deposition of the entire Paleozoic, Mesozoic, and lower Tertiary rocks (Tibetan Sedimentary Series) occurred in the northern zone. However, toward the south in the intermediate zone, it is difficult to estimate with reasonable confidence how much of the Paleozoic or Mesozoic rocks were deposited. Today only the lower Paleozoic rocks are

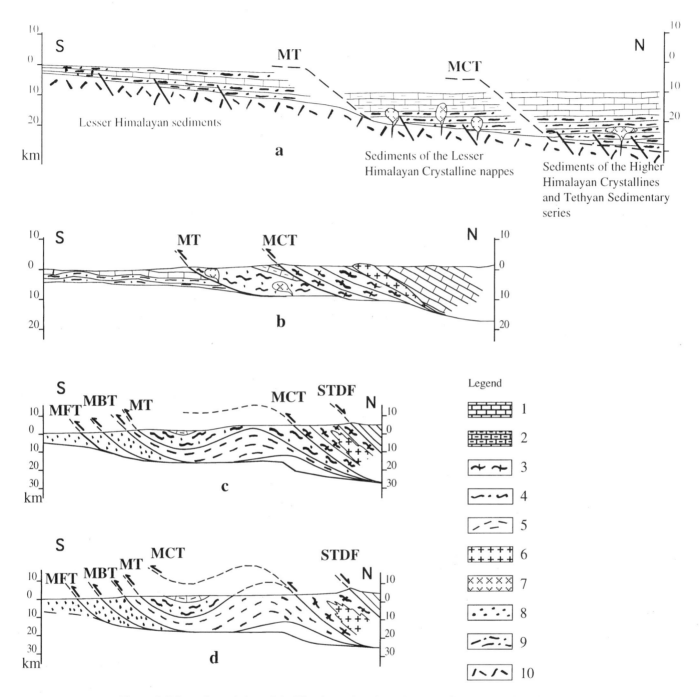

Figure 6. Schematic evolution of the Himalayan domain. a: A schematic reconstruction of the sedimentary basin in the northern edge of the Indian continental marginal sea showing the respective positions of the sedimentary deposits of the three zones and the positions of the proto Main Central thrust (MCT) and the Mahabharat thrust (MT). b: Evolution of the thrust tectonics along the MCT and the MT. c and d: Evolution of the Lesser Himalayan nappes and frontal thrusts. 1. Tibetan Sedimentary Series of the Higher Himalaya. 2. Sedimentary Series (Paleozoic) of the Lesser Himalayan nappes. 3. Higher Himalayan Crystallines. 4. Metamorphic rocks of the Lesser Himalayan nappes (Bhimpedi group). 5. Lesser Himalayan metasediments and sediments (Phulchauki Group). 6. Tertiary Himalayan granites. 7. Cambrian-Ordovician granites. 8. Siwalik sediments. 9. Pelitic and arenaceous sediments of the Indian continental marginal sea. 10. Indian shield. MBT, Main Boundary thrust; MFT, Main Frontal thrust; STDF, South Tibetan detachment fault.

preserved and are found only in three isolated areas in the Lesser Himalayan crystalline nappes. It is less-well known whether any Paleozoic or Mesozoic rocks were deposited over the larger part of the southern zone (Lesser Himalayan zone). Although there is scant and inconclusive evidence, some authors regard the upper part of the Lesser Himalayan sediments (e.g., Upper Nawakot Group in central Nepal) as lower Paleozoic (Stöcklin, 1980); it is likely that there was little or no deposition in the entire southern zone during the early Paleozoic, and the marine to terrestrial upper Paleozoic and Mesozoic sediments were deposited only in small, isolated basins (e.g., Tansen Group, Sakai, 1983). Therefore, although the lower Paleozoic rocks of the Lesser Himalayan crystalline nappes (the Phulchauki Group) and the Tibetan Sedimentary Series of the north were contemporaneous, and were deposited in the same peri-Gondwanian marginal basin, they were deposited in different environments, and as a result, have different facies characteristics.

The postcollision intracrustal subduction of the leading northern edge of the Indian plate and the sediment cover led to high-grade metamorphism (Eo-Himalayan metamorphism that preceded movement on the Main Central thrust) that reached peak temperatures of 670 to 750 °C and pressures of 7.5 to 10 kbar (England et al., 1992). Toward the south, the rocks of the intermediate zone somewhat away from the leading edge were not metamorphosed to the same degree as those of the northern part. Whereas the ca. 500 Ma granite intrusions of the northern zone may have been transformed into augen gneisses and orthogneisses, the granites of the intermediate zone remained little affected by the deformation and metamorphism. The sediments deposited on the southernmost part of the basin along the continental margin now belonging to the Lesser Himalaya, were least affected by the metamorphism.

SUMMARY

The tectonic evolution of the Lesser Himalayan nappes may be summarized as follows.

During the Himalayan orogeny, the Main Central thrust, a major intracontinental thrust that formed following the India-Eurasia collision, was followed by the development of a new thrust (the Mahabharat thrust) farther south (Fig. 6, A and B). The Main Central and Mahabharat thrusts are splays of the same thrust system and merge at depth to the decollement along which the intracrustal subduction of the Indian plate occurred. At least 100 km of crustal shortening has been accommodated along the Main Central thrust (Brunel, 1975; Gansser, 1966) and a significant amount of shortening must have occurred along the Mahabharat thrust. The Main Boundary thrust and other frontal thrusts (Main Frontal thrust), which developed subsequently, also merge at the decollement level (Fig. 6C).

The movement along the Mahabharat thrust brought intermediate-zone rocks over low-grade metamorphosed to unmetamorphosed Lesser Himalayan sediments. The Main Central thrust brought metamorphic rocks of amphibolite facies along with slivers of basement rocks of Indian crust over low- to medium-grade rocks of the intermediate zone (Fig. 6B). That the Lesser Himalayan crystallines were not strongly metamorphosed under the Higher Himalayan Crystallines nappe coverage probably implies that the crystallines thickness was somewhat reduced and quickly eroded. The rock units forming stacks of thrust sheets were later folded in large-scale structures, and after erosion were preserved along the synclinal cores in the Lesser Himalaya (Fig. 6C). Thus the rocks belonging to the Lesser Himalayan crystalline nappes have not come from the Higher Himalayan Crystallines or the Main Central thrust zone, but represent a separate unit characterized by its own stratigraphy, lithology, and metamorphism. The root zones of these crystalline nappes therefore are not in the Higher Himalaya. In most cases (Fig. 6), the thrust tectonics and erosion have not allowed the root zones of these nappes to be preserved.

ACKNOWLEDGMENTS

The authors thankfully acknowledge the fruitful discussions with P. G. DeCelles (University of Arizona), and A. Pêcher (Université Joseph Fourier). We thank Peter Copeland (University of Texas) for critically going through the manuscript. The manuscript has largely benefited from the reviews of A. Macfarlane and R. Sorkhabi. The authors are, however, responsible for the content of the paper.

REFERENCES CITED

Amatya, K., and Jnawali, B., compilers, 1996, Geological map of Nepal: Kathmandu, Department of Mines and Geology/International Center for Integrated Mountain Development (DMG/ICIMOD/CDG/UNEP), scale 1:1,000,000, 1 sheet.

Arita, K., 1983, Origin of the inverted metamorphism of the Lower Himalayas, central Nepal: Tectonophysics, v. 95, p. 43–60.

Arita, K., Ohta, Y., Akiba, C., and Maruo, Y., 1973, Kathmandu region, in Hashimoto, S., Ohta, Y., and Akiba, C., eds., Geology of the Nepal Himalayas: Tokyo, Saikon Publishing Co. Ltd., 286 p.

Arita, K., Shiraushi, K., and Hayashi, D., 1984, Geology of western Nepal and a comparison with Kumaon, India: Hokkaido University Journal of Faculty of Science, ser. IV, v. 2, p. 1–20.

Auden, J. B., 1935, Traverses in the Himalaya: Geological Survey of India Records, v. 69, p. 123–167.

Bashyal, R. P., 1986, Geology of Lesser Himalaya, far western Nepal, in Le Fort, P., Colchen, M., and Montenat, C., eds., Évolution des domaines orogéniques d'Asie méridionale (de la Turquie à l'Indonésie): Nancy, France, Sciences de la Terre, Mémoire 47, p. 31–42.

Bordet, P., 1961, Recherches géologiques dans l'Himalaya du Népal, région du Makalu: Paris, France, Éditions du Centre National de la Recherche Scientifique, 275 p.

Bordet, P., Cavet, J., and Pillet, J., 1959, Sur l'existence d'une faune d'âge silurien dans la région de Kathmandou (Himalaya du Népal): Paris, Académie des Sciences, Comptes Rendus, v. 248, sér. D, p. 1247–1249.

Bordet, P., Cavet, J., and Pillet, J., 1960, La faune silurienne de Phulchauki, près de Kathmandu (Himalaya du Népal): Société Géologique de France,

Bulletin, sér. 7, v. 2, p. 3–14.

Brown, R. L., and Nazarchuk, J. H., 1993, Annapurna detachment fault in the Greater Himalaya of central Nepal, *in* Treloar, P. J., and Searle, M. P., eds., Himalayan tectonics: Geological Society of London Special Publication 74, p. 461–473.

Brunel, M., 1975, La nappe du Mahabharat, Himalaya du Népal central: Paris, Académie des Sciences, Comptes Rendus, v. 280, sér. D, p. 551–554.

Brunel, M., and Kienast, J. R., 1986, Étude pétro-structurale des chevauchements ductiles himalayens sur la transversale de l'Everest-Makalu (Népal oriental): Canadian Journal of Earth Sciences, v. 23, p. 1117–1137.

Brunel, M., Chaye d'Albissin, M., and Locquin, M., 1985, The Cambrian age of magnesites of east Nepal as determined through the discovery of paleobasidiospores: Geological Society of India Journal, v. 26, p. 255–260.

Burchfiel, B. C., Chen Zhiliang, Hodges, K. V., Liu Yuping, Royden L. H., Deng Changrong, and Xu Jiene, 1992, The South Tibetan detachment system, Himalayan orogen: Extension contemporaneous with and parallel to shortening in a collisional mountain belt: Geological Society of America Special Paper 269, 41 p.

Colchen, M., Le Fort, P., and Pêcher, A., 1986, Notice explicative de la carte géologique Annapurna-Manaslu-Ganesh (Himalaya du Népal) au 1:200.000ème: Paris, Éditions du Centre National de la Recherche Scientifique, 138 p.

Dangol, V., Upreti, B. N., Dhital, M. R., Wagner, A., Bhattarai, T. N., Bhandari, A. N., Pant, S. R., and Sharma, M. P., 1993, Engineering geological study of a proposed road corridor in eastern Nepal: Katmandu, Tribhuvan University, Department of Geology Bulletin, Special Issue 3, p. 91–107.

Deniel, C., 1985, Apport des isotopes du Sr, du Nd et du Pb à la connaissance de l'origine des leucogranites himalayens. Exemple du Manaslu (Himalaya, Népal) [Ph.D. thesis]: Universiet de Clermont-Ferrand, France, 114 p.

Einfalt, H. C., Hoehndorf, A., and Kaphle, K. P., 1993, Radiometric age determination of the Dadeldhura granite, Lesser Himalaya, far western Nepal: Bulletin Suisse de Minéralogie et de Pétrographie, v. 73, p. 97–106.

England, P., Le Fort, P., Molnar, P., and Pêcher A., 1992, Heat sources for Tertiary metamorphism and anatexis in the Annapurna-Manaslu region central Nepal: Journal of Geophysical Research, v. 97, no. B2, p. 2107–2128.

Fuchs, G., 1981, Geologic-tectonical map of the Himalaya: Geological Survey of Austria, scale 1:2,000,000, 1 sheet.

Fuchs, G., and Frank, W., 1970, The geology of west Nepal between the rivers Kali Gandaki and Thulo Bheri: Jahrbuch der Geologischen Bundesanstalt, Sonderband 18, 103 p.

Gansser, A., 1964, Geology of the Himalayas: London, Interscience Publishers, John Wiley and Sons, 289 p.

Gansser, A., 1966, The Indian ocean and the Himalaya: A geologic interpretation: Eclogae Geologicae Helveticae, v. 59, p. 832–848.

Hagen, T., 1969, Report on the geological Survey of Nepal, Volume 1, Preliminary reconnaissance: Zürich, Denkschriften der Schweizerischen Naturforschenden Gesellschaft, Mémoires de la Société Helvétique des Sciences naturelles 86, 185 p.

Hashimoto, S., 1959, Some notes on the geology and petrography of the southern approach to Mt. Manaslu in the Nepal Himalaya: Sapporo, Faculty of Science Hokkaido University, ser. 4, v. 10, p. 95–110.

Hashimoto, S., Ohta, Y., and Akiba, C., eds., 1973, Geology of the Nepal Himalayas: Tokyo, Saikon Publishing Co. Ltd., 286 p.

Hayashi, D., Fujii, Y., Yoneshiro, T., and Kizaki, K., 1984, Observations on the geology of the Karnali region, west Nepal: Nepal Geological Society Journal, Special Issue 4, p. 29–40.

Heim, A., and Gansser, A., 1939, Central Himalaya: Geologic observations of the Swiss expedition, 1936: Zürich, Mémoires de la Société Helvétique des Sciences naturelles 73, 246 p.

Ishida, T., 1969, Petrography and structure of the area between the Dudh Kosi and the Tamba Kosi, east Nepal: Geological Society of Japan Journal, v. 75, p. 115–125.

Johnson, M. R. W., and Rogers, G., 1995, Age of metamorphism of the Kathmandu Complex, Nepal: Himalaya-Karakorum-Tibet Workshop, 10th, Ascona, Switzerland, Abstracts, 3 p.

Kizaki, K., 1994, An outline of the Himalayan upheaval: A case study of the Nepal Himalayas: Kathmandu, Japan International Cooperation Agency (JICA), 127 p.

Le Fort, P., 1975, Himalaya, the collided range. Present knowledge of the continental arc: American Journal of Science, v. 275A, p. 1–44.

Le Fort, P., 1989, The Himalayan orogenic segment, *in* Şengör, A. M. C., ed., Tectonic evolution of the Tethyan region, Proceedings, NATO advanced study institute, Istanbul, 23 September–2 October 1985 (NATO ASI series C, Volume 259): Dordrecht, The Netherlands, Kluwer Academic Publishers, p. 289–386.

Le Fort, P., Debon, F., and Sonet, J., 1983, The lower Paleozoic "Lesser Himalayan" granitic belt: Emphasis on the Simchar pluton of central Nepal, *in* Shams, F. A., ed., Granites of Himalayas, Karakorum and Hindu Kush: Lahore, Pakistan, Punjab University, p. 235–255.

Le Fort P., Debon, F., Pêcher A., Sonet J., and Vidal P., 1986a, The 500 Ma magmatic event in southern Asia, a thermal episode at Gondwana scale, *in* Le Fort, P., Colchen, M., and Montenat, C., eds., Évolution des domaines orogéniques d'Asie méridionale (de la Turquie à l'Indonésie): Nancy, France, Sciences de la Terre, Mémoire 47, p. 191–209.

Le Fort, P., Pêcher, A., and Upreti, B. N., 1986b, A section through the Tibetan Slab in central Nepal (Kali Gandaki valley): Mineral chemistry and thermobarometry of the Main Central Thrust Zone, *in* Le Fort, P., Colchen, M., and Montenat, C., eds., Évolution des domaines orogéniques d'Asie méridionale (de la Turquie à l'Indonésie): Nancy, France, Sciences de la Terre, Mémoire 47, p. 211–228.

Lombardo, B., Pertusati, P., and Borghi, S., 1993, Geology and tectono magmatic evolution of the eastern Himalaya along the Chomolungma-Makalu transect, *in* Treloar, P. J., and Searle, M. P., eds., Himalayan tectonics: Geological Society of London Special Publication 74, p. 341–355.

Macfarlane, A. M., 1992, The tectonic evolution of the core of the Himalaya, Langtang National Park, central Nepal [Ph.D. thesis]: Cambridge, Massachusetts Institute of Technology, 233 p.

Macfarlane, A. M., 1995, An evaluation of the inverted metamorphic gradient at Langtang National Park, central Nepal Himalaya: Journal of Metamorphic Geology, v. 13, p. 595–612.

Maruo, Y., and Kizaki, K., 1983, Thermal structure in the nappes of the eastern Nepal Himalayas, *in* Shams, F. A., ed., Granites of Himalayas, Karakorum and Hindu Kush: Lahore, Pakistan, Punjab University, p. 271–286.

Morrison, C. W. K., and Oliver, G. J. H., 1993, A study of illite crystallinity and fluid inclusions in the Kathmandu Klippe and the Main Central Thrust zone, *in* Treloar, P. J., and Searle, M. P., Himalayan tectonics: Geological Society of London Special Publication 74, p. 525–540.

Pandey, M. R., Tandukar, R. P., Avouac, J. P., Lavé, J., and Massot, J. P., 1995, Interseismic strain accumulation on the Himalayan crustal ramp (Nepal): Geophysical Research Letters, v. 22, p. 751–754.

Pêcher, A., 1991, The contact between the Higher Himalaya Crystallines and the Tibetan Sedimentary Series: Miocene large scale dextral shearing: Tectonics, v. 10, p. 587–598.

Pêcher, A., and Le Fort, P., 1986, The metamorphism in central Himalaya, its relations with the thrust tectonic, *in* Le Fort, P., Colchen, M., and Montenat, C., eds., Évolution des domaines orogéniques d'Asie méridionale (de la Turquie à l'Indonésie): Nancy, France, Sciences de la Terre, Mémoire 47, p. 285–309.

Pognante, U., and Benna, P., 1993, Metamorphic zonation, migmatization and leucogranites along the Everest transect of eastern Nepal and Tibet: Record of an exhumation history, *in* Treloar, P. J., and Searle, M. P., eds., Himalayan tectonics: Geological Society of London Special Publication 74, p. 323–340.

Rai, S. M., Guillot, S., and Le Fort, P., 1997, Pressure-temperature evolution in the Kathmandu and Gosainkund crystalline nappes (central Nepal): Himalaya-Karakorum-Tibet Workshop, 12th, Roma, Italy, Abstracts: Milano, Università degli Studii, p. 127–128.

Sakai, H., 1983, Geology of the Tansen Group of the Lesser Himalaya in Nepal: Kyushu University, Memoire of the Faculty of Science, ser. D (Geology), v. 25, p. 27–74.

Schärer, U., and Allègre, C. J., 1983, The Palung granite (Himalaya); high-resolution U-Pb systematics in zircon and monazite: Earth and Planetary Science Letters, v. 63, p. 423–432.

Schelling, D., 1992, The tectonostratigraphy and structure of the eastern Nepal Himalaya: Tectonics, v. 11, p. 925–943.

Sharma, T., and Kizaki, K., 1989, Metamorphism and thermal history of the Jaljala Synclinorium, central west Nepal Himalaya: Nepal Geological Society Journal, v. 6, p. 21–34.

Sharma, T., Kansakar, R., and Kizaki, K., 1984, Geology and tectonics of the region between Kali Gandaki and Bheri rivers in central west Nepal: University of the Ryukyus, Bulletin of the College of Science, v. 38, p. 57–102.

Srivastava, P., and Mitra, G., 1994, Thrust geometries and deep structure of the outer and lesser Himalaya, Kumaon and Garhwal (India): Implications for evolution of the Himalayan fold-and-thrust belt: Tectonics, v. 13, p. 89–109.

Stöcklin, J., 1980, Geology of the Nepal and its regional frame: Geological Society of London Journal, v. 137, p. 1–34.

Stöcklin, J., and Bhattarai, K. D., 1980, Geological map of Kathmandu area and central Mahabharat range: Kathmandu, United Nations Development Programme, scale 1:250,000, 1 sheet.

Talent, J. A., Goel, R. K., Jain, A. K., and Pickett, J. W., 1988, Silurian and Devonian of India, Nepal and Bhutan: Biostratigraphic and paleobiogeographic anomalies: Cour. Fortschritte-Institut Senckenberg, v. 106, p. 1–57.

United Nations Economic and Social Commission for Asia and the Pacific Cooperation (ESCAP) Department of Mines and Geology (DMG), 1993, Atlas of the mineral resources of the ESCAP region, Geology and mineral resources of Nepal: Explanatory Brochure, Volume 9: Bangkok, 107 p.

Upreti, B. N., 1990, An outline geology of far western Nepal: Journal of Himalayan Geology, v. 1, p. 93–102.

Upreti, B. N., and Dhital, M. R., 1996, Landslide studies and management in Nepal: Kathmandu, International Centre for Integrated Mountain Development (ICIMOD), 87 p.

Valdiya, K. S., 1980a, Geology of Kumaun Lesser Himalaya: Dehra Dun, India, Wadia Institute of Himalayan Geology, 291 p.

Valdiya, K. S., 1980b, The two intracrustal boundary thrusts of the Himalaya: Tectonophysics, v. 66, p. 323–348.

Valdiya, K. S., 1981, Tectonics of the central sector of the Himalaya, in Gupta, H. K., and Delany, F. M., eds., Zagros, Hindu Kush, Himalaya geodynamic evolution: American Geophysical Union Geodynamic series 3, p. 87–110.

Valdiya, K. S., 1986, Correlations of Lesser Himalayan formations of Nepal and Kumaon, in Le Fort, P., Colchen, M., and Montenat, C., eds., Evolution des domaines orogéniques d'Asie méridionale (de la Turquie à l'Indonésie): Nancy, France, Sciences de la Terre, Mémoire 47, p. 361–383.

MANUSCRIPT ACCEPTED BY THE SOCIETY FEBRUARY 3, 1998

Geological Society of America
Special Paper 328
1999

Evolution of a Neogene fluvial system in a Himalayan foreland basin, India

Rohtash Kumar, Sumit K. Ghosh, and Satish J. Sangode
Sedimentology Group, Wadia Institute of Himalayan Geology, P.O. Box 74, Dehra Dun 248 001, India

ABSTRACT

Pliocene-Pleistocene evolution of the Himalayan foreland (Siwalik) basin is documented from a 2.4-km-thick fluvial succession in the Haripur sub-basin, Himachal Pradesh, India. Variations in deposit architecture, paleoflow orientations, and mineralogy observed within the succession are related to tectonic activity along Main Boundary thrust and Intra-Foreland thrust. The Dhok Pathan Formation (ca. 6 to 5.5 Ma) of the Middle Siwalik sub-group is at the base of the succession. It contains thick multistoried gray sheet sandstones and minor mudstones interpreted to be deposits of a major trunk drainage system. The gradual upsection addition of buff ribbon sandstone and a substantial increase in overbank mudstones in the overlying Tatrot Formation of the Upper Siwalik sub-group, starting at ca. 4.8 Ma, marks the inception of piedmont drainage in this area. Pre-Tertiary-clast–bearing conglomerate, derived mainly from the Lesser Himalayan zone formations, first occurs at 1,375 m (3.36 Ma) in the succession and substantially increases in abundance at 1,685 m (2.6 Ma), at the base of the Pinjor Formation. Tertiary-clast–bearing syntectonic conglomerates from the Sub-Himalayan Tertiary belt first appear in the succession at 2,100 m (1.77 Ma) and persist through the top of the section at about 0.5 Ma.

Differences in sandstone framework composition and paleoflow orientation indicate the presence of three distinct drainage systems at various times during basin filling. The southeasterly flowing axial trunk drainage was joined by a southwesterly flowing transverse trunk drainage at 5.5 Ma and was completely displaced by largely south flowing piedmont drainage in the study area at about 1.77 Ma. Upsection variations in the fluvial architecture are interpreted to record: (1) movement of the Main Boundary thrust at about 5.5 Ma and tilting of the basin to the southwest; (2) inception of piedmont drainage around 4.8 Ma during initiation of the Intra-Foreland thrust; (3) enhanced activity along the Intra-Foreland thrust at 1.77 Ma, forming a small depression that filled with syntectonic Tertiary-clast–bearing conglomerate; and (4) southward tilting of the basin and displacement of the transverse trunk drainage by piedmont drainage at about 1.77 Ma.

INTRODUCTION

Foreland basins are located between strongly deformed cover rock of the orogenic zone and relatively undeformed rock cover of the craton. These basins are underlain by continental crust and contain detritus derived from the erosion of the uplifted orogenic zone. These deposits record temporal and spatial variation in sedimentation related to basin subsidence and tectonic activity in the marginal fold-thrust belt (e.g., McLean and Jerzykiewicz, 1978; Beer and Jordan, 1989; and Johnson and

Kumar, R., Ghosh, S. K., and Sangode, S. J., 1999, Evolution of a Neogene fluvial system in a Himalayan foreland basin, India, *in* Macfarlane, A., Sorkhabi, R. B., and Quade, J., eds., Himalaya and Tibet: Mountain Roots to Mountain Tops: Boulder, Colorado, Geological Society of America Special Paper 328.

Pierce, 1990). The control of hinterland thrusting on the evolution of fluvial architecture in foreland basins is well documented. However, the role of intrabasinal tectonic deformation on basin sedimentation is more poorly understood.

The Siwalik foreland basin evolved due to continent-continent collision of the Indian and Eurasian plates. The sedimentary fill of this basin has been well studied in the Potwar Plateau, Pakistan (Johnson et al., 1985; Burbank and Raynold, 1988; Willis 1993a, 1993b, and references therein), but there are few studies that provide long, well-documented records of the Siwalik Group of India. Schumm and Rea (1995) suggested three phases of uplift in the Himalayan belt, at 12–10 Ma, 9–8 Ma, and 4–3 Ma, on the basis of sedimentation rates in the Bengal fan. The first two phases have been related to activity along the principal thrusts in the Himalayan orogenic belt, the Main Central thrust and Main Boundary thrust. The third phase, however, may be related to proximal partitioning within the foreland basin, such as reported from the other foreland basins (DeCelles and Hertel, 1989; Zoetemeijer et al., 1990; Meyers et al., 1992). The impact of tectonism during the Pliocene-Pleistocene on sedimentation rates and patterns within the Indian Himalayan foreland basin has not been well documented. The study evaluates the role of intrabasinal deformation, fluvial architecture, sediment dispersal patterns, and sedimentary processes that form the Pliocene-Pleistocene Siwalik sediments in the Haripur sub-basin (Fig. 1).

HARIPUR SUB-BASIN

Geology and measured section

The Haripur sub-basin is bounded by the Yamuna River to the east and Markanda River in the west (Fig. 1). The Middle Siwalik sub-group is exposed in the southern part of the study area along the Himalayan Frontal fault. These strata are transitionally overlain by the Upper Siwalik sub-group toward the north. The Upper Siwalik sub-group is divided into the Tatrot, Pinjor, and Boulder Conglomerate Formations (Srivastava et al., 1988; Nanda et al., 1991). In the northern part of the study area, the Upper Siwalik sub-group has been overthrusted by the Lower Siwalik sub-group (Nahan Formation) across the Nahan thrust (Intra-Foreland thrust). Farther north, the Lower Siwalik sub-group is overthrusted along the Main Boundary fault by Lower Tertiary sediments of the Subathu and Dagshai Formations and other, pre-Tertiary, Lesser Himalayan zone formations along the Main Boundary thrust (Medlicott, 1864; Valdiya, 1980).

This study describes a 2.4-km-thick sedimentary succession through the Middle and Upper Siwalik sub-groups (Fig. 2, a and b), from the base in the Dhok Pathan Formation to the Boulder Conglomerate Formation. The sedimentary section was measured and sampled along the Somb Nadi River and its eastern tributary, Jamni Khol, in the Haripur area (Fig. 1, a and b).

Paleomagnetic sampling and analysis

Samples from 200 paleomagnetic sites in red, brown, yellow, and grayish-brown overbank siltstone and mudstone were obtained throughout the succession (Fig. 2, a and b). Triplicate oriented samples were taken from each site by standard methods (Johnson et al., 1975).

We employed a progressive thermal demagnetization on all 800 specimens from 200 sites at the intervals of 25, 50, and 100 °C to 700 °C; monitoring of low-frequency magnetic susceptibility measurements was on Bartingtons MS-2 unit. The efficacy of thermal demagnetization on hematite-bearing redbeds has long been recognized in Siwalik mudstones (Tauxe et al., 1980; Tauxe and Badgely, 1988) and elsewhere (Irving and Opdyke, 1965; Dunlop, 1970). The vector endpoint plots (Fig. 3) for the representative specimens indicated the removal of the viscous remanent component (acquired during the present Earth's magnetic field) after 200 °C, and the blocking temperature for a strong secondary component at ~450 °C. The natural remanent magnetism (NRM) intensities are in a range of 10E-1 to 10E-2 A/m, sufficient to be analyzed on a DSM-2 spinner magnetometer (Schonstedt, USA). The details of all paleomagnetic results were described in Sangode et al. (1996).

A sharp fall in the intensity decay curves at 500 °C is observed in most of the sites. Previous studies (Collinson, 1974) have attributed this fall to the presence of specularite, a black polycrystalline hematite. Detailed work on similar redbeds of the Siwalik Group in the Potwar Plateau (Tauxe et al., 1980) supports the presence of specularite in these sediments.

The site mean direction for each horizon was calculated using the statistics of Fisher (1953). The paleolatitudes (λp) and paleolongitudes (ϕp) of the virtual geomagnetic pole (VGP) were deduced using the derivations given by Butler (1992). Using the tectonic-tilt corrections, the mean directions for each site were calculated from a set of unit vectors after determining the direction cosines of each unit vector. Having calculated the mean directions, the dispersion estimates were done by a precision parameter (K) and the confidence limit with a probability level of 95% ($\alpha95$) for each site. The approximate estimate of the angular standard deviation (sd) by direct analogy with the Gaussian statistics was performed. When the antipode of the reverse polarity mean is compared with the normal polarity mean in this investigation (Fig. 4), the directions are 1° apart for the selected sites, suggesting an excellent pass of the reversal test. This indicates the reliability of the Characteristic Component of NRM (ChRM) directions as the primary directions.

The paleolatitudes of the VGP (λp) were plotted with their site locations on the studied sedimentary column (Fig. 5) for the identification of the observed magnetic zonations on a standard geomagnetic polarity time scale (GPTS; Cande and Kent, 1995). Thus, 18 magnetic polarity reversals were estimated after plotting the paleolatitudes of the VGP on the analyzed section.

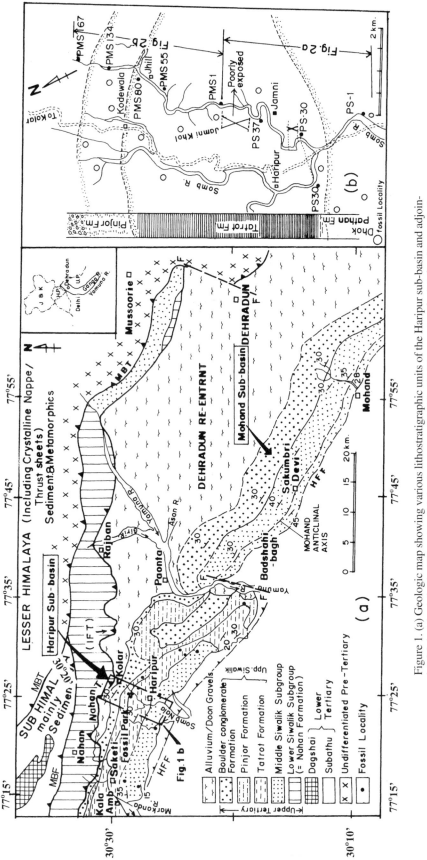

Figure 1. (a) Geologic map showing various lithostratigraphic units of the Haripur sub-basin and adjoining Mohand sub-basin. These two sub-basins are separated by the Yamuna tear fault (after Kumar et al., 1991). (b) Traverse line and paleomagnetic sample sites of the measured section.

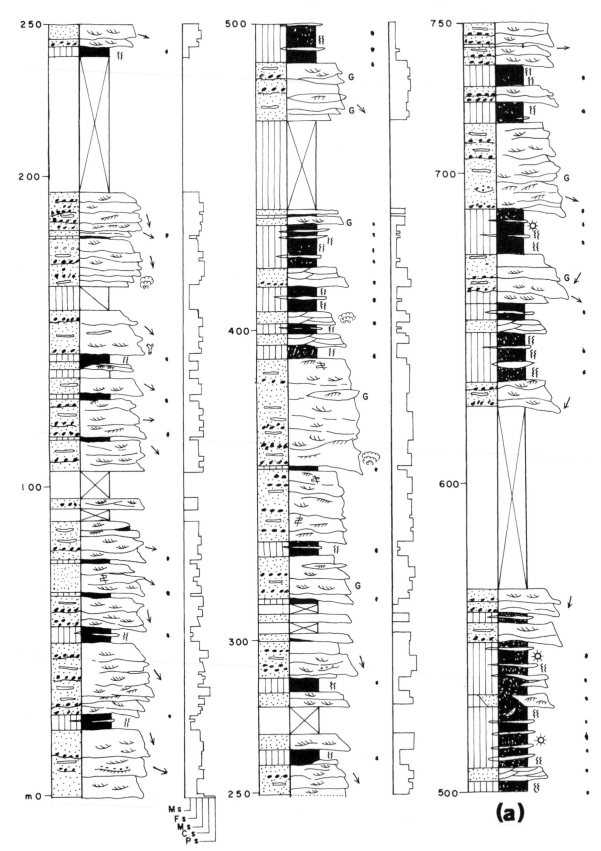

Figure 2 (above and on next three pages). Detailed sedimentary log of the measured sections: (a) along the Somb Nadi, (b) along its eastern tributary, Jamni Khol. For location see Figure 1b.

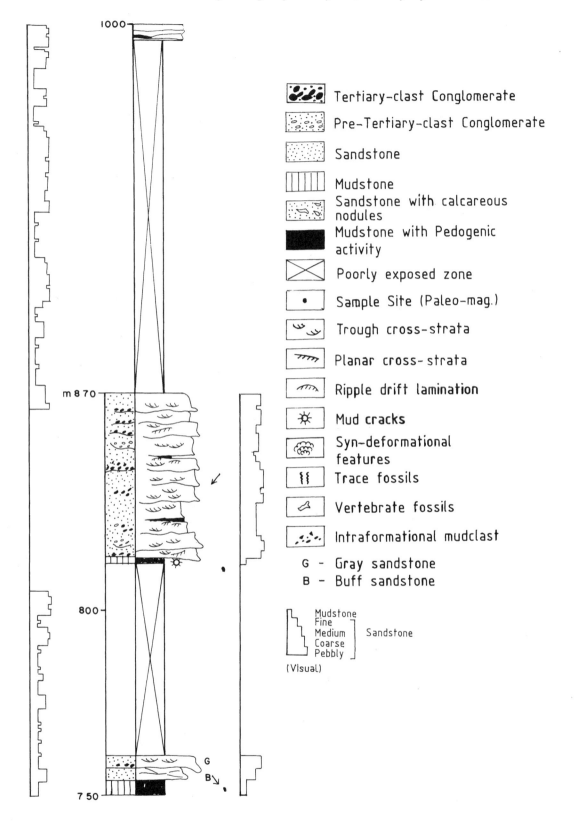

Tertiary-clast Conglomerate

Pre-Tertiary-clast Conglomerate

Sandstone

Mudstone

Sandstone with calcareous nodules

Mudstone with Pedogenic activity

Poorly exposed zone

Sample Site (Paleo-mag.)

Trough cross-strata

Planar cross-strata

Ripple drift lamination

Mud cracks

Syn-deformational features

Trace fossils

Vertebrate fossils

Intraformational mudclast

G - Gray sandstone
B - Buff sandstone

Mudstone
Fine
Medium   Sandstone
Coarse
Pebbly

(Visual)

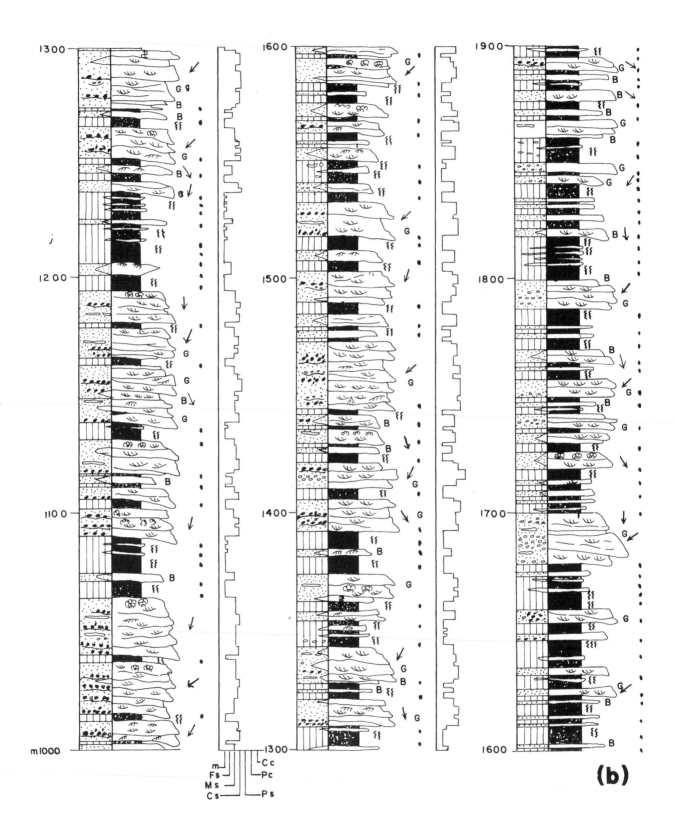

(b)

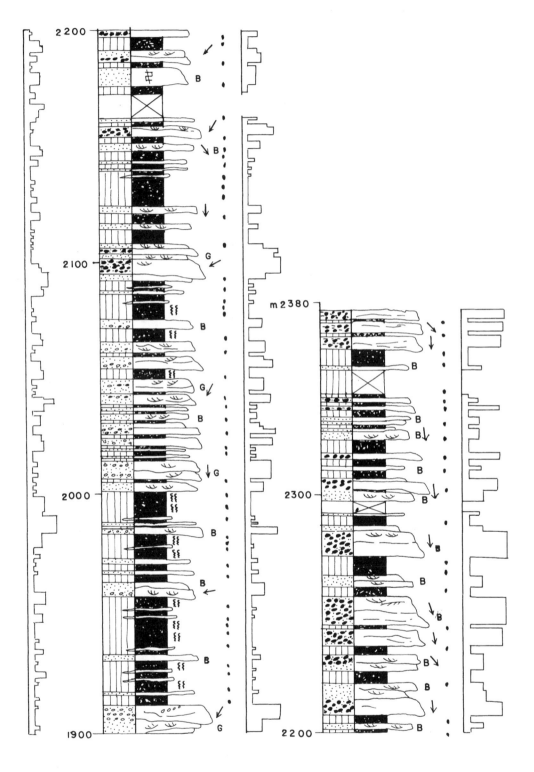

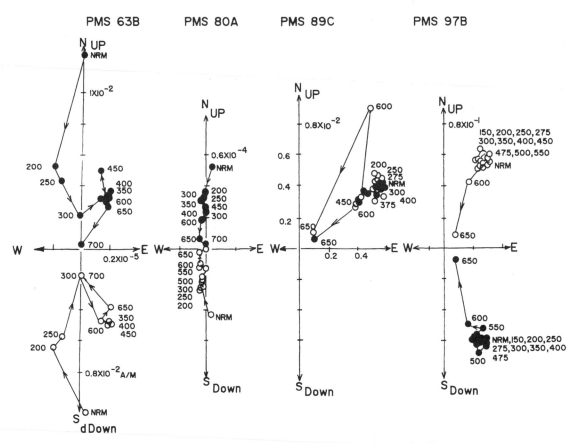

Figure 3. Representative vector end point plots in the Haripur sub-basin samples. Note the component removed at 200 °C directed near the present Earth's magnetic field. The secondary component removed near 300 °C makes an overlapping coercivity spectra with the Earth's components. Another strong secondary component is unblocked at around 450 °C. Both the vertical and horizontal components in all the samples pass toward the origin, indicating a primary, hard component.

Estimation of ages

The recently modified GPTS of Cande and Kent (1995) has been adopted for the estimation of time on the observed polarity events. Because the terminologies of the older GPTS (Mankinen and Dalrymple, 1979) are more conversant with the earlier work in the Siwalik basin, they are followed by equivalent chronological events of Cande and Kent (1995) in brackets.

A long normal polarity zone begins at 1300 m in the Upper Siwalik sub-group lithotype (Fig. 5). This zone is divided by a short polarity reversal, and is followed by a long reversed polarity zone including three short normal events. This pattern is characteristic of the Gauss-Matuyama long normal and long reversal in the Neogene epoch of the GPTS. Tuffaceous mudstones at the Pinjor type locality in the adjoining Chandigarh area of the Punjab Sub-Himalaya are near the Gauss-Matuyama boundary (Mehta et al., 1993). A bentonitic tuff in the meausured Haripur section is 32 m below this same apparent magnetic polarity transition (Fig. 5). On this basis we placed the Gauss-Matuyama boundary (C2An.1n to C2r.2r at 2.58 Ma) at ~1,685 m (Fig. 5).

Several mammalian vertebrate fossil localities that support

our proposed paleomagnetic dates were reported from the study area by Srivastava et al. (1988) and Nanda et al. (1991). The occurrences of diagnostic faunas of the study area are listed in Table 1. Middle Siwalik fauna are represented by suidae species *Dicoryphochoeras titan,* and *Hippohyus* cf. *H. Grandis,* typical of the Dhok Pathan Formation elsewhere in India. The Upper Siwalik fauna is represented at Haripur by *Equus, Rhinoceros, Cervus,* and *Bos* (Nanda et al., 1991). Earlier workers marked the Tatrot-Pinjor faunal boundary at the Pinjor type section, characterized by the appearance of *Equus* and cervids with antlers and the absence of *Hipparion,* near the Gauss-Matuyama magnetic polarity transition (Opdyke et al., 1979; Tandon et al., 1984; Ranga Rao et al., 1988).

A summary of magnetic polarity chronological events and formation boundaries is as follows.

1. The Gauss-Gilbert boundary (base of C2An.3n; 3.58 Ma) is at 1,300 m.

2. The Gauss-Matuyama boundary (C2An.1n-C2r.2r; 2.58 Ma) is at 1,685 m and correlates with the Tatrot-Pinjor faunal boundary.

3. The Reunion event (C2r.1n; 2.15–2.14 Ma) extends from 1,880 to 1,915 m.

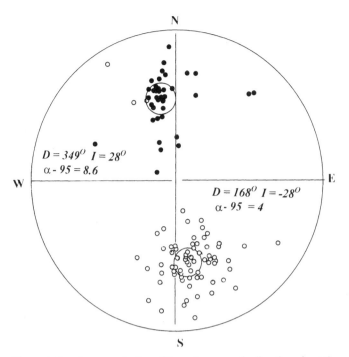

Figure 4. Equal-area projection of the paleomagnetic directions from the studied section, after correction for bedding tilt. D = declination, I = inclination, α = confidence level.

4. The Olduvai normal event (C2n; 1.95–1.77 Ma) extends from 1,990 to 2,078 m.

5. The Jaramillo normal event (Clr.1n; 1.07–0.99 Ma) extends from 2,204 to 2,227 m.

6. The Brunhes normal event (Cln; 0.78 Ma) begins at 2,250 m.

SEDIMENTOLOGY

Sedimentation patterns

There are profound changes in channel-body geometry and the percentage of overbank to channel deposits through the Siwalik succession in the Haripur sub-basin. The lower 400 m (Dhok Pathan Formation) is thickly bedded (>40 m), multistoried gray sandstone containing minor intervening overbank mudstones (Fig. 2a). The overbank/channel deposit thickness ratio is generally less than 0.2, but locally can be as high as 1 (Fig. 6).

Gray sandstone bodies are as thick as 40 m and contain multiple, vertically stacked channel deposits separated by internal erosion surfaces (Fig. 7). The lower contacts of sandstone bodies are generally erosive and nearly planar, and the upper contact grades into overlying mudstone deposits. Lag deposits of calcrete, mudballs, mud pellets, and extrabasinal quartzite clasts overlie basal erosional surfaces of the sandstone bodies.

Sandstone bodies contain large-scale trough cross-strata (as thick as 2 m). Sandstone fines upward and cross-sets decrease in thickness (from 2 m to 20 cm) upward within sandstone bodies. These sandstone bodies generally have sheet-like geometries

(width/depth or W/D >15), although ribbon (W/D <15) sand bodies are locally present. The intervening massive mudstones are brown to gray and contain calcrete nodules. Immature paleosols and bioturbation features are commonly observed in the mudstone.

At the boundary between the Dhok Pathan and Tatrot Formations (400–600 m; 5.5–5 Ma), the thick gray multistoried sandstone bodies are replaced by both minor sheet and ribbon-shaped bodies and the proportion of overbank mudstone increases (Figs. 2a, 6, and 8). The thickness of trough cross-strata also decreases. The average trough cross-strata set thickness is <20 cm. Lateral accretion beds in channels are common. In places, channel bodies pass laterally into mudstone channel fills. Overbank deposits have mature paleosol profiles and well-developed mudcracks.

There are three types of sandstone bodies in the Tatrot Formation (600–1,500 m; 5–3.07 Ma): (1) major gray sheet bodies (W/D >100), (2) minor gray sheet bodies (W/D > 15 < 100), and (3) ribbon bodies, both gray and buff (W/D < 15).

Buff ribbon sandstone bodies first occur at 760 m (4.8 Ma) in the succession (Fig. 2a). These buff sandstone bodies (Fig. 9) are associated with higher proportion of overbank deposits (overbank/channel deposits ratio >5; Fig. 6) and are dominated by small-scale trough cross-strata and parallel laminations. The size of buff sandstone bodies increases upsection. Gray and buff sandstone initially interfinger, but buff sandstones are only present above 2,100 m (1.77 Ma; Figs. 2b and 5). A distinct conglomerate body is present at 1,375 m (3.36 Ma) and is associated with overbank mudstones (overbank/channel deposit ratios >10) (Fig. 6). This conglomerate consists of subrounded to subangular clasts (mainly quartzite) derived from the then-uplifted Outer Lesser Himalayan terrain (Kumar and Ghosh, 1991). Conglomerate beds substantially increase in abundance above 1,670 m (2.6 Ma; Figs. 2b and 5).

Mudstones are more abundant, and the overbank/channel deposit ratio exceeds 5 near the Tatrot-Pinjor Formation boundary at 1,685 m (Fig. 6). In the Pinjor Formation, minor gray sheet sandstone bodies remain common, but the frequency of buff sandstone increases. Buff sandstones also increase in thickness, are locally multistoried, and are accompanied by pre-Tertiary-clast-bearing conglomerates. The single to multistoried conglomerates bodies are stratified, transverse imbricated, and are composed of subangular to subrounded clasts, mainly quartzite with subordinate limestone, phyllite, slate, chert, granitoid, and rare basic igneous rocks. Clast size ranges from 10 to 15 cm; the largest clasts are 20 cm.

At the contact between the upper part of the Pinjor Formation and the Boulder Conglomerate Formation (2,100 m; 1.77 Ma), the conglomerate clast composition changes from quartzite derived from the Lesser Himalaya zone to reworked sub-Himalayan, lower Tertiary sandstone clasts (Fig. 2b). The conglomeratic layers are 1–6 m thick in the basal part of the Boulder Conglomerate Formation, stratified, imbricated, and composed of subrounded to subangular clasts embedded in buff sandy-muddy matrix and interbedded with buff sandstones and abun-

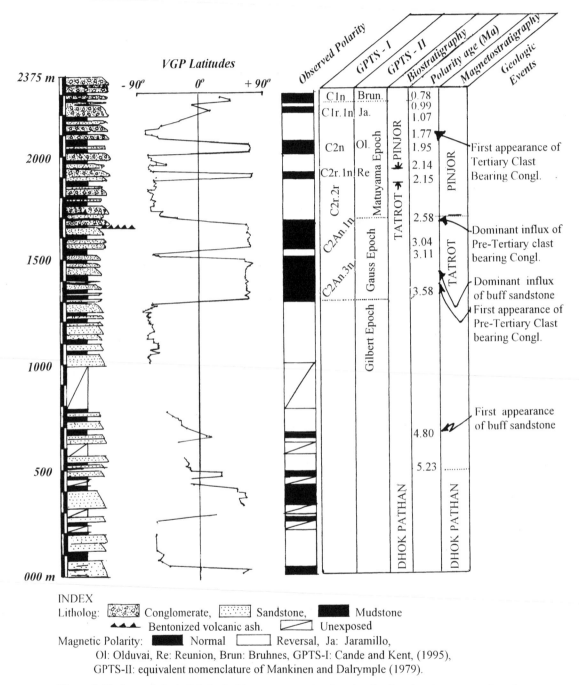

INDEX
Litholog: [░░] Conglomerate, [▒▒] Sandstone, [■■] Mudstone
▲▲▲ Bentonized volcanic ash. [◹] Unexposed
Magnetic Polarity: [■] Normal [ ] Reversal, Ja: Jaramillo,
Ol: Olduvai, Re: Reunion, Brun: Bruhnes, GPTS-I: Cande and Kent, (1995),
GPTS-II: equivalent nomenclature of Mankinen and Dalrymple (1979).

Figure 5. Haripur sub-basin lithological log summary showing the plot for virtual geomagnetic pole
(VGP) paleolatitude and the observed magnetic polarity. The geomagnetic polarity time scale (GPTS)
nomenclature is from both the recently modified version (GPTS-I: Cande and Kent, 1995) and from an
older version (GPTS- II: Mankinen and Dalrymple, 1979). The biostratigraphic divisions are after
Nanda et al. (1991).

TABLE 1. SALIENT FEATURES OF HARIPUR SUB-BASIN

	Stratigraphic Status (Thickness, age range)	Lithology	Fauna*
Lower Siwalik Sub-Group	Nahan Formation (1250 m)	Fine- to medium-grained gray indurated multi-storied sandstones with yellow and brown pedogenic mudstone	–
Upper Siwalik Sub-Group (1875 m)	Boulder Conglomerate Formation (300 m; 1.7 to 0.5 Ma)	Thickly bedded massive to stratified Tertiary-clast bearing conglomerate; interstratified buff fine- to medium-grained sandstones, brown mudstones	–
	Pinjor Formation (390 m; 2.6 to 1.7 Ma)	Stratified pre-Tertiary clast–bearing conglomerate; fine- to medium-grained gray and buff sandstones with variegated overbank mudstones, buff sandstones gradually increase in upsection.	*Equus sivalensis; Bos acutifrons; Rhinoceras* sp.; *Cervus* sp.; *Elephas.*
	Tatrot Formation (1185 m; 5.23 to 2.6 Ma)	Fine- to medium-grained gray multistoried sandstones, ribbon gray and buff sandstones, variegated overbank mudstones	*Archidiskon planifrons, Stegodon insignis*
Middle Siwalik Sub-Group	Dhok Pathan Formation (500 m; ~6 to 5.23 Ma)	Thickly bedded gray multi-storied fine- to medium-grained sandstones, rare overbank mudstone; gradual upsection increase in mudstone	*Dicoryphochoerus titan;* Hippophyus cf. *H. gandis;* Propotamochoerus cf. *P. salinus*

*After Nanda et al., 1991.

dant mudstones (overbank/channel deposit ratio >5; Fig. 6). The size of the conglomerate bodies, clast size (up to 50 cm), and angularity all increase upsection, and conglomerates have abundant muddy matrix and are weakly imbricated (Fig. 10).

Compositional variability

Sandstones in the Siwalik Group at Haripur are lithic arenites (53.5%), sublithic arenites (37.3%), subarkoses (4.6%), and lithic graywackes (4.6%). Composition variations in the Siwalik sandstones can be examined by comparing changes in the ratio of quartz (Q), feldspar (F), and rock/lithic fragments (L). The gray sandstones are medium- to fine-grained lithic arenites having an average QFL ratio of 55:6:39. Buff sandstones are mostly fine grained and less-commonly medium-grained sublithic arenites to lithic arenite; the average QFL ratio is 70:1:29 (Table 2). Rock/lithic grain types of the gray and buff sandstones show large differences. Buff sandstones have abundant sedimentary lithics (Ls), mainly siltstone, shale, and limestone, and rare metamorphic grains (Lm) and mica. Gray sandstones have abundant metamorphic grains (Lm), mainly quartz-mica tectonite, phyllite, and metaquartzite. They contain moderate proportions of sedimentary

grains (Ls), mostly sandstone, siltstone, shale, and chert, as well as less-common acid-plutonic igneous rock fragments (Li). Mica, mainly biotite and chlorite, is abundant in the gray sandstones, and the heavy fraction contains kyanite, garnet, and sillimanite.

There is considerable variation in QFL proportions and lithic grain-type proportions in the section. The amount of quartz relative to lithics dramatically increases between 300 to 1,000 m, whereas feldspar increases more gradually over the basal 700 m (Fig. 11). Between 300 and 800 m there is more Lm than Ls, whereas Ls dominates over Lm above 800 m. The percentage of Ls increases substantially in the buff sandstone. Li almost disappears above 300 m and reappears between 800 and 1,200 m (Fig. 11). There is a relative increase in Ls, to a maximum of 84%, and a decrease in Lm (16 %) in the upper two-thirds of the section. From 1,800 to 2,100 m quartz and feldspar increase, whereas the lithic fragments decrease gradually. Farther upsection, above 2,100 m, quartz decreases and lithic fragments increase (Fig. 11).

Paleoflow variability

Paleoflow measurements were made on 266 sets of trough cross-strata and more than 2,000 clast imbrications. Paleoflow

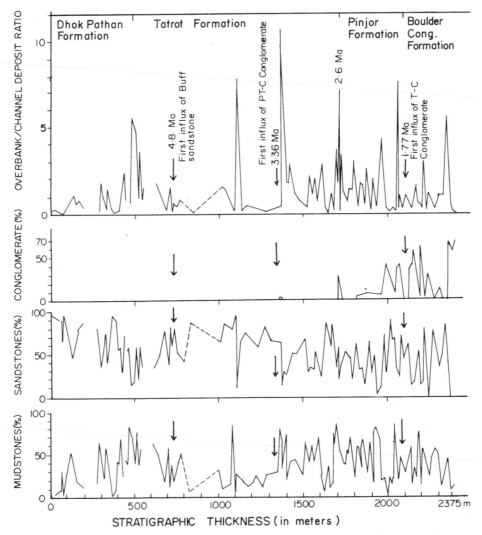

Figure 6. Upsection variation in percentage of overbank mudstones, channel sandstone, conglomerate, and ratio of overbank/channel deposits.

was mainly toward the southeast (Fig. 11) in the basal 500 m (5.23 Ma) of the succession (all gray sandstones), although there is a secondary mode toward the northeast. From 500 to 1,450 m (5.23 to 3.2 Ma), paleoflow directions of the buff and the gray sandstones are almost perpendicular to each other; the gray sandstone to the southwest and the buff sandstone to the southeast. In the upper part of the succession (1,450 to 2,375 m; 3.2 Ma to 0.5 Ma), paleoflow was mainly toward the south-southeast for trough cross-strata and south-southwest for imbricated clasts, with high variance.

DEPOSITIONAL SYSTEMS

Changes in fluvial architecture, the amount of mudstone relative to channel sandstone, paleoflow orientations, and mineralogy reveal changes in the depositional environment. Prior to 5.5 Ma (the basal 400 m), sediments are multistoried gray sheet sand-

stones that have abundant erosional surfaces, no lateral accretionary surfaces, and low paleocurrent variability. Few overbank mudstones are preserved. These are interpreted to have been deposited in a braided river system (e.g., Rust and Jones, 1987; Kumar, 1993). The size of cross-bed sets (up to 2 m) and bank-derived intraclasts lags indicates a major river system, possibly of the magnitude of the present Ganga River. The southeast paleoflow direction parallels that of the present Ganga River.

The abundance of mudstone increases and the sizes of the sandstone bodies decrease between 400 and 1,600 m (5.5–2.8 Ma). Lateral accretion surfaces and channel plug deposits in the sandstone bodies, and the abundance of overbank mudstone suggest a meandering river environment. The paleoflow was initially toward the east, but subsequently shifted toward the southwest. Relatively small trough cross-strata, mature paleosols, and mud cracks suggest a low flow-magnitude river system (cf. Kumar and Tandon, 1985; Kraus, 1987). Above 600 m,

Figure 7. Multistoried sandstone bodies in the Dhok Pathan Formation, Haripur sub-basin. Sandstone bodies are gray, large-scale trough cross stratified and separated by erosion surfaces (ES).

Figure 8. The transition interval of Dhok Pathan and Tatrot Formations dominated by overbank mudstone deposits (spanning 400–600 m; Fig. 2a). The gray ribbon sandstone body (GS) is comparatively thin and merges laterally into siltstone and/or mudstone with mud cracks.

Figure 9. Outcrop showing both ribbon and sheet sandstone bodies. The ribbon sandstone body (R) is buff, tapers laterally (arrow), and is overlain by the levee (L) deposits. The profile is capped by the gray sheet sandstone (S).

Figure 10. Massive, poorly sorted, mud-matrix-supported Tertiary-clast–bearing conglomerate in the upper part of the Boulder Conglomerate Formation.

the increased size of the gray sandstone bodies, the absence of internal lateral accretionary surfaces, and the decrease in mudstone content indicate a braided river environment. Buff ribbon sandstone bodies, which first appear at 760 m (4.8 Ma), show no evidence of lateral accretion. The smaller size of these sandstone bodies indicates low-magnitude rivers that have laterally

fixed channels. The frequency and size of buff sandstone bodies increase above 1,450 m (3.2 Ma), which suggests a gradual increase in magnitude of piedmont drainage. Paleoflow directions in the piedmont drainage were almost perpendicular to the transverse trunk drainage.

At 1,375 m (3.36 Ma), pre-Tertiary-clast–bearing conglomerates first appear in multistoried gray sandstone bodies, and are interpreted to record the return of the southwesterly flowing, major transverse trunk drainage. The abundance of conglomerate deposits increases upsection to 2,100 m, within both the gray and buff sandstones. Buff sandstones are more abundant than gray sandstones. This interval is interpreted to record interfingering of gravelly braided transverse trunk stream and piedmont stream(s).

At 2,100 m (1.77 Ma), the sediments in the section coarsen, gray sandstone is rare, and Tertiary clasts appear in the conglomerates. Upsection, conglomerates become massive, mud-matrix supported, and are composed only of reworked lower Tertiary sandstone clasts. This suggests rapid deposition in the proximal part of alluvial-fan debris flows.

TABLE 2. A COMPARISON OF GRAY AND BUFF SANDSTONES OF SIWALIKS

Areas	Age (Ma)	Sandstone composition	Carrier(s)
Potwar Plateau, northern Pakistan*	8.1	Gray - $Q_{28}F_{12}L_{60}$	Trunk stream (*Paleo-Indus*)
		Buff - $Q_{50}F_{11}L_{39}$	Piedmont stream
Haripur Sub-Basin Northern India	~6 to 0.5	Gray - $Q_{55}F_6L_{39}$	Trunk stream (*Paleo-Ganga*)
		Buff - $Q_{70}F_1L_{29}$	Piedmont stream

*Data from Behrensmeyer and Tauxe, 1982.

TECTONIC IMPLICATIONS

The temporal variation of the fluvial architecture of Siwalik Group sediments is strongly influenced by tectonism (e.g., Parkash, et al., 1980; Johnson et al., 1985; Tandon, 1991; Kumar, 1993; Willis, 1993b; Kumar and Ghosh, 1994, and others). The controlling factors are uplift, sediment supply, and basinal subsidence. Two-dimensional theoretical models predict the interplay between the timing of tectonic uplift, basin subsidence, and change in basin depositional rates (e.g., Beaumont, 1981; Flemings and Jordan, 1989, 1990, and others).

The Haripur sub-basin received at least 400 m of thick (>40 m), multistoried gray sheet sandstone bodies prior to 5.5 Ma. Southeasterly flow directions and the preponderance of metamorphic lithic grains suggest axial trunk (paleo-Ganga River) flow derived from north of the Main Central thrust (Fig. 12). The presence of detritus derived from the Lesser Himalayan zone is attributed to activity on the Main Boundary thrust along the northwestern margin of this part of foreland basin.

At 5.5 Ma, the fluvial architecture changed to thinly bedded gray sheet and ribbon bodies and abundant overbank mudstones. Paleoflow pattern changed from southeast to southwest, reflecting the replacement of an southeasterly flowing axial drainage system by southwesterly transverse trunk drainage. Changes in sandstone composition are interpreted to reflect a tectonic reorganization of drainage patterns. This drainage reorganization (Fig. 12) resulted in widening of interfluve area that filled with huge overbank mudstones, recording a period of tectonic uplift and rapid basin subsidence (e.g., Heller et al., 1988; Paola, 1988). Southwestward basin tilting, due to the tectonic rejuvenation of the Main Boundary thrust along the northeastern margin of the basin, resulted in accumulation of a coarse gravel sheet near the thrust in the adjoining Mohand sub-basin (Fig. 1a; Kumar and Ghosh, 1994, 1995). This tectonism produced an increase in subsidence rate and accumulation space in the distal Haripur sub-basin.

Buff ribbon sandstone bodies are interfingered with gray sandstone beginning at 760 m (4.8 Ma). Gray and buff sandstones have distinct compositions (QFL percent), lithic fragment types, and mica content. The composition of buff sandstone suggests that the detritus was derived from the uplifted lower Tertiary sub-Himalayan sedimentary belt located along the northern flank of the Haripur sub-basin (Fig. 12). Similar river systems of differing scale are also documented at about 8.1 Ma within the Khaur area of the Potwar Plateau (Behrensmeyer and Tauxe, 1982). The gray and buff sandstone systems differ in sand-body size, lithofacies, paleocurrent orientation, and sandstone composition. The buff sandstone is interpreted to be the result of piedmont drainage draining only frontal areas, whereas blue-gray sandstone is interpreted to be major trunk drainage that drained both frontal and interior areas of the Himalaya.

The distinct changes in provenance and drainage patterns indicate the appearance of piedmont drainage because of partitioning of the northern fringe of the Haripur sub-basin along the Intra-Foreland thrust (Nahan thrust) starting at 4.8 Ma (Fig. 12). This correlates with increases in the Bengal fan sedimentation rates between 3 and 4 Ma (Schumm and Rea, 1995). Furthermore, the gray sandstones deposited by transverse trunk drainage were gradually replaced by buff sandstones laid down by the piedmont drainage of much smaller dimension. Following a brief interval of interfingering between these systems, gray sandstones disappear from this basin around 1.77 Ma (Fig. 12). This suggests gradual uplift of the lower Tertiary sedimentary belt along the Intra-Foreland thrust.

The pre-Tertiary-clast–bearing conglomerate of this basin first appears at 1,375 m (3.6 Ma). This conglomerate was deposited in a thick gravel sheet that was southwesterly prograding toward the souhwest, from the Mohand sub-basin to the east (Kumar and Ghosh, 1995). This suggests that activity along the Main Boundary thrust ceased, with simultaneous decrease in basinal subsidence in the Mohand sub-basin, causing southwesterly progradation of the gravel sheet from the Mohand sub-basin (proximal) to the Haripur sub-basin (distal). A similar type of gravel-sheet migration in other foreland basins was reported by Heller et al. (1988) and Paola (1988).

Syntectonic (Tertiary-clast bearing) conglomerate replaces post-tectonic (pre-Tertiary-clast–bearing) conglomerate at 2,100 m (1.77 Ma). The compositional shift is interpreted as a consequence of rapid uplift along the Intra-Foreland thrust, which resulted in the formation of a rapidly subsiding narrow depression. This has also caused southward tilting of the basin.

CONCLUSIONS

The fluvial system of the Haripur sub-basin, a part of the Siwalik foreland basin, evolved primarily through the interplay of extra-basinal (Main Boundary thrust) and subsequent intra-basinal (Intra-Foreland thrust) tectonic activity. Due to this interplay, the basin underwent the following tectono-sedimentary changes: (1) prior to 5.5 Ma, sediments composed thickly bedded, multistoried sheet to thinly bedded sheet and ribbon sandstone bodies; (2) there was replacement of southeasterly flowing axial trunk drainage by a southwesterly flowing trans-

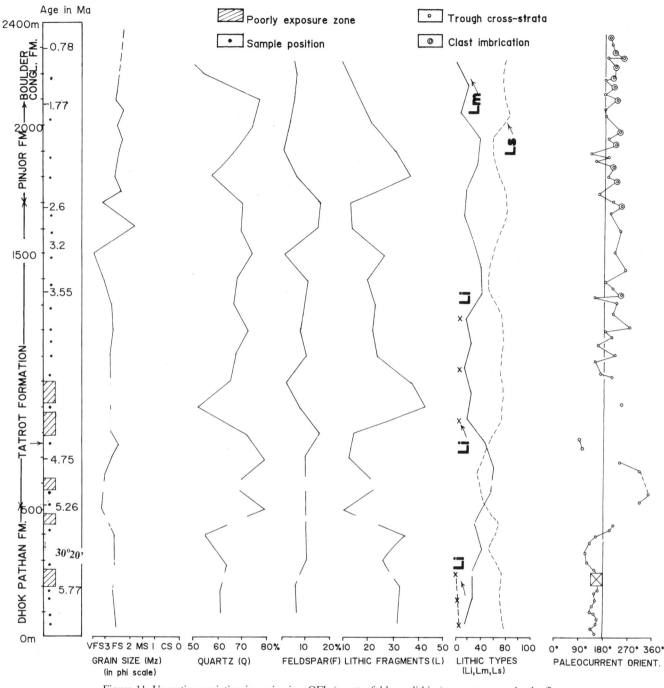

Figure 11. Upsection variation in grain size, QFL (quartz, feldspar, lithics) percentage, and paleoflow orientation.

verse trunk drainage, due to accelerated tectonic activity along the Main Boundary thrust at about 5.5 Ma; (3) around 4.8 Ma, gray sandstone transverse trunk drainage was gradually replaced by buff sandstone piedmont drainage; (4) the appearance of syntectonic (reworked lower Tertiary) conglomerates started at 1.77 Ma. After a brief interval of interfingering of the buff and gray systems, the transverse trunk drainage was completely displaced from this basin at around 1.77 Ma.

ACKNOWLEDGMENTS

We thank V. C. Thakur, Director, Wadia Institute of Himalayan Geology (WIHG), for his constant encouragement during this work. We are grateful to our colleagues from WIHG, N. R. Phadtare, R. K. Mazari, and V. Raiverman for fruitful discussions and critical comments on the early version of manuscript. J. Bridge, B. Willis, and an anonymous reviewer provided

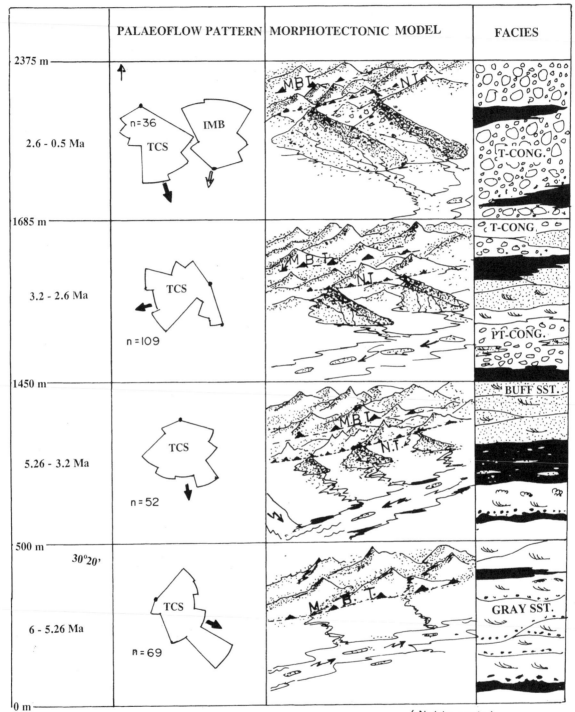

Figure 12. Conceptual tectono-sedimentary model of the Haripur sub-basin (for explanation, see text). MBT—Main Boundary thrust, NT—Nahan thrust, IMB—imbrication, TCS—trough cross-stratification, SST.—sandstone, P-T CONG.—conglomerate with pre-Tertiary clast, T-CONG—conglomerate with Tertiary clast.

useful comments. J. Quade is thanked for his valuable comments for all-round improvement of the manuscript. Financial assistance was provided to Kumar by the organizers of the 11th Himalayan-Karakorum-Tibet workshop (National Science Foundation Grant EAR-9628265).

REFERENCES CITED

Beaumont, C., 1981, Foreland basins: Royal Astronomical Society Geophysical Journal, v. 65, p. 291–329.

Beer, J. A., and Jordan, T. E., 1989, The effect of Neogene thrusting on deposition in the Bermejo Basin, Argentina: Journal of Sedimentary Petrology, v. 59, p. 330–345.

Behrensmeyer, A. K., and Tauxe, L., 1982, Isochronous fluvial systems in Miocene deposits of northern Pakistan: Sedimentology, v. 29, p. 331–352.

Burbank, D. W., and Raynolds, R. G. H., 1988, Stratigraphic keys to the timing of deformation; an example from the northwestern Himalayan foredeep, *in* Kleinspehn, K., and Paola, C., eds., New perspectives in basin analysis: New York, Springer-Verlag, p. 331–351.

Butler, R. F., 1992, Palaeomagnetism: Magnetic domains to geologic terranes: London, Blackwell Science Publication, 310 p.

Cande, S. C., and Kent, D.V., 1995, Revised calibration of the geomagnetic polarity time scale for the Late Cretaceous and Cenozoic: Journal Geophysical Research, v. 100, p. 6093–6095.

Collinson, D. W., 1974, The role of pigment and specularite in the remanent magnetism of red sandstones: Royal Astronomical Society Geophysical Journal, v. 38, p. 253–264.

DeCelles, P. G., and Hertel, F., 1989, Petrology of fluvial sands from the Amazonian foreland basin, Peru and Bolivia: Geological Society of America Bulletin, v. 101, p. 1552–1562.

Dunlop, D. J., 1970, Hematite: Intrinsic and defect ferromagnetism: Science, v. 169, p. 858–860.

Fisher, R. A., 1953, Dispersion on a sphere: Royal Society of London Proceedings, ser. A, v. 217, p. 295–305.

Flemings, P. B., and Jordan, T. E., 1989, A synthetic stratigraphic model of foreland basin development: Journal of Geophysical Research, v. 94, p. 3851–3866.

Flemings, P. B., and Jordan, T. E., 1990, Stratigraphic modeling of foreland basins: Interpretating thrust deformation and lithospheric rheology: Geology, v. 18, p. 430–434.

Heller, P. L., Angevine, C. L., Winslow, N. W., and Paola, C., 1988, Two-phase stratigraphic model of foreland-basin sequence: Geology, v. 16, p. 501–504.

Irving, E., and Opdyke, N. D., 1965, The palaeomagnetism of the Bloomsberg redbeds and its possible application to the tectonic history of the Appalachians: Royal Astronomical Society Geophysical Journal, v. 9, p. 153–167.

Johnson, E. A., and Pierce, F. W., 1990, Variation in fluvial deposition on an alluvial plain: An example from the Tongue River Member of the Fort Union Formation (Palaeocene), southeastern Powder River basin, Wyoming, U.S.A.: Sedimentary Geology, v. 69, p. 21–56.

Johnson, N. M., Opdyke, N. D., and Lindsay, E. H., 1975, Magnetic polarity stratigraphy of Pliocene/Pleistocene terrestrial deposits and vertebrate faunas, San Pedro Valley, Arizona: Geological Society of America Bulletin, v. 86, p. 5–12.

Johnson, N. M., Stix, J., Tauxe, L., Cerveny, P. F., and Tahirkheli, R. A. K., 1985, Palemagnetic chronology, fluvial processes and tectonic implications of the Siwalik deposits near Chinji village, Pakistan: Journal of Geology, v. 93, p. 27 -40.

Kraus, M. J., 1987, Integration of channel and flood plain suites II. Vertical relations of alluvial paleosols: Journal of Sedimentary Petrology, v. 57, p. 602–612.

Kumar, R., 1993, Coalescence megafan: Multistorey sandstone complex of the

late orogenic (Mio-Pliocene) Sub-Himalayan belt, Dehra Dun, India: Sedimentary Geology, v. 85, p. 327–337.

Kumar, R., and Ghosh, S. K., 1991, Sedimentological studies of the Upper Siwalik Boulder Conglomerate Formation, Mohand area, district Saharanpur, U.P.: Journal of Himalayan Geology, v. 2, p. 159–167.

Kumar, R., and Ghosh, S. K., 1994, Evolution of the Mio- Pleistocene alluvial fan system in the Siwalik foreland basin, Dehra Dun, Indial, *in* Kumar, R., Ghosh, S. K., and Phadtare, N. R., eds., Siwalik foreland basin of India: Himalayan Geology, v. 15, p. 143–159.

Kumar, R., and Ghosh, S. K., 1995, Sedimentation and source terrain history of the Mio-Pleistocene foreland basin, Doon Valley: Symposium on recent advances in geological studies of Northwest Himalaya and the foredeep [abs.]: Lucknow, Geological Survey of India, p. 351–352.

Kumar, R., and Tandon, S. K., 1985, Sedimentology of Plio-Pleistocene late orogenic deposits associated within intra-plate subduction of Upper Siwalik Subgroup of a part of Punjab Sub-Himalaya, India: Sedimentary Geology, v. 42, p. 105–158.

Kumar, R., Ghosh, S. K., Virdi, N. S., and Phadtare, N. R., 1991, Siwalik foreland basin (Dehra Dun–Nahan sector), *in* Excursion guide: Dehra Dun, India, Wadia Institute of Himalayan Geology, Special Publication No. 1, p. 1–61.

Mankinen, E. A., and Dalrymple, G. B., 1979, Revised geomagnetic polarity time scale for the interval 0–5 M.Y. BP.: Journal of Geophysical Research, v. 84, p. 615–629.

McLean, J. R., and Jerzykiewicz, T., 1978, Cyclicity, tectonic and coal: Some aspects of fluvial sedimentology in the Brazeav-Paskappo Formations, Coal Valley area, Alberta, Canada, *in* Miall, A. D., ed., Fluvial sedimentology: Canadian Society of Petroleum Geologists Memoir 5, p. 441–468.

Medlicott, H. B., 1864, On the geological structure and relationship of the southern portion of the Himalayan between the rivers Ganga and Ravee: Geological Survey of India Memoir 3, 212 p.

Mehta, Y. P., Thakur, A. K., Nand Lal, Shukla, B., and Tandon, S. K., 1993, Fission-track age of zircon separates from tuffaceous mudstone of the Upper Siwalik Subgroup of Jammu-Chandigarh sector of Panjab Sub-Himalaya: Current Science, v. 64, p. 519–521.

Meyers, J. H., Suttner, L. J., Furer, L. C., Moy, M. T., and Soreghan, M. J., 1992, Intrabasinal tectonic control on fluvial sandstone bodies in the Colverly Formation (Early Cretaceous) west-central Wyoming, USA: Basin Research, v. 4, p. 315–333.

Nanda, A. C., Sati, D. C., and Mehra, G. S., 1991, Preliminary report on the stratigraphy and mammalian faunas of the Middle and Upper Siwalik, west of Yamuna, Paonta, Himachal Pradesh: Journal of Himalayan Geology, v. 2, p. 151–158.

Opdyke, N. D., Lindsay, E. H., Johnson, G. D., Johnson, N. M., Tahirkheli, R. A. K., and Mirza, M. A., 1979, Magnetic polarity stratigraphy and vertebrate palaeontology of the Upper Siwalik sub-group of Northern Pakistan: Palaeogeography, Palaeoclimatology, Palaeoecology, v. 27, p. 1–34.

Paola, C., 1988, Subsidence and gravel transport of alluvial basins, *in* Kleinspehn, K. L. and Paola, C., eds. New perspectives in basin analysis: New York, Springer-Verlag, p. 231–243.

Parkash, B., Sharma, R. P., and Roy, A. K., 1980, The Siwalik Group (molasse)— Sediments shed by collision of continental plate: Sedimentary Geology, v. 25, p. 127–159.

Ranga Rao, A., Agarwal, R. P., Sharma, U. N., Bhalla, M. S., and Nanda, A. C., 1988, Magnetic polarity stratigraphy and vertebrate palaeontology of the Upper Siwalik sub-group of Jammu hills, India: Geological Society of India Journal, v. 31, p. 361–385.

Rust, B. R., and Jones, B. G., 1987, The Hawkesbury Sandstone south of Sydney, Australia. Triassic analogue for the deposits of large braided rivers: Journal of Sedimentary Petrology, v. 57, p. 222–233.

Sangode, S. J., Kumar, R., and Ghosh, S. K., 1996, Magnetic polarity stratigraphy of the Siwalik sequence of Haripur area (H.P.), NW Himalaya: Geological Society of India Journal, v. 47, p. 683–704.

Schumm, S. A., and Rea, D. K., 1995, Sediment yield from disturbed earth systems: Geology, v. 23, p. 391–394.

Srivastava, J. P., Verma, S. N., Joshi, V. K., Verman, B. C., and Arora, R. K., 1988, Review of the some of the recent biostratigraphic work on the Siwalik rocks of northwestern Himalaya for Neogene-Quaternary boundary and for the establishment of Saketi fossils park: Geological Survey of India Special Publication, v. 11, p. 233–241.

Tandon, S. K., 1991, The Himalayan foreland basin: Focus on Siwalik basin, *in* Tandon, S. K., Pant, C., and Cashyap, S. M., eds., Sedimentary basins of India, tectonic context: Nainital, Gyanodaya Prakashan, p. 171–201.

Tandon, S. K., Kumar, R., Koyama, M., and Nitsuma, N., 1984, Magnetic polarity stratigraphy of the Upper Siwalik sub-group east of Chandigarh, Punjab sub-Himalaya, India: Geological Society of India Journal, v. 25, p. 45–55.

Tauxe, L., and Badgley, C., 1988, Stratigraphy and remanence acquisition of a palaeomagnetic reversal in alluvial Siwalik rocks of Pakistan: Sedimen-

tology, v. 35, p. 697–715.

Tauxe, L., Kent, D. V., and Opdyke, N. D., 1980, Magnetic components contributing to the NRM of Middle Siwalik red beds: Earth and Planetary Science Letters, v. 47, p. 279–284.

Valdiya, K., 1980, Geology of Kumaun Lesser Himalaya: Dehra Dun, India, Wadia Institute of Himalayan Geology, 288 p.

Willis, B., 1993a, Ancient river systems in Himalayan foredeep, Chinji village area, northern Pakistan: Sedimentary Geology, v. 88, p. 1–76.

Willis, B., 1993b, Evolution of Miocene fluvial systems in the Himalayan foredeep through a two kilometer-thick succession in northern Pakistan: Sedimentary Geology, v. 88, p. 77–121.

Zoetemeijer, R., Desegaulex, P., Cloetingh, S., Roure, F., and Moretti, I., 1990, Lithospheric dynamics and tectonic-stratigraphic evolution of the Ebro Basin: Journal of Geophysical Research, v. 95, p. 2701–2711.

MANUSCRIPT ACCEPTED BY THE SOCIETY FEBRUARY 3, 1998

Geological Society of America
Special Paper 328
1999

Stratigraphic and structural framework of Himalayan foothills, northern Pakistan

Kevin R. Pogue
Department of Geology, Whitman College, Walla Walla, Washington 99362
Michael D. Hylland
Utah Geological Survey, 1594 West North Temple, Suite 3110, Salt Lake City, Utah 84116
Robert S. Yeats
Department of Geosciences, Oregon State University, Corvallis, Oregon 97331
Wali Ullah Khattak and Ahmad Hussain
Geological Survey of Pakistan, P.O. Box 1355, Shami Road, Peshawar, Pakistan

ABSTRACT

We present a geological synthesis of northern Pakistan between the Main Boundary and Main Mantle thrusts based on new stratigraphic and structural information. The Hazara (Dakhner) Formation and its metamorphosed equivalents form the basal Proterozoic sedimentary sequence in the Himalayan foothills of northern Pakistan. These units were deformed and metamorphosed prior to the deposition of the overlying Phanerozoic section. The Paleozoic section of the Peshawar basin was preserved in a half graben created during late Paleozoic rifting. Paleozoic rocks were mostly removed from elongate northeast-trending highlands bounding the half graben on the north and south. Whereas the northern highland was submerged by the Late Triassic, large parts of the southern highland remained subaerial until the Middle Jurassic.

The Hissartang fault of the Attock-Cherat Range is interpreted as being continuous with the Nathia Gali fault of Hazara. Both are the first faults north of the Salt Range thrust to expose Proterozoic rocks in their hanging walls. The Panjal fault of Hazara and the Khairabad fault of the Attock-Cherat Range are also interpreted to be a single continuous fault. The Panjal-Khairabad fault forms the southern limit of rocks that were metamorphosed by the Himalayan collision. Between the Panjal-Khairabad fault and Main Mantle thrust, there is no evidence for a Himalayan fault comparable to the Main Central thrust of the central Himalaya of India and Nepal. The absence in Pakistan of a Main Central thrust analog as well as other stratigraphic and structural contrasts precludes the extrapolation of central Himalayan tectonic subdivisions to northern Pakistan.

INTRODUCTION

The Himalaya of northern Pakistan consists of three major tectonic provinces separated by the Main Boundary thrust and Main Mantle thrust (Fig. 1). South of the Main Boundary thrust the Kohat and Potwar Plateaus expose unmetamorphosed Mesozoic and Tertiary sedimentary rocks and Neogene foredeep sedi-

ments deformed by folds and thrust faults. North of the Main Boundary thrust, the Main Mantle thrust separates rocks of the Indian plate on the south from the Kohistan island-arc terrane, which was accreted to Asia ca. 100 Ma (Treloar et al., 1992). The rocks between the Main Boundary and Main Central thrusts record a transition from the unmetamorphosed fold and thrust belt to the south to high-grade metamorphic rocks in the footwall

Pogue, K. R., Hylland, M. D., Yeats, R. S., Khattak, W. U., and Hussain, A., 1999, Stratigraphic and structural framework of Himalayan foothills, northern Pakistan, *in* Macfarlane, A., Sorkhabi, R. B., and Quade, J., eds., Himalaya and Tibet: Mountain Roots to Mountain Tops: Boulder, Colorado, Geological Society of America Special Paper 328.

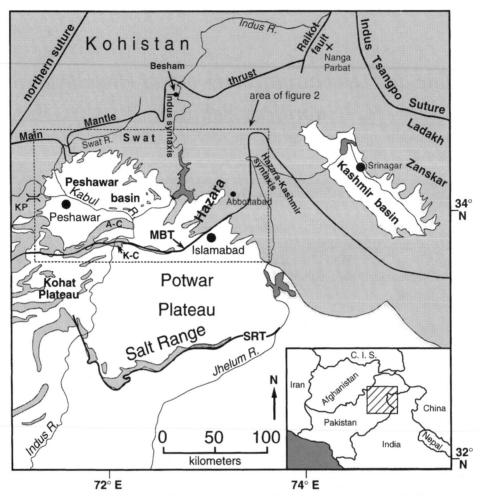

Figure 1. Location map of the Himalaya of northern Pakistan and northwestern India showing selected major faults. KP is Khyber Pass; A-C is Attock-Cherat Range; K-C is Kala Chitta Range; MBT is Main Boundary thrust; SRT is Salt Range thrust. Locations of faults are from Gansser (1981), Yeats and Lawrence (1984), Baker et al. (1988), Lawrence et al. (1989), and Baig (1990).

of the Main Mantle thrust. This region will be referred to herein as the Himalayan foothills; the topography between the Main Boundary and the Main Mantle thrusts gradually rises in elevation northward toward the high Himalayan peaks. The studied area is bounded on the east by the Main Boundary or Murree thrust, and on the west by inadequately mapped mountains near the Afghanistan border (Fig. 2).

The stratigraphic and structural synthesis presented here was prompted by the publication of new geologic maps (Bossart et al., 1988; Lawrence et al., 1989; Baig, 1990; Hylland, 1990; Hussain et al., 1990; DiPietro and Lawrence, 1991; Greco, 1991; Pogue, 1994) and the discovery, in the newly mapped areas, of stratigraphic and structural relationships that facilitate correlations with adjacent areas mapped previously (Fig. 3; Latif, 1970; Meissner et al., 1974; Calkins et al., 1975). Stratigraphic interpretations are based on generalized stratigraphic columns (Fig. 4) derived from the new maps presented herein and stratigraphic information from Latif (1974), Meissner et al. (1974), Calkins et

al. (1975), Hussain et al. (1990), DiPietro and Lawrence (1991), and Pogue et al. (1992a).

The foothills region can be divided into three tectonic blocks, bounded by major Himalayan faults (Fig. 2). The southern block is referred to as the Kala Chitta–Margala block after the Kala Chitta Range and Margala Hills, which form prominent escarpments along the southern boundary of the block. The central and northern blocks are referred to as the Nathia Gali–Hissartang block and the Panjal-Khairabad block, respectively, after the faults that form their southern boundaries.

STRATIGRAPHY

Panjal-Khairabad block

Proterozoic formations. Thick intervals of unfossiliferous low-grade metasedimentary rock underlie Paleozoic rocks throughout the Panjal-Khairabad block. Previously workers

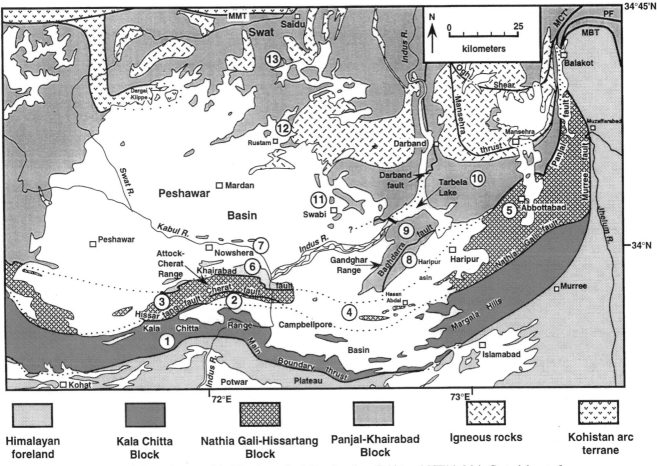

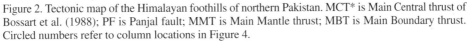

Figure 2. Tectonic map of the Himalayan foothills of northern Pakistan. MCT* is Main Central thrust of Bossart et al. (1988); PF is Panjal fault; MMT is Main Mantle thrust; MBT is Main Boundary thrust. Circled numbers refer to column locations in Figure 4.

assigned these rocks to a variety of formations (Fig. 5). The following stratigraphic information details a refined and regionally applicable stratigraphic nomenclature for the Proterozoic rocks of the Himalayan foothills. Correlations based on new stratigraphic information (Fig. 4) and radiometric ages also permit a further refinement of the ages of these units (Fig. 6).

With the exception of Early Proterozoic crystalline rocks exposed near Besham (Baig, 1990; DiPieto et al., this volume), the oldest exposed rocks in the Panjal-Khairabad block are marble, carbonaceous phyllite, and graphitic schist of the Gandaf Formation. The Gandaf Formation is named for the village of Gandaf, located 3 km north of Tarbela dam (Fig. 7), where it consists of more than 500 m of carbonaceous and calcareous phyllite and schist and carbonaceous marble containing interbedded muscovite-chlorite-quartz schist. The Gandaf Formation is also exposed in a 100-m- to 1-km-wide belt in the hanging wall of the Baghdarra fault in the Gandghar Range (Fig. 7), where it has a transitional contact with overlying Manki Formation slate and argillite.

The Manki Formation consists of more than 1,000 m of argillite, slate, phyllite, and argillaceous meta-siltstone that overlies the Gandaf Formation in the Gandghar Range and forms the oldest exposures in the Attock-Cherat Range. In the northern Attock-Cherat Range (Fig. 4, column 6) and in the footwall of the Baghdarra fault in the Gandghar Range (Fig. 4, column 8), the Manki Formation is overlain by more than 500 m of limestone and argillite of the Shahkot Formation, Utch Khattak Formation, and Shekhai Formation (Hussain, 1984; Yeats and Hussain, 1987). Limestone of the Shahkot Formation has a gradational contact with the underlying Manki Formation. The limestone is overlain by 100–150 m of slate and argillite that are identical to the Manki Formation. A 10–70 m interval of lenticular blocks of stromatolitic limestone in a matrix of calcareous mudstone forms the base of the overlying Utch Khattak Formation. The upper Utch Khattak Formation is slate and argillite, similar to the upper Shahkot Formation. The Shekhai Formation is composed of a basal 1-m-thick bed of quartzite overlain by a thick sequence of dolomitic and arenaceous limestone and marble.

On the northwestern flanks of the Gandghar Range, in the hanging wall of the Baghdarra fault, arenaceous and dolomitic marble and calcareous and dolomitic quartzite are between the Manki Formation and Tanawal Formation (Fig. 4, column 9; Fig. 7). These rocks are named the Sobrah Formation for exposures

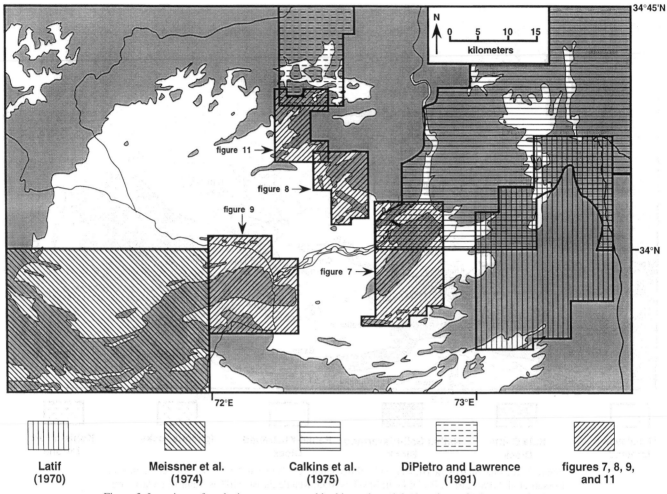

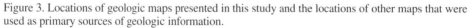

Figure 3. Locations of geologic maps presented in this study and the locations of other maps that were used as primary sources of geologic information.

near Sobrah village, 5 km south-southwest of Tarbela dam. The Sobrah Formation has a maximum thickness of more than 200 m near Tarbela dam, but thins abruptly and is locally absent in adjacent areas.

The Tanawal Formation is a metaclastic unit having a protolith of feldspathic sandstone, siltstone, and shale. Typical lithologies range from quartzite and argillite near Tarbela dam to schistose quartzite and quartz-mica schist near Mansehra. The thickness of the Tanawal Formation north of Swabi (Fig. 8) exceeds 3,000 m (Fig. 4, column 11). The Tanawal Formation unconformably overlies the Gandaf Formation west of the Darband fault, the Sobrah or Manki Formation between the Darband and Baghdarra faults, and the Shekhai Formation east of the Baghdarra fault (Figs. 4 and 7).

Paleozoic and Mesozoic formations. More than 3,500 m of Paleozoic strata are exposed along the northeastern margin of the Peshawar basin (Pogue et al., 1992a; Fig. 4, column 11). Unconformably overlying the Tanawal Formation, the dolomite-dominated Ambar Formation forms the base of the Paleozoic section. Although the Ambar is unfossiliferous, an Early Cambrian age

can be inferred from its stratigraphic position and lithologic similarity with the Sirban Formation of the Lower Cambrian Abbottabad Group (Fig. 6). The overlying fossiliferous Ordovician through Carboniferous section is dominated by lithologies typical of shallow-water epicontinental sedimentation (Pogue et al., 1992a). Lower Paleozoic rocks correlative with the Peshawar basin section are exposed between Abbottabad and Tarbela Lake in the cores of several synclinal structures (Fig. 4, column 10). On the basis of correlations with the Panjal volcanics of Kashmir, the Permian is represented by the Malandrai Greenschist, Duma Formation, and Karapa Greenschist (Fig. 4, column 12; Pogue et al., 1992b; DiPietro et al., this volume; Wardlaw and Pogue, 1995). The only confirmed Mesozoic rocks in the Panjal-Khairabad block are Upper Triassic limestones of the Kashala Formation exposed in the northern Peshawar basin (Pogue et al., 1992a).

Nathia Gali–Hissartang block

Proterozoic formations. The oldest rocks exposed between the Panjal and Nathia Gali faults belong to the Hazara Formation.

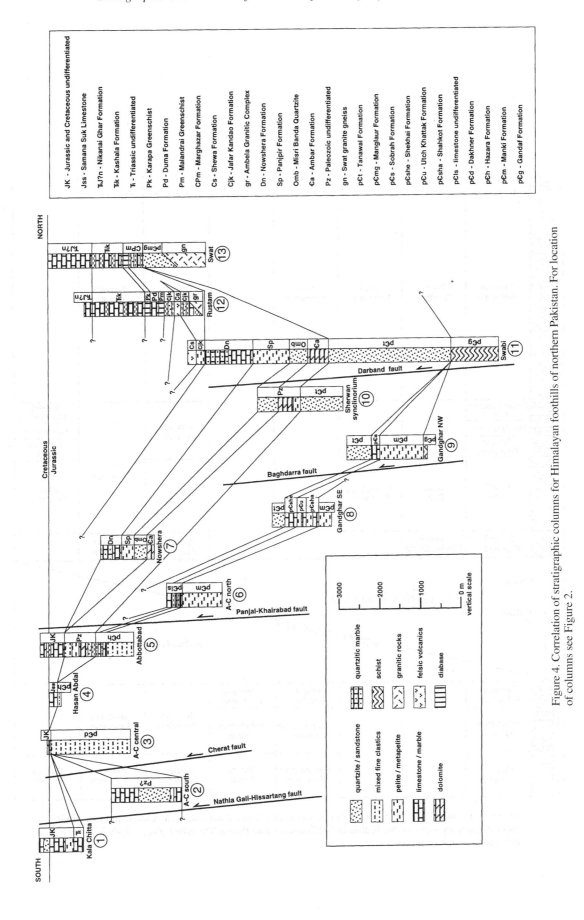

Figure 4. Correlation of stratigraphic columns for Himalayan foothills of northern Pakistan. For location of columns see Figure 2.

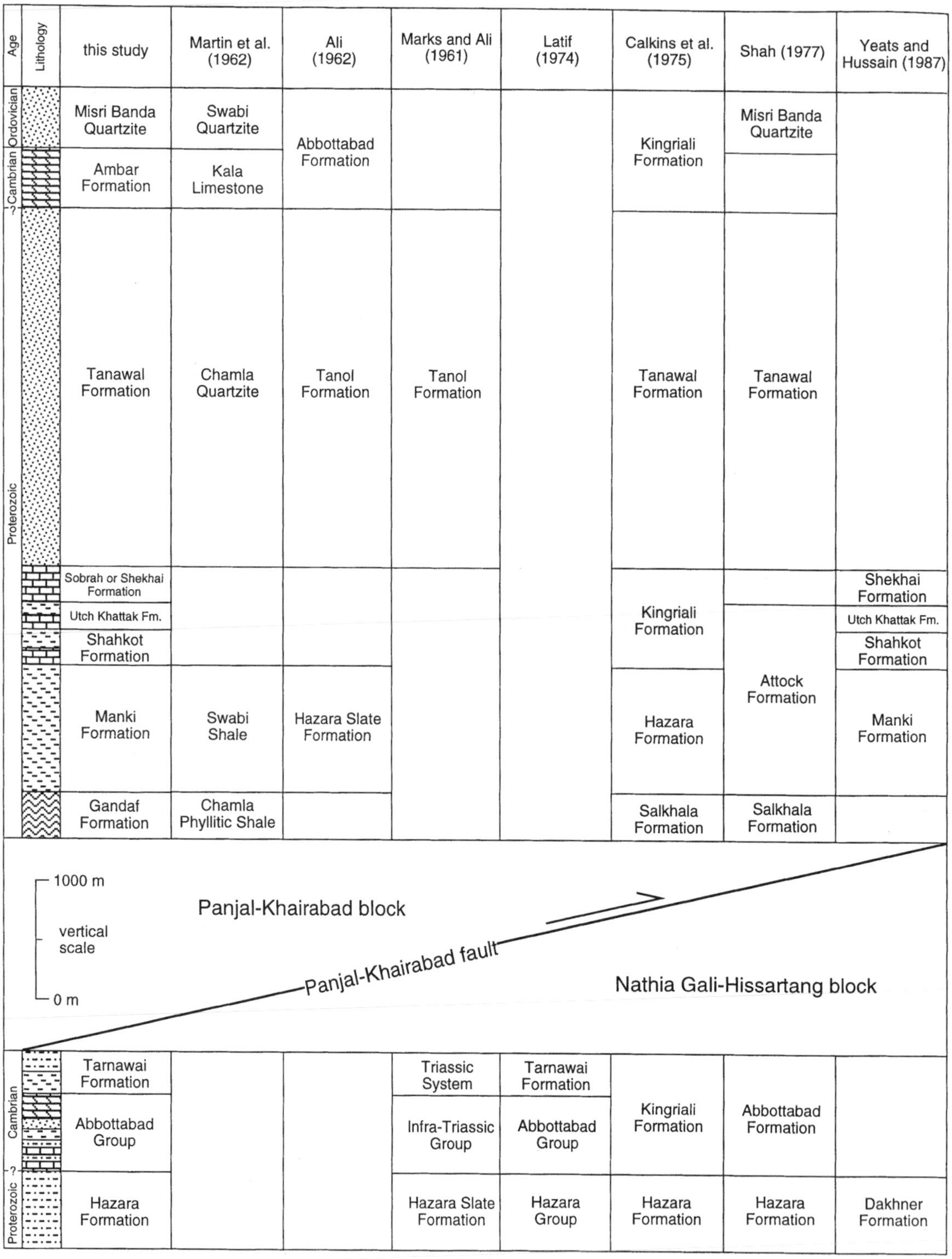

Age	Lithology	this study	Martin et al. (1962)	Ali (1962)	Marks and Ali (1961)	Latif (1974)	Calkins et al. (1975)	Shah (1977)	Yeats and Hussain (1987)
Cambrian Ordovician		Misri Banda Quartzite	Swabi Quartzite	Abbottabad Formation			Kingriali Formation	Misri Banda Quartzite	
?		Ambar Formation	Kala Limestone						
Proterozoic		Tanawal Formation	Chamla Quartzite	Tanol Formation	Tanol Formation		Tanawal Formation	Tanawal Formation	
		Sobrah or Shekhai Formation					Kingriali Formation		Shekhai Formation
		Utch Khattak Fm.							Utch Khattak Fm.
		Shahkot Formation							Shahkot Formation
		Manki Formation	Swabi Shale	Hazara Slate Formation			Hazara Formation	Attock Formation	Manki Formation
		Gandaf Formation	Chamla Phyllitic Shale				Salkhala Formation	Salkhala Formation	

1000 m

vertical scale

0 m

Panjal-Khairabad block

Panjal-Khairabad fault

Nathia Gali-Hissartang block

Age	Lithology	this study			Marks and Ali (1961)	Latif (1974)	Calkins et al. (1975)	Shah (1977)	Yeats and Hussain (1987)
Cambrian		Tarnawai Formation			Triassic System	Tarnawai Formation			
		Abbottabad Group			Infra-Triassic Group	Abbottabad Group	Kingriali Formation	Abbottabad Formation	
?									
Proterozoic		Hazara Formation			Hazara Slate Formation	Hazara Group	Hazara Formation	Hazara Formation	Dakhner Formation

Figure 5. History of nomenclature for Proterozoic and lower Paleozoic sedimentary and low-grade metasedimentary rocks of the Nathia Gali–Hissartang and Panjal-Khairabad blocks. Lithologic symbols are the same as in Figure 4.

unit	inferred age	lower limit	upper limit	references
Tarnawai Formation	Early Cambrian	The Tarnawai Formation is Early Cambrian in age based on Hyolithids and sponge spicules obtained from the Hazira Member.		Latif (1972) Latif (1974)
Abbottabad Group	Early Cambrian	Late Proterozoic - unconformably overlies upper Proterozoic Hazara Formation.	Early Cambrian - underlies Tarnawai Formation.	Latif (1974)
Ambar Formation	Cambrian	Late Proterozoic - unconformably overlies Tanawal Formation. Lithologically similar to Sirban Dolomite of Abbottabad Group.	Early Ordovician - overlain by Lower Ordovician Misri Banda Quartzite.	Pogue et al. (1992a)
Tanawal Formation	Late Proterozoic	Late Proterozoic - unconformably overlies Manki Formation.	Cambrian - intruded by Upper Cambrian Mansehra Granite.	LeFort et al. (1980)
Sobrah Formation	Late Proterozoic	Late Proterozoic - unconformably overlies Manki Formation.	Cambrian - overlain by Tanawal Formation.	new formation name
Shekhai Formation	Late Proterozoic	Late Proterozoic - unconformably overlies Utch Khattak Formation.	Cambrian - overlain by Tanawal Formation.	Hussain (1984) Hylland (1990)
Utch Khattak Formation	Late Proterozoic	These units are locally rich in stromatolites but are otherwise unfossiliferous. They are lithologically identical to the Miranjani Limestone and Langrial Limestone of Latif (1969) which occur as carbonate intervals within the Hazara Formation.		Hussain (1984) Hylland (1990)
Shahkot Formation				
Dakhner Formation	Late Proterozoic	Identical in lithology and stratigraphic position with the Hazara Formation.		Yeats and Hussain (1987)
Hazara Formation	Late Proterozoic	Late Proterozoic - based on Rb/Sr whole-rock ages.	Early Cambrian - unconformably underlies Abbottabad Group.	Crawford and Davies (1975)
Manki Formation	Late Proterozoic	Early Proterozoic - overlies Gandaf Formation.	Cambrian - unconformably underlies Tanawal Formation.	Hussain (1984) Yeats and Hussain (1987) Hylland (1990)
Gandaf Formation	Early Proterozoic	Early Proterozoic or Archean - overlies Karora Formation which unconformably overlies Archean Besham Complex.	Early Proterozoic - intruded by lower Proterozoic granitic rocks of the Kotla Complex in the Indus syntaxis.	DiPietro et al. (this volume)

Figure 6. Inferred ages of Cambrian and older sedimentary and low-grade metasedimentary rocks of the Nathia Gali–Hissartang and Panjal-Khairabad blocks.

Near the southern limit of exposure of the Hazara Formation, sandstone and shale are the dominant lithology. The relative percentage of shale and the grade of metamorphism increase northward. In the vicinity of the Panjal fault, the unit consists of weakly metamorphosed pelitic rock and graywacke. East of Haripur, the upper part of the Hazara Formation contains two algal limestone horizons that Latif (1969) referred to as the Langrial Limestone and Miranjani Limestone (Fig. 4, column 5). Latif (1969) also noted beds of gypsum in the Hazara Formation southeast of Abbottabad. The Dakhner Formation of the Attock-Cherat Range is lithologically identical to the southern, shallow-water facies of the Hazara Formation (Yeats and Hussain, 1987). The exposed thickness of both the Hazara and Dakhner Formations exceeds 1,000 m.

Cambrian formations. Near Abbottabad, an unconformity-bounded sequence dominated by dolomite and shale overlies the Hazara Formation (Fig. 4, column 5). Latif (1970, 1974) subdivided these rocks into the Kakul Formation, Sirban Formation, and Tarnawai Formation. The Kakul and Sirban Formations compose the Abbottabad Group. The oldest unit of the Abbottabad Group is the Tanakki Conglomerate, which is the basal member of the Kakul Formation. The Tanakki Conglom-

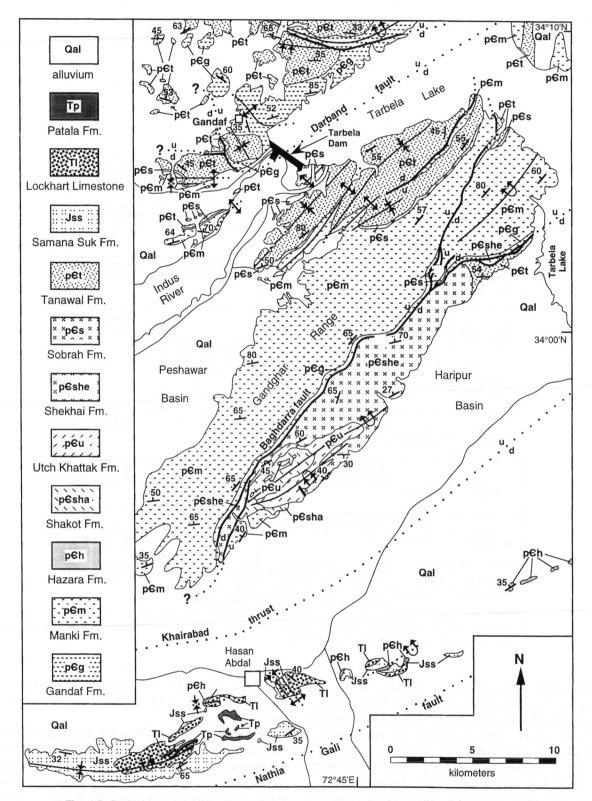

Figure 7. Geologic map of the Gandghar Range and vicinity. See Figure 3 for location.

erate consists of angular to subangular pebble- to boulder-sized clasts, derived primarily from the underlying Hazara Formation, in a siltstone matrix. The remainder of the Kakul Formation consists of sandstone and shale interbedded with carbonate. Resistant dolomite of the overlying Sirban Formation forms the most conspicuous outcrops of the Abbottabad Group. The Tarnawai Formation consists of a lower Galdanian Member com-

posed of siltstone and mudstone and an upper Hazira Member, which is primarily glauconitic and phosphatic shale and siltstone (Latif, 1974). The Tarnawai Formation is Early Cambrian in age, on the basis of fossils recovered from the Hazira Member (Fig. 6; Latif, 1972). Latif (1974) also considered the Abbottabad Group to be Early Cambrian on the basis of its unconformable contact with the underlying Proterozoic Hazara

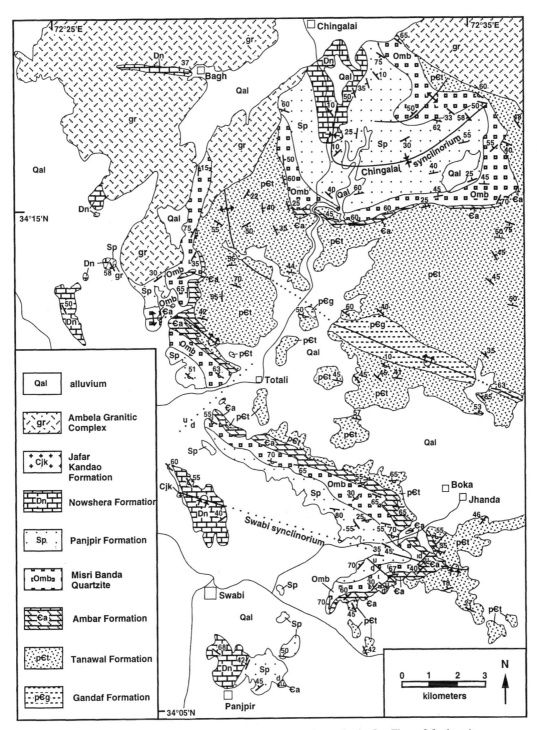

Figure 8. Geologic map of the Swabi area, northeastern Peshawar basin. See Figure 3 for location.

Formation and conformable contact with the overlying Lower Cambrian Tarnawai Formation.

Paleozoic(?) formations. On the southern flank of the Attock-Cherat Range, an enigmatic sequence of rocks is exposed in the structural block bounded by the Cherat and Hissartang faults (Fig. 9; Fig. 4, column 2). The oldest of the units, the Darwaza Formation, consists of carbonate overlain by argillite. Unconformably overlying the Darwaza Formation are interbedded quartzite and argillite of the Hissartang Formation, that are in turn overlain by limestone of the Inzari Formation. Similarities of quartzite and argillite of the Hissartang Formation with the upper Misri Banda Quartzite and argillite of the lower Panjpir Formation prompted Yeats and Hussain (1987) to suggest a correlation with these Paleozoic rocks near Nowshera (Fig. 4, column 7).

Mesozoic formations. In Hazara, Proterozoic or Lower Cambrian strata in the Nathia Gali–Hissartang block are overlain by Jurassic strata (Calkins et al., 1975; Shah, 1977; Fig. 4, columns 4 and 5). Northeast of Abbottabad, interbedded shale and sandstone of the Datta Formation form the base of the Mesozoic section. The overlying Shinawari Formation consists of shale interbedded with limestone. The Middle Jurassic Samana Suk Formation consists of as much as 300 m of pelloidal and oolitic limestone (Calkins et al., 1975). The Jurassic section thins dramatically southwest of Abbottabad, and the Datta Formation and Shinawari Formation are absent in outcrops near Hasan Abdal (Fig. 7; Fig. 4, column 4). In the Attock-Cherat Range, the only rocks of Jurassic age are discontinuous outcrops of Samana Suk Formation in fault-bounded blocks along the Cherat fault (Hussain et al., 1990).

In Hazara, strata of purely Jurassic age are overlain by Upper Jurassic to Lower Cretaceous shale and sandstone of the Chichali Formation and Lumshiwal Sandstone (Fig. 4, column 5; Calkins et al., 1975; Shah, 1977). These units form a marker horizon in northeastern Hazara but are absent southwest of Abbottabad, where the Samana Suk Formation is overlain by Paleocene Lockhart Limestone. In Hazara, the Lumshiwal Sandstone is

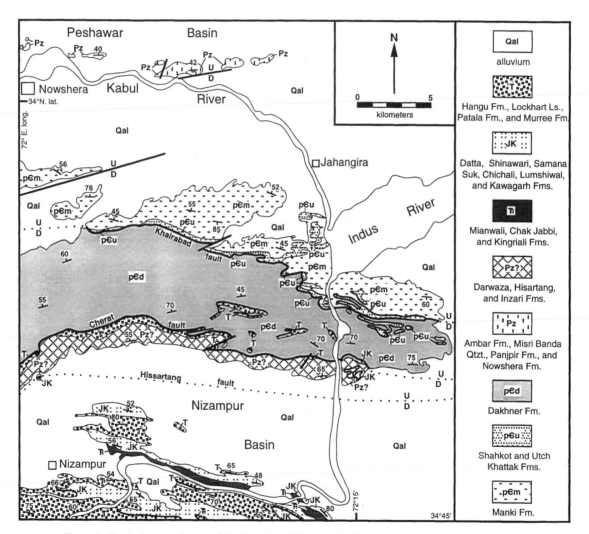

Figure 9. Geologic map of parts of the Nowshera hills, Attock-Cherat Range, and Kala Chitta Range, simplified from Hussain et al. (1990). See Figure 3 for location.

overlain by 100 m of the Upper Cretaceous Kawagarh Limestone (Calkins et al., 1975). Cretaceous rocks are absent near Hasan Abdal, but Upper Cretaceous limestone unconformably overlies the Dakhner Formation in the central Attock-Cherat Range (Yeats and Hussain, 1987; Fig. 4, columns 3 and 4).

Tertiary formations. An unconformity marked by a 1–2-m-thick laterite forms the base of the Paleocene section throughout the Nathia Gali–Hissartang block (Hylland, 1990). This laterite and overlying sandstone, shale, coal, and limestone have been assigned to the Hangu Formation and Lockhart Limestone (Shah, 1977). Paleocene rocks unconformably overlie Upper Cretaceous limestone north and east of Abbottabad, the Jurassic Samana Suk Formation near Hasan Abdal, and the Proterozoic Dakhner Formation and Paleozoic(?) Inzari Limestone in the Attock-Cherat Range. Shale and limestone of the upper Paleocene–lower Eocene Patala Formation overlie the Lockhart Limestone throughout the Nathia Gali–Hissartang block. Shale of the Patala Formation is the youngest bedrock in the Hasan Abdal area (Fig. 7). A thin interval of limestone of early Eocene age mapped by Latif (1970) as Margala Hills Limestone conformably overlies the Patala Formation in Hazara. In the Attock-Cherat Range, the Margala Hill Limestone is missing and the Patala Formation is overlain unconformably by shale and sandstone that are probably correlative with the Miocene Murree Formation.

Kala Chitta–Margala block

The oldest exposed rocks in the Kala Chitta–Margala block are limestone and marl of the Lower Triassic Mianwali Formation that crop out in the northern Kala Chitta Range (Fig. 9; Fig. 4, column 1; Hussain et al., 1990). Overlying the Mianwali Formation are Middle to Upper Triassic limestone and dolomite of the Chak Jabbi and Kingriali Formations. East of the Kala Chitta Range, the oldest outcrops are limestone of the Middle Jurassic Samana Suk Formation. The stratigraphic succession of Jurassic, Cretaceous, and Paleocene strata of the Kala Chitta–Margala block is similar but thicker than that of the Nathia Gali–Hissartang block. In the Kala Chitta–Margala block in southern Hazara, Paleocene strata are overlain by lower Eocene Margala Hills Limestone followed by marl and limestone mapped by Latif (1970) as lower Eocene Lora Formation. In the Kala Chitta Range, similar lower Eocene rocks were divided by Meissner et al. (1974) into a lower Sakesar Limestone and an upper Shekhan Limestone. Lower to middle Eocene mudstone and clay interbedded with sandstone, conglomerate, and marl are the youngest bedrock in the Kala Chitta–Margala block. These rocks were mapped as Kuldana Formation in southern Hazara (Latif, 1970) and as Mami Khel Clay in the Kala Chitta Range (Meissner et al., 1974).

Correlation and stratigraphic framework of pre-Tertiary strata

Proterozoic. Stratigraphic relationships between the Hazara (Dakhner) Formation and Manki Formation indicate that these units were originally deposited as a laterally continuous section in a northward-deepening marine environment (Fig. 10). Lithologies and sedimentary structures indicative of shallow-marine deposition are common in the Dakhner Formation and in the Hazara Formation south of Haripur. Gypsum beds in the Hazara Formation documented by Latif (1969) represent a facies that is transitional with the evaporite-dominated Salt Range Formation, which underlies the Paleozoic section south of the Main Boundary thrust. Proterozoic rocks beneath the Kala Chitta Range are therefore inferred to be transitional between evaporites of the Salt Range Formation and shallow-water marine clastics of the Dakhner Formation (Fig. 10). The pelitic facies of the Hazara Formation north of Abbottabad has undergone low-grade metamorphism and is indistinguishable from the Manki Formation. The contrasts in lithology and metamorphic grade between the formations are obvious, however, south of Haripur, where the Panjal-Khairabad fault has juxtaposed the Manki Formation and the shallow-water facies of the Hazara (Dakhner) Formation (Figs. 7 and 9). The northward progression of facies of the Hazara Formation thus records a transition from evaporites of the Salt Range Formation to low-grade metapelite of the Manki Formation.

In the central Gandghar Range, graphitic phyllite of the Gandaf Formation is thrust over Proterozoic limestone along the Baghdarra fault (Fig. 7). There is a gradual transition up-section in the hanging wall of the Baghdarra fault from this graphitic phyllite to slate of the Manki Formation. In the northwestern Gandghar Range, the Manki Formation is overlain by discontinuous limestone of the Sobrah Formation followed by Tanawal Formation quartzite (Fig. 4, column 9). Across the Indus River, on the northwest side of the Darband fault, the Sobrah Formation is absent, and graphitic phyllite, schist, and marble of the Gandaf Formation are overlain directly by quartzite of the Tanawal Formation (Fig. 4, column 11). The contrast in lithologies below the Tanawal on either side of the Darband fault could be the result of pre-Tanawal (Proterozoic) displacement on the Darband fault.

The Shahkot and Utch Khattak Formations are essentially thick carbonate interbeds within the upper part of the Manki Formation (Fig. 4, column 8). In the southeastern Gandghar Range (Fig. 7), both formations include an upper argillite or slate identical to the underlying Manki Formation. These units are interpreted as correlative with the Miranjani Limestone and Langrial Limestone of Latif (1969).

The Shekhai and Sobrah Formations form a southward-thickening limestone lens at the base of the Tanawal Formation (Fig. 10). They are separated from the underlying Utch Khattak or Manki Formations by an unconformity marked by a thin interval of quartzite. In the Gandghar Range, both formations are overlain by quartzite of the Tanawal Formation. The southward thickening of the Shekhai Formation at the expense of the Tanawal Formation suggests that the two formations may be separate facies of the same stratigraphic interval.

The Tanawal Formation is interpreted as a clastic wedge derived from the erosion of a Proterozoic highland. The absence of the Tanawal Formation in all sections south of the Panjal-

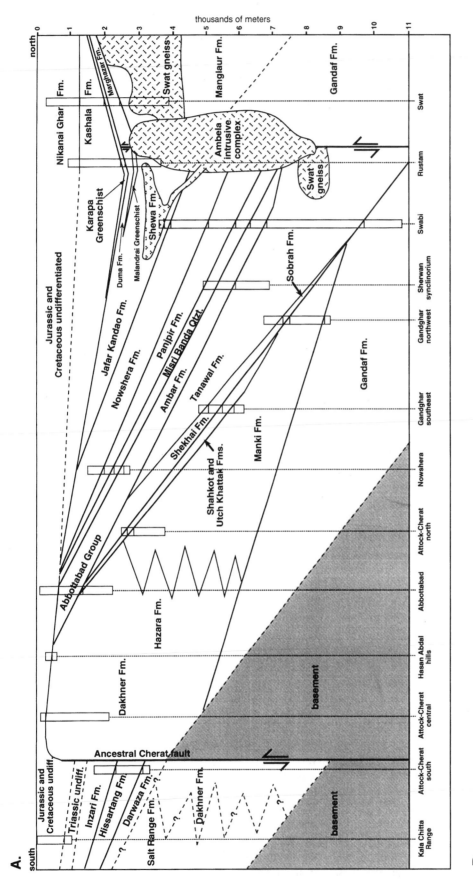

Figure 10. A: Interpretation of pre-Late Cretaceous stratigraphic framework of Himalayan foothills of northern Pakistan. The figure is diagrammatic and is not intended to represent a pre-Cretaceous cross section at any specific location. The shaded area is Precambrian crystalline basement. The columns superimposed on the diagram are the same as in Figure 4 and are located in Figure 2. The horizontal positions of the columns have been adjusted to compensate for the effects of Himalayan shortening and therefore do not reflect present-day distances or relative positions. Columns north of the Panjal-Khairabad fault, such as the Attock-Cherat Range north column, are therefore positioned to the north of those that are south of the fault, such as the Abbottabad column, regardless of current geographic locations (Fig. 2). B: Simplified and unexaggerated version of A.

Khairabad fault indicates dramatic southward thinning of the 1,000-m-thick sections exposed north of Swabi (Fig. 8) and northwest of Abbottabad (Calkins et al., 1975).

Paleozoic. The base of the Paleozoic section throughout the foothills is an angular unconformity marked by a conglomerate. Proterozoic and Cambrian tectonic events uplifted, tilted, and weakly metamorphosed the Tanawal, Manki, and northernmost Hazara Formations prior to deposition of the overlying Ambar Formation or Abbottabad Group. A Late Cambrian event removed the Ambar Formation in the Chingalai synclinorium (Pogue et al., 1992a).

Paleozoic rocks exposed within the Panjal-Khairabad block were preserved in a half graben created during late Paleozoic rifting (Fig. 10). Pogue et al. (1992b) proposed a now-concealed northeast-striking normal fault to account for late Paleozoic uplift and removal of lower Paleozoic strata in Swat. A similar structure is proposed to account for the absence of Paleozoic rocks from much of the Nathia Gali–Hissartang block (Fig. 10). The axis of the uplift, where Jurassic or Cretaceous strata overlie Proterozoic Dakhner or Hazara Formation, can be traced from the central Attock-Cherat Range northeastward through Hasan Abdal to southern Hazara. Uplift can be constrained as being younger than the Lower Cambrian Tarnawai Formation, the youngest unit beneath the unconformity, and older than the Jurassic strata that overlie the unconformity. Throughout most of its length, the fault responsible for the uplift has been concealed by younger thrusting along the Nathia Gali fault. In the Attock-Cherat Range, however, fault-bounded rocks of probable Paleozoic age are preserved in the hanging wall of the Hissartang fault (Figs. 4 and 9). These rocks, represented by the Darwaza, Hissartang, and Inzari Formations, are interpreted as a former southward continuation of Paleozoic strata exposed in the southern Peshawar basin (Fig. 10). The Cherat fault separates the Attock-Cherat Paleozoic(?) section on the south from Proterozoic Dakhner Formation, overlain by Cretaceous strata on the north (Fig. 9; Yeats and Hussain, 1987; Hussain et al., 1990). The position of the Cherat fault is consistent with that proposed to account for late Paleozoic uplift. Latest Cretaceous motion of the Cherat fault documented by Yeats and Hussain (1987) may represent the reactivation of an older rift-related structure. In Figure 10, retrodeformation of late Paleozoic displacement on the Cherat fault implies that the Cambrian stratigraphy in the Abbottabad area is transitional between the Ambar Formation and part of the Paleozoic(?) section of the Attock-Cherat Range. This is not the case, however. In Hazara, due to the northeasterly strike of Cambrian facies, the Abbottabad Group, which has been correlated with Cambrian strata of the Salt Range (Latif, 1984; Stöcklin, 1986), is preserved on the north side of the late Paleozoic uplift.

Mesozoic. The oldest Mesozoic rocks exposed north of Cherat fault are Upper Triassic (Carnian) marbles of the Kashala Formation, which were deposited following thermal subsidence of the late Paleozoic rift highlands of Swat (Pogue et al., 1992b). The southern uplift, associated with the Cherat fault, remained subaerial throughout the Triassic, because no Triassic rocks overlie upper Proterozoic or Cambrian strata along the length of the uplift. Transgression of the southern highland commenced in the Early Jurassic when the Datta Formation was deposited on the Abbottabad Group and Tarnawai Formation in Hazara. The highland was mostly inundated by the Middle Jurassic, when limestone of the Samana Suk Formation was deposited on the Proterozoic Hazara Formation throughout southern Hazara. Unnamed Late Cretaceous limestone overlying the Proterozic Dakhner Formation in the central Attock-Cherat Range (Yeats and Hussain, 1987) indicates that some parts of the uplift remained subaerial throughout the Early and middle Cretaceous. Mesozoic formations exposed in the Kala Chitta–Margala block were deposited south of late Paleozoic uplifts and reflect deposition in deeper water than their type sections in the Salt and Surghar Ranges (Fatmi, 1973; Yeats and Hussain, 1987).

STRUCTURE

Structural framework of the foothills

Panjal-Khairabad block. The Panjal fault diverges from the Murree fault near Balakot and strikes generally southwestward between Mansehra and Abbottabad before it is buried by Haripur basin alluvium (Fig. 2). The fault is inferred to extend southwestward beneath alluvium, so that it intervenes between exposures of Manki Formation in the southern Gandghar Range and exposures of the Hazara Formation in the hills near Hasan Abdal (Fig. 7).

Stratigraphic throw along the Khairabad fault of the northern Attock-Cherat Range as mapped by Yeats and Hussain (1987) and Hussain et al. (1990) is identical to that along the Panjal fault to the northeast. North of the fault, metapelite of the Manki Formation is overlain by Proterozoic limestone. South of the fault, unmetamorphosed Proterozoic Dakhner Formation is overlain by Upper Cretaceous limestone (Fig. 9). The Khairabad fault is concealed beneath alluvium of the southern Peshawar basin west of the Attock-Cherat Range until it emerges in the hills south of the Khyber Pass (Fig. 2).

All pre-Cenozoic rocks north of the Panjal-Khairabad fault have been metamorphosed. The original foliations of the Manki Formation and the Gandaf Formation were probably imparted during the Proterozoic (Baig et al., 1988). Pre-Cenozoic rocks younger than these formations remained unmetamorphosed until the early Tertiary. In general, the grade of metamorphism increases from south to north in the Panjal-Khairabad block. The color alteration index of Peshawar basin conodonts recovered by Pogue et al. (1992a) documents a northward increase in peak metamorphic temperatures from 300 °C to 400 °C. Between the Peshawar basin and the Main Mantle thrust, the metamorphic grade increases gradually but dramatically (DiPietro and Lawrence, 1991).

The structure of the southern part of the Panjal-Khairabad block is dominated by south- or southeast-vergent folds that deform bedding and bedding-parallel foliation in the low-grade metamorphic rocks. Bedding and foliation strike generally northnortheast east of Mansehra on the western limb of the Hazara-Kashmir syntaxis and northeastward north of Abbottabad (Calkins et al., 1975). In the southern Gandghar Range, the Indus syntaxis accounts for a gradual 45° rotation of strike to a general east-west orientation that is maintained farther west in outcrops in the northern Attock-Cherat Range and Nowshera area (Figs. 7 and 9; Hussain et al., 1990). Rocks on the northern margin of the Peshawar basin have been subjected to multiple folding episodes. The structure of the Chingalai synclinorium (Fig. 8) was produced by early northwest-trending folds that were refolded along northeast-trending axes. In Swat, DiPietro and Lawrence (1991) recognized four distinct folding episodes. The first three episodes with north-trending fold axes were refolded along east-trending axes, producing the gneiss-cored domes of central Swat. The north-trending folds die

out south of the garnet isograd, where major folds trend to the east and are south vergent. In the vicinity of Rustam, Himalayan folds wrap around and are locally backfolded against the northwestern margin of the Ambela Granitic Complex (Fig. 11).

The east- and east-southeast–trending folds in the northern Peshawar basin near Swabi (Fig. 8) abruptly rotate to the northeast along the west shore of Tarbela Lake as they approach the Indus syntaxis (Fig. 7). On either side of the Indus River gorge, from Tarbela dam to Besham, bedding and foliation are similarly diverted to become parallel with the axis of the syntaxis (Calkins et al., 1975).

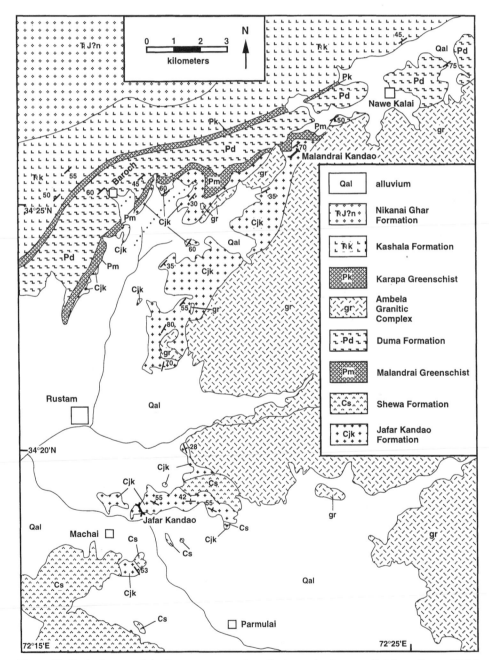

Figure 11. Geologic map of the Rustam area, northern Peshawar basin, compiled from Pogue (1994) and unpublished mapping by Irshad Ahmad. See Figure 3 for location.

The structure of the region east of the Indus River between Darband and Mansehra is dominated by tight to isoclinal south-vergent folds of the Tanawal Formation and Mansehra Granite (Calkins et al., 1975; Treloar et al., 1989b). Fold axes abruptly swing northward between Mansehra and Balakot on the western flank of the Hazara-Kashmir syntaxis (Calkins et al., 1975; Bossart et al., 1988).

The Panjal-Khairabad block is notable for the absence of internal imbrication. The Paleozoic stratigraphy and metamorphic grade of the Nowshera and Swabi areas are very similar (Pogue et al., 1992a), precluding a Himalayan fault of large displacement beneath the intervening alluvium. Recent geologic mapping of the area between Swabi and the Main Mantle thrust (Figs. 8 and 11; DiPietro and Lawrence, 1991; DiPietro et al., this volume) revealed no evidence for the Main Central thrust of Coward et al. (1988), the Alpurai thrust of Treloar et al. (1989a), or any other major Himalayan fault. The only important Himalayan faults west of the Indus River between the Panjal-Khairabad fault and the Main Mantle thrust are late Quaternary faults in the southern Peshawar basin (Yeats and Hussain, 1989).

Nathia Gali–Hissartang block. The first fault north of the Salt Range to bring Precambrian rocks to the surface was named the Nathia Gali fault by Latif (1984). Throughout southern Hazara, the Nathia Gali fault places the Proterozoic Hazara Formation over Mesozoic and Tertiary limestone (Latif, 1970). The Nathia Gali fault splits from the Murree fault 5 km south of Muzaffarabad and then abruptly turns westward 10 km farther south (Fig. 2; Greco, 1991). The fault strikes southwestward through Hazara before it is concealed beneath alluvium of the Haripur basin (Fig. 2; Latif, 1970). It extends westward beneath the alluvium of the Campbellpore basin south of outcrops of Hazara Formation in the hills near Hasan Abdal (Figs. 2 and 7) before emerging from the alluvium in the southern Attock-Cherat Range as the Hissartang fault, where it thrusts Paleozoic(?) Darwaza Formation over the Jurassic Samana Suk Formation (Figs. 2 and 9; Yeats and Hussain, 1987; Hussain et al., 1990). The correlation of the Nathia Gali fault with the Hissartang fault is based on similarities of the stratigraphy of footwall rocks exposed in the Margala Hills and Kala Chitta Range and on the restriction of outcrops of Proterozoic strata to areas north of the faults. The displacement of Tertiary strata across the Hissartang fault at the western end of the Attock-Cherat Range is small compared to the displacement of pre-Tertiary strata observed in outcrops to the east. This relationship led Yeats and Hussain (1987) to conclude that the majority of the displacement on the fault occurred during the Cretaceous. West of the Attock-Cherat Range, the fault is concealed by alluvium of the Peshawar basin before it emerges north of Kohat (Fig. 2; Meissner et al., 1974).

With the exception of the northern exposures of the Hazara Formation, rocks of the Nathia Gali–Hissartang block are unmetamorphosed. North of Abbottabad, pelitic rocks of the Hazara Formation were gently folded and weakly metamorphosed prior to deposition of the overlying Tanakki Conglomerate (Baig and Lawrence, 1987; Baig et al., 1988). This metamorphism is subtle or absent in the Hazara Formation south of Abbottabad and in the Dakhner Formation.

The trends of folds and strikes of thrust faults within the Nathia Gali–Hissartang block generally parallel the strike of the nearest segment of the Nathia Gali or Hissartang faults (Latif, 1970; Hussain et al., 1990). In Hazara, the folds have been generated by at least two distinct phases of northwest-southeast–oriented compression. The first southeast-vergent phase was associated with southeast-directed thrusting along the Nathia Gali fault and its hanging-wall imbricates. The second phase produced north-vergent backfolds that locally fold the Nathia Gali fault and its imbricates so that they dip to the south and appear as normal faults in outcrop (Latif, 1970; Calkins et al., 1975). Evidence for a backfolding episode is lacking in the hanging wall of the Hissartang fault in the Attock-Cherat Range, where faults and folds are consistently south vergent.

Kala Chitta–Margala block. North of Islamabad, Mesozoic and Tertiary strata of the Margala Hills are thrust southeastward over Miocene Murree Formation along the Main Boundary thrust. In this area, the Main Boundary thrust (also known as the Murree fault) is composed of multiple thrust faults that merge toward the northeast to form a single north-striking fault along the western flank of the Hazara-Kashmir syntaxis (Latif, 1970; Yeats and Lawrence, 1984; Greco, 1991). West of the Margala Hills, the Main Boundary thrust zone strikes east along the southern flank of the Kala Chitta Range and the northern boundary of the Kohat Plateau (Fig. 2; Meissner et al., 1974). The unmetamorphosed Mesozoic and Tertiary strata exposed between the Main Boundary thrust and the Nathia Gali–Hissartang fault have been deformed by multiple episodes of north-south compression that produced both south- and north-vergent coaxial folds and associated thrust faults. Backfolding of formerly south-vergent structures has produced moderate to steep southward dips on the constituent faults of the Main Boundary thrust zone in the Margala Hills and in the Kohat area (Latif, 1970; Coward et al., 1988).

Structure discussion

Deformational history of the foothills. Pelitic rocks of the Gandaf Formation, Manki Formation, and northern Hazara Formation were deformed, weakly metamorphosed, uplifted, and eroded prior to deposition of the Lower Cambrian Abbottabad Group. The intrusion of the Mansehra and Swat granites into the Tanawal Formation and older units in the northern part of the Panjal-Khairabad block during the Cambrian (Le Fort et al., 1980) could have occurred either during the late stages of this event or could be part of an unrelated episode of tectonism. The Tanawal Formation was probably derived from a highland produced during Late Proterozoic and/or Early Cambrian tectonism. Removal of the Cambrian Ambar Formation and deposition of Lower Ordovician conglomerate and feldspathic sandstone in the northern Peshawar basin provides evidence for Late Cambrian tectonism (Pogue et al., 1992a).

Beginning in the Carboniferous, the foothills region was affected by extensional tectonics that eventually climaxed in rifting during the Permian (Pogue et al., 1992b). Normal faulting on the landward side of the rift produced elongate northeast-trending highlands in central Swat, the central Attock-Cherat Range, and southern Hazara. Erosion of the uplifted fault blocks produced major unconformities in Swat, where Carboniferous or Permian rocks overlie Proterozoic strata (Pogue et al., 1992b), and in the Attock-Cherat Range and southern Hazara, where Jurassic and Cretaceous limestone overlie Proterozoic rocks (Latif, 1980; Yeats and Hussain, 1987).

Renewed tectonism commenced during the Late Cretaceous with initial motion along the Cherat and Hissartang faults in the Attock-Cherat Range (Yeats and Hussain, 1987). Widespread compressional tectonics related to the obduction of the Kohistan island arc may have begun as early as 62 Ma (Klootwijk et al., 1985), and was certainly underway by 50 Ma (Patriat and Achache, 1984). According to DiPietro and Lawrence (1991), early west-vergent folds in the northern Panjal-Khairabad block in Swat were produced during initial oblique convergence of the western margin of the Indian plate with Kohistan. Kyanite-grade metamorphism in Swat was attributed by DiPietro and Lawrence (1991) and DiPietro (1991) to Eocene subduction of the Swat sequence to depths of 35–45 km beneath the Main Mantle thrust. Lower grade rocks exposed as far south as the northern Attock-Cherat Range were metamorphosed at approximately the same time, but at substantially shallower depths. The accretion of the Kohistan arc is responsible for the large-scale south-vergent folds in Swat and south-vergent folds and thrust faults north of Mansehra (Treloar et al., 1989a; DiPietro and Lawrence, 1991). After the emplacement of Kohistan, the deformation front migrated southward and rocks previously subducted and metamorphosed were thrust over unmetamorphosed rocks along the Panjal-Khairabad fault. This chronology was supported by Treloar et al. (1992), who suggested that motion of the Panjal-Khairabad fault prior to 20 Ma was largely responsible for uplift and exhumation of the high-grade metamorphic rocks south of the Main Mantle thrust. The deformation front continued to migrate southward during the Miocene, producing south-vergent folds and thrust faults between the Main Boundary thrust and the Panjal-Khairabad fault. The Hissartang and Nathia Gali faults were reactivated during this time, although displacement was small compared to pre-Paleocene displacement (Yeats and Hussain, 1987). Major displacement along the Main Boundary thrust zone began between 10 Ma and 5 Ma (Treloar et al., 1992). The major south- or southeast-vergent structures of the foothills were subsequently folded about north-trending axes during the development of the Hazara-Kashmir and Indus syntaxes (Bossart et al., 1988). Offset river gravels, tilted terraces, and airphoto lineaments suggest recent motion along north-striking faults associated with the Indus syntaxis (Yeats and Hussain, 1989; Baig, 1990). Left-stepping pressure ridges adjacent to Quaternary faults (Yeats and Hussain, 1989) and an east-trending zone of seismicity in the southern Peshawar basin (Seeber et al., 1981) also attest to continuing tectonism in the foothills region.

Correlation with tectonic subdivisions of the central Himalaya. Much effort has been expended in attempts to extrapolate the tectonic subdivisions proposed by Gansser (1964) for the central Himalaya to the northwestern Himalaya in Kashmir and Pakistan. The problems involved with such attempts were summarized by Yeats and Lawrence (1984), who proposed a unique set of subdivisions for the Himalaya of northern Pakistan. Despite the efforts of Yeats and Lawrence (1984), recent workers have continued to apply central Himalayan tectonic nomenclature to northern Pakistan. A primary concern of some studies has been to locate the Pakistani equivalent of the Main Central thrust. The Main Central thrust of Gansser (1964, 1981) is at the base of a thick slab of Precambrian crystalline basement that has been transported a large distance to the south over unmetamorphosed or very low grade metamorphic rocks. The amount of shortening on the Main Central thrust is such that it is very difficult to correlate the sedimentary cover of the hanging wall (the Tethyan Himalaya) with sedimentary rocks of the footwall (the Lesser Himalaya). Greco et al. (1989) considered a prominent mylonite zone exposed in the Kaghan valley north of the Hazara-Kashmir syntaxis to be a northwestern extension of the Main Central thrust. As mapped by Bossart et al. (1988) and Greco et al. (1989), the Main Central thrust–correlative mylonite zone strikes northward on the west side of the syntaxis near Balakot (Fig. 2), where it is interpreted to turn to the west and merge with the Oghi shear of Coward et al. (1988). Greco et al. (1989) therefore considered the Oghi shear as the tectonic equivalent of the Main Central thrust of the central Himalaya. Coward et al. (1988) considered the Mansehra thrust, which also converges with the mylonite zone of Bossart et al. (1988) and Greco et al. (1989), to be the Pakistani Main Central thrust. Both Coward et al. (1988) and Greco et al. (1989) based their correlations on the sharp increases in metamorphic grade across the faults. However, neither the jump from chlorite to biotite grade at the Mansehra thrust nor the jump from garnet to kyanite grade at the Oghi shear is comparable to the dramatic increase in metamorphism across the Main Central thrust in the central Himalaya. Furthermore, the presence of Tanawal Formation intruded by Mansehra granite in the hanging wall and footwall of both the Mansehra thrust and Oghi shear precludes the dramatic shortening that would be expected across the Main Central thrust. Rather than being major tectonic boundaries, the Oghi shear, Mansehra thrust, and other similar faults north of Mansehra are local thrusts that imbricate a portion of the Indian plate that was formerly subducted beneath Kohistan along the Main Mantle thrust. The entire metamorphic terrane was then thrust to the south over unmetamorphosed rocks along the Panjal-Khairabad fault. The contrast in stratigraphy and grade of metamorphism across the Panjal-Khairabad fault implies dramatic shortening, and led Pogue et al. (1992a) to suggest that the Panjal-Khairabad fault is the Pakistani analog to the Main Central thrust. However, although the stratigraphic relationships across the two faults are analogous, the Panjal-Khairabad fault does not bring high-grade metamorphic basement to the surface, nor does it mark the base of a topographic step in the manner of the Main Central thrust. Thus, while the Panjal-Khairabad fault shares some characteristics with the Main Central thrust, it is not the western continuation of that structure. The absence of a major crustal-scale thrust fault in northern Pakistan similar to the Main Central thrust of the central Himalaya may be related to decreased shortening due to oblique convergence of the Pakistani Himalaya near the western edge of the Indian plate.

Pogue et al. (1992a) considered Paleozoic and Mesozoic rocks exposed in the Peshawar basin to be the western Himalayan counterpart of the Tethys Himalaya of the central Himalaya. However, central Himalayan Tethyan sections are often unmetamorphosed and unconformably overlie or are faulted against crystalline basement of the High Himalaya, whereas the Tethyan rocks of the Peshawar basin consist of greenschist facies metamorphic rocks that unconformably overlie Proterozoic metasediments that are more typical of the Lesser Himalaya (Gansser, 1964). The foothills region therefore contains no terrane comparable to the High Himalaya, and the metasedimentary rocks exposed north of the Panjal-Khairabad fault constitute a metamorphosed hybrid of Gansser's (1964) Tethyan and Lesser Himalaya.

Pogue et al. (1992a) and Treloar et al. (1992) correlated rocks in the footwall of the Panjal-Khairabad fault with the Lesser Himalaya of northern India and Nepal on the basis of presence of thick intervals of Proterozoic sedimentary rocks, the absence of Ordovician through Carboniferous strata, and the structural position of the rocks north of the apparent westward continuation of the Main Boundary thrust. However, upper Paleozoic rocks of Gondwana affinity typical of the Lesser Himalaya are not present in northern Pakistan except south of the Main Boundary thrust in the Salt Range. Furthermore, exposures of Proterozoic sedimentary rocks in the foothills are bounded on the south by the Nathia Gali–Hissartang fault, a major structure that has no counterpart in the Lesser Himalaya. The foothills region is bounded on the south by the Main Boundary thrust, which like its namesake in the central Himalaya, thrusts older rocks southward over deformed foredeep strata. However, Tertiary molasse of the Murree Formation crops out extensively north of the Main Boundary thrust near Peshawar, and exposures of pre-Murree rocks in the Pakistan Himalaya are not limited to regions north of the Main Boundary thrust as they are in the Himalaya of northern India. The observations outlined here make it apparent that the central Himalayan tectonic subdivisions of Gansser (1964) and their bounding structures cannot be extrapolated to northern Pakistan.

SUMMARY AND CONCLUSIONS

Pre-Cenozoic sedimentary rocks and the protoliths for metasedimentary rocks exposed between the Main Boundary thrust and Main Mantle thrust were originally deposited in an epicontinental marine environment near the north- or northwest-facing margin of continental India. Proterozoic rocks represented by the Hazara (Dakhner) Formation, Manki Formation, and Gandaf Formation form the base of the sedimentary section and record a northward transition from evaporite of the Salt Range Formation to pelitic sediment deposited in deeper water to the north. The Shahkot and Utch Khattak Formations are carbonate intervals within the upper part of the pelite-dominated basal Proterozoic section. The Tanawal Formation was derived from erosion of a highland produced during the early stages of a Late Proterozoic through Early Ordovician phase of tectonism. The Tanawal Formation thins dramatically southward and is replaced by carbonate of the Shekhai

Formation. Early Paleozoic tectonism is indicated by an angular unconformity at the base of the Paleozoic section, the intrusion of the Mansehra Granite, and the local removal of Cambrian strata. Paleozoic shallow-marine strata are preserved in half grabens created during late Paleozoic extensional tectonism that climaxed with Permian rifting. Paleozoic rocks were largely or completely eroded from northeast-trending highlands on the landward side of the rift. Thermal subsidence of the rifted margin eventually submerged the highlands and led to deposition of Mesozoic shallow-water carbonates. Compressional tectonism commenced in the Late Cretaceous with initial motion on thrust faults in the Attock-Cherat Range. Reverse motion on the Cherat fault during this time may represent reactivation of a normal fault formed during late Paleozoic rifting. Rocks north of the Panjal-Khairabad fault were deformed and metamorphosed during Eocene subduction of northern India beneath the Kohistan island-arc terrane. Following uplift and exhumation, rocks metamorphosed beneath Kohistan were thrust southward over unmetamorphosed rocks along the Panjal-Khairabad fault. Significant contrasts in stratigraphy and metamorphism on either side of the Panjal-Khairabad fault indicate that shortening on this structure exceeds that of any other single fault in the foothills region. The migration of the deformation front toward the foreland produced south- or southeast-vergent folds and thrust faults in unmetamorphosed strata south of the Panjal-Khairabad fault and reactivated Late Cretaceous structures such as the Hissartang fault. The Hissartang fault is the westward continuation of the Nathia Gali fault, a major structure that thrusts Proterozoic rocks in the axis of a late Paleozoic rift highland southward over Mesozoic strata. Fundamental differences in stratigraphy, metamorphism, and relative displacement preclude the extension of the faults and tectonic subdivisions of the central Himalaya of India and Nepal to the northwestern Himalaya of Pakistan.

ACKNOWLEDGMENTS

Financial support for this research was provided by U.S. National Science Foundation grants to Joseph DiPietro, Robert D. Lawrence, and Robert S. Yeats (EAR-9316021, INT-86-09914, EAR 86-17543, and INT 86-42445). The study benefitted from discussions and/or field excursions with Joe DiPietro, Arif Ghauri, Anita Harris, Said Rahim Khan, Robert Lawrence, Robert Lillie, Robert Stamm, R. A. K. Tahirkheli, Peter Vail, and Bruce Wardlaw. Assistance in the field was provided by Imtiaz Ahmad, Sajjad Ahmad, Gulzar Aziz, Elisa Weinman Pogue, Mohammed Riaz, and Peter Sak. The manuscript benefitted from reviews by David Pivnik and Jay Quade. The field experience was greatly enhanced by the kindness, generosity, and hospitality of the Pathan villagers of the Northwest Frontier Province of Pakistan.

REFERENCES CITED

Ali, C. M., 1962, The stratigraphy of the southwestern Tanol area, Hazara, West Pakistan: Punjab University Geological Bulletin, no. 2, p. 31–38.
Baig, M. S., 1990, Structure and geochronology of pre-Himalayan orogenic events

in the northwest Himalaya, Pakistan, with special reference to the Besham area [Ph.D. dissertation]: Corvallis, Oregon State University, 300 p.

Baig, M. S., and Lawrence, R. D., 1987, Precambrian to early Paleozoic orogenesis in the Himalaya: Kashmir Journal of Geology, v. 5, p. 1–22.

Baig, M. S., Lawrence, R. D., and Snee, L. W., 1988, Evidence for late Precambrian to Early Cambrian orogeny in Northwest Himalaya, Pakistan: Geological Magazine, v. 125, p. 83–86.

Baker, D. M., Lillie, R. J., Yeats, R. S., Johnson, G. D., Yousuf, M., and Hamid Zamin, A. S., 1988, Development of the Himalayan frontal thrust zone: Salt Range, Pakistan: Geology, v. 16, p. 3–7.

Bossart, P., Dietrich, D., Greco, A., Ottiger, R., and Ramsay, J. G., 1988, The tectonic structure of the Hazara-Kashmir syntaxis, southern Himalayas, Pakistan: Tectonics, v. 7, p. 273–297.

Calkins, J. A., Offield, T. W., Abdullah, S. K. M., and Ali, S. T., 1975, Geology of the southern Himalaya in Hazara, Pakistan and adjacent areas: U.S. Geological Survey Professional Paper 716–C, 29 p.

Coward, M. P., Butler, R. W. H., Chambers, A. F., Graham, R. H., Izatt, C. N., Khan, M. A., Knipe, R. J., Prior, D. J., Treloar, P. J., and Williams, M. P., 1988, Folding and imbrication of the Indian crust during Himalayan collision: Royal Society of London Philosophical Transactions, ser. A, v. 326, p. 89–116.

Crawford, A. R., and Davies, R. G., 1975, Ages of pre-Mesozoic formations of the Lesser Himalaya, Hazara district, northern Pakistan: Geological Magazine, v. 12, p. 509–514.

DiPietro, J. A., 1991, Metamorphic pressure-temperature conditions of Indian plate rocks south of the Main Mantle thrust, Lower Swat, Pakistan: Tectonics, v. 10, p. 742–757.

DiPietro, J. A., and Lawrence, R. D., 1991, Himalayan structure and metamorphism south of the Main Mantle thrust, Lower Swat, Pakistan: Journal of Metamorphic Geology, v. 9, p. 481–495

Fatmi, A. N., 1973, Lithostratigraphic units of the Kohat-Potwar province, Indus basin, Pakistan: Geological Survey of Pakistan Memoirs, v. 10, p. 1–80.

Gansser, A., 1964, Geology of the Himalayas: London, Interscience Publishers, 273 p.

Gansser, A., 1981, The geodynamic history of the Himalaya, *in* Gupta, H. K. and Delany, F. M., eds., Zagros–Hindu Kush–Himalaya geodynamic evolution: American Geophysical Union Geodynamics Series 3, p. 111–121.

Greco, A., 1991, Stratigraphy, metamorphism, and tectonics of the Hazara-Kashmir syntaxis area: Kashmir Journal of Geology, v. 8–9, p. 39–65.

Greco, A., Martinotti, G., Papritz, K., and Ramsay, J. G., 1989, The crystalline rocks of the Kaghan Valley (NE-Pakistan): Eclogae Geologicae Helvetiae, v. 82, p. 629–653.

Hussain, A., 1984, Regional geological map of Nizampur covering parts of Peshawar, Mardan, and Attock districts, Pakistan: Geological Survey of Pakistan Geologic Map Series 14, 1 sheet, scale 1:50,000.

Hussain, A., Yeats, R. S., and Pogue, K. R., 1990, Geologic map of the Attock-Cherat Range and adjoining areas, N.W.F.P. and Punjab, Pakistan: Geological Survey of Pakistan N.W.F.P. Map Series1 sheet, scale 1:100,000.

Hylland, M., 1990, Geology of the southern Gandghar Range and Kherimar hills, northern Pakistan [M.S. thesis]: Corvallis, Oregon State University, 77 p.

Klootwijk, C. T., Conaghan, P. J., and Powell, C. M., 1985, The Himalayan arc: Large-scale contiental subduction, oroclinal bending and back-arc spreading: Earth and Planetary Science Letters, v. 75, p. 167–183.

Latif, M. A., 1969, The stratigraphy of southeastern Hazara and parts of Rawalpindi and Muzaffarabad districts of West Pakistan and Azad Kashmir [Ph.D. thesis]: London, University of London, 316 p.

Latif, M. A., 1970, Explanatory notes on the geology of southeastern Hazara, to accompany the revised geological map: Jahrbuch der Geologischen Bundesanstalt, Sonderband, v. 15, p. 5–20.

Latif, M. A., 1972, Lower Paleozoic (Cambrian?) Hyolithids from Hazira Shale, Pakistan: Nature, Physical Science, v. 240, p. 92.

Latif, M. A., 1974, A Cambrian age for the Abbottabad Group of Hazara, Pakistan: Punjab University Geological Bulletin, no. 10, p. 1–20.

Latif, M. A., 1980, Overstep by Thandiani Group, Jurassic, over older rock sequences in Hazara: Punjab Geological Society Contributions to the Geology of Pakistan, v. 1, p. 1–7.

Latif, M. A., 1984, Age of the Salt Range Formation in the light of the broader set-

ting of Himalayan geology: Kashmir Journal of Geology, v. 2, p. 39–51.

Lawrence, R. D., Kazmi, A. H., and Snee, L. W., 1989, Geologic setting of the emerald deposits, *in* Kazmi, A. H., and Snee, L. W., eds., Emeralds of Pakistan: Geology, gemology, and genesis: New York, Van Nostrand Reinhold, p. 13–38.

Le Fort, P., Debon, F., and Sonet, J., 1980, The "Lesser Himalayan" cordierite granite belt, typology and age of the pluton of Manserah (Pakistan): Peshawar University Geological Bulletin, v. 13, p. 51–61.

Marks, P., and Ali, C. M., 1961, The geology of the Abbottabad area, with special reference to the infra-Trias: Punjab University Geological Bulletin, v. 1, p. 47–55.

Martin, N. R., Siddiqui, S. F. A., and King, B. H., 1962, A geological reconnaissance of the region between the lower Swat and Indus Rivers of Pakistan: Punjab University Geological Bulletin, v. 2, p. 1–13.

Meissner, C. R., Master, J. M., Rashid, M. A., and Hussain, M., 1974, Stratigraphy of the Kohat quadrangle, Pakistan: U.S. Geological Survey Professional Paper 716–D, 30 p.

Patriat, P., and Achache, J., 1984, India-Eurasia collision chronology has implications for crustal shortening and driving mechanisms of plates: Nature, v. 311, p. 615–621.

Pennock, E. S., Lillie, R. J., Zaman, A. S. H., and Yousaf, M., 1989, Structural interpretation of seismic reflection data from eastern Salt Range and Potwar Plateau, Pakistan: American Association of Petroleum Geologists Bulletin, v. 73, p. 841–857.

Pogue, K. R., 1994, Stratigraphic and structural framework of Himalayan foothills, northern Pakistan [Ph.D. thesis]: Corvallis, Oregon State University, 148 p.

Pogue, K. R., Wardlaw, B. R., Harris, A. G., and Hussain, A., 1992a, Paleozoic stratigraphy of the Peshawar basin, Pakistan: Correlations and implications: Geological Society of America Bulletin, v. 104, p. 915–927.

Pogue, K. R., DiPietro, J. A., Khan, S. R., Hughes, S. S., Dilles, J. A., and Lawrence, R. D., 1992b, Late Paleozoic rifting in northern Pakistan: Tectonics, v. 11, p. 871–883.

Seeber, L., Armbruster, J. G., and Quittmeyer, R. C., 1981, Seismicity and continental subduction in the Himalayan arc, *in* Gupta, H. K., and Delaney, F. M., eds., Zagros–Hindu Kush–Himalaya geodynamic evolution: American Geophysical Union Geodynamics Series 3, p. 215–242.

Shah, S. M. I., ed., 1977, Stratigraphy of Pakistan: Geological Survey of Pakistan Memoirs, v. 12, 138 p.

Stöcklin, J., 1986, The Vendian–Lower Cambrian salt basins of Iran, Oman, and Afghanistan: Stratigraphy, correlations, paleogeography, *in* Le Fort, P., Colchen, M., and Montenat, C., eds., Orogenic evolution of southern Asia, Sciences de la Terre Memoire 47, p. 329–345.

Treloar, P. J., Broughton, R. D., Williams, M. P., and Khan, M. A., 1989a, Deformation, metamorphism, and imbrication of the Indian plate south of the Main Mantle thrust, north Pakistan: Journal of Metamorphic Geology, v. 7, p. 111–125.

Treloar, P. J., Williams, M. P., and Coward, M. P., 1989b, Metamorphism and crustal stacking in the north Indian plate, north Pakistan: Tectonophysics, v. 165, p. 167–184.

Treloar, P. J., Coward, M. P., Chambers, A. F., Izatt, C. N., and Jackson, K. C., 1992, Thrust geometries, interferences, and rotations in the northwest Himalaya, *in* McClay, K. R., ed., Thrust tectonics: New York, Chapman and Hall, p. 325–342.

Wardlaw, B. R., and Pogue, K. R., 1995, Permian of Pakistan, *in* Scholle, P. A., and Peryt, T. M., eds., The Permian of northern Pangaea: Sedimentary basins and economic resources: New York, Springer-Verlag, p. 215–224.

Yeats, R. S., and Hussain, A., 1987, Timing of structural events in the Himalayan foothills of northwestern Pakistan: Geological Society of America Bulletin, v. 99, p. 161–176.

Yeats, R. S., and Hussain, A., 1989, Zone of late Quaternary deformation in the southern Peshawar basin, Pakistan, *in* Malinconico, L. L., and Lillie, R. J., eds., Tectonics of the western Himalayas: Geological Society of America Special Paper 232, p. 265–274.

Yeats, R. S., and Lawrence, R. D., 1984, Tectonics of the Himalayan thrust belt in Northern Pakistan, *in* Haq, B. U., and Milliman, J. D., eds., Marine geology and oceanography of Arabian Sea and coastal Pakistan: New York, Van Nostrand Reinhold Co., p. 177–198.

MANUSCRIPT ACCEPTED BY THE SOCIETY FEBRUARY 3, 1998

Geological Society of America
Special Paper 328
1999

Triangle zone in the Himalayan foreland, north Pakistan

Ishtiaq A. K. Jadoon* and Wolfgang Frisch
Institute of Geology, Tübingen University, Sigwartstrasse 10, Tübingen D-72076, Germany
Tariq M. Jaswal
Oil and Gas Development Corporation of Pakistan, W-Blue Area, Islamabad, Pakistan
Arif Kemal
Pakistan Oil Limited, Rawalpindi, Pakistan

ABSTRACT

Surface geology and seismic reflection profiles reveal the geometry of a triangle zone in the Himalayan foreland of Pakistan. Surface expression of the triangle zone is the Soan syncline (monocline), the northern foreland-dipping steep limb of which is located above a bedding-parallel backthrust in the Tertiary molasse strata. The hinterland-dipping Khairi-Murat thrust is located on the proximal end of the triangle zone. The steep Dhurnal backthrust becomes shallower to the south and dies out at a depth of about 2 to 4 km. At this depth, it merges with a north-dipping blind thrust that propagates upsection as a ramp from a layer of Eocambrian evaporites at a depth of about 8 km and forms a flat along a pelitic horizon in Miocene molasse strata. The two faults bound a blind, tapered wedge of allochthonous strata (core wedge) inserted below the backthrust. Coherent and discoherent reflections above and below the Dhurnal backthrust show the undeformed planar and deformed (pop-ups) geometry of the foot-wall and hanging wall outside and inside the wedge.

We interpret the three-dimensional geometry of the triangle zone in terms of a core wedge having flat-ramp-flat geometry and internal as well as external pop-ups. The presence of blind faults of smaller lateral extent (about 10 km) and shortening (about 2 km) indicates the occurrence of more than one hydrocarbon trap in the triangle zone.

Published magnetostratigraphy limits the formation of the triangle zone between 2.1 to 1.9 Ma. On the basis of cross-section balancing, we calculate horizontal contraction of 4.5 km and rock uplift of about 2.8 km along the core wedge. The shortening and rock uplift rates amount to about 22 mm/yr and about 14 ± 2 mm/yr, respectively. The presence of hydrocarbons (the Dhurnal oil field) in such young structural traps in the Salt Range has important bearings for the exploration of oil and gas in the Himalayan foreland.

INTRODUCTION

The Himalayan foreland basin in north Pakistan (Fig. 1) is one of the first areas in the world explored for hydrocarbons (Khan et al., 1986). The first commercial discovery of oil was made in 1914 at Khaur from Eocene limestone of the Potwar Plateau (Fig. 2). Here, the surface expression is that of a buried mountain front. A typical traverse may start from the axis of the Soan syncline across the Khairi-Murat Range. Along this traverse, autochthonous flat strata along the axis of the Soan syncline are tilted increasingly northward above a south-dipping passive backthrust (Jaswal, 1990; Jaswal et al., 1997) in the Tertiary

---

*Present address: Schlumberger Overseas S.A., POB 8746, Doha, Qatar;
jadoon@doha.geoquest.slb.com.

Jadoon, I. A. K., Frisch, W., Jaswal, T. M., and Kemal, A., 1999, Triangle zone in the Himalayan foreland, north Pakistan, *in* Macfarlane, A., Sorkhabi, R. B., and Quade, J., eds., Himalaya and Tibet: Mountain Roots to Mountain Tops: Boulder, Colorado, Geological Society of America Special Paper 328.

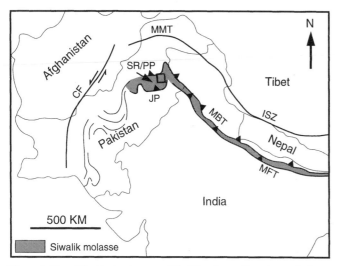

Figure 1. Simplified tectonic map of the Himalayas. Box shows the location of Figure 2. CF = Chaman fault; ISZ = Indus suture zone; MBT = Main Boundary thrust; MFT = Main Frontal thrust; MMT = Main Mantle thrust; JP = Jhelum Plain; SR/PP = Salt Range–Potwar Plateau.

molasse strata. In the Khairi-Murat Range to the north, allochthonous Eocene platform strata are emplaced over molasse strata along the north-dipping, foreland-vergent Khairi-Murat thrust. The geology between backthrust and forethrust is complex, and there are moderate to steep dips of poor seismic resolution. Seven shallow wells to 431 m depth (Kamran and Ranke, 1987) were drilled between 1930 and 1933 in this area (Fig. 2). More recently, after the discovery of the Dhurnal oil field (Fig. 2) in 1984, exploration efforts have been renewed to further evaluate the petroleum potential of this area.

Structural geometries similar to those just described are recognized as triangle zones (Gordy et al., 1977), and are common features near thrust fronts throughout the world (Price, 1986; Vann et al., 1986; Ramos, 1989; Sanderson and Spratt, 1992; Lawton et al., 1994; Jadoon et al., 1992, 1994). A triangle zone is generally defined as an area bounded by a backthrust at the foreland margin of a thrust belt and a floor thrust that terminates updip at the backthrust. The space between the two thrusts is occupied by a deformed (core) wedge of competent allochthonous strata. The sequence above the backthrust is called a roof sequence (Banks and Warburton, 1986). These structures have become increasingly important as they are recognized as sites of significant hydrocarbon accumulations (Jones, 1982; Müller et al., 1988; Ramos, 1989).

Recently, the triangle zone geometry of the Dhurnal oil field was recognized on the basis of interpretation of industry seismic reflection profiles (Jaswal, 1990; Jaswal et al., 1997). In this triangle zone, the Dhurnal backthrust in Figure 2 is recognized as a passive backthrust at the foreland margin of the thrust belt (Jaswal, 1990). In this chapter, we use seismic reflection profiles combined with surface geology and well data to draw three cross sections across the Khairi-Murat Range to show along-strike and across-strike variations in structural style and geometry of the triangle zone. Age data are used (e.g., Burbank and Raynolds, 1984; Raynolds and Johnson, 1985) to constrain the timing of evolution of the Khairi-Murat triangle zone and to provide estimates of shortening and uplift rates due to the deformation of the core wedge.

TECTONIC SETTING

The Himalayan collision system represents an active collision orogen between the Indian and Eurasian subcontinents (e.g., Le Fort, 1975). The ongoing collision since about 55 Ma (Powell, 1979; Klootwijk et al., 1985; Beck et al., 1995) involves continuous uplift, erosion, and deposition of sediments in the adjacent foreland basins (Treloar et al., 1991; Raynolds and Johnson, 1985). Sedimentary strata in the foreland are detached and translated along the Salt Range thrust over the Jhelum plain in Pakistan (Yeats and Lawrence, 1984; Yeats et al., 1984; Coward and Butler, 1985; Treloar et al., 1992).

The Salt Range–Potwar Plateau represents a broad (about 130 km across strike) zone of Himalayan foreland thrusting in north Pakistan (Fig. 1). Seismic reflection profiles were used to draw balanced cross sections of the zone (Leathers, 1987; Lillie et al., 1987; Baker et al., 1988; Pennock et al., 1989; Jaswal et al., 1997). These cross sections reveal the gross geometry of the area, including depth and presence of the main decollement in the Eocambrian evaporites. The distribution of foreland thrusting that includes a gentle topography (envelope <1°), broad width (about 130 km), lack of internal deformation, and symmetrical structures is compatible with thrust wedges developed over a weak decollement (Davis and Engelder, 1985; Jaume and Lillie, 1988; Davis and Lillie, 1994).

The broad Salt Range–Potwar Plateau has two parts. To the south, the Salt Range is located at the leading edge of an emergent thrust sheet (Yeats et al., 1984; Lillie et al., 1987; Baker et al., 1988). The 90-km-wide thrust sheet remains undeformed in the central Salt Range. To the north, the thrust sheet is imbricated. This imbricated part, called the North Potwar deformed zone, has an emergent and a buried thrust front in the western and eastern parts of the deformed zone, respectively (Jaswal, 1990). A few studies provide some ideas about the evolution of the North Potwar deformed zone (Treloar et al., 1992; McDougall et al., 1993; Baig, 1995; Jamshed, 1995). Jaswal (1990), Jaswal et al. (1997), and Jadoon et al. (1997) used seismic reflection profiles to work out the structural complexities of the deformed zone; however, structure and kinematics of the zone are as yet unresolved. Here we show cross sections of the buried mountain front in the eastern North Potwar deformed zone to complement the earlier studies. These cross sections, constrained by seismic reflection profiles, show the internal geometry of a triangle zone above the evaporites. This work, particularly useful for hydrocarbon exploration in north Pakistan, increases our understanding of the triangle-zone geometry. Tight age constraints on the clastic sedimentation and thrusting (e.g., Raynolds, 1980; Burbank and Raynolds, 1984, 1988; Johnson et al., 1986) pro-

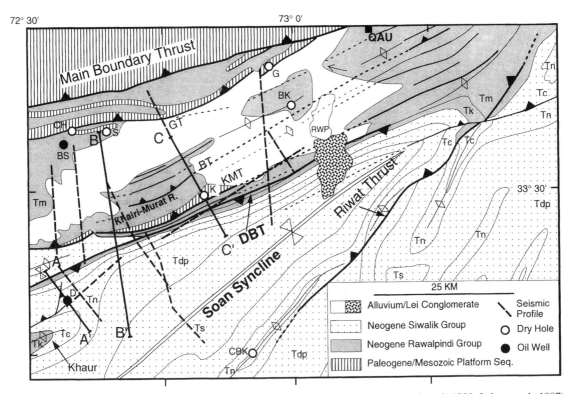

Figure 2. Geologic map of the eastern part of North Potwar deformed zone (based on Pennock et al., 1989; Jadoon et al., 1997). Note field relationship of Lei Conglomerate with the north flank of the Soan syncline and the Dhurnal backthrust. Lei Conglomerate is based on Naeem and Bhatti (1985) and Burbank and Raynolds (1988). Lines AA′, BB′, and CC′ show the location of cross sections in Figures 5 through 7. These lines and dashed lines show locations of seismic profiles. BT = Bokra thrust; DBT = Dhurnal backthrust; GT = Golra thrust; KMT = Khairi-Murat thrust. Tertiary formations (Fm): Ts = Soan Fm.; Tdp = Dhok Pathan Fm.; Tn = Nagri Fm.; Tc = Chinji Fm.; Tk = Kamlial Fm.; Tm = Murree Fm. Wells: BK = Bokra; BS = Bhal Syedan; CBK = Chak Beli Khan; CH = Chirrat; D = Dhurnal; G = Golra; S = Sadkal; K = Khairi-Murat. QAU = Quaid-i-Azam University, RWP = Rawalpindi.

vide additional support on the development of the triangle zone and the accumulation of hydrocarbons in a structural trap.

SEISMIC REFLECTION PROFILES, WELL DATA, AND GENERAL OBSERVATIONS

Industry seismic reflection profiles and well data from the eastern North Potwar deformed zone were made available by the Oil and Gas Development Corporation of Pakistan (OGDC) with the permission of the Ministry of Petroleum and Natural Resources, Pakistan (Fig. 2). Most of data are from 1977 to 1993. Basal lines recorded and processed by the OGDC in 1993 are from the OGDC–Zaver Petroleum's joint north Potwar concession. These data were used to draw three parallel cross sections to resolve the structural geometry of the buried mountain front in the eastern North Potwar deformed zone, north of the Soan syncline (monocline). A representative stratigraphic column based on the Dhurnal well (Jaswal, 1990; Ahmed et al., 1993) (Fig. 3) shows stratigraphic thicknesses and producing horizons.

Distribution of industry seismic profiles and well data have provided a good basis for the interpretation of the triangle zone in the eastern North Potwar deformed zone. Most of the seismic lines located in Figure 2 include data of 5 to 6 s two-way travel-time, yet the basement can be seen near 4 s two-way traveltime. The stratigraphic column above the basement is divided into four major units on the basis of their seismic signatures. These include the crystalline basement, the Eocambrian evaporites, the Cambrian to Eocene platform sequence, and the Tertiary molasse strata, including the Rawalpindi and Siwalik Groups (Figs. 3 and 4). Seismic data show clear reflections from distinct stratigraphic and tectonic units below the Soan syncline. Seismic reflections from the core wedge are generally less distinct and are very poor to the north of the Khairi-Murat thrust. However, reflections related to the Khairi-Murat thrust can be clearly recognized in all of the seismic profiles (Fig. 4), comparable to seismic signatures of similar structures reported elsewhere (e.g., Bally et al., 1966; Müller et al., 1988).

Generally the top of the basement is characterized by a strong, continuous, subhorizontal reflection overlain by a zone of transparent seismic signature representing the Eocambrian evaporites. The Cambrian to Eocene platform strata are imaged by a series of continuous strong reflections (Fig. 4). The semicontinuous reflections above the platform sequence represent the molasse strata. Seismic data are tied with composite seismic pro-

AGE	FORMATION	SM/PAT	DESCRIPTION	THICKNESS	OIL
PLEIST-OCENE / HOLOCENE	POTWAR SILT	· · · · · Ts · · · · · 3200 m/s			
MIOCENE — Siwalik Group	SOAN (0.7 Ma)		Conglomerate, sandstone, claystone	>450 m	
	DHOK PATHAN (5.1 Ma)		Claystone, sandstone	600 m	
	NAGRI (7.9 Ma)		Sandstone, shale	518 m	
	CHINJI (10.1 Ma)		Sandstone, shale	1313 m	
Rawalpindi Group	KAMLIAL (13.1 Ma)	Tr 4000 m/s	Sandstone	393 m	
	MURREE		Shale, sandstone	1713 m	
EOCENE	MAMIKHEL		Shale		
	CHORGALI		Dolomite, shale, ss	234 m	●
	SAKESAR		Limestone		●
PALEOCENE	PATALA	P-E	Limestone, Shale		●
	LOCKHART		Limestone	193 m	
	HANGU		Sandstone, shale		
PERMIAN	WARGAL	4500 m/s	Limestone		●
	AMB		Sandstone, shale		◗
	SARDHAI		Shale	652 m	
	WARCHA		Sandstone, shale		◗
	DANDOT		Sandstone, shale		
	TOBRA		Sandstone, siltstone		
INFRA-CAMBR	SALT RANGE FORMATION	SRF 4700 m/s	Dolomite, shale, salt	>100	
PRE-CAMB	BASEMENT OF INDIAN SHIELD	PC 6000 m/s	Biotite schist		

Figure 3. Simplified stratigraphic column of the North Potwar deformed zone based on Dhurnal-3 well (after Kamran and Ranke, 1987; Jaswal, 1990; Ahmed et al., 1993). SM/PAT = Symbols and Patterns. Approximate seismic velocities are estimated from thicknesses from the well data, sonic logs, and conversion of stacking velocities from seismic lines to interval velocities. Age determination of the Siwaliks is based on magnetostratigraphy and fission-track dating (Raynolds, 1980; G. Johnson et al., 1982; N. Johnson et al., 1982). Filled dots = hydrocarbon production, half-filled dots = hydrocarbon shows. Ts =Tertiary Siwalik Group and Potwar Silt, Tr = Tertiary Rawalpindi Group, P-E = Permian through Eocene, SRF = Salt Range Formation, PC = Precambrian, ss = sandstone.

files from the Salt Range–Potwar Plateau (Lillie et al., 1987; Pennock et al., 1989; Jaswal, 1990) and the Dhurnal well (Figs. 2 and 3). A nearly complete stratigraphic section from Nagri through the Eocambrian Salt Range Formation was drilled to a depth of 4,890 m in the Dhurnal well (Fig. 3).

Interpretation of the seismic data shows that the Eocambrian Salt Range Formation plays an important role in shaping the geometry of structures in the triangle zone. These strata overlie the basement and have a general thickness of about 2 km in the central Salt Range–Potwar Plateau (Lillie et al., 1987). These are reported to thin out to 500 m in the eastern Salt Range–Potwar Plateau (Pennock et al., 1989). The evaporites show an average thickness of 1100 m below the Soan syncline (Jaswal, 1990) and thin out to the east and north (Figs. 5, 6, and 7). The Eocambrian

evaporites do not retain their thickness and provide an effective gliding plane. Flow of the evaporites from below the synclines into the anticlines is observed in the triangle zone (Figs. 5 and 7).

SEISMIC INTERPRETATION AND GEOMETRY OF THE TRIANGLE ZONE

Cross sections in Figures 5, 6, and 7 show the three-dimensional geometry of the triangle zone in the North Potwar deformed zone. The sections illustrate the basement at a depth between 6 and 7 km that dips to the north with an average angle of about 3°. A basement normal fault having a hanging wall down to the north displacement and a throw of about 600 m is interpreted to be below the Khairi-Murat triangle zone (Fig. 4). We consider the fault responsible for deformation in that it produced an obstruction against the southward-translating strata along the decollement. The mechanisms of normal fault development by bending of the rigid continental crust below the Salt Range–Potwar Plateau and thrusting of the Salt Range above a normal fault were discussed by Lillie et al. (1987), Baker et al. (1988), and Jaswal et al. (1997).

All of the sedimentary strata above the basement are detached from basement along a decollement in the Eocambrian evaporites. The decollement serves as the floor thrust. A blind thrust moves upsection from the floor thrust and merges into the Dhurnal backthrust (roof thrust). A core wedge of Cambrian to Neogene strata is thrust toward the foreland between the bounding floor and backthrust. The Kamlial and Siwalik formations (Fig. 3) along the Dhurnal backthrust are passively uplifted, tilted, and exposed due to the underthrusted core wedge. The geometry of the tectonic wedge is established by recognizing the backthrust and blind thrusts, and locating the hanging-wall and footwall cutoff points of critical strata across the blind thrusts. Horizontal reflections below the Soan syncline and the core wedge are interpreted to represent autochthonous strata (Fig. 4).

The core wedge shows a decreasing amount of shortening to the east (Figs. 5–7). The Khairi-Murat thrust soles out in the basal decollement at a depth of about 9 km. In each case (Figs. 6 and 7) it shows a constant displacement of about 11 km. The displacement of 11 km of the thrust is consistent with its laterally extensive surface trace in the North Potwar deformed zone (Jaswal, 1990). The north-dipping Khairi-Murat thrust and the south-dipping Dhurnal backthrust converge upward and bound a 2–6-km-wide zone of complex geology at the surface. Similar expression of triangle zones is observed in other fold and thrust belts (Jones, 1982; Müller et al., 1988; Ramos, 1989; Sanderson and Spratt, 1992; Skuce et al., 1992; Lawton et al., 1994).

Variations typical for triangle zones are observed by comparing cross-sections AA′, BB′, and CC′ in Figures 5, 6, and 7. An interpretation of seismic reflection profiles (Fig. 4) shows a flat-ramp-flat geometry for the core wedge. This geometry is modified by pop-ups (terminology from Butler, 1982), backthrusts, and ductile flow of the evaporites (Figs. 5 and 7). The role of salt as an effective decollement horizon, its tendency to flow, and its influ-

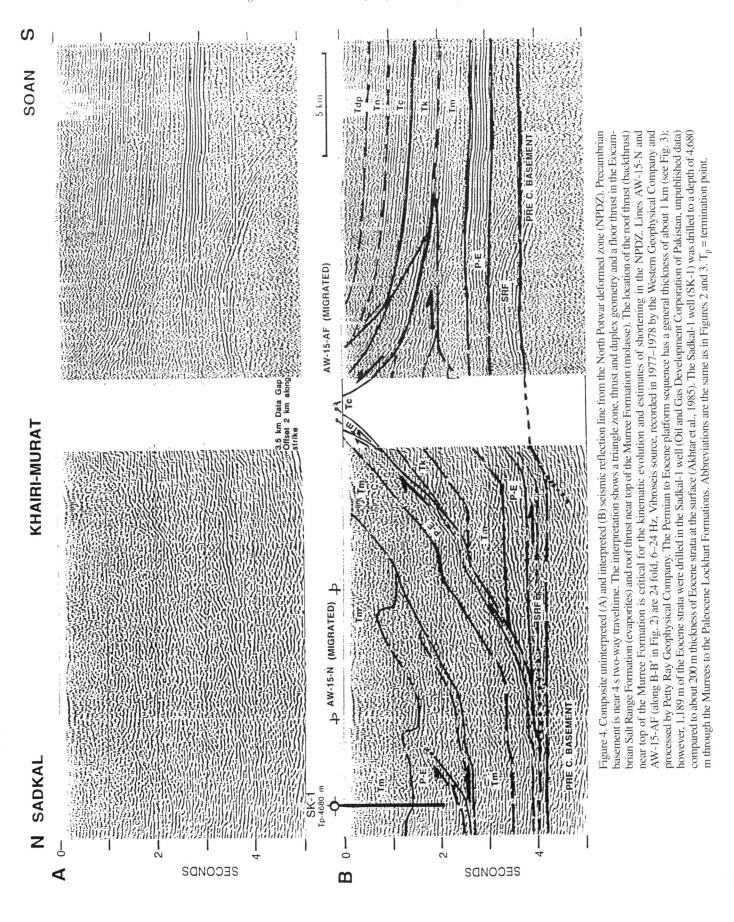

Figure 4. Composite uninterpreted (A) and interpreted (B) seismic reflection line from the North Potwar deformed zone (NPDZ). Precambrian basement is near 4 s two-way traveltime. The interpretation shows a triangle zone, thrust and duplex geometry and a floor thrust in the Eocambrian Salt Range Formation (evaporites) and roof thrust near top of the Murree Formation (molasse). The location of the roof thrust (backthrust) near top of the Murree Formation is critical for the kinematic evolution and estimates of shortening in the NPDZ. Lines AW-15-N and AW-15-AF (along B-B' in Fig. 2) are 24 fold, 6–24 Hz, Vibroseis source, recorded in 1977–1978 by the Western Geophysical Company and processed by Petty Ray Geophysical Company. The Permian to Eocene platform sequence has a general thickness of about 1 km (see Fig. 3); however, 1,189 m of the Eocene strata were drilled in the Sadkal-1 well (Oil and Gas Development Corporation of Pakistan, unpublished data) compared to about 200 m thickness of Eocene strata at the surface (Akhtar et al., 1985). The Sadkal-1 well (SK-1) was drilled to a depth of 4,680 m through the Murrees to the Paleocene Lockhart Formations. Abbreviations are the same as in Figures 2 and 3. T_p = termination point.

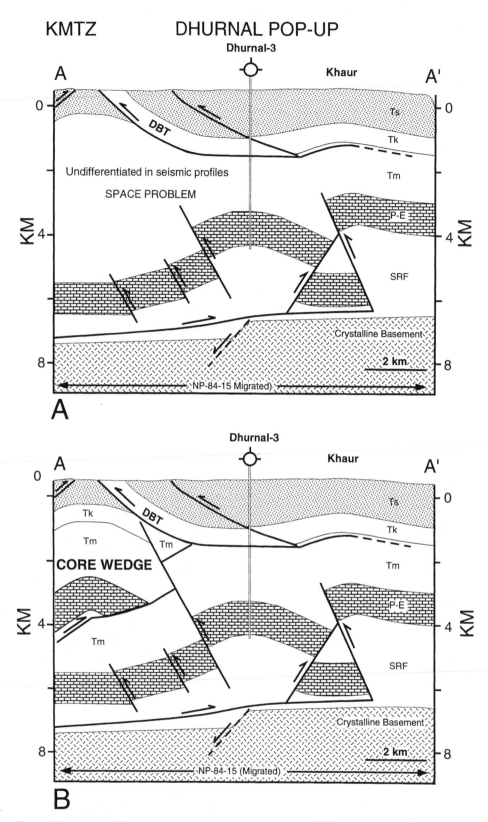

Figure 5. Section AA′ (Fig. 2), based on the seismic reflection profile NP-84-15 (Jaswal, 1990) in Figure 3. A: The geometry of the triangle zone with fault tip line Dhurnal pop-up, the Dhurnal backthrust, and the basement are based on strong reflections, whereas a zone of poor reflections is shown uninterpreted. B: Complete interpretation, suggesting the presence of a core wedge. Thickness of the core wedge is predictable based on seismic reflection interpretations and surface geology. KMTZ = Khairi-Murat triangle zone. Other abbreviations as in Figures 2 and 3.

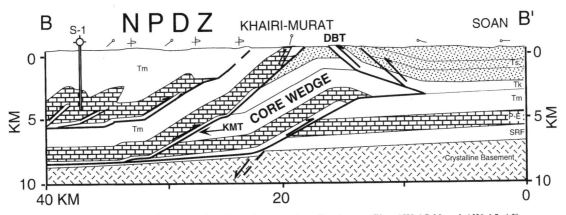

Figure 6. Section BB′ (Fig. 2), based on the seismic reflection profiles AW-15-N and AW-15-AF (Fig. 4). Notice undeformed footwall block of the core wedge, unlike Figure 5. KMT = Khairi-Murat thrust; NPDZ = North Potwar deformed zone; DBT = Dhurnal backthrust; S-1 = Sadkal-1 well. Other abbreviations as in Figures 2 and 3.

KHAIRI-MURAT TRIANGLE ZONE

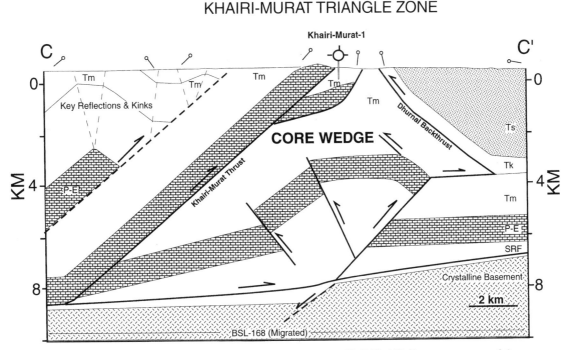

Figure 7. Section CC′ (Fig. 2), based on seismic reflection profile BSL-168. Pop-up geometry of the core wedge, backthrusting, and ductile deformation at deeper levels is similar to sand-box modeling (Mulugeta and Koyi, 1987; Koyi, 1995). Abbreviations as in Figures 2 and 3.

ence on the mechanics of thrusting and thrust geometries in the Salt Range–Potwar Plateau was described by Yeats et al. (1984), Jaume and Lillie (1988), and Davis and Lillie (1994).

Figure 5A, based on the interpretation of clear reflections in the seismic profile along line A-A′ (Fig. 2; Jaswal, 1990), illustrates the development of a pop-up below the backthrust as a fault tip-line structure. Here we interpret a core wedge of the platform and molasse strata filling the space in the zone of undifferentiated reflections (Fig. 5B). A basement normal fault or a basement warp provides an irregular surface below the deformed wedge.

The overall geometry of the symmetrical structures in this cross section is consistent with deformation over a weak decollement (Davis and Engelder, 1985).

The Dhurnal backthrust generally merges into the blind thrust at a depth of about 3.5–4 km. However, in Figure 5 it merges into the blind thrust at a depth of about 2 km. This is due to deformation in the footwall strata of the core wedge that involves about 2 km uplift along blind thrusts. As a result, deformation extends more than 11 km from the backthrust surface trace to the south, as compared to about 5 km in other sections discussed below.

Figure 6 shows a flat-ramp-flat geometry of the core wedge between the Dhurnal backthrust and the Khairi-Murat thrust. At depth, the backthrusts have gentler dips and meet the tip point of the blind floor thrust. The flat in the footwall of the core wedge remains undeformed in this section, implying eastward termination of the Dhurnal pop-up. The horizontal contraction along the core wedge is about 4.5 km. However, the maximum offset between cutoff points is about 5.5 km.

Figure 7 shows a modified geometry of the core wedge from flat-ramp-flat into a pop-up by the presence of backthrusts and ductile flow of the evaporites. The shortening of the core wedge is about 2 km. Decrease in shortening (relative to the previous section) implies eastward termination of the structure, consistent with flat but poor reflections along the strike (longitudinal seismic profile, southwest Rawalpindi, in Fig. 2). Experimental modeling suggests sequential evolution of the thrust systems as detachment, folding, and thrust faulting (Dixon and Tirrul, 1991). Similar work shows the dominance of ductile deformation at deeper levels of the crust (Koyi, 1995) and backthrusting during the incipient evolution of a thrust (Mulugeta and Koyi, 1987).

DEVELOPMENT OF THE TRIANGLE ZONE

The Himalayan foreland in north Pakistan is an active thrust system. Age constraints on the development of structures (e.g., Raynolds 1980; Burbank and Raynolds, 1984; Johnson et al., 1986; Burbank and Raynolds, 1988) are an essential tool for section restoration, dating of migration, and an understanding of accumulation of hydrocarbon reserves.

Magnetostratigraphic control suggests that the northern limb of the Soan syncline was developed between 2.1 and 1.9 Ma (Burbank and Raynolds, 1984). Cross sections in this chapter show the development of the northern limb of the Soan syncline by uplift and rotation of the Siwalik strata along the Dhurnal backthrust. Nearly vertical Siwalik strata, as young as 2.1 Ma, along the northern limb of the Soan syncline and the thrust stack in the eastern North Potwar deformed zone are truncated and overlain by the generally undeformed Lei Conglomerate (Figs. 2 and 8B; Naeem and Bhatti, 1985; Burbank and Raynolds, 1988). The base of the Lei Conglomerate is interpreted to be 1.9 Ma (Burbank and Raynolds, 1984; Raynolds and Johnson, 1985); this is supported by a 1.6 ± 0.2 Ma date of an ash bed based on zircon fission-track analysis in the Lei Conglomerate (G. Johnson et al., 1982). Because the Dhurnal backthrust is kinematically related to the formation and motion of the core wedge (Fig. 8), the development of the triangle zone in the eastern North Potwar deformed zone can be dated between 2.1 and 1.9 Ma.

RATES OF SHORTENING AND UPLIFT

Balanced cross sections and the available age constraints on the development of the Khairi-Murat triangle zone permit calculation of the amount of shortening, uplift, and exhumation due to the motion of the core wedge in the Khairi-Murat triangle zone.

Shortening can be measured by correlating the hanging-wall and footwall cutoffs in the balanced cross sections, whereas rock uplift may be calculated as the rise of a particular stratigraphic horizon from its regional level (Fig. 8). Specifically, surface uplift is a measure of the elevation change of the Earth's surface with respect to a reference level, whereas exhumation is a measure of the uplift of a rock mass relative to the local Earth's surface (England and Molnar, 1990; Treloar et al., 1991). The amount of exhumed material equals the amount of overburden removed by either erosion or normal faulting.

The geometry of the triangle zone shows that about 5.5 km of net slip (between cutoff points) has occurred along the core wedge and the Dhurnal backthrust (Fig. 8A). This is divided into 4.5 km of horizontal contraction and 2.8 km of rock uplift along the core wedge. A partially restored cross section shows about 6 km of rock uplift, including the amount removed by erosion, along the Dhurnal backthrust (Fig. 8B). This is due to the combined effects of upward motion and uplift of the core wedge and the Dhurnal backthrust above hinterland- and foreland-dipping ramps, respectively (Fig. 8, B and C).

The restored geometry of the triangle zone shows that about 4.5 km of horizontal contraction has occurred along the core wedge. Considering the deformation to have occurred between 2.1 and 1.9 Ma, the rate of structural contraction is calculated to be about 22 mm/yr. This number exceeds the shortening estimates of 9–18 mm/yr in the Salt Range–Potwar Plateau (Leathers, 1987; Baker et al., 1988; Jaswal, 1990; Jadoon et al., 1997), 7.1 mm/yr for the Riwat thrust in Figure 2 (Jadoon and Frisch, 1997), and 10–15 mm/yr in the sub-Himalaya in India (Lyon-Caen and Molnar, 1985). These differences may be attributed to the episodic accretion and stick-slip mode of decollement propagation, illustrated by sand-box modeling (Mulugeta and Koyi, 1992). Strain partitioning and episodic deformation are supported by chronology of clastic sedimentation and thrusting from the Salt Range–Potwar Plateau (Burbank et al., 1986; Johnson et al., 1986).

The sequential restoration provides insight into the amount of rock uplift and exhumation related to the evolution of the Khairi-Murat triangle zone (Fig. 8). It shows about 2.8 km of rock uplift along the core wedge (Fig. 8A) and about 6 km of uplift along the Dhurnal backthrust (Fig. 8B), similar to findings of Burbank and Beck (1991). Variations in the amount of uplift are related to the irregular geometry of the core wedge. Considering that deformation was between 2.1 and 1.9 Ma, a rate of rock uplift of 14 ± 2 mm/yr can be calculated along the core wedge, close to the 15 mm/yr of uplift along northern limb of the Soan syncline calculated by Burbank and Raynolds (1984). High rates of uplift and denudation of as much as 10 mm/yr are not unusual in the Himalayan foreland (Burbank and Beck, 1991) and the Nanga-Parbat region (Zeitler, 1985).

Having restored the geometry of the core wedge, a space remains open that can be filled by about 45 km^2 of eroded strata along the leading edge of the Dhurnal backthrust (Fig. 8B). This amount, added to about 8 km^2 of eroded strata in the core wedge,

NORTH POTWAR DEFORMED ZONE

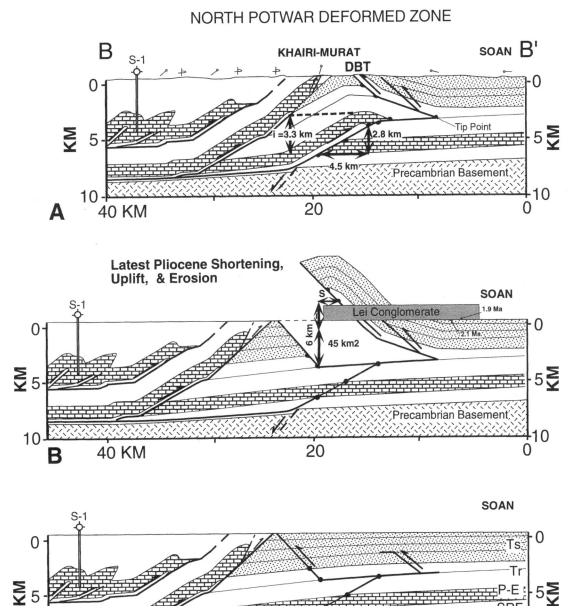

Figure 8. Sequential development of the Soan syncline triangle zone. A: Complete cross section. Note 4.5 km of shortening and about 2.8 km of uplift along the core wedge. B: Partially restored cross section of the core wedge. Timing constraints on the Siwalik strata and Lei Conglomerate are from Burbank and Raynolds (1984) and Raynolds and Johnson (1985). Note about 6 km of uplift and smaller amount of shortening (S) along the leading edge of the Dhurnal backthrust. Variation in shortening and uplift is a function of core wedge geometry and the Dhurnal backthrust, discussed in the text. C: Fully restored cross section of the core wedge. Restoration suggests shortening and uplift rates of 22 mm/yr and 14 ± 2 mm/yr, respectively, along the core wedge. Patterns as in Figure 5; abbreviations as in Figures 2 and 3.

is in agreement with the estimated minimum of 60 km² along the northern limb of the Soan syncline by Burbank and Beck (1991). However, our more precisely restored geometry of the triangle zone (Fig. 8C) refutes the values of 200 km² or more of erosion proposed by Burbank and Beck (1991).

HYDROCARBON POTENTIAL

Triangle zones are recognized as key structures for the exploration of hydrocarbons (Jones, 1982). The Salt Range–Potwar Plateau is currently producing moderate amounts of hydrocarbons (Khan et al., 1986; Raza et al., 1989; Kemal, 1991). The Dhurnal oil field, discovered in 1984 (Ahmed et al., 1993), produces hydrocarbons from a triangle zone setting (Jaswal, 1990). Dhurnal, the largest oil field of Pakistan, was producing 19,000 barrels of oil per day during its peak production in 1989 (Ahmed et al., 1993). Estimated recoverable reserves of oil in the pop-up are 49 million barrels. The structure is located in the triangle-zone geometry on the foreland side of the core wedge.

Figure 9A shows the length and shortening of some thrusts in the Khairi-Murat triangle zone. It shows three sets of structures from the buried fault tip line (e.g., Dhurnal and Khaur) to the exposed Khairi-Murat thrust (Figs. 2, 5, and 6). Along the fault tip line, small-scale blind faults are observed that have about 2 km of shortening and structural relief. The blind thrusts appear to link with increasing displacement. The linking process of smaller thrusts into a larger thrust with increasing displacement is similar to the observations of Elliot (1976) and Davison (1994), as illustrated in Figure 9B.

The presence of a linked fault system in the Khairi-Murat

triangle zone implies the existence of more than one hydrocarbon trap, and these are yet to be explored. Structural traps related to propagating blind thrusts having small displacement are capable of retaining moderate to large quantities of hydrocarbons, similar to the Dhurnal oil field (Fig. 5) and the Sui gas field (Jadoon et al., 1994). In this chapter we have illustrated the potential of the core wedge as a structural trap between the north-dipping Khairi-Murat thrust and the south-dipping Dhurnal backthrust. Numerous oil and gas fields throughout the Alberta foothills in Canada are bounded by such structures (Jones, 1982).

CONCLUSIONS

In this chapter we interpreted the three-dimensional geometry and structural evolution of a triangle zone underlain by evaporites. In this system, the Dhurnal oil field is a fault tip line pop-up structure (Jaswal, 1990) on the foreland side of the core wedge below the south-dipping Dhurnal backthrust and the north-dipping Khairi-Murat thrust on the proximal end of the core wedge. To the east, the wedge contains an excessive amount of evaporites in its core, and its geometry is dominated by a pop-up between the north-dipping blind thrust and the south-dipping backthrusts. The mechanism of thrusting with symmetrical structures is compatible with deformation over a weak decollement (Davis and Engelder, 1985).

Deformation above the backthrust, in the northern limb of the Soan syncline, was between 2.1 and 1.9 Ma and is tightly constrained by the magnetostratigraphy and fission track dating (Burbank and Raynolds, 1984; Raynolds and Johnson, 1985). Because the northern limb of the Soan syncline is related to the

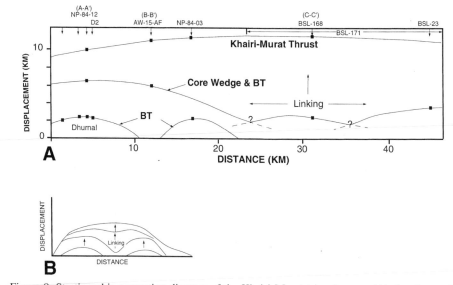

Figure 9. Stratigraphic separation diagram of the Khairi-Murat triangle zone (A) showing variable length and shortening from fault tip line to the Khairi-Murat thrust. Fault length and displacement are based on seismic reflection interpretation. Minor thrusts appear to link and develop large-magnitude thrusts similar to a fault-linking mechanism illustrated in B (Davison, 1994). See Figure 2 for locations of the seismic lines, and Figures 5–7 for the cross sections. D1 to D3 = Dhurnal wells, BT = blind thrusts. Abscissa distance is perpendicular to profile lines.

insertion of a wedge of allochthonous strata below the foreland sequence, we conclude that the triangle zone was developed during the 2.1–1.9 Ma time span. Its development involves 4.5 km of shortening and about 2.8 km of uplift. The high rates of shortening and uplift (22 mm/yr and 14 ± 2 mm/yr, respectively) can be attributed to episodic accretion and a stick-slip mode of decollement propagation in the Salt Range which is supported by magnetostratigraphic data (Johnson et al., 1986; Burbank and Raynolds, 1988). The potential of hydrocarbons in such a young structural trap has important bearings for the exploration of oil and gas in the Himalayan foreland sedimentary basin.

Structural variation in the triangle zone shows the presence of blind thrusts of smaller lateral extent (about 10 km) and about 2 km of shortening. These thrusts appear to link to form a single large thrust (e.g., the Khairi-Murat thrust) at advanced stages of development. The presence of small-magnitude blind thrusts implies: (1) the presence of more than one structural trap in the Khairi-Murat triangle zone, and (2) the existence of closure in unexplored structures.

ACKNOWLEDGMENTS

This work on the North Potwar deformed zone is carried out with cooperation of the Oil and Gas Development Corporation of Pakistan (OGDC). We gratefully acknowledge the management of the OGDC for release of seismic lines and well data with permission of the Ministry of Petroleum and Natural Resources, Pakistan. I. Jadoon gratefully acknowledges a Post Doctoral Research Fellowship (1994–1995) by the Alexander von Humboldt Stiftung of Germany, Tübingen University, for facilities during the research tenure, and Quaid-i-Azam University for an extraordinary leave. Special thanks are extended to N. K. Siddique (Pakistan Petroleum Limited), and A. Bhatti (Geological Survey of Pakistan) for providing geologic maps. The cooperation of many others, including K. A. Ali, S. M. Ali, and R. Ahmed (Pakistan), and R. Girbacea, and P. Zweigel (Tübingen), is gratefully acknowledged. R. S. Yeats, R. Sorkhabi, and M. Yoshida are acknowledged for constructive criticism.

REFERENCES CITED

Ahmed, S. N., McGann, G. M., and Aizad, T., 1993, Dhurnal oil field, Potwar basin, Pakistan: Pakistan Journal of Petroleum Technology, v. 2, p. 1–18.

Akhtar, K., Bajwa, M. S., Kausar, A. B., Bhatti, A. K., and Khan, A. A., 1985, Geological map of Fatehjang (sheet no. 43C/10): Geological Survey of Pakistan, Quetta, scale 1:50,000.

Baig, S., 1995, Structural study of the Main Boundary Thrust System in northwest Himalaya, Pakistan [M.Ph. thesis]: Islamabad, Pakistan, Quaid-i-Azam University, 75 p.

Baker, D. M., Lillie, R. J., Yeats, R. S., Johnson, G. D., Yousaf, M., and Zaman, A. S. H., 1988, Development of the Himalayan thrust zone: Salt Range, Pakistan: Geology, v. 16, p. 3–7.

Bally, A. W., Gordy, P. L., and Stewart, G. A., 1966, Structure, seismic data, and orogenic evolution of southern Canadian Rocky Mountains: Canadian Petroleum Society Bulletin, v. 14, p. 337–381.

Banks, C. J., and Warburton, J., 1986, "Passive-roof" duplex geometry in the frontal structures of the Kirthar and Sulaiman mountain belt, Pakistan: Journal of Structural Geology, v. 8, p. 229–237.

Beck, R. A., Burbank, D. W., Sercombe, W. J., Riley, G. W., Barndt, J. K., Berry, J. R., Afzal, J., Khan, A. M., Jurgen, H., Metje, J., Cheema, A., Shafique, N. A., Lawrence, R. D., and Khan, M. A., 1995, Stratigraphic evidence for an early collision between northwest India and Asia: Nature, v. 373, p. 55–58.

Burbank, D. W., and Beck, R. A., 1991, Rapid, long-term rates of denudation: Geology, v. 19, p. 1169–1172.

Burbank, D. G., and Raynolds, R. G. H., 1984, Sequential late Cenozoic structural disruption of the northern Himalayan foredeep: Nature, v. 311, p. 114–118.

Burbank, D. W., and Raynolds, R. G. H., 1988, Stratigraphic keys to the timing of thrusting in the terrestrial foreland basins: Applications to the northwest Himalaya, *in* Kleinspehn, K. L., and Paola, C., eds., Frontiers in sedimentary geology: New Perspective in Basin Analysis: New York, Springer-Verlag, p. 331–351.

Burbank, D. W., Raynolds, R. G. H., and Johnson, G. D., 1986, Late Cenozoic tectonics and sedimentation in the northwestern Himalayan foredeep: II. Eastern limb of the northwest syntaxis and regional synthesis, *in* Allen, P., and Homewood, P., eds., Foreland basins: International Association of Sedimentalogists Special Publication 8, p. 293–306.

Butler, R. W. H., 1982, The terminology of structures in thrust belts: Journal of Structural Geology, v. 4, p. 239–245.

Coward, M. P., and Butler, R. W. H., 1985, Thrust tectonics and deep structures of the Pakistan Himalayas: Geology, v. 13, p. 417–420.

Davis, D. M., and Engelder, T., 1985, The role of salt in fold-and-thrust belts: Tectonophysics, v. 119, p. 67–88.

Davis, D. M., and Lillie, R. J., 1994, Changing mechanical response during continental collision: Active examples from the foreland thrust belts of Pakistan: Journal of Structural Geology, v. 16, p. 21–34.

Davison, I., 1994, Linked fault systems; extensional, strike-slip and contractional, *in* Hancock, P. L., ed., Continental deformation: London-New York, Pergamon Press, p. 121–142.

Dixon, J. M., and Tirrul, R., 1991, Centrifuge modelling of fold-thrust structures in a tripartite stratigraphic succession: Journal of Structural Geology, v. 13, p. 3–20.

Elliot, D., 1976, The energy balance and deformation mechanism of thrust sheets: Royal Society of London Philosophical Transactions, ser. A, v. 283, p. 289–312.

England, P., and Molnar, P., 1990, Surface uplift, uplift of rocks, and exhumation of rocks: Geology, v. 18, p. 1173–1177.

Gordy, P. L., Frey, F. R., and Norris, D. K., 1977, Geological guide for the C. S. P. G. and 1977 Waterton-Glacier Park field conference: Calgary, Canadian Society of Petroleum Geologists, 93 p.

Jadoon, I. A. K., and Frisch, W., 1997, Hinterland-vergent tectonic wedge below the Riwat thrust, Himalayan foreland, Pakistan: Implications for hydrocarbon exploration: American Association of Petroleum Geologists Bulletin, v. 81, p. 438–448.

Jadoon, I. A. K., Lawrence, R. D., and Lillie, R. J., 1992, Balanced and retrodeformed geological cross-section from the frontal Sulaiman Lobe, Pakistan: Duplex development in thick strata along the western margin of the Indian plate, *in* McClay, K., eds., Thrust tectonics: London, Chapman and Hall, p. 343–356.

Jadoon, I. A. K., Lawrence, R. D., and Lillie, R. J., 1994, Seismic data, geometry, evolution, and shortening in the active Sulaiman fold-and-thrust belt of Pakistan: American Association of Petroleum Geologists Bulletin, v. 78, p. 758–774.

Jadoon, I. A. K., Frisch, W., Kemal, A., and Jaswal, T. M., 1997, Thrust geometries and kinematics in the Himalayan foreland (North Potwar Deformed Zone), North Pakistan: Geologische Rundschau, v. 86, p. 120–131.

Jamshed, S. Q., 1995, Structural interpretation of north eastern Potwar Deformed Zone and the Main Boundary Thrust in Pakistan [M.Ph. thesis]: Islamabad, Pakistan, Quaid-i-Azam University, 46 p.

Jaswal, T. M., 1990, Structure and evolution of the Dhurnal oil field, Northern Potwar Deformed Zone, Pakistan [MS thesis]: Corvallis, Oregon State University, 63 p.

Jaswal, T. M., Lillie, R. J., and Lawrence, R. D., 1997, Structure and evolution of the Northern Potwar Deformed Zone, Pakistan: American Association of Petroleum Geologists Bulletin, v. 81, p. 308–328.

Jaume, S. C., and Lillie, R. J., 1988, Mechanics of the Salt Range-Potwar Plateau, Pakistan. A fold-and-thrust belt underlain by evaporites: Tectonics, v. 7, p. 57–71.

Johnson, G. D., Zeitler, P., Naeser, C. W., Johnson, N. M., Summers, D. M., Frost, C. D., Opdyke, N. O., and Tahirkheli, R. A. K., 1982, The occurrence and fission-track ages of late Neogene and Quaternary volcanic sediments, Siwalik Group, northern Pakistan: Palaeogeography, Palaeoclimatology, Palaeoecology, v. 37, p. 63–93.

Johnson, G. D., Raynolds, R. G., and Burbank, D. W., 1986, Late Cenozoic tectonics and sedimentation in the northwestern Himalaya Foredeep: I. Thrust ramping and associated deformation in the Potwar region, *in* Allen, P., and Homewood, P., eds., Foreland basins: International Association of Sedimentalogists Special Publication 8, p. 273–291.

Johnson, N. M., Opdyke, N. D., Johnson, G. D., Lindsay, E. H., and Tahirkheli, R. A. K., 1982, Magnetic polarity stratigraphy and ages of Siwalik Group rocks of the Potwar Plateau, Pakistan: Palaeogeography, Palaeoclimatology, Palaeoecology, v. 37, p. 17–42.

Jones, P. B., 1982, Oil and gas beneath east-dipping thrust faults in the Alberta Foothills, *in* Powers, K., eds., Rocky Mountain Association of Geologists Guidebook, v. 1, p. 61–74.

Kamran, M., and Ranke, U., 1987, Pakistan oil data: Islamabad, Hydrocarbon Development Institute of Pakistan (unpublished report), 128 p.

Kemal, A., 1991, Geology and new trends for petroleum exploration in Pakistan, *in* Ahmed, G., Kemal, A., Zaman, A. S. H., and Humayon, M., eds., New directions and strategies for accelerating petroleum exploration and production in Pakistan: Pakistan, Ministry of Petroleum and Natural Resources, p. 16–57.

Khan, M. A., Ahmed, R., Raza, H. A., and Kemal, A., 1986, Geology of petroleum in Kohat-Potwar depression, Pakistan: American Association of Petroleum Geologists Bulletin, v. 70, p. 396, 414.

Klootwijk, C. T., Conaghan, P. J., and Powell, C. M., 1985, The Himalayan Arc; large-scale continental subduction, oroclinal bending, and back-arc spreading: Geologische Rundschau, v. 67, p. 37–48.

Koyi, H., 1995, Mode of internal deformation in sand-wedges: Journal of Structural Geology, v. 17, p. 293–300.

Lawton, D. C., Spratt, D. A., and Hopkins, J. C., 1994, Tectonic wedging beneath the Rocky Mountain foreland basin, Alberta, Canada: Geology, v. 22, p. 519–522.

Leathers, M., 1987, Balanced structural cross-section of the western Salt Range and Potwar Plateau: Deformation near the strike-slip terminus of an overthrust sheet [M.S. thesis]: Corvallis, Oregon State University, 271 p.

Le Fort, P., 1975, Himalayas the collided range. Present knowledge of the continental arc: American Journal of Science, v. 275-A, p. 1–44.

Lillie, R. J., Johnson, G. D., Yousaf, M., Zamin, A. S. H., and Yeats, R. S., 1987, Structural development within the Himalayan foreland fold-and-thrust belt of Pakistan, *in* Beaumont, C., and Tankand, A. J., eds., Sedimentary basins and basin-forming mechanisms: Canadian Society of Petroleum Geologists Memoir 12, p. 379–392.

Lyon-Caen, H., and Molnar, P., 1985, Gravity anomalies, flexure of the Indian plate, and the structure, support, and evolution of the Himalaya and Ganga basin: Tectonics, v. 4, p. 513–538.

McDougall, J. W., Hussain, A., and Yeats, R. S., 1993, The Main Boundary Thrust and propagation of deformation into the foreland fold-and-thrust belt in northern Pakistan near the Indus River, *in* Treloar, P. J., and Searle, M., eds., Himalayan tectonics: Geological Society of London Special Publication 74, p. 581–588.

Müller, M., Nieberding, F., and Wanninger, A., 1988, Tectonic style and pressure distribution at the northern margin of the Alps between Lake Constance and the River Inn: Geologische Rundschau, v. 77, p. 787–796.

Mulugeta, G., and Koyi, H., 1987, Three-dimensional geometry and kinematics of experimental piggyback thrusting: Geology, v. 15, p. 1052–1056.

Mulugeta, G., and Koyi, H., 1992, Episodic accretion and strain partitioning in a model sand wedge: Tectonophysics, v. 202, p. 319–333.

Naeem, M. M., and Bhatti, M. A., 1985, Geological map of Islamabad (sheet no. 43G/2): Quetta, Geological Survey of Pakistan, scale 1:50,000.

Pennock, E. S., Lillie, R. J., Zaman, A. S. H., and Yousaf, M., 1989, Structural interpretation of seismic reflection data from eastern Salt Range and Potwar Plateau: American Association of Petroleum Geologists Bulletin, v. 73, p. 841–857.

Powell, C. M., 1979, A speculative tectonic history of Pakistan and surroundings: Some constraints from the Indian Ocean, *in* Farah, A., and DeJong, K. A., eds., Geodynamics of Pakistan: Quetta, Geological Survey of Pakistan, p. 1–24.

Price, R. A., 1986, The southeastern Canadian Cordillera: Thrust faulting, tectonic wedging, and delamination of the lithosphere: Journal of Structural Geology, v. 8, p. 239–254.

Ramos, V. A., 1989, Andean foothills structures in northern Magallanes Basin, Argentina: American Association of Petroleum Geologists Bulletin, v. 73, p. 887–903.

Raynolds, R. G. H., 1980, The Plio-Pleistocene structural and stratigraphic evolution of the eastern Potwar Plateau, Pakistan [Ph.D. thesis]: Hanover, New Hampshire, Dartmouth College, 265 p.

Raynolds, R. G. H., and Johnson, G. D., 1985, Rates of Neogene depositional and deformational processes, northwest Himalayan foredeep margin, Pakistan, *in* Snelling, N. J., ed., The chronology and the geological record: Geological Society of London Memoir 10, p. 297–311.

Raza, H. A., Ahmed, R., Alam, S., and Ali, S. M., 1989, Petroleum zones of Pakistan: Journal of Hydrocarbon Research, v. 1, no. 2, p. 1–20.

Sanderson, D. A., and Spratt, D. A., 1992, Triangle zone and displacement transfer structures in the eastern front ranges, southern Canadian Rocky Mountains: American Association of Petroleum Geologists Bulletin, v. 76, p. 828–839.

Skuce, A. G., Goody, N. P., and Maloney, J., 1992, Passive-roof duplexes under the Rocky Mountains foreland basin, Alberta: American Association of Petroleum Geologists Bulletin, v. 76, p. 67–80.

Treloar, P. J., Rex, D. C., and Williams, M. P., 1991, The role of erosion and extension in unroofing the Indian Plate thrust stack, Pakistan Himalaya: Geological Magazine, v. 128, p. 465–478.

Treloar, P. J., Coward, M. P., Chambers, A. F., Izatt, C. N., and Jackson, K. C., 1992, Thrust geometries, interferences, and rotations in the northwest Himalaya, *in* McClay, K. R., ed., Thrust tectonics: London, Chapman and Hall, p. 325–342.

Vann, I. R., Graham, R. H., and Hayward, A. B., 1986, The structure of mountain fronts: Journal of Structural Geology, v. 8, p. 215–227.

Yeats, R. S., and Lawrence, R. D., 1984, Tectonics of the Himalayan thrust belt in northern Pakistan, *in* Haq, B. U., and Millimann, J. D., eds., Marine geology and oceanography of Arabian Sea and coastal Pakistan: New York, Van Nostrand Reinhold, p. 177–198.

Yeats, R. S., Khan, S. H., and Akhtar, M.. 1984, Late Quaternary deformation of the Salt Range of Pakistan: Geological Society of America Bulletin, v. 95, p. 958–966.

Zeitler, P. K., 1985, Cooling history of the N. W. Himalaya, Pakistan: Tectonics, v. 4, p. 127–151.

MANUSCRIPT ACCEPTED BY THE SOCIETY FEBRUARY 3, 1998

Geological Society of America
Special Paper 328
1999

Frontal structural geometries and detachment tectonics of the northeastern Karachi arc, southern Kirthar Range, Pakistan

Daniel D. Schelling
Energy and Geoscience Institute, University of Utah, 423 Wakara Way, Salt Lake City, Utah 84108

ABSTRACT

The Karachi arc is an east-vergent fold-thrust belt along the western margin of the Indian subcontinent that protrudes eastward into the lower Indus River basin. Between Thano Bhula Khan and Sehwan Sharif, the eastern Karachi arc is characterized by north-south–trending, parallel to en echelon, doubly plunging anticline-syncline pairs that are generally asymmetric and dominantly east vergent. Anticlinal forelimbs and/or overturned synclinal hinges are frequently cut by north-south–trending thrust faults that record displacements of as much as 1,000 m. The projection of folds and thrust faults to depth suggests a thin-skinned tectonic style for the Karachi arc, the detachment surface being located within shale sequences of the Goru Formation at a depth of 2 to 4 km below sea level. Tear faults, which are interpreted as thin-skinned structures, allow along-strike change in structural accommodation to east-west tectonic shortening across the Southern Kirthar Range. The northern boundary of the Karachi arc is along the Lake Manchhar tear-fault system, which separates a southern Kirthar structural province characterized by an emergent imbricate-fan structural geometry from a central Kirthar structural province characterized by a passive roof duplex structure. Most of the deformation undergone by the northeastern Karachi arc postdates deposition of the Miocene to Pleistocene Manchhar Group, and sub-Holocene river terraces have been uplifted along the topographic front of the southern Kirthar Range. Tectonic deformation within the eastern Karachi arc is therefore believed to be of Pliocene-Pleistocene to Holocene age.

Despite being located adjacent to a transpressional plate boundary, the Karachi arc has undergone virtually no identifiable strike-slip–related deformation, indicating (1) that there has been significant strain partitioning along the Ornach Nal–Chaman transform fault system, and (2) that the Karachi arc remains unaffected by the northward underthrusting of the Indian subcontinent beneath the Himalayan orogenic arc.

INTRODUCTION

Located along the western margin of the Indian subcontinent and to the east of the Ornach Nal and Chaman transform fault systems, the Sulaiman and Kirthar Ranges of Pakistan define a north-south–trending fold and thrust belt which connects the Himalayan continental collision zone to the northeast with the Makkran accretionary wedge system to the southwest (Fig. 1).

Together, the Kirthar and Sulaiman Ranges represent the deformed western margin of the Indian subcontinent, which has undergone dominantly transpressional deformation since the initial collision of the Indian subcontinent with the Afghan plate during the Late Cretaceous or Paleogene (Abdel-Gawad, 1971; Powell, 1979; Sarwar and De Jong, 1979; Lawrence et al., 1981; Bannert et al., 1992; Bender and Raza, 1995). The northern sector of the Sulaiman-Kirthar mountain system, the Sulaiman

Schelling, D. D., 1999, Frontal structural geometries and detachment tectonics of the northeastern Karachi arc, southern Kirthar Range, Pakistan, *in* Macfarlane, A., Sorkhabi, R. B., and Quade, J., eds., Himalaya and Tibet: Mountain Roots to Mountain Tops: Boulder, Colorado, Geological Society of America Special Paper 328.

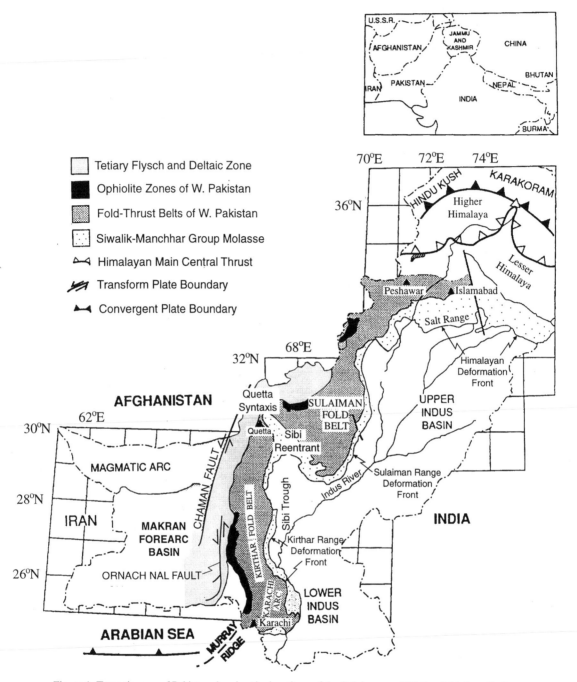

Figure 1. Tectonic map of Pakistan showing the locations of the Sulaiman and Kirthar fold-thrust belts. The Karachi arc is located where the Southern Kirthar Range protrudes into the Lower Indus River basin just north of Karachi. (Modified after Klootwijk et al., 1981.)

Range, is offset to the east relative to the southern sector, the Kirthar Range, the two mountain systems being separated by the north-south–trending Sibi trough (Fig. 1). The Kirthar Range can be subdivided into central and northern sectors, located to the immediate west of the Sibi trough, and a southern sector, the Southern Kirthar Range, which is to the south of the Sibi trough. The eastern part of the Southern Kirthar Range, the Karachi arc,

protrudes eastward into the Lower Indus basin (Figs. 1 and 2).

During the past 10 years a number of publications have documented the structural styles and evolution of the Sulaiman and Northern Kirthar Ranges of Pakistan (e.g., Banks and Warburton, 1986; Humayon et al., 1991; Jadoon et al., 1992, 1993, 1994). Thin-skinned structural styles have generally been identified in the Sulaiman and Northern Kirthar Ranges, including the recog-

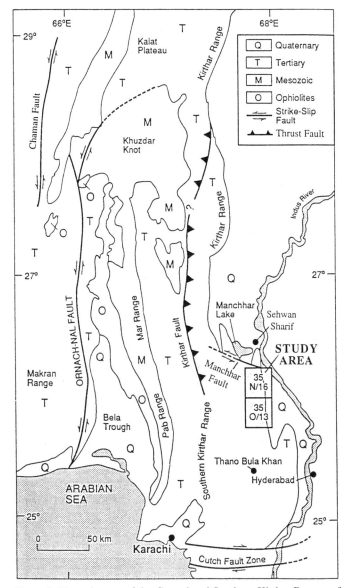

Figure 2. Tectonic map of the Central and Southern Kirthar Ranges of southern Pakistan showing the location of the study area and the Survey of Pakistan, 1:50,000-scale topographic base maps 35N/16 and 35O/13. (Geologic map modified after Sarwar and DeJong, 1979.)

nition of multiple detachment horizons and both active and passive roof duplex structural systems (Banks and Warburton, 1986; Humayon et al., 1991; Jadoon et al., 1992, 1993, 1994). However, the structural geometries and evolution of the Southern Kirthar Range and the Karachi arc remain virtually unknown; publications dealing with the geology of the Southern Kirthar Range have generally discussed only the large-scale structural features of the region (e.g., Hunting Survey Corporation, Ltd., 1961; Bannert et al., 1992; Bender and Raza, 1995). In addition, the structural relationships between the Southern and Central Kirthar Ranges, and between the Karachi arc to the south and the Sibi trough to the north, are poorly understood.

During the fall of 1991 a one-month period was spent in the field in the northeastern sector of the Karachi arc, between Thano Bhula Khan to the south and Sehwan Sharif to the north (Fig. 2), to conduct a structural and stratigraphic study of the region for Texaco Frontier Exploration Co. Two Survey of Pakistan topographic quadrangles, numbers 35N/16 and 35O/13 (Figs. 2, 3, and 4), were mapped during the field season, and traverses were made along three transects to collect detailed structural data for the construction of balanced cross sections across the study area. The results of the field work and structural analysis are presented in this chapter.

STRUCTURE OF THE NORTHEASTERN KARACHI ARC

The northeastern Karachi arc is characterized by the presence of roughly north-south–trending, parallel to en echelon folds and thrust faults (Figs. 3 and 4). Folds mapped within the study area are generally asymmetric, overturned, doubly plunging structures, which are frequently cut by underlying thrust faults and which generally display pronounced kink-band structural geometries (Fig. 5). Most of the folds and thrust faults within the region define east-vergent structural systems. All of the kilometer-scale asymmetric folds observed in the study area have overturned forelimbs in the regions of greatest fold amplitude, and in each case the forelimbs become vertical and then upright with decreasing dips as they are traced to both the north and the south along the fold axes (Fig. 6). Overturned fold limbs generally dip between 45° and 90°, although dips as low as 20° have been observed locally along overturned fold limbs.

The largest fold mapped in the northeastern Karachi arc is the Ranikot anticline, a dominantly east vergent, asymmetric structure that can be traced for a distance of more than 100 km between Sehwan Sharif in the north and Thano Bhula Khan to the south (Fig. 2). To the north, in the vicinity of cross-section line N-N′, where the Ranikot anticline has undergone its greatest structural uplift, the Upper Cretaceous Pab Sandstone and Mughalkot Formation are exposed in the core of the anticline (Fig. 3). To the south, along cross sections C-C′ and S-S′, the Paleocene Ranikot Formation is exposed within the erosionally breached core of the Ranikot anticline (Figs. 4 and 5). The east limb of the Ranikot anticline is vertical to overturned throughout the study area and has been cut by a series of east-vergent thrust faults, including the Kirthar Frontal thrust, the easternmost emergent thrust fault of the Southern Kirthar Range. Hanging-wall splay thrusts off of the Kirthar Frontal thrust, including the Rahman Dhoro thrust in the north and the Ranikot thrust in the south, branch with the Kirthar Frontal thrust between cross-sections N-N′ and C-C′ (Figs. 3 and 4), and these thrust faults are therefore believed to branch with the Kirthar Frontal thrust at depth as well. Both the Ranikot thrust and the Rahman Dhoro thrust offset the overturned east limb of the Ranikot anticline.

South of cross section C-C′ both the Ranikot thrust and the Kirthar Frontal thrust become blind thrust faults (Fig. 4), and tec-

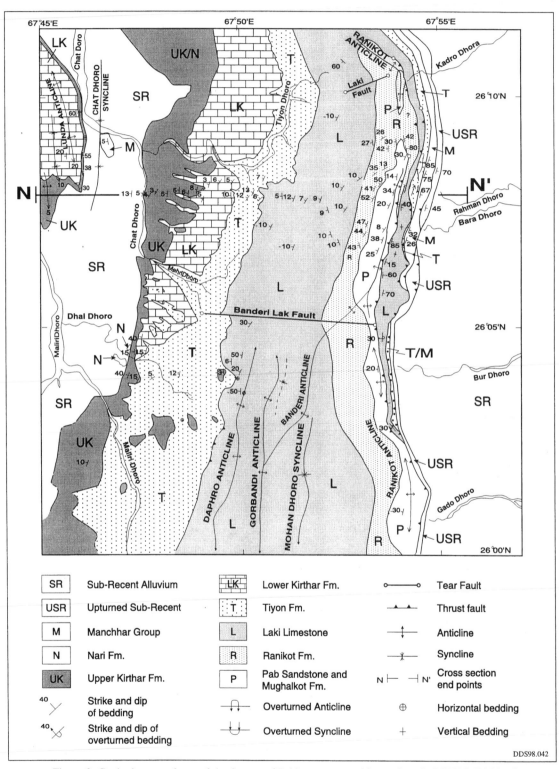

Figure 3. Geologic map of part of the Survey of Pakistan topographic quadrangle 35N/16. Width of map = 20 km. Quadrangle location within the Southern Kirthar Range is shown in Figure 2.

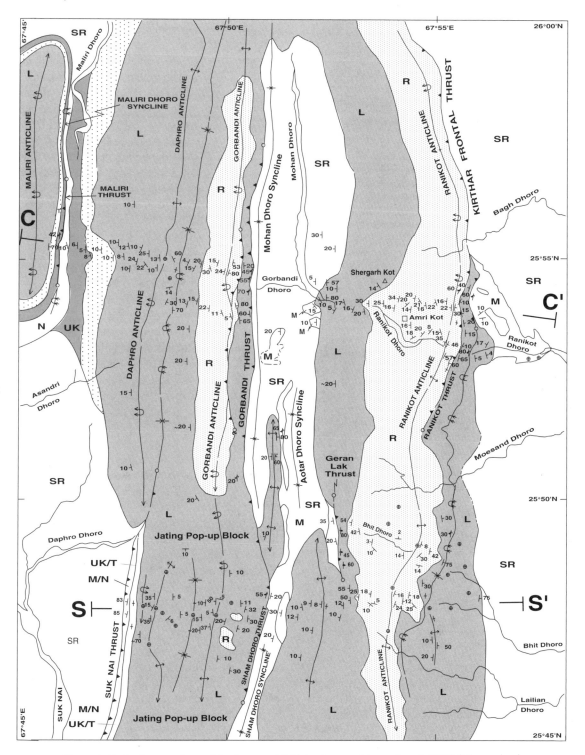

Figure 4. Geologic map of part of the Survey of Pakistan topographic quadrangle 35O/13. Legend as in Figure 3. Width of map = 22 km. Quadrangle location within the Southern Kirthar Range is shown in Figure 2.

Figure 5. Looking north across the Geran Lak (Pass) at a kink fold and subvertical limestone sequences belonging to the Laki Formation. Structure is located along the west limb of the Ranikot anticline in the vicinity of cross-section S-S′ (Fig. 4). GT = Geran Lak thrust, a west-vergent thrust fault that cuts the west limb of the Ranikot anticline north of cross-section line S-S′. The Ranikot Formation (R) is exposed along the crest of the Ranikot anticline in the Bhit Dhoro Valley to the right. The cliff of vertical limestones is ~120 m high.

Figure 6. Looking south along the east limb and crest of the Daphro anticline in the vicinity of cross-section line C-C′ (Fig. 4). The overturned, west-dipping, east limb in the foreground straightens and becomes east dipping and upright to the south. The Daphro Dhoro (ephemeral stream) on the left occupies a synclinal trough, and the Daphro Ridge on the right is formed by subhorizontal Laki Formation limestones on the crest of the Daphro anticline. The length of the anticline is ~10 km.

tonic shortening across the Ranikot anticline–Kirthar Frontal thrust system is accommodated almost entirely by folding at the erosion surface. However, just to the north of cross-section S-S′ the west limb of the Ranikot anticline becomes overturned and is cut by the west-vergent Ganderi Lak thrust (Fig. 5); in the vicinity of cross-section S-S′ the generally asymmetric, east-vergent Ranikot anticline becomes a symmetric structural feature.

The Chat Dhoro, Maliri Dhoro, Mohan Dhoro, Aotar Dhoro, and Sham Dhoro synclines, located to the west of the Ranikot

anticline (Figs. 3 and 4), are active piggy-back basins within which sub-Holocene and Holocene alluvium has been deposited directly upon Eocene through Miocene sedimentary sequences. To the west of these asymmetric, east-vergent synclines a series of east-vergent anticlines and a single structural pop-up block have been mapped, including the Lumba anticline, the Maliri anticline, the Gorbandi anticline, the Daphro anticline, and the Jating pop-up block (Figs. 3 and 4). All of the anticlines are underlain by east-vergent thrust faults; the Jating pop-up block is bounded on the east by the east-vergent Sham Dhoro thrust and on the west by the west-vergent Suk Nai thrust. With the exception of the Gorbandi anticline, along the crest of which the Ranikot Formation is exposed (Fig. 4), all of the structural uplifts mapped to the west of the Ranikot anticline are capped by the erosion-resistant, Eocene age Laki or Kirthar Limestones.

There is little question that the stratigraphy of the northeastern Karachi arc has played a critical role in determining the structural styles and geometries that have developed in the region. The Jurassic through Cenozoic sedimentary section of the northeastern Karachi arc (Fig. 7) is composed of a series of mechanically competent and incompetent units that appear to have defined the locations of regional and local detachment horizons as well as the structural geometries of large- and small-scale folds. Mechanically competent stratigraphic units within the Karachi arc include: (1) the Jurassic Chiltan Limestone, which is not exposed within the eastern Karachi arc but is described elsewhere in the Kirthar Range and within the Lower Indus basin (Williams, 1959; Quadri and Shuaib, 1986; Banks and Warburton, 1986; Bender and Raza, 1995); (2) the combined Cretaceous Pab Sandstone, Mughalkot Formation, and the Parh Limestone; (3) the Eocene Laki Limestone; and (4) the Eocene Kirthar Limestone. These mechanically competent units are separated by shale- and marl-rich stratigraphic sequences that have allowed both interbed slip between the more competent sequences and the development of low-angle thrust faults and detachment surfaces (decollements). The thickest shale-rich sequence in the Southern Kirthar Range is the Lower Cretaceous Goru Formation (Fig. 7), which reaches an estimated thickness of 2,700 m in the Lower Indus basin directly to the east of the Karachi arc (Bender and Raza, 1995). The shale-rich, Paleocene Ranikot Formation, which is between the overlying Laki Formation and the underlying Pab Sandstone (Fig. 7), reaches an estimated thickness of 1,100 m in the study area. The mechanically incompetent Eocene Tiyon Formation separates the massive limestones of the Laki and Kirthar Formations. In addition to these thicker, shale- and marl-rich stratigraphic sequences, both the Kirthar and Laki Limestones include thin, incompetent layers that have allowed significant interbed slip and the development of buckle folds in the northeastern Karachi arc.

Structural geometries of folds and thrust faults within the study area indicate that the northeastern Karachi arc is underlain by one or more detachment surfaces along which all of the mapped thrust faults are believed to flatten at depth. Detachment-related thrust-transferal systems and tear faults, which have allowed differential accommodation to east-west tectonic shorten-

Age	Lithology	Stratigraphy	Estimated Thickness
Recent		Alluvium	up to 15 m
Pleistocene to Miocene		Manchhar (Siwalik) Group	up to 375 m
Oligocene		Nari Fm.	Approx. 150 m
Eocene		Kirthar Fm.	
Eocene		Tiyon Fm.	75 - 210 m
Eocene		Laki Fm.	200 - 350 m
Paleocene		Ranikot Fm.	600 - 1200 m
Cretaceous		Pab Ss.	250 - 400 m
Cretaceous		Mughalkot Fm.	
Cretaceous		Parh Ls.	
Cretaceous		Goru Fm.	up to 2,700 m
Cretaceous		Sembar Fm.	
Jurassic		Chiltan Ls.	?

Figure 7. Simplified stratigraphic column for the Southern Kirthar Range. (Modified after Schelling and Rine, 1991.)

ing from north to south within the Southern Kirthar Range, have also been recognized. The recognition of a detachment-related structural development for the Southern Kirthar Range has been based, in part, upon the construction of three balanced cross sections across the study area, which are discussed individually in the following.

Balanced structural cross section S-S′

In contrast to the generally east vergent, asymmetric character of structures mapped in the northeastern Karachi arc, cross-section S-S′ has been constructed across two locally symmetric structural uplifts, the Ranikot anticline to the east and the Jating pop-up block to the west (Fig. 8). The Ranikot anticline along cross-section S-S′ is ~4 km wide and includes a broad crestal region, characterized by relatively low dip angles, flanked by steeply dipping to vertical or overturned fold limbs (Figs. 5 and 8). Projection of fold geometries to depth (Fig. 9) requires that a

detachment surface underlie the Ranikot anticline at a maximum depth of ~2.5 to 3 km below sea level, or ~2.5 km stratigraphically below the base of the Laki Limestone. Although it is possible that detachment surfaces may exist locally within the Paleocene Ranikot Formation, it is known that the Ranikot anticline includes both the Cretaceous Pab Sandstone and the underlying Mugalkhot Formation along its crest to the north (Fig. 3), and therefore it is almost certain that the detachment surface that underlies the Ranikot anticline is located within the Goru Formation, a shale-dominated unit that has an estimated thickness of ~2,500 to 2,700 m in the adjacent Lower Indus basin (Williams, 1959; Bender and Raza, 1995). Furthermore, constraints from structural geometries of the Ranikot anticline to the north, and from the Jating pop-up block to the west, suggest that the detachment surface underneath the Ranikot anticline along cross-section S-S′ is located close to the maximum depth of detachment determined for the Ranikot anticline along cross-section S-S′. Accordingly, balanced cross-section S-S′ has been constructed with a detachment surface beneath the Ranikot anticline located within the shale sequences of the Goru Formation at a depth of ~2.5 km below sea level (Fig. 8).

West of the Ranikot anticline cross-section S-S′ crosses the Jating pop-up block, a structural pop-up block bounded by divergent thrust faults; the east limb of the Jating pop-up block is cut by the east-vergent Sham Dhoro thrust, and the steeply dipping to overturned west limb of the pop-up block is cut by the west-vergent Suk Nai thrust (Figs. 4 and 8). The crest of the Jating pop-up block is capped by a 4.5-km-wide zone of subhorizontal, erosion-resistant Laki Limestones that have been deeply incised by the south-flowing Jating Dhoro (Dhoro = ephemeral stream). As with the Ranikot anticline to the east, fold and fault geometries projected to depth indicate that a detachment surface must exist beneath the Jating pop-up block at a depth of 3 to 4 km below sea level, or within the shale-rich sequences of the Goru Formation. Balanced cross-section S-S′ has therefore been constructed with a detachment surface located within the Goru Formation across the entire cross section.

Because of the clear indications that structural geometries observed at the erosion surface are related to detachment faults located within the Goru Formation, it is difficult to determine whether the sub-Goru Formation stratigraphic section has undergone significant deformation within the northeastern Karachi arc. However, balanced cross-section construction suggests that the Ranikot anticline and the Jating pop-up block are underlain by a broad structural high at the Chiltan Limestone stratigraphic level in the vicinity of cross-section S-S′. It is therefore probable that the Chiltan Limestone has undergone limited east-vergent compressional deformation within the frontal sectors of the Karachi arc.

On both the east and west sides of the Ranikot anticline the Miocene to Pleistocene Manchhar Group (a lateral equivalent to the Siwalik Group mapped elsewhere in northern and central Pakistan) directly overlies the Eocene Laki Limestone with an erosional unconformity. However, vertical to overturned expo-

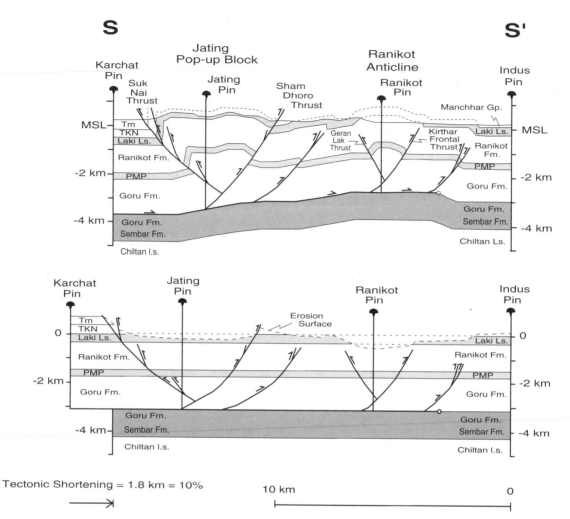

Figure 8. Balanced and restored structural cross-section S-S′ (Fig. 4). The following formations have been treated as single stratigraphic units for cross-section construction: (1) the Tiyon, Kirthar, and Nari Formations (TKN); (2) the Pab Sandstone, the Mughalkot Formation, and the Parh Limestone (PMP); and (3) the Goru and Sembar Formations. Tm = Manchhar Group. MSL is mean sea level. FM. = Formation. Gp. = Group. Ls. = Limestone.

sures of the Eocene Tiyon and Kirthar Formations and the Oligocene Nari Formation have been mapped between the overlying Manchhar Group and the underlying Laki Limestones along the faulted west limb of the Jating pop-up block (Figs. 4 and 8). The clear erosional unconformity along the base of the Manchhar Group suggests that the lack of a Tiyon-Kirthar-Nari stratigraphic section east of the Jating pop-up block may be the result of Miocene-Pliocene erosion rather than the result of nondeposition. In addition, along the west limb of the Jating pop-up block, stratigraphic bedding surfaces within the Manchhar Group are subvertical, and the Manchhar Group has been thrust over sub-Holocene alluvium of the Suk Nai Valley (Figs. 4 and 8). Deformation and uplift across the Jating pop-up block can therefore be clearly dated as post-Manchhar, or of probable Pliocene-Pleistocene age.

Restoration of balanced cross-section S-S′ indicates that

the Jating pop-up block and the Ranikot anticline have accommodated ~1.8 km of east-west horizontal tectonic shortening, or ~10% shortening, between the Indus pin in the east and the Karchat pin in the west (Fig. 8).

Balanced structural cross section C-C′

Balanced cross-section C-C′ (Fig. 10) crosses the central part of the study area in the vicinity of the Ranikot and Amri Kot forts (Fig. 4). Along cross-section C-C′ the Ranikot anticline displays a pronounced asymmetry, having a steeply overturned east limb and a gently (less than 30°) dipping west limb. Erosion-resistant Laki Limestones form an impressive dip slope along the back (west) limb of the anticline in the vicinity of cross-section C-C′, as they do along most of the Ranikot anticline's 100 km length. The forelimb of the Ranikot anticline along cross-section C-C′ is cut by

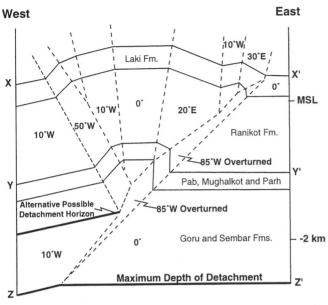

Figure 9. Projection to depth of the Ranikot anticline along cross-section line S–S′ using a kink-fold (dip-domain) geometry to determine the maximum depth of a detachment surface below the anticline. The amplitude of the Ranikot anticline has decreased to zero at the location of stratigraphic horizon Z–Z′, which marks the maximum depth for an underlying detachment. A possible alternative detachment horizon above horizon Z–Z′ is shown directly beneath the Pab Sandstone–Parh Limestone sequence. Fm(s). = Formation(s). Gp. = Group.

the Kirthar Frontal thrust, the Ranikot thrust, and a third splay thrust sandwiched between the Ranikot and Kirthar Frontal thrusts (Figs. 10 and 11). Fault and fold structural geometries across the Ranikot anticline, along cross-section C–C′, indicate that the Ranikot anticline is underlain by a detachment surface located beneath the Pab Sandstone and the Mughalkot Formation that must be above an estimated depth of ~3 km below sea level. Therefore, cross-section C–C′ has been constructed with a detachment surface located within the Cretaceous Goru Formation beneath the Ranikot anticline. The angular fold mapped within the Laki Limestones to the east of the Ranikot anticline has also been interpreted as being related to a splay thrust from the detachment surface located within the Goru Formation.

Geometric relationships between the Ranikot anticline and its associated forelimb-cutting thrust faults along cross-section line C–C′ indicate that the Ranikot anticline developed as a fault-propagation fold, as appears to be the case with virtually all of the asymmetric folds mapped within the northeastern Karachi arc. In addition, to the immediate south of cross-section line C–C′, the west-dipping Ranikot thrust is located along the overturned, steeply west dipping contact between the older but structurally overlying Ranikot Formation and the younger but structurally underlying Laki Limestones. Therefore, the Ranikot thrust has been interpreted as having developed as a hanging wall splay thrust from the Kirthar Frontal thrust after the initial development of the Ranikot anticline as an overturned structure. Sequential, schematic structural cross sections illustrating the

probable structural evolution of the Ranikot anticline, the Kirthar Frontal thrust, and the Ranikot thrust are shown in Figure 12.

West of the Ranikot anticline, along cross-section C–C′, three asymmetric, east-vergent anticlines have been mapped. The easternmost of these anticlines, the Gorbandi anticline, has a steeply west dipping, overturned forelimb that is cut by the Gorbandi thrust and an associated hanging-wall splay thrust. Fault and fold structural geometries along the Gorbandi anticline and fault system are similar to those observed along the Ranikot anticline directly to the east; the Gorbandi anticline is therefore believed to have undergone a structural evolution similar to that illustrated for the Ranikot anticline in Figure 12.

The Daphro anticline (Fig. 6), located directly to the west of the Gorbandi anticline, has a significantly tighter fold geometry than either the Gorbandi or the Ranikot anticlines. This anticline, which is cut by an east-vergent thrust fault directly to the north of cross-section line C–C′, has a structural geometry that requires the existence of a detachment surface within the Ranikot Formation. Therefore, although a regional detachment horizon for the northeastern Karachi arc has been identified as existing within the Cretaceous Goru Formation, there is clear evidence for the development of a secondary detachment horizon within the Ranikot Formation. It appears that the east-vergent Maliri anticline, located to the west of the Daphro anticline, has also formed above a structural detachment within the Ranikot Formation.

A detachment-related structural accommodation zone must exist between the entirely east-vergent Gorbandi-Daphro anticlinal structural system to the north and the Jating pop-up block to the south. Apparently, deformation related to the west-vergent Suk Nai thrust system in the south is transferred to the east-vergent Daphro anticline–thrust system to the north between cross-sections S–S′ and C–C′.

East of the Ranikot anticline, in the vicinity of cross-section C–C′, the Manchhar Group is observed to directly overlie the Laki Limestone, as was noted for the area to the east of the Ranikot anticline in the vicinity of cross-section S–S′. In addition, subvertical exposures of the Manchhar Group have been observed in both the hanging wall and footwall of the Kirthar Frontal thrust in the vicinity of cross-section C–C′ (Fig. 11). Therefore, there is little question that uplift and thrust motion across the Ranikot anticline–Kirthar Frontal thrust system postdate deposition of at least part of the Miocene through Pleistocene Manchhar Group sedimentary section. West of the Gorbandi anticline, within the Maliri syncline and along the eastern flanks of the Maliri anticline, exposures of the Tiyon and Kirthar Formations have been mapped above the Laki Limestones (Fig. 4). It is probable that the lack of a Tiyon-Kirthar sedimentary section on the east side of the Ranikot anticline is the result of post-Oligocene erosion rather than the nondeposition of these sequences.

Restoration of balanced cross-section C–C′ indicates that the Ranikot, Gorbandi, and Daphro anticlines have accommodated ~2.6 km of east-west, horizontal tectonic shortening, or ~13% shortening, between the Indus pin in the east and the Maliri pin in the west (Fig. 10).

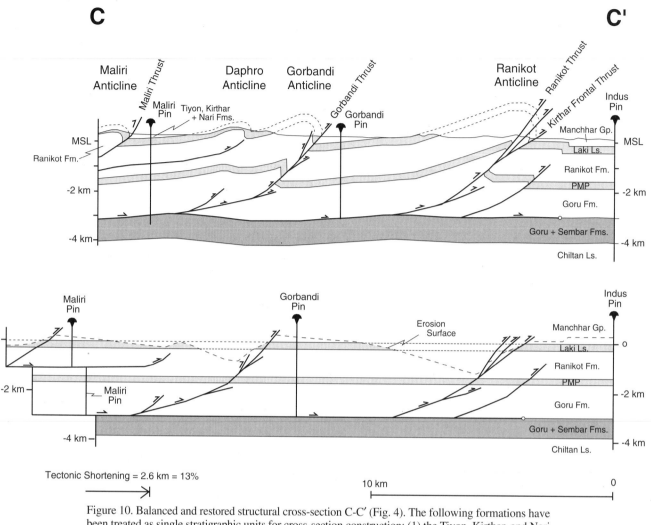

Figure 10. Balanced and restored structural cross-section C-C' (Fig. 4). The following formations have been treated as single stratigraphic units for cross-section construction: (1) the Tiyon, Kirthar, and Nari Formations; (2) the Pab Sandstone, the Mughalkot Formation, and the Parh Limestone (PMP); and (3) the Goru and Sembar Formations. MSL is mean sea level. Fm(s). = Formations(s). Gp. = Group. Ls. = Limestone.

Balanced structural cross section N-N'

Structural cross section N-N' (Fig. 13) crosses the northern part of the study area within the Survey of Pakistan topographic quadrangle 35N/16 (Fig. 3). Along this cross section the Ranikot anticline is broader than elsewhere in the study area, and a distance of ~14 km separates the Kirthar Frontal thrust to the east from the trough of the Chat Dhoro syncline to the west. In addition, the crest of the Ranikot anticline has undergone greater structural uplift in the vicinity of cross-section N-N' than elsewhere in the region; the Cretaceous Pab Sandstone and Mughalkot Formation are exposed in the core of the structure (Figs. 3, 13, and 14). As observed to the south along cross-section C-C', the east limb of the Ranikot anticline along cross-section N-N' is overturned, west dipping, and has been cut by a series of east-vergent thrust faults, including the Kirthar Frontal thrust and the Rahman Dhoro thrust

(Fig. 13). Just to the south of cross-section N-N' the Manchhar Group is overturned in the hanging wall of the Kirthar Frontal thrust and sub-Holocene conglomerates are upturned in the footwall of the Kirthar Frontal thrust (Fig. 14), implying a Pleistocene-Holocene age for deformation and uplift along the Ranikot anticline–Kirthar Frontal thrust structural system. In the same area, overturned Pab Sandstone has been thrust upon overturned Laki Limestones along the Rahman Dhoro thrust (Fig. 14), suggesting that the Rahman Dhoro thrust developed after the initial formation of the overturned, asymmetric Ranikot anticline. A series of small anticlines, having wavelengths of less than 1 km, have been mapped between the Kirthar Frontal thrust and the Rahman Dhoro thrust in the northern study area, one of which is shown along cross section N-N'.

The overall structural geometry of the Ranikot anticline differs between cross-sections N-N' and C-C'. Rather than having

Figure 11. Looking north at overturned, west-dipping beds belonging to the Ranikot Formation (R), the Ranikot thrust (RT), overturned and west-dipping Laki Formation limestones (L), vertical sedimentary sequences belonging to the Manchhar Group (M), gently east- dipping, sub-Holocene conglomerates (SR), and the Kirthar Frontal thrust (KF). This photograph was taken in the vicinity of cross-section line C-C'. Topographic relief is ~600 m.

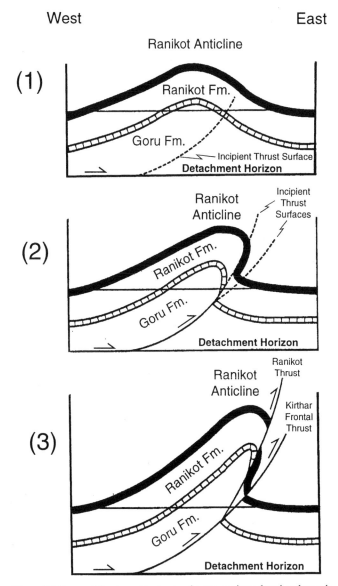

Figure 12. Sequential, schematic structural cross sections showing the probable structural evolution of the Ranikot anticline and the Ranikot and Kirthar Frontal thrust systems, beginning with (1) the initiation of a fold above a basal detachment within the Goru Formation, followed by (2) the formation of an overturned, asymmetric, fault-propagation fold cored by a blind thrust, and continuing to (3) the present-day structural geometry of an overturned fold cut by multiple forelimb thrust faults. Fm. = Formation.

a uniformly west dipping west limb, as observed along cross-section C-C', along cross-section N-N' the Ranikot anticline has a relatively steep west limb adjacent to the crest of the structure. The west limb then flattens to dips of 10° or less to the west along a pronounced kink-band boundary (Fig. 13). Projection of the Ranikot surface structure to depth suggests that a detachment surface exists within the Goru Formation at a depth of 2 to 2.5 km below sea level, or ~2 to 2.5 km beneath the base of the Laki Limestone. This estimated depth to a detachment surface is in close agreement with that calculated for the Ranikot anticline and the Jating pop-up block along cross-sections S-S' and C-C'. The steep west limb of the Ranikot anticline along cross-section N-N' has been interpreted as being underlain by blind back thrusts (Fig. 13), similar to the Geran Lak thrust mapped to the north of cross-section S-S'.

The monotonous dips of 5° to 15° to the west over a distance of ~10 km along the back limb of the Ranikot anticline, along cross-section line N-N', (Figs. 3 and 13) suggest that the Goru Formation detachment surface dips ~5° to 15° to the west beneath the Ranikot anticline back limb. The gentle westward dip of the detachment surface in this location is believed to be the result of the entire Cretaceous and Jurassic sedimentary section having been uplifted and tilted to the west, although whether the deformation of the Jurassic-Cretaceous section predates or postdates the development of the Ranikot anticline is difficult to determine.

The rapid change in structural geometries between the Ranikot anticline to the north, as observed along cross-section N-N', and the combined Ranikot, Gorbandi, and Daphro anticlinal systems to the south, was accommodated in part by the development of the Banderi Lak fault (Fig. 3). The Banderi Lak fault cuts across only the crest and backlimb of the Ranikot anticline, and

apparently dies out in the vicinity of the Rahman Dhoro thrust to the east. To the west, the Banderi Lak fault dies out within the Maliri Dhoro–Chat Dhoro syncline, which is continuous between cross-sections C-C' and S-S'. To the immediate south of the Banderi Lak fault a series of four, detachment-related anticlines have been mapped, including the Daphro, Gorbandi, and Ranikot anticlines; to the immediate north of the fault deformation is restricted to the development of only the detachment-related Ranikot anticline (Fig. 15). Therefore, the Banderi Lak fault has been interpreted as a thin-skinned tear fault that exists only above the Goru

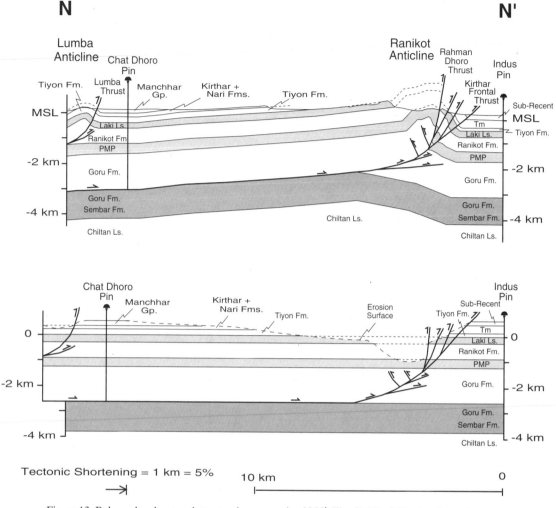

Figure 13. Balanced and restored structural cross-section N-N' (Fig. 3). The following formations have been treated as single stratigraphic units for cross-section construction: (1) the Kirthar and Nari Formations; (2) the Pab Sandstone, the Mughalkot Formation and the Parh Limestone (PMP); and (3) the Goru and Sembar Formations. Tm = Manchhar Group. MSL is mean sea level. Fm. = Formation. GP = Group. Ls = Limestone.

Formation detachment surface (Fig. 15). The Banderi Lak fault has clearly allowed differential accommodation of east-west tectonic shortening, as well as differential degrees of tectonic shortening, between the northern and southern sides of the fault.

Along the west limb of the Ranikot anticline, in the vicinity of cross-section N-N', an ~150-m-thick section of Eocene Kirthar Limestone and Oligocene Nari Formation has been mapped above the Tiyon Formation. The Nari Formation is overlain unconformably by the Manchhar Group in this location. However, along the east limb of the Ranikot anticline, a distance of ~12 km to the east, the Manchhar Group directly overlies the Tiyon Formation. Given the unconformable and erosional contact between the overlying Manchhar Group and the underlying sedimentary sequences, it is probable that the Kirthar and Nari Formations were eroded off of the eastern flank of the Ranikot anticline prior to the uplift of this structure. This erosional unconformity may

indicate the presence of an outer foredeep bulge in the vicinity of the Ranikot anticline in late Oligocene or early Miocene time, the uplift resulting from thrust loading along the western margin of the Indian platform. It is also possible that this early phase of uplift involved contractional deformation of the Jurassic and Cretaceous section at depth, similar to that shown along cross-sections N-N' and S-S' beneath the Goru Formation detachment surface.

Restoration of balanced cross section N-N' (Fig. 13) indicates that the Ranikot anticline has accommodated ~1 km of east-west, horizontal tectonic shortening, or ~5% shortening, between the Indus pin in the east and the Chat Dhoro pin in the west.

DISCUSSION

Geologic mapping in the northeastern Karachi arc, along with structural analysis and balanced cross-section construction,

Figure 14. Looking south along the overturned and faulted east limb of the Ranikot anticline south of cross-section line N–N'. The Pab Sandstone (P) has been thrust over the overturned, west-dipping Laki Formation (L) along the Rahman Dhoro thrust. The Laki Limestone is stratigraphically overlain by the erosionally thinned and overturned Tiyon Formation. The overturned, west-dipping Manchhar Group (M) unconformably overlies the Tiyon Formation. The Kirthar Frontal thrust is located along the valley in the background, which separates the overturned Manchhar Group (M) from upturned, east-dipping, sub-Holocene conglomerates (SR). Deformation of post-Manchhar, sub-Holocene conglomerates indicates Pleistocene or Holocene deformation along the Ranikot anticline–Kirthar Frontal thrust system.

indicates that the frontal sector of the Southern Kirthar Range is underlain by a regional structural detachment located within the Cretaceous Goru Formation at a stratigraphic depth of 2 to 3 km beneath the base of the Laki Limestone. Orientations of both large- and small-scale structures within the study area, combined with stereoplots of poles to bedding (Fig. 16), indicate that the northeastern Karachi arc has undergone deformation as a result of roughly east-west–oriented, horizontal compressional stress. This interpretation is supported by the presence of east-west–oriented slickensides observed along bedding planes within the Pab Sandstone, along the crest of the Ranikot anticline, indicating east-west–oriented, bedding-parallel slip during the formation of the Ranikot anticline. In addition, despite the local existence of roughly symmetric compressional structures within the study area (e.g., the Jating pop-up block), there is no question that the Karachi arc is a dominantly east-vergent structural system impinging upon the Lower Indus basin.

Despite the fact that the Southern Kirthar Range lies alongside the transform plate boundary between the Indian subcontinent and the Afghan plate (Fig. 1), and that the Kirthar Range has an orientation subparallel to that of the adjacent Ornach Nal–Chaman transform fault system (Fig. 2), there is virtually no evidence within the frontal sector of the Southern Kirthar Range for any left-lateral strike-slip motion; all deformation within the northeastern Karachi arc appears to be the result of roughly east-west–oriented compressional stress. Therefore, there must be a significant degree of strain partitioning along the Ornach Nal–Chaman transform fault system and across the Kirthar

Range, strike-slip deformation being restricted to those areas directly adjacent to the Ornach Nal–Chaman fault system, and the compressional component of the overall transpressional deformation being transmitted farther toward the interior of the Indian subcontinent (toward the Lower Indus basin) than the strike-slip component.

In addition, the lack of any identifiable north-south–oriented component of deformation (including both north-south compressional and strike-slip deformation) within the northeastern Karachi arc implies that the south-vergent compressional deformation related to the northward underthrusting of the Indian subcontinent along the Himalayan orogenic arc has had virtually no effect on the Karachi arc or the Southern Kirthar Range. However, the southern sector of the Sulaiman Range, where the Sibi Lobe is sandwiched between the Indus basin to the east and the Sibi trough to the west, has a clearly documented component of south-directed overthrust deformation (Humayon et al., 1991; Jadoon et al., 1993). It is suggested here that the Sibi Lobe is the southernmost expression, in Pakistan, of south-directed overthrusting related to the collision of the Indian subcontinent with Eurasia.

Horizontal tectonic shortening across the frontal sector of the northeastern Karachi arc, estimated at 1.0 to 2.6 km, or 5% to 13%, is significantly less than that documented for the Sulaiman Range to the north (Humayon et al., 1991; Jadoon et al., 1992, 1994) and for the southern sector of the Himalayan arc within Pakistan, India, and Nepal (Lyon-Caen and Molnar, 1985; McDougall and Hussain, 1991; Schelling, 1992; Schelling and Arita, 1991). This is partly because tectonic shortening within the northeastern Karachi arc has been calculated for only the frontal structures of the fold and thrust belt, whereas estimates for tectonic shortening across the Sulaiman Range and the southern Himalaya have generally been based upon cross sections constructed across wider sections of the deformation belts. However, it is almost certain that the Southern Kirthar Range as a whole, which belongs to a dominantly transpressional structural system, has undergone less horizontal tectonic shortening than those areas that have been subjected to north-south tectonic shortening along the dominantly compressional Himalayan structural system (e.g., the Salt Ranges of Pakistan and the Siwalik Hills of India and Nepal). In any case, it is clear that the northeastern Karachi arc, as the frontal-most structural system of an emergent imbricate fan, has accommodated only a small amount of the total, east-west tectonic shortening undergone by the Southern Kirthar Range. Therefore, east-west tectonic shortening across the Southern Kirthar Range may be comparable to that estimated for the Sulaiman Range to the north, which is located within a similar, transpressional structural setting.

The east-vergent, emergent imbricate-fan structural geometry of the northeastern Karachi arc may explain both the eastward protrusion of the Karachi arc into the Lower Indus basin, relative to the Central Kirthar Range, and the southward termination of the Sibi trough. Along the eastern flanks of the northern Kirthar Range, Banks and Warburton (1986) documented the existence of a passive-roof duplex, a west-vergent thrust system

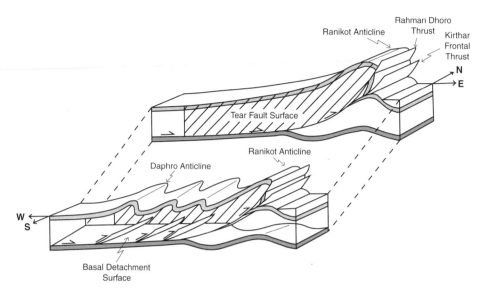

Figure 15. Schematic diagram showing the change in structure across the Banderi Lak fault. This tear fault terminates along the Rahman Dhoro thrust to the east, along the west limbs of the Daphro and Ranikot anticlines to the west, and is believed to terminate along a basal detachment surface within the Goru Formation at depth. The Banderi Lak fault allows differential accommodation of east-west tectonic shortening from north to south.

at the surface overlying an east-vergent tectonic wedge at depth. In addition, within the Central Kirthar Range, a major, west-vergent fault system (the Kirthar fault in Fig. 2) has been documented (Sarwar and De Jong, 1979; Bannert et al., 1992). The west-vergent Kirthar fault system appears to die out to the south at approximately the same latitude as the northern boundary of the Karachi arc. It is probable, then, that the transition from the Northern and Central Kirthar Ranges to the Southern Kirthar Range coincides with a structural transition zone that separates passive-roof duplex structural geometries to the north from the east-vergent, imbricate-fan structural geometries of the Southern Kirthar Range and the Karachi arc to the south (Fig. 17). The Manchhar fault is therefore interpreted here as a tear fault that separates the uplifted, east-vergent, emergent imbricate fan of the Karachi arc in the south from the relatively undeformed Sibi trough to the north.

CONCLUSIONS

Geologic mapping within the northeastern Karachi arc indicates that the region is characterized by north-south–trending, parallel to en echelon, doubly plunging anticline-syncline pairs that are generally asymmetric and dominantly east vergent. Large-scale anticlines are generally located within the hanging walls of thrust faults which offset anticlinal forelimbs and/or adjacent, overturned synclinal hinges and which record displacements to 1,000 m.

Analysis of large-scale structural geometries and the construction of balanced cross sections indicate that the northeastern Karachi arc is underlain by a regional detachment surface located within shale sequences of the Cretaceous Goru Formation at a depth of 2 to 4 km below sea level. Most thrust faults mapped within the northeastern Karachi arc are believed to be splays off the Goru Formation detachment surface, although local thrust-detachment horizons have been identified within the Paleocene Ranikot Formation. Structural geometries of fold-fault systems further suggest that anticlines within the northeastern Karachi arc developed as fault-propagation folds, and that hanging-wall splay thrusts generally formed after the initial development of overturned forelimbs along large-scale anticlines. Thin-skinned tear faults have been identified within the study area that allow along-strike changes in accommodation to compressional deformation and in amounts of tectonic shortening.

Horizontal, east-west tectonic shortening across the frontal structures of the northeastern Karachi arc has been estimated to range from 1.0 to 2.6 km, or between 5% and 13%. Most of the deformation undergone by these frontal structures postdates deposition of the Miocene to Pleistocene Manchhar Group, indicating a Pliocene-Pleistocene to Holocene, eastward propagation of the Karachi arc structural system.

Despite being located alongside the western transpressional plate boundary of the Indian subcontinent, the northeastern Karachi arc has undergone deformation under a dominantly east-west–oriented compressional stress regime and has undergone virtually no identifiable north-south–oriented strike-slip deformation. Therefore, it appears that there has been significant strain partitioning along the Ornach Nal–Chaman transform fault system, the east-west compressional component of the overall transpressional deformation being transmitted farther toward the interior of the Indian sub-

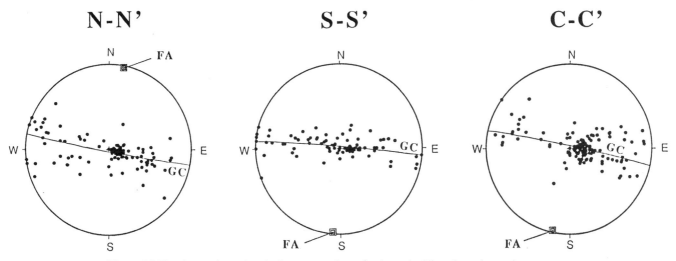

Figure 16. Equal-area, lower hemisphere stereoplots of poles to bedding along the northern transect (N-N′), the southern transect (S-S′), and the central transect (C-C′). FA is best-fit fold axis; GC is best-fit great circle containing poles to bedding. Stereoplots created utilizing Stereonet v. 3.75 (Allmendinger, 1988).

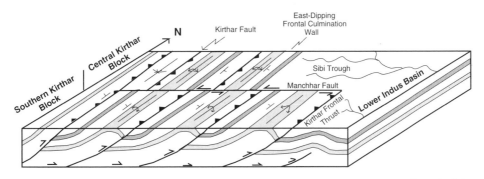

Figure 17. Schematic block diagram illustrating the structural relationships between the Central Kirthar Range, the Southern Kirthar Range, the Sibi trough and the Manchhar fault. The Manchhar fault has been interpreted as a tear fault that separates the east-vergent imbricate fan of the Karachi arc from the west-vergent structural system of the Central Kirthar Range (located above a passive-roof duplex) and from the relatively undeformed Sibi trough.

continent than the strike-slip component. In addition, the Southern Kirthar Range and the Karachi arc appear to remain unaffected by south-vergent compressional deformation related to the northward underthrusting of the Indian subcontinent beneath the Himalayan arc.

Whereas the Southern Kirthar Range and the Karachi arc are characterized by an east-vergent, emergent imbricate-fan structural geometry, the frontal structural systems of the Northern and Central Kirthar Ranges display a well-documented passive-roof structural style. The Manchhar fault has therefore been interpreted as a thin-skinned tear fault located along an east-west–oriented structural transition zone that separates the Southern Kirthar Range from the Central Kirthar Range, and the eastward-protruding Karachi arc from the relatively undeformed Sibi trough.

ACKNOWLEDGMENTS

This chapter presents the results of a study conducted for Texaco Frontier Exploration Company during the fall of 1991. Permission from John Kovacs of Texaco to publish this paper is gratefully acknowledged. Geological field mapping and structural analysis benefited from ongoing discussions with James Rine of the University of South Carolina and Arshad Bhutta of the Geological Survey of Pakistan, both of whom were in the field with me in Pakistan. The geological field work upon which this paper is based could not have been conducted without the assistance of the numerous employees of Business Security Technology, Ltd. In particular, Neil Don Paul, Assif Ali Bhatti, and Ibrahim Bhatti were essential companions during my traverses across the rugged terrain of the southern Kirthar Mountains. I am also grateful for the assistance of Muhammad Sadiq Gobol of Amri Kot, and Bake Shah of Bajara, both of whom assisted throughout the duration of the field program. R. Lawrence and R. Lillie provided many helpful comments in their reviews of the original manuscript.

REFERENCES CITED

Abdel-Gawad, M., 1971, Wrench movements in the Baluchistan Arc and relation to Himalayan–Indian Ocean tectonics: Geological Society of America Bulletin, v. 82, p. 1235–1250.

Allmendinger, R. W., 1988, Stereonet v. 3.75: _____.

Banks, C. J., and Warburton, J., 1986, "Passive-roof" duplex geometry in the frontal structures of the Kirthar and Sulaiman mountain belts, Pakistan: Journal of Structural Geology, v. 8, p. 229–237.

Bannert, D., Cheema, A., Ahmed, A., and Schaffer, U., 1992, The structural development of the Western Fold Belt, Pakistan: Geologisches Jahrbuch, Reihe B, Heft 80, 60 p.

Bender, F. K., and Raza, H. A., 1995, Geology of Pakistan: Berlin, Gebruder Borntraeger, 414 p.

Humayon, M., Lillie, R. J., and Lawrence, R. D., 1991, Structural interpretation of the eastern Sulaiman foldbelt and foredeep, Pakistan: Tectonics, v. 10, p. 299–324.

Hunting Survey Corporation, Ltd., 1961, Reconnaissance geology of part of West Pakistan: Toronto, Ontario, Canada, Colombo Plan Cooperative Project, 550 p.

Jadoon, I. A. K., Lawrence, R. D., and Lillie, R. J., 1992, Balanced and retro-deformed geological cross-section from the frontal Sulaiman lobe, Pakistan: Duplex development in thick strata along the western margin of the Indian plate, *in* McClay, K., ed., Thrust tectonics: London, Chapman and Hall, p. 343–356.

Jadoon, I. A. K., Lawrence, R. D., and Lillie, R. J., 1993, Evolution of foreland structures, an example from the Sulaiman thrust lobe of Pakistan, SW of the Himalayas, *in* Treloar, P. M., and Searle, M., eds., Himalayan tectonics: Geological Society of London Special Publication 74, p. 589–603.

Jadoon, I. A. K., Lawrence, R. D., and Lillie, R. J., 1994, Seismic data, geometry, evolution, and shortening in the active Sulaiman fold-and-thrust belt of Pakistan, southwest of the Himalayas: American Association of Petroleum Geologists Bulletin, v. 78, p. 758–774.

Klootwijk, C. J., Naziruollah, R., De Jong, K. A., and Ahmed, H., 1981, A paleomagnetic reconnaissance of northeastern Baluchistan, Pakistan: Journal of Geophysical Research, v. 86, p. 289–306.

Lawrence, R. D., Khan, S. H., DeJong, K. A., Farah, A., and Yeats, R. S., 1981, Thrust and strike slip fault interaction along the Chaman transform zone, Pakistan, *in* McKlay, K., and Price, N., eds., Thrust and nappe tectonics: Geological Society of London Special Publication 9, p. 363–370.

Lyon-Caen, H., and Molnar, P., 1985, Gravity anomalies, flexure of the Indian Plate, and the structure, support and evolution of the Himalaya and the Ganga Basin: Tectonics, v. 4, p. 513–538.

McDougall, J. W., and Hussain, A., 1991, Fold and thrust propagation in the western Himalaya based on a balanced cross section of the Surghar Range and Kohat Plateau, Pakistan: American Association of Petroleum Geologists Bulletin, v. 75, p. 463–478.

Powell, C. M., 1979, A speculative history of Pakistan and surroundings: Some constraints from the Indian Ocean, *in* Farah, A., and De Jong, K., eds., Geodynamics of Pakistan: Quetta, Geological Survey of Pakistan, p. 5–24.

Quadri, V., and Shuaib, M., 1986, Hydrocarbon prospects of Southern Indus Basin, Pakistan: American Association of Petroleum Geologists Bulletin, v. 70, p. 730–747.

Sarwar, G., and De Jong, K. A., 1979, Arcs, oroclines, syntaxes: The curvatures of mountain belts in Pakistan, *in* Farah, A., and De Jong, K., eds., Geodynamics of Pakistan: Quetta, Geological Survey of Pakistan, p. 341–349.

Schelling, D., 1992, The tectonostratigraphy and structure of the eastern Nepal Himalaya: Tectonics, v. 11, p. 925–943.

Schelling, D., and Arita, K., 1991, Thrust tectonics, crustal shortening, and the structure of the far-eastern Nepal Himalaya: Tectonics, v. 10, p. 851–862.

Schelling, D., and Rine, J., 1991, Geology of Block 17, Southern Kirthar Mountains (Western Sindh, Pakistan): University of South Carolina, Earth Sciences and Resources Institute Technical Report 91-12-391, 110 p.

Williams, M. D., 1959, Stratigraphy of the Lower Indus Basin, West Pakistan, *in* Proceedings of the 5th World Petroleum Congress, New York, section 1, paper 19, p. 377–394.

MANUSCRIPT ACCEPTED BY THE SOCIETY FEBRUARY 3, 1998

Geological Society of America
Special Paper 328
1999

Large-scale erosional processes at the southern flank of the Ganesh Himal range, central Nepal

C. F. Uhlir and J.-M. Schramm

University of Salzburg, Institute of Geology and Paleontology, Hellbrunnerstrasse 34/III, Salzburg 5020, Austria

ABSTRACT

An area of complex landslides is between the villages of Jarlang and Burang on the southeastern slope of Ankhu Khola valley, within the Ganesh Himal's southern flanks in central Nepal. Slow rotational rockslides within deeply weathered mica quartzites and schists have destabilized the head scarp composed of compact augen gneiss in Jarlang, causing rockslides from the main scarp. Successions of small rockslides ($<10^6$ m^3) have generated rather uniform deposits, whereas large, long-runout landslides ($>10^6$ m^3) have generated stratified deposits that have thin shear horizons.

The recent erosional processes within the colluvial deposits, forced by rapid weathering of the deposits, include gully erosion and successive rotational and translational slides along the gully margins. The triggering event for the gullying and later gravitational slumping at Burang and Jarlang in 1954 was nine days of intense rainfall. The higher landslide activity within the Jarlang gully system is explained by reactivation along shear horizons in older landslide deposits.

The yearly amount of mass wasting of both gullies divided by the area of the Ganesh Himal watershed yields an average rate of erosion of 6 mm/yr. This indicates that large-scale landsliding, and subsequent rapid erosion of the landslide deposits, could be the major denudation process within the Higher Himalayan range during interglacial time.

INTRODUCTION

The Himalayas contain some enormous erosional features that pose serious problems for habitation of mountain hillslopes and for depositional areas downsteam. This chapter describes one area within such features and the complex processes that have led to the current rapid degradation of the slopes. The current high rates of uplift in the Himalayas (e.g., Mugnier et al., 1996; Burbank, 1992), coupled with seasonally intense monsoonal precipitation, force intensive fluvial dissection of the Himalayan range, producing instability of slopes and a wide range of mass movements. The main type of mass movement within the crystalline rocks of the Lesser and Higher Himalayan zones are slow mountain creeps and fast rockslides (landslides) on various scales, as apparent in

detailed geologic maps of Heuberger (1986), Weidinger et al. (1996), and Uhlir (1997). The mass movement events are generally thought to have occurred in the early postglacial or interstadials, and to correlate with the retreat of the valley glaciers and seismic activity.

The study area is at the southern flank of the Ganesh Himal's main ridge, 55 km northwest of Kathmandu on the southeastern slope of Ankhu Khola valley, at ~lat 28°05′ N and 85°05′ E (Fig. 1). Topographically, this area is situated in the "mid stage" of Thouret (1981), between 870 and 3,500 m, and undergoes very large extremes of monsoonal climate, including typical precipitation of 3,000 to 4,000 mm within three months. The subtropical stage, between 500 and 1,500 m in elevation and underlain by ferralitic soil, is not present in the interior Ankhu Khola valley.

Uhlir, C. F., and Schramm, J.-M., 1999, Large-scale erosional processes at the southern flank of the Ganesh Himal range, central Nepal, *in* Macfarlane, A., Sorkhabi, R. B., and Quade, J., eds., Himalaya and Tibet: Mountain Roots to Mountain Tops: Boulder, Colorado, Geological Society of America Special Paper 328.

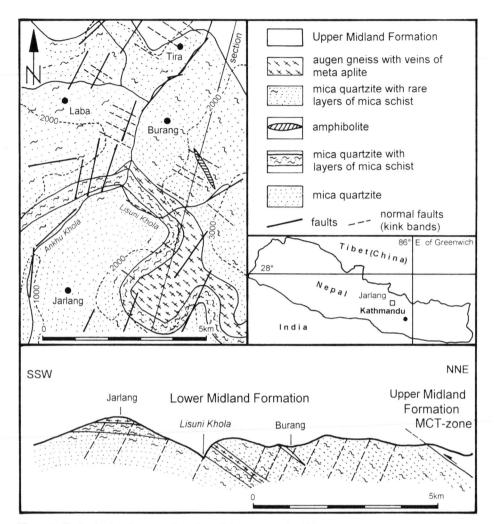

Figure 1. Geologic sketch map and section of the upper and middle Ankhu Khola valley, after Pêcher (1977). MCT is Main Central thrust.

An area of complex landslides is located between the villages of Jarlang and Burang on Ankhu Khola's southeastern slope (Figs. 1 and 2). This area contains a wide range of mass movement features within both bedrock and colluvial cover. The colluvial cover is as thick as 80 m and is composed of landslide debris partially covering disintegrated rock of slow rotational rockslides. The landsliding and associated processes have been active for at least 400 yr.

The main hillslope factors (Table 1) promoting the slides in bedrock are as follows. (1) Foliation dips roughly parallel to the slope. A zone of shear faults cuts the scarps at 20–50 m intervals. (2) Thin layers of interstratified mica schist weaken compact mica quartzites. (3) In Jarlang, a 120-m-thick layer of compact augen gneiss overlies the succession of mica quartzite and mica schist.

The principal factors promoting slides within the thick and oversteepened colluvium are fast weathering processes within the debris and, in Jarlang, the presence of a succession of shear

plains. Deforestation does not seems to be a significant factor (Marston and Miller, 1987).

The main factors triggering slides are of a cyclic nature and include very high annual monsoonal precipitation (Thouret, 1981), catastrophic rainstorms every 30 to 60 yr (Carson, 1985; Marston and Miller, 1987), and major seismic activity every 250 to 500 yr (Bilham et al., 1995). As a result of all these processes, about one-quarter of the area's farmland has been devastated and five hamlets destroyed within the past 40 yr.

GEOLOGIC AND TECTONIC SETTING

The lithology of the slide area is dominated by psammitic and pelitic metasediments and discontinuous horizons of augen gneiss and amphibolite (Table 2). The rocks belong to the lower Midland Formation (lower Nawakot Group of Stöcklin, 1980) and are on the northern limb of the Kuncha Gorkha anticline. They are a part of the inverted metamorphic suite related to

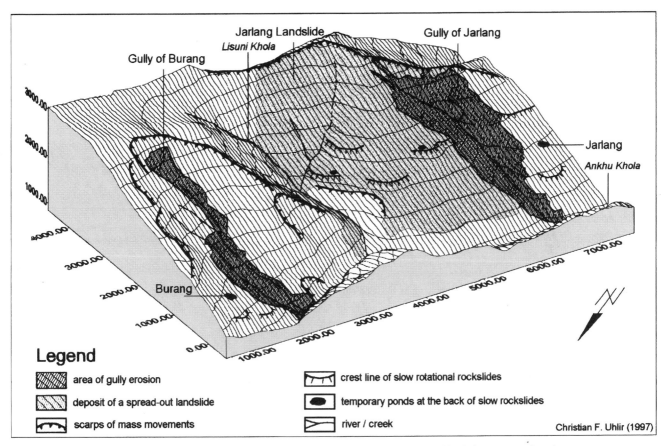

Figure 2. Perspective view of the Burang-Jarlang landslide area (z axis = altitude in meters, referred to sea level; x, y axes = distance in meters, not related to any projection).

overthrusting of the Tibetan slab along the Main Central thrust (Pêcher, 1977). This inverted metamorphism within the lower Midland Formation of Le Fort (1975) progresses from greenschist facies (south) to low-grade amphibolite facies (north).

The tectonic features in the study area were created during several stages of deformation (Pêcher, 1977). The most important structures are: (1) schistosity S_1 dipping 10°–30° to the north or northeast, roughly parallel to primary bedding S_0, (2) simple folds, their b axes dipping parallel to the dip of S_1, (3) schistosity S_2 folding S_1, generally dipping 10°–15° steeper than S_1, and (4) kink bands, described as normal faults by Bogacz and Krokowski (1986), that have a 60°–70° southwest to south-southwest dip; and (5) series of faults that strike northnortheast.

SUCCESSION OF MASS MOVEMENTS

Mass movement in the study area begins with deep-seated, slow, rotational rockslides within the mica quartzites and schists, typically creating temporary ponds at the back of the slide masses. These slides, promoted by river dissection, destabilize the materials upslope, causing rockslides from the scarps.

In the most cases these rockslides are minor (<10^6 m^3), but at Jarlang, large landslides (>10^6 m^3, see Abele, 1974; Heim, 1932), also called long-runout or spread-out landslides (Schaller, 1991), develop in the overlying augen gneiss. The Jarlang landslide event occurred more than 300–400 yr ago, as interpreted from the state of the vegetation (Uhlir, 1996), and about 45 yr ago, according to a witness report, a small rockfall (<10^6 m^3) originated from the southwestern part of the Jarlang landslide's head scarp (Table 1).

Witnesses report that in 1954, after nine days of continuous heavy rainfall at the end of the summer monsoon, a series of landslides and rockfalls occurred throughout the Ganesh Himal region. The biggest events were gravity slumps within colluvium at average slope angles of 25° close to the villages of Burang and Jarlang. Southwest of Burang, within the deposits of small rockfalls (<10^6 m^3), and in the village area of Jarlang, within the deposits of the Jarlang landslide, 1.07 km^2 of farmland including five hamlets slid down rapidly enough to kill 300 people. No damming of the Ankhu Khola river was reported in these cases. Since this catastrophe, both slide areas remain active, and there have been multiple types of landslides (Brown et al., 1992).

Gullying within both slide areas has since led to successive

**TABLE 1. TYPES OF MASS MOVEMENTS
AT THE JARLANG AND BURANG LANDSLIDE AREAS**

Types of Mass Movements	Velocity	Promoting Factors	External Triggering	Activity
Spread out land-slides generated by rock slides and falls (Jarlang only)	Extremely rapid (as much as 90 m/s)	Schistosity, jointing, faults	Seismic events, self triggering	Inactive- episodic
Rock slides and rock falls generating debris flow	Extremely rapid (as much as 30 m/s)	Schistosity, jointing, faults	Seismic events, self triggering, monsoonal precipitation	Inactive- episodic
Rotational rock slides (successive)	Extremely to very slow	Schistosity, weathering, river dissection	Water saturation	Episodic- permanent
Rock fall	Extremely rapid (as much as 15 m/s)	Schistosity, jointing slope angle >40°	Wind, precipitation, seismic events, self triggering	Episodic- permanent
Successive rotational (wedge-shaped) debris slides	Slow to moderate (1.5 m/yr to 1.5 m/month)	Gullying, weathering	Water saturation, slope undercutting	Episodic
Successive translational debris slides (Jarlang only)	Slow to moderate (1.5 m/yr to 1.5 m/month)	Preexisting flat failure surface of fine grained nature, gullying	Water saturation	Episodic
Debris avalanches	Very rapid (as much as 10 m/s)	Debris accumulation within the gully	Water saturation	Episodic
Gullying		Weathering	Monsoonal precipitation	Permanent
Debris creep	Slow to very slow	Slope undercutting, debris accumulation	Water saturation	Episodic- permanent

rotational and translational slides along the side scarps. The gully at Burang (Fig. 3) was enlarged before 1978 by a 70-m-wide, 400-m-long rotational slide along the northeastern flank, on the basis of evidence from aerial photography. Since this event, this gully has remained mostly stable, except for small slips along the southeastern flank and small-scale talus creep within the gully.

The gully at Jarlang (Figs. 4 and 5) was enlarged by the same mechanism to a giant torrential gully system that notched a new valley within only 40 yr. The slide grew from an original width of 300 m to 1.2 km at present, and covers an area of 2.68 km². The total volumetric loss is now 1.46×10^8 m³. The suggestion of Thouret (1981) of an average yearly loss of mate-

rial of 2.5×10^6 m³, when added to the estimated volume of the initial 1954 event, results in nearly the same figure.

The sketch maps of the development of the Burang and Jarlang gullies (Fig. 6) show the history of enlargement and give an idea of the area expected to be damaged during the next 10 yr. The gully at Burang has an endangered area of 0.25 km², and that of the gully at Jarlang is nearly 1 km². The difference in activity of the Burang and Jarlang colluvium is explained by the lithology of the colluvial deposits. The colluvium at Burang consists of a succession of small rockfall deposits with rather uniform grain sizes (Uhlir, 1996). The colluvium at Jarlang is composed of a succession of strongly fractured and shattered rock (partially cataclastic), having partial preservation of the

TABLE 2. ROCKS INVOLVED IN MASS MOVEMENTS AT THE JARLANG LANDSLIDE AREA*

Sample[†]	Parent Rock	Behavior of Fracturing	Structure	Compressive Strength[§] (Uniaxial) (N/mm^2)
U10J	Meta-aplite	Blocky and splintery	Medium-grained, compact granitic structure	>160
U11J	Orthogneiss	Blocky and splintery	Medium-grained, compact granitic structure	>160
U16J	Muscovite biotite quartzite	Brittle and splintery	Fine-grained, layered, with mica-rich layers	<10
U28J	Muscovite biotite quartzite	Brittle and splintery	Fine-grained, thin-layered, with mica-rich layers	30–124
U29J	Muscovite biotite quartzite	Platy and brittle	Fine-grained, compact, with mica-rich layers	50–135
U31J	Muscovite biotite quartzite	Brittle and splintery	Fine-grained, fine-layered	<10

*Uhlir (1996).
†For sample locations see Figure 8.
§Compressive strength estimated using the Schmidt Hammer.

original rock structure. These compact layers, which have stable slope angles of as much as 50° in dry condition, are interlayered with fine-grained, pulverized shear zones (or "kakirites"; Heitzmann, 1985; Fig. 7). These shear zones within the old Jarlang landslide deposits are reactivated by the gullying, and result in translational slides along the central scarp and northeastern side scarps. Open cracks behind the scarp of the gully (Fig. 8) confirm the possibility of continued growth similar to the past 40 yr. In the next several years, rockslides (<10^6 m^3) from above the gully may also be expected.

Jarlang landslide deposit

The 15–50-m-thick deposit of the old Jarlang landslide, covering the slow rotational rockslides, encompasses an area of 12 km^2 (Fig. 2). The volume of the landslide is more than 2.5 × 10^8 m^3. The maximum elevation from crown to toe is about 2,000 m. The head scarp follows a fault zone that dips 85° to the west-northwest, which is interrupted by kink bands that dip 70° to the south-southwest. The landslide deposit consists mainly of augen gneiss and secondarily of mica quartzite and schist, all of the lower Midland Formation.

Outcrops within the gully at Jarlang and along the Lisuni

Khola River support the theory that big, long-runout landslides travel en bloc and spread out along thin shear zones that lubricate the movement. Several theories on the lubrication of landslides were discussed by Schaller (1991). The thickness of the shear zones increases with distance from the head scarp, from about 20 cm near head scarp to 1.5 m near the toe (Fig. 7), and 5 m at the Lisuni Khola creek. The main part of the Jarlang landslide (Fig. 2) traveled along the Lisuni Khola valley down to the Ankhu Khola valley, as evidenced by relics of landslide deposit. Near the head scarp three thin shear layers, embedded in intensely shattered rock, form an uneven sliding plane. Small obstacles will be overcome by the generation of additional shear zones within the sliding mass. The backside trough of the slow rotational rockslides is filled by successive overridings of the sliding mass (Fig. 9).

Subsurface weathering of the shear zones has changed the fine-grained pulverized material of augen-gneiss composition to a sandy, silty clay. Partial chemical alteration was observed. Thin sections of the sand fraction show mainly unaltered feldspar and quartz. X-ray diffraction analysis of the silty and clayey fraction showed that quartz dominates the silty fraction and the fraction smaller than 20 μm is composed of kaolinite, chlorite, illite, and unaltered feldspar. Vermiculite is common

Figure 3. The gully of Burang in 1994 showing partial reforestation on its northeastern flank (for scale, cf. Fig. 6).

Figure 4. The gully of Jarlang in 1994 showing destruction of terraced farmland (for scale, cf. Fig. 8).

Figure 5. Wedge-shaped slides on the southwestern flank of the gully at Jarlang (for scale, cf. Fig. 8).

within the debris at the surface of the gully at Jarlang. Swelling clay minerals, such as montmorillonite or mixed layer chlorite/montmorillonite, were not detected within the altered shear horizons (Uhlir, 1996), but they are present in the A horizon of the surrounding soils (Thouret, 1981) and in old soil horizons within the gully at Burang (Table 3). These clayey horizons at different levels provide slip planes of the translational debris slides on the northwestern side scarp and below the head scarp at the Jarlang gully, and therefore are causal factors for the rapid growth of this erosional complex. At the Burang gully, old soil horizons function as slip planes for small-scale translational debris slides.

CONCLUSIONS

Thick landslide and rockslide debris is common as colluvial cover on crystalline rock sequences of the Lesser and Higher Himalayan zones. The stability of those deposits is reduced by weathering produced by the extremely abundant monsoonal precipitation. Catastrophic rainstorms trigger debris slumps, resulting in massive gully erosion and major mass wasting. The yearly loss of material of the colluvial deposits at Jarlang and Burang divided by the area of the Ankhu Khola River's watershed yields an average rate of erosion of 6 mm/yr. This rate is comparable to estimates of long-term erosion rates from other rapidly denuding parts of the Himalaya, such as nearby Langtang (2.9 mm/yr; Hejl et al., 1997) and the Nanga Parbat area of Pakistan (5 mm/yr; Zeitler et al., 1993). Our results show that relatively rare, large-scale landslides can displace masses of as much as 15 km³ (Masch et al., 1981), and that fast erosion of their deposits is the major mechanism for denudation of the Lesser and Higher Himalayan crystalline zones during interglacial times.

ACKNOWLEDGMENTS

We thank B. N. Upreti and M. P. Sharma from the Tribhuvan University, Kathmandu, for legal support and recommendations essential for obtaining base maps and aerial photographs, A. M. Bassett and W. Vetters for discussions on the geology and petrology of central Nepal, and T. Devkota for field assistance and his services as translator. J. Quade and S. D. Ellen provided helpful reviews of our manuscript. Financial support from the Stiftungs- und Foerderungsgesellschaft der Paris Lodron Universitaet Salzburg, the Federal Ministry of Science, Research and the Arts in Austria, and the Austrian Science Foundation (FWF grant no. P9433-GEO) is gratefully acknowledged.

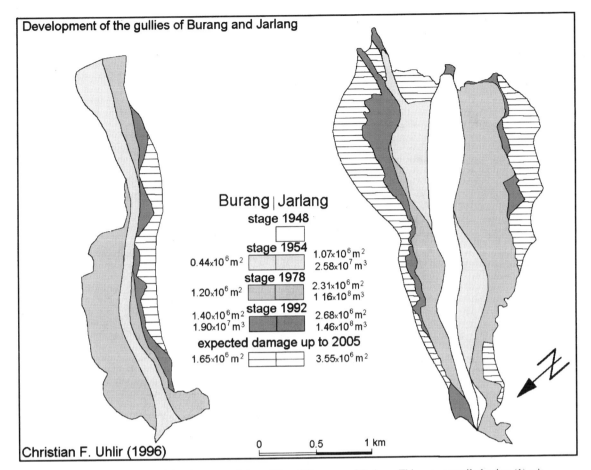

Figure 6. Sketch maps of development of the gullies of Burang and Jarlang. This was compiled using (1) witness reports, (2) the topographic map 71 H4 1:63360 (1966), which is based on aerial photographs from 1954, (3) aerial photographs from 1978 and 1992, and (4) ground surveys during 1993–1994.

Figure 7. Shear horizon, 1.5 m thick, consisting of cataclastic and pulverized material (kakirite). The bedrock below the shear zone is shattered mica quartzite from a slow rotational rockslide. The material above the shear zone consists of intensely shattered and disintegrated augen gneiss.

REFERENCES CITED

Abele, G., 1974, Bergstürze in den Alpen, ihre Verbreitung, Morphologie und Folgeerscheinungen: Wissenschaftliche Alpenvereinshefte, v. 25, p. 1–230.

Bilham, R., Bodin, P., and Jackson, M., 1995, Entertaining a great earthquake in Western Nepal: Historic inactivity and geodetic test for the development of strain: Nepal Geological Society Journal, v. 11 special issue, p. 73–88.

Bogacz, W., and Krokowski, J., 1986, Mesoscopic structural studies of postmetamorphic deformations and tectonic evolution of the Central Nepal Himalaya, *in* Saklani, P. S., ed., Himalayan thrust and associated rocks (Current Trends in Geology, Volume 9): New Delhi, India, Today and Tomorrow's Printers and Publishers, p. 233–264.

Brown, W. M., Cruden, D. M., and Dennison, J. S., 1992, The Directory of the world landslide inventory: U.S. Geological Survey Open-File Report 92-427, p. 1–216.

Burbank, D. W., 1992, Causes of recent Himalayan uplift deduced from deposited patterns in the Ganges Basin: Nature, v. 357, p. 680–683.

Carson, B., 1985, Erosion and sedimentation processes in the Nepalese Himalaya: International Centre for Integrated Mountain Development (ICIMOD), Occasional Paper no. 1, p. 1–39.

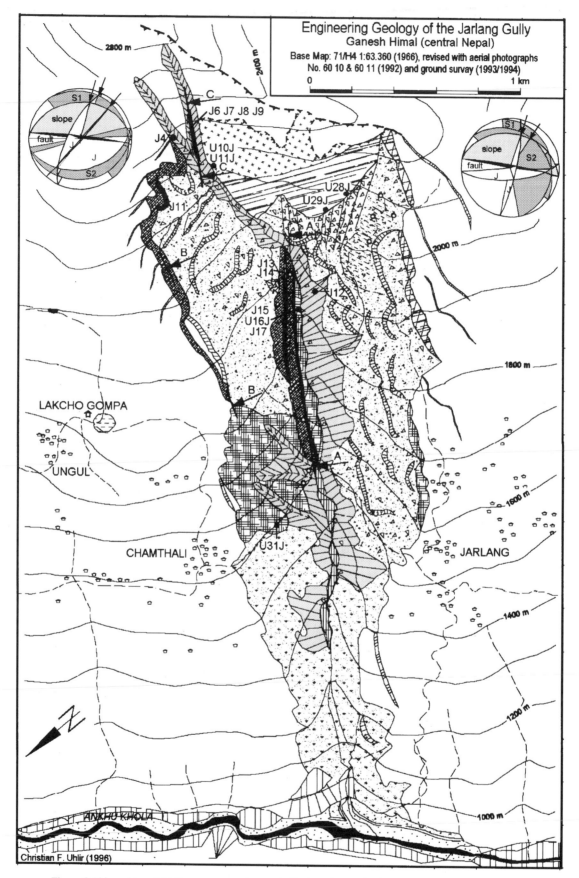

Figure 8 (this and top right figure on opposite page). Engineering geologic map of the gully of Jarlang.

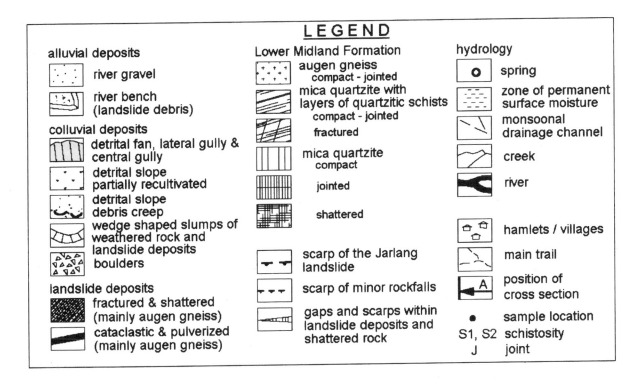

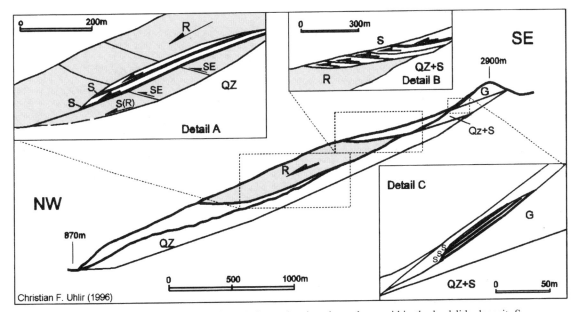

Figure 9. Cross sections of the gully at Jarlang, showing shear planes within the landslide deposit. S, shear horizon; SE, secondary shear horizons; R, rockslide; QZ, quartzite; QZ+S, quartzite and mica schists; G, augen gneiss. Location of sections are shown in Figure 8.

TABLE 3. CLAY-SIZE MINERALS AT THE JARIANG GULLY

Sample*	Clay-size Minerals (2µ)
J6, J8, J9	Illite, chlorite, kaolinite, albite, microcline
J13, J14	Illite, kaolinite, albite
J7, J11, J4	Illite, chlorite, kaolinite, albite, microcline
J15, J17	Illite, kaolinite, vermiculite, mixed-layer illite/montmorillonite
B5[†]	Illite, chlorite, kaolinite, mixed-layer chlorite/montmorillonite, mixed-layer illite/montmorillonite
B6[†]	Illite, chlorite, kaolinite, montmorillonite, mixed-layer chlorite/montmorillonite

*See Figure 8 for sample locations.
[†]Taken from the center of the Burang gully from old soil horizons at 1,700 m altitude.

Heim, A., 1932, Bergstuerze und Menschenleben: Zürich, Fretz und Wasmuth, 218 p.

Heitzmann, P., 1985, Kakirite, Kataklasite, Mylonite—Zur Nomenklatur der Metamorphite mit Verformungsgefügen: Eclogae Geologicae Helvetiae, v. 78, p. 273–286.

Hejl, E., Schramm, J.-M., and Weidinger, J. T., 1997, Long-term exhumation at the Tsergo Ri landslide area (Langthang Himal, Nepal)—Information from apatite fission-track data [abs.]: 12th Himalaya-Karakorum-Tibet Workshop: Rome, Accademia Nazionale dei Lincei and Società Geografica Italiana Róma, p. 149–150.

Heuberger, H., 1986, Der Bergsturz vom Khumdschung, Mount-Everest-Gebiet, Nepal: Material und Technik, v. 3, p. 175–181.

Le Fort, P., 1975, Himalaya: The collided range. Present knowledge of the continental arc: American Journal of Science, v. 275A, p. 1–44.

Marston, R. A., and Miller, M. M., 1987, Mass wasting in the Manaslu-Ganesh and Langtang-Jugal Himals, *in* Marston, R. A., ed., Environment and society in the Manaslu-Ganesh region of the Central Nepal Himalaya. A final report of the 1987 Manaslu-Ganesh Expedition: Moscow, Foundation for Glacier and Environmental Research, p. 47–57.

Masch, L., Erismann, T., Heuberger, H., Preuss, E., and Schröcker, A., 1981, Frictional fusion on the gliding planes of two large landslides: Bulletin de Liaison des Laboratoires des Ponts et Chaussées, Spécial v. 10, p. 11–14.

Mugnier, J. L., Huyghe, P., Leturmy, P., and Delcaillau, B., 1996, Plio-Quaternary increase of sediment supply in syn-orogenic basins of Himalayas: Tectonic control or climatic effect? [abs.]: 11th Himalaya-Karakorum-Tibet Workshop: Flagstaff, Northern Arizona University, p. 107–108.

Pêcher, A., 1977, Geology of the Nepal Himalaya: Deformation and petrography in the Main Central Thrust zone, *in* Ecologie et géologie de l'Himalaya, C.N.R.S., Colloque internationale 268, Paris: Paris, Centre de la Recherce Scientifique, p. 301–318.

Schaller, P. J., 1991, Analysis and implications of large Martian and terrestrial landslides [Ph.D. thesis]: Stanford, California Institute of Technology, 604 p.

Stöcklin, J., 1980, Geology of Nepal and its regional frame: Geological Society of London Journal, v. 137, p. 1–34.

Thouret, J. C., 1981, Géodynamique des grands versants de l'Ankhu Khola, Népal Central [in French and English]: Paris, Centre National de la Recherche Scientifique (CNRS), 281 p.

Uhlir, C. F., 1996, Geological studies on slope dynamics in the Ganesh Himal (Central Nepal) [Doctoral thesis]: Salzburg, University of Salzburg, 92 p.

Uhlir, C. F., 1997, Report on the engineering geological, morphological and hazard mapping for the alignment of the high voltage power line from Namche Basar to Lukla in Solukhumbu (East Nepal): Unpublished report for ÖKO HIMAL Salzburg (Austria), 22 p.

Weidinger, J. T., Schramm, J.-M., and Surenian, R., 1996, On preparatory causal factors, initiating the prehistoric Tsergo Ri landslide (Langthang Himal, Nepal): Tectonophysics, v. 260, p. 95–107.

Zeitler, P. K., Chamberlain, C. P., and Smith, H. A., 1993, Synchronous anatexis, metamorphism, and rapid denudation at Nanga Parbat (Pakistan Himalaya): Geology, v. 21, p. 347–350.

MANUSCRIPT ACCEPTED BY THE SOCIETY FEBRUARY 3, 1998

Geological Society of America
Special Paper 328
1999

Search for buckling of the southwest Indian coast related to Himalayan collision

Rebecca Bendick and Roger Bilham
CIRES, Campus Box 216, University of Colorado, Boulder, Colorado 80309

ABSTRACT

Microseismicity and moderate earthquakes occurring throughout Peninsular India indicate that stresses associated with the Himalayan collision may result in weak deformation of the subcontinent. One geometric response to stress in a thin elastic plate is the creation of buckles, a feature of the oceanic plate south of the Indian continent, but not normally a feature of continental deformation. Geomorphic studies of the Malabar coastline identify erosional and accretional coastlines, and occasionally invoke vertical neotectonics as an underlying cause for their observed distribution. In support of these geological observations are numerous historical accounts that suggest that coastal features have changed in the past 500 yr. We investigated several locations along the southwest coast of India where uplift or subsidence has been reported. We found that evidence for recent vertical motions is ambiguous along much of the coast but geologic, geomorphic, and tide-gauge data near Mangalore (13°N) confirm previous studies that require uplift relative to points to the north and south. Quaternary rates are lower than current rates indicated by tide-gauge data (≈3 mm/yr) and spirit-leveling data (≈6 mm/yr), but both are consistent with recent strain rates observed geodetically in southern India (<10 nanostrain/yr). Although the apparent wavelength of warping (200 km) along the west coast of India is symptomatic of buckling, the known rheological structure of India is not conducive to its development.

INTRODUCTION

The ocean floor south of India is characterized by a series of east-west–oriented buckles (Weissel and Haxby, 1984) having a wavelength of 220 ± 20 km. These have been attributed to northerly or northeasterly compressional stresses in the Indian plate generated by the collision of the Indian plate with southern Tibet (Zuber, 1987). Although these buckles diminish in amplitude northward, we hypothesize that intraplate seismic activity in India may be in part related to the incipient formation of related buckles in the continental crust. Stress orientations on the Indian continent (Gowd et al., 1992) and mantle flow velocities inferred from seismic tomography (Rai et al., 1992) are oriented approximately northeast, parallel to inferred Nuvel 1 plate motions (DeMets et al., 1994) and plate motions observed by global positioning system (GPS) geodesy (Freymuller et al., 1996). The horizontal deformation rate in southern India in the past 130 yr has been measured geodetically to be less than 10 nanostrain/yr (Paul et al., 1995); corresponding tilt rates are 10–20 nrad/yr on approximate east-west axes revealed by spirit leveling (Nagar and Singh, 1991).

This scenario is contrary to the general assumption that plates behave as essentially rigid bodies but, as we have seen elsewhere (Burg et al., 1994; Jin et al., 1994), continental plates are subject to applied stresses close to their elastic strength, and some configurations may produce internal deformation. Buckling usually requires a layered lithosphere. In typical models, a weak subsurface low-velocity layer reduces the effective elastic thickness of the crust allowing it to buckle at stresses less than its fracture strength (Turcotte and Schubert, 1982).

Bendick, R., and Bilham, R., 1999, Search for buckling of the southwest Indian coast related to Himalayan collision, *in* Macfarlane, A., Sorkhabi, R. B., and Quade, J., eds., Himalaya and Tibet: Mountain Roots to Mountain Tops: Boulder, Colorado, Geological Society of America Special Paper 328.

Vertical deformation is invoked in published analyses of coastal and offshore morphology, most notably in arches and sub-basins (of ~400 km wavelength) mapped in seismic sections by Biswas (1989), and in interpretations of the Malabar coastline that invoke tectonic explanations for erosion and accretion (Nair, 1987; Ramasamy, 1989). Recent contributions by Subrahmanya (1996) also highlight a region of Quaternary uplift along an axis from Mangalore to Madras. Coastal instability is described in several historical texts and has been inferred from archeological excavations of harbors constructed since the fifteenth century B.C. (Rao, 1989). In the Appendix we give a detailed account suggestive of rapid emergence of parts of the coast in a cata-strophic event (cf. Cochin, 1341 A.D.).

We identified 10 sites along the Malabar coast of India which had associated vertical motions described either in the historical or scientific literature (see Appendix). We visited each of these sites to examine evidence for tectonic deformation. In some locations, such as Cochin and Alleppy, historical accounts of emergence or submergence were refuted by local historians or were otherwise interpretable in terms of seashore erosion or accretion. For the majority of the sites, we made qualitative observations regarding the lack of robust sea-level markers such as clear marine terraces or exposed bedrock. The entire Malabar coast was observed to be particularly unsuited to the preservation of tectonic vertical motions because of vast quantities of monsoon-transported sand. We then analyzed tide-gauge data for cities along the Indian coast available for the years 1950 to the present.

RESULTS

Quaternary basins and coastal warping

An intriguing aspect of the western coast of India is the presence of several Quaternary basins that do not extend far inland but that have apparent east-west axes that plunge west-ward beneath the continental shelf (Fig. 1). The north-south spacing of these basins is of the order of several hundred kilometers and they thus suggest incipient buckling of the form we seek. The crest of one of the east-west anticlines separating these basins is found at Warkallai (Varkala, lat 8°44′N). Most of the Malabar coastline is characterized by straight sandy beaches, southward transport being driven by prevailing currents and winds (Soman, 1980). However, between Quilon and Warkallai (20 km north of Trivandrum), Tertiary sediments rise from below sea level to form a 60-m-high sea cliff capped by laterite that would be actively eroded were it not now protected by a charnockite block seawall. This exposed Tertiary sequence over-lies the Precambrian basement farther north, at depths to 250 m in a series of boreholes drilled for aquifer exploration purposes (Fig. 2, Raghava Rao, 1975).

Subrahmanya (1996) identified a region of apparent uplift across the Indian Peninsula at ~13°N that also corresponds to one of the antiforms separating Quaternary basins along the west coast of India. This region of uplift is represented by a

major east-west–trending drainage divide, significant micro-seismicity, and a gravity high. Mapped paleochannels indicate that rivers north of this divide, the Tungabhadra and the Penner, have been migrating northward during the Quaternary. River channels south of the divide, including the Palar, Ponnatyar, Cauvery, Gurupur, and Nethravathi, are moving southward. Ramasamy (1989) reported analogous evidence associated with an axis of upwarping between Cochin and Madurai and claimed that seismicity was concentrated along this as well as the Man-galore-Madras line.

Cocoanut Island, at lat 13°28′N, is the most northerly island of the St. Mary Islands group, and consists of vertical columnar basalt (93 Ma; Subrahmanya, 1996) that has several step-like levels that have been interpreted to represent marine terraces. The central part of the island is an extensive shell bank overlain by a thin soil development that supports shrubs and coconut trees. The terrace levels are nowhere precisely horizontal, suggesting that the erosional surfaces may have exploited cooling joints orthog-onal to the vertical columns. Subrahmanya (1996) distinguished levels at 1.5 m, 3 m, 6 m, and 10 m both on the main island and on other islands to the west and south. The ages of these inferred marine terraces are unknown.

The island's western beaches are shelly; the eastern beaches are fine calcareous sands. The highest point of the

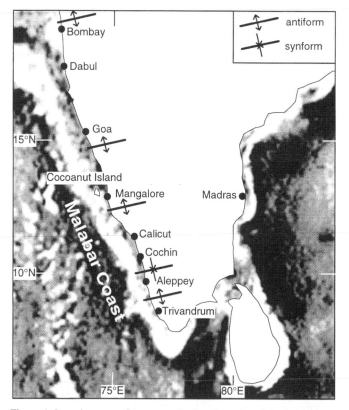

Figure 1. Location map. Quaternary basins along the Malabar coast are mapped with 200–450 km spacing. Geoid swells with ≈250 km wave-length (white = high) in the Bengal Fan are faintly visible in SEASAT imagery east and southeast of Madras (13°N).

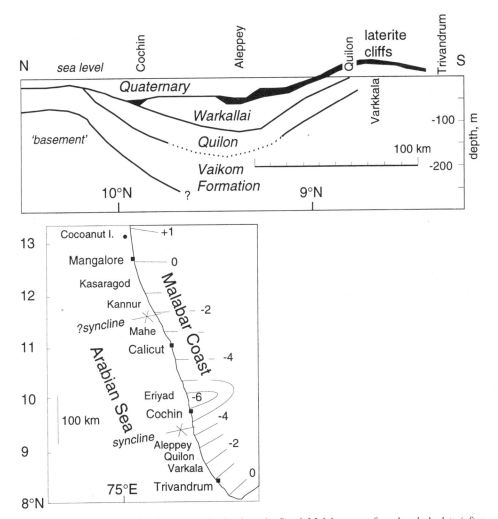

Figure 2. A section through a Quaternary basin along the South Malabar coast from borehole data (after Raghava Rao, 1975; redrawn by Soman, 1980). Laterites (black shading) exposed at Quilon are submerged 50 m below Aleppey. The lower panel shows locations mentioned in text and leveling data from Nagar and Singh (1991). Contours are in millimeters/year. Over a 200 km distance, the vertical uncertainty is approximately 0.1 mm/yr for the 120 yr interval of measurements.

shell deposit approximates the 3 m basalt terrace. We excavated a 2.5 m trench to sea level through the shell deposit ~40 m east of the eroding largest beach, 5 m east of the highest berm. The basal layer, approximately at mean sea level, consisted of basalt cobbles. The shells were fragmented and stratified with textural variations among layers. Upper levels included color changes mixed with occasional thin matrices of mud that may represent former soils. However, numerous mud banks along the coasts are activated in large storms, and these mud layers may be derived from such deposits. Carbon-14 analysis of shelly material yielded ages of 3,150 ± 800 yr (UCL-401) for a sample taken at the base of the trench (0.25 m above sea level) and 2,800 ± 200 yr (UCL-399) for the uppermost sample (2.25 m above sea level). If the age of these materials represents the time of their deposition, we infer an uplift rate of 0.78 ± 0.09 mm/yr.

Historical accounts of emergence and submergence

We reproduce a number of accounts in the Appendix that suggest abrupt coastal events in the past 700 yr: earthquakes, emergence, and subsidence. In particular, several eighteenth and nineteenth century writers discussed the presence of offshore post-sixteenth century ruins at Calicut (11°15′N), and the creation of new land at Cochin (9°59′N) in 1341 A.D. In each of the cases we found no outstanding morphological evidence for vertical motions of the coastline, but found considerable evidence for accretion and erosion. All of the sites that we investigated were characterized by extremely low relief, mainly sandy beaches with few outcrops of bedrock. The new land created at Cochin is representative of many of the sites. It is no more than 1 m above sea level and consists exclusively of sandy soil and debris. Other historical accounts of submerged temples, such as at Calicut, we found to be substantiated neither by local historians nor by physical evidence.

Tide-gauge data

Tide-gauge data (Fig. 3) are available for Bombay, Mangalore, Cochin, and Madras for the years 1950 to the present. Subrahmanya (1996) presented a preliminary analysis using annual means for sea level that indicates uplift of Mangalore and Madras relative to global mean sea level. We extend this analysis to monthly data contributed to the Permanent Service for Mean Sea Level. The data were inspected first for abrupt offsets in the vertical datum of tide gauges. Where these coincided with known changes in operating parameters of gauges, we adjusted the local datum by subtracting from following data, the difference in the constant terms of least squares linear fits to the preceding and following three years of data. For example, a data gap at Mangalore in 1960 required a −37 ± 2 mm offset, and a change in gauge location in 1976 required a +48 ± 1 mm offset. Six months of overlapping data in 1976 from the old and new gauges at Mangalore made this adjustment more certain than the 1960 inferred offset (Fig. 4). In order to examine sea levels independent of eustatic global changes, the monthly data were compared with data from Bombay, which reveal an approximately linear sea-level fall of 0.19 ± 0.02 mm/yr since 1880. To suppress annual variations in the sea-level data, we applied a Gaussian tapered 2 yr window to each series, reducing the annual variance from more than 200 mm to ~20 mm. There are clear differences in the behavior of the selected sites. If we assume that the Bombay record characterizes eustatic sea level for the region and that the longest time series are most representative of secular trends, then Mangalore is rising 2.66 ± 0.13 mm/yr, Madras is stationary (0.04 ± 0.8 mm/yr), and Cochin is sinking at 2.48 ± 0.11 mm/yr. The 40 yr

trend at Cochin is nonlinear, which renders linear trend analysis here suspect (Figs. 3 and 5). The least-squares linear trend for Cochin depends much on the subset of the time series selected for analysis, and subsidence of 3 mm/yr prior to 1961 is replaced by an emergence signal of ≈2 mm/yr since then.

A more accurate estimate of relative motion may be obtained by first differencing the monthly values of overlapping sections of tide-gauge data, and then estimating trends in the difference curves. The Bombay minus Mangalore series is shown in Figure 4 with an evident rise of Mangalore of 1.95 ± 0.13 mm/yr. Improved rejection of local oceanic noise is typically obtained when the tide-gauge sites that are differenced are relatively close together. The proximity of gauges is especially important in India because a surge in sea level occurs at the time of the monsoon, which is not synchronous along the Indian coast. Hence, a significant annual oceanic origin may remain following this method of analysis. Data from Mangalore and Cochin might be expected to provide the clearest evidence for relative vertical tectonic activity, because they are the closest of the two gauges, and are on the peaks and troughs of Quaternary structures (Fig. 5). According to this analysis, Mangalore is rising at 3.22 ± 1.1 mm/yr relative to Cochin, yet even for these data, the phase shift of the monsoon northward is sufficient to aggravate the noise level in simple differences. In theory, were we to seek additional improvements in signal to noise ratio, we might ignore the two to three months of data during which the monsoon perturbs sea level. We have not attempted this because this approach may mimic an annual thermal signal that we otherwise suppress by including all the data.

DISCUSSION

Quaternary basins and coastal warping

The borehole data from the two structural basins mapped on the Malabar coast do not permit an unequivocal interpretation of the structural development of the coastal basin, but it would appear that the Miocene Vaikom beds (>100 m of gravels, clays, and thin lignite beds) that overly the basement were folded after deposition. The same may be true of the overlying Quilon formation, which has a maximum thickness of 70 m. The Pliocene Warkallai formation is 60 m thick and consists of lignites, clays, sands, and laterite, interpreted by Soman (1980) as shallow-water littoral deposits of upper Miocene age. These beds have a laterite cap of varying thickness and are unconformably overlain by Quaternary sediments.

If we assume that deformation of the 120 m amplitude basin (assuming north-south symmetry) started at the beginning of the Quaternary (1.8 Ma), the minimum rate of basin growth is ~0.07 mm/yr and the wavelength is ~180 km along the coast. If this is interpreted as a buckle associated with Himalayan collision, this represents an almost negligible shear strain rate (≈0.7 nanostrain/yr). Had the deformation between Eriyad and Quilon started in the late Pleistocene, the

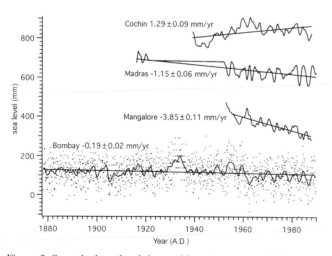

Figure 3. Smoothed sea-level data and least-squares trends in sea level from four tide gauges on the coast of India. The monthly mean data for Bombay shown as dots are illustrative of typical annual variance at all of the gauges. Cochin data are not well represented by a linear trend.

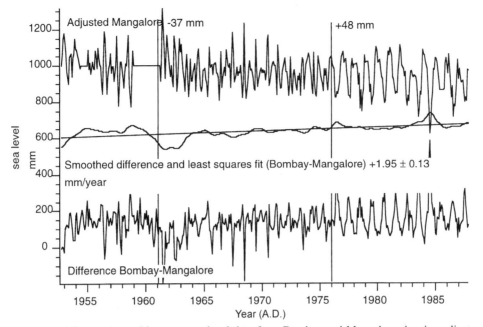

Figure 4. Differenced monthly mean sea-level data from Bombay and Mangalore showing adjustments made in 1960 and 1976. Note the substantial change in character of annual sea level obtained from the new Mangalore tide gauge in 1976.

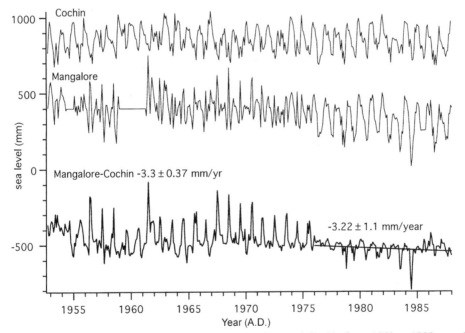

Figure 5. Differences in sea-level data between Mangalore and Cochin from 1953 to 1988 reveal residual annual spikes caused by the phase lag of the annual monsoon. The mean fit to all the data differs little from the mean trend obtained from improved post-1976 data.

strain rate would be roughly an order of magnitude larger. In contrast, Prabhakara Rao (1968) estimated a sedimentation rate in the Warkalli formation of ≈4 mm/yr, requiring a Tertiary subsidence rate almost two orders of magnitude larger. Vertical deformation data for the period 1860–1980 (Fig. 2) indicate that the Cochin region subsided 6 ± 0.1 mm/yr rela-

tive both to Mangalore and the southern tip of India (Nagar and Singh, 1991). Paulose and Narayanaswamy (1968) claimed that a second basin of deposition hosts Tertiary sediments between Kannur (Cannanore) and Kasargod, although this apparently is not associated with significant recent vertical deformation.

Uplift at 13°N

Dates derived from shelly deposits on Cocoanut Island indicate a maximum rate of uplift of 0.78 ± 0.09 mm/yr. However, we consider it doubtful that these dates represent the emplacement of the island deposit. The shelly mixture contains organisms from several different provenances, indicating a mixed ecological assemblage typical of storm deposits of historical time (Ellis, 1924). Thin mud layers found at several levels are also characteristic of storm wash.

Tide-gauge data

The residual secular variations evident in differenced sea-level data are partly of oceanic origin, partly related to local tectonics, and partly related to tide-gauge instability. Notwithstanding these limitations, the gauge data for the period considered are consistent: Mangalore rises 1.95 ± 0.13 mm/yr relative to Bombay and 3.22 ± 1.1 mm/yr relative to Cochin. The difference in rate between Mangalore and Cochin is clearly above the oceanic noise level on the Malabar coast, although we are unable exclude the possibility that the tide gauge at Cochin is sinking relative to the region inland. A change in rate at Cochin in 1961 may signify vertical instability of the gauge. Despite its apparent emergence after a gap in 1961 with an exponential decay between 1961 and 1963, it is unlikely that the Bangalore gauge continues to rise with respect to its local surroundings, in that the same emergence rate applies to the two installations (pre- and post-1976).

The leveling data for the past century indicate a subsidence rate for Cochin relative to Mangalore of 6 ± 0.1 mm/yr, confirming a broad region of subsidence consistent with the tide-gauge results. The possibility that bench-mark instability along the 400 km line Malabar coast should show a systematic variation of the form shown in Figure 2 is slight. Moreover, the contoured leveling data presented by Nagar and Singh (1991) are evidently unconstrained by the tide-gauge data (Singh, 1997, personal communication), and are linked only to the tide gauge at Bombay which, according to the leveling data, rises at 5 ± 0.1 mm/yr relative to Mangalore.

CONCLUSIONS

Geomorphological evidence for buckling of the Indian continent along the Malabar coast is limited and ambiguous. Portions of the Malabar Coast have advanced and retreated, but its dynamic morphology may be as easily attributed to coastal processes of erosion and deposition as to vertical motions. Specific historical accounts of subsidence and uplift are attributed to littoral processes causing coastal advance and retreat. The shallow slope of the coastal zone, the scarcity of bedrock, and the difficulty in dating laterite exposures provides few opportunities to find clear geologic indicators of recent vertical motion along the coast. Reported terrace levels in columnar joints on offshore islands permit an ambiguous interpretation, and associated constructional terraces are interpreted as storm deposits of reworked sea-floor materials.

Some evidence remains compelling: the drainage divide along the Mangalore-Madras axis reported by Subrahmanya (1996) and the tide-gauge and leveling data presented here. The tide-gauge and leveling data suggest that Mangalore, for the past few decades at least, has been rising at >3 mm/yr relative to Cochin, 300 km south. This rate is more than an order of magnitude larger than onshore rates prevailing during the formation of Quaternary basins along the Indian coast. If the observed uplift is real, it would be sufficient to drive the weak but concentrated microseismicity observed at $13 \pm 1°N$. Independent confirmation of localized uplift is potentially available through the future application of modern geodetic techniques (GPS and absolute gravimetry).

Observational uncertainties currently prevent the conclusive geological confirmation of long-wavelength active continental deformation. It is likely that the Indian craton, lacking a pronounced low-velocity layer, is too thick to buckle under the stresses imposed by collision. Hence, the presence of localized uplift at 13°N, and subsidence at 10°N may have an alternative physical mechanism.

ACKNOWLEDGMENTS

We thank our colleagues, A. Radhakrishna, K. Subrahmanya, Gyanesh Sharma, G. C. Suresh, John Paul, V. K. Gaur, and Dr. Valdiya and Dr. Cochhar in Bangalore, Mangalore, and Calicut for hosting our visit to Malabar. Claudio Vita-Finzi, University College, London, kindly estimated the ages of materials from Cocoanut Island, and provided thoughtful interpretations of their implications, and reviewed the manuscript. The study was funded by the National Science Foundation, grant INT-94 23240.

APPENDIX

The Malabar coast abounds with legends of sunken temples, earthquakes, and submarine ruins. We reproduce accounts that have been interpreted by some authors as subsidence of the Calicut region and emergence of the Cochin region. Field inspection of these two areas leads us to conclude that erosion and accretion could equally explain the observations. We conclude by appending a summary of historical earthquakes not found in standard catalogues of Indian events. The magnitudes of most of these events are unknown, except perhaps for the 1881 Bay of Bengal earthquake. The most intriguing of these accounts is the Dabul tsunami of September 1524, experienced in deep water on the continental shelf between Goa and Bombay by the fleet of Vasco da Gama.

Cochin 9°59′50″

Historical accounts indicate the emergence of part of the coast of the island of Vaipin, north of Cochin, in 1341 A.D. Commemorative plaques near the Portuguese fort record the 1341 event as a storm, although on what authority it is not clear. Newbold (1846) wrote the following about Cochin.

The most remarkable changes are to be found in the vicinity of Cochin. On its northern side we find the island of Vaypi, which was thrown up by the sea about the year 1341. The soil upon this new formation resembles that of the flat districts of Malabar, which consists of sea-sand and calcareous matter combined with clay, said to be washed down from the Ghauts. The production of this island had so strong an effect on the minds of the Hindus, that they marked the geological phenomenon by commencing from it the new era, termed Puduvepa (New Introduction). Contemporaneous with the appearance of the island of Vaypi, the waters which during the rainy season are discharged from the Ghauts, broke through the banks of the river Cochin, and overwhelmed a village of the same name, with such impetuosity as to sweep it away, and formed in that district a river, a lake, and a harbour so spacious that very large ships can now lie in security on the north-east side of Cochin, where the river runs into the sea.

The emergence of new land at Vaipin Island gave rise to the Hindu Era "Puduvepa" or "Putuveppa" (meaning "new deposit"; Logan, 1887, p. 158). The era is associated with the sudden appearance of a coastal tract and the impounding of waters behind the coastal bar. This lends itself to a possible interpretation of coastal uplift, or of storm-related accretion. The southwest portion of Vaypin Island, which we visited in 1995, is now known by the name of Puduvepa. Three coastal beach ridges were visible in front of the western-facing seawall, at ≈50 m intervals with <50 cm of relief above the mud-filled swales between them. The ridges appear as storm beaches of sand near the present shore (no or few shells); a covering of trees and bushes IS inland. A remarkable feature of the island elsewhere is its absence of relief. Numerous channels and ponds are found inland and ancient beach ridges that have been mapped throughout the island show no tendency to form terraces. At high tide in December we found that sea level was less than 1 m (3 ft) below any part of the southern part of the island.

Hamilton (1727) hinted that the marine coast at Cochin had eroded many kilometers by 1703.

The first Europeans that settled at Cochin were the Portugeze, and there they built a fine City on the River's Side, about 3 leagues from the Sea: but the Sea gaining on the Land yearly, it is not now 100 Paces from it.

The absence of marine terraces indicates to us the absence of continued uplift, and evidence for erosion and accretion suggests that the "Puduvepa" event was not emergence of the coast but accretion of additional land to the island during the 1341 storm (see Appendix Figure 1).

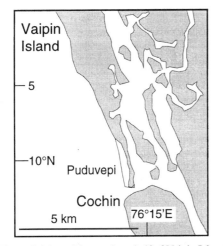

Appendix Figure 1. Map of the southern half of Vaipin Island, accessible by ferry from Cochin. The southwest corner of the island is known as Puduvepi.

Calicut (Khozikode) 11°15′

A number of historical accounts suggest that part of the old Portuguese city of Calicut may be currently submerged. Hamilton (1727, p. 177) wrote the following (note that Chess-trees were two pieces of wood projecting on each side of the ship to confine the lower corners of the mainsail. His ship was the *Albermarle*).

On Anno 1703 about the Middle of February, I called at *Calecut* in my Way to *Surat*, and standing into the Road, I chanced to strike on some of the Ruins of the sunken Town built by the *Portugeze* in former Times. Whether that Town was swallowed up by an Earthquake as some affirm, or whether it was undermined by the Sea, I will not determine; but so it was, that in 6 Fathoms at the main Mast, my Ship, which drew 21 Foot water, sat fast afore the Chess-tree. The Sea was smooth, and, in a short Time, we got off without damage.

Stanhope (1785, p. 109) wrote the following in his memoirs.

Calicutt, which is now an inconsiderable village, was formerly a magnificent city, and the residence of a powerful Prince. According to the tradition of the natives, it was overwhelmed near 200 years ago by a sudden rising of the sea, and all its inhabitants perished. We anchored on the spot where the ancient city stood and as we went ashore at low water, the foundations of the buildings were discernible to the naked eye.

Newbold (1846, p. 252) repeated oral legends and invoked eustatic sea-level rise, or a storm surge, as a possible mechanism.

In some places, as on the Coromandel coast, tracts formerly inhabited have disappeared under the sea. The bank on which stood the old city of Calicut (the landing place of Albuquerque) a little to the south of the present site, is now buried under the sea, but it does not appear at all clear whether in this, or other cases of submergence, the cause was a sinking of the land, or a change in the configuration of the coast by a sudden rise of the sea. It is said that the remains of an old factory are to be seen in the surf off Pukaad, and those of Pagodas in the surf at Tricanapulyon on the coast of Travancore.

Logan (1887, p. 75) had difficulty in reconciling the nineteenth century anchorages with the location of the city.

The entrance and exit to and from the anchorages (2–3 miles offshore), particularly from the southward, is encumbered by a reef known as the Coote Reef, from one of the Honourable Company's vessels having grounded on it. This is probably also the reef alluded to by Captain Alexander Hamilton as "The ruins of a sunken town built by the Portuguese." That the sea has encroached at Calicut cannot be doubted, but that a Portuguese fort once stood where the Coote Reef now is cannot be believed, although the tradition alluded to by Captain Hamilton has great currency on the coast.

The shoreline near Cochin is straight, sandy, and essentially featureless. Numerous widely separated shoals are mapped offshore on Survey of India hydrographic charts 218, 219, and 259 (scale 1:300,000). The present Customs Port Office at Calicut appears to be located at the end of the screw pile jetty described by Logan (1887), which is currently in disrepair (as in 1881), but in 1887 extended to 4 m of water. It is not known whether tidal records were obtained on this jetty at any time. The Port Officer was unable to confirm rumors of offshore ruins, although he did mention that vague reports had been related to him about submarine structures 15 km to the north beyond Kappad beach. On following this lead we found that this beach is interrupted by scattered rock outcrops that show possible wave-cut terraces at ≈1 m and perhaps 3–5 m. Local villagers expressed no knowledge of submarine ruins. A historical marker at Kappad beach commemorating the landing of Vasco de Gama in 1498 has been relocated inland twice, according to local villagers, suggesting that the coast has retreated. Logan (1887) also offered evidence for the erosion of the coast near Calicut in the marine exhumation of the grave of Shaikh Mammu Koya, but cautions that the erosion could have been minor and followed by annual coastal accretion.

According to Logan (1887, p. 319–320) the Portuguese fort at Calicut, "square in form with bastions at the corners facing the sea," was constructed in 1513 by an engineer named Thomas Fernandez with assistance from the local Zamorin "south of the city on the northern bank of the Kalayi River at the southern extremity of Calicut . . . flanked on two sides by water." The fort was abandoned during hostilities in 1525 (Logan, 1887, p.326), but its subsequent history remains unknown. If the fort had been constructed on an estuarine sand bar it could easily have collapsed during an erosional phase of the river or the sea, and its ruins might now be covered by subsequent accretion. If these were the submerged ruins that Hamilton and Stanhope encountered, the anchorage they would have used would have been much different from that used today.

The coastal region inland from Calicut is flat and close to sea level. Significant subsidence in this region (e.g., more than 1 m) would thus bring a large region close to marine flooding. Had an earlier tract of Calicut been submerged, it would have had to have been constructed on a coastal terrace below the present coastal plain. In that we find no evidence for multiple terrace levels above the present level, a lower marine terrace is unlikely, but not impossible. We are unable to bring further evidence to bear on the existence or nonexistence of a submerged offshore ruin, but geomorphic evidence for the coast at Calicut to be subsiding is decidedly weaker than evidence for shoreline structures being undermined and submerged by repeated accretion and erosion.

Earthquakes

The following Malabar earthquakes were encountered in our search through colonial materials. Except for the 1881 earthquake, the events were not listed in Mallet (1853), Gangopadhay (1988), or Dunbar et al., (1992).

Dabul: September 1524. Two apparently independent descriptions of a tsunami, related either to a major earthquake on the Arabian Sea, Bay of Cambay, or Macran coast, or to an offshore submarine slump, afflicted Vasco Da Gama's fleet three weeks before his death as the newly appointed Viceroy of India. In the fifteenth century, the town of Dabul at 17°34′ was a major trading port near Ratnagari roughly midway between Goa and Bombay (Yule and Burnell, 1903). Logan (1887, p. 322) wrote about the event.

On 11th (or 21st) Sept 1524 Vasco da Gama as Viceroy of India arrived at Goa with 3000 men in 14 ships. On reaching the land at Dabul and with the wind becalmed during the watch at daybreak, the sea trembled in such a manner, giving such great buffets to the ships, that all thought they were on shoals, and struck sails, and lowered boats into the sea with great shouts, and cries and discharge of cannon. On sounding they found no bottom, and they cried to God for mercy, because the ships pitched so violently that the men could not stand upright and the chests were sent from one end of the ship to the other. The trembling came, died away, and was renewed each time during the space of a Credo. The subterranean disturbance lasted about an hour, in which the water made a great boiling up, one sea struggling with another. When daylight was fully come, they saw the land. Da Gama maintained his presence of mind during this, and reassured his men by telling them that even the sea trembled at the presence of the Portugese.

The recitation of the Latin Credo (fast) has a duration of fewer than three min. If the sea waves resulted from an earthquake its moment release must have been considerable, similar perhaps to the 1819 Rann of Cutch event. An independent account of the same event indicating that Vasco da Gama recognized the tsunami as the effects of an earthquake can be found in Kerr (1824), who cited (Astl. I, 54. b.) as his source.

While in the Gulf of Cambaya, in a dead calm, the ships were tossed about in so violent a manner that all on board believed themselves in imminent danger of perishing, and began to consider how they might escape. One man leapt overboard, thinking to escape by swimming, but was drowned; and such as lay sick of fevers were cured by the fright. The viceroy, who perceived that the commotion was occasioned by the effects of an earthquake called aloud to his people, "courage my friends, for the sea trembles from the fear of you who are on it."

Cochin 1784. Newbold (1846) wrote, "In 1784 a strong concussion was felt."

Calicut 1881–1882. Logan (1887, p. 34) wrote the following.

Calicut 30 Dec 1881 midnight Bay of Bengal (R.D. Oldham, Rec. Geol. Suv. India, 17, 47-53, 1884). Felt throughout India (Arracan and Malabar Coasts, Nicobar Islands, Kathmandu) but very weakly in Calicut. The tsunami was recorded around the Bay of Bengal.
Calicut 31 Dec 1881 7:10 AM Madras Time Felt by persons at rest.
Calicut 28 Feb 1882 6:16 Madras time Furniture, roof tiles and window frames shook audibly for a second. Total duration 4–5 secs felt at Telichery and Nilgiri.

Allatur. Logan (1887, p. 34) wrote, "14 Oct 1882 14:00 near Palghat 'tables and boxes rattled audibly for about 1 sec.'"

Trivandrum 1823–1856. Logan, 1887, p. 34) listed the following.

Trivandrum Feb 1823
Trivandrum Sept 12 1841
Trivandrum Nov 20 1845
Trivandrum March 17 1856
Trivandrum Aug 11 1856 5:51:25
Trivandrum Aug 22 1856 16:25:10
Trivandrum 1 Sept 1856 12:15:00

REFERENCES CITED

Biswas, S. K., 1989, Hydrocarbon exploration in western offshore basins of India, *in* Recent geoscience studies in the Arabian Sea off India. Papers presented in the Seminar held on September 23–25, 1987, at Mangalore Karnataka: Geological Survey of India Special Publication 24, p. 185–194.

Burg, J. P., Davy, P., and Martinod, J., 1994, Shortening of analogue models of the continental lithosphere: New hypothesis for the formation of the Tibetan plateau: Tectonics, v. 12, p. 475–483.

DeMets, C., Gordon, R., and Voght, P., 1994, Location of the Africa-Australia-India triple junction and motion between the Australian and Indian plates: Results from an aeromagnetic investigation of the central Indian and Carlsburg ridges: Geophysical Journal International, v. 119, p. 893–930.

Dunbar, P. K., Lockridge, P. A., and Whiteside, L. S., 1992, Catalog of significant earthquakes 2150 B.C.–1991 A.D. including quantitative casualties and damage. U.S. Department of Commerce, National Oceanic and Atmospheric Administration, National Geophysical Data Center, Report SE-49, September 1992 (U.S. Government Printing Office: 1992-673-025/60-17).

Ellis, R. H., 1924, A short account of the Laccadive Islands and Minicoy: Madras, Government Press (1924 reprint), 123 p.

Freymuller, J., Bilham, R., Burgmann, R., and Larson, K., 1996, Motion of the Indian Plate 1991-5 and deformation in the Lesser Himalaya: Geophysical Research Letters, v. 23, p. 3107–3110.

Gangopadhay, 1988, Bibliography of Indian earthquakes: Geological Society of India, Miscellaneous Publication 60, p. 135.

Gowd, T. N., Srirama Rao, S. V., and Gaur, V. K., 1992, Tectonic stress field in the Indian Subcontinent: Journal of Geophysical Research, v. 97, p. 11,879–11,888.

Hamilton, A., 1727, A new account of the East Indes, with numerous maps and illustrations, with introduction and notes by Sir William Foster, Volume 1: New Delhi, Argonaut Press (1930 reprint), 273 p.

Jin, Y., McNutt, M. K., and Zhu, Y., 1994, Evidence from gravity and topography data for folding of Tibet: Nature, v. 371, p. 669–674.

Kerr, R., 1824, A general history and collection of voyages and travels, arranged in systematic order: Forming a complete history of the origin and progress of navigation, discovery, and commerce, by sea and land, from the earliest ages to the present time. Volume 2: Blackwood, Edinburgh, and

T. Cadell, p. 445.

Logan, W., 1887, Malabar (2 volumes): New Delhi, Asia Educational Services (1995 reprint) 759 p.

Mallet, R., 1853, Catalogue of recorded earthquakes from 1606 B.C. to A.D. 1850: British Association for the Advancement of Science, 22nd Meeting Report, 112 p.

Nagar, V. K., and Singh, A. N., 1991, Recent vertical motion in India: Dehra Dun, Survey of India.

Nair, M. M., 1987, Coastal geomorphology of Kerala: Geological Society of India Journal, v. 29, p. 450–458.

Newbold, T. J., 1846, Summary of the geology of Southern India, Part 4: Royal Asiatic Society of London Journal, v. 8, p.____.

Paul, J., Blume, F., Jade, S., Kumar, V., Swathi, P. S., Ananda, M. B., Gaur, V. K., Bürgmann, R., Bilham, R., Namboodri, B., and Mencin, D., 1995, Microstrain stability of Peninsular Indian 1864–1994: Indian Academy of Science Proceedings, v. 104, p. 131–146.

Paulose, K. V., and Narayanaswamy, S., 1968, The Tertiaries of the Kerala Coast: Geological Survey of India, Memoirs, v. ____, p. ____.

Prabhakar Rao, G., 1968, Age of the Warkallai Formation and the emergence of the present Kerala coast: National Institute of Science Bulletin, v. 38, p. 449–456.

Raghava Rao, K. V., 1975, Groundwater exploration, development and long term aquifer management in Kerala: Proceedings Symposium. Mineral Resources of Kerala and their utilization: Trivandrum, p. 5–15.

Rai, S. S., Ramesh, D. S., Srinagesh, D., Suryaprakasam, K., Mohan, G., Rajagopala Sarma, P. V. S. S., Satyanarayana, Y., and Gaur, V. K., 1992, Seismic tomography of the South Indian shield: Current Science, v. 62, p. 213–226.

Ramasamy, S. M., 1989, Morpho-tectonic evolution of east and west coasts of Indian Peninsula, *in* Recent geoscientific studies in the Arabian Sea off India: Geological Society of India Special Publication 24, p. 333–339.

Rao, S. R., 1989, Excavation of submerged ports—Dwarka, A case study, *in* Marine archaeology of Indian Ocean countries: Calcutta, Geological Society of India, p. 47–52.

Soman, K., 1980, Geology of Kerala: Trivandrum, Centre for Earth Science Studies Professional Paper 8.

Stanhope, P. D., 1785, Genuine memoirs of Asiaticus in a Series of Letters to a Friend during five years residence in different parts of India:, three of which were spent in the service of the Nabob of Arcot, interspersed with Anecdotes of several well known characters and containing an impartial account of the confinement and death of Lord Pigot and of the share the Nabob of Arcot had in that memorable transaction: Hugli, N. L. Chowdhury and Co., p. 124

Subrahmanya, K. R., 1996, Active intraplate deformation in South India: Tectonophysics, v. 249, p. 267–282.

Turcotte, D., and Schubert, G., 1982, Geodynamics: Applications of continuum physics to geological problems: New York, Wiley and Sons, 450 p.

Weissel, J., and Haxby, W., 1984, A tectonic tour of the Indian Ocean via the SEASAT satellite: Eos (Transactions, American Geophysical Union), v. 65, p. 185.

Yule, H., and Burnell, A. C., 1903, Hobson-Jobson: A glossary of colloquial Anglo-Indian words and phrases and of kindred terms, etymological, geographical, and discursive: New Delhi, John Murray (1995 reprint), p. 1021.

Zuber, M. T., 1987, Compression of oceanic lithosphere: An analysis of intraplate deformation in the central Indian Ocean: Journal of Geophysical Research, v. 92, p. 4817–4826.

MANUSCRIPT ACCEPTED BY THE SOCIETY FEBRUARY 3, 1998

Index

[Italic page numbers indicate major references]

Printed in U.S.A.